After 69 CE – Writing Civil War in Flavian Rome

Trends in Classics – Supplementary Volumes

Edited by
Franco Montanari and Antonios Rengakos

Associate Editors
Evangelos Karakasis · Fausto Montana · Lara Pagani
Serena Perrone · Evina Sistakou · Christos Tsagalis

Scientific Committee
Alberto Bernabé · Margarethe Billerbeck
Claude Calame · Jonas Grethlein · Philip R. Hardie
Stephen J. Harrison · Richard Hunter · Christina Kraus
Giuseppe Mastromarco · Gregory Nagy
Theodore D. Papanghelis · Giusto Picone
Tim Whitmarsh · Bernhard Zimmermann

Volume 65

After 69 CE – Writing Civil War in Flavian Rome

Edited by
Lauren Donovan Ginsberg and Darcy A. Krasne

DE GRUYTER

ISBN 978-3-11-073688-5
e-ISBN (PDF) 978-3-11-058584-1
e-ISBN (EPUB) 978-3-11-058474-5
ISSN 1868-4785

Library of Congress Control Number: 2018962690

Bibliographic information published by the Deutsche Nationalbibliothek
The Deutsche Nationalbibliothek lists this publication in the Deutsche Nationalbibliografie;
detailed bibliographic data are available on the Internet at http://dnb.dnb.de.

© 2020 Walter de Gruyter GmbH, Berlin/Boston
This volume is text- and page-identical with the hardback published in 2018.
Editorial Office: Alessia Ferreccio and Katerina Zianna
Logo: Christopher Schneider, Laufen
Printing and binding: CPI books GmbH, Leck

www.degruyter.com

John Penwill
D · M

Contents

Acknowledgements —— IX
Introduction —— 1

Part I: Lucanean Lenses

Marco Fucecchi
Flavian Epic: Roman Ways of Metabolizing a Cultural Nightmare? —— 25

Raymond Marks
Sparsis Mauors agitatus in oris: Lucan and Civil War in *Punica* 14 —— 51

John Penwill †
How It All Began: Civil War and Valerius's *Argonautica* —— 69

Part II: Narrating *Nefas* in Statius's *Thebaid*

Federica Bessone
Signs of Discord: Statius's Style and the Traditions on Civil War —— 89

Timothy Stover
Civil War and the Argonautic Program of Statius's *Thebaid* —— 109

Marco van der Schuur
Civil War on the Horizon:
Seneca's *Thyestes* and *Phoenissae* in Statius's *Thebaid* 7 —— 123

Part III: Leadership and Exemplarity

Alice König
Reading Civil War in Frontinus's *Strategemata*:
A Case-Study for Flavian Literary Studies —— 145

Neil W. Bernstein
Inuitas maculant cognato sanguine dextras:
Civil War Themes in Silius's Saguntum Episode —— 179

Steve Mason
Vespasian's Rise from Civil War in Josephus's *Bellum Judaicum* —— 199

Leo Landrey
Embroidered Histories:
Lemnos and Rome in Valerius Flaccus's *Argonautica* —— 227

Part IV: Family, Society, and Self

Claire Stocks
Band of Brothers:
Fraternal Instability and Civil Strife in Silius Italicus's *Punica* —— 253

William J. Dominik
Civil War, Parricide, and the Sword in Silius Italicus's *Punica* —— 271

Alison Keith
Engendering Civil War in Flavian Epic —— 295

Jean-Michel Hulls
A Last Act of Love? Suicide and Civil War as Tropes in Silius Italicus's *Punica* and Josephus's *Bellum Judaicum* —— 321

Part V: Ruination, Restoration, and Empire

Eleni Hall Manolaraki
Domesticating Egypt in Pliny's *Natural History* —— 341

Darcy A. Krasne
Valerius Flaccus's Collapsible Universe: Patterns of Cosmic Disintegration in the *Argonautica* —— 363

Siobhan Chomse
Instability and the Sublime in Martial's *Liber Spectaculorum* —— 387

Bibliography —— 411
Notes on Contributors —— 443
Thematic Index —— 447
Index of Passages —— 463

Acknowledgments

This volume originates from an international conference, "Writing About Civil War in Flavian Rome," held at the 8th Celtic Conference in Classics in Edinburgh, Scotland in the summer of 2014. The three days of the panel included 30 papers on Flavian literature's diverse responses to civil war. As only a subset of these are included in the present volume, we would like to single out for thanks the remaining panelists from Edinburgh, whose contributions of scholarship and insight at the conference implicitly and explicitly informed the subsequent shape of the project: Paolo Asso, Antony Augoustakis, Pramit Chaudhuri, Daniela Galli, Randall Ganiban, Dustin Heinen, Martijn Icks, Nicholas Rupert, Carey Seal, Étienne Wolff, and Andrew Zissos. In addition to those that read papers, moreover, we also want to thank the participants who attended the sessions and contributed to the spirited dialogue and debate, whether on campus at the University of Edinburgh or up the road at the Abbey Bar, where conversation often continued into the night. As Anton Powell, founder of the CCC, once said, there is a special correlation between pub and publication, and the Abbey demonstrated the veracity of this idea. Indeed, Anton Powell himself deserves a special mention, not just for his continued commitment to the CCC and its unique format, but for his own enthusiastic participation in our panel and his encouragement to publish its papers; and we also thank Douglas Cairns, Anton Powell's co-organizer of the CCC in 2014, for organizing the event and its logistics. Another to whom we owe a special debt of gratitude is Antony Augoustakis, who has provided much advice as this project developed. We also wish to thank the editorial team at De Gruyter and the *Trends in Classics* series, and the anonymous reviewers for their many suggestions that strengthened the volume in uncountable ways. Additionally, we are grateful to our supportive colleagues at Columbia University, the University of Cincinnati, and the University of Missouri-Columbia; and we consider ourselves particularly lucky that Darcy Krasne had Ray Marks, a fellow Flavianist, as a colleague at Mizzou throughout much of this project.

We were also fortunate to receive material and financial support for this project from a variety of sources. The librarians and staff at the John Miller Burnam Classics Library of the University of Cincinnati, the Arthur and Janet C. Ross Library of the American Academy of Rome, and the various libraries and reading rooms of the University of Missouri, Columbia University, and UCLA all helped us with access to important materials throughout the project's development; Sally Krasne also helped with procuring materials from UCLA and travel logistics leading up to the conference. Key financial support came from the American Academy of Rome, the Louise Taft Semple Fund of the Department of Classics at the

University of Cincinnati, and the Tytus Scholars Program at the University of Cincinnati. Finally, we wish to thank the writing group through which we, the editors, first began to collaborate as graduate students; without the creation of that group and the support of its members, the interactions that brought about this volume might never have happened.

On a different note, it was with great sadness that we learned of John Penwill's passing as this project neared its conclusion. John was a characteristically enthusiastic participant in the original conference and a tireless supporter of the volume as it developed. We know that he was hard at work on changes to his essay that he had told us included additional bibliography that he was keen to engage with, such as Armitage's important new work, *Civil Wars: A History in Ideas* (2017). Unfortunately and understandably, he was not able to pass along these revisions before his death. We are grateful to Frances Mills for her communication with us during a difficult time and for her help in ascertaining the status of John's paper. In honor of his memory, we have printed the latest version of his essay that he had sent to us with minimal changes; and for his deep engagement with our CCC panel and this volume and for his myriad contributions to the wider field of Flavian literature, we dedicate this volume to John Penwill.

Introduction

"Even those Romans who tried hardest not to speak of civil war found themselves reliving it in their writings."

Armitage 2017a, 59

nec iam recentia saeuae pacis exempla sed repetita bellorum ciuilium memoria captam totiens suis exercitibus urbem, uastitatem Italiae, direptiones prouinciarum, Pharsaliam Philippos et Perusiam ac Mutinam, nota publicarum cladium nomina, loquebantur. prope euersum orbem etiam cum de principatu inter bonos certaretur, sed mansisse C. Iulio, mansisse Caesare Augusto uictore imperium; mansuram fuisse sub Pompeio Brutoque rem publicam: nunc pro Othone an pro Vitellio in templa ituros? utrasque impias preces, utraque detestanda uota inter duos, quorum bello solum id scires, deteriorem fore qui uicisset. erant qui Vespasianum et arma Orientis augurarentur, et ut potior utroque Vespasianus, ita bellum aliud atque alias cladis horrebant.

Tac. *Hist.* 1.50.2–4

Their talk was no longer of the recent atrocities of a bloody peace, but resorting to the memory of civil wars, they spoke of a city repeatedly captured by its own armies, of the devastation of Italy, of the plundering of the provinces, of Pharsalia, Philippi, and Perusia, and Mutina, names notorious for public disaster. They said that the world had been nearly overturned even when the struggle for the principate was waged between honest men, but that the empire had remained when Gaius Julius won and had remained when Caesar Augustus won; that the Republic would have remained under Pompey and Brutus; but now—should they go to the temples to pray for Otho, or for Vitellius? Prayers for either would be impious and vows for either detestable when, in the struggle between the two, the only thing you could know for sure was that the worse man would win. There were some who were looking to Vespasian and the armies in the East, and yet although Vespasian was a better option than either of the other two, they shuddered at another war and another massacre.

1 Writing Civil War, Writing 69 CE

Although outside the chronological boundaries of this volume, Tacitus's narrative of the civil wars that gave rise to the Flavian dynasty has largely shaped modern investigation into these events and their cultural impact on Flavian Rome.[1] It is Tacitus, for example, that seems to have led Paul Jal to conclude his landmark

---

[1] The best recent historical overviews of the era, Wellesley 2000 and Morgan 2006, both rely heavily on Tacitus despite the richness of the parallel tradition. Tacitus's *Histories* have also been the subject of increasing interest with new commentaries (e.g., Damon 2003 and Ash 2007b) and a host of monographs (see especially Ash 1999; Joseph 2012; Master 2016).

https://doi.org/10.1515/9783110585841-001

study of Roman civil war with 69 CE on the grounds that the conflicts of that year inaugurated a fundamentally different kind of *bellum ciuile* that changed both the mechanisms and stakes for waging civil war, and others have followed suit.[2] Moreover, the brief Tacitean vignette quoted at the outset of this chapter is a useful heuristic in its compressed illumination of several important truths concerning writing about civil war after the wars of 69 CE,[3] linking the wars of that year not just to Rome's wider history of discordant conflict but to its literary representations of that discord. Thus we, too, begin with Tacitus.

The first truth evident in Tacitus's account is the enduring legacy of the Republic's civil wars in the Roman cultural imagination, particularly the sense of *Discordia*'s cyclical, iterative nature. The political strife of Rome's past remained a key yardstick against which later cataclysms were measured and a key allusive matrix through which to view future events. The points of comparison evoked here bring together not only the wars themselves, but the civil warriors who wage them, the devastation those warriors leave in their wake, and the moral judgment that attends Roman discussions of civil war. *Bellum ciuile* is simultaneously a historically attested event from the final century of the Roman Republic and a wider conceptual framework through which Romans understood themselves. Each new instantiation, facsimile, and shadow of civil war bears traces of those that came before and adds to the sense of civil war as Rome's inescapable curse, constant and yet somehow worse with each generation. It is precisely through the act of remembering that the Romans of 69 CE recognize and name the devastation around them as *bellum ciuile*.

The second truth is that any attempt to write civil war becomes an intertextual project.[4] As Petronius's poet Eumolpus reminds his audience, any singer of *bella ciuilia* must be *plenus litteris* ("filled with literature," Petr. 118.6). This remains the case half a century later for Tacitus, as well; scholars have noted, for example, that as his anonymous Romans catalogue public disasters in order to highlight the era's most devastating conflicts, they simultaneously allude to the literary incarnations of these conflicts. For instance, the chronological displacement of *Perusia ac Mutinam* has been read by some as an allusion to Lucan's own catalogue of chaos (*Perusina fames Mutinaque labores*, Luc. 1.42).[5] Likewise,

---

[2] Jal 1963, 14, 489ff.
[3] For the programmatic status of this passage in Tacitus's *Histories*, see Ash 2010; Breed *et al.* 2010b, 11; Joseph 2012, 53–62. See also below on the dialectical difference between "writing about civil war" and "writing civil war."
[4] And not just in the Roman world. See, e.g., Healy/Sawday 1990, esp. 3–4, on literature and England's civil war.
[5] Paratore 1951, 354–55 n. 21, and Damon 2010, 378–79.

some have seen in Tacitus's marked omission of a conjunction between *Pharsaliam* and *Philippos* an allusion to the wider literary conflation of the two battle sites in Lucan's epic and earlier poetry.[6] Following Cynthia Damon, we might ask, "is Tacitus suggesting that these Romans of 69 CE have read their Lucan and realized that the grim story he told continued after his death?"[7] Perhaps so.

But though Lucan may indeed be a particular intertextual target for Tacitus, the historian also incorporates into his brief *synkrisis* elements which Jal first identified as constitutive of a wider narrative tradition of civil war at Rome, a tradition that both includes and transcends the influence of an individual poet like Lucan.[8] These include the language of savagery and impiety, the image of a world turned upside-down, the idea of geographic escalation such that a war within a single city can become a World War, and the idea of iterative cycles, to name just a few. And so it seems that Tacitus's Romans are not simply "remembering" the Republic's civil wars (which, of course, they had not been alive to see); rather, they are mediating that *repetita ... memoria* through Rome's literature of civil war, drawing on its recurring tropes and figures as well as its key texts.[9] In other words, even as Tacitus's anonymous Romans seek to understand 69 CE as a new instantiation of Rome's old problem, they shape their perception of these events according to a well-developed and recognized literary schema. To narrate the *nefas* of 69 CE requires not only a memory of the past, but a memory of the literature of that past.

A final point is that, even as they replayed the struggles of Rome's earlier history, the civil wars of 69 CE stood somewhat apart, not least because Empire and Rome's new dynastic system had changed the stakes. As Tacitus portrays it, the newest iteration of what used to be a war concerned with the stability of *imperium* or even the *res publica* was now seen simply as a battle between questionable men who hunted a throne; the inevitable result was that another general with another foreign army would bring about further destruction. The inherent distancing, both political and geographical, that this result of imperial expansion imposes on Rome's civil strife can be seen most clearly in the Roman people's ideological detachment from the struggle: as the *populus Romanus* contemplates the ways in which their present recalls their knowledge of the past, they also see in that repetition a significant degeneration.

---

[6] See Joseph 2012, 57–62. For the poetic *topos*, see Verg. G. 1.489–92; Ov. Met. 15.823–24; Man. 1.907–14; Luc. 1.680 and 695.
[7] Damon 2010, 378.
[8] Jal 1963, 60–69 and 231–488.
[9] See especially Joseph 2012, 62.

However, the Tacitean story is not the only story to be told. Rather, Flavian literature itself—a rich era of literary output sandwiched between Lucan's iconoclastic *Bellum Ciuile* and Tacitus's equally seductive *Histories* of *bella ciuilia*—offers a fertile field for investigating Rome's literary response to the crisis of the year 69 CE.[10] And it is to this literature that we now turn.

2 The Flavian Moment

The Flavian era was populated not by those whose memories of civil strife had dimmed in the course of the extended internal peace of the Julio-Claudian era, nor by those under the apparently halcyon rule of Nerva and Trajan that came about without civil strife, but by those whose recollection was fresh and whose dominant experience of civil strife was as an imperial and recursive phenomenon. Each of the successive civil wars of 69 CE placed a new emperor on an increasingly destabilized and bloodied throne; the year's series of *bella ciuilia* rivaled the trauma of the late Republic in subsequent cultural memory, and Romans even saw their own city disfigured towards the end of that infamous struggle, as Flavian and Vitellian forces vied for total domination. This final chapter culminated in the burning of the Capitoline, an act which would haunt Rome as "the most grievous and most disgusting crime" to have occurred since Romulus slew Remus.[11] The authors of Flavian Rome thus write for a contemporary audience of survivors, both those who survived the conspiracies and uprisings that brought an end to Julio-Claudian Rome and those who survived the civil wars that would follow. And they write in an era that must now acknowledge civil strife as an ineradicable part of Imperial Rome's DNA.

It is, of course, unfortunate that nearly all Flavian historiography has been lost, leaving the modern reader with no contemporary prose history through which we might explore a particularly Flavian historical narrative of *bellum ciuile*.[12] And yet, as the papers in this volume testify, the idea of civil war suffuses

---

10 Our use of the term "Flavian literature" in this volume consistently refers to all texts produced between 70 and 96 CE under the dynasty that the wars of 69 CE brought to power.

11 *id facinus post conditam urbem luctuosissimum foedissimumque rei publicae populi Romani accidit* (Tac. *Hist.* 3.72.1). On the strategic symbolism of the Flavian occupation of the Capitoline and its subsequent cultural memory, see especially Heinemann 2015; see also Landrey in this volume.

12 Our primary understanding of the major Flavian historians, Pliny the Elder, Cluvius Rufus, and Fabius Rusticus, again comes from Tacitus. On their influence, see Cizek 1972, 8–15; Griffin 1984, 15 and 235–37; Ripoll 1999; Champlin 2003, 39–44; Degl'Innocenti Pierini 2007, 146–55.

and shapes much more of Flavian literature than just its vanished historical narratives. While Jal stopped short of analyzing the wealth of literature produced in the wake of those events, recent commentaries on Flavian authors—especially the three major epics of the period—often draw attention to their allusions to the history and prior literature of civil war, and studies of individual genres and texts frequently explore these allusions in more detail.[13] But despite the acknowledged prevalence of this theme and despite the current renaissance in Flavian studies that has brought this era to the forefront of new work on Latin literature, no single study has brought together the generically diverse and heterogeneous perspectives of its authors on the topic of *bellum ciuile*.[14]

The Flavian contribution to Rome's civil war literature is also often overlooked in larger studies of civil war as a literary theme, from Jal onwards, despite ever increasing interest in both the historical phenomenon of civil war and its artistic representation throughout Rome's history.[15] To take but one example, an important inspiration for this volume and the conference from which it originated was a conference held at Amherst College in 2005, "See How I Rip Myself: Rome and Its Civil Wars," which subsequently became the volume *Citizens of Discord: Rome and its Civil Wars* (Breed et al. 2010a). That volume catalyzed new work on

---

13 A bibliography for the subject would be too vast to be useful, but a peek inside the indices of recent companions to Silius Italicus (Augoustakis 2010b), Valerius Flaccus (Heerink/Manuwald 2014), and Statius (Dominik et al. 2015), as well as the indices of the many recent collected volumes of essays and commentaries on individual books of Flavian epic, demonstrates the prevalence of civil war as an important theme.

14 Ahl 1984b and Henderson 1998 remain key predecessors both in the study of Roman literature's fascination with civil war as a theme and in their attention to Flavian Rome's particular contribution to this literary tradition.

15 The civil wars of antiquity and the literary tradition which springs from them have increasingly become a hot topic over the past two decades. In terms of dedicated monographs or edited collections, see especially Price 2001; Nappa 2005; Batstone/Damon 2006; Osgood 2006; McNelis 2007; Breed et al. 2010a; Dinter 2012; Grillo 2012; Joseph 2012; Wienand 2012; Osgood 2014; Börm et al. 2016; Welch 2015; Lange 2016; Ginsberg 2017; Lange/Vervaet *forthcoming*, Lowrie/Vinken *in progress*. In addition to these, the anticipated volumes that will emerge from three separate 2017 conferences will continue to refine our understanding of Roman civil war and its legacy: Lowrie and McCormick's "Civil War: Discord Within," at the University of Chicago; Havener and Gotter's "A Culture of Civil War? *Bellum civile* in the Late Republic and Early Principate," at the University of Konstanz; and Hinge, Kemezis, Lange, Madsen, and Osgood's "Cassius Dio: The Impact of Violence, War, and Civil War," at Aalborg University. Moreover, although not focused on Rome exclusively, Armitage's recent groundbreaking cultural history of civil war (Armitage 2017a) devotes two of his six chapters to Rome's unique contribution to the phenomenon and its various discourses, and Rome plays an equally large role in his epilogue on literature's role in the process.

the topic with questions still at the core of studies of Roman civil war: why did Romans repeatedly subject themselves to civil war and how, in turn, did civil war insinuate itself into Rome's worldview and Rome's understanding of its identity? Though its focus was not on literature exclusively (unlike our present volume), it featured many groundbreaking pieces that explored literary reflections of civil war and the various textual strategies through which Romans commemorated their propensity for *discordia*. Nevertheless, within its admirably broad chronological boundaries and selection of authors lies an important gap. For when the volume turns to the Year of the Four Emperors, absent are any texts written in the decades immediately following the outbreak of civil war in 69 CE. It is our contention, however, and one shared by our volume's contributors, that Flavian literature represents an important chapter to writing civil war at Rome, one worthy of the focused attention which this volume brings.

Writing civil war—if not necessarily writing *about* civil war—was an inescapable project in Flavian Rome, whether as the subject of a head-on engagement or as a voice that can be heard in the erasures and unfilled spaces of a textual enterprise. Through linguistic, thematic, or historical engagement with Rome's civil war past, Flavian authors repeatedly—if not always explicitly—create a space for themselves as the next chapter of the wide-ranging and long-standing tradition of civil war literature at Rome. At the same time, we also see them forging an identity for themselves as authors of a new Flavian era, with its own rich diversity of approaches and perspectives, including literature that provides strategies of recuperation and healing as it seeks ways of moving beyond Rome's iterative curse of civil war.

The essays collected in this volume aim to shine a spotlight on these neglected Flavian voices within Rome's literary tradition of civil war. In doing so, we privilege an approach that confronts the multi-generic corpus of Flavian literature, over and against the still too common definition of "Flavian literature" primarily in terms of Flavian epic, one that brings together a heterogeneous collection of ancient authors and genres. The papers, which emerge from a multi-day panel held at the 8th Celtic Conference in Classics in 2014, also incorporate diverse approaches both to the literary strategies used to narrate civil war and to the significance of writing (about) civil war after its brutal reemergence in 69 CE. Moreover, as we examine the representation of civil war through a Flavian lens, we also probe what precisely might constitute that lens, as well as the degree to which the periodization advanced with the term "Flavian" remains meaningful given the era's diverse literary output.[16] The result is a fresh overview of the theme of civil war in Flavian literature, which no two papers approach from the same angle or with the same preconceptions. In this way, we hope to push to the fore themes that are truly indicative of the contemporary cultural and literary climate, in addition to noting fissures that resist such a chronological schematization, the sorts of discordant or non-homogeneous note that such periodization often attempts to suppress.

3 Defining Civil War and Its Literature

Readers might at this point expect a degree of specificity in terms of what we (the editors and our various contributors) mean by "civil war," especially in light of a host of new works on the subject.[17] Amid the broad swath of approaches and scholarly questions that has continually grown over the past two decades, the idea of defining, naming, and thereby framing what civil war is (and is not) has remained a consistent thread.[18] What is the difference, for example, between civil war, sedition, revolution, or another form of violent political strife? Is there a conceptual difference between *bellum ciuile* and *bellum internum*? What is the role of individual motivations and passions within a larger armed conflict? Is civil war an escalation from *seditio* or private *ira*, or is it a question of perspective, given that successful civil warriors often coopt the language of justified revolution upon victory? And how can we articulate the apparently inevitable slippage between categories?

It turns out that answering such questions and thereby defining discrete and limiting parameters for "civil war" is nearly impossible in practice. In his awardwinning investigation into the mechanisms and logic that underpin violence in civil war, Kalyvas urges a more inclusive view.[19] He queries, for example, how one might differentiate between the macro-level (public, ideological, collective) political violence that underpins civil war and the micro-level violence between

---

16 For an interrogation of what might constitute the "Flavian" aspect of Flavian literature, see König in this volume. On limits of periodization when it comes to Flavian Rome and its literature, see also Dominik *et al.* 2009, 1; Boyle/Dominik 2005, 1–3; Manuwald/Voigt 2013, 4–5; Wilson 2013.
17 See above (n. 15).
18 For attempts to differentiate terminologically between civil war and associated acts of internal violence at Rome, see Armitage 2017a, 64ff. and 222–23. See also Jal 1963, 7–14 and 20–34; Brunner *et al.* 1984, 667–70; Rosenberger 1992; Börm 2016, 16ff.; Osgood 2015, 1683.
19 For his own definition of civil war (which he productively decouples from his study of the broader and more fluid phenomenon of civil war violence), see Kalyvas 2006, 17.

intimates (families, neighbors, friends), which may be divorced from the motivations driving wider civil conflict, but nonetheless remain part of its origin, impact and trauma.[20] In the end, civil war's fusing of public and private, personal and political, individual and collective problematizes our desire to name and frame.[21] Thus, within the wider conceptual category of "civil war," what appears to be a just revolution to some might seem to be illegal sedition or conspiracy to others; and when looked at retrospectively one's position might shift again due to hindsight, as we can see most famously in the Romans' own understanding of the demise of the Gracchi brothers in light of what came later.[22] In every case, moreover, micro-actions might consist mostly of individuals taking advantage of wider social chaos to pursue personal and even familial hatreds or rivalries absent of political or ideological motivations. And on the larger scale, civil wars often occur alongside of or give rise to wars between separate political entities; this is a truth already enshrined in myth, most notably in the legend of the sons of Oedipus. As David Armitage notes in his landmark monograph *Civil Wars: A History in Ideas*, "civil war" has been such a conceptually generative and fertile topic for exploration because "there has never been a time when [its] definition was settled to everyone's satisfaction or when it could be used without question or contention."[23] Thus while it may appear advantageous to avoid the notion that every instance of internal discord can be properly termed "civil war" and to define *bellum ciuile* through strict criteria such as the engagement of armies and the activity of the populace,[24] it is equally important to see how with every new experience of civil war, our understanding of what it means concomitantly evolves. For this reason, as Armitage notes, civil war has remained undertheorized and resistant to schematization.[25]

---

20 Kalyvas 2006, 3–5, 16–19, 330–63, and *passim*.
21 See also Armitage 2017a, 12–14. Osgood's 2014 study of the so-called *Laudatio Turiae* is an extended case study in how the desire to demarcate the limits of civil war with definitions that require pitched battles between citizens does not correspond to the experience of those who lived through them or to the way in which they were commemorated in art and literature.
22 Armitage 2017a, 48. On these issues see also Börm 2016, 16ff. On the Gracchi specifically, see Wiseman 2010.
23 Armitage 2017a, 12. Armitage's monograph will remain essential reading for any serious inquiry into civil war. See also, however, the varied responses to his monograph assembled in *Critical Analysis of Law* 4.2 (2017), especially Lange 2017 and Straumann 2017, as well as the reply by Armitage himself (Armitage 2017b).
24 Börm 2016, 17, pursues this line of reasoning admirably, though even he acknowledges its limitations when it comes to the specific case studies of the volume (Börm *et al.* 2016).
25 Armitage 2017a, 7.

Rome's literature of civil war well embodies and illustrates this conceptual richness and the difficulty inherent in attempting to define *bellum ciuile* or confine its resonances; and the discrete conceptual and representative strata extend across the verbal and the thematic as well as the historical and the cultural.[26] We find here a wealth of symbol systems, vocabulary, metaphors, and tropes, which cumulatively, over time, create a trans-generic literary tradition and paradigmatic mode of expression. Indeed, under the early empire, Roman literature had already established for itself a paradigmatic vocabulary—what Federica Bessone terms a *koiné*—of civil war.[27] Included in this linguistic code are terms like *nefas* and *scelus* which emphasize the unspeakable, twisted nature of internal discord; conversely, we see a large-scale problematization of value terminology within the context of *bellum ciuile* and a focus on linguistic paradox, as concepts like *fides* or *pietas* are redefined to celebrate kin-slaughter.

Individual pre-Flavian authors contribute phrases which transcend their status as intertexts to become themselves *topoi* for civil war; so, for example, echoes of Horace's seventh epode, especially its indignant opening (*quo, quo scelesti ruitis?*), reverberate across the subsequent literary tradition. Likewise, what began as a general lament for strife in Book 5 of Vergil's *Aeneid* (*quis furor iste nouus? quo nunc, quo tenditis ... heu, miserae ciues?*, *A.* 5.670–71)—itself perhaps indebted to Horace—would be ossified through its varied receptions into a rallying cry against civil war's frenzy (Tib. 1.10.33; Ov. *Met.* 3.531; Sen. *Phoen.* 557, *Thy.* 339; Petr. 108.14.1) and would become a veritable catch-phrase for Lucan (*quis furor, o ciues*, Luc. 1.8; cf. 1.681, 7.95)—and for his successors, in turn. In other words, we see not only individual and cumulative receptions of specific moments in Horace, Vergil, Ovid, Lucan, Seneca, and others, but also the simultaneous establishment of a Roman poetics of civil war.

The developed system analogizes between different types of discord, from suicide and fratricide on the micro-level to cosmic dissolution on the macro-level. Indeed, Michèle Lowrie has recently argued that this symbolic discourse, of and surrounding civil war, is one of Rome's original contributions to the history of concepts precisely because while, "as a political concept, *bellum ciuile* may be restricted to warfare among citizens, its consistent analogical extension from the soul to the cosmos commutes it into a figure of thought that fights internally against conceptual confinement."[28] Thus, when we speak of Flavian literature's

---

26 See especially Jal 1963, 15 and 60ff., on what would become the Flavian authors' literary and linguistic inheritance.
27 Bessone, p. 90.
28 Lowrie 2016, 352.

representation of civil war, we necessarily take a broad view both of the term *bellum ciuile* and of the ways in which the wider concept might manifest itself throughout the various genres, prosaic and poetic, that make up the era's surviving literary output.

4 Organization and Thematic Overview

We have organized the volume into five sections, each of which highlights a different approach, focus, theme, or trope. Our first two sections take us into the killing fields of Rome's two surviving epics of civil war, one Neronian, the other Flavian. The literature of the Flavian age marks an especially crucial stage in the reception of Rome's poetics of civil war through its rapid canonization of Lucan's *Bellum Ciuile*, a discordant and iconoclastic poem that Flavian authors seem to have seen as prophetic for the horrors of the *bella ciuilia* of 69 CE that the Neronian *uates* himself did not live to experience, as well as an ideal—or at least unavoidable—vehicle for capturing civil war's violence.[29] Accordingly, in recognition of the *Bellum Ciuile*'s signal impact on subsequent literature, our first section, "Lucanean Lenses," contains three papers on the Flavian response to Lucan and its echoes or refashionings of Lucanean themes, scenes, and language. While elements of this Flavian response to Lucanean poetics are hardly absent from the rest of the volume, these three papers cumulatively offer an overarching and multivocal investigation of how Flavian literature uses its intertextual dialogue with Lucan to produce a socio-historical commentary on Rome's most recent civil wars and the new era that followed.

Our second section, "Narrating *Nefas* in Statius's *Thebaid*," turns to Flavian literature's own most sustained engagement with the theme of civil strife and balances the previous section's broader approaches to Lucanean reception with its focus on the minutiae of Statius's poetics of civil war. The three papers investigate the poet's methods of intensifying the already-overt civil war that permeates his epic, probing his language and compositional practices from three distinct points of view: style, ecphrasis, and genre. Each also explores how Statius's allusive appropriations retroactively crystalize and heighten the *bellum ciuile* within the earlier texts on which he draws to craft his own linguistic systems, his own deconstructive intertextuality, and his own mode of generic interplay.

---

[29] See especially Stover 2012, 3: "Lucan's nightmarish visions of *bellum civile* had burst forth into the 'here and now' of historical reality, creating the impression that Lucan's challenge to epic and the civil war's challenge to empire were somehow related, were in some way symptoms of the same disease."

The remaining three sections each explore a trope of civil war literature that transcends individual works and their genres to become a dominant theme in Flavian Rome's literature of civil war. The first of these, "Leadership and Exemplarity," draws out and expands on this pair of intersecting themes through four papers on Frontinus's *Strategemata*, Silius's *Punica*, Josephus's *Bellum Judaicum*, and Valerius Flaccus's *Argonautica*. The question of leadership becomes a locus of tension in Flavian literature, whether we think in terms of the statesman who holds political power or of the general with an army at his back. Perhaps most interesting are the moments in which the one is pitted against the other, as civil warfare challenges the structures and hierarchies of a state at peace. What does it mean to be a leader in times of civil upheaval? Under what circumstances can would-be leaders undertake criminal action and still be viewed as a positive *exemplum*? Do different virtues of leadership appear in contexts of civil warfare as opposed to war against a foreign population? How do traditional virtues such as *pietas* and *fides* persist as exemplary in a society at war with itself? And, finally, what lasting value do *exempla* drawn from *bellum ciuile* have for a state at peace, especially if these *exempla* are animated by a fundamental confusion between virtue and vice? These four papers respond in diverse ways to the above set of questions as they take us from wars waged on the battlefields of history to struggles inside a discordant community.

This point brings us to our fourth section, "Family, Society, and Self," which tackles similar questions but with a focus on individuals and the bonds between them, familial and otherwise. The four papers included here investigate a set of prominent themes that are familiar as substitutive *loci* for or spurs to civil war: fraternity, inheritance, suicide, and gender. How do fraternal bonds and the question of inheritance replicate in miniature the tensions and fissures within wider civil war narratives? Or, indeed, the opposite: how can these sites of potential familial conflict offer strategies for ameliorating the passions that underlie *bellum ciuile*? What role do women play—as wives, mothers, daughters, or indeed, abstract personifications—in catalyzing and perpetuating social *discordia*, especially as Flavian literature confronts the Augustan inheritance of displacing the guilt of civil war onto the Republic's "women out of control"? Finally, how does society-wide mass suicide (whether actuated through literal suicide or through the killing of family members) literalize civil war's destructive properties while at the same time offering an alternative avenue for its progress?

The final section, "Ruination, Restoration, and Empire," expands outward from the individual, constituent parts of society to examine the grand structures of reality (the entirety of Rome, the entirety of the *orbis*, and even the entirety of the cosmos) and the ways in which they are constructed and dismantled within the confines of a single text. The three papers, which treat Pliny the Elder, Valerius Flaccus, and Martial, each confront the interrelationship of *urbs* and *orbis* from a different angle, providing productively conflicting images of the relationship between reconciliation, restoration, and ruination. Threading among the chapters, we encounter questions of how a world consumed by war returns to peace, what the changing shape of Roman *imperium* (both geographical and ideological) means for Rome's future, and how the enormity of civil war's effects—and the enormity of the Roman *orbis*—can be contained within a single text. Does cohesion imply stability? Does enormity inevitably lead to collapse?

Such an arrangement of the volume into five parts is meant neither to imply a homogeneity to the interpretive strategies and arguments contained within each section nor to preclude essays within one section from being meaningfully in dialogue with those of another, but rather to emphasize that specific dimension of each individual paper in the context of a dialogue with the other chapters in its section. For this reason, we conclude our introduction with a synthetic and in-depth look at some of the core themes that cut across these categories.

4.1 Modes of Allusion

As we mentioned at the outset of our introduction, writing civil war is a fundamentally intertextual project in which previous texts (and previous civil wars) are woven together into new contexts. It thus comes as no surprise to see textual interaction as a primary concern that runs through our various papers, and certainly Lucan and Lucanean poetics cannot but loom large (as explored in our first section of papers). This does not, however, imply a uniformity to allusive readings, and we also see other models emerge which filter Flavian literature's negotiation of civil war's literary memory through other texts, including those of fellow Flavian authors. In addition, the Flavian intertextuality (and intratextuality) traced throughout this volume is polyvalent not just in its literary models, but in its modes of allusion: style, structure, and history itself each become a focus through which allusion produces meaning.

For Marco Fucecchi (ch. 2), Flavian Rome's reception of Lucan must be read in terms of Lucan's own expansion of civil war as a theme from his predecessors. Fucecchi traces an "antiphrastic" mode of intertextuality through which Lucan, Vergil, and other poetic predecessors are pitted agonistically against one another and against themselves; the end result is a response to the *Aeneid* built out of a Lucanean critique of Vergil's oblique and reticent treatment of *bellum ciuile*, but a response that simultaneously questions Lucan's nightmarish presentation of a civil war without end. Marco van der Schuur (ch. 7), by contrast, reads Statius's *Thebaid* as a continuation of Seneca's *Phoenissae* (an intertextual relationship also highlighted to different ends in Federica Bessone's chapter, ch. 5) that brings to fruition that play's expected but unachieved fraternal strife by drawing on the "cosmic framework" of another Senecan text, the *Thyestes*, which successfully achieved an open-ended cycle of familial bloodshed and revenge. Both contributors see the Flavian poets as "moving beyond" the texts that are their models (an image also employed by Alison Keith, ch. 14), such that they imbue their model texts with new Flavian meanings. But where van der Schuur locates the successful development of deferred civil war within the borders of Statius's text, Tim Stover (ch. 6) demonstrates how the *Thebaid* can instead retroject an enhanced discourse of civil war back onto a slightly earlier Flavian epic, Valerius's *Argonautica*. Focusing on a single passage of the *Thebaid*, the ecphrastic description of the long-ago creation of Harmonia's necklace, Stover sees Statius as extracting from the *Argonautica* a rarified quintessence of civil war and thereby eliminating any of the earlier epic's ambiguity. Neil Bernstein (ch. 9), meanwhile, proposes not just a reception, but a progressive and developing interaction between Flavian texts that likewise serves to heighten and evoke civil war, adducing a parallel between Silius's Saguntum episode and the duel between Polynices and Eteocles in Statius's *Thebaid* that is most likely a case of "bidirectional" influence between texts that are being composed more or less simultaneously.

In addition to this diversity of models for intertextual reception, we also see a multitude of allusive modes. Bessone (ch. 5), for example, moves us beyond the macro-level of textual interaction to the micro-level of style as she examines how Statius receives a pre-existing symbol-system of tropes, linguistic keywords, and stylistic markers from a wide array of predecessors and adapts them to his own increasingly destabilized and "perverse" poetics of civil war. Alice König (ch. 8) looks at how Frontinus may use the very structure of his exemplary catalogue in allusive ways, allowing his complex system of reference, citation, excerpting, and juxtaposition to evoke for his reader additional historical narratives to the micro- and macro-tales he chooses to tell; and she argues for the availability of such additional narratives for a Flavian audience (just as for a modern critical ear) regardless of authorial intention. And Leo Landrey (ch. 11) demonstrates one way in which history itself can serve as an intertext, showing how Thoas's innovative escape from Lemnos in Valerius's *Argonautica* would recall for its Flavian audience Domitian's similar path as he escaped the burning of the Capitoline during the conflict between Flavian and Vitellian forces; this moment of historical intertextuality then opens up a wider meditation on the traditional role of the Capitoline as guarantor of poetic immortality.

4.2 Traumas of Civil War

The question of whether civil war remains equally problematic for the authors of the Flavian period as it did for those who witnessed the fall of the Republic looms large, as does the perennial question of whether civil war—or any aspect of it—can be viewed as healing and restorative. König (ch. 8) introduces the possibility that, for Frontinus at least, civil war may have been a less conspicuous and troubling part of cultural discourse than modern scholarship assumes; and Fucecchi (ch. 2) argues that even while civil war itself is a negative event, the Flavian epicists variously suggest that its repetitive occurrence results in a stronger Rome that can better withstand future outbreaks. Ray Marks (ch. 3), meanwhile, proposes that Silius shows those who have successfully made it through their own civil strife helping to halt the unchecked spread of civil war abroad. In both of these latter two cases, the experience of civil war is not itself positive but nevertheless helps to mitigate its own future negativity. On the flip side, John Penwill (ch. 4) argues that the continued existence of autocratic and power-hungry individuals ensures the ongoing recurrence of civil war, and that Valerius sees the newly-instantiated Flavian regime as just one temporary break from such perennial strife in a historical trajectory composed of vicissitudes. Darcy Krasne (ch. 17), much like Penwill, sees Valerius as embedding ongoing Roman civil war into Jupiter's Book 1 *Weltenplan* (V. Fl. 1.531–60), and both draw strongly on Lucanean intertexts to facilitate their readings; but where Penwill argues for visible Flavian analogues with Valerius's characters and circumstances, Krasne argues more globally for the poet's construction of an entire cosmos to which such self-directed aggression, inward collapse, and kin-strife are endemic.

4.3 Fragmentation and Restoration

Fragmentation seems to be an inevitable result of civil war's disintegrative impact, but in Flavian literature it likewise butts up against an interest in construction and restoration. Several chapters look both at this process and at the further dialogues that are produced by the resulting juxtaposition of fragments. To begin on the most literal level, two contributors explore Flavian literature's concern with the topographic scars on Rome's landscape and the Flavian program of urban restoration. Landrey (ch. 11) sees in the *Argonautica*'s praise of Hypsipyle a lament for the Capitoline's destruction, a "ghost beneath the text that pulls on its readers' minds"[30] and anticipates yet further need for the restoration and amelioration of civil war's topographic traumas. In a similar vein, Siobhan Chomse (ch. 18) turns our attention to Flavian Rome's most famous topographic landmark: the Colosseum. In her eyes, Martial's commemoration of this structure looks to the ruination of Nero and his Rome and to the *bellum Neronis* which brought the Flavians to power, while simultaneously prefiguring the fragility of the Colosseum as a site of permanence, order, and imperial power.

We also see such concern for fragmentation and restoration on a more metaphorical level within the structures of individual works of literature. Chomse further argues that as Martial engages with the Flavians' stone *monumentum*, he simultaneously constructs his own literary *monumentum* of epigrammatic bricks that in turn range from the (micro)cosmic, containing worlds and multitudes, to the fragmentary, slivers of text torn from Lucan in particular. König (ch. 8) points out the potential for seeing traces of civil war not just within Frontinus's individual *exempla* but also between them, as the organization of his stratagems—each torn individually from the anchoring context of their own narratives—builds up grander structures that replay Rome's history of civil war in piecemeal and unpredictable fashion. Stover (ch. 6) sees Statius as breaking apart Valerius's *Argonautica* to provide individual ingredients for his "witch's brew"[31] of *nefas* (simultaneously Harmonia's necklace and the entire *Thebaid*). Krasne (ch. 17) picks out long-term and permanent loci of civil war and cosmic instability that exist within Jupiter's seemingly stable cosmos, in Valerius's *Argonautica*, arguing that the teleological thrust of humankind within the epic is a cyclical, seemingly inescapable, and ever-expanding progression of civil war that echoes throughout Rome's own *imperium sine fine*. Eleni Manolaraki (ch. 16) argues that Pliny's discussion, in his *Natural History*, of Egyptian flora and fauna and beliefs endeavors to integrate the Roman empire's formerly-diverse parts into a unified and synthesized whole, working against depictions of the empire as a patchwork fabric of dubiously-reconciled adversaries.

4.4 Rome Abroad

Manolaraki sees in Pliny's universalizing approach a goal of reducing the otherness of Egypt, traditionally a site for the externalization of Roman civil war[32] but now the site of Vespasian's assumption of *imperium*; and similar Flavian

---

30 Landrey, p. 236.
31 Stover, p. 110, quoting Chinn 2011, 81.
32 See, e.g., Lowrie 2015.

tendencies to diminish differences between Italy and the rest of the world are likewise explored by other contributors. In Fucecchi's view (ch. 2), the epic poets use universalizing strategies to downplay the uniqueness of civil war as a strictly Roman phenomenon, while in König's reading (ch. 8), such universalizing is the result (perhaps intended, perhaps not) of Frontinus's imbrication in his *Strategemata* of *exempla* drawn indiscriminately from domestic, foreign, and civil wars, from all periods and all places.

König's reading, in turn, directs us to a noticeable blurring between foreign and domestic spheres, over and above a more general tendency to Romanize non-Roman characters through behavior, name, or circumstance. In particular, as though in anticipation of debates over the parameters of "civil war" such as we have surveyed above, Flavian literature problematizes how *bellum ciuile* can even be coherently defined in the wake of 69 CE, when the categories of domestic and foreign, *bellum ciuile* and *bellum externum*, had been disturbed by the year-long war among provincial legions and ethnically diverse auxiliaries culminating with an accession made outside Italy.[33] Accordingly, many of the studies in this volume find slippage or even outright conflation between *bellum internum* and *externum*, as well as complex interrogations of ethnicity. In addition to Frontinus, we have already seen how, in Manolaraki's argument, Pliny the Elder downplays the ethnic Otherness of Egypt while simultaneously refiguring Egypt from a site of *bellum ciuile* in its Republican past to a site of fertile integration with the rest of the Flavian empire. On the other hand, Steve Mason's reading of Josephus (ch. 10) sees the Jewish author as building his people and nation into what we might see as the Flavian era's equivalent of Augustan Egypt—a great and old foreign power that mirrors and matches Rome and also serves as a safe exterior locus onto which to displace war, but that is, at the same time, itself prone to internal conflict. Chomse (ch. 18) explores how Martial's epigrams turn the Colosseum into a staging-ground for Flavian imperialism and world wars, replicating foreign diversity within this bounded Roman space; but these wars, as she shows, also look provocatively to Lucan's text, to civil war, and, in so doing, might recall for their audience the most recent fighting that took place in Rome.

The same discourse of domestic and foreign, Roman and Other, also animates this volume's readings of the *Punica*, which together identify an array of Silian approaches to the familiar strategy of situating anxieties externally, a strategy which William Dominik (ch. 13) labels "geographical distancing."[34] Marks (ch. 3) examines how Silius models his sea-battle between Romans and Syracusans, in

---

[33] This phrase was borrowed from an early draft of Eleni Manolaraki's chapter.
[34] Dominik, p. 273.

Punica 14, on Lucan's episode of foreign conflict within civil war, the sea-battle between Caesar and the Massilians. But Marks finds no one-to-one correspondence between the two sets of Romans and their foreign opponents; rather, Silius capitalizes on Lucan's embedded *bellum externum* to create tensions within ethnic and intertextual identities by modelling his own Romans on Lucan's Massilians, his Syracusans on the troops of Lucan's Caesar. Bernstein (ch. 9) likewise demonstrates that the idea of foreignness can be problematic, showing that distancing strategies can also be externally motivated: as he argues, although the Spanish Saguntum boasts a plethora of ties through kinship and treaty with Rome, it "choose[s] to die in a state of deracination"[35] by symbolically severing its ties with Rome before committing mass suicide, in a contradiction of the dominant discourse between the opponents whose war has occupied it and who see it as one of Rome's many "alter-egos"[36] in the poem. As discussed further below, both Jean-Michel Hulls (ch. 15) and Alison Keith (ch. 14) identify pervasive and complex intersections of gender and ethnicity, inherited from but developed beyond that established in Augustan literature, that serve to displace the Roman experience of civil war onto a series of Others while also complicating Rome's own identity. And moving from the war's fields of battle to its commanders, Claire Stocks (ch. 12) examines how Silius displaces the concept of brotherhood as a site of instability and discord onto the Carthaginian Other, arguing that Silius devotes special attention to Hannibal's relationships with his brothers Mago and Hasdrubal, over and above the more famous fraternal bonds of the Scipios, to articulate domestic, Roman anxieties about brotherly contests, especially between brothers who hold (or aspire to hold) political power.

4.5 Discourses of Gender

This tension and slippage between Roman and Other likewise brings us to a consideration of gendered discourses. As Keith demonstrates (ch. 14), Roman literature since the time of Horace and Vergil was engaged in a complex mapping of civil war onto a gendered system that sought to displace the guilt for discord's recurrence onto the women of Roman society. Moreover, the concomitant rise in public prominence of imperial women and their not-infrequent scandalous ends invited that very gendered system to be negotiated and renegotiated in the literature that would follow. Keith's essay takes us through many core examples of

---

35 Bernstein, p. 182.
36 Dominik, p. 274.

this Flavian expansion in gendering civil war, from the central role of the Furies in all three epic poems to the focus on episodes of discord that threaten the masculine structures of the state. A similar interest in such gendered discourse underpins many of the papers in this volume. Fucecchi (ch. 2) sees Flavian epic's wider focus on feminized violence as part of a Lucanean reception that turns, for example, Argia's traditional female virtue into "a negative pattern originating from the darkest side of the Neronian *Pharsalia*,"[37] (e.g., Erictho). Stover (ch. 6), in his focus on Harmonia's disastrous necklace, points to the role of marriage as a site of and catalyst for discord in the epics of Statius and his predecessor Valerius Flaccus (an observation also made by Keith); using the ecphrasis of the necklace's creation as a starting point, Stover then analyzes how these two epic poets create a "palpable sense of dread at the horrific kin-killing that will be unleashed by the marriage"[38] of Medea, Harmonia, and Argia, in turn. Finally, as Hulls (ch. 15) tackles instances of mass-suicide in two Flavian authors, he notes a gendering of violence and survival. In Silius's Saguntum, the protagonists who catalyze violence are all female (Fides, Tisiphone, Tiburna), but it is almost exclusively men who perpetrate the act of kin-killing; the Saguntine women, moreover, take on masculine attributes as they direct violence against their own bodies. In Josephus's text, suicide and the drive to it is considered the height of *andreia* while survival is depicted as unmanly; but as a woman leads the survivors of the mass-violence to safety, Josephus points to her masculine qualities. Mason (ch. 10) also dwells briefly on Josephus's dialectic of gender in his parallel account of the Roman and Judaean civil wars, which portrays the Flavians as repeatedly overcoming opponents who exhibit a negative femininity and excessive lust for power, luxury, and plunder—although it is notable that whereas such traits are straightforward in their Roman opponents (Vitellius and his men), they are deceptive in the Judaeans (the army of John of Gischala), who combine effeminate lust with a masculine approach to slaughter.

4.6 Origins and Endings

The question of gendered agency in instigating and perpetuating civil war points us to a wider question at the heart of many papers: what are the origins of civil war, and how does it proceed to infect both Romans and others? The fraught question of its endpoint, by contrast, is less frequently confronted head-on (or it

---

[37] Fucecchi, p. 48.
[38] Stover, p. 114.

is seen as unceasing), attention instead being turned, in several chapters, to Flavian authors' different strategies of mitigating the trauma of civil war's ongoing recurrence. Penwill (ch. 4) sees the origin not of civil war itself, but its international spread, as attendant on the voyage of the Argo and her opening of the seas, as evidenced by Jupiter's apostrophe to the goddess Bellona proclaiming a path made for her through the waves (V. Fl. 1.545–46); and through the marital union of the geographically-opposed Thessaly and Colchis, foreign war irrevocably becomes civil war.[39] Krasne (ch. 17), however, in addressing the same poem, reads civil war as innate to both the cosmos itself and the human race that inhabits it. Dominik (ch. 13) argues that Silius situates multiple points of Roman civil war's genesis throughout the events of the Second Punic War, from the defeat at Cannae to the eventual defeat of Hannibal, while also painting the portrait of a *populus Romanus* that already possessed the necessary character to descend into— and welcome—civil strife. Bernstein (ch. 9), Bessone (ch. 5), Keith (ch. 14), Landrey (ch. 11), and van der Schuur (ch. 7) note various instances of the direct divine instigation of civil strife on a more localized level, in a pervasive resurrection and reimagining of Juno and Allecto's instigation of war in the *Aeneid*; among them are Fides and Tisiphone instigating mass suicide at Saguntum in Silius's *Punica*; Fama announcing Polynices' Argive marriage at Thebes in Statius's *Thebaid*; Tisiphone provoking civil war at Thebes in stages throughout *Thebaid* 7; and the efforts of Venus and Fama on Lemnos in Valerius's *Argonautica* (or Venus and the human Polyxo in Statius's recounting of the same events).

Marks (ch. 3) connects a city's internal equilibrium to its ability to triumph (or fail) in foreign war, but also to its leaders' ability to stem civil strife elsewhere: just as civil war spreads from one society to another like a sickness (an image also profitably used by Fucecchi, ch. 2, and parallel to the interpersonal contagion of civil strife explored by Keith, ch. 14),[40] so too can its successful abatement have a ripple-effect. The end of the actual text, in connection with the civil war it contains, also receives some scrutiny: as discussed above, van der Schuur (ch. 7) argues that Statius produces civil war within his text in a fashion that completes the open-ended text of Seneca's *Phoenissae*, while heightening the apparent potential for multiple outcomes within his own text (including the successful aversion of war); and Penwill (ch. 4) situates the potential for endless civil war in the

---

[39] Stover, too, sees the marriage of Jason and Medea as an inceptive moment of "original sin" (p. 115), at least in the refining hands of Statius.

[40] One might be tempted to see a metaphorical parallel for such a spread of civil war in König's suggestion that Frontinus's sporadic groupings of civil war *exempla* result from a sort of mental contagion, as "one civil war story made him think of another" (p. 165).

(seemingly?) endless text of Valerius's *Argonautica*, which is, for him, itself constructed as a recollection of the endless *Bellum Ciuile*.

Attention is also paid to the specific origin of the civil wars of 69 CE, or at least to the *bellum ciuile* waged by Vespasian. Complicating the image of Josephus as a Flavian mouthpiece, Mason (ch. 10) shows how the historian draws unexpected attention to Vespasian's agency and strategy in initiating a new civil war against Vitellius, one which he suggests was driven by personal animosity and ὀργή (a convenient synonym for our well-known *furor*?); at the same time, Josephus offers a counter-narrative to the Flavian foundation-myth of spontaneous acclamation in Alexandria which becomes, in the historian's narrative, another example of shrewd Vespasianic stage-direction. Mason's chapter thus allows us to interrogate the myths of origin promoted by the Flavian dynasty and their attempts to control how the "end" of the civil wars of 69 CE would be remembered.

4.7 The Imperial Family

So, too, several papers tackle Flavian literature's engagement with the imperial family whom these civil wars brought to power. On Mason's reading, Josephus gives us a character-portrait of a Vespasian who is wily, dogged, and distrustful, at times appearing as a foil to Josephus himself. Penwill (ch. 4) views the *Argonautica*'s opening encomium to Vespasian as bringing Rome's new *princeps* into a productive tension with Jason, a man whose quest is driven by an initial drive to avoid civil war and yet who finds himself continually in a Lucanean narrative. Dominik (ch. 13) sees Silius as hinting at the apotheosized Vespasian in his closing divinization of Scipio, with the result that Silius's earlier destabilizations of the positivity of apotheosis, particularly the apotheosis of the "key figure and symbol of civil war,"[41] Julius Caesar, also color the poet's generally-positive images of Vespasian and his dynasty. Moving from Vespasian to his sons, Stocks (ch. 12) views the *Punica*'s focus on brothers-in-arms as responding to a wider imperial iconography of fraternal harmony that was championed by Augustus and rejuvenated by Vespasian in an attempt to solidify power, as well as, more generally, "the complications involved in the combination of family and state";[42] and Keith (ch. 14), too, sees the widespread "displacement of responsibility" for internecine strife in the Flavian epics as reflective of "the Vespasianic family

---

[41] Dominik, p. 292.
[42] Stocks, p. 255.

narrative"[43] that promoted masculinity and the stern *mos maiorum* through legislation and rhetoric. Landrey (ch. 11), meanwhile, as mentioned above, reads into Valerius's Lemnian slaughter a sustained allusion to Domitian's escape from the burning Capitoline, weaving memories of the young Flavian prince into his overtly mythological narrative. But the Flavian *gens* and the civil wars that brought it to power can also be conspicuously ignored, as König (ch. 8) argues of Frontinus's near-total (but not absolute) erasure of contemporary *exempla* from his collection of military stratagems. Indeed, such a resounding silence makes the few exceptions speak all the more loudly, and through their placement and content, they seem to prompt readers to "reflect a little more closely on what it means to be a successful Roman *imperator* ... in the Flavian present,"[44] with all the unexpressed but looming potential of civil war that such a role, by now, inevitably calls to mind.

What emerges from these intersecting but divergent readings is a polyphonous corpus of literature that betrays a pervasive concern for Rome's Flavian future and the civil wars of its recent past. No collection such as the one we offer here could be the final word on the subject of civil war in Flavian literature nor be exhaustive in its coverage; indeed, we anticipate that this volume will raise as many questions as it set out to answer. Through these 17 papers, we aim to foster dialogue and debate while setting the stage for reintegrating the Flavian era into wider discussions of Rome's literature of civil war and for articulating Flavian Rome's particular contribution to that literature.

Lauren Donovan Ginsberg / Darcy A. Krasne

---

43 Keith, p. 320.
44 König, p. 174.

Part I: **Lucanean Lenses**

Marco Fucecchi
Flavian Epic: Roman Ways of Metabolizing a Cultural Nightmare?

The nightmare alluded to in the title is obviously civil war: the original sin, the curse, the ancestral crime (*scelus*) of the Roman people, as it is represented by some of the most important voices of Augustan literature.[1] In fact, when recalling the horrors and tragedies of the recent past, Horace and Vergil mostly display gratitude towards the Princeps who restored peace and morality. Some decades later, under Nero, Lucan's *Pharsalia* brings again to the fore the internecine strife that sanctioned the end of the Republican age, thus reopening deep wounds that the *Aeneid* had left unhealed. Moreover, after the so-called "year of the four Emperors" (69 CE), civil war still proves to be a crucial and topical issue: the Flavian epic revival highlights the pervasiveness of such an archetypal theme of the Roman culture, but it also tries to settle accounts with it.

Vergil's *Aeneid* starts well before Rome's foundation myth (i.e., Romulus's fratricide) and traces the nightmare back to the time of the Trojans and Latins. The notion of civil war is deeply rooted in the conflict between these two seeds from which the Romans will spring (Books 7–12). However it also has a broader reach, such that it even affects the poem's first half. During Troy's final night, Aeneas and his comrades take the shields of their Greek victims and, soon after, become the target of the Trojan defenders: *hic primum ex alto delubri culmine telis* | *nostrorum obruimur oriturque <u>miserrima caedes</u>* | *armorum facie et Graiarum errore iubarum* ("Now's the first time we are crushed by our own side's volleys of missiles launched from the shrine's high roof. It's the start of a pitiful slaughter caused by the misjudged look of our arms, by our helmets with Greek crests,"

This article develops and enhances some ideas in the paper I delivered at the conference *Letture e lettori di Lucano* (University of Salerno, 27–29 March 2012), now published as Fucecchi 2015. Together with the analysis of new passages, I intend to give a more balanced as well as nuanced assessment of complex issues which my current research focuses on.

1 For the notion of Rome's original *scelus* in Augustan poetry, see, e.g., Hor. *Epod.* 7.18, *Carm.* 1.2.29; Verg. *Ecl.* 4.13, *G.* 1.406. See Bessone 2011, 59–60, as well as, in this volume, Bessone (pp. 91, 102–3, 105) and, more specifically on gender relations, Keith (pp. 297–300). By contrast with this Augustan theme, the Republican sources recollected by Wiseman 2010 (Varro, Lucretius, Sallust, and Cicero) display a perception of civil war as a "recent and anomalous phenomenon" (25) that can be traced back no earlier than to the age of the Gracchi.

https://doi.org/10.1515/9783110585841-002

Verg. *A.* 2.410–12).[2] The same pathetic phrase (*miserrima caedes*) occurs only once again in the poem, during the account of the war in Latium when, after Camilla's death, the Italic cavalry is forced to withdraw hastily (Verg. *A.* 11.879–86):

> qui cursu portas primi inrupere patentis,
> hos inimica super mixto premit agmine turba,   880
> nec miseram effugiunt mortem, sed limine in ipso
> moenibus in patriis atque inter tuta domorum
> confixi exspirant animas. pars claudere portas,
> nec sociis aperire uiam nec moenibus audent
> accipere orantis, oriturque miserrima caedes   885
> defendentum armis aditus inque arma ruentum.

> Gates have been opened. The first wave of fugitives bursts within, sprinting, pressed by a raging mob of the foe, mixed in with their own lines. Failing to flee a pathetic death on their very own thresholds: on their homeland's walls or in safe rooms within their own houses. Skewered by spear-thrusts, they gasp out their souls. Some rash individuals slam the gates shut. They don't dare keep escape within city defences open to comrades who plead for admittance. A hideous slaughter follows. The swords that the fugitives rush on are swords of defenders blocking their access.

In both cases, amid the blinding frenzy of war, the defenders of a besieged city are led to desperately engage in battle with their own comrades and, unconsciously, end up helping their enemies: the Trojans wrongly believe that they are fighting against a platoon of the Greek invaders, while the citizens of Laurentum deliberately prevent their own troops from entering the gates of the city, striking them as if they and their pursuers were one and the same thing.

Obviously, Vergil also engages in the *Aeneid* with the implications of the civil war theme for his own time. The *ecphrasis* of the battle of Actium on Aeneas's shield (*A.* 8.675–728), being the most conspicuous foray into the future of the whole poem, finds itself at odds with the two previous examples. Thanks to the ostentatious appropriation of a leitmotif in Augustan propaganda, the internecine struggle for power between Mark Antony and Octavian becomes the final act of a *bellum externum*: next to Romans dressed like Egyptians (Verg. *A.* 8.685), true foreign enemies like Cleopatra now begin to appear, as well as monstrous divinities like Anubis, who fight against the Olympian gods (Verg. *A.* 8.698–708).

---

[2] *miserrima caedes*, "*quia inter ciues*," as Servius *ad loc.* explains. *Error* (confusion, mistake) here stands out as a word-theme: at first, an *error* causes the Greek soldiers to be overpowered by the Trojans; soon after, instead, Aeneas and his comrades become victims of the *error* of their fellow citizens. Translations of the *Aeneid* are from Ahl 2007.

The above passages are representative of the *Aeneid*'s different ways of indirectly approaching and foreshadowing a delicate issue such as civil war, an issue that it almost never tackles explicitly but that constantly flows under its surface.[3] In fact, the way such implications sporadically emerge within the text reveals a twofold strategy. On the one hand, the poet's attempt to exorcize this nightmare seeks to reassure readers, leading them to appreciate the world peace finally achieved by Augustus. At the same time, however, mostly when representing characters as being unaware of the consequences of their actions, Vergil hints at the risk that any war might restlessly shimmer into a civil conflict, leading to a sudden, undesirable setback in the difficult recovery from the disease contracted by Roman society. Intentional or not, the final effect of these suggestions could be considered an ancient acknowledgment of the return of the repressed.[4]

By contrast, Lucan is anything but reticent and indirect. He rewinds the tape and the nightmare happens again in all its cruel reality: his empathic narrative technique erases any epic distance. Making readers relive the "collective suicide," i.e., the collapse of the Roman Republic, is a paradoxical way to problematize the topicality of civil war, which is controversially presented as the hard but necessary premise of political change and the inevitable step towards the instauration of monarchy. Civil war led to the birth of the Empire, just as Jupiter's power was the result of his victory over the Giants.[5] But what do these words imply? Perhaps a poem at war with itself. The traumatic process of constructing an empire inevitably contrasts with the final result, which, despite its magnificence, cannot completely obliterate its origin: the perception of this result will be inevitably influenced by the process itself.

Moreover, Lucan's *Pharsalia* also seems to display a prophetic quality, as an involuntary anticipation of the events of 69 CE: in this sense, it represents a modern, provocative interlocutor for the Flavian epic poems, which constantly deal with this topic at various levels. In fact, Valerius Flaccus, Statius, and Silius draw largely upon this new classic of the epic genre (along with Ovid's *Metamorphoses*) in order to mark their own position within the canon and forestall the reductive

---

3 On the civil war theme (and its ambiguities) in the *Aeneid*, see Giusti 2016, 37–55.
4 Hardie 2016, 14, notes that "repression is a recurrent response in Augustan poetry to the problem of the irrational, but the repressed has a way of returning."
5 *quod si non aliam uenturo fata Neroni | inuenere uiam magnoque aeterna parantur | regna deis caelumque suo seruire Tonanti | non nisi saeuorum potuit post bella gigantum, | iam nihil, o superi, querimur; scelera ipsa nefasque | hac mercede placent* ("But if the Fates could find, to bring forth Nero, no other way, and eternal kingdoms cost gods dearly, nor heaven be slave to its Thunderer unless the savage Giants had lost the wars—by god, we don't complain; those crimes, the guilt, are pleasing at this price," Luc. 1.33–38). Translations of Lucan's *Pharsalia* are from Fox 2012.

label of Vergilian imitators. Unlike Lucan, however, they prefer to look at civil war from a relatively more distant viewpoint, i.e., through the filter of myth or ancient Roman history (earlier than the 1st c. BCE),[6] and tend to embed civil war within a larger context. Such a twofold strategy, which I suggest ultimately aims to neutralize (or even exorcize) the negative force originating from the *Pharsalia* and its explicit provocation, enables these post-Vergilian epicists to position themselves as post-Lucanean voices as well.

In Flavian epic poetry, civil war is still represented as a tragic phenomenon constantly affecting human societies in different ages and contexts, an almost inevitable step in the process of their socio-political growth.[7] However, it always looks framed, almost relativized, by other events; it is, in effect, finally overcome so as to prevent readers from thinking that it is a definitive and inescapable end, after which there is no tomorrow. This seems to apply to the *Thebaid* in particular, where—after eleven books dominated by the forces of evil (with only rare, though illuminating, examples of humanity and virtue)—the epilogue stages Theseus's restoration of moral order (*pietas*, *fides*, etc.) in Thebes, dramatizing the final victory of epic over tragedy. But the same could be probably said of Silius's and Valerius's epic narratives, where civil war is not expected to have a programmatic function. Scipio's final triumph in the *Punica* sanctions Carthage's defeat as well as the (only temporary) end of the internal discord that is already emerging in Rome. The seed of future internecine strife, displayed by the rivalry between the consuls, has also caused the disaster of Cannae, i.e., the worst defeat suffered by Rome during the Second Punic War. However, this tragic event, situated at the very center of Silius's poem, is endowed with the underlying meaning of a collective *deuotio*, a sacrifice that paves the way to the final victory.

For his part, Valerius Flaccus's Jason, a young apprentice-leader, chooses not to stir up an internal revolt against his uncle Pelias and instead accepts the mission imposed by the Thessalian tyrant. Once arrived in Colchis, he is involved in a fratricidal contest between the king Aeetes and his brother Perses. Without actually affecting the traditional plot,[8] this unprecedented war provides a new setting for Medea's falling in love with the Greek hero. The latter accomplishes his task (the conquest of the Golden Fleece) by taking advantage of the gods' support, as is usually the case in epic poetry. Nonetheless, Jason also relies upon his

---

[6] See, e.g., Marks 2010b and Dominik in this volume.
[7] See, in particular, the chapters by Keith and Dominik in this volume.
[8] The king of Colchis will not keep his promise to give Jason the Golden Fleece, and in Book 7, the Greek hero will still have to deal with Aeetes' monsters, just as in Apollonius's poem.

own human qualities: strength and heroic prowess, but also firmness, self-sacrifice, sagacity, and diplomatic wisdom.

To sum up: after Lucan (and after the crisis of 69 CE leading to the advent of the Flavian dynasty), civil war positions itself as a constant presence in epic poetry, which is also symptomatic of the need to "metabolize," in my terminology, this nightmare of Roman history and culture.

Even so, Flavian epic's revival is not characterized by nostalgia, nor is it only interested in rediscovering the "better past." The act itself of distancing civil war from the immediate present does not imply neutralizing the apocalyptic consequences of the *Pharsalia* nor envisaging a totally unproblematic future. On the contrary, the Flavian epicists take into due account Lucan's delegitimization of the Augustan myths as well as his way of giving voice to doubts and obsessions that undermine the ideology of the *Aeneid*. In fact, these "belated" poets often warn of the risk of relapsing into that notorious nightmare, foregrounding at the same time the cohesive role played by moral values (and exemplified by the behavior of paradigmatic leaders) as a deterrent to the collapse of society.

In this chapter, I illustrate some aspects of the earliest reception of the *Pharsalia* to show how the epic poems of the late 1st c. CE—while paying homage to Vergil's authority—actually seem to go well beyond him (and, to some extent, beyond Augustus as well) by responding to some issues raised by Lucan.[9] The way in which the Flavian epicists look at Lucan as the new counterclassical model of the Neronian age shows to what extent they aim to both assert their own primacy in the genre as well as indirectly celebrate the advent of a new age and a new ruling dynasty. For this purpose, instead of surveying the presence of (Lucanean-style) civil war in Flavian epic, it will be even more useful to see how Silius, Valerius, and Statius respectively react to the numerous tangential allusions to their own subject matter that are scattered throughout their Neronian model. The manifold ways in which they incorporate and even "correct" Lucan's references to the Second Punic War and to the Argonautic and Theban myths represent important indirect responses to the *Pharsalia* and its irredeemable darkness. Once exploited in order to contest the primacy of the (more reticent) *Aeneid*, the corrosive potential of civil war as an epic theme looks as though it has been finally absorbed and even framed into new constructions aimed at inverting Lucan's negative polarity. After surviving the last civil war of 69 CE, the Flavian epicists may perhaps feel authorized in approaching the *Pharsalia* from this inclusive and corrective viewpoint.

---

[9] Like Ovid (to quote the words used by Barchiesi 2001), Lucan too proves to be a "mighty source of alternative energy" for the Flavian epicists, a source whose potential they can exploit to (partially) redeem themselves from their own belatedness (see also Hershkowitz 1998b).

1 Silius and Lucan: Cannae (and Pharsalus)

In Silius's *Punica*, the interaction between Vergilian and Lucanean models brings about the coexistence of Republican nostalgia, in particular the longing for the ancient virtues that made Rome stronger and bigger, together with an awareness of the difficult evolution of the state, characterized by an alternating sequence of light and dark: the traumatic age of civil war ended by Augustus's advent and the consequent period of peace; the crisis of the Julio-Claudian dynasty, with its autocratic developments modelled upon Oriental-style despotism; and finally, the ascent of the Flavian emperors with the restoration of peace, morality and order. Neronian epic, in particular, appears to be most directly responsible for Silius's peculiar interest in the theme of internecine strife, which retroactively affects the treatment of the second war against Carthage, providing the narrative with a "threatening subplot."[10]

The Cannae episode represents perhaps the most relevant example or, even better, the structural hub of this strategy. The account of the tragic Roman defeat occupies the core of the poem's architecture, i.e., Books 8 to 10. This stands in sharp contrast with the distribution of narrative material in Livy's third decade, where the year 216 BCE, culminating in the battle of Cannae, covers the second half of Book 22. In situating the Cannae episode halfway through his *Punica*, Silius is probably alluding to Ennius's *Annales*,[11] in which that battle also lies at the center of the poem's structure. From a slightly different viewpoint, however, the Flavian author may also be responding to the "provocative" centrality that Lucan attributes to the battle of Pharsalus: a centrality through which the Neronian poem—with its antagonistic emulative gesture—may have challenged the architecture of Ennius's historical epic itself.

In fact, Silius's triad of books devoted to Cannae features a large number of allusions which embrace the whole complex of Lucan's *Pharsalia*.[12] However,

---

10 See Dominik in this volume.
11 Ennius seems to have included the account of Cannae in his Book 8, i.e., at the core of the central triad (Books 7–9) devoted to the Second Punic war in the poem's first edition of fifteen books. See Skutsch 1985, 366; Fucecchi 2006b, 313 n. 12.
12 The debt of Silius's Cannae episode towards Lucan's *Pharsalia* starts from the outset of the latter: e.g., the whole prophetic section containing the negative omens as well as the words of the soldier announcing Rome's defeat (Sil. 8.622–76) joins together the series of prodigies in Luc. 1.522–83 and the prophecy of the frenzied *matrona* (Luc. 1.673–95) to finally reach the eve of the battle at Pharsalus (7.151–84): see Marks 2010a, 135. More generally, about the problematic relationship between Lucan's civil war and some episodes of Silius's *Punica* (respectively the fall

there is a particularly strong relationship with Lucan's account of Pharsalus in Book 7, both in terms of the overall episode as well as in terms of numerous affinities between the main characters. The "Roman Hannibal"[13] and Caesar share the same outrageous confidence in victory, which serves to stir up the warlike fury of their soldiers. Compare, for example, Caesar's exhortation to his troops (*uos tamen hoc oro, iuuenes, ne caedere quisquam | hostis terga uelit: ciuis qui fugerit esto. | sed, dum tela micant, non uos pietatis imago ulla nec aduersa conspecti fronte parentes | commoueant*, "But I implore you, men, don't cut down any enemy in the back! Whoever flees, count him your fellow citizen. But as long as weapons flash, don't let any shadow of piety move you, not even if you see your father in the enemy's front ranks," Luc. 7.318–22) with Hannibal's to his allies (*dextram Ausonia si caede cruentam | attolles, hinc iam ciuis Carthaginis esto*, "if any of you lift up a hand red with Roman blood, he shall be henceforth a citizen of Carthage," Sil. 9.210–11).[14] Then, after the battle, the leaders both walk across the battlefield looking proudly at the spectacle of the carnage (*iuuat Emathiam non cernere terram | et lustrare oculis campos sub clade latentes*, "[Caesar] likes that he can't see Emathia's ground and that his eyes take stock of fields hidden beneath a massacre," Luc. 7.794–95; cf. *lustrabat campos et saeuae tristia dextrae | facta recensebat pertractans uulnera uisu*, "[Hannibal] was riding over the battlefield, reviewing his dreadful handiwork and feasting his eyes upon wounds," Sil. 10.450–51). Another important affinity ties the Roman consuls at Cannae, Paulus and Varro, to the strange couple formed by Pompey and Cicero. In both cases the resigned voice of good sense (that of Pompey and Paulus, respectively) is inevitably condemned to be overpowered by demagogic folly, while readers begin to understand the ruinous consequences of internecine contest.[15]

However, what does the overlap of the two tragic episodes actually mean for Silius? Are we to believe that the battle of Cannae is implicitly to be considered a

---

of Saguntum and the conquest of Syracuse by Marcellus), see Bernstein, Marks, and Dominik in this volume.

13 The title of Claire Stocks's recent monograph (Stocks 2014) enables me both to point to the "Caesarian" (i.e., Lucanean) character of Silius's Hannibal (this is mostly true until his victory at Cannae at least, but see also Sil. 17.605–15) and to refer to the "Hannibalic" trait Lucan injects into his Caesar so as to present him as the perfect heir to Rome's worst enemy.

14 Translations of Silius's *Punica* are from Duff 1934.

15 See especially Cicero's words (Luc. 7.62–85) and Varro's reported speech (Sil. 9.1–7; cf. also Liv. 22.43–44). Furthermore, we should not forget the chain of internecine murders between father and sons in the episode of Satricus, Solymus, and Mancinus that immediately precedes the battle (Sil. 9.66–177 with Fucecchi 1999). In general, for the interrelation between Lucan and Silius, see Meyer 1924, Brouwers 1982, and Marks 2010a.

proleptic announcement of the crisis leading to Pharsalus (and Philippi)? This is probably true, but—in my view at least—it is only one side of the issue. The fact that such a tragic event suggests and effectively introduces the seeds of civil strife—resulting in the dispute between the two consuls—does not reflect its full meaning. The Roman defeat at Cannae also has to provide the example of a paradigmatic sacrifice, a kind of collective *deuotio*, which—while sanctioning the symbolic martyrdom of the heroic Paulus—ends up absolving Varro himself and his irrational conduct. In fact, the painful episode culminates in a celebration of the recovered harmony within the social body: when coming back to Rome—like a helmsman who survived a shipwreck, while the crew perished (Sil. 10.608–12)— Varro receives solidarity from the Senate, led by Fabius Maximus *Cunctator*, and the Roman people, and he is restored to his place within the community. Thus, Cannae's defeat proves to have produced (almost immediately) the necessary "antibodies" that will lead Rome to the final victory against the Carthaginians and enable her to face the difficult trials of both the near and distant future.[16]

Roman culture had long since begun the "sanctification" of that terrible carnage: from Polybius (6.58) to Cicero (*Off.* 3.47) to the resigned voice of Horace's Hannibal (*Carm.* 4.4.61–76). Silius goes even a step further: such an extreme sacrifice, as a κτῆμα ἐς αἰεί, will sanction Rome's dignity to gain world primacy in the future. This concept emerges for the first time in Jupiter's words to Venus (Sil. 3.584–90), where the name of Paulus features with those of Marcellus and Fabius in the series of heroes who are to make Rome "more glorious for her calamities" (*nobilior ... malis*, Sil. 3.584). These heroes, "by their defeats (*per uulnera*), will gain for Latium an empire so great, that their descendants will be unable to overthrow it, for all their luxury and degenerate hearts" (*hi tantum parient Latio per uulnera regnum, | quod luxu et multum mutata mente nepotes | non tamen euertisse queant*, Sil. 3.588–90).[17]

Thereafter, the same motif will resonate twice at Cannae. At the core of the event (Sil. 9.346ff.), the narrator invites Rome to "bless those wounds" (*adora uulnera*, Sil. 9.350) which will forever bring her glory: "For never shalt thou be greater than then" (*nam tempore, Roma, | nullo maior eris*, Sil. 9.351–52).[18] Then, at the end of the central triad of books, he comments on the first signs of Rome's

---

[16] For an opposing view, see Dominik in this volume.
[17] Cf. Verg. *A.* 12.435–36 (Aeneas to Ascanius): *disce, puer, uirtutem ex me uerumque laborem, | fortunam ex aliis* ("learn from me, lad, what courage involves and the meaning of effort. Others can teach you of Fortune"). Troy's destruction is the prerequisite for a great future (Aeneas is a "patient" hero, the hero of grief).
[18] "Later victories"—the voice continues—"shall sap thy strength, till naught but the story of thy defeats (*sola cladum ... fama*) shall preserve thy fame" (Sil. 9.353).

rebirth: troops made up of child soldiers and deserters condemned to undergo forced military service in Sicily (*haec tum Roma fuit. post te cui uertere mores | si stabat fatis, potius, Carthago, maneres*, "such was Rome in those days; and, if it was fated that the Roman character should change when Carthage fell, would that Carthage were still standing!" Sil. 10.657–58). This is both a challenging and celebratory claim. In fact, Carthage will definitively fall, and the victorious Rome, too, will understand the unpleasant meaning of moral decline. However, the tragic experience of Cannae has taught the Romans how to suffer and learn from their mistakes so as to raise their heads again: this is also a way of showing to what extent the *Punica* highlights the worst Roman defeat ever, both as the principal reason for the victory over Carthage and as the fundamental premise of a great future. The heroic expiatory sacrifice performed by a single leader (Paulus) stands out as a paradigm for both the troops and the generations to follow. Grief and pain are the necessary preconditions for apotheosis: this is true for the Second Punic War as well as the remainder of Roman history, afflicted by the disease of civil war.

At the same time, such an encomiastic paradox, which invites us to look at Cannae's tragic carnage as the first step of Rome's resurrection, is a typically Flavian way of reacting to Lucan's provocative rereading of this military disaster in merely consolatory terms. At the beginning of *Pharsalia* Book 2, while marching to the theater of civil war between Marius and Sulla, the respective troops address their just complaint to the cruel gods: *o miserae sortis, quod non in Punica nati | tempora Cannarum fuimus Trebiaeque iuuentus* ("What a pitiful lot to not be born in the times of the Punic Wars, to fight at Cannae and Trebia!" Luc. 2.45–46). Drawing upon Aeneas's *makarismos* of the fallen at Troy in Vergil,[19] the Roman soldiers lament being condemned to fight in a war where glory has no place and death itself is meaningless. It would be better to satiate the ghost of Hannibal and its thirst for posthumous vengeance, as the narrator will explicitly say when commenting on Curio's defeat in Africa.[20] Accordingly, from Lucan's perspective,

---

[19] *o terque quaterque beati, | quis ante ora patrum Troiae sub moenibus altis | contigit oppetere!* ("Greater by three, even four times, the blessing chance gave those with the fortune to die beneath Troy's mighty ramparts under their fathers' gaze!" Verg. A. 1.94–96). It is worth noticing that Aeneas pronounces these words during "the archetypal episode of an outbreak of *furor* suppressed," as Hardie 2016, 4–5, defines the storm scene which opens the *Aeneid*.

[20] *excitet inuisas dirae Carthaginis umbras | inferiis fortuna nouis, ferat ista cruentis | Hannibal et Poeni tam dira piacula manes. | Romanam, superi, Libyca tellure ruinam | Pompeio prodesse nefas uotisque senatus. | Africa nos potius uincat sibi* ("Fortune, wake the spiteful ghosts of fallen Carthage for these grim new sacrifices! May they appease cruel Hannibal and the Punic shades!

even the tragic Roman defeat at Cannae is a relatively positive counterpart to the slaughter of civil war, as it represents a better way to die: a noble, even glorious sacrifice whose meaning, however, is confined to the narrow, sterile sphere of lament. If Cannae can no longer be conceived of as the nadir of Roman history, it is only because the following tragedy of civil war—whose climactic point is represented by the battle of Pharsalus—shows that there is much worse.

For Silius, too, Cannae is a synonym of civic tragedy: the rivalry between the two consuls, Paulus and Varro, provides a first eloquent example of the consequences of internal discord. Yet the unlucky battle is neither the beginning of the end for Rome nor only to be evoked as a (paradoxical) consolatory term of reference. As a collective *deuotio*, Cannae will open up the road to the *Urbs*'s rejuvenation. By making Rome's worst defeat both the perturbing signal of the imminent crisis and the greatest victory of the Roman spirit of self-sacrifice, the *Punica* invites readers to look more confidently at the future. As the first manifestation of the dangerous disease which will nearly destroy the body of the state, Cannae undoubtedly anticipates Pharsalus (together with the succession fights of 69 CE). However, after tracing the nightmare of civil war back to the more glorious period of Republican history (and thus expanding the "negative" influence of the Neronian *Pharsalia*), the *Punica* also shows that it still is possible to rise up again. Thanks to this Flavian resemiotization, Cannae's defeat provides the antidote which will allow Rome to survive the civil wars of the future, even those that Lucan could not forecast.

2 Geographical Explorations and Political Expansion: the Argonautic Alternative to Civil War

Valerius Flaccus's *Argonautica*, probably the earliest among the Flavian epic poems,[21] takes us from Republican history to the most ancient Greek myth and once again raises the problem of its later reception and interpretation. The primacy of the Apollonian version of the Argonautic saga was contested in Rome by the time of Catullus 64, if not earlier.[22] In the early Imperial Age, Valerius Flaccus's poem

---

Gods above, what a sin to make Libyan soil the site of a Roman ruin, for Pompey, to serve the Senate's will. Instead, let Africa conquer us for herself," Luc. 4.788–93).

21 Stover 2012.
22 Before Catullus (64.11), the Argo seems to have been already presented as the "first ship" in the *Argonautica* of Varro Atacinus (Ov. *Am.* 1.15.21–22).

plays an important role in that contest: not only because it shares with Catullus the emphasis given to the Argo as the first ship (which is typical of the Roman poetic tradition), but also because it grants unusually ample space to war, and civil war in particular. At the outset of the heroic age, fratricidal strife for power already appears as an endemic phenomenon, encompassing the whole world (which is still a non-Roman world): from Thessaly, the western starting point of this myth, to Colchis in the far east. The voyage of the Argo links these two extreme poles, where civil war is constantly about to happen (e.g., in Greece, where Jason decides, however, not to settle accounts with Pelias immediately) or is actually taking place (when Jason lands in Colchis, Perses has already launched his attack on Aeetes' kingdom). Thus the Flavian poet almost provides a mythical background for Lucan's claustrophobic image of the future world invaded and torn by (Roman) civil war.

If great emphasis is laid upon the opening of the seas as the primeval factor of war's diffusion throughout the world according to Jupiter's plan (*uia facta per undas | perque hiemes, Bellona, tibi*, "for you, Bellona, has a path been fashioned through the billows and through storms," V. Fl. 1.545–46),[23] we need to say that Valerius's remarkable interest in this topic does not fundamentally destabilize the traditional Argonautic plot, at least so far as we can tell from the state of tradition.[24] The narrative representation of the Colchian war in Book 6 is probably the most impressive result of the poet's engagement in reshaping the saga, and (as in Silius's *Punica*) it may be considered a tribute to Lucan's poem, which challenges the "inclusive" ambitions of the new Flavian epics. Within such a context, Jason has more opportunities to display his heroic stature, which is undeniably enhanced in comparison with his Apollonian *alter ego*.[25] However, the Colchian (fratricidal) war does no more than cause a delay and produces only indirect, though not negligible, consequences.[26] Medea enters the narrative as a pivotal character who will again play a decisive role. Such an element ends up reducing the distance between the old and the new Jason: thus, as is the case for the

---

[23] Translations of Valerius's *Argonautica* are from Mozley 1934.
[24] For a good assessment of the unfinished (rather than incomplete) state of Valerius's *Argonautica*, see Hershkowitz 1998b, 1–35.
[25] Hershkowitz 1998b; Stover 2012. Cf. Hunter 1993a and Clauss 1993 on Apollonius's Jason.
[26] At 6.427–54 Juno's intervention sanctions the inefficacy of war as way of resolving the impasse and leaves room for a fundamental change: Medea's involvement in the action. More specifically on civil war in Valerius's *Argonautica* (as well as its ensuing engagement with Lucan's poem), see Buckley 2010 and the chapters by Keith, Krasne, Landrey, Penwill, and Stover in this volume.

Hellenistic model, the Flavian *Argonautica* will also have to deal with the task of defining the character of the epic hero and his set of qualities.

Apollonius's poem was more centered on the opposition between two types of leadership, respectively embodied by Heracles, the champion of archaic, individual, and old-fashioned heroism, and Jason, portrayed as a modern exemplary hero. The Flavian remake of the Greek myth still presupposes such a difference, but it rather stages a dialectic negotiation between these two patterns. The result of this negotiation is inevitably influenced by the distinctive set of Roman or, rather, quintessentially Flavian values. From the outset, Valerius's Jason is credited with a great reputation for his virtue, which is a major source of concern for his uncle Pelias.[27] The young son of Aeson stands as the first exponent of a new generation of post-Herculean (rather than merely anti-Herculean) heroes who exploit their human qualities to the limits, without relying upon superhuman powers or miraculous devices of divine origin.[28] More explicitly than in Apollonius, this Flavian Jason expects to be involved in warfare (i.e., a war in an unknown land, against a foreign enemy), and eventually he will be, like the Vergilian Aeneas, although in an unpredictable way. As a consequence, the protagonist of Valerius's *Argonautica* represents the example of a "collective" leader who slightly differs from his Greek counterpart: he rather recalls the traditional figure of the *dux*, with whom Roman readers were quite familiar. The new hero displays both individual and public virtues, such as prowess, on the one hand, and diligent, assiduous activity (*industria*), firmness and self-sacrifice (*constantia*), and practical understanding and sagacity (*prudentia*) on the other.

Valerius's Jason has to face delicate situations and choices which call for a high sense of responsibility, great strength, diplomatic wisdom, and even the ability to deal with danger verging on recklessness. Such a difficult path starts

---

27 *sed non ulla quies animo fratrisque pauenti | progeniem diuumque minas. hunc nam fore regi | exitio uatesque canunt pecudumque per aras | terrifici monitus iterant; super ipsius ingens | instat fama uiri uirtusque haud laeta tyranno* ("yet had his mind no rest, through dread of his brother's offspring and the threats of heaven; for the soothsayers foretold that through him destruction should come upon the king, and the victims at the altar repeated their fearful warnings: moreover, above all the great renown of the hero himself weighed upon his mind, and prowess never welcome to a tyrant," V. Fl. 1.26–30).
28 Such a fundamental concept is already mirrored by Jason's first reaction when Pelias orders him to undertake the voyage: *nunc aerii plantaria uellet | Perseos aut currus et quos frenasse dracones | creditus, ignaras Cereris qui uomere terras | imbuit et flaua quercum damnauit arista* ("had he but Perseus' winged sandals now or the car and the fabled teams of dragons of him who first set the mark of the ploughshares upon lands that knew not Ceres, and preferred the golden ear to the acorn," V. Fl. 1.67–70).

the moment he receives Pelias's order. Before venturing into the unknown sea, the Flavian hero, unlike his Apollonian counterpart, already shows how to live under a tyrant. While perfectly understanding Pelias's rage and his dissimulated intention (V. Fl. 1.64–66),[29] Jason is said to immediately reject the idea of stirring up a revolt against his uncle and, displaying confidence in divine support, decides to face the challenge imposed (*heu quid agat? populumne leuem ueterique tyranno | infensum atque olim miserantes Aesona patres | aduocet*, "alas! what is he to do? shall he summon to his aid a fickle populace, already girding at their aged lord, and the elders that long since have pitied Aeson?" V. Fl. 1.71–73; cf. *tandem animi incertum confusaque pectora firmat | religio*, "at last, his trust in heaven gives strength to his doubting, troubled heart," V. Fl. 79–80).[30]

By undertaking the sea voyage, Jason rejects the idea of rebelling against the tyrant in order to defend his own rights. Thus he accepts the mantle of his heroic duties, which includes the leadership of a dangerous, collective enterprise. This does not only mean giving up his personal political ambitions for the moment. When leaving his homeland, Jason abandons his beloved parents to the tyrant's rage: in so doing, he also leaves the moral responsibility for internecine hatred and slaughter entirely to his uncle Pelias, as suggested by the words the ghost of Cretheus addresses to Aeson (*sed tibi triste nefas fraternaque turbidus arma | rex parat et saeuas irarum concipit ignes*, "but against thee the violent king prepared a deadly crime and arms, brother against brother, and is nursing the fierce fires of his passion," V. Fl. 1.747–48).

Jason's instinctive enthusiasm for glory (V. Fl. 1.76ff.) tempers the bitterness of Pelias's order and actually contributes to relativizing risks and consequences of embarking upon the adventure over the seas.[31] At the start, none other than Hercules can be Jason's term of reference with regard to heroism, in that the younger character aims to follow in the footsteps of his greater model, displaying strength and self-sacrifice.[32] After leaving aside the prospect of civil strife, the

---

[29] See Hershkowitz 1998b, 246–47.
[30] See Ripoll 1998, 203–4, and Zissos 2008, 123 *ad* 1.71–73.
[31] In fact, Jason never fails to display his concerns, which will lead him to plan his revenge against Pelias: to take his son, Acastus, aboard the Argo and make him participate in that dangerous expedition (see V. Fl. 1.150ff.). See also Jason's worried invocation to the sea gods, which aims to avert their rage from his enterprise (V. Fl. 1.194–202).
[32] After all, Jason's (apparently awkward) way of thinking about his parents' safety when it is too late and they are abandoned to Pelias's mercy (V. Fl. 1.693ff.) may be construed, to some extent, as a "Herculean" feature: in fact, as Seneca's *Hercules Furens* shows, when Hercules sets out to accomplish the last of his labors, he leaves his wife Megara with their sons and his father

commander of the Argo feels as if he is about to undertake a Herculean (though not individual) endeavor that will bestow eternal fame upon him. Therefore, his first public act as leader—just after fulfilling his religious tasks (i.e., praying to Neptune and taking auspices and prophecies)—is to announce that he is leaving Thessaly with confidence, since he has the gods on his side; he is listening to Jupiter's voice and not that of a perfidious tyrant, like Pelias (or Eurystheus) (V. Fl. 1.244–47):

> non mihi Thessalici pietas culpanda tyranni
> suspectiue doli: deus haec, deus omine dextro   245
> imperat; ipse suo uoluit commercia mundo
> Iuppiter et tantos hominum miscere labores.

> Not mine is it to blame the Thessalian tyrant for the honour he doth his kin, or his suspected wiles; it is the god, the god that by this fair omen enjoins this on us; Jupiter himself hath willed the fellowship of men throughout his world, and their union in such mighty tasks.

Indeed, as Jupiter's plan well explains (V. Fl. 1.531–60, 563–67), the Argonautic mission is part of a divine project, which aims to favor the shifting of world power from Asia to Greece as well as to test a new model of leadership.[33] Jason is called upon to embody the prototype of a young multifaceted leader, combining traditional heroic values with *savoir-faire*, discretion, diplomatic skills, and even dissimulation, not to mention problem-solving.[34]

As mentioned earlier, Jason is not interested in taking immediate revenge upon Pelias or in fighting against him. However, by involving the tyrant's son Acastus in the expedition, the leader of the Argonauts intends to exact partial revenge on his uncle and make him share the same concerns Aeson and Alcimede have (V. Fl. 1.154–55).[35] While standing before Acastus, Jason delivers an adulatory speech, which aims at gratifying his interlocutor's self-pride and enthusiasm

---

Amphitryon to Lycus's mercy. Unlike Hercules, however, Jason assumes command over the whole crew, with its burden of responsibilities.

[33] For the recurrent theme of the succession of empires, starting from the beginning of Herodotus's *Histories*, see also Plb. 29.21 (quoting Demetrios of Phaleron); D.S. 2.24ff.; Just. *Epit*. 1.3.5–6 (= Pompeius Trogus); D.H. 1.2–4.1. On the Jovian program, see Stover 2012, 28–30.

[34] The set of "diplomatic skills" appears quite early in Latin literature as a key feature in the depiction of the military and political Roman leader. This may also recall Ennius's portrait of the "good companion" (*Ann*. 268–86): "humanities" are implicated in the construction of a new (cultivated) model of leader.

[35] We should not forget that Jason's wish is accompanied by a positive *augurium* directly stemming from Jupiter (V. Fl. 1.156–60).

through honorable (though improbable) comparisons with heroes of a "superior" category, like Telamon or the Dioscuri (V. Fl. 1.164–67):

> ... non degeneres, ut reris, Acaste,
> uenimus ad questus: socium te iungere coeptis   165
> est animus neque enim Telamon aut Canthus et Idas
> Tyndareusque puer mihi uellere dignior Helles.

'Nay, Acastus,' says the leader, 'I am not come, as thou deemest, to utter ignoble plaints; I am minded to make thee partner of our enterprise; I hold not Telamon nor Canthus nor Idas nor Tyndareus' son more worthy than thou art to seek the fleece of Helle'.

Such a malicious approach, by means of Jason's invitation to Acastus to share burdens and honors with him (*socium te iungere coeptis*), finds a sort of natural complement in the last part of Jason's speech, in which the hero anticipates the glorious return of the Argo and puts before Acastus's eyes the image of himself feeling regret for not taking part in the enterprise (V. Fl. 1.170–73):

> nunc forsan graue reris opus, sed laeta recurret   170
> cum ratis et caram cum iam mihi reddet Iolcon,
> quis pudor heu nostros tibi tunc audire labores,
> quae referam uisas tua per suspiria gentes!

At this time perchance thou thinkest the labor too heavy: yet when the vessel shall speed joyfully home, and give me back my loved Iolcos, ah! how shalt thou sigh as I tell of all the nations we have seen!

The two-verse exclamation at 1.172–73, situated at the very close of the speech in sharp relief, represents the climactic point of Jason's previous exhortation (V. Fl. 1.168–69):

> o quantum terrae, quantum cognoscere caeli
> permissum est, pelagus quantos aperimus in usus!

Lo! what mighty tracts of land, what vast expanse of sky it is granted us to know! To what great ends are we opening the paths of the sea!

The voyage of the Argo will literally open up a world: this is the most important goal attained by Jason and his companions alongside the conquest of the Golden Fleece, which represents the official aim of the expedition ordered by Pelias. The boastful tenor of Jason's words is prompted by a tendentiously persuasive strategy: while trying to gain his interlocutor's trust, Jason aims first to obtain a "safe-conduct" as well as a first revenge on Pelias.[36] However, the leader of the Argonauts also seems to be aware (perhaps to a higher degree than Pelias himself) of the potential implications of his undertaking: Jason's attitude looks like a form of progressivism in a broader cultural sense (i.e., enhancement of geo-ethnographical knowledge), but also proves to be tinged with political imperialism. Such a behavior certainly aims at stirring up Acastus's thirst for glory, but it also reflects Jason's own expectations. As I have been arguing, this image conveniently adheres to heroic ethics as well as to the plan Jupiter will soon enunciate; moreover, it sounds like an indirect confirmation of Jason's wise, as well as diplomatic, choice not to pursue immediate vengeance through civil war.

Some years ago, Andrew Zissos[37] convincingly showed that such a display of self-confidence echoes a typically imperial propaganda motif, which was already employed by Lucan at the beginning of the *Pharsalia*: *heu, quantum terrae potuit pelagique parari | hoc quem ciuiles hauserunt sanguine dextrae* ("Oh, how much of earth and sea might have been gained with all the blood our citizens' hands have drained," Luc. 1.13–14). In fact, Jason does not explicitly speak of conquering lands and seas but euphemistically alludes to the opening of vast horizons for human knowledge, as is well demonstrated by the presence of *cognoscere* instead of *parari*, together with the addition of *quantum caeli*. Yet, it is difficult to resist the idea that this Flavian Latin heir of the ancient Greek hero—who is rejecting the option of civil strife to embark upon a dangerous heroic adventure—is giving voice, for the first time and from the mythical past, to the imperialistic alternative of expansion and conquest, which the disenchanted narrator of Lucan's poem bitterly pointed out as a neglected target in the final years of the Roman Republic.

Zissos rightly remarks that the Lucanean echo throws a dark shadow over Jason's proud boast: when undergoing Pelias's orders, the commander of the Argo still does not know that, once in Colchis, he will be involved in civil strife. Yet I am not comfortable with the idea that Jason's words should be entirely destabilized by irony, nor would I read Valerius's allusion as an implicit endorsement of the pessimism displayed by the narrating voice of the *Pharsalia*. Rather, I would take a step further and consider the possibility that, although his principal aim is to take the tyrant's son with him on board the first ship, the young commander of the Argonauts, as a new (pre-Roman) model of a "collective" leader, is also sharing his own dream with Acastus. Admittedly, Valerius depicts

---

36 See also Jason's "triumphant" satisfaction when Acastus appears right before the Argo leaves the shore (*ductor ouans laetusque dolis agnoscit Acastum*, V. Fl. 1.485).
37 Zissos 2004a, who follows in the footsteps of Pollini 1984.

Jason as being engaged in dissimulation, but we should not fail to observe a fundamental difference with the egotistic attitude of Pelias the tyrant: the young hero also seems to display sincere enthusiasm for the prospect of writing, with the help of the gods, the foundational myth of (imperial) expansionism; a myth whose necessary premises are the provisional renunciation of personal ambitions and vengeance in his own homeland, the consequent rejection of internecine feuds and the ambition to attain glory by reaching new fields of conquest. Thus, from the remote past, Jason also seems to give a positive and Flavian answer to Lucan's pessimism.

In Colchis, Jason and his comrades come across the civil war for power between King Aeetes and his brother Perses and actually become involved in it. Aeetes manipulates Jason's will by promising to give back the Fleece if the Argonauts help him to defeat his enemy. Although reluctantly, the Greek hero accepts the proposal of a tyrant once again and takes Aeetes' side in order to achieve his own goal. While doing so, he displays metaliterary awareness of the unprecedented nature of the war which he is embarking upon, as well as its character of quasi-Herculean labor (V. Fl. 5.542–45):

> 'ergo nec hic nostris derat labor arduus actis'
> excipit Aesonides 'et ceu nihil aequore passis
> additus iste dies? ueniant super haec quoque fato
> bella meo?'   545

> 'This hard task also then was among our destined deeds,' Jason begins, 'and as though we had suffered naught upon the sea this day is set thereto. Let then this war too be added to my fate.'

We cannot say if Jason, in this circumstance, still believes in divine support or not. He seems to rather rely upon his own heroic firmness and sense of duty. Be that as it may, the gods are actually guiding the hero's choice: an apparently awkward choice, but legitimized by Juno's explicit statement to Minerva that the Argonauts' aid to Aeetes is part of her plan (V. Fl. 5.288–90). Jason's participation in the conflict will obviously be ineffectual because Aeetes has no intention of keeping his word. However, it will at least indirectly lead the hero to seducing Medea, the strongest ally he could hope to have on his side in this situation and the ultimate resource mobilized by Juno in order to enable the Argonauts to accomplish their mission.[38]

Finally, the dangerous alliance with the perfidious tyrant turns into an opportunity for success. Jason acquires the Golden Fleece after showing heroic prowess, endurance, and diplomatic sensitivity, but he also comes back home with another (even more precious) prize: Medea, the mighty ally upon whom, as Jupiter anticipates, the future of Aeetes' kingdom will depend again. Certainly, when looking at the mysterious pictures of the temple of the Sun in Book 5, readers (unlike the internal characters of the narrative) can easily guess the dark future which is in store. However, at this stage of the myth's development, at least, another issue is at stake, which involves Jason's behavior as a new model of leader as well as the dynamics of politics and international relationships. Although we do not know how Valerius imagines the end of the poem, nevertheless, to quote Idmon's reassuring words, *ratis omnia uincet* after all.

Thus, in view of the peculiar epic-historical character of the Colchian episode, Jason's attitude towards Aeetes, and perhaps even his success in gaining the favor of the tyrant's daughter (thanks to the gods' help), could probably be considered as an indirect way of foreshadowing from the mythical past the tactic displayed by Rome in the numerous "wars for succession," which upset Eastern client kingdoms like Armenia during the first century CE.[39] In such circumstances, Rome was used to siding with one competitor or another alternatively, in order to keep the political situation of the whole area under control.

To sum up, in this new Flavian version of the Argonautic saga, two opposite forms of Lucanean reception co-exist. The "negative" one enhances the pervasive role of civil war as a global evil: from the very outset of the heroic age, Valerius provides an indirect anticipation of the idea of his contemporary, Roman world involved in civil war. The "positive" reception of Lucan's poem, by contrast,

---

38 The conquest of the Golden Fleece may be the only target of Juno and Minerva, whose plan runs parallel to Jupiter's (macro-)program about the shifting of world power; however, see Krasne in this volume for discussion of other divine motivations.
39 Think, for instance, of the Roman-Parthian War of 58–63 CE, when the Imperial legate Cn. Domitius Corbulo momentarily succeeded in installing Tigranes VI on the throne of Armenia (59–61 CE) after deposing the Arsacid Tiridates, who was supported by the Parthian king Vologaeses (e.g., Tac. *Ann.* 13.36–38). However, a few years later (66 CE), Tiridates I was crowned in Rome by Nero. The plan to encircle the new Parthian Armenia with a string of forts and clients was brought about under the Flavians: "Vespasian … strengthened the fortifications of the Iberian capital Mtskheta in 75 and before 96 a centurion of the XII Fulminata (now a Cappadocian legion) left a record of his presence (possibly a diplomatic mission?) under Domitian in southwestern Albania" (Wheeler 2007, 243).

which counteracts the effects of the former, starts with Jason's refusal to stir up civil war in his homeland as a means of resolving the internal conflict for power. Then, it continues with the hero's "Herculean" choice to accept being involved in a war between two brothers in a foreign kingdom: this paves the way for the accomplishment of Jupiter's plan. The corrosive irony of Lucan's recrimination is thus recognized but, at the same time, incorporated into a new discourse on the heroic origins of expansionism and imperialism, where it undergoes reinterpretation. The Flavian poet tries to exorcize the negative potential of the civil war theme by representing the Argonautic myth also as a truly positive response to Lucan: a myth of conquest, the opening of the seas (as a deterrent to internal fighting), and the way in which a young apprentice-leader begins to learn how to successfully tame (and even take advantage of) a tyrant's rage.

3 Redemption from Tragedy: "Positive" Recollections of Lucan's *Pharsalia* in Statius's *Thebaid* 12

In Lucan's counter-classical epic, the mythical Greek archetype of fratricidal strife—the Theban war between Eteocles and Polynices—is relived for the last time in Roman Republican history. The plot of the *Pharsalia* is rich in Theban implications which constantly emerge throughout the poem, creating an almost systematic network of allusions. Some decades later, when writing his own Latin epic version of the Greek tragic myth, Statius takes such allusions into account and, setting them in a proper Theban context, also enhances their narrative function. Once (re-)integrated into the primary level of narration, the scattered traces of "Lucan's *Thebaid*" become more than mere tangential digressions.

Recollections of the Neronian poem mostly contribute to the negativity of the first eleven books of Statius's epic, which stage the progressive, compelling domination of evil and *furor* over Earth. Once more, we start with a negative kind of appropriation that even reconstructs the mythical background to the *Pharsalia*, taking its catastrophic message at face value. However, this does not cover the whole of Lucan's influence on the Flavian *Thebaid*. The first eleven books also contain rare examples of humanity, as well as luminous manifestations of virtues such as heroic constancy and self-sacrifice, which stand out vividly against the gloomy background and owe something to Lucanean patterns. For instance, Adrastus's flight from the battlefield, as a symbolic sublimation of defeat, reminds us of Pompey's own flight at Pharsalus; Menoeceus's *deuotio* recalls that of Cato; and Argia's heroic conjugal *pietas* makes us think about Cornelia after her husband's defeat.

A similar combination, though in inverse proportion, can also be noticed in Statius's Book 12, which finally reaffirms human values by staging the defeat of *furor* and impiety. The intervention of Theseus, who embodies a new virtuous prototype of monarch and champion of *clementia*, comes to break the demonic power of Creon; at the same time, his intervention almost seems to mark the end of Lucan's negative influence over Statius's plot. But though tragedy cedes to epic, the thread of Lucanean negative intertextuality remains visible: for instance, the hubristic way in which Creon, the new tyrant of Thebes, refuses to allow the burial of the dead foes offers a perfect synthesis of the impious challenge issued to religious as well as human laws by the same character in Sophocles' *Antigone* and its "actualization" in Roman history as displayed by Lucan's Caesar, the arrogant winner of Pharsalus.[40]

However, despite these residual traces of negativity, it is worth noting that the macroscopic reversal leading to reconciliation, justice, and humanity brings about a peculiarly positive way of recollecting Lucan's text, which consists of localized signs of so-called "antiphrastic intertextuality." By adopting this particular technique of allusion, Statius seems to emulate Lucan's tendentious (and antiphrastic) way of rereading and commenting on Vergil's *Aeneid*, providing for his part a (counter-)imitation of the *Pharsalia*.[41] Thus, the sophisticated, inclusive (and Flavian) literary strategy enacted by the poet of the *Thebaid* contributes to injecting new meaning into the images and narrative situations of the Neronian model.

An emblematic example is the *Pathosformel* of wives and relatives desperately looking through the battlefield for the remains of their loved ones, while the dispute rages over Creon's ban. Statius places great emphasis on the nocturnal spectacle of *pietas* offered by Argia and Antigone, respectively wife and sister of Polynices. The former arrives under Thebes' walls without displaying any fear: "She spoke and entering the shelter of a shepherd's hut nearby, she rekindles the breath of her flagging torch and breaks wildly into the dread field" (*dixit, tectumque aggressa propinquae | pastorale casae reficit spiramina fessi | ignis, et*

---

[40] The way Statius's Creon vents his rage against the corpses of the Argive princes and forbids burning them (Stat. *Theb.* 12.94–95, with Pollmann 2004) goes even beyond the example of his most recent epic predecessor, i.e., Lucan's Caesar after the battle of Pharsalus (Luc. 7.794–99). See also Ambühl 2015, 259–61, and Lanzarone 2016, 496.

[41] On Lucan's antiphrastic technique of allusion, see Narducci 1979, 31–79, and Conte 1994b, 446.

horrendos irrumpit turbida campos, Theb. 12.267–69).[42] Desperation intensifies her courage and, more than pain and sorrow, the simile which follows, that of Ceres menacingly looking for the lost Persephone,[43] highlights the upsetting, almost terrifying nature of the image. Argia seems almost to gain superhuman size in her resemblance to a goddess who is demanding vengeance; and the help provided to Ceres in the simile by the grumbling Enceladus (*Theb.* 12.274–75), buried under Mt. Etna, may also remind us of another goddess, *Gaia*, who in Gigantomachic iconography is often represented vainly begging Zeus to spare her children.[44] Like Ceres and mother Earth, Polynices' wife is expressing her grief as well as asking for vengeance.

Argia is like a woman possessed, a true Maenad (Stat. *Theb.* 12.282–90):

> nocte sub infesta, nullo duce et hoste propinquo,
> sola per offensus armorum et lubrica tabo
> gramina, non tenebras, non circumfusa tremescens
> concilia umbrarum atque animas sua membra gementes,   285
> saepe gradu caeco ferrum calcataque tela
> dissimulat, solusque labor uitasse iacentes,
> dum funus putat omne suum, uisuque sagaci
> rimatur positos et corpora prona supinat
> incumbens, queriturque parum lucentibus astris.   290

> In hostile night, without a guide and with enemy close by, [Argia] makes her lonely way. Stumbling on weapons and grass slippery with gore, she fears not the darkness or the assembly of shades gathered all around her, souls lamenting their lost limbs. Often in her blind passage she tramples on steel and weaponry, feigning unawareness. Her one concern is to avoid the fallen, as she thinks that every body is hers and scans them keenly as they lie, turning them on their backs and bending over them complaining of the dim starlight.

Finally, thanks to Juno's intercession with the Moon, Argia finds Polynices. At first she recognizes his cloak, her own handiwork, "though the fabric is hidden and the blood-soaked purple languishes" (Stat. *Theb.* 12.314–15). Argia calls upon the gods: she imagines that nothing else remains of her beloved, when, finally, he appears, nearly trampled into the dust (*Theb.* 12.315–17). At this point, fury turns into grief. The young wife falls prostrate about his face, seeking his departed soul with kisses, and, pressing the blood from his hair and clothing,

---

[42] Translations of Statius's *Thebaid* are from Shackleton Bailey 2003.
[43] Stat. *Theb.* 12.270–77 with Pollmann 2004, 151–52.
[44] The most important sources are listed in Moore 1988, 171–77. As regards the literary tradition of Gaia's pain over her children's death, see Hes. *Th.* 858; Hor. *Carm.* 3.4.73–75, with Nisbet/Rudd 2004, 77 *ad loc.*

gathers it up to treasure: in her mourning, Argia literally engages herself (with all her body) in recollecting any residual trace of life in Polynices' corpse (*tum corpore toto* | *sternitur in uultus animamque per oscula quaerit* | *absentem, pressumque comis ac ueste cruorem* | <u>*seruatura*</u> *legit*, Stat. *Theb.* 12.318–21).

Then she moves into a mournful lament for the dead (*Theb.* 12.322ff.). The protest against fate for deceiving her husband's legitimate aspirations (*ad debita regna profectum*, Stat. *Theb.* 12.322) is followed by regret for having roused Polynices' warlike fury and pushed her own father Adrastus to help him in this unfortunate enterprise (*Theb.* 12.336–37). But the most touching note comes soon after, when Argia bitterly rejoices to see the whole of Polynices' body (*sed bene habet, superi, gratum est, Fortuna; peracta* | *spes longinqua uiae:* <u>*totos inuenimus artus*</u>, "But it is well, High Ones; I thank you, Fortuna. The distant hope of my journey is accomplished. I have found his body whole," Stat. *Theb.* 12.338–39). Before finding her husband's corpse, Argia is afraid of having to collect dispersed limbs, i.e., the same pitiful duty which—as Lucan has shown—many widows and mothers have to deal with during (civil) war.[45]

In fact, the very way in which Argia comments on her desperate, almost "furious," search for Polynices' body throughout the Theban field, as well as its final positive outcome (*totos inuenimus artus*, Stat. *Theb.* 12.339), risks activating by contrast another, much more terrible Lucanean pattern: that of Erictho, the Thessalian witch of *Pharsalia* 6, who is used to running through the battlefields by night in search of human corpses, and whom we encounter while she is sifting through the plain of Pharsalus hoping "to mutilate the slaughtered carcasses of kings and to steal the ashes of the Hesperian nation and the bones of nobles, and to own *so many* souls" (*caesorum truncare cadauera regum* | *sperat et Hesperiae cineres auertere gentis* | *ossaque nobilium tantosque adquirere manes*, Luc. 6.584–86). The more this antiphrastic technique of allusion[46] avoids dissimulating its own negative (i.e., Lucanean) matrix, the more it sounds convincing. From Statius's viewpoint, Argia (the very prototype of conjugal devotion as well as virile heroism) obviously represents a pious version of Lucan's monster as long as we think of her looking for Polynices' remains.

Things completely change a few lines later, when Argia herself announces her will to take revenge on the remains of Eteocles, her hateful brother-in-law. At this point, metaphor changes into reality: the heroic, even "demonic fury" of conjugal *pietas*, which might indirectly remind us of Erictho, effectively shifts towards the literal imitation of the Neronian (counter) model (Stat. *Theb.* 12.341–43):

---

[45] See, for example, Luc. 2.166–73, with Fantham 1992, *ad loc.*
[46] See above.

> ... qua parte, precor, iacet ille nefandus
> praedator? uincam uolucres (sit adire potestas)
> excludamque feras.
>
> Where, I pray, does that villainous robber lie? Given access, I shall outdo the birds and shut out the wild beasts.

This last detail even prefigures an extremization of Erictho's character, which is in line with the typically Flavian tendency to juxtapose conflicting patterns so as to "saturate" the paradigm. Argia declares her will to prevent wild beasts and birds of prey from dismembering Eteocles' corpse before she is able to reach it: she definitely does not want to lose such a cruel privilege. By contrast, according to Lucan's representation, Erictho usually waits until the beasts have finished their job (Luc. 6.550–53):

> et, quodcumque iacet nuda tellure cadauer,   550
> ante feras uolucresque sedet; nec carpere membra
> uolt ferro manibusque suis, morsusque luporum
> expectat siccis raptura e faucibus artus.
>
> Whatever corpses lie out on the naked ground she seizes before the beasts and birds; not wanting to pick the bones with iron or her own hands, she waits and snatches the pieces from the thirsty jaws of wolves.

In my view, this passage from Lucan's Thessaly, with its horrific nocturnal landscape and perturbing inhabitants, is as crucial for understanding Statius's image as the Homeric intertext noted by Karla Pollmann, Hecuba's desire to rend and eat Achilles' liver.[47]

When Antigone arrives (*Theb.* 12.349ff.), she is surprised to find an *altera ego* in the Argive princess and sadly has to admit that her fraternal love has been overcome by conjugal loyalty.[48] Their pious rivalry only leads to a final, greater collective lament, when the two women are said to "share Polynices' limbs between them" (*Theb.* 12.385–88):

---

[47] τοῦ ἐγὼ μέσον ἧπαρ ἔχοιμι | ἐσθέμεναι προσφῦσα ("I wish I could set teeth in the middle of his liver and eat it," Hom. *Il.* 24.212–13, transl. Lattimore), with Pollmann 2004, *ad loc.* Hecuba will later take successful revenge upon Polymestor, the Thracian king who killed her son Polydorus, after Troy's fall, when she blinds him by tearing out his eyes (cf. Eur. *Hec.* 1035–55 and Ov. *Met.* 13.561–64).

[48] On the encounter between the fratricides' sister and Polynices' widow, see Keith (pp. 318–19) in this volume.

> ... hic pariter lapsae iunctoque per ipsum   385
> amplexu miscent auidae lacrimasque comasque,
> partitaeque artus redeunt alterna gementes
> ad uultum et cara uicibus ceruice fruuntur.

> Here both collapse and with joint embrace eagerly mingle tears and hair over the body, dividing the limbs between them; then they go back to his face, lamenting by turns, and enjoy his beloved neck in alternation.

Such competition between Polynices' wife and sister paradoxically evokes the atmosphere of another stock piece of Homeric epic: two enemies fighting over a corpse.[49] At the same time, the imagery of the body's dismemberment and mutilation (*partitae artus*, *Theb.* 12.387), which runs throughout Statius's episode, can most likely be traced more closely back to Lucan's poem.

In the heroic portrait of Argia, the traditional examples of female virtues merge with a negative pattern originating from the darkest side of the Neronian *Pharsalia*. By drawing upon an absolute specimen of impiety like the Lucanean Erictho, Statius manages to construct a hypercharacterized—and typically Flavian—model of conjugal devotion, where grief and lament meet with emphatic pugnacity and desire for vengeance.

4 Conclusions

Flavian epic poets do not aim merely to return to Vergil, but to respond to Lucan's provocative challenge of building a whole (anti-)epic on civil war by incorporating such a delicate subject into larger contexts. The *Aeneid* traces back to Roman prehistory the origin of civil war, although Vergil gestures towards such a nightmarish theme in both Aeneas's account of Troy's last night and the war between Trojans and Latins only subtly and indirectly: the Augustan poet takes care not to reopen still fresh wounds. The nightmare, however, casts its dark shadow over Rome's foundational act itself (the internecine strife between Romulus and Remus) and reaches the contemporary age: the ecphrasis of Aeneas's shield, with Octavian's victory against Mark Antony in the battle of Actium, hints *a posteriori* at the event which sanctions the *Urbs*'s refoundation.

---

49 See, for example, Hector and Patroclus fighting over the dead Cebrion, a son of Priam in Hom. *Il.* 16.759–64, or the subsequent fights for Sarpedon's body (*Il.* 16.508–683) and the dead Patroclus himself (*Il.* 17.233–318). Valerius Flaccus had already exploited the Homeric pattern (rejected by Vergil) in the war narrative of the *Argonautica* (V. Fl. 6.345–66).

After Lucan's provocative reenactment of the internecine strife which led to the collapse of the Roman Republic, Valerius Flaccus, Statius, and Silius capitalize on Vergil's idea of indirectly sketching an "archaeology" of civil war by concentrating on ancient myths or even periods of Roman history, like the Second Punic War, that still far predate the events narrated in the *Pharsalia*. However, unlike Vergil and under the influence of their Neronian predecessor, the three Flavian epicists, by tackling the civil war theme much more explicitly and extensively, increase its pervasiveness in time and space. On the one hand, they seem to exploit Lucan's corrosive delegitimization of the Augustan myth in order to go beyond Vergil and his slight reticence in reassuring readers about the final restoration of peace. At the same time, they apparently seek to encompass the destructive force of the topic by relativizing its paradigmatic and absolute meaning. While suggesting the worldwide diffusion of civil war, their stories do not necessarily aim to relive the nightmare as though it were still (necessarily and inevitably) affecting the historical present. Despite constantly hinting at the danger of relapse, they rather dramatize examples of the nightmare itself in which it is finally overcome.

While paying homage to the *Aeneid*, the Flavian epicists display perfect knowledge of the new Neronian (counter-)classic of the genre, whose almost prophetic quality was proved true by the conflicts of 69 CE, a few years after the death of its author. By incorporating and outdoing the model of Lucan's antagonistic and iconoclastic epic, Valerius, Silius, and Statius manage to gain autonomy from Vergil's authority. At the same time, they offer idiosyncratic examples of the Imperial (and, particularly, Flavian) tendency towards cultural integration and inclusiveness.[50] While sharing the same will to redeem their belatedness and go beyond their greatest model, they also seem to display an awareness of living in the most affluent and civilized era. After running the risk of relapsing into the nightmare of civil war—which proves to be endemic in the field of myth as well as in that of Roman (and even pre-Roman) history—the Flavian age is now ready to compete with Augustan grandeur.

---

50 See in this volume the remarkable observations by Manolaraki about the case of Pliny the Elder.

Raymond Marks
Sparsis Mauors agitatus in oris: Lucan and Civil War in *Punica* 14

Since the studies of Ahl, Davis, and Pomeroy and McGuire, the theme of civil war in Silius's *Punica* has received regular attention.[1] It is especially evident in the Cannae Books (8–10), where allusions and references to civil war abound, but they have been identified elsewhere too, showing that civil war is an epic-wide preoccupation.[2] One notable pattern that has emerged from this research is Silius's use of the theme in close connection with the defeat and/or fall of major cities and peoples in the poem. One such city is Rome, especially at Cannae but also in her defeats leading up to it at the Ticinus, the Trebia, and Lake Trasimene in Books 4 and 5. There is also the Spanish city of Saguntum, whose fall in Book 2 is attended by internecine slaughter and suicide. And in the second half of the epic, the theme informs Carthage's declining fortunes, which end with her final defeat at Zama in Book 17, as well as those of Capua in Books 11 and 13.

Another city that should be included in the group but is often overlooked in discussions of civil war in the epic is Syracuse, in *Punica* 14. In that book, the Roman general Marcus Claudius Marcellus invades Sicily and wages a campaign against the Carthaginians and their allies on the island. He lands at Zancle and storms the city of Leontini (Sil. 14.110–77) and then marches to Syracuse, which becomes the site of most of the book's action: he blockades the city (Sil. 14.178–91), lays siege to it (Sil. 14.292–352), fights a sea battle against the Syracusans and their Carthaginian allies (Sil. 14.353–579), and, after a plague (Sil. 14.580–617), takes the city (Sil. 14.618–84). Of these events, the sea battle is especially noteworthy as it marks a significant departure from the historical record. Livy (Liv. 25.27) tells us that a Carthaginian fleet, led by Bomilcar, lay facing a Roman fleet off Cape Pachynus but decided not to engage the Romans there and left.[3] In Silius's version of events, however, there is a fully developed sea battle (Sil. 14.353–579), which, as has long been acknowledged, is extensively modeled

---
1 Ahl *et al.* 1986; McGuire 1995; McGuire 1997.
2 See, e.g., Fucecchi 1999; Marpicati 1999; Marks 2008; Tipping 2010, 31–41. Allusions to Lucan's *Bellum Ciuile* throughout the epic also attest to Silius's interest in this theme. For more, see Wezel 1873, 89–95; Steele 1922, 326–30; Meyer 1924; Häußler 1978, 161–77; Brouwers 1982; Marks 2010a; Marks 2010c.
3 For more on Silius's deviation from Livy here, see Burck 1984a, 31.

after the sea battle at Massilia in Lucan's *Bellum Ciuile* (Luc. 3.509–762).[4] But why does Silius invent this battle? The answer, I propose, lies in its Lucanean intertext: Silius invents the battle precisely so that he may allude to the sea battle in *Bellum Ciuile* 3 and, in doing so, invites us to read his text in close relation to Lucan's and, with that, to consider the ways in which the events at Syracuse speak to the theme of civil war.

But why should civil war be so foregrounded here? One motivating factor might be the historical fact that the Syracusans were divided in their support of the Romans and the Carthaginians and were thus divided among and against themselves. Early in Book 14, Silius traces the origin of this internal division to the reign of Hieronymus, the grandson and successor of Hiero II (Sil. 14.85–109), and later observes how it led Syracuse to switch from the Roman to the Carthaginian side in the war (Sil. 14.279–93).[5] Another consideration may be that Silius wishes to bring Syracuse's story in line with those of other cities that are likewise associated with civil war in the epic: again, Saguntum and Rome in the first half of the epic, Capua and Carthage in the second half. For one of the lessons that Silius's use of the civil war theme in these instances impresses upon us is that the decline and/or fall of these cities is ultimately due not to external factors, such as the aggressive actions of their enemies on the outside, but to internal conditions, such as civil strife, within the cities themselves.[6] By alluding extensively to Lucan in *Punica* 14, then, Silius may want to suggest a similar interpretation regarding the fall of Syracuse. But that is not all. If we take a closer look at the events at Syracuse in the *Punica* and the events at Massilia in the *Bellum Ciuile*, it becomes clear that Silius is not simply using Lucan to associate Syracuse with civil war, but to distance Marcellus and the Romans from it as well. Consequently, he not only distinguishes Rome as she is now in the second half of the *Punica* from her

---

[4] So Wezel 1873, 92–95; Meyer 1924, 37–48; Brouwers 1982, 76–78; Burck 1984a, 31–44; Spaltenstein 1990, 312–30. Many of the parallels discussed in this chapter have already been identified in these works and in those cited in n. 2, above. I regret that I cannot acknowledge the contributions of these scholars in connection with every instance of allusion cited hereafter. For the possibility that Silius may have drawn on other models for his sea battle as well, see Burck 1984a, 31 n. 111.

[5] Verbal parallels with Lucan in the former passage may also suggest the idea of civil war: *non cernere terra(m)* (Sil. 14.100 = Luc. 7.794); *noua saeuit in armis | libertas i a c t a t que i u g u m* (Sil. 14.106–7) = *s e r u i t i u m f u g i s s e ... | ... saeuis libertas subditur armis* (Luc. 4.577–78).

[6] For more, see Marks 2005a (Rome); Cowan 2007 (Capua); and Marks 2010a (Rome & Carthage). Saguntum is a different matter; for while she is ultimately responsible for her fall—her citizens commit suicide and engage in internecine violence—she, nevertheless, remains a model of *fides*. On this, see p. 61 below, as well as Bernstein and Hulls in this volume.

former "civil war" self in the first half, but shows us how a city, when it moves beyond civil war, may serve as a positive force in the world, containing and checking civil strife wherever and whenever it flares up abroad. In this respect, Silius's Rome stands in marked contrast to Lucan's Rome, whose civil war spreads and infects cities outside of the *ciuitas Romana*, including Massilia.

1 Opening Phase: Sil. 14.353–93

On first glance, I admit, it is hard to see how Silius's program of allusion to *Bellum Ciuile* 3 should lead us to such an interpretation, as broad structural and thematic similarities between them appear to identify the Syracusans, who are beset by civil strife, with the Massilians, who wish to avoid it, and to identify Marcellus and the Romans, who are not involved in civil war, with Lucan's Caesarians, who are. Indeed, one cannot fail to observe that Silius's Romans besiege Syracuse just as Lucan's Caesar besieges Massilia and that the Syracusans successfully foil the Roman siege just as the Massilians successfully foil the Caesarian siege (Sil. 14.292–352; Luc. 3.453–508).[7] Also, Syracuse and Massilia are ethnically related, both being Greek colonies and being frequently identified as such by their respective poets, whereas Silius's Romans and Lucan's Caesarians are both Roman.[8] What is more, there is the sea battle, which, for being modeled after Lucan's, only seems to reinforce these parallels: in *Punica* 14 the besieged city of Syracuse is defeated at sea by their besieger, the Romans, just as the Massilians are defeated at sea by their besieger, the Caesarians, in *Bellum Ciuile* 3.

And yet Silius goes to great lengths to destabilize these very correlations in his account of the battle itself. Consider the opening phases of both sea battles, which are quite similar structurally and thematically. Each poet describes how the combatants row out into the harbor to face each other (Sil. 14.353–59 = Luc. 3.521–37) and then offers a general description of the initial engagement,

---

[7] Also, note that Silius alludes to Lucan several times in connection with Marcellus's arrival at Syracuse and subsequent siege: *Ephyraea* ad *moenia* u e r t i t (Sil. 14.180) = *Ephyraeaque moenia seruat* (Luc. 6.17); *diu non* s u m p s e r i t, *hostem* (Sil. 14.296) = *diu non* c r e d i d i t *hostem* (Luc. 4.653); *correptae* rapido *in cineres abiere ruinae* (Sil. 14.315) = *corripuisse* faces aut iam quatiente *ruina* (Luc. 1.494) and *in immensas cineres abiere* cauernas (Luc. 5.135); a f f i x o uicina *in robora* f e r r o | *sustulerant* sublime *ratem* (Sil. 14.328–29) = m e r s o uiolata *in robora* t e l o (Luc. 3.435) and *robora* … | namque *ratem* uacuae *sustentant* undique cupae (Luc. 4.419–20); aggere ualli (Sil. 14.335 = Luc. 6.31).
[8] For Syracuse and Massilia as Greek, see pp. 62–63 below.

each detailing the churning of the waves and the din of battle (Sil. 14.360–84 = Luc. 3.538–55).[9] Now, for reasons I indicated previously, we might expect the Carthaginians and, especially, the Syracusans to play the role of the Massilians and the Romans that of the Caesarians, but Silius suggests otherwise. When he describes the Carthaginian fleet's crescent-shaped formation, he alludes not to the Massilian fleet in Lucan's text, but to the Caesarian fleet, which adopts a similarly crescent-shaped formation: *ac simili curuata sinu diuersa ruebat | classis et artabat lunato caerula gyro* ("And the opposing fleet was speeding on in a similar, curved shape and was reducing the sea's expanse with its crescent ring," Sil. 14.369–70) = *lunata classe recedunt | ordine contentae gemino creuisse Liburnae* ("The Liburnians, content to have risen up with two rows of oars, hang back in their crescent array," Luc. 3.533–34).[10] As the opening phase continues, Silius again identifies the Carthaginians with Lucan's Caesarians by a structural and thematic parallel. After the general description of the battle's engagement, Silius turns his attention to the Carthaginian commander Himilco (Sil. 14.384–407); at the corresponding moment in *Bellum Ciuile* 3, Lucan turns his attention to the Caesarian commander Brutus (Luc. 3.556–66). Granted, the situations are different in that Himilco is here trying to avoid being rammed whereas Brutus instructs his helmsman to let his ship be rammed so that they may engage in close-quarter fighting on the decks. Even so, the similar sequence of events and the similarly timed appearances of Himilco and Brutus—each of whom is a commander, is the first named individual in his respective battle, and is or is about to be rammed—invite comparison between them.[11]

But the comparison is still more fully developed than that. In 14.384–93, Silius describes Himilco's massive, slow ship, which towers above all others

---

[9] Specific parallels include: *tum uocibus aequor | personat, et clamat scopulis clamoris imago* (Sil. 14.364–65) = *miscentur in aethere uoces, | remorumque sonus premitur clamore* (Luc. 3.540); *increpuere tubae* (Sil. 14.373) = *potuere tubae* (Luc. 3.542; cf., e.g., Prop. 4.11.9, Luc. 1.432, V. Fl. 6.28); *sternitur effusis pelagi media area telis* (Sil. 14.378) = *emissaque tela | aera texerunt uacuumque cadentia pontum* (Luc. 3.545–46); *ast aliae latere atque incussi roboris ictu | detergent remos, aliae per uiscera pinus | tramissis ipso retinentur uulnere rostris, | quo retinent* (Sil. 14.381–84) = *ut primum rostris crepuerunt obuia rostra* (Luc. 3.544) and *ast alias ... | seque tenent remis* (Luc. 3.565–66). Also, note: *tam uasto ad proelia nisu | incumbunt proni positisque in margine puppis* (Sil. 14.375–76) = *stat quisque suae de robore puppis | pronus in aduersos ictus* (Luc. 3.570–71) and *incumbit prono lateri* (Luc. 3.648).

[10] The Roman fleet, though, similarly (note *simili*, Sil. 14.369) attempts an enveloping maneuver: Sil. 14.366–68 (cf. Luc. 3.532–33). I am using the following editions: Delz 1987 (Silius); Shackleton Bailey 1997 (Lucan). All translations are my own.

[11] The passages are also linked by verbal parallelism: *residentis puppe magistri* (Sil. 14.401) = *residenti puppe magistro* (Luc. 3.558).

(Sil. 14.384–91), and contrasts it with the Romans' light and easily maneuverable ships (Sil. 14.392–93). We encounter a similar passage toward the beginning of Lucan's account of the sea battle (Luc. 3.525–37), where he relates the disposition of the Caesarian fleet, which includes larger and smaller ships. Tellingly, Brutus's ship, described at the end of the passage, is a massive vessel that towers above others in its fleet, much like Himilco's in *Punica* 14: *celsior at cunctis Bruti praetoria puppis | uerberibus senis agitur molemque profundo | inuehit* ("But the praetorian ship of Brutus, loftier than the others, is moved by its six rows of oars and conveys its mass on the sea," Luc. 3.535–37) = *medias inter sublimior ibat | terribilis uisu puppis, qua nulla per omne | egressa est Libycis maior naualibus aeuum* ("Moving in their midst was [Himilco's] ship, frightful to behold, than which no larger vessel ever set forth from Libyan dockyards," Sil. 14.384–86).[12] As Silius's description of Himilco's ship continues, we encounter another parallel that associates it with Lucan's Caesarians: *sed quater haec centum numeroso remige pontum | pulsabat tonsis* ("But this ship was striking the sea with four hundred oars," Sil. 14.387–88). The words *remige* and *pulsabat tonsis* echo Lucan's description of the Caesarian and Massilian fleets rowing out to meet each other: *paribusque lacertis | Caesaris hinc puppes, hinc Graio remige classis | tollitur: impulsae tonsis tremuere carinae* ("With equal effort Caesar's ships rise up from this direction, the fleet with its Greek oars from that direction: their hulls, driven on by oars, trembled," Luc. 3.525–27). But the words *quater ... remige* in Silius's description of Himilco's ship also call to mind ships with four tiers of oars, which are among the Caesarian fleet and are described only a few lines later by Lucan: *quasque quater surgens extructi remigis ordo | commouet* ("And ships which are moved by four rising tiers of oars," Luc. 3.530–31).

Silius's Romans and Lucan's Massilians are associated with each other by allusion as well. The Romans' lighter, swifter ships, referred to at the end of the Silian passage, correspond to the light, swift ships of the Massilians that Lucan mentions shortly after his description of Brutus's ship: *procurrunt leuitate agili docilesque regentis | audiuisse manum Latio cum milite puppes* ("The ships carrying Latin soldiers speed forward, agile and light, taught to obey the hand of their pilot," Sil. 14.392–93) = *sed Grais habiles pugnamque lacessere pinus | et temptare fugam nec longo frangere gyro | cursum nec tarde flectenti cedere clauo* ("But the Greeks have ships nimble enough to initiate an attack and take flight, to change

---

12 The verb *agitur* (Luc. 3.536) and the detail of the mass of Brutus's ship (*molem*, Luc. 3.537) may have also influenced the description of Himilco's ship *lento se robore agebat* (at Sil. 14.390). But also note a parallel with Luc. 3.535–36 at Sil. 14.487–88 (a Roman ship): *ipse adeo senis ductor Rhoeteius ibat | p u l s i b u s*.

course without swerving widely, and to respond quickly to the rudder when it turns," Luc. 3.553–55). Also, the Silian phrase *audiuisse manum* (Sil. 14.393), which refers to the easy maneuverability of the Roman ships, echoes a phrase that appears in Lucan's description of a Massilian helmsman named Telo: *derigit huc puppem miseri quoque dextra Telonis, | qua nullam melius pelago turbante carinae | audiuere manum* ("Also, a ship was guided here by the hand of wretched Telo than which no hand was obeyed more by ships when the sea was turbulent," Luc. 3.592–94). As we can see, from the beginning of the sea battle in *Punica* 14, Silius encourages us to identify the Carthaginians and Syracusans with Lucan's Caesarians and the Romans with Lucan's Massilians, not the other way around. And even though Himilco's and Brutus's fortunes diverge considerably over the course of the battle—Himilco eventually flees defeated (Sil. 14.559–61), while Brutus is victorious (Luc. 3.761–62)—it is perhaps indicative of Silius's purpose to identify them that the last named individual we see in his sea battle is Himilco, just as the last named individual we see in Lucan's is Brutus.

2 The Sea Battle: Sil. 14.394–561

After the opening phase, allusions to the sea battle in *Bellum Ciuile* 3 continue, although many of them do not allow us to match up a side in one conflict with a specific side in the other.[13] But in several instances where combatants can be matched up, correlations between Romans and Massilians and between Carthaginians and Caesarians tend to be maintained. Consider when the hand of a Roman pilot, who is trying to ram Himilco's ship, is pinned to the helm by an arrow: *nec deinde regenda | puppe manus ualuit flectenti immortua clauo* ("And, then, his hand, dying while at the turning helm, could not guide the ship," Sil. 14.402–3). The words *flectenti clauo* recall their use in reference to the Massilians' swift ships, to which I referred above (*flectenti ... clauo*, Luc. 3.555), and the fate of the pilot echoes that of the aforementioned Massilian helmsman Telo, whose hand, after he is struck in the chest while trying to ram a Caesarian ship, steers the ship off course as he dies: *auertitque ratem morientis dextra magistri* ("And the hand of the dying pilot steered the ship aside," Luc. 3.599). This Telo, moreover, is probably the inspiration for a Roman named Telo, who is killed when a spear

---

[13] E.g., Sil. 14.427–28, 476–80 = Luc. 3.681–88; Sil. 14.503–4 = Luc. 3.676–77; Sil. 14.518–21 = Luc. 3.565–70, 574; Sil. 14.539–41 = Luc. 3.647–50; Sil. 14.543–49 = Luc. 3.670–79, 691; Sil. 14.550 = Luc. 3.660–61; Sil. 14.551 = Luc. 3.578; Sil. 14.552–54 = Luc. 3.694–96; Sil. 14.557–58 = Luc. 3.541.

pierces him in the head in 14.442–43. The dying hand of the Roman pilot (*manus immortua*, Sil. 14.403) has an additional antecedent in one of two Massilian twin brothers, whose hand is likewise *immortua*, after being chopped off as he tries to grab the side of a Caesarian ship to board it: *deriguitque tenens strictis immortua neruis* ("And his hand, holding on, grew stiff in death, its muscles contracted," Luc. 3.613).[14] The parallelism continues when another Roman, Taurus, next tries to take over the helm for the wounded pilot (Sil. 14.404–7) but is struck by an arrow; Taurus has a model in a Massilian named Gyareus, who, when trying to take over for Telo, is gored by a grappling hook (Luc. 3.600–2).[15] The death of a Carthaginian named Sciron, on the other hand, points to a correlation between Silius's Carthaginians and Lucan's Caesarians. He is killed when gored by a ship's beak (Sil. 14.481–87); an unidentified combatant at Massilia is similarly killed when crushed between the beaks of two clashing ships (Luc. 3.652–61). Verbal parallels, though, suggest that Silius has in mind the death of a Caesarian named Catus as well: *terga simul pariter missis et pectora telis | transigitur; medio concurrit pectore ferrum* ("He is pierced in the back and the chest by spears equally thrown at the same time; the spear-tips meet in the middle of his chest," Luc. 3.587–88) = *transigitur ualida medius, dum se alleuat, alni | cuspide Marmarides Sciron* ("Sciron, a Marmarid, while lifting himself up, is pierced through the middle by the powerful beak of a ship," Sil. 14.481–82).

In one instance Silius appears to deviate from this pattern by identifying a Carthaginian with a Massilian, but in the end, he upholds it by a surprising twist. The context is a fire spreading through the ship of Himilco (Sil. 14.423ff.), who is, as we have seen, Brutus's Silian counterpart. At one point, a member of its crew, Sabratha, prays to Hammon, the tutelary god of the vessel, that he strike a Roman with his spear (Sil. 14.436–41); he does, piercing Telo in the head (Sil. 14.442–43). The name Telo, as was noted above, is inspired by a Massilian of the same name (Luc. 3.592–99). But as the narrative continues, Lucan's Telo becomes a model for a Carthaginian, the ship's helmsman, Bato. As the fire consumes the vessel and Himilco safely abandons the ship (Sil. 14.444–51), Silius turns his attention to this Bato, whose fate is anticipated in terms reminiscent of the aforementioned Massilian: *proxima nudarunt miserandi fata Batonis | desertam ductore ratem* ("The subsequent death of pitiable Bato left the ship bereft of its pilot," Sil. 14.452–53) = *derigit huc puppem miseri quoque dextra Telonis* ("Also, the hand of wretched

---

14 But also compare Sil. 14.484: *portatur rigido, miserandum, immortua rostro* (Sciron).
15 Also, note: *dumque ad opem accurrit ceu capta nauita puppe* (Sil. 14.404) = *dum cupit in sociam Gyareus erepere puppem* (Luc. 3.600).

Telo steers the ship this way," Luc. 3.592). Both, moreover, are skilled helmsmen and are similarly described as such (Sil. 14.453–57 = Luc. 3.593–96).[16]

We might leave the matter there, conceding that this marks a deviation from the pattern established in the opening phase of the conflict—for Bato is Carthaginian, but his Lucanean model is Massilian—were it not for what happens next. Seeing no way to escape the fire, Bato calls on Hammon to witness his death and commits suicide (Sil. 14.458–61):

> "accipe nostrum,
> Hammon, sanguinem," ait "spectator cladis iniquae."
> atque acto in pectus gladio dextra inde cruorem   460
> excipit et large sacra inter cornua fundit.

"You, Hammon," he says, "who look upon this unjust misfortune, receive our blood." And, after driving a sword in his chest, he catches the blood and pours it liberally between the god's horns.

On first glance, Bato's suicide appears to be a noble, pious act; after all, he is willing to go down with his ship and even offers himself as a sacrifice to Hammon. And yet we hear in the phrase *spectator cladis iniquae* (Sil. 14.459) a rebuke of the god, suggesting that, from the pilot's perspective, Hammon is indifferent to his suffering or, perhaps, simply powerless to alleviate it.[17] If so, Bato is not only to be contrasted with his fellow Carthaginian Sabratha, who, differently, invoked the god and successfully secured his aid, but also stands in a sympathetic relation to Sabratha's (and Hammon's) victim, the Roman Telo.[18] Of course, an affinity between the two has a sound intertextual basis, as we have seen: Telo and Bato are both the poetic progeny of the same figure in *Bellum Ciuile* 3, the Massilian Telo. Bato's identification with Lucan's Telo, then, is less of a deviation than it appears; for, in the end, as he renounces his god and takes his own life, he becomes, as it were, less Carthaginian and more Roman and Massilian.[19]

---

16 Among parallels between the passages, note: *pelago* (Sil. 14.454 = Luc. 3.593); *quid ... quid* (Sil. 14.455) = *seu ... seu* (Luc. 3.595); *crastinus* (Sil. 14.455) = *crastina* (Luc. 3.595); *nec peruigilem tu fallere uultum | ... Cynosura, ualeres* (Sil. 14.456–57) = *nec lux est notior ulli* (Luc. 3.594).
17 Similarly, Duff 1934, 307, who translates, "Ammon, who lookest idly on at our cruel defeat." Also, cf. Spaltenstein 1990, 320: "'Spectator' 459 implique 'sans agir'."
18 For a detailed analysis of the contrasting scenes involving Sabratha and Telo, see Burck 1984a, 37.
19 We might also compare Bato with another Massilian, the father of Argus, who, seeing his son dying, commits suicide (Luc. 3.741–51) and, like Bato, does so by stabbing himself with a *gladius* (*acto in pectus gladio*, Sil. 14.460; *per uiscera missi | ... gladii*, Luc. 3.748–49). This suicide, which caps off Lucan's sea battle, would seem to confirm that Massilia has been drawn into civil strife, suicide being a recognized analogue of civil war, but it also testifies to the Massilians'

There are, however, a few instances in which the pattern we have been observing is clearly violated. In two cases Silius's Romans are identifiable with Lucan's Caesarians. A Roman ship sinks in a manner reminiscent of the sinking of a Caesarian ship (Sil. 14.411–13 = Luc. 3.627–33), and verbal parallels link another Roman ship (or, possibly, the ship of a Roman ally), sunk by a Sicilian named Podaetus, to Brutus's ship at Massilia: *et iam turrigerum* demerserat aequore Nessum ("And he had already sunk the Nessus, a turreted ship," Sil. 14.500) = *et iam turrigeram* Bruti comitata carinam | uenerat in fluctus Rhodani cum gurgite classis ("And a fleet, accompanying Brutus's turreted ship, had already come with the Rhône's waters to the sea," Luc. 3.514–15). Also, a Carthaginian named Lilaeus is identified by allusion with Lucan's Massilians. When his hand is cut off while he lays hold of an enemy ship (Sil. 14.489–91), we are reminded of the Massilian twin, mentioned above, who loses his hand while grabbing onto an enemy ship (Luc. 3.609–13), or of those Massilians who, when climbing onto one of their own ships, have their hands cut off by fellow Massilians who fear they may capsize it (Luc. 3.661–69). Verbal parallels point to still another Massilian, named Lycidas: *quam rapidis puppem manibus frenare Lilaeus | dum temptat, saeua truncatur membra bipenni* ("While Lilaeus tries quickly to grab on and slow that ship down, his limbs are cut off by a violent axe-blow," Sil. 14.489–90) = *ferrea dum puppi rapidos manus inserit uncos, | adfixit Lycidan* ("While a grappling hook was quickly digging its claws into the ship, it impaled Lycidas," Luc. 3.635–36).[20]

---

unwillingness to accept that state of affairs; for, ever since Caesar first threatened their city, the Massilians have been prepared to kill themselves rather than to be participants in and victims of his civil war (see pp. 60–61 below). The father's suicide, therefore, while motivated by grief for his son Argus, also reflects the Massilians' moral objection to the Caesarian cause. In light of the parallelism between the Massilian father's fate and Bato's, we are perhaps meant to read the latter's rebuke of Hammon in similar terms, namely, as a renunciation of the Carthaginians' cause on par with the Massilians' rejection of Caesar's civil war.

20 While I focus in this chapter on allusions in Silius's sea battle to Lucan's in *Bellum Ciuile* 3, I should point out that Silius alludes to other moments in the *Bellum Ciuile* as well: Sil. 14.368 = Luc. 6.42; Sil. 14.374 = Luc. 9.349; Sil. 14.381 = Luc. 3.494, 6.137 (cf. V. Fl. 2.534, Stat. *Theb.* 6.943); Sil. 14.411 = Luc. 6.232 (cf. Prop. 4.4.91, Sil. 9.327); Sil. 14.420 = Luc. 8.8, 702 (cf. Sil. 12.622); Sil. 14.449 = Luc. 2.106 (cf. Verg. *A.* 9.687, Stat. *Theb.* 5.260, Sil. 5.423); Sil. 14.474 = Luc. 1.547; Sil. 14.483 = Luc. 1.692; Sil. 14.488 = Luc. 9.149; Sil. 14.540 = Luc. 9.649; Sil. 14.574 = Luc. 6.421; Sil. 14.579 = Luc. 3.175, 6.294.

3 Checking Civil War Abroad

It is not necessarily surprising that Silius's Romans and Carthaginians/Sicilians are not always identifiable with Lucan's Massilians and Caesarians, respectively. Such one-to-one correspondences between texts are rarely maintained in such a neat and tidy fashion when a poet alludes extensively to another, as Silius does to Lucan here. Another complicating factor in this instance is that both poets are describing similar events, sea battles, and hence share a considerable amount of vocabulary and thematic content. And yet we cannot overlook the relative consistency with which Silius cultivates the correlations we have observed nor the fact that they are set forth in the opening phase of the battle, which, for coming at the beginning, takes on a kind of programmatic force. What is more, the instances in which Silius deviates from the pattern, identifying Romans with Caesarians or Carthaginians with Massilians, are few, and one of them, as we have seen, may not represent a deviation at all. But why does our poet identify his Romans with Lucan's Massilians and his Carthaginians and Sicilians with Lucan's Caesarians, and not the other way around?

Silius's aim is to draw ethical distinctions between his combatants, distinctions that may not be self-evident on first read but that, on closer inspection, reveal themselves in proportion as the combatants resemble or are differentiated from Lucan's. Consider Syracuse and Massilia. Both cities are similar in several ways: they are both Greek colonies, are besieged, and suffer defeat. But they are fundamentally dissimilar on a moral level, and Silius's program of allusion to Lucan, whereby they are not identified with each other, invites us to reflect on that difference. As was noted above, Silius's Syracusans are involved in civil strife from the beginning and are faithless not only among themselves, but to their former ally, Rome, whose cause they abandon to join the Carthaginians. Lucan's Massilians, by contrast, are initially not involved in civil war and try to avoid it despite Caesar's efforts to draw them in: they take seriously their alliance with Rome and regard it as a violation of *fides* to fight on behalf of either side in the war (Luc. 3.300–55). Silius, in fact, draws this very distinction between the two cities when describing the efforts of two pro-Carthaginian ringleaders, Hippocrates and Epycides, to rouse the Syracusans to oppose the Romans (Sil. 14.279–91). These brothers, who were born of a Carthaginian mother and a Sicilian father (Sil. 14.287–90), exhibit vices inherited from both sides of the family: *geminaque a stirpe parentum | astus miscebant Tyrios leuitate Sicana* ("And, as a consequence of their mixed parentage, they combined Tyrian cunning and Sicilian fickleness," Sil. 14.290–91). Silius's reference to their Sicilian *leuitas* takes us back to Lucan's Massilians and in such a way as to remind us of their *fides* and lack of Greek *leuitas: Phocais in dubiis ausa est seruare iuuentus | non Graia leuitate fidem signataque iura, | et causas, non fata, sequi* ("In this time of uncertainty the Phocaean youth did not exhibit Greek fickleness; it dared to keep its faith, to abide by signed treaties, and to follow principles, not fortune," Luc. 3.301–3).

Consistent with Massilia's differentiation from Syracuse is her identification with another of Silius's "civil war" cities, Saguntum.[21] This connection is made, in fact, by the Massilians themselves in Lucan's *Bellum Ciuile*. When addressing Caesar, they say that they prefer to remain neutral in the war, but, if besieged, are not afraid to follow Saguntum's example in the Second Punic War: *nec pauet hic populus pro libertate subire | obsessum Poeno gessit quae Marte Saguntum* ("Nor is this people afraid to suffer for the sake of freedom what Saguntum endured when it was besieged by the Carthaginians," Luc. 3.349–50). They are prepared, they go on to say, to emulate the Saguntines by destroying themselves rather than to let their city be taken (Luc. 3.351–55). Silius's Saguntum does not fail to live up to this image. Of his "civil war" cities, it is the only one that does not exhibit disunity or a crisis of *fides*, but is, rather, a model of *fides*, and so much so that it destroys itself to remain loyal to Rome and to preserve *fides* among her own people (Sil. 2.526–707), just as the Massilians are willing to do. Silius even has the goddess Fides herself inspire the Saguntines to hold out against the Carthaginians during the siege (Sil. 2.475–525).[22] It might also be noted that several times in the *Punica* Silius alludes to the words Lucan's Massilians use when professing their willingness to emulate the Saguntines and thus implicitly endorses the identification of the cities with one another: *obsessum Poeno gessit quae Marte Saguntum* (Luc. 3.350) = *nec nunc obsessa demum et fumante Sagunto* (Sil. 2.284); *at puer obsessae generatus in ore Sagunti* (Sil. 3.66); *hic super excisam primori Marte Saguntum* (Sil. 11.143); *quid uos, quis claro deletum est Marte Saguntum* (Sil. 17.328). Silius's program of allusion to *Bellum Ciuile* 3 in the sea battle of *Punica* 14, therefore, not only sets Syracuse's *perfidia* in contrast to Massilia's *fides* but reinforces the Massilians' likeness to Silius's faithful Saguntines.

An ethical divide separates Silius's Romans from Lucan's Caesarians as well. In *Bellum Ciuile* 3 Caesar turns a deaf ear to the Massilian's request to remain neutral and forces war, civil war, upon them with the avowed intention of destroying them (Luc. 3.358–72). In *Punica* 14, on the other hand, the Roman commander Marcellus tries to avoid conflict at Syracuse: when he reaches the city, he makes

---

21 For Silius's Saguntum and civil war, see the contributions of Bernstein, Hulls, Keith, and Stocks elsewhere in this volume.
22 Fides' intervention is clearly a fiction, but Saguntum's self-destructive demise otherwise has historical basis (e.g., Liv. 21.14; V. Max. 6.6.ext.1; D.S. 25.15).

diplomatic overtures in hopes of easing tensions (Sil. 14.181–83), and when he does attack, he does so reluctantly and only because he feels he has no alternative (Sil. 14.292–97). Also, when he takes the city at the end of the book, he shows remarkable restraint by checking the wrath of his troops and sparing the city unnecessary bloodshed (Sil. 14.665–75), and for his clemency he is praised by the Syracusans and by the poet himself (Sil. 14.679–83).[23] An important consequence of this contrast between Silius's Romans and Lucan's Caesarians, to say nothing of the Romans' corresponding identification with the Massilians, is that it allows us to measure the distance between the two Romes in Silius's epic, the "civil-war-esque" Rome of *Punica* 4–10 and Rome as she is in Books 11–17, a city that has pulled herself together, exhibits unity and a sense of collective purpose, and, importantly, wins one victory after another, including here in Book 14 at Syracuse.[24] Post-Cannae Rome exemplifies, then, a more positive formulation of that lesson to which I referred earlier: that stable, harmonious conditions within a city are critical to its success in war against foreign adversaries on the outside.

The "foreignness" of Rome's adversary in this instance further informs our understanding of Rome's victory at Syracuse and its relation to the theme of civil war and to Lucan's text. Syracuse's Greek origins, culture, and traditions are repeatedly noted throughout the book.[25] This fact, when read in connection with Silius's program of allusion to *Bellum Ciuile* 3, invites us to compare Massilia, which is similarly figured as a Greek "other" in that epic.[26] But while Syracuse and Massilia are both seen as alien, foreign, and outside the sphere of Roman

---

23 In portraying Marcellus in this way, Silius follows Cicero's "sterilized" version of Syracuse's fall (*Ver.* 2.4.116, 120–23) rather than Livy's (25.31), who indicates that the event was attended by much violence and looting. For details, see Burck 1984a, 53–60; Ripoll 2000b, 153–56.

24 Marcellus, incidentally, did not behave this way in his earlier appearance in *Punica* 14. From the moment he landed in Sicily and attacked Leontini (Sil. 14.110–47), he was swift, aggressive, and ruthless, and tellingly, we encounter several allusions to Lucan there: *atque u b i cuncta uiro caedesque e x p o s t a tyranni* (Sil. 14.114) = *ut scelus hoc S u l l a e caedesque ostensa placeret* (Luc. 2.192); *proelia campos* (Sil. 14.125) = *proelia Campi* (Luc. 7.306; cf. V. Fl. 5.221); *femineum credas maribus concurrere uulgus* (Sil. 14.129) = *pectora femineum ceu Bruti funere uulgus* (Luc. 7.39); *pigro luctandi studio certamen in umbra | molle pati docta et gaudens splendescere oliuo | stat, mediocre decus uincentum, ignaua iuuentus* (Sil. 14.136–38) = *spem mundi petitis: Grais delecta iuuentus | gymnasiis aderit studioque ignaua palaestrae* (Luc. 7.270–71); *e i c i t a n - g u s t o uiolentius ore Propontis* (Sil. 14.145) = *Euxinumque ferens p a r u o r u a t ore Propontis* (Luc. 9.960). To a certain extent, then, Marcellus's evolution in the book is mimetic of Rome's in the epic, a further indication that Book 14 is, as Stocks 2014, 150–62, observes, "the *Punica* in miniature."

25 Sil. 14.39–44, 50–54, 93–95, 180, 281–86, 301, 338, 341, 505–11, 562, 642, 647–48.

26 Luc. 3.301–2, 340, 355, 358, 388, 463, 478, 497, 516, 526, 553, 561, 583, 586, 610, 667, 697, 728, 753.

cultural influence, there is an important difference between them: Syracuse is, additionally, portrayed as eastern, exotic, and decadent (Sil. 14.654–65), whereas Massilia is not.[27] This portrait of Syracuse, especially given that it appears in connection with her fall, is moralizing in tone, suggesting that her downfall is, in part, attributable to her luxurious ways.[28] More than that, however, Syracuse's "foreignness" calls attention to one of the central ideas in Lucan's epic, to which Massilia's story, among others, testifies: that civil war has the potential to regenerate itself, to spread, and to infect non-Roman "others."[29] This idea is central, in fact, to Silius's treatment of the Sicilian campaign in *Punica* 14 as well, and we find evidence thereof in an allusion to Lucan in the book's programmatic proem.

In the proem, Silius calls on the Muses to turn their attention to Sicily (Sil. 14.1–2) and other locales (3–8). Here he anticipates the theaters of war to which his narrative turns in this and subsequent books of the epic: in addition to Syracuse (4) in Book 14, there will be military operations in Italy (3–4), Macedonia (5), and Greece (5) in Book 15, and across the Sardinian sea (6) in Libya (7) in Book 17 and Spain (8) in Books 15 and 16. Silius concludes as follows: *sic poscit sparsis Mauors agitatus in oris. | ergo age, qua litui, qua ducunt bella, sequamur* ("So demands Mars, stirred up in far-flung lands. Come on, then. Let us follow where the war-trumpets, where wars lead," Sil. 14.9–10). The phrase *Mauors agitatus* echoes a similar collocation, *Mauors agitans*, in *Bellum Ciuile* 7, where Julius Caesar, urging on his men at the battle of Pharsalus, is compared to Mars driving the Bistones before him (Luc. 7.567–71):

---

[27] There may also be an allusion to Lucan in the Silian passage that underlines this difference. Among Syracuse's riches are elegantly crafted statues of the gods, which contrast with the crude, rustic images of gods found in the grove at Massilia: *simulacra deorum | numen ab arte datum seruantia* (Sil. 14.662–63) = *simulacraque maesta deorum | arte carent* (Luc. 3.412–13). But on *simulacra deorum*, also cf. Lucr. 5.75, 6.419; Cic. *Cons.* fr. 10.41 (Courtney); Tib. 2.5.77; Sil. 3.30. Also, note that Silius refers to Syracuse's temples thereafter in a way that recalls temples in Alexandria in *Bellum Ciuile* 10: *templa uetustis | ... d e i s* (Sil. 14.672–73) = *templa uetusti | n u m i - n i s* (Luc. 10.15–16).

[28] Compare the faithless city of Capua, whose decadence is likewise seen as a factor contributing to her demise: Burck 1984b, 48–49; Cowan 2007, 35–36, 40–41. Also, note that Silius focuses on Capua's wealth and luxury in connection with the city's fall (Sil. 13.351–56), much as he does in Syracuse's case, and that that passage and a similar treatment of the subject in Sil. 11.38–43 echo Luc. 1.160–65, where moral decline is identified as one of the causes of civil war (Marks 2010a, 143). For more on the relationship between Capua and Syracuse in the *Punica*, see Marks 2005b, 259–62.

[29] Hence, the civil war becomes a world war. For more, see Bexley 2014.

> quacumque uagatur,
> sanguineum ueluti quatiens Bellona flagellum
> Bistonas aut Mauors agitans, si uerbere saeuo
> Palladia stimulet turbatos aegide currus, 570
> nox ingens scelerum est.

> Wherever he ranges about, just as Bellona brandishing her bloody whip or Mars driving forth the Bistones, if with furious lashings he drives on his team, alarmed by Pallas's aegis, there is a vast gloom of wickedness.

The parallel succinctly reinforces the theme of "civil war abroad"; for Pharsalus testifies to the reach of the Roman civil war beyond Italy, just as Massilia does earlier in that epic and just as Syracuse testifies to the reach of the Punic War beyond Italy in the *Punica*. But the allusion also hints at an important difference between the two scenarios: in the *Bellum Ciuile* Lucan's Caesar spreads civil war abroad—note the active participle *agitans*—whereas Silius's Romans are drawn into a civil war conflict abroad by others, namely, the Syracusans—note the passive participle *agitatus*. Moreover, Silius's Romans stand in marked contrast to Caesar because they are involved neither in civil war nor in anything evocative thereof (as they were, say, in the first half of the epic), but rather, are involved in a conflict with a foreign foe, which is itself involved in civil strife, as we have seen.

The Romans' victory at Syracuse, therefore, signals a reverse of the situation in Lucan's epic: instead of spreading civil war abroad, they are now in the position of checking it and putting a stop to it, which they in effect do by taking the city. The outcome of events at Syracuse points, then, to the possibility that one may halt civil war's regenerative, totalizing force. Add the fact that Silius puts such emphasis on the clemency Marcellus exhibits toward the vanquished Syracusans when he takes the city (Sil. 14.665–75, 679–83), and it may be that the poet is also suggesting that a good, powerful individual like Marcellus can be instrumental in this process of checking civil strife abroad, just as a wicked, powerful individual like Lucan's Caesar can be instrumental in perpetuating and spreading it.[30] Two allusions to *Bellum Ciuile* 2, in fact, speak to this point. First, when

---

30 In this respect Silius's anticipation of Rome's civil war future from the perspective of the Second Punic War might remind us of the Sallustian idea of *metus hostilis*, according to which Rome's moral decline was a consequence of her defeat of Carthage in the Third Punic War; Marcellus would thus represent simultaneously Rome as she was before that decline and a way to counteract or resist it after its onset. Silius's positive assessment of Marcellus's leadership, though, is also shaped by his historicizing treatment of the Second Punic War as a whole, which

Marcellus makes his final push to take Syracuse and has his men storm its walls, we are reminded of Domitius Ahenobarbus when at Corfinium he sends his men out to destroy a bridge so as to check Caesar's advance: *i n f u n d u n t rapidum conuulsis moenibus agmen* ("They pour their army swiftly over the ruined walls," Sil. 14.638) = *d e u o l u i t rapidum nequiquam moenibus agmen* ("In vain, he had his army hasten down from the walls," Luc. 2.491).[31] Although Domitius's plan, unlike Marcellus's, proves unsuccessful (note *nequiquam*)—Caesar forces Domitius's men to retreat (Luc. 3.500–4)—the allusion, nevertheless, figures Marcellus's offensive maneuver as if it were a defensive one, and one with the specific aim of halting Caesar's progress and, with that, the spread of his civil war. As Domitius explains to his troops before sending them out (Luc. 2.487–90):

> hoc limite bellum
> haereat, hac hostis lentus terat otia ripa.
> praecipitem cohibete ducem: uictoria nobis
> hic primum stans Caesar erit.   490

Let the war be stuck at this boundary; let the enemy linger and, inactive, waste his time on this bank. Keep this rash leader in check: for us it will be a victory if Caesar is first held up here.[32]

The second allusion comes when Marcellus, taking Syracuse, restrains his troops from sacking the city: *propere r e u o c a t a militis ira | iussit stare domos* ("He quickly checked his soldiers' wrath and ordered the houses to be left standing," Sil. 14.671–72). This recalls Pompey when he first takes the field and tries to rouse his troops with a speech (Luc. 2.528–30):

> iamque secuturo iussurus classica Phoebo
> t e m p t a n d a s que ratus moturi militis iras
> alloquitur tacitas ueneranda uoce cohortes.   530

---

invites us to see his virtues and those of other leaders, especially Scipio, as Flavian virtues or prefigurations thereof. For more, see Marks 2005b, 252–69, 276–88.

[31] The Lucanean line is also alluded to in a "civil-war-esque" moment in Valerius's *Argonautica*, Cyzicus's battle with the Argonauts: *saeuit acerba fremens t a r d u m que a moenibus agmen | increpitat* (V. Fl. 3.229–30).

[32] Lucan here may have also influenced Hannibal's assessment of Fabius's delaying tactics *inuentum, dum se cohibet terimurque sedendo, | uincendi genus* (Sil. 7.151–52).

On the next day, Pompey, planning to give the trumpet signal, thinks that he should incite the wrath of his soldiers who are about to march and in a lofty tone addresses his silent cohorts.

The contrast between Pompey and Marcellus that the allusion develops, the former spurring his men on to fight, the latter reining them in, complements Marcellus's identification with Domitius in the previous allusion and combines with it to clarify the civil war "message" we are to draw from the conclusion of *Punica* 14: the siege of Syracuse marks an attempt to curb civil strife, and Marcellus's clemency exemplifies the good a powerful individual can do in achieving that end.[33]

While I have argued that Silius uses the theme of civil war in *Punica* 14 to point to positive developments in Rome's story at this point in his epic, I do not wish to suggest that he is blind to its darker realities in Roman history. Indeed, we cannot forget that while the events at Syracuse look back to those at Massilia in an allusive sense, evoking Lucan's *Bellum Ciuile*, they also look forward to civil war in a chronological sense, being figured in terms of a civil war event in Rome's future, the siege of Massilia. This is not to discount the fact that Silius has produced a historically revisionist version of events that conveys a constructive moral lesson, but it is also not to deny the possibility that what happened at Syracuse, in Silius's eyes, may have contributed, in some measure, to Rome's future civil wars. Antony Augoustakis, in fact, raises this very point in a recent discussion of a Sicilian named Daphnis, whose death in the sea battle occasions a lengthy reflection on his legendary ancestor, Daphnis, the founder of bucolic poetry (Sil. 14.462–76). Reading the passage in connection with Syracuse's fall at the end of the book, he argues that "Daphnis' presence marks the transition from

---

[33] When referring to Marcellus's moral example for future ages, Silius also evokes by allusion the Caesarian Curio when he inquires about the legend of Antaeus: *et dabit antiquos ductorem noscere m o r e s* (Sil. 14.683) = *nominis antiqui cupientem noscere c a u s a s* (Luc. 4.591). The parallel hints at an identification of Marcellus's victory over Syracuse with Hercules' over Antaeus in Africa, which is recounted immediately thereafter (Luc. 4.593–655), but also implies a contrast between Marcellus and Curio, who, though emboldened by Hercules' success, will be defeated and killed during his African campaign and ends up resembling more closely the vanquished Antaeus. Shortly thereafter, Silius concludes the book by praising the emperor for checking the rapacity of provincial administrators throughout the world (Sil. 14.684–88) and thus compares him with Marcellus. But an echo of Lucan may also suggest a comparison with Cato: *ni cura uiri, qui nunc dedit otia mundo, | effrenum arceret populandi cuncta furorem* (Sil. 14.686–87) = *otia solus agam? procul hanc arcete furorem* (Luc. 2.295). The parallel, incidentally, lends support to the reading *furorem*, which is transmitted in the MSS, over *pudorem*, the emendation of Håkanson 1979, 35 printed by Shackleton Bailey.

the pastoral world of Greek Sicily to the imperial realities of an island destined to be ruled by the Romans after the Second Punic War."[34] Augoustakis's observation helpfully sets forth the wider historical context in which civil war will one day flourish and to which Silius's allusions, as we have seen, look ahead; for one of those imperial realities of which he speaks will be the spread of civil war abroad, whether to Sicily, Massilia, Pharsalus, or beyond.

---

[34] Augoustakis 2012, 134.

John Penwill†
How It All Began: Civil War and Valerius's *Argonautica*

Since the accession/usurpation of Galba in 68 CE exposed the *arcanum imperii*, that one could become *princeps* elsewhere than at Rome (Tac. *Hist.* 1.4), Rome would thereafter live always in the shadow of civil war. No matter what its shortcomings, the Julian regime had at least brought stability, and if *principatus* was the price to be paid for *pax*, Rome had been prepared to pay it.[1] But the Year of Four Emperors showed that this was a flawed bargain, that *principatus* in fact was the prize for which the ambitious were only too willing to abandon *pax* and (re)create the horrors of Lucan's vision of civil war.[2]

For Valerius Flaccus's monarchs (and this applies particularly to Pelias in Thessaly and Aeetes in Colchis), the power they hold is always a potential prize to be won by another and must therefore be defended in the face of actual or perceived threats. It is a principle enshrined in heaven, as Jupiter's reference to the battles by which he attained and subsequently retained power attests (V. Fl. 1.563–65).[3] Prophecies and the entrails of sacrificed beasts have warned Pelias that Jason, his brother Aeson's son, would bring about his destruction, and so he devises a mission for him which will get him out of the way, hopefully forever (V. Fl. 1.26–37).[4] Likewise, in Book 5, the shade of Phrixus appears to Aeetes

---

I would like to thank all those who heard earlier versions of this paper for their questions and comments, and particularly the editors of this volume, Darcy Krasne and Lauren Donovan Ginsberg, for their patience and encouragement.

---

[1] For the attitude of the Roman upper classes to the establishment and conduct of the Augustan principate, see esp. Tac. *Ann.* 1.2 (written of course from a Trajanic/Hadrianic perspective). Cf. Davis 1999, 3–6.

[2] The civil wars of 68/69 proved the final end to any confidence Romans might have had that the Augustan settlement had put an end to civil war for good. Cf. Krasne 2011, 105: "Against the background of civil war, a new dynasty had again emerged to replace the old, following the pattern of civil wars which had first generated and then repeatedly marred, or threatened to mar, the principate." See further n. 31 below.

[3] Cf. the observation of the Athenian delegate in Thucydides' Melian dialogue, who likewise universalizes: "Our opinion of the gods and our knowledge of men lead us to conclude that it is a general and necessary law of nature to rule wherever one can" (Th. 5.105, transl. Warner). Statius at *Theb.* 1.142–64 reduces the motivation of Eteocles and Polynices to *nuda potestas* (150)—not wealth, not moral principle, but power pure and simple. See Hardie 1993a, 95.

[4] On the significance of the intrafamilial conflict between Pelias and Aeson in Valerius's version of the Argonaut saga, see now Seal 2014, 127–30.

in a dream, warning that if the Golden Fleece is removed from the kingdom it will cause the collapse of his regime: *tunc tibi regnorum labes luctusque supersunt* ("then there remains for you the fall of your kingship and grief," V. Fl. 5.236).[5] Hence in spite of warnings that the continued presence of the Fleece will bring disaster to his people (5.259–62), Aeetes refuses to give it up. When his half-brother Perses objects and receives popular support in doing so, Aeetes accuses him of plotting to overthrow him, and within the space of three lines we are suddenly in the middle of a full-scale civil war. As Aeetes puts it to Jason in the course of seeking his support in the conflict, Perses is simply manifesting a universal truth (*sceptri sic omnibus una cupido*, "so much is the scepter the sole object of everyone's desire," V. Fl. 5.536), and when Jupiter gives his outline of future events in Colchis, the *sceptrum* is precisely what Perses will get (*uictorque domos et sceptra tenebit*, "victorious he will possess both palace and scepter," V. Fl. 5.684).[6] The civil conflict in Colchis mirrors that in Thessaly; at both ends of the earth, tyrants fear violent overthrow, particularly at the hands of close relatives, and will take any measures to ensure their survival.[7] The *bella* are always *plus quam ciuilia*.

Which of course brings us to Lucan. For Lucan, the ultimate cause of the civil war between Caesar and Pompey was the same principle: as sure as night follows day, *nulla fides regni sociis, omnisque potestas | impatiens consortis erit* ("there will be no trust between allies in rulership, and no power will brook a partner," Luc. 1.92–93), and the power-sharing arrangement supposedly cemented by Pompey's marriage to Julia was therefore bound to fail. At first Jason resists the operation of this principle; his initial reaction to Pelias imposing the quest for the Golden Fleece on him is to contemplate taking advantage of this and staging a coup, calling on the partisans of Aeson for support. But as a young and idealistic hero (like the heroes of the *Iliad* whose motivation is the pursuit of glory rather than the recovery of Helen), he rejects this in favor of the glory that will be his if the quest succeeds (V. Fl. 1.73–78). But the brute fact of the matter is that had he

---

5 The text used for quotations from Valerius is that of Ehlers 1980; critical apparatus, where relevant, is adapted from Liberman 1997–2002. Translations, unless otherwise stated, are my own.
6 On the interconnectedness between the *sceptrum* and civil war elsewhere in Flavian epic, see Dominik in this volume.
7 On tyrants in the *Argonautica* see Cowan 2014, who draws attention to "the remarkable prominence of the figure of the tyrant" in the poem (231) and the way in which "civil war and its domestic analogue, kin-killing, pervade [it]" (244). Cf. Zissos 2003, 673–77, who sees in this preoccupation with tyranny the hallmarks of "a narrative that manifests an immense charge of anxiety" with respect to contemporary Roman politics; the point is further developed at Zissos 2009, 354–62.

pursued the Lucanic rather than the heroic course, he would have saved his family's lives. His moment of sudden (*subitus*) panic at 1.693–99 as he confronts the possible (and, as we will shortly discover, actual) consequences of leaving his family at the mercy of Pelias serves right at the beginning of the expedition to undermine, and I would say fatally undermine, any positive aspects of the heroic impulse by which he and his fellow-Argonauts are motivated. And by the time we get to the end, the undermining is complete. The success of Jason's quest has relied on the assistance of Medea, without whose magic arts he could never have performed the tasks imposed by Aeetes nor seized the Fleece from its guardian dragon. Now in possession of the Fleece and married to Medea, he finds himself trapped on the island of Peuce, besieged by a fleet commanded by his new brother-in-law, Absyrtus. Far from bringing peace and harmony, the marriage, as in the *Bellum Ciuile*, has a toxic effect. In the *Argonautica*, the union of Thessaly and Colchis, at opposite ends of the earth at the beginning, binds the two together in transcontinental conflict, a conflict that will last through history down to Valerius's own time. That between Pompey and Caesar is but one manifestation of it. The most recent is the Flavians' overthrow of Vitellius.

That Lucan has finally taken over the quest saga that the *Argonautica*'s Apollonian paradigm shows it "should have been"[8] is clearly demonstrated by the way in which the *Argonautica*'s ending echoes that of the *Bellum Ciuile*.[9] Both

---

[8] Hardie 1993a, 83: "Valerius Flaccus's *Argonautica* is a version of the archetypical Greek myth of the questing journey." Clauss 2014, 102–5, sees Valerius's incorporation of the Flavians (specifically, Vespasian) into the Argonautic myth as wholly positive, replacing the Julii as "the apex of universal history"; as will be apparent, I have serious reservations about this interpretation.

[9] The ending of the *Argonautica* is extensively discussed at Hershkowitz 1998b, 1–34, and Monaghan 2002, 150–90. Hershkowitz devotes her opening chapter to an analysis of the ending and provides many excellent insights, but she is unable to escape from the assumption, based on Quintilian's enigmatic *multum in Valerio Flacco nuper amisimus* ("we have recently lost much in Valerius Flaccus," *Inst.* 10.1.90), that "the poet died before he could complete his epic" (2). Monaghan proposes that the assumption that the poem is unfinished rests on erroneous and anachronistic preconceptions about closure. She focuses her attention on the characterization of Medea and argues that Valerius shuts off his narrative before she morphs from an epic to a tragic character, the tipping point of which is her complicity in the murder of Absyrtus—an act which in Apollonius she advocates in the speech following the equivalent of her final Valerian one (A.R. 4.410–20). This to me seems the right conclusion, but arrived at for the wrong reason. The central character in the epic is Jason, not Medea, and it is Jason's dilemma, to which Medea is a contributor, that is the key focus in this final part of the final book. Any argument as to whether or not the *Argonautica* is complete must be grounded on that—as well as on those perceptive if all-too-obvious principles enunciated by Jamie Masters with respect to the end of Lucan's *Bellum Ciuile*: one, that the best evidence for where a work is supposed to end is where it does in fact end, and two, that it is up to those who claim a work is unfinished to prove their case (Masters

poems end abruptly with their protagonist surrounded by forces vastly superior in number and seemingly no way out; and both seem to break off at the end of a book considerably shorter than the average, giving the clear impression that the work is unfinished. First, Lucan (10.535–39, 542, 543–46):

> dum parat in uacuas Martem transferre carinas,   535
> dux Latius tota subitus formidine belli
> cingitur: hinc densae praetexunt litora classes.
> hinc tergo insultant pedites. uia nulla salutis,
> non fuga, non uirtus; uix spes quoque mortis honestae ...
> ...
> captus sorte loci pendet ...
> ...
>   ... respexit in agmine denso
> Scaeuam perpetuae meritum iam nomina famae
> ad campos, Epidamne, tuos, ubi solus apertis   545
> obsedit muris calcantem moenia Magnum.

As he is preparing to take the fighting up to the enemy ships, the Latian commander [*sc.* Caesar] is suddenly surrounded by war in all its terror. On the one side a thick mass of ships is lining the water's edge, and on the other infantry are leaping at his rear. There is no avenue of rescue, not in flight, not in heroic action; scarcely even the hope of an honorable death. ... Trapped by the nature of the place, he is left hanging. ... He looked back in the massed column and saw Scaeva, already winner of a name of everlasting glory on your fields, Epidamnus, where with the walls breached he alone beset the rampart-trampling Magnus.

Compare Valerius (V. Fl. 8.261–63, 306, 463b–67):

1992, 216–59). See Penwill 2013, 30–31 with n. 7. Ripoll 2008, 180–83, following Nesselrath 1998, postulates that the final event in the poem would have been a duel between Jason and Absyrtus (a possibility also aired by Hershkowitz 1998b, 9). But Valerius has closed this particular avenue by bringing on an overwhelming number of Colchians (the whole population excluding the royal family, V. Fl. 8.280–82) who are only kept at bay by Juno's intervention; unlike Turnus in *Aeneid* 12, Absyrtus holds the position of strength and has no motive for agreeing to resolve the issue by single combat. Toohey 1993, 201, postulates that by the second half of the poem Jason has become the analogue for Domitian rather than Vespasian, and that to continue would require the narration of an event that would horrify Minerva and threaten what he terms "the ideological substrate of the *Argonautica*" that is embodied in Domitian's special relationship with this goddess (Suet. *Dom.* 15.3; cf. Mart. 7.1), concluding that Valerius might have found "premature silence a preferable means for ending his poem." Unfortunately, Toohey's argument is based on the second half of the *Argonautica* being composed during the reign of Domitian, which does not accord with current scholarly opinion (following Stover 2012, 7–26).

> Absyrtus subita praeceps cum classe parentis
> aduehitur profugis infestam lampada Grais
> concutiens diramque premens clamore sororem ...
> ...
> cum subitas uidere rates ...
> ...
> maestus at ille [sc. Iason] minis et mota Colchidos ira 463b
> haeret, et hinc praesens pudor, hinc decreta suorum
> dura premunt. utcumque tamen mulcere gementem 465
> temptat et ipse gemens et †temperat dictis:
> "mene aliquid meruisse putas? me talia uelle?"

463b L] om. V || mota Ehlers] noto L || 466 gemens et dictis temperat iras M² || 467 ita interpunxit Mozley; alii aliter || mene L] mane V || meruisse] metuisse Barth

Absyrtus came rushing towards them with a fleet suddenly procured from his father, shaking a hostile torch at the fugitive Greeks and assailing his sister with shouts of "*dira*" ...
...
When they [sc. the Minyae] saw these ships suddenly appear ...
...
But the gloom-filled Jason is stopped in his tracks by the Colchian woman's threats and surging anger; on the one side shame, aroused by the one confronting him, on the other, his companions' demands, both weigh heavily on him. Nevertheless he tries in whatever way he can amid his own grief to calm her distress and say something to assuage her <anger>: "Do you think I have deserved something? that this is the sort of thing I want?"

Caesar is trapped on Pharos, an island at one of the mouths of the seven-branched Nile, while Jason is trapped on Peuce, an island at the mouth of the seven-branched Danube;[10] and as Caesar is brought to his final moment through his involvement with Cleopatra and consequent intervention in the grubby civil conflict in Alexandria, so Jason is brought to his through Medea, now poised to involve him in her own version of *bella plus quam ciuilia*. And in Jason's case there is a moral dilemma also, as he is caught between his duty to his followers and that to his wife, both of whom express their feelings about the situation and about Jason himself in no uncertain terms. The impasse is complete, and Valerius does nothing to resolve it. Like Caesar, Jason is left hanging; and, as for Caesar, there is for Jason no *fuga*, no *uirtus*, and certainly no *spes mortis honestae*.[11]

---

[10] The iteration of the "seven-branched" motif is significant; V. Fl. 8.187 clearly alludes to Luc. 8.445. Pellucchi 2012, 234, notes the elaborate construction of Valerius's line; the intention is surely to make the allusion patent.

[11] It should be stressed that this interpretation of the *Argonautica*'s ending does not depend for its validity on the proposition that the *Bellum Ciuile*'s ending is likewise intentional. The text of

This is the final and perhaps the most telling allusion to Lucan in the *Argonautica*. But Lucan has, in fact, been there right from the very first lines of Book 1 (V. Fl. 1.1–4):

> prima deum magnis canimus freta peruia natis
> fatidicamque ratem, Scythici quae Phasidis oras
> ausa sequi mediosque inter iuga concita cursus
> rumpere flammifero tandem consedit Olympo.

> Seas first traversed by great sons of gods we sing, and the oracular ship, which after daring to make for the shores of Scythian Phasis and to force its way between the rocks moving against it finally settled on Olympus.

Note first the unusual first person plural *canimus*, very rarely used in an initial declaration of intent. The other surviving example is the second line of the *Bellum Ciuile* (Luc. 1.1–2):

> bella per Emathios plus quam ciuilia campos
> iusque datum sceleri canimus ...

> Wars more than civil across Emathian plains and legality conferred on crime we sing ...

Zissos, in his commentary, suggests that its appearance in Valerius "probably constitutes a nod to Lucan,"[12] but in my view it is more than just a nod, occurring as it does in the same metrical *sedes* in line 1 of his poem as it does in Lucan's line 2. Then there is the echo of Lucan's treatment of the Argonautic expedition in his catalogue of *semina Martis* ("seeds of warfare") that originate in Thessaly (Luc. 6.400–1):

> prima fretum scindens Pagasaeo litore pinus   400
> terrenum ignotas hominem proiecit in undas.

> First to cleave the sea from Pagasaean shore a pine-tree cast land-locked humanity out into unknown waves.

Lucan's epic as received by Valerius was one that ended at line 546 of Book 10, and it is with *that* text that Valerius is setting up an intertextual relationship. Cf. van der Schuur in this volume, who explores Statius's similar engagement with the end of Seneca's *Phoenissae*, another possibly unfinished Neronian text of civil war.
12 Zissos 2008, 74.

Note here the emphasis on primacy, together with the echo of *fretum scindens* in *freta peruia*—and all this in the very first line.¹³

The Lucanic ending is in fact the final element in a series of allusions to and evocations of Lucan that permeate the *Argonautica*. In his 2012 book *Epic and Empire in Vespasianic Rome*, Tim Stover takes a positive view of these allusions, arguing that the poem is one of "renewal and rebirth" and that it represents through the "rehabilitation of the epic genre" from Lucan's challenge an expression of support for and relief at Vespasian's "refoundation of the imperial project" after the disastrous civil wars of 68–69 CE.¹⁴ My own view is that this is far from being the case. Prophecy, and particularly prophecy that looks beyond the ending of the poem, is significant here, and I start with the paired prophecies of Mopsus and Idmon at V. Fl. 1.207–39.¹⁵ Mopsus's tone recalls that of the possessed

---

13 For a full discussion of the encomium that follows, see Penwill 2013, 32–37, with bibliography there cited.

14 Stover 2012, 1–4 and *passim*; more recently, Stover 2014. Cf. Mitousi 2014, 155: "[T]he innovative voyage of the Argo stands for the Flavian dynastic enterprise." The main difficulty I have with Stover's position is the function of Valerius's allusions to Lucan, which, as will be apparent, I regard not as "rehabilitation of the epic genre" but as an imposition of the Lucanic world-view onto the supposedly positive legend of the quest for the Golden Fleece. Buckley 2010, 434, tries to have it both ways: "I aim to show that Valerius Flaccus combines the appeal to a 'traditional' Homeric-Virgilian narrative technique with Lucan's *Bellum Civile* to forge an innovatory approach to epic for a new ruling dynasty: an approach that *both* encodes a positive 'new beginning' *and* signals its awareness that this is just another story in the cycle of Roman power—power gained by civil war" (italics original). Cf. Krasne 2011, 152–61, who discusses the issue of whether the *Argonautica*'s attitude to the Flavian regime is optimistic, pessimistic, or somewhere in between by reference to the image of the Dioscuri as parallels for Titus and Domitian (further on which, see Wood 2016 and Stocks in this volume). In his more recent study, Stover 2014 portrays Jason as an old-style epic hero, winning the admiration of Medea by his feats of arms on the battlefield (V. Fl. 6.575–760, on which see also Fucecchi 2014, 124–28). Jason may be as comfortable in this role as he was in the Cyzicus episode (V. Fl. 3.80–86), but this story requires more than that: Jason can only succeed in his performance of the tasks imposed by Aeetes with Medea's help, and the heroic value system receives its final death-knell early in Book 8 as Medea teases Jason by suggesting that he might care to seize the Fleece from the guardian dragon while it is fully awake. Jason is scared (*trepido*, V. Fl. 8.59) and reduced to silence in awe of her (*ille silet, tantus subiit tum uirginis horror*, V. Fl. 8.67). (For an interpretation more generous to Jason, cf. Ripoll 2008, 175–77.) Zissos 1999, 290–91, notes the fact that Valerius alludes to three possibilities for overcoming the dragon available in the tradition, which serves to throw the version he chooses (and more importantly the two he rejects) into higher relief.

15 On these prophecies and their relationship to each other, see Feeney 1991, 316–17; Groß 2003, 39–63; Zissos 2004a, 26–35; Zissos 2004b, 319–23; Galli 2007, 150; Krasne 2011, 126–27; Cowan 2014, 247–48, with further bibliography there cited.

matrona at Luc. 1.674–95;[16] like her he is filled with the god, like her he presents a series of vivid images, like her he is transported in both space and time. His visions include the storm and its calming, the loss of Hylas, Pollux wounded by Amycus, Jason's ploughing and sowing, conflict over the Fleece, Medea's escape from Corinth, and her murder of the children and of Creusa. Idmon's prophecy is far more generalized: there will be toil, certainly, but then eventual success and a return to parental embrace (with a tear or two shed for the ones who don't make it back).[17] What we have here, I suggest, are two models for reading the *Argonautica*:[18] one which gives attention to detail and is alive to the dubious moral status of the enterprise, to the individual suffering involved, and to the grim future beyond the end of the poem; the other a bland and anodyne view that it is nothing but a basic quest narrative in which hard work produces a successful outcome. The former one might call the Lucanic reading, the latter the Caesarean, and it is instructive to apply them retrospectively to the encomium where, notoriously for the dating of its composition, many of the verbs are in the future tense. An Idmonian/Caesarean reading will dwell on the toil and achievement narrative of *Iudaea capta*, to be rendered in graphic detail by Domitian (V. Fl. 1.12–14), and see in the foretelling of Vespasian's catasterism the accolade of a loyal citizen exercising his mantic powers as priest of Apollo.[19] A Mopsian/Lucanic reading would focus more on the Lucanic intertext and on the fact that Vespasian's star is said specifically to be of use to ships from Greece, Sidon, and Egypt, presumably in their voyages west, and recall that this reflects (in reverse order) the route Vespasian himself took as he made his move on Rome. Civil war and the no longer *arcanum imperii* lurk here. The point is in fact reinforced by Neptune at V. Fl. 1.644–45: *ueniant Phariae Tyriaeque carinae | permissumque putent* ("let ships of Pharos and Tyre come and think it permitted so to do").[20] That is one of

---

16 Hershkowitz 1998b, 26–27; Fuà 2002, 109–14; Zissos 2004a, 29.
17 Zissos 2004a, 26–35, in his lengthy analysis of this passage, usefully draws attention to what he terms the "vatic dissonance" between Mopsus and Idmon, relating their prophecies not only to the group of three given at Luc. 1.584–695 (Arruns, Figulus, and the unnamed *matrona* mentioned above) but also to the Phemonoe episode of Luc. 5.67–236, where the priestess first gives Appius false information about the functioning of the oracle but then under the inspiration of Apollo finally reveals the truth. The parallels are not exact (there is a good deal of *parturient montes* about the oracle as ultimately delivered), but to link the misleading part of Phemonoe's discourse to Idmon and the frenzied climax to Mopsus enriches our understanding of the relationship between Valerius's two prophets and our awareness of the Lucanic allusions.
18 For another internal model of reading in the epic, see Landrey in this volume.
19 Zissos 2008, 80–81.
20 On Neptune's remark and its implications, cf. M. Davis 1989, 64.

the futures to which the *Argonautica* looks forward. Absyrtus's pursuit and blockade of the Argonauts is but the first in a long series of naval operations that are enabled by this opening up of the seas and by the existence of the Argo as a blueprint.[21] That the poem ends with the blockade still in place invites us to contemplate its implications not just for history but for the present. It is pertinent to note here that Idmon is said to foresee his own death, foreshadowing the fact that he and his ideology will be killed off before the poem comes to an end. The relative space given to the two in Book 1 is also instructive: Mopsus gets sixteen lines, Idmon four.

Later in Book 1, we have the prophecy of Jupiter (V. Fl. 1.531–60):[22]

```
tum genitor: "uetera haec nobis et condita pergunt
ordine cuncta suo rerumque a principe cursu
fixa manent; neque enim terris tum sanguis in ullis
noster erat cum fata darem, iustique facultas
hinc mihi cum uarios struerem per saecula reges.         535
atque ego curarum repetam decreta mearum.
iam pridem regio quae uirginis aequor ad Helles
et Tanai tenus immenso descendit ab Euro
undat equis floretque uiris nec tollere contra
ulla pares animos nomenque capessere bellis              540
ausa manus. sic fata locos, sic ipse fouebam.
accelerat sed summa dies Asiamque labantem
linquimus et poscunt iam me sua tempora Grai.
inde meae quercus tripodesque animaeque parentum
hanc pelago misere manum. uia facta per undas            545
perque hiemes, Bellona, tibi. nec uellera tantum
indignanda manent propiorque ex uirgine rapta
ille dolor, sed—nulla magis sententia menti
fixa meae—ueniet Phrygia iam pastor ab Ida,
qui gemitus irasque pares et mutua Grais                 550
dona ferat. quae classe dehinc effusa procorum
bella, quot ad Troiae flentes hiberna Mycenas,
quot proceres natosque deum, quae robora cernes
oppetere et magnis Asiam concedere fatis!
```

---

21 One of the functions of the ship-building scene (V. Fl. 1.121–29) is to suggest that anyone with the necessary skills can duplicate this work. This comes to dramatic fulfilment in Book 8, where after impotently watching the Argo sail off with Medea and the Fleece because they have no means of pursuit (V. Fl. 8.136–39), the Colchians suddenly turn up at Peuce with a fleet large enough to transport the entire population (V. Fl. 8.259–84). They certainly prove to be faster learners than Pelias's Thessalians, who likewise impotently watch the Argo sailing off with Acastus across what is, to them, a medium as impossible as the air (V. Fl. 1.700–8).
22 On this passage and Jupiter's role in the epic, see also Krasne in this volume; on the influence of Lucan on Jupiter's prophecy, see also Fucecchi in this volume.

> hinc Danaum de fine sedet gentesque fouebo 555
> mox alias. pateant montes siluaeque lacusque
> cunctaque claustra maris, spes et metus omnibus esto.
> arbiter ipse locos terrenaque summa mouendo
> experiar, quaenam populis longissima cunctis
> regna uelim linquamque datas ubi certus habenas." 560

Then [spoke] the Father: "All these things, established in ancient times, are now moving forward in their own order; from the very beginning of their course, all remain fixed. For nowhere on earth were there blood-relations of ours when I was allotting destinies, and so I was able to exercise impartiality when I was deciding on those who would rule in various places through the ages. And I shall here repeat the decrees I made with such care. For a long time now has the region that stretches down from the measureless East to the sea of virgin Helle, and as far as the Tanais, abounded in horses and excelled in men; no group has dared to raise equal spirit against them or seize their fame in war. Such was the favor I used to show their lands and destinies. But their final day is rapidly approaching, and we are abandoning tottering Asia; the Greeks are now demanding their time of me. That is why my oaks, my tripods and the spirits of their forefathers have sent this band to sea. And it is for you, Bellona, that a way has been forged through waves and storms. It is not just resentment over the fleece that lingers, nor that closer pain arising from an abducted maiden, but—and no decision is more firmly fixed in my mind—a shepherd will come from Phrygian Ida to bring equal anguish and anger to the Greeks as payback. What wars will you see pour forth from the fleet led by her suitors! how many winters bewailed by Mycenae! how many leaders and sons of gods, what heroes will you see fall and Asia yield to my high destinies! After that, the end of the Danai is settled, and I shall soon be favoring other races. Let mountains, forests, lakes, and all boundaries of the sea be there for the taking; let hope and fear be there for all. Myself as controller, by changing the locations of earthly hegemonies, will experiment to see who gets the longest rule over all peoples and where I can confidently leave the reins of government once they have been handed over."

As many commentators have observed, this is (in Stover's words) "clearly modelled on the prophecy offered by Vergil's Jupiter in *Aeneid* 1."[23] That is certainly true in the formal sense, and there is indeed a significant intertextual relationship established; and as with the corresponding prophecy of Jupiter in Book 3 of Silius Italicus's *Punica*, its meaning and significance are determined by that relationship.[24] Here, too, the differences constitute the crucial element. First of all, in the *Aeneid* the prophecy is given by way of reassurance to an anxious Venus pleading

---

[23] Stover 2012, 28. Cf. Hardie 1993a, 83; Zissos 2008, 305. See most recently Ganiban 2014, whose essay, like mine, draws attention to the differences imposed by Valerius on the Vergilian paradigm, and Davis 2015, 159.
[24] On Silius, see Penwill 2013, 46–52. In no case are these pronouncements of Jupiter included simply because it is a requirement of the epic genre that they be there, as suggested by, e.g., Franchet d'Espèrey 1998, 220, and Kleywegt 2005, 289.

the cause of her son. What prompts the *Argonautica*'s prophecy is both similar and radically different: it is a father pleading the cause of his son, but in this case the father is the Sun-god, the son is Aeetes, and what the father is pleading for is the *abandonment* of the Argonautic enterprise (V. Fl. 1.505–27), not its success. And whereas Venus pleads for fulfilment of Jupiter's promise that Aeneas's descendants will rise to world domination (Verg. *A.* 1.234–36), here the Sun-god portrays Aeetes as pacifist and unambitious, making Phrixus part of his family and sharing the kingdom with him rather than joining with him in a war against Greece.[25] Secondly, in the face of the Sun-god's plea that his son be left alone and that peace prevail, Jupiter is forced into asserting his authority as he outlines the plans he laid down from the beginning of his rule, and what he has to say will not please his immediate audience. Jupiter specifically states that the opening up of the seas which the Argonautic enterprise will bring about is to facilitate not commerce but war and conflict (*uia facta per undas | perque hiemes, Bellona, tibi*, "it is for you, Bellona, that a way has been forged through waves and storms," V. Fl. 1.545–46).[26] Peace is not part of Valerius's Jupiter's grand plan in the way that it was for Vergil's Jupiter (Verg. *A.* 1.291–96). Thirdly, the prophecy proceeds through a series of hegemonic shifts, from the eastern realms of Aeetes and Troy, through the Greeks as a consequence of their success in the quest for the Fleece and victory in the Trojan War, and finally to—well, who? Jupiter says that after the Greeks have had their time of supremacy he will favor "other nations" (*gentesque fouebo | mox alias*, V. Fl. 1.555–56) and "test" them to see whom he can trust to put in charge of the world (V. Fl. 1.558–60):

---

25 The motif of an appeal to Jupiter by the Sun-god is as old as the *Odyssey* (12.377–83), where Helios demands vengeance for his cattle slaughtered by Odysseus's crew. There Zeus agrees (motivated at least in part by Helios's threat to withdraw to Hades if he doesn't), promising to destroy Odysseus's ship. In this case, however, Jupiter refuses the Sun-god's request (which specifically asks for the ship to be turned back, not destroyed—*flecte ratem motusque*, "turn the ship and its course," V. Fl. 1.525); that even this milder resolution is rejected reinforces the significance Jupiter attaches to the success of the Argonautic enterprise and its historical consequences. It is also worth noting with Ganiban that in this instance the Sun-god makes no threat, reflecting the fact that in Valerius he has become a more liminal and subservient figure (Ganiban 2014, 254–56) (although it should be pointed out that chronologically the *Odyssey* episode occurs a generation later than the *Argonautica* one—perhaps now that the Trojan War has been fought and won, Zeus/Jupiter can grant the Sun-god some indulgence!).
26 On the negative aspects of the development of sea-navigation, cf. Ganiban 2014, 253 and 258. Seal 2014, 115–24, argues persuasively for a "causal relation between navigation and internecine strife" which becomes particularly prominent in the second half of the *Argonautica* and prefigures the importance of controlling the sea in the ultimate rise to power of Augustus and Vespasian. Both navigation and civil war are features of the age of Jupiter.

> arbiter ipse locos terrenaque summa mouendo
> experiar, quaenam populis longissima cunctis
> regna uelim linquamque datas ubi certus habenas.   560

> Myself as controller, by changing the locations of earthly hegemonies, will experiment to see who gets the longest rule over all peoples and where I can confidently leave the reins of government once they have been handed over.

Mozley considerately adds a footnote to his Loeb translation to say that "this is obviously meant to be a prophecy of the Roman Empire,"[27] but to my mind it is anything but obvious; nor do I agree with commentators such as Zissos who say that it is "oblique" or "implied."[28] In fact the contrast with the *Aeneid*'s Jupiter (and indeed the *Punica*'s) in this regard is stark. In the *Aeneid*, Jupiter spends his entire speech unfolding details of Roman history, declaring in the midst of it all, "*imperium sine fine dedi*" ("I have already given them power without end," Verg. *A.* 1.279). No experimentation here! And as if to reinforce the perception of his Jupiter's vagueness about Rome, Valerius has him giving specific details about the Trojan War, its cause, and its conduct at V. Fl. 1.548–54, saying of it, moreover, *nulla magis sententia menti | fixa meae* ("no decision is more firmly fixed in my mind," V. Fl. 1.548–49). This ought to mean that the Trojan War is the great watershed of history, that as in the *Aeneid*, Rome will emerge from the ashes of Troy and become the great imperial power, but there is nothing of that in what Valerius's Jupiter has to say.[29] The world, with its mountains, forests, lakes, and

---

27 Mozley 1934, 44 n. 2.
28 Zissos 2008, 321; cf. Taylor 1994, 220: "A Roman audience ... would have no difficulty in recognizing these 'gentes ... alias' as the Roman nation." Possibly so, but this if anything draws further attention towards the omission of Romans in general and Flavians in particular from the prophecy. Clauss 2014, 107, argues that Valerius's Jupiter's refusal to identify the ultimate possessor of power in the world is an indication that Vergil's Jupiter got it wrong and that "the Julio-Claudians can be said to have failed to live up to Jupiter's expectations." This would make the Flavians simply the next stage in the experiment, which is hardly flattering. On the "pointed omission of Rome" in Jupiter's prophecy see Ganiban 2014, 259–61, with bibliography there cited. Kleywegt 2005, 326, suggests that "VF is subtle enough not to name the future world empire, suggesting that as yet Jupiter has not made up his mind about the exact nature of his decision," but there seems to me little subtlety about this passage.
29 Wacht 1991, 15, cites V. Fl. 2.571–73, where the narrative voice speaks of the future "race of the Aeneadae and the glories of a better Troy" (*et genus Aeneadum et Troiae melioris honores*, V. Fl. 2.573) to support his contention that the *gentes aliae* of V. Fl. 1.555–56 are indeed the Romans: "Unter den 'gentes aliae' ... ist also einzig Rom von Valerius ausdrücklich benannt." That the Romans do come to dominate the world is an obvious historical fact for one living in the first century CE; this makes it all the more striking that they are not mentioned as other races are in Jupiter's detailed *Weltenplan*. It is also open to question whether indeed we are living in a "better

seas, is there for the taking, but who gets it all is unspecified. The obvious implication is that we are still in the experimental phase;[30] and the obvious implication of *that* is that the cycle of civil war is still very much with us. Hence the universal motivation of hope and fear (*spes et metus omnibus esto*, V. Fl. 1.557): hope that the regime in place for the time being will prove both benign and long-lasting, fear that with each pivotal moment of succession the horror of civil war will manifest itself once more.[31] For Vergil's Jupiter, Augustus was an end; for Valerius's, Vespasian is not.

Fourthly, there is the aftermath. In the *Aeneid*, Jupiter sends Mercury down to Carthage to make Dido and her people receptive to the arrival of the Trojan boat-people. In the *Argonautica*, on the other hand, Jupiter is given a second speech in which he addresses those sons of his who are members of the *Argo*'s crew, Hercules and the Dioscuri (V. Fl. 1.563–67). This is couched very much in terms of "reward for effort," which Jupiter relates to his own wars for supremacy against Titans and Giants; this recalls not just the *labor omnia uicit* ideology of the *Georgics*' Jupiter and what I earlier termed the Idmonian view of history (and note that Idmon appropriates the phrase in his *ratis omnia uincet* at V. Fl. 1.236), but also Lucan's analogy between those cosmic battles and the civil wars that eventually led to Nero's ascendancy (Luc. 1.33–45). Civil war, not the (re)conquest of Judaea, was the *labor* that brought Vespasian to power and, as Mart. 5.5.7–8 attests, civil war was likewise the subject of Domitian's alleged epic;[32] and our thoughts are led to Vespasian here by the repeated motif of

---

Troy." The Troy of the *Argonautica* was ruled by the tyrannical Laomedon (on Laomedon as tyrant, see Cowan 2014, 236–37) who in his perfidious treatment of Hercules brings about the first sack of his city. Are the present rulers of Rome, who came to power through civil war, really any different? Cf. Zissos 2003, 668–77.

30 Criado 2013, 196–97, usefully draws attention to the fact that an important precursor of Valerius's Jupiter in this respect is Ovid's Pythagoras (*Met.* 15.420–52), who includes the rise and fall of hegemonies as part of the never-ending cycle of metamorphosis. The list culminates with Rome, but the implication is that Rome herself will one day be replaced. See also Hardie 1993a, 95; Ganiban 2014, 259 n. 32.

31 Bernstein 2014, 164: "The Flavians' momentary provision of security does not imply that the system that they oversee provides permanent stability." For Wacht 1991, 10, it is simply an issue of power: "soll allen Völkern Hoffnung auf Vorherrschaft, aber auch Furcht vor Unterdrückung zuteil werden." Manuwald 2009, 587–91, and Manuwald 2013, 33–34, draws attention to the fact that humans have no knowledge of Jupiter's grand plan; we can only surmise its nature on the basis of what we observe happens in the world, and that does not inspire confidence. On the allusion to Lucan 7.211 in this phrase, cf. Stover 2012, 38–40; Ganiban 2014, 260–61. Yet another indication that the future is Lucanic rather than Vergilian.

32 Cf. Penwill 2000, 67–69.

catasterism and the shining light for mariners that the Dioscuri will become (V. Fl. 1.568–73).

That Jupiter's prophecy should say nothing about Rome's ascendancy and the Flavian rise to power is extraordinary—the latter particularly, given Vergil's Jupiter's focus on the Julians. But before considering the further implications of this, we need to revisit Jason on Peuce, at the moment when the Colchians turn up uninvited to gatecrash the wedding party.

The Minyae, who only a little while ago had been so supportive of Jason in his intention to marry Medea, now insist that she should be given back, and one of their motives for doing so is what they learn from Mopsus about the future consequences of *not* doing so (V. Fl. 8.395–99):

> quemque suas sinat ire domos nec Marte cruento   395
> Europam atque Asiam prima haec committat Erinys.
> namque datum hoc fatis, trepidus supplexque canebat
> Mopsus, ut in seros irent magis ista nepotes
> atque alius lueret tam dira incendia raptor.

> Let him [*sc*. Jason] allow each to go to his own home and let not this Fury [*sc*. Medea] be the first to join Europe and Asia in bloody war. For this was ordained by the Fates, this did Mopsus, terrified and beseeching, prophesy: that these things would work through to the next generation and a second abductor pay penalty for such an appalling conflagration.

Mopsus finally reveals the will of Jupiter, that the abduction of Helen that will lead to the Trojan War will be a direct consequence of Jason's abduction of Medea.[33] And the Minyae want none of it. We have, of course, already heard Jupiter say that the Trojan War is the cornerstone of his plans for the unfolding of human history, and living as we do in that history, we know that it is unavoidable. Yet for a fleeting moment, as Jason's first inclination is to give in to his companions' demands as he did on Lemnos (V. Fl. 2.384–92), we glimpse the possibility of another world, another history, in which the Trojan War and everything that arises from it does not take place. The Mopsian voice begs for that, as did the Sun-god back in Book 1. But Jason is now married to Medea and thus inexorably linked to the future that Mopsus himself foretold earlier in Book 1, a future that has been confirmed by other prophecies, dreams, works of art, and divine conversations.[34] The Fury will be let loose; the *prima* of V. Fl. 8.396, the last occurrence of the word

---

[33] On the historical nexus between the abduction of Medea and the Trojan War, to which Herodotus, the father of history, gives his *imprimatur*, see Zissos 2002, 85–87.
[34] On the devices Valerius employs to foreshadow Medea's tragic future beyond the *Argonautica*, see Davis 2010, 7–11, and Davis 2014, *passim*.

in the poem, links back to the first word of the first line of the first book of the epic. This is where it all begins. All we can do is leave Jason on Peuce staring into the abyss, frozen in that eternal moment, forever on the brink of fratricide and all it will lead to.

So what are the implications for Vespasian? I return to the encomium. The remarkable thing here is that only one exploit of Vespasian's is evoked, that of opening up the Caledonian ocean (V. Fl. 1.7–9). It was not something he did while emperor, but while in the service of another. (It is also a fiction, but that's another story.)[35] Both of these elements serve to link him with Jason, whose opening up of the Black Sea was undertaken in the service of Pelias.[36] In the course of his quest, Jason, who initially rejects civil war as a means of avoiding the deadly mission on which Pelias proposes to send him, becomes embroiled in three *bella plus quam ciuilia*[37]—these being the Lemnian episode (wives versus husbands), Cyzicus (guests versus hosts), and the Colchian civil war (half-brother versus half-brother, where the fighting is specifically compared to that of a Roman civil war at 6.402–6)—and at the end is faced with a fourth (brother-in-law versus brother-in-law), although as we have seen, the text does not go there. Civil war, the opportunistic exploitation of the chaos of 69, is what has now propelled Jason's avatar, Vespasian, one-time loyal servant of SPQR in Britain, Africa, and Judaea, onto the world stage as emperor and self-proclaimed founder of a dynasty (note *genitor* at 1.16). Having succeeded in the quest for his own Golden Fleece (or maybe that should be golden bough)[38] by making that journey from Alexandria to Rome, he now becomes recipient of ostentatiously over-the-top flattery of the

---

35 See Zissos 2008, 82–84.
36 For a detailed argument in support of the proposition that Jason symbolizes Vespasian, see Taylor 1994, 223–26. Whether this is as positive for Vespasian as she claims is another matter. Cf. Toohey 1993, 194: "As Aeneas was an imperial prototype, so must Jason be. Whether this is for Vespasian, Titus, or Domitian does not matter terribly. … We witness in Jason a generic imperial prototype."
37 On the ways in which Valerius has grafted civil war (and particularly *Roman* civil war) motifs on to the traditional Argonaut saga see McGuire 1997, 103–13, and more recently, Seal 2014, 126–35, and Davis 2015, 159–67.
38 The golden bough is, of course, the talisman of power at Verg. A. 6.136–48 which the would-be empire-builder Aeneas must pluck to receive confirmation that fate is on his side. It is worth noting that whenever it is plucked another grows in its place, which hints at a succession of hegemonies more along the lines of Valerius's Jupiter's vision than that of his Vergilian counterpart. It is also worth noting that there is in the mythological tradition a golden fleece, often a lamb (E. *Or.* 998–1000, Acc. *trag.* 206–13 [=*Atr.* VIII R³]) but for Seneca a golden ram specifically (Sen. *Thy.* 223–35), that performs a similar function, to confer kingship of Mycenae on its possessor. This, unlike the golden bough, can be and was stolen in the pursuit of power.

kind that Lucan dished out for Nero (Luc. 1.33–66). It is as if Valerius is addressing Vespasian in the first days of his principate, at the equivalent of Jason's wedding to Medea where everyone is congratulating him, and offering a Mopsian warning if he but care to read it.

The prophecy of Jupiter reinforces the point: who gets to rule longest over all peoples has not yet been decided; the apparent certainties of the Julian regime have resolved (or dissolved) into never-ending experimentation, as the tumultuous year of four emperors and Vespasian's own emergence from it attest. One usurpation provides the blueprint for another, and Vespasian's star will be there to act as a guide. A new invasion of Colchians is an ever-present possibility, and the moral compromises necessary to ward against it can and do lead to a descent into tyranny from which there is no way out. The ever-present risk is that it will all end on Peuce, where the companions who were once so supportive turn against you, the gods you thought were favorable desert you[39] and what you imagined was the guerdon of success turns out to be a raging Fury. Remember what happened to your four predecessors. Led to Peuce in the first instance by taking bad advice (the uninformed decision of the helmsman Erginus to seek an alternative route),[40] by his own vanity (the desire to show himself to all lands as he returns in triumph, *cunctis redeuntem ostendere terris*, V. Fl. 8.199), and through a series of deceptions (the lies Jason tells Medea about where they are actually heading), Jason's final moment in the poem, the climax of his quest, finds him desperately trying to control a situation that has all so suddenly become toxic, uttering that despairing cry with which the poem concludes (V. Fl. 8.467): *mene aliquid meruisse putas, me talia uelle?* The Fleece, *uellus*, lurks in that final word and haunts both Jason and us as we exit the poem; read another way, taking *me* as ablative, taking *uelle* as the imperative of *uello*, and replacing the question mark with one of exclamation, it becomes Jason's final plea to Medea for help:

---

[39] Note that Pallas, given first priority by Jason in the preparations for the wedding ceremony, is here said to be *inuita iam* ("now unwilling," V. Fl. 8.224).
[40] Valerius emphasizes that the reason behind the decision is baseless, resting as it does on the fact that both Erginus and Jason are ignorant of Jupiter's decree that once a ship had passed safely through, the Clashing Rocks would clash no more (V. Fl. 4.708–10). In Apollonius's version, Jason is instructed by Phineus that the Argonauts must seek an alternative route home (A.R. 2.421); Valerius's Phineus issues no such instruction. In Seneca's *Medea* (454–56), as implicitly at Pi. *P.* 4.251–57, the Argo returns the way it came, which further adds to the sense that Valerius is marking Erginus's advice as wrong. Cf. Lazzarini 2012, 189–91; Pellucchi 2012, 221–42. Zissos 2004b, 330–31, with n. 60, approves the substitution of Erginus for Ancaeus, but I incline to the view that in this instance the departure from Apollonian precedent is a negative.

"Pluck such things from me" or "Fleece me of such things."[41] As with Pompey's trampling the walls in a final, futile act of Remus-style defiance in the *Bellum Ciuile* (*calcantem moenia Magnum*, "the rampart-trampling Magnus," Luc. 10.546),[42] the Flavian *Argonautica* ends with an impassioned and equally futile plea for history to be changed. But under Jupiter's grand plan it is the Scaevas and Caesars and their future generation counterparts, dedicated to the acquisition and maintenance of power, who will predominate, and the civil wars of the year of four emperors are merely one more stage in its implementation. This, I would argue, is the post-Lucan, post-69 verdict on Caesar and Caesarism that informs Valerius's epic.

---

41 On the etymological link between *uellus* ("fleece") and *uello* ("pluck") see *OLD* s.v. *uellus¹*.
42 That the image of Pompey trampling the ramparts evokes Remus as archetype of intra-familial conflict at Rome is argued by Rossi 2005, 256. Cf. Penwill 2009, 90–95 (with n. 30).

Part II: **Narrating *Nefas* in Statius's *Thebaid***

Federica Bessone
Signs of Discord: Statius's Style and the Traditions on Civil War

Today, style is not a fashionable object in Latin studies, much less in studies of Flavian poetry. The re-evaluation of "Silver epic" has been more a claim of its cultural relevance and contemporary resonances than an acknowledgment of the merit to be found in its strictly formal qualities; scholarly interest has focused on structure and narrative technique, ideology or implicit literary history, rather than on linguistic micro-structures.[1] Even the style which is perhaps the most dense and provoking, that of Statius, is still often labeled as "mannerist" and "baroque" rather than acknowledged for its peculiarities; and scholars still rely on catch-all generalizations like hyperbole and paradox to describe its unusual qualities rather than engaging in detailed investigations of its internal mechanisms and technical characteristics. Yet the diction of Statius and the other poets is worth being "re-discovered." As much detailed work has now been done in commentaries,[2] it is time, I believe, to build on this volume of observations, reflecting more broadly on the formal characteristics of Statian poetry. One of the future tasks of criticism will be that of outlining the "anatomy" of this style—to recall the Flaubertian title of Gian Biagio Conte's essay on *enallage* in Vergil.[3]

Civil war is not only the central theme of the *Thebaid*, it is also the decisive impulse for the creation of its poetic style: the intra-familial struggle for power is a conceptual knot which is fertile ground for Statius's expressive, as well as ideological, elaboration. From the architecture of the epic to the single *iunctura*—from the organism to the verbal cell—the concept of internal conflict determines the form of the poem, as if inscribed in its DNA. The very configuration of the epic genre is thus violently overthrown: this negative poetic gesture reverses the conventions of celebratory epos—that which sings of κλέα ἀνδρῶν—and, even more than the *Bellum Ciuile*, systematically perverts the language of epic.

Hyperbole and paradox are indeed a mark of Statius's poetry, one that the *Thebaid* shares with the *Achilleid* and the *Siluae*: an idiosyncratic manner of representing the world in words. In the *Siluae*, linguistic excess becomes the sign of celebratory exaltation, a rhetoric of wonder that transforms contemporary reality

---
1 Exceptions are, e.g., Vessey 1986 and Sacerdoti 2012 (on which see Bessone 2015).
2 Among the latest, Micozzi 2007 is especially interested in this aspect (cf. 16–17), as well as Briguglio 2017; see also Dewar 1991; Smolenaars 1994; Parkes 2012; Augoustakis 2016; Gervais 2017.
3 Conte 2007a, 5–63 (= 2007b, 58–122).

into "the best of all possible worlds," even superior to myth; in the *Achilleid*, the oxymoronic contact between the protagonist's heroic greatness and his erotic deviation—and the resulting clash of generic registers—produces effects of irony and even epic parody, in wording as well as in theme, in a poem that is as provoking and transformative as Ovid's *Metamorphoses*.

In the *Thebaid*, scandals of language embody and replicate the ethical scandal of a conflict between equals. Even at a stylistic level, this epic of *nefas* follows Vergil truly from a distance and approaches the rhetorical inventions of Lucan and the lessons of tragedy, Greek, Roman, and Senecan: Statius appropriates these earlier poetic expressions of an upset world and adds to that his pursuit of an almost unprecedented verbal density, where polysemy and plural ambiguities open vertiginous perspectives of meaning. In this paper, I suggest some possible future research directions for a study of Statian style, offering a sample analysis of a few verses taken from the culminating point of the *Thebaid*, the brothers' duel.

1 Roman Rhetoric: The Deprecation of Civil Wars between History and Myth

As he explores the theme of civil war, Statius elaborates a peculiar poetic style, in which different traditions of Greek and Roman culture are reshaped. In particular, the interpretative tradition of Rome's civil conflicts perpetuates itself within the *Thebaid*, as the mythological poem repurposes thought-schemes and expressive patterns employed in earlier reflections on Roman history. Intellectual approaches and elements of diction link Statius's work to historiography as well as to epic and other genres, almost as if there were for Statius a pre-existing Roman *koiné* for civil struggles, whether mythical or historical.

I have shown elsewhere how, from the beginning of the poem, Statius adopts a deprecating rhetorical stance towards civil war.[4] The first apostrophe by the narrator, addressed to the Theban brothers, *quo tenditis iras,* | *a, miseri?* ("alas you wretches, to what end do you stretch your wrath?" *Theb.* 1.155–56),[5] recalls passionate interrogative moves like the onset of Horace's seventh *Epode* (*quo, quo scelesti ruitis? aut cur dexteris* | *aptantur enses conditi?*, "where, where are you rushing to in this evil madness?" Hor. *Epod.* 7.1–2) or Lucan's proemial apostrophe

---

4 Bessone 2011, 58–61.
5 Translations from the *Thebaid* are by Shackleton Bailey 2003 (with my adaptations in italics); translations from Lucan are by Duff 1928; from Horace's *Epodes*, by Rudd 2004.

(*quis furor, o ciues* ... ?, "what madness was this, my countrymen?" Luc. 1.8), and also *Patria*'s reproach to Caesar at the Rubicon (*quo tenditis ultra?* | *quo fertis mea signa, uiri?*, "whither do ye march further? and whither do ye bear my standards, ye warriors?" Luc. 1.190–91). These are emphatic moves, contrasting the necessity of external aggressions with the absurdity of internal violence. Seneca *rhetor*, in the *Controuersiae*, employs similar moves for an episode of fraternal strife that is modelled on the *fratrum fabulosa certamina* (Sen. *Con.* 1.1.23); even Tacitus appropriates this repertoire of rhetorical formulas, where a sacrilege like the burning of the Capitol, in the struggle between Vitellians and Flavians in 69 CE, provokes a passionate comment in the historian (Tac. *Hist.* 3.72.1).[6]

As early as the τις-Rede in Book 1, modeled on that of Lucan's second book,[7] Statius applies to the Theban story interpretative categories that have been elaborated in the Roman historical context. Confronted with the pact of alternation that preludes the brothers' war, the anonymous man interrogates himself using the pattern of multiple explanations. These are the same interrogatives formulated by Horace in the seventh *Epode*, where the *persona loquens* hypothesizes that the catalyst for civil war is *furor*, a *uis acrior*, or a *culpa* ("is it blind frenzy that hurries you along, or some stronger force, or is it guilt?" *Epod.* 7.13–14), and answers that the *acerba fata* and fraternal *scelus* ("a cruel fate and the crime of a brother's murder," *Epod.* 7.17–18) have haunted the Romans since Romulus's fratricide, a sacrilege which casts a shadow over the destiny of Rome's *nepotes*.[8]

The well-known formula *quis furor...?*, inaugurated by Vergil for the civil rebellion of the Trojan women, and exploited by Ovid in Pentheus's warning to his fellow citizens, is consecrated at the beginning of the *Bellum Ciuile* as the distinctive mark of the conflict between equals.[9] This formula then becomes a leitmotif of the *Thebaid*, and Statius draws attention to its complex Lucanean heritage. A quasi-citation from the *Bellum Ciuile* occurs in the description of the work of Fama in Book 2: here Lucan's whole formulation is to be found, just inverted in the order of the interrogative sentences; it suggests that the news spread in Thebes of Polynices' wedding in Argos is already equivalent to an announcement of the war between brothers (*Theb.* 2.211–13):

---

6 See Berti 2007, 314 n. 1 and 318–25.
7 *Theb.* 1.173–85; cf. Luc. 2.67–232.
8 See Bessone 2011, 59–60, with bibliographical references. Cf. Hor. *Epod.* 7.13–20.
9 On the tradition of this formula see Roche 2009 on Luc. 1.8 (cit. above); cf. *quis furor iste nouus?* (Verg. *A.* 5.670–71); *quis furor, anguigenae, proles Mauortia, uestras* | *attonuit mentes?* (Ov. *Met.* 3.531–32), with Barchiesi/Rosati 2007, *ad loc.*; Sen. *Thy.* 339; *Phoen.* 557; *quis furor, o caeci, scelerum? ciuilia bella* | *gesturi metuunt ne non cum sanguine uincant* (Luc. 7.95–96); Petr. 108.14.1; Tib. 1.10.33 is also a relevant anti-militarist matrix. See also Georgacopoulou 2005, 22–23.

> hospitia et thalamos et foedera regni
> permixtumque genus (quae tanta licentia monstro,
> quis furor?) et iam bella canit.

> she chants of guests and weddings, pacts of royalty and mingling of families, and now (such licence has the monster, such is her madness!) of war.

Notice *bella canit*: Fame herself, to whom the expressions of reproval by the *Bellum Ciuile*'s narrator refer, contributes from afar to set the civil war in motion, as a delighted epic poet instead of a scandalized one.[10]

The same language (*quis furor?*) recurs in the opening of Jocasta's speech to Eteocles in Book 11, before the duel. Here, Lucan's appeal to his fellow citizens (*o ciues*) is updated for the imperial age. A synonym for *furor*, namely *regni ... Eumenis*, appears, the f/Fury that is coeval with the reign of Thebes (and perhaps with absolute power in itself) (*Theb.* 11.329–32):

> quis furor? unde iterum regni integrata resurgit
> Eumenis? ipsi etiam post omnia, comminus ipsi   330
> stabitis? usque adeo geminas duxisse cohortes
> et facinus mandasse parum est?

> What madness is this? Whence once more does the Fury of our kingdom rise again full-blown? Will you yourselves when all is done, yourselves stand face to face? Is it too little to have led two armies and delegated your crime?

Here, moreover, *parum est?* is yet another echo of Horace's seventh *Epode* (*parumne campis atque Neptuno super | fusum est Latini sanguinis ... ?* "Has too little Latin blood been shed on land and sea ... ?" *Epod.* 7.3–4).

From deprecation to dissuasion. Another key passage in the poetic tradition on civil wars is Anchises' warning to Caesar and Pompey in *Aeneid* 6 (Verg. *A.* 6.832–35):[11]

> ne, pueri, ne tanta animis adsuescite bella
> neu patriae ualidas in uiscera uertite uires;
> tuque prior, tu parce, genus qui ducis Olympo,
> proice tela manu, sanguis meus!   835

---

10 *Bella canit* is productively compared by Gervais 2017 with Luc. 1.1–2, *bella ... canimus*.
11 Translations from the *Aeneid* are by Ahl 2007.

> No, my boys, no! Don't accustom your spirits to wars of such huge scope, / Don't use your strength and your vigour to disembowel your country! / You be the first to show pity, you, who are sprung from Olympus! / Throw down the sword in your hand, son of my blood!

Lucan had already alluded to that model, showing the ineffectiveness of Anchises' dissuasion while condemning Caesar's disobedience to it. In the *Bellum Ciuile*'s proem, the image of the "imperial people turn*ing* their victorious right hands against their own vitals" (*populumque potentem | in sua uictrici conuersum uiscera dextra*, Luc. 1.2–3) shows that Anchises' warning not to turn one's vigor against the country's *uiscera* (*neu ... in uiscera uertite*, Verg. A. 6.833) has been disregarded; above all, the new, sarcastic recalling of Vergil's passage in the invective against Caesar in Book 7 underlines, as Narducci observed, that "far from laying down arms first, *Caesar* keeps" raging against the *patriae uiscera* "even when Pompey has already acknowledged his victory."[12]

Within the literary tradition of the theme of civil wars at Rome, there is a continual osmosis between historical epic and mythological poetry: before Lucan, Seneca had, in the *Phoenissae*, twice recalled Anchises' admonition in Jocasta's words. In the tragedy, Jocasta invites Eteocles to desist "first" (*prior*) as being the first to bear responsibility for the fratricidal conflict: *tu pone ferrum, causa qui ferri es prior* ("Do thou put by the sword, who art the sword's first cause," Sen. Phoen. 483).[13] Shortly before, she had likewise addressed to Polynices an apostrophe modelled on that of Anchises: *iunge complexus prior, | qui tot labores totque perpessus mala | longo parentem fessus exilio uides* ("Come thou first to thy mother's arms, thou who hast endured so many toils, so many misfortunes, and, worn with long exile, seest thy mother at last," Sen. Phoen. 464–66). Seneca has his Jocasta echo the Vergilian *prior* twice and shows her pathetically uncertain on which one of the two sons to embrace "first" (*misera quem amplectar* prius? Sen. Phoen. 460). The double echo of this key moment in Vergil's *Aeneid* stresses that, here, both fighters are equally near in blood to the character trying to persuade them, their mother: the strife between brothers is a familial crime even more impious than that between son-in-law and father-in-law.

Statius engages with the whole intertextual tradition spanning from Vergil to Seneca and Lucan when he lets Anchises' warning be recalled not by Jocasta, but by Adrastus. In addressing the brothers, the king of Argos invokes the closer

---

[12] Narducci 2002, 223–24, referencing Luc. 7.721–23: *tu, Caesar, in alto | caedis adhuc cumulo patriae per uiscera uadis, | at tibi iam populos donat gener* ("While *you*, Caesar, *are* still treading on corpses piled high and marching over the very life of *your* country, *you* receive from *your* kinsman nations as a gift").

[13] Translations of Seneca's *Phoenissae* are by Miller 1929².

kinship relation he has with Polynices, as father-in-law with son-in-law, but he emphasizes that not even Eteocles is far from him in blood; Statius thus exploits further details from the Vergilian model, with new disturbing effects (*Theb.* 11.429–35):

> tamen ille rogat: "spectabimus ergo hoc,
> Inachidae Tyriique, nefas? ubi iura deique?   430
> bella ubi? ne perstate animis. te deprecor, hostis
> (quamquam, haec ira sinat, nec tu mihi sanguine longe),
> te, gener, et iubeo; sceptri si tanta cupido est,
> exuo regales habitus, i, Lernan et Argos
> solus habe!"   435

> Yet he beseeches: "Sons of Inachus and Tyrians, shall we then watch this wickedness? Where is right and the gods, where war? Persist not in your passion. I pray you desist, my enemy – though did this anger permit, you too are not far from me in blood; you, my son-in-law, I also command. If you so much desire a sceptre, I put off my royal raiment, go, have Lerna and Argos to yourself."

Statius repeats many formal elements of the Vergilian passage: the negative imperative with *ne*; *animis* (albeit in a different syntactical function); the anaphora of the second person pronoun (*tuque prior, tu*), here in the accusative (*te ... te*) and referring once to each of the two brothers; a degree of intensity in the warning to these two belligerents, based on the speaker's kinship relation with one of the two. Also worthy of note is that the image of "blood" (*sanguis*) is here associated with the supposed *hostis*, who (as Adrastus emphasizes) is himself linked by affinity to Adrastus: this increases the legitimacy of the latter's request and the *pathos* of the announced refusal. Moreover, in Statius, the gradation of intensity is not expressed by the comparative *prior*,[14] but by the ascending *climax* from the verb of supplication to that of command (*te deprecor ... te, gener, et iubeo*). Nor is there any Vergilian invitation to lay down arms (*proice tela manu, sanguis meus*, *A*. 6.834), such as will later be echoed in Antigone's speech to Polynices (*conprime tela manu ... | frater*, "Brother, hold your weapons," *Theb.* 11.363–64); rather, Adrastus's speech underlines the new theme of lust for power (*sceptri si tanta cupido est*).[15]

---

14 The memory of Vergil's *prior*, however, seems to emerge again when Eteocles hits first in the duel: *rex impius aptat | tela et funestae casum prior occupat hastae* (*Theb.* 11.499–500).
15 For the *sceptrum* as an important locus of discord elsewhere in Flavian literature, see Dominik (this volume).

Even another potential family conflict is suggested, that between Adrastus and Polynices for the reign of Argos: strife between *socer* and *gener*, as in *Aeneid* 6. Adrastus renounces kingship so that Polynices can "reign alone" (*i, Lernan et Argos | solus habe!*): this recalls the leitmotif of indivisible kingship and is yet another example of Statius's tendency to multiply the images of civil war, at every level (human, divine, infernal, even animal), and on every occasion offered by the poem.

2 Inversion and Perversion, Paradoxes, Ambiguity: The Epic of *Nefas* and Its Language

One of the most pervasive and typical gestures of Statius's poetry is that of inversion; in this, the poet of the *Thebaid* learns from Lucan. Paradox informs the text at every level, its hermeneutic force laying bare the aporia created by conflict between equals. This includes a paradoxical application of similes and a "paradoxical" use of intertextuality, reversing well-known models, in a stylistic correlative of distorted reality. Conventional epic diction and the linguistic registers that it appropriates—such as the legal or the religious—are continually twisted and deformed.

2.1 Intertextual Inversions

Allusive inversions express, at an intertextual level, the character of an "unnatural" epic, which reverses traditional paradigms so as to represent a subverted world of values. The poem's first extended simile compares the discordant brothers to two oxen intolerant of the yoke (*Theb.* 1.131–38); Statius inverts the Homeric simile that likens the concordant work of the two Ajaxes to a yoke of oxen (Hom. *Il.* 13.701–8) and thus programmatically announces, through the intertextual antiphrasis, his inversion of the epic of κλέα ἀνδρῶν.[16] Almost at the other end of the poem, the apostrophe to the brothers (*Theb.* 11.574–79), who have died upon one another in the duel, reverses that of Vergil to Euryalus and Nisus (*A.* 9.446–49), the friends who died for one another: the promise of poetic memory is here overturned into a paradoxical promise of oblivion.[17] Framing the

---

16 More on this in Bessone *forthcoming*.
17 Bessone 2011, 80–89, with further bibliography.

story of Eteocles and Polynices, an ostentatious antiphrastic gesture indicates Homer and Vergil as discarded authorities: in Statius, as in Lucan, the writing of civil war is also an internal war inside the epic code.

2.2 Linguistic Perversions: The Language of Law and War

Moving from the use of allusive art to that of poetic language, the *Thebaid* exhibits a perversion of the conventional language of military epic and its type-scenes. The duel between the brothers is an extreme example of this. In the brief exchange that precedes it, Polynices stresses that his brother's sole respect for pacts is his respect for war pacts (*Theb.* 11.392–95):

> nec mitior ille,
> "tandem," inquit, "scis, saeue, fidem et descendis in aequum?
> o mihi nunc primum longo post tempore frater,
> congredere: hae leges, haec foedera sola supersunt."   395

> No gentler is the other: "At length, bully," he says, "do you know the meaning of good faith and come down onto the level? Now for the first time in so long you are my brother: fight me. These are the only terms, the only covenants that remain."

Here, the overlap of legal language and the language of war is full of sarcasm and extends to amphiboly: *descendis in aequum* suggests a respect for "equity" (or a coming down to "just pacts," *in ius*, as Lactantius Placidus glossed *in aequum* here), but at the same time it is the military phrase for "coming down to the battlefield, taking the field," the "equal and plain field" which allows an equitable strife. *Congredere*, too, is polysemous: the only possible encounter between brothers, that which is now at last accomplished, is not an "agreement," but an "engagement" on the field.

The ambiguity of the language thus emphasizes the perversion of familial bonds into bonds of war. A duel which is executed with all due ceremony, but between brothers, is an atrocious paradox: here, respect for the norms of war—and of the epic genre—coincides with the breaking of the laws of nature.[18]

---

[18] An atrocious amphiboly occurs also in Eteocles' preceding utterance, *ne incesse moras, grauis arma tenebat* | *mater* ("chide not the delay, my mother's weight was holding my arms," *Theb.* 11.390–91); Jocasta holds back his weapons with the weight of her body and authority, but her description as a *grauis … mater* cannot but suggest the image of pregnancy and childbirth, creating a paradoxical short circuit. She who tries to hold back her son's weapons is the mother who has literally given birth to war, the *impia belli* | *mater* (*Theb.* 7.483–84), as Statius defined

2.3 Sacral Language and *Nefas*, Prayer and Impiety

Sacral language is also subjected to perversion in this episode. After the interventions of Adrastus and Pietas, who is driven away by Tisiphone, the duel resumes (*Theb.* 11.499–508):

> instaurant crudele nefas; rex impius aptat
> tela et funestae casum prior occupat hastae.   500
> illa uiam medium clipei conata per orbem
> non perfert ictus atque alto uincitur auro.
> tunc exul subit et clare funesta precatur:
> "di, quos effosso non inritus ore rogauit
> Oedipodes flammare nefas, non improba posco   505
> uota: piabo manus et eodem pectora ferro
> rescindam, dum me moriens hic sceptra tenentem
> linquat et hunc secum portet minor umbra dolorem."

Again they start the cruel atrocity. The impious king makes ready his darts and is first to take the chance of a deadly spear. The weapon makes to drive through the mid orb of the shield but fails to carry its impact through and is overcome by the deep-set gold. Then the exile advances and loudly utters a deadly prayer: "Gods whom gouged Oedipus asked not in vain to fan the flame of crime, I make no excessive plea. I shall purify my hands and tear open my breast with the same steel, providing that in death he leaves me holding the sceptre and bears this grief with him, an inferior shade."

The oxymoronic *instaurant ... nefas* constrains in a sacrilegious union a verb that has a ritual import with the prime synonym of fratricidal impiety.[19] *Instaurare*, "introduced by Vergil to poetry, is properly used of renewing a ritual, and thence of renewing such things as war, which (at least initially) have a ceremonial aspect."[20] Here, Statius perverts Vergil's language into the style of a sacrilegious

---

her in Book 7. A similar amphiboly is in Tacitus's initial description of Livia: *Liuia grauis in rem publicam mater, grauis domui Caesarum nouerca* (Tac. *Ann.* 1.10.5); cf. Severy 2003, 149 and n. 80.

19 There is an analogous effect in Cic. *Ver.* 1.11 *scelus illud pristinum renouauit et instaurauit*. Cf. Stat. *Theb.* 11.232–33, *ipse instaurari sacrum male fortis agique | imperat, et magnos ficto premit ore timores* ("He himself, too steadfast, orders the rite renewed and carried through, hiding dire misgivings with a feigned countenance"): almost an anticipation of the stubborn impiety with which the duel will be resumed and brought to an end.

20 So Harrison 1991 on Verg. *A.* 10.543–44 *instaurant acies* ("The battle-lines were renewed," his translation).

epic—almost introducing into epos the tragic Seneca's taste for the staging of crime as a *rituel peruerti*.[21]

The language of prayer is also overturned, through disturbing ambiguities. The reference to Oedipus's prayer (*Theb.* 11.504–5), for example, suggests that Polynices is praying to infernal deities, including the Furies who preside over the fight. Here, observing the perversion of language can have consequences on textual criticism. At line 505, the reading of P, *flammate*, is corrected by the *recentiores* and by Heinsius into *flammare*, introducing an infinitive construction not unparalleled in Statius but eliminating the imperative, which is a constant feature of prayers in the *Thebaid*.[22] Here, indeed, an imperative is missed, as Polynices' *uota* are otherwise expressed only at the end, in the subordinate clause introduced by *dum* (507). *Flammate*, however, is not convincing either; such figurative language seems too flamboyant for direct speech, yet conversely the verb—a favorite with Statius—appears bland when juxtaposed against *nefas*. The other manuscripts have the alternative reading *firmate*, which forms with *nefas* an unprecedented and pregnant *iunctura*. If we accept *firmate* (printed by early editors like Gronovius and Barth), Polynices interprets the missed blow of his brother (*non perfert ictus*, *Theb.* 11.502) as a favorable omen, a sign that Oedipus's evil prayer has been fulfilled and that his own can now be fulfilled as well. In the religious language that constitutes normal epic vernacular, an omen is followed by asking the gods to "confirm the portent" (*firma* or *firmate omen*).[23] If we take *firmate* as the correct reading, then, in a violent deviation, Polynices asks the gods to "confirm the *nefas*." There is an ascending climax from *instaurant nefas* (*Theb.* 11.499), spoken by the narrator: by appropriating that word, Polynices now consciously takes upon himself, before the very gods, the whole responsibility of the epic's *nefas*. A progression from Oedipus's perverse prayer to the Fury

---

21 Dupont 1995, 231–73; cf. e.g., *seruatur omnis ordo, ne tantum nefas | non rite fiat* (Sen. *Thy.* 689–90).

22 I owe this observation to Colacicco 2014, a doctoral thesis of the Università di Salerno that I supervised as a second tutor; the author bases herself on the list in Dominik 1994a, 306–7 (31 prayers, from which she omits 6.197–201, 8.588–91, 9.506–10, and 11.248–49).

23 Cf. *Iuppiter omnipotens, precibus si flecteris ullis, | aspice nos, hoc tantum; et si pietate meremur, | da deinde augurium, pater, atque haec omina firma* (Verg. *A.* 2.689–91), with Casali 2017 (and cf. *A.* 8.78 *adsis o tantum et propius tua numina firmes*); [Nox] *adsistas operi tuaque omina firmes* (Stat. *Theb.* 1.504); *nosco te, summe deorum. | adsis o firmesque tuae, pater, alitis omen* (Sil. 4.126–27); *"firmemus prospera" dixit | "omina, nec uotis superi concordibus absint, | cornigerumque Iouem Tarpeiumque ore uocemus"* (Sil. 16.259–61). For *omen/omina firmare*, cf. moreover *sic aquilae clarum firmauit Iuppiter omen* (Cic. *Mar.* fr. 3.13 Soubiran); *omine quo firmans animum sic incipit ipsa* (Verg. *G.* 4.386).

in Book 1, *da ... nefas* (*Theb.* 1.85–86), can also be noticed: *firmate nefas*, uttered by the son, looks like the accomplishment of the father's promise: *da, Tartarei regina barathri,* | *quod cupiam uidisse nefas, nec tarda sequetur* | *mens iuuenum: modo digna ueni, mea pignora nosces* ("Queen of Tartarus' pit, grant the wickedness I would fain see. Nor will the young men's spirit be slow to follow. Come you but worthy, you shall know them my true sons," *Theb.* 1.85–87). Polynices' final invocation thus caps a sequence initiated by Oedipus and continued by Pluto and Tisiphone (*ede nefas, Theb.* 8.68; *impelle nefas, Theb.* 11.110).[24]

Linguistic perversions do not end here. Again at *Theb.* 11.505–6, *non improba posco* | *uota* expresses a conventional claim: "my prayer is not excessive, immoderate, disproportionate," where *improbus* indicates what exceeds the right measure;[25] here, however, the strong and morally charged meaning of *improbus*, "evil," conflicts with the meaning peculiar to prayer and creates a paradoxical effect. In the same way, at line 506, *piabo manus* has a paradoxical resonance, as it refers the verb of expiation and purification to a gesture that is defined by tradition as an indelible contamination, one impossible to purify.[26]

2.4 Perversion of Epic Conventions ("Not Knowing that One's Own Blood is Being Spilt")

Finally, we turn to a striking example of how conventional epic language can be emptied and refilled with a clashing content, thus offering a seemingly unchanged wrapping to an atrociously overturned meaning. A frequent motif in the *Thebaid* is that of the warrior who, in the heat of the fight, does not perceive his wounds (*nescit*).[27] In the brothers' duel, that motif radically changes. In this

---

24 See Bessone 2011, 98.
25 So, e.g., Argia's *improba non sunt* | *uota: rogos hospes planctumque et funera posco* ("my prayer is not inordinate. A stranger, I ask a pyre, a lament, a corpse," *Theb.* 12.260–61).
26 This impossibility of purification goes back to A. *Th.* 679–82: ἀλλ' ἄνδρας Ἀργείοισι Καδμείους ἅλις | ἐς χεῖρας ἐλθεῖν· αἷμα γὰρ καθάρσιον. | ἀνδροῖν δ' ὁμαίμοιν θάνατος ὧδ' αὐτοκτόνος– | οὐκ ἔστι γῆρας τοῦδε τοῦ μιάσματος ("It is enough that Cadmean men go to battle with the Argives; such blood purifies itself. But the death of two men of the same blood killing each other—that pollution can never grow old," transl. Sommerstein, modified).
27 *Theb.* 3.330–35 (the wounded bull, in a simile for Tydeus); *iam cruor, et tepido signantur tempora riuo.* | *nescit adhuc Capaneus* (*Theb.* 6.783–84); (the lion, in a simile for Capaneus) *qualis ... leo ... praedam uidet et sua uulnera nescit* (*Theb.* 7.670–74) with Smolenaars 1994, *ad loc.* (quoting Luc. 1.212); *sed caede noua iam lubrica tellus* | *armaque seminecesque uiri currusque soluti* | *impediunt laeuumque femur, quod cuspide fixum* | *regis Echionii, sed dissimulauerat ardens,* | *siue ibi nescierat* (*Theb.* 9.200–4) with Dewar 1991 (quoting Lucr. 3.642ff.).

scene, the image of blood produces, from the beginning, the most disturbing effects. At *Theb.* 11.515–17, *exsultat fratris credens hunc ille cruorem | (credit et ipse metu), totis iamque exsul habenis | indulget* ("The other exults, believing it his brother's *blood*, as does he himself in his fear. And now the exile gives full licence to his reins"), the topical motif of the exultation (*exultat*) of the victorious warrior who believes he has struck the enemy changes under our eyes into the impious joy of the brother who sheds his brother's blood, in line with the image created by Vergil in the *Georgics*: *gaudent perfusi sanguine fratrum, | exilioque domos et dulcia limina mutant | atque alio patriam quaerunt sub sole iacentem* ("they steep themselves in their brothers' blood and glory in it; they barter their sweet homes and hearths for exile and seek a country that lies beneath an alien sun," Verg. *G.* 2.510–12, transl. Fairclough).[28] The first true flowing of blood is equated to the full consummation of the consanguineous crime: *sic auidi incurrunt; necdum letalia miscent | uulnera, sed coeptus sanguis, facinusque peractum est* ("so avidly they run at one another. Not yet do they mingle death-dealing strokes, but bloodshed has begun and the evil deed is done," *Theb.* 11.535–36). Human *furor* here reaches its culmination and surpasses even the Furies themselves (*Theb.* 11.537–38).

Statius offers at this point a supreme exercise in style, a whole hexameter segment (down to the semiseptenarian *caesura*) that is perfectly ambiguous, being legible in two overlapping and clashing meanings (*Theb.* 11.539–40):

> fratris uterque furens cupit adfectatque cruorem
> et nescit manare suum.   540
>
> Each furiously desires and seeks his brother's blood and knows not that his own is flowing.

The text plays on the ambiguity of *nescire*, between the neutral and the ethically charged senses of "not knowing"—"not to perceive" or "not to realize," "not to feel" physically or "to ignore" morally—and it exploits the amphiboly of *suum*, "his own"—that is, "of his own body" or "of his own kin." The *topos* of the combatant insensitive to pain thus becomes confused with the paradox of the brother oblivious to the blood tie, a paradox given epigrammatic form by the placement of *fratris* and *suum* at the extremes of the sentence, simultaneously antithetical and synonymical. Physical insensitivity here becomes ethical indifference, and

---

28 Cf. *crudeles gaudent in tristi funere fratris* (Lucr. 3.72); *perfudere manus fraterno sanguine fratres* (Catul. 64.399).

conventional epic language changes into the language of impiety, thus revealing an unexpected and atrocious side.[29]

2.5 The Wars of the Womb: Fratricide and Incest[30]

The narrative has reached its climax. Eteocles and Polynices face each other on the field, and the poet also faces his supreme task. The two lines that depict the duelists are a stylistic *tour de force* (*Theb.* 11.407–8):[31]

> stat consanguineum campo scelus, unius ingens
> bellum uteri, coeuntque pares sub casside uultus.

> Kindred crime stands in the field, the mighty battle of a single womb; beneath their helmets twin faces meet.

Statius re-writes in reverse the astonished wait that precedes the duel between Aeneas and Turnus (Verg. *A.* 12.707–9):

> stupet ipse Latinus
> ingentis, genitos diuersis partibus orbis,
> inter se coiisse uiros et cernere ferro.

> Latinus himself is astonished, / Speechless that two huge men, born in different parts of the circling / Globe should be coming together and settling issues with iron.

The amazement at the strife between "two huge men, born in different parts of the circling globe" cedes its place here to the scandal of a "mighty war" between two brothers, born from the "same womb" (*unius ingens bellum uteri*).[32] The geographical horizon of the *Aeneid* has narrowed, in the *Thebaid*, to Oedipus's

---

29 Statius may be elaborating on A. *Th.* 718 (ἀλλ' αὐτάδελφον αἷμα δρέψασθαι θέλεις; "You want to shed the blood of your own brother?" transl. Sommerstein). For the motif of blood in civil strife cf. Luc. 7.95–96 (quoted above, n. 9).
30 This section can be fruitfully read in connection with Lauren Donovan Ginsberg's analysis of the incest theme in Seneca's *Phoenissae* and its crucial nexus with Polynices' assault on his mother-city (see Ginsberg 2018).
31 Notice the contrast with *stant gemini fratres, fecundae gloria matris,* | *quos eadem uariis genuerunt uiscera fatis:* | *discreuit mors saeua uiros* ("Twin brothers fought there, the pride of a fertile mother; but the same womb gave them birth for different deaths. The cruel hand of death made distinction between them," Luc. 3.603–5).
32 For discussion of a similar inversion of this *Aeneid* passage in Silius's *Punica*, see Bernstein in this volume (pp. 192–93).

house: Statius's epic, as it reaches its culminating point, turns into a tragedy that is consummated inside the family—even inside the same womb.

Vergil sets up a wordplay on *ingentes, genitos*, bringing the para-etymological meaning of *ingens*, "native," near to *genitos*, which is determined, on the contrary, by *diuersis partibus orbis*. We do not know if the pseudo-etymology could suggest at the same time that the heroes "born in different parts of the circling globe" were, however, originally "native" of the same land, Italy—where the Trojans' forefather Dardanus had come from. What is certain is that Statius pushes to the extreme the idea of civil conflict that is, at most, only hinted at in Vergil's passage and radicalizes the impiety of the fight.

The two lines of the *Thebaid* are articulated into three compact segments. The first segment, down to the bucolic diaeresis, is tied up by chiastic alliteration and assonance: *stat consanguineum campo scelus* (*Theb.* 11.407). Statius learns from Vergil the monumental effect of that initial monosyllable: *stat* is, in the *Aeneid*, the sign of firmness, most of all that of the hero ready for the fight.[33] In the *Thebaid*, however, traditional epic language is transformed: the subject of *stat* is an abstract singular noun, which substitutes the two fighters with their personified crime: "on the field there stands," like a statue, not a pair of heroes or armies, but a single symbolic monument to the consanguineous crime.[34]

The phrase *consanguineum ... scelus* is in its turn an emblem that summarizes not only the fratricide, but the incest it originates from, by a tragic consequentiality. At the same time, this field (*stat ... campo*) is the very field of Mars in which, from the dragon's teeth sown by Cadmus, the mass of the Spartoi, the earth-born warriors, *stetit*, "has risen" and "has deployed in battle array."[35] A single image thus epitomizes different phases of the tragedy of Thebes, from the evil "augury" of the *terrigenae* (now accomplishing itself in their descendants),[36] to the consanguineous crime of incest, to the brothers' duel.

The following apposition, *unius ingens | bellum uteri*, is framed by alliteration and is divided by enjambment into the anticipated adjectives on one side, in

---

33 Traina 1997 on Verg. *A.* 10.467 and 12.663.
34 Cf. Franchet d'Espèrey 1999, 240. This use of *stare* is anticipated in Jocasta's speech (*Theb.* 11.330–31, quoted above, §1). Cf. also *stupeo et exsanguis tremo, | cum stare fratres hinc et hinc uideo duos | sceleris sub ictu* (Sen. *Phoen.* 528–30).
35 *Quis satis Thebas fleat? | ferax deorum terra, quem dominum tremit! | e cuius aruis eque fecundo sinu | stricto iuuentus orta cum ferro stetit*, "who could lament Thebes enough? O land, fertile in gods, before what lord dost thou tremble now? The city from whose fields and fecund bosom a band of youth stood forth with swords ready drawn" (Sen. *Her. F.* 258–61).
36 Cf. *fraternasque acies fetae telluris hiatu | augurium seros dimisit ad usque nepotes?* (*Theb.* 1.184–85).

oxymoronic contact with each other, and the corresponding substantives, in chiastic order, on the other. The sons "are" the war: the abstract for the concrete was already visible in Jocasta's self-definition as *impia belli | mater*, in Book 7 (*Theb.* 7.483),[37] but here the effect is intensified by the stylistic pressure, with disruptive force.

There is a well-known contact between this juncture and Manilius's *Thebana ... | bella uteri* (Man. 5.463–64).[38] What must still be stressed, I believe, is that the relevant passage of the *Astronomica* is a survey of tragic subjects, made in a style that imitates the *stilus cruentus* of the tragic genre (Man. 5.458–67):[39]

> quin etiam tragico praestabunt uerba coturno,
> cuius erit, quamquam in chartis, stilus ipse cruentus,
> nec minus hae scelerum facie rerumque tumultu   460
> gaudebunt. uix una trium memorare sepulcra
> ructantemque patrem natos solemque reuersum
> et caecum sine nube diem, Thebana iuuabit
> dicere bella uteri mixtumque in fratre parentem,
> quin et Medeae natos fratremque patremque,   465
> hinc uestes flammas illinc pro munere missas
> aeriamque fugam natosque ex ignibus annos.

> Offspring of Cepheus will also furnish words for the buskin of tragedy, whose pen, if only on paper, is drenched in blood; and the paper no less will revel in the spectacle of crime and catastrophe in human affairs. They will delight to tell of scarce one burial accorded three; the father belching forth the flesh of his sons, the sun fled in horror, and the darkness of a cloudless day; they will delight to narrate the Theban war between a mother's issue, and one who was both father and brother to his children; the story of Medea's sons, her brother and her father, the gift which was first robe and then consuming flame, the escape by air, and youth reborn from fire. (transl. Goold)

Hübner's commentary observes that *bella uteri* looks like a metonymy drawn from the language of tragedy (and likewise, *sepulcri/a* in reference to Thyestes, eater and "tomb" of his sons).[40] We do not know which tragic models stand behind the Manilian definition, but we can recognize that Statius's expression presupposes the distinctly tragic matrix of the Theban myth. Greek and Roman

---

[37] Cf. *Theb.* 7.526–27: *adnuite, aut natum complexa superstite bello | hic moriar*, and, with *nefas*, *Theb.* 7.514: *nupsi equidem peperique nefas, sed diligo tales*.
[38] See Venini 1970.
[39] See Baldini Moscadi 1993, esp. 80–84, and Feraboli *et al.* 2001, 516–17: both refer to Accius as a possible model. Here I print the text of Goold 1977; line 461 is particularly tormented (see Hübner 2010, *ad loc.*).
[40] Hübner 2010 on Man. 5.463–64 and 461.

tragedy supplies the *Thebaid* with a rich source of figurative language to express the tangled *nefas* of intrafamilial and political strife.

And yet *unius ingens bellum uteri* is not only a metonymy, where "war of the womb" stands for "war between brothers." This womb is that of Jocasta (the mother of all familial conflicts), the symbolic place around which there gathers, and from which is generated, the whole tragedy of Oedipus's house.[41] In Seneca's *Oedipus*, line 371 (*natura uersa est; nulla lex utero manet*, "Nature is inverted; no law abides / In the womb") is a motto for the whole work.[42] "Oedipus has inverted nature, and breached all laws of the womb":[43] the sons of that womb now breach, with fratricide, another natural law.

Adjectives play a fundamental role here. In tension with each other, *unius* and *ingens* increase one another's effect: the war is so much greater as it severs what once was undivided; and, by an *enallage*, the force of *ingens* extends to that "single" maternal womb, so extraordinarily capacious as to contain a war. The entire tradition of Greek and Roman tragedy has exercised its style on the images of unity, duplicity, capacity of Jocasta's womb. Sophocles uses such imagery several times, in the *Oedipus Tyrannus*; so does Seneca in his own *Oedipus*. In these two plays, even before the fight between Eteocles and Polynices, Jocasta's womb is the "double field" (διπλῆν ἄρουραν, S. *OT* 1257) of Oedipus and his sons, or "the same bounteous harbor [that] was sufficient for" (ᾧ μέγας λιμὴν αὐτὸς ἤρκεσεν, S. *OT* 1208, transl. Jebb) Oedipus as child and husband, or "this teeming womb which bore husband and sons" (*hunc ... uterum capacem, qui uirum et gnatos tulit*, Sen. *Oed*. 1038–39);[44] and Oedipus is the one who "sows together with his father" the "woman sown by him as well."[45] These are different and complementary manners of emphasizing the impious multiplicity of the functions of the same female organ, for different generations of family members.

Even before engendering the war between the brothers, the womb of the mother and wife of Oedipus (son and rival of his father, brother and father of his sons) has been the site of the confusion, the mixing, and the conflict between different familial functions. *Unius ingens bellum uteri* thus becomes, like

---

[41] See also in his *aliquod ius exsecrabile castris | huic utero est* (*Theb*. 7.484–85) and *hostem | quem peperi* (*Theb*. 7.490–91).
[42] Töchterle 1994 on 371: "ein Motto des ganzen Stückes"; cf. Mastronarde 1970, 301; Motto/Clark 1974, 84. Translations from Seneca's *Oedipus* are by Boyle 2011.
[43] Boyle 2011 on 371–72.
[44] Cf. also *uno auia partu liberos peperit uiro, | sibi et nepotes* ("at one birth the grandmother bore children to her husband and grandchildren to herself," Sen. *Phoen*. 136–37).
[45] τοῦ πατρὸς | ὁμόσπορος ("heir to his father's bed," S. *OT* 459–60); ἔχων δὲ λέκτρα καὶ γυναῖχ' ὁμόσπορον ("possessing his bed and the wife who bore his children," S. *OT* 260).

consanguineum ... scelus, another "total" emblem of the tragic history of Thebes and its repeated internal conflicts—literally, intrauterine conflicts. In the oracle related by Creon in Seneca's *Oedipus*, the "wars" of Oedipus's sons are put on a level with Oedipus's "war" with himself, as a consequence of his impious return into his mother's womb: *tecum bella geres, natis quoque bella relinques, | turpis maternos iterum reuolutus in ortus* ("you will wage wars with yourself, bequeath wars to your sons, / For foul reversion to the maternal birthplace," Sen. *Oed.* 237–38). The obscure and brilliant phrase *tecum bella geres* perhaps does not refer solely to the self-destructive search for Laius's killer by Oedipus, nor to his self-blinding, but, with the density of oracular language, grasps more deeply the core of Thebes' peculiar tragedy: its every act of generation is an act of self-destruction.[46]

Even this symbol goes back to the beginnings of the city, to the war between the brothers generated by the womb of the same mother, the earth. Already in the *Thebaid*'s proem, Cadmus the founder is "the frightened farmer sowing in impious furrows the battles of a covered Mars" (*trepidum ... Martis operti | agricolam infandis condentem proelia sulcis*, *Theb*. 1.7–8, my transl.).[47] The images of sowing sons and wars,[48] of earthly or maternal furrows, of the field as a womb or the womb as a field, tie up in a symbolic unity the successive stages of a cursed history that is condemned to repeat itself and can be recognized altogether in each of its new embodiments.

Ingens is another crucial term here: Statius uses it in all its para-etymological force, already exploited by Vergil, Ovid, and then by the author of the *Octauia*.[49] The war is not only "big," not only "inborn," "native" of Jocasta's womb, but it is, so to say, "innate," "connatural" with it; and it is a war that takes place "inside" and "against" the family (*in + gens*, with the preposition taken in a local or a hostile sense).[50]

---

46 Particularly interesting in this connection is the image of Bellona in the Eclogues of Calpurnius Siculus: *dum populos deus ipse reget, dabit impia uinctas | post tergum Bellona manus spoliataque telis | in sua uesanos torquebit uiscera morsus | et modo quae toto ciuilia distulit orbe, | secum bella geret* (Calp. *Ecl.* 1.46–50); for the phrase cf. also *quaeris Alcidae parem? | nemo est nisi ipse: bella iam secum gerat* (Sen. *Her. F.* 84–85).
47 See now Briguglio 2017, *ad loc.* Cf. *post consanguineas acies sulcosque nocentes* (*Theb*. 4.436), and see Parkes 2012 for numerous intertexts behind the *fetus ager* of *Theb*. 4.435. Cf. also the parallel myth of Jason's sowing at Ov. *Met.* 7.123–30 and Ov. *Met.* 7.141–42.
48 Cf. also πατροκτόνον Οἰδιπόδαν, | ὅστε ματρὸς ἁγνὰν | σπείρας ἄρουραν, ἵν' ἐτράφη | ῥίζαν αἱματόεσσαν | ἔτλα ("the parricide Oedipus, who went so far as to sow a root of blood in the sanctified field of his mother, in the place where he was given life," A. *Th.* 752–56).
49 See Keith 1991; Hinds 1993, 41, with bibliography in n. 71; Ginsberg 2011.
50 Cf. *ingentes ... tumultus* (*Theb*. 4.438), in the fraternal strife of the *terrigenae* (*Theb*. 4.434–42).

In coining the oxymoronic *unius ingens*, Statius seems to keep in mind the *Bellum Ciuile*, where, the Vulteius episode is described as a civil war inside the civil war, a doubly paradoxical strife inside the same faction of Roman citizens: *concurrunt alii totumque in partibus unis | bellorum fecere nefas* ("Others met in combat; and there the horrors of civil war were enacted in full by one faction alone," Luc. 4.548–49). Statius radicalizes Lucan's rhetoric: *unius ingens* is substituted for *totum in unis*, and the summative *nefas* of a single party becomes the "huge war of a single womb." From the internal war to the intra-uterine war: in the *Thebaid*, the consanguineous crime is taken to absolute extremes, and the style of the *Bellum Ciuile* is strengthened with the force of tragic *lexis*.

Finally, the third and last segment, *coeuntque pares sub casside uultus* (*Theb*. 11.408). The perversion of conventional epic language is evident here.[51] The norm of *epos* wants the fights to be equal: on the surface, *coeuntque pares* describes a proper duel. With the same phrase, though negated, Lucan defines the imparity of Caesar and Pompey's forces (*nec coiere pares*, "The two rivals were ill-matched," Luc. 1.129).[52] But the epic norm is here transgressed from the inside, and in a clamorous way: from an equal fight to a fight between equals, even between kinsmen. In general, civil war is a war in which the weapons of the contenders are equal, on par with each other: this is the scandal at the end of *Georgics* 1 (*ergo inter sese paribus concurrere telis | Romanas acies iterum uidere Philippi*, "so it was that Philippi beheld for a second time Roman armies clash in the shock of matching arms," *G*. 1.489–90, transl. Fairclough), in Anchises' speech in *Aeneid* 6 (*illae autem paribus quas fulgere cernis in armis, | concordes animae nunc*, "Those, though, the souls that you see all ablaze in identical armour, / Hearts so harmonious now," *A*. 6.826–27), and in the proem of the *Bellum Ciuile* (*infestisque obuia signis | signa, pares aquilas et pila minantia pilis*, "how standards confronted hostile standards, eagles were matched against each other, and pilum threatened pilum," Luc. 1.6–7).

But here we are beyond that. Fighting at a par, here, are the faces that are *pares*, similar to each other, of two brothers: faces unrecognizable under the helmets (those, at least, perhaps differing from one another), symbolizing blindness

---

51 A further perverse effect seems suggested by the contact between *uteri* and *coeuntque pares*: the fight between equals looks like a variant of the sexual union between close relatives—a sort of replica, as well as a logical consequence, of it.
52 Cf. *ite in bella pares* (Ov. *Ars* 3.3) with Gibson 2003; *OLD* s.v. *par, paris*, a., 13. The juncture with *coire* recurs also in a non-hostile sense: e.g. (with *par* as a substantive), *ut coeat par | iungaturque pari* (Hor. *Ep*. 1.5.25–26).

towards the blood relationship.[53] Even more than in the *Bellum Ciuile*, in the *Thebaid* the fight between *pares* is an impious perversion of the epic code.

For this atrocious play on the ambiguity of *pares*, Statius has an Ovidian model in Themis's prophecy on the tragedies of Thebes: "*nam iam discordia Thebae | bella mouent*" *dixit* "*Capaneusque nisi ab Ioue uinci | haud poterit, fientque pares in uulnere fratres*" ("'Civil war', she said, 'embroils / Thebes now and save by Jove's might Capaneus / Shall not be conquered: brothers shall be paired / In wounds," Ov. *Met.* 9.403–5, transl. Melville). As in the oracular language, *pares* oscillates between the predicative function, in the epic sense of an "equal" strife, and the attributive function, that describes and condemns at the same time a cursed strife between two "equals": two brothers who fulfil their equality in a perverse way, giving death to each other.

In this perverse epic, even traditional epic language becomes the linguistic sign of perversion. As on the plain of Thebes, so too on the planes of style and the generic tradition the civil war of the *Thebaid* is engendered through a creative gesture of self-destruction.

---

53 Cf. ... *sed ut secundum uota Parthorum sua | Urbs haec periret dextera? | neque hic lupis mos nec fuit leonibus, | numquam nisi in dispar feris* (Hor. *Epod.* 7.9–12), with Mankin 1995 and Watson 2003 on 11–12 on in *dispar feris*; *illa rationis expertia et a nobis immanitatis crimine damnata abstinent suis, et tuta est etiam inter feras similitudo* (Sen. *Cl.* 1.26.4).

Tim Stover
Civil War and the Argonautic Program of Statius's *Thebaid*

The description of Harmonia's necklace at *Thebaid* 2.269–305 is a passage rich in programmatic significance.[1] On the one hand, the very existence of the necklace offers an etiology for the civil discord at the heart of the poem. On the other hand, the nature of the necklace's composition provides auto-referential commentary on the manner in which Statius's epic is constructed: what goes into making the necklace is what goes into making the text.[2] Indeed, the etiological and programmatic nature of the ecphrasis is marked from the outset. The phrase *longa est series* ("long is the sequence," *Theb.* 2.267), used to introduce the description of the necklace, echoes the words Statius employs when choosing where to begin his song, i.e., *longa retro series* ("far back goes the tale," *Theb.* 1.7).[3] The necklace takes us back to the poem's opening and thus back to the very beginning of things.[4] Consequently, if we wish to investigate how—perhaps even why—Statius writes about civil war in the *Thebaid*, a good place to begin is with the description of this "beauteous curse" (*decorum ... nefas, Theb.* 2.294–95).[5]

In what follows, I focus particularly on how in this passage Statius advertises engagement with Valerius's *Argonautica* as an important element of his poetic program, an aspect of the ecphrasis that has been overlooked in previous readings.[6] I thus seek to complement a number of important recent studies on the

---

I am grateful to Lauren and Darcy for inviting me to be part of such a wonderful panel in Edinburgh and thankful for their very helpful comments on earlier drafts of this paper.

1 See Feeney 1991, 363–64; McNelis 2007, 50–75; Chinn 2011. Given its obvious meta-poetic and programmatic charge, it is odd that this passage has not received more attention, something noted also by McNelis 2007, 52 n. 12. While still true, the previous statement was truer when I gave the oral version of this paper in Edinburgh in 2014. But see now Cannizzaro 2017, whose excellent article covers much of the same ground as I do and whose findings partially overlap with my own. It is fascinating that two readers of the *Thebaid* independently honed in on the same passage and came to similar conclusions about it. Things in the world of Flavian epic are moving rapidly indeed!
2 See McNelis 2007, 51.
3 On the echo, see Mulder 1954, 194. Text and translation of the *Thebaid* come from Shackleton Bailey 2003.
4 On the etiological dimensions of the *Thebaid*'s proem, see Pollmann 2004, 17.
5 On the necklace as the impetus for war, see McNelis 2007, 55.
6 In my view Valerius's *Argonautica* antedates the whole of Statius's *Thebaid*, which was likely begun ca. 80 CE, since it was composed (but left unfinished) between 70 CE and late 79 CE or early 80 CE. For a full discussion of the date of Valerius's poem, see Stover 2012, 7–26.

https://doi.org/10.1515/9783110585841-006

Argonautic and/or Valerian aspects of Statius's *Thebaid*.[7] In general, I suggest that Statius here signals a tendentious mode of reading Valerius that privileges the darker aspects of his predecessor's poem. If this means that, in the process, Valerian ambivalence is obliterated in favor of using Valerian material as building blocks for an unmitigated "catalog of lust and madness," as Denis Feeney describes the *Thebaid*,[8] well so be it.[9] Indeed, Helen Lovatt suggests that one of the hallmarks of Statius's engagement with Valerius is his desire to undo the potentially positive dimensions of his epic predecessor, "to re-make Valerius in his own image, to take him down to the underworld with him."[10] Valerius, in fact, may have invited this type of poetic *aemulatio* ("rivalry") from his epic successor by giving civil war such a prominent role in his *Argonautica*, where it is nevertheless subordinated to the main theme of the narrative.[11] As if in answer to this, Statius announces in *Thebaid* 2 that Argonautic material—specifically *Valerian* Argonautic material—plays a prominent role in his poem on civil war, but as only one ingredient among the many that make up his textual "witch's brew," as Christopher Chinn has suggestively dubbed the description of Harmonia's necklace.[12] That is, the *Thebaid* responds to the *Argonautica*'s recontextualization of civil war by re-contextualizing Argonautic material within a narrative dominated by the theme of civil war. But Statius's response to Valerius goes further than this. When Statius incorporates Valerius into his epic "cauldron," he attempts to boil him down, as it were, in order to reduce his predecessor to an author whose work is not only useful seasoning for a poem on unmitigated *nefas* ("unspeakable crime"), but whose work is primarily *about* unmitigated *nefas*. And as we shall see, Statius's sorcery vis-à-vis Valerius relies heavily on the witch whose presence in the *Argonautica* does more than any other to darken the mood, shading the poem's epic triumphalism and steering the narrative toward the tragic and nefarious: Medea.[13]

---

[7] See Fucecchi 2007; Stover 2009; Parkes 2014a; Parkes 2014b; Lovatt 2015; Cannizzaro 2016.
[8] See Feeney 1991, 364.
[9] On ambivalence as a fundamental feature of Valerius's *Argonautica*, see Zissos 2004a; Stover 2009, 449–50; Buckley 2010; Stover 2012, 42–46; Buckley 2014; Cowan 2014.
[10] See Lovatt 2015, 422–23 (quotation from 423).
[11] On Valerius's engagement with civil war, see Buckley 2010; Stover 2012; Seal 2014.
[12] See Chinn 2011, 81.
[13] Medea's presence in the ecphrasis has long been noted, but in a manner that differs from my primary focus here. Statius's description of the necklace shares a number of similarities with Seneca's depiction of Medea preparing her noxious wedding gifts for Creusa (Sen. *Med.* 771–844). On this, see Mulder 1954, 195.

1 The Golden Fleece

After being informed that Vulcan fashioned a *dirum monile* ("dire necklace," *Theb.* 2.266) for Harmonia's wedding out of anger at the illicit love affair between Venus and Mars, we get a description of the necklace's constituent elements (*Theb.* 2.276–88):

> ibi arcano florentes igne zmaragdos
> cingit et infaustas percussum adamanta figuras
> Gorgoneosque orbes Siculaque incude relictos
> fulminis extremi cineres uiridumque draconum
> lucentes a fronte iubas; hic flebile germen   280
> Hesperidum et dirum <u>Phrixei uelleris aurum</u>;
> tum uarias pestes raptumque interplicat atro
> Tisiphones de crine ducem, et quae pessima ceston
> uis probat; haec circum spumis lunaribus unguit
> callidus atque hilari perfundit cuncta ueneno.   285
> non hoc Pasithea blandarum prima sororum,
> non Decor Idaliusque puer, sed Luctus et Irae
> et Dolor et tota pressit Discordia dextra.

> Around it he sets a circle of emeralds flowering with hidden fire, adamant stamped with ill-omened shapes, Gorgon eyes, ashes of a thunderbolt end left on Sicilian anvil, crests shining from the heads of green serpents; here is tearful fruit of the Hesperides and the dire gold of Phrixus's fleece. Then he entwines various harms, a chieftain torn from Tisiphone's black hair and the most noxious of the powers that attest the Girdle. These he cunningly smears about with lunar spume and over the whole spreads gay poison. Not Pasithea, chief of the charming sisters, nor Beauty, nor the Idalian boy shaped it, but Mourning and Anger and Grief and Strife with all the power of her hand.

I begin with an analysis of line 281, since it is here that Valerius's epic enters the ecphrasis. The phrase *Phrixei uelleris* echoes V. Fl. 6.150, where these words occupy the same metrical position: *inpulit et dubios <u>Phrixei uelleris</u> ardor | Centoras et diros magico terrore Choatras* ("Frenzy kindled by the fleece of Phrixus urged to the fray also the doubting Centors and the Choatrae feared for horrid magic," V. Fl. 6.150–51).[14] Here we learn that two peoples, the Centors and Choatrae, were

---

14 The collocation *Phrixeum uellus* in reference to the Golden Fleece is quite common. However, a search using the PHI database reveals that the genitive phrase *Phrixei uelleris* is found in this metrical position only at V. Fl. 6.150 and Stat. *Theb.* 2.281, so the connection between Statius and Valerius here is a strong one. Citations of Valerius are taken from the editions of Liberman 1997 and Liberman 2002. Translations are those of Mozley 1934, with slight occasional alterations to modernize his diction.

inspired to come to Colchis and to participate in war against its king Aeetes because they were desirous of obtaining the Golden Fleece for themselves. Statius alludes to a passage in Valerius where an explicit connection is made between the ultimate goal of Argo's voyage—the Golden Fleece—and war, or more specifically civil war. This is so because the fighting in Valerius's Colchis arises from a dispute between Aeetes and his brother Perses. Consequently, like the fighting in Statius's Thebes, the Colchian war in Valerius's *Argonautica* is a matter of *fraternas acies* ("fraternal warfare," Stat. *Theb.* 1.1; cf. *fraterna … Erinys*, V. Fl. 4.617). Statius's allusive gesture thus prompts us to recall that in Valerius's poem, the Golden Fleece is indeed at the center of civil discord between brothers: as Valerius describes at 5.259–77, the civil war begins when Aeetes and Perses disagree over whether the fleece should be kept in Colchis or returned to Greece. Of course, the civil war in Colchis is one of the most radical innovations to the Argonautic legend made by Valerius.[15] So Statius's allusion here is pointed. The passage cited and the themes it conjures up paint Valerius as a poet predominately of civil war. On Statius's tendentious reading of Valerius, the Golden Fleece is primarily a symbol of internecine conflict, a triggering mechanism for conflict between brothers.[16] As a result, the "dire gold of Phrixus's fleece" (*dirum Phrixei uelleris aurum,* Stat. *Theb.* 2.281) is revealed to be a perfect ingredient for Vulcan's "dire necklace of Harmonia" (*dirumque monile | Harmoniae,* Stat. *Theb.* 2.266–67). Evident here, too, is the manner in which Statius seeks to exploit the darker aspects of his Flavian predecessor's text for his poem of fratricidal madness.

Another effect of Statius's allusion to the passage in *Argonautica* 6 cited above is that it indirectly evokes Medea. It does so because immediately after we are introduced to the magic-practicing Choatrae, we learn that one of them, a certain Coastes, has come to Colchis not for war, but rather to see Medea, whose expertise in sorcery impresses him: *maximus hos inter Stygia uenit arte Coastes. | sollicitat nec Martis amor, sed fama Cytaeae | uirginis et paribus spirans Medea uenenis* ("Mightiest among them in Stygian arts Coastes comes: it is not love of war that excites him, but the fame of the Cytaean maid and Medea breathing poisons to match his own," V. Fl. 6.155–57). This gels nicely with yet another verbal echo of Valerius's text contained in *Thebaid* 2.281, one that prompts us to reflect on Medea as an agent of *nefas* in the *Argonautica*, a character whose presence in the narrative casts a shadow over Argo's triumphant voyage. Statius's line ending

---

[15] See Fucecchi 2006a, 11.
[16] Statius's allusion thus implicitly renders the Valerian Golden Fleece disconcertingly similar to the mysterious golden fleeced ram that triggers discord between Thyestes and his brother Atreus in Seneca's *Thyestes* (223–41); see also Penwill in this volume, p. 83 n. 38.

uelleris aurum recalls a line ending of Valerius's: *ipsi inter medios rosea radiante iuuenta | altius inque sui sternuntur uelleris auro* ("Midmost of them all in rosy radiance of youth they [i.e., Jason and Medea] recline on a loftier couch and upon the gold of their own fleece," V. Fl. 8.257–58). These lines conclude Valerius's description of the wedding of Jason and Medea, a context of obvious similarity to the description of Harmonia's necklace in *Thebaid* 2. For it is the fact that Argia is wearing the necklace during her *wedding* to Polynices that prompts Statius to describe its construction and checkered past (*Theb.* 2.265–68). The ill-omened nature of this marriage ceremony has been ably elucidated by McNelis.[17] However, what has been overlooked is that this feature of Statius's text also mirrors the Valerian passage. As the wedding procession approaches the temple of Minerva, a shield falls from its roof, snuffing out the fire of the bridal torches, and a trumpet blast is heard from within the shrine (*Theb.* 2.249–64). Statius's emphasis on Minerva's dissatisfaction with the wedding rituals recalls this same goddess's displeasure with the marriage of Jason and Medea in *Argonautica* 8. As Jason builds an altar to Minerva in preparation for the wedding, we are informed that the goddess, who hitherto had been a staunch ally of Jason's, is "now displeased" (*inuitae iam Pallados*, V. Fl. 8.224).[18] Why is Valerius's Minerva suddenly unhappy? One reason, advanced by Langen and Mozley, is that she has foreknowledge of the awful events to come as a result of this union.[19] Indeed, Valerius foregrounds divine displeasure at the ill-omened marriage and its destructive consequences: during the rituals accompanying Jason and Medea's wedding, we are made, along with Mopsus, to see visions of horror—infanticide in particular—that will result from this union (V. Fl. 8.247–51):

> sed neque se pingues tum candida flamma per auras
> explicuit nec tura uidet concordia Mopsus
> promissam nec stare fidem, breue tempus amorum.
> odit utrumque simul, simul et miseratur utrumque   250
> et tibi tum nullos optauit, barbara, natos.

---

17 See McNelis 2007, 53.
18 The adjective *inuitae* is obelized by Liberman 2002, 147, with discussion at 371–72. For arguments in defense of the reading, see Spaltenstein 2005, 434, and Pellucchi 2012, 280–81.
19 See Langen 1896–97, 535, and Mozley 1934, 428 n. 2. Spaltenstein 2005, 434, is skeptical of this interpretation: for him the reference to Minerva's unhappiness with the nuptials stems only from her virginal nature and opposition to the ways of Venus. Spaltenstein's view, however, need not be mutually exclusive with the readings advanced by Langen and Mozley, but rather can be complementary with them. On this, see Pellucchi 2012, 281.

> But no bright flame won its way upward through the odorous air, nor does Mopsus see concord in the frankincense or lasting loyalty, but a brief term of love. Both of them does he hate, and both at the same time pity, nor any more does he desire children for you, barbarian maiden.

As with the wedding of Argia and Polynices in Statius's *Thebaid*, here too what should be a joyous celebration is tarnished by bad omens, Minerva's displeasure, and a palpable sense of dread at the horrific kin-killing that will be unleashed by the marriage.[20]

Statius's allusions to Valerius have several effects. For one thing, the evocation of the murderously disastrous relationship between Jason and Medea adds still further to the aura of dread surrounding what should be a happy moment in Argos. Also, Statius once again advertises that his appropriation of Valerius is guided by a desire to extract from the *Argonautica* its darkest energy. In fact, Statius here draws our attention to a passage in Valerius's poem where the outward appearance of present happiness is vitiated by the horror to come. It is also interesting that Statius specifically echoes a moment that sees the not-so-happily married couple "reclining upon the gold of their own fleece" (V. Fl. 8.257–58, cited above). Once again, Statius has highlighted in Valerius a passage where the poem's narrative of epic achievement—the successful retrieval of the Golden Fleece—is darkened by the tragic kin-killing to come. It is as if for Statius the outward voyage was only a relatively unimportant prelude to the *nefas* that will be unleashed by Medea: it is her negative energy and the criminality associated with it that Statius wishes to exploit. Like the Scythian Coastes in *Argonautica* 6, Statius, too, has come to Valerius's Colchis looking for Medea, as it were. The intertexts activated by Statius's allusive gestures reveal why the Golden Fleece is an appropriate ingredient for Vulcan to use in fashioning Harmonia's necklace. In tendentiously mining Valerius's *Argonautica* for his poetics of unmitigated *nefas*, Statius struck gold.[21]

---

[20] For excellent discussions of how Valerius darkens the mood of the marriage ceremony in contrast to Apollonius's depiction of the event as overwhelmingly joyous, see Salemme 1991, 76–84, and Pellucchi 2012, 271–78. However, Valerius may well have been inspired to foreground the tragic consequences of the marriage by a statement found in Apollonius's account of the wedding (A.R. 4.1165–67). There, as the couple weds, we are informed that "it is a fact that we tribes of suffering men never plant our feet firmly upon the path of joy, but there is ever some bitter pain to keep company with our delight" (transl. Hunter 1993b).

[21] On the *Thebaid* as quintessentially a poem of *nefas*, see Ganiban 2007.

2 Mars and Venus

There are several other points of contact between the description of Harmonia's necklace in *Thebaid* 2 and the wedding of Jason and Medea in *Argonautica* 8; these connections further advertise a sustained level of engagement with Valerius's narrative on Statius's part. For example, Jason's splendor as he approaches his bride is likened to Mars furtively approaching Venus: *qualis sanguineo uictor Gradiuus ab Hebro | Idalium furto subit aut dilecta Cythera* ("similar to Gradivus was he, when he comes in triumph from blood-stained Hebrus and steals into Idalium or beloved Cythera," V. Fl. 8.228–29).[22] Of course, it was anger over the illicit love affair between Mars and Venus that prompted Vulcan to fashion for Harmonia the necklace that in *Thebaid* 2 adorns the neck of Argia (Stat. *Theb.* 2.269–73). If one reads the Valerian passage through a Statian lens, the seemingly positive simile designed to highlight Jason's attractiveness and impressive physique instead assumes an ominous connotation.[23] In Statius's *Thebaid*, the love affair of Mars and Venus functions as a kind of "original sin" whose destructive effects are far-reaching. As an earthly instantiation of this divine relationship, the union of Jason and Medea becomes a symbol—perhaps *the* symbol—of conjugal turmoil and familial dysfunction in the human realm.

Thus Jason and Medea, or more properly, Valerius's Jason and Medea, assume an etiological dimension vis-à-vis Statius's *Thebaid*: their marriage led to the moment in *Thebaid* 2 that I have been discussing, in two different senses. On the one hand, Valerius's depiction of the wedding of Jason and Medea is highlighted as an important literary model for the wedding of Argia and Polynices. On the other hand, the world-historical significance accorded to Argo's voyage in Valerius's poem (V. Fl. 1.531–60) is here boiled down by Statius to an "original sin" on par with the illicit union of Mars and Venus. For Statius, the originative power of Argo's precedent-setting maiden voyage is important because of the originative power of the precedent set by the *maiden*'s voyage. The murderous energy produced by the ill-starred marriage of Jason and Medea is a perfect ingredient indeed for Harmonia's necklace, and for Statius's poem of *nefas*.[24]

---

[22] On the simile, which has no parallel in Apollonius's poem, see Shelton 1971, 508–9; Gärtner 1994, 226–29; Ripoll 1998, 172–76; Pellucchi 2012, 272–74. Of particular relevance here is Gärtner's astute observation that the reader is made to think of Hephaestus's retaliation against Aphrodite and Ares as recounted in *Odyssey* 8; see Gärtner 1994, 228.
[23] For other ways in which the simile carries negative connotations, see Pellucchi 2012, 272–74.
[24] Statius's usage of the periphrasis *Idalius ... puer* (*Theb.* 2.287) to describe Cupid during the ecphrasis on Harmonia's necklace may also point to Valerius's depiction of the wedding of Jason

It is worth pausing over another detail in the Valerian wedding scene alluded to by Statius's usage of the phrase *uelleris aurum*. Valerius informs us that Venus clothes Medea in a robe and places a crown on her head: *ipsa suas illi croceo subtegmine uestes | induit, ipsa suam duplicem Cytherea coronam | donat et arsuras alia cum uirgine gemmas* ("Venus clothes the girl with her own robe of saffron texture, and gives to Medea her own twofold crown and the jewels destined to burn upon another bride," V. Fl. 8.234–36). Medea marries Jason while wearing the crown that will kill her rival Creusa in Corinth, something unparalleled in other accounts of their union.[25] We are thus once again made to see the tragedy to come. Moreover, in more general terms, Medea is married while adorned with a divine gift that will do harm to yet another bride in the future, and thus the parallel with the situation in *Thebaid* 2 is striking: the necklace worn by Argia during her ill-omened marriage to Polynices will one day adorn the neck of Eriphyle, to whom it will bring "laments and disasters" (*gemitus ... clades, Theb.* 2.303). And although we are not told who fashioned the crown that Valerius's Venus gives to Medea—could it have been her husband?—the Valerian Vulcan did (at the very least) fashion a *representation* of this crown and its destruction of Creusa on the Temple of the Sun in Colchis: *deficit in thalamis turbataque paelice coniunx | pallam et gemmiferae donum exitiale coronae | apparat, ante omnes secum dequesta labores* ("His wife, distressed in her chamber and moved to anger by her rival, prepares a robe and the deadly gift of a jeweled crown, first bewailing all her sufferings," V. Fl. 5.446–48). The *nefas* in Corinth anticipated by the ecphrasis in *Argonautica* 5 and alluded to again during the wedding in *Argonautica* 8 is not actualized in Valerius's poem. But it *is* there, and Statius hones in on this absent presence. The crown given to Medea was not

---

and Medea. There the adjective *Idalius* is employed twice (V. Fl. 8.225, 229). These are the only uses of this epithet in Valerius's poem, and Statius only uses the word two other times in the *Thebaid* (5.63 and 12.16). The former is especially interesting for my purposes, since it is found in the same line as a reference to Venus's "girdle" (*ceston*), on which more below.

25 On Valerius's innovation in having Medea marry Jason while wearing the crown that one day will kill her Corinthian rival, see Shelton 1971, 510; Spaltenstein 2005, 436–37; Lazzarini 2012, 233; Pellucchi 2012, 289–90. Valerius may well be making explicit something that is intertextually implicit in Apollonius's epic, wherein "the gifts women bestow at Medea's own wedding foreshadow in their nature and in the vocabulary used to describe them the deadlier ones she herself will give another bride in Euripides' [*Medea*]" (Knight 1991, 250). On the Valerian Venus's usurpation of Juno's traditional role as *pronuba* ("preparer of the bride"), see Salemme 1991, 78; Bernstein 2008, 59 n. 89; Pellucchi 2012, 275–76. This too is ominous, since Venus is no fan of Medea and her family, hostility that again takes us back to her illicit affair with Mars: Vulcan only discovered he was being cuckolded because Sol, progenitor of Medea's family line, snitched (V. Fl. 6.467–68 with Wijsman 2000, 186–87).

designed to cause harm, like Harmonia's necklace was. But it can be converted into a destructive force by a devotee of the dark arts who is determined to poison it. A fitting image, I suggest, for the way Statius engages with the work of his Flavian predecessor, a tendentiously deconstructive reading of the *Argonautica* that reveals the darkness visible in Valerius's text and repurposes it for its own epic designs.[26]

3 The *cestos* of Venus

Another detail in Statius's description of the ingredients used in Harmonia's necklace that points to Valerius's poem is the reference to the *cestos* ("girdle") of Venus (*Theb.* 2.282–85):

> tum uarias pestes raptumque interplicat atro
> Tisiphones de crine ducem, et quae pessima ceston
> uis probat; haec circum spumis lunaribus unguit
> callidus atque hilari perfundit cuncta ueneno.   285

> Then he [sc. Vulcan] entwines various harms, a chieftain torn from Tisiphone's black hair and the most noxious of the powers that attest the Girdle. These he cunningly smears about with lunar spume and over the whole spreads gay poison.

Of course this mysterious item (*cestos*) figures prominently in *Iliad* 14, where Hera borrows it from Aphrodite in order to seduce Zeus, and it is understandable that most readers of these lines see here a reference primarily to Homer.[27] But as Marco Fucecchi has noted, we must also allow for the intervention of Valerius, in whose epic the *cestos* of Venus plays a significant role in compelling Medea to fall in

---

26 On the topic of poisoning jewelry, it is worth noting that when she marries Jason, Medea is also wearing a necklace that she herself has poisoned and that, along with the robe and crown given to her by Venus, will one day be used to kill Creusa in Corinth: *ipsumque monile ueneris | implicat* ("and she fills with poisons even her necklace," V. Fl. 8.18–19). The notion that the "wedding gifts" sent to Creusa comprised a robe, a crown, and a necklace almost certainly derives from Seneca (*Med.* 570–74), where a necklace is mentioned along with the more traditional (i.e., Euripidean) robe and crown. On Seneca's innovation in this regard, see Costa 1973, 120–21, and Hine 2000, 166–67. On Valerius's imitation of Seneca here, see Spaltenstein 2005, 388 and Pellucchi 2012, 63.
27 See Mulder 1954, 201, and Chinn 2011, 82. For a stimulating and wide-ranging discussion of Aphrodite's "girdle" in the *Iliad* and its relations to actual Greek magical practices, see Faraone 1990.

love with Jason.[28] In fact, it appears that Statius once again has Valerius's text specifically in mind: his use of the collocation *spumis lunaribus* (*Theb.* 2.284) echoes a phrase in Valerius's *Argonautica* (*lunam spumare*, V. Fl. 6.447).[29] This phrase is employed by Valerius in a description of Medea's unrivaled bewitching powers, a description that comes immediately before Venus's girdle is introduced into the narrative with the sequence beginning at V. Fl. 6.455.[30] For at this point in the *Argonautica*, Juno approaches Venus in order to ask the goddess of love if she may borrow the powerful object, a request that Venus grants (V. Fl. 6.469–74):

> tum uero optatis potitur, nec passa precari
> ulterius dedit acre decus fecundaque monstris   470
> cingula, non pietas quibus aut custodia famae,
> non pudor, at contra leuis et festina cupido
> adfatusque mali dulcisque labantibus error
> et metus et demens alieni cura pericli.

> Now at last she has what she desires: suffering no further prayer Venus gives Juno the dangerous ornament, the girdle fruitful in dire issues, that knows not piety nor care of good repute nor honor, but rather fickleness and hot desire, and inducement to ill and sin that allures the wavering, and fear and the distracting terror of another's peril.

One of the first things to note about this item, referred to here as *cingula*, is that Valerius parts ways with Homer by intensifying its negative effects.[31] In fact, these lines read like a more expansive version of Statius's abbreviated characterization of the *cestos*'s noxious powers (*quae pessima ceston | uis probat*, *Theb.* 2.283–84). It is thus likely that Statius had Valerius's *cingula* in mind. For as Mulder notes Homer's *cestos* has seductive power,[32] but not the kind of destructive and debilitating force that would justify its inclusion in Harmonia's necklace, whereas Valerius's version does. Its destructive power is on prominent display later in *Argonautica* 6. Juno delivers the *cingula* to Medea as she stands on the walls of Colchis watching Jason fight in the civil war (V. Fl. 6.668–71):

> interdum blandae derepta monilia diuae
> contrectat miseroque aptat flagrantia collo,
> quaque dedit teneros aurum furiale per artus,   670
> deficit.

---

28 See Fucecchi 1997, 114.
29 See Spaltenstein 2005, 133.
30 On the civil war resonances of Medea's powers and lunar spume in Valerius's epic, see also Krasne in this volume, pp. 379–84.
31 See Langen 1896–97, 447; Salemme 1991, 51; Fucecchi 1997, 14–16.
32 See Mulder 1954, 201.

> Meanwhile she handles the necklace plucked from the winsome goddess, and fits it, flashing fire, about her hapless neck, and where she has set the maddening gold upon her tender limbs there her strength fails.

In addition to emphasizing the debilitating effects of the *cingula*, perhaps the most remarkable thing about this piece of "maddening gold" (*aurum furiale*) is that it turns out to be... a necklace (*monilia*)! This is both un-Homeric and quite unusual in general, although not wholly unique to Valerius, as Langen demonstrates.[33] One effect of this narrative choice, however, is to bring the Statian and Valerian texts into even closer contact, as Fucecchi notes.[34] Statius's reference to the destructive power of Venus's *cestos* during his description of Harmonia's *dirum monile* ("dire necklace," *Theb.* 2.266) thus slyly acknowledges the object's metamorphosis from a "girdle" with seductive power in Homer's *Iliad* to a "necklace of insanity" in Valerius's *Argonautica*.[35]

Moreover, in Valerius the use of Venus's *cestos* is actually connected to her affair with Mars, the triggering event for the fabrication of Harmonia's necklace in *Thebaid* 2. At *Argonautica* 6.467–68 Venus eagerly lends Juno her *cestos* to be used for Medea's destruction because she desires revenge against Sol for revealing to Vulcan her involvement with Mars: *sensit diua dolos, iam pridem sponte requirens | Colchida et inuisi genus omne excindere Phoebi* ("the goddess perceived her craft, but for long had she sought herself to destroy the Colchian land and all the hated race of the Sun").[36] On the one hand, it is Valerius's intervention between Homer and Statius that makes the *cestos* appropriate as an ingredient for Harmonia's necklace. On the other hand, we see here again Statius advertising an affinity with the darker aspects of Valerius's poem. For of the various meanings one can ascribe to Venus's necklace in Valerius's *Argonautica*, chief among them is that it is a conspicuous symbol of divine intervention that leads to recklessness, the subversion of *pietas*, fratricidal madness, and the desire for revenge. Statius knows indeed where to look in Valerius to find material suitable for his own epic constructions.

Given what I have been suggesting about the nature of the *Thebaid*'s engagement with Valerius's *Argonautica*, it is tempting to end my discussion at this point, with Statius's evocation of Medea standing on the walls of Colchis viewing

---

[33] See Langen 1896–97, 447–48. See also Salemme 1991, 59 n. 19; Wijsman 2000, 255–56.
[34] See Fucecchi 1997, 224–25.
[35] I call the Homeric *cestos* a "girdle" for simplicity's sake, but see Faraone 1990 on the difficulty of determining its exact nature.
[36] See the useful notes on Valerius's elaboration of Venus's hatred of the Colchians at Fucecchi 1997, 112–13; Wijsman 2000, 186–88; Spaltenstein 2005, 138–39.

a civil war while wearing a "necklace of insanity" given to her by a vengeful god hell-bent on her destruction. But I want to conclude with an examination of yet another allusion to Valerius's *Argonautica* in Statius's description of Harmonia's necklace. At the very end of the ecphrasis, Statius lists various personified abstractions that had a hand in fashioning the object: *non Decor Idaliusque puer, sed Luctus et Irae | et Dolor et tota pressit Discordia dextra* ("nor Beauty, nor the Idalian boy shaped it, but Mourning and Anger and Grief and Strife with all the power of her hand," *Theb.* 2.287–88). The list of figures echoes a similar one in Book 2 of the *Argonautica* (V. Fl. 2.204–8):

> adcelerat Pauor et Geticis Discordia demens
> e stabulis atraeque genis pallentibus Irae   205
> et Dolus et Rabies et Leti maior imago
> uisa truces exerta manus, ut prima uocatu
> intonuit signumque dedit Mauortia coniunx.

Fear and insensate Strife from her Getic lair, dark-browed Anger with pale cheeks, Treachery, Frenzy, and towering above the rest Death, her cruel hands bared, come hastening up at the first sound of the Martian consort's pealing voice that gave the signal.

The scene, of course, is the island of Lemnos, where Venus does her best impression of a Fury in order to inspire the women of the island to kill the men (V. Fl. 2.101–6, 196–98).[37] The Valerian intertext is perfectly suited for this programmatic moment in Statius's *Thebaid*. Harmonia's necklace causes divinely inspired madness and awful suffering within the family. The horror triggered by this madness also centers on the women of Thebes, as the list of successive Theban women who have worn the object suggests: Harmonia, Semele, Jocasta, Argia, and soon enough Eriphyle (*Theb.* 2.289–305). By evoking Valerius's Lemnos episode, Statius points yet again to the kind of material he finds useful in his predecessor. If one is looking for *nefas* in Valerius's epic, Lemnos, Argo's first port of call, is a great place to look.[38] Clearly, Statius found quite a lot of inspiration there. He of course composes his own version of the Lemnian massacre in *Thebaid* 5, a passage that has long been regarded as engaging directly with Valerius's depiction of the same events.[39] Like Statius's own version of the Lemnian

---

[37] On Venus-as-Fury in Valerius's epic, see Hardie 1993a, 43–44, and Elm 1998. The "infuriating" power of Harmonia's necklace is further enhanced if we allow for the intervention of Vergil's description of the snake thrown by Allecto at Amata, which morphs into a "golden necklace" (*tortile ... aurum*, *A.* 7.351–52). On this passage's significance for Statius's description of Harmonia's necklace, see Lovatt 2001, 106 n. 11.
[38] On Valerius's Lemnos episode, see also Landrey and Keith in this volume.
[39] See Vessey 1970, 52; Feeney 1991, 375–76; Poortvliet 1991a, 68–69; Parkes 2014b, 329–30.

massacre (and indeed like the *Thebaid* as a whole), Valerius's Lemnos episode is characterized by hellish energy, betrayal, insanity, familial dysfunction, and civil discord. Thus we see again how Statius's programmatic ecphrasis offers an allusive "snapshot" of the kind of Valerian material suitable for Statius's poetry of *nefas*.

4 Conclusion

The foregoing discussion brings me to my final points. In Valerius's Lemnos episode, Statius found in his predecessor an *epyllion*, as it were, whose themes more fully resonated with the horror he sought to conjure up than anything else in Valerius's poem. Thus the allusions to Valerius in the description of Harmonia's necklace reveal Statius's approach to his Flavian predecessor. It is a tendentious approach that extracts from the *Argonautica* primarily the macabre, the nefarious, the dysfunctional, and then uses them as ingredients for his epic of *fraternas acies*. It is telling that Statius is drawn especially to places like Hypsipyle's Lemnos and Medea's Corinth. It reflects a way of reading Valerius's *Argonautica* as a text whose narrative present, the triumphant voyage of Argo, is haunted by both the past (Lemnos) and the future (Corinth). We have seen that, in Valerius's poem, Venus's *cestos* is used on Medea because of the goddess's desire for revenge against Sol; we have also seen that this leads to a wedding during which Jason and Medea are likened to Mars and Venus, a passage alluded to by Statius during his programmatic ecphrasis. Surely it is not a coincidence, then, that Valerius's Lemnian massacre is the direct result of the love affair between Venus and Mars. The women of Lemnos stop worshipping Venus because of her mistreatment of Vulcan, who has a special connection to the island (V. Fl. 2.95–100):

> Lemnos cara deo (nec fama notior Aetne   95
> aut Lipares domus): has epulas, haec templa peracta
> aegide et horrifici formatis fulminis alis
> laetus adit. contra Veneris stat frigida semper
> ara loco, meritas postquam dea coniugis iras
> horruit et tacitae Martem tenuere catenae.   100

> Lemnos is dear to the god (neither Aetna nor his Liparean home is more renowned): here the banquets, here too is the temple where he loves to repair when he has completed the aegis or forged wings for the dire thunderbolt. But there Venus's altar stands always cold, since the day when the goddess trembled before her husband's righteous anger, while Mars lay bound in the silent fetters.

This chain of causality has no parallel in Apollonius's account, where we are given no indication at all as to why the Lemnian women decided to neglect Aphrodite's worship, thereby provoking her wrath (A.R. 1.614–15).[40] It is a unique feature of Valerius's poem then that both the hellish events on Lemnos and those to come in Corinth derive from the very same "original sin" that prompted Vulcan to fashion Harmonia's necklace, which in turn causes the tragic events recounted in Statius's *Thebaid*.[41] These are the kinds of narrative sequences that Statius seeks to exploit, as his allusively programmatic ecphrasis indicates, and with which he finds avenues for driving Valerius, like some latter-day Amphiaraus, down to hell with him. Valerius's *Argonautica* is, in my view, far from an unmitigated "catalog of lust and madness," but there is plenty of lust and madness to go around. Indeed, Statius's allusive gestures prompt us to reflect upon the fact that portions of Valerius's epic issue from the exact same source as Harmonia's necklace. Readers may disagree about the ultimate meanings of Valerius's poem, but one thing is for sure. For a poet like Statius, who knows what he wants to extract from his predecessor, who knows how best to boil things down for his "witch's brew," Valerius's *Argonautica* may well offer a recipe for writing about civil war.

---

40 See Poortvliet 1991a, 83, and Seal 2014, 130.
41 In fact, Statius seems cunningly to acknowledge this feature of Valerius's narrative. As she begins to recount the horrific events on Lemnos, Statius's Hypsipyle refers to Venus's *cestos* (*Theb.* 5.63). Statius thus indirectly links this item—used against Medea in retaliation for Sol's revelation of Venus's affair with Mars (V. Fl. 6.467–68)—to the subsequent massacre, thereby obliquely conjuring up the cause of Venus's wrath in the Valerian account.

Marco van der Schuur
Civil War on the Horizon: Seneca's *Thyestes* and *Phoenissae* in Statius's *Thebaid* 7

Statius's *Thebaid* shows its debt to Senecan tragedy right from the moment that the figure of Oedipus enters the stage, immediately following the proem. This Oedipus is a Senecan Oedipus:[1] he has exacted his punishment of self-blinding on himself, just as Seneca's Oedipus had at the end of the play that bears his name,[2] and has achieved the state of limbo desired by Seneca's Oedipus.[3] The reader's Senecan impression of the character is reinforced when Oedipus concludes his invocation of Tisiphone to incite fraternal strife between his sons with the following words: *da, Tartarei regina barathri, | quod cupiam uidisse nefas. nec tarda sequetur | mens iuuenum: modo digna ueni, mea pignora nosces* ("Queen of Tartarus's pit, grant the wickedness I would fain see. Nor will the young men's spirit be slow to follow. Come you but worthy, you shall know them my true sons," Stat. *Theb.* 1.85–87).[4] These lines echo the words Oedipus utters at the end of the first half of Seneca's *Phoenissae*. There, Seneca's Oedipus, too, suspects that his sons will be true to their father in their criminality: *aliquid facite propter quod patrem | adhuc iuuet uixisse. facietis, scio: | sic estis orti* ("achieve something to make your father glad that he lived till now! You will do it, I know: you were born

---

I would like to thank the readers (both at home and abroad) of the dissertation chapters on which this contribution is based for their comments. Versions of this paper have been presented both at the Civil War Panel in Edinburgh as well as the *Latinistendag* 2015 in Amsterdam. I would like to thank the editors, De Gruyter's anonymous readers, and Hans Smolenaars for their helpful comments on this chapter, and Lauren Donovan Ginsberg in particular for sharing some of her work on *Phoenissae* prior to publication.

1 Cf. Vessey 1973, 72: "The Oedipus of the *Thebaid* is the Senecan Oedipus; it is as if Statius was continuing the story from the point at which the tragedian had left it." See also Delarue 2000, 144. See Smolenaars 2008 for more on the various Theban traditions (Senecan and others) on which Statius draws in his portrayal of Oedipus and Jocasta in Book 1 of the *Thebaid*.
2 Cf. *scrutatus lumina dextra* (Stat. *Theb.* 1.46) with *scrutatur ... lumina* (Sen. *Oed.* 965) and *nil, parricida dexterae debes tuae* (Sen. *Oed.* 1002). Parallel noted by Heuvel 1932, ad *Theb.* 1.46. See also Vessey 1973, 72.
3 Cf. *longa ... morte* (Stat. *Theb.* 1.48) with *morere, sed citra patrem* (Sen. *Oed.* 951) and *mors eligatur longa* (Sen. *Oed.* 949). Parallels noted by Heuvel 1932, ad *Theb.* 1.48.
4 For Seneca, I follow the text of Zwierlein; for Statius, that of Shackleton Bailey; for Vergil, that of Mynors. All translations of Seneca and Statius are from the Loeb editions of Fitch and Shackleton Bailey. Translations of Vergil are my own.

to it," Sen. *Phoen.* 336–38).⁵ However, the Theban plays are not the only Senecan intertext invoked here. A Fury setting in motion a cycle of crime within a royal family or igniting strife between brothers inevitably reminds the post-Senecan reader of the Fury from the prologue of Seneca's *Thyestes*, setting in motion the renewed strife between the brothers Atreus and Thyestes.⁶ In the third choral ode of the *Thyestes*, the chorus expresses the fear that the conflict between both brothers will turn into a *bellum ciuile* (Sen. *Thy.* 562); it is with these words that Seneca makes this Greek myth into part of the Roman discourse on civil war, our theme here.⁷

From the very start of the epic, Statius's *Thebaid* is alert to the importance of the theme of fraternal strife in Senecan tragedy.⁸ In this chapter, I will zoom in on Statius's engagement with the *Thyestes* and *Phoenissae* in Book 7 of his *Thebaid*. This is a pivotal book in Statius's epic: the *fraternas acies* that the poet had announced in the poem's opening line are finally brought about. Seneca's *Thyestes* and *Phoenissae* also find themselves teetering on the brink of civil war, but unlike the *Thebaid*, they do not cross that ledge: the *Thyestes* threatens to turn into a civil war but ultimately does not; the *Phoenissae* breaks off just before the conflict between Eteocles and Polynices actually breaks out (Sen. *Phoen.* 664).⁹ But even though civil war does not actually erupt in these plays, civil war is very much present through the metaphors of fraternal strife, cosmic dissolution, and incest.¹⁰

---

5 See Delarue 2000, 150–51; Ganiban 2007, 28–29. See now also Davis 2016, 66–67, for a comparable discussion of these and other allusions to Seneca's Theban plays.
6 See Feeney 1991, 347 n. 116, on *Thyestes* as the clearest prototype for Statius's cosmic disruption at the beginning of his epic. See also Frings 1992, 16–18, and Delarue 2000, 256–69, on the role of the *Thyestes*, as well as other Senecan tragedies, in Statius's treatment of Oedipus and Tisiphone's intervention at Thebes. Criado 2000, 26–30, emphasizes the general importance of the models of Aeschylus's *Eumenides* and Seneca's *Thyestes* and *Hercules Furens* to the overture of Statius's epic. On the importance of both *Thyestes* and the Theban plays to the *Thebaid*, see also Davis 2016, 66–72.
7 Lowrie 2016, 333–34.
8 The monographs of Frings 1992; Criado 2000; and Bessone 2011 all make Statius's interaction with Senecan tragedy an integral element of their discussion of the *Thebaid*. For the most recent discussions of Statius and Senecan tragedy, see Augoustakis 2015 and Davis 2016, 66–72. The former also comments on the increased scholarly interest in both Senecan tragedy and Flavian epic and provides a brief overview of the history of the quest for and interpretation of the correspondences between Seneca and Statius (Augoustakis 2015, 377, with n. 1).
9 Of course, as Hans Smolenaars and others have discussed with me, the plot of Euripides' tragedy with the same name does move beyond the point where Seneca's *Phoenissae* breaks off, and Statius's engagement with this play continues beyond the Jocasta scene. However, my focus here is on Statius as a Latin poet, responding to the Latin poetic tradition.
10 Lowrie 2016 and Ginsberg 2018.

Statius's treatment of the outbreak of fraternal strife can be read as a poetic commentary on Seneca's apparent reluctance to write of warfare between brothers. Moreover, Statius's response to these two tragedies is closely connected to some of the larger questions of Flavian literature. The *Thyestes* and *Phoenissae* challenged Statius not only as a poet in the long-standing tradition of generic interaction between epic and tragedy but also as a voice in the Roman discourse on civil war.

Let us start with literary history. Although both the relative and the absolute dating of Seneca's tragedies is a complex matter, it is highly probable that the *Thyestes* and *Phoenissae* are the last two plays that Seneca wrote.[11] If this is indeed the case, it is tempting to assume that these tragedies contain Seneca's final thoughts on the tragic genre and its interaction with other genres, including epic.[12] They would thus subsequently provide an open challenge to poets following after Seneca, working in either epic or tragedy. Statius himself is keenly aware of this generic challenge posed by Seneca and responds to it.[13] Statius rises to the challenge Senecan tragedy posed in other ways, as well, responding to themes and tensions, parallels and contrasts, that are present in Seneca's tragic *oeuvre*.[14] A further point that is relevant to Statius's reception of Senecan tragedy as a poetic oeuvre is the apparently unfinished nature of the *Phoenissae*, which has no

---

[11] For in-depth discussion of the relative dating of Seneca's tragedies see Fitch 1981; Dingel 2009. Both scholars argue that the *Thyestes* and *Phoenissae* are probably Seneca's final tragedies. On the dating of *Thyestes*, see also Nisbet 1990.

[12] On Seneca's tragic intertextuality and (meta)poetics, see, e.g., Schiesaro 2003; Littlewood 2004; Hinds 2011; Seo 2013, 94–121; Trinacty 2014. An early attempt to insert Seneca's use of Furies into the epic tradition can be found in Gilder 1997. See Schiesaro 2003 in particular on Seneca's engagement with concerns of the epic genre. I explore these intertextual generic interactions further in my dissertation. More generally speaking, my intertextual thinking is particularly indebted to Hardie 1989, Hardie 1993a, and Hinds 1998, in that I read Seneca and Statius as poets tendentiously rewriting and commenting on the works of their predecessors. See Smolenaars 1994, xxvi–xlii, on Statius's technique of multiple imitation (see also the bibliography in n. 14), obviously an inspiration for my Statian pages.

[13] As has been observed by Augoustakis 2015, 377: "Just as Seneca grafts the tragic genre with epic overtones, and, as Schiesaro has pointed out, makes the two genres project a troubling shadow onto each other, so Statius exploits the interaction between the two genres to underscore the inescapability from the *nefas* that overshadows the *Thebaid*'s perverted epic landscape."

[14] This technique is a variant of the one discussed by Hardie 1989 (so-called "combinatorial allusion"), who argues that Flavian poets respond to themes and tensions in Vergil's *Aeneid* by simultaneously alluding to two parallel or contrasting passages in Vergil's epic. See also Hardie 1990 for a comparable technique in Ovid's response to Vergil in his Theban books. See also Seo 2013, 122–84, and Micozzi 2015 on Statius's highly reflexive and manipulative take on the literary tradition he has inherited.

choral odes and seems to break off in the middle of a discussion between Jocasta, Eteocles and Polynices. The critical consensus is that the play is unfinished, but there have been some notable voices of dissent.[15] I will argue that Statius's reception of the *Phoenissae* anticipates these scholarly debates by several centuries.[16]

If the *Thyestes* and *Phoenissae*—two plays preoccupied with the threat of civil war—do indeed constitute Seneca's final words as a tragic poet, they must have seemed, just as Lucan's epic,[17] prophetic to their post-69 CE audience of the events that shortly followed their author's death. Just as the Flavian Emperors had to carry on beyond the civil wars from which their dynasty had emerged, so the Flavian epicists had to find a way to continue the epic tradition following the destruction wrought by Lucan's epic.[18] I argue here that Seneca's (presumably final) civil war-tinged tragedies, *Thyestes* and *Phoenissae*, presented Statius with a similar challenge, a *non plus ultra* that Statius dares to move beyond.[19]

1 *Thyestes* and the Discourse of Civil War

Seneca and Statius could both draw on a long tradition of Roman thinking on civil war, a tradition that would be carried on long after them. Both the phenomenon and the concept of civil war had been with the Romans since the days of Sulla.[20] In Roman thinking of the late Republic and early Empire, the struggles between the brothers Eteocles and Polynices, Atreus and Thyestes, served as crucial tragic metaphors for Romans to think about their own civil wars,[21] laying the

---

15 See especially Frank 1995, 1–16, for the case against the *Phoenissae* as a finished play; Tarrant 1978, 229–31, argues that the play is complete. Hirschberg 1989, 7–8, with reference to earlier scholarship, discusses the possibility that the unfinished nature of the *Phoenissae* is due to the manuscript transmission, adducing the play's absence of choral odes as an argument against this hypothesis. For further discussion see below.
16 For Flavian epicists prefiguring 20th century interpretative debate see Hardie 1989, 3.
17 Stover 2012, 3.
18 See Stover 2012, 2–3 (and *passim*), on Valerius Flaccus's attempts to meet this challenge and Walter 2014 on the Flavian reinvention of epic, starting from Valerius and responding to Stover's approach. See also Fucecchi in this volume.
19 For this twin challenge to Flavian epicists presented by the Annaei, compare Krasne's discussion in this volume of Valerius's *Argonautica* as a response to the treatment of Argonautic myth both Lucanean and Senecan.
20 On the emergence and development of the concept of civil war in Roman thinking, and on civil war as something peculiarly Roman, see now the overview in Armitage 2017a, 31–90.
21 See Petrone 1996. See also Korneeva 2011, 35–41, with further references. On Seneca's *Thyestes* as a predecessor to Statius's *Thebaid* as poetry about fraternal strife, see Frings 1992. Narducci

groundwork for Statius and Seneca's looking at the very Roman concern of civil war through the lens of Greek myth.[22] More generally, Romans often thought of civil war in terms of war within the family and fraternal strife.[23] This notion became even more salient after the emergence of the Principate. A historian like Tacitus could conceive of the violence involved in the struggle for succession within the imperial family and the violence against citizens involved in the Principate in general as "a continuation of civil war by other means."[24] In addition to this, Tacitus combined the threat of civil war looming beneath the surface of the Principate with allusions to the tragic strife between family members in his portrayal of dynastic conflict within the imperial family.[25] He was anticipated, however, by the Flavians. For example, as Lauren Donovan Ginsberg has recently argued, the pseudo-Senecan *Octavia* similarly explores the unsettling similarities between Principate and civil war.[26] The theme of fraternal rivalry recurs in a more subdued key in Silius's *Punica*, which offers its readers several examples of the complex dynamics involved in fraternal relationships, including that of Titus and Domitian.[27] Statius's portrayal of the conflict between Eteocles and Polynices has also been read as a reflection on the supposed rivalry between Titus and Domitian.[28]

In his *Thyestes*, Seneca fuses Greek myth and Roman thinking by calling the conflict between Atreus and Thyestes *bellum ciuile*.[29] But fraternal strife, the dissolution of family bonds, is just one of the many ways in which civil war manifests itself. It also dissolves the unity of the human body and soul, turning its various parts against each other, or even the compact of the cosmos itself. As Michèle Lowrie has argued, both Seneca's third choral ode and the *Thyestes* as a whole, drawing on the larger tradition of Roman thinking on civil war, show how

---

2002, 19, and Ambühl 2015, 33, comment on the importance of the theme of civil war in Seneca's *Phoenissae* and its intertextuality with Lucan's *Bellum Ciuile*, both with further references. On (Statius's) Thebes as a mirror for Roman concerns see, among others: Ahl 1986; Hardie 1990; Henderson 1991; Dominik 1994b; Janan 2009; Bessone 2011; McAuley 2016, 297–344. On Statius and Lucan, see now Ganiban 2011 and Roche 2015, with further references.

22 On this similarity between Seneca and Statius see Petrone 1997, 19, and Franchet d'Espèrey 1999, 21: "Stace ... a choisi le mythe, comme Sénèque dans ses tragédies."
23 See Petrone 1996, 15–100, for a comprehensive account.
24 See Keitel 1984. For the phrasing, Armitage 2017a, 72.
25 See Klaassen 2014, 172–78, for discussion and further references.
26 Ginsberg 2017, 3 and *passim*.
27 See Stocks in this volume.
28 Dominik 1994b in particular.
29 Lowrie 2016, 341: "Seneca reverses a common trope: in Latin literature, killing within the family often stands for civil war. Here the strife between the brothers is called civil war and it extends throughout the city."

civil war results in dissolution and discord everywhere, "an existential threat at all levels."[30]

Pervasive as fraternal strife and cosmic dissolution may be in the *Thyestes*, an actual civil war never takes place within the play, even though, to the characters of the play, this is by no means certain from the beginning. Atreus's first impulse is to summon all of his armies in his hunt for Thyestes (Sen. *Thy.* 180–89), before settling for guile instead of military force by tempting his exiled brother into a power-sharing deal. Following Thyestes' return and the apparent reconciliation between both brothers in the third act, we arrive at the third choral ode (Sen. *Thy.* 546–622). The chorus's description of the situation before the reconciliation, of Mycenae as a city prepared for war between the brothers (*Thy.* 552–59), makes Atreus's call for war much more real than when we first heard it.[31]

However, a clear allusion to the threat of civil war can also be found here through an allusion to Vergil. When the chorus asks *otium tanto subitum e tumultu | quis deus fecit?* ("What god has created sudden calm / out of such uproar?" Sen. *Thy.* 560–61), they allude to Tityrus's *deus nobis haec otia fecit* ("A god has created this calm for us," Verg. *Ecl.* 1.6).[32] As Tarrant points out, Seneca, through his direct reference to the *arma ciuilis ... belli* (Sen. *Thy.* 562) directly afterwards, "makes explicit a connection that remains below the surface of Vergil's poem." In addition to this, Seneca returns to the *Aeneid* in the following line with *pallidae natos tenuere matres* ("ashen-faced mothers clasped their children," Sen. *Thy.* 563), which echoes Vergil's *trepidae matres pressere ad pectora natos* ("frightened mothers pushed their sons to their breasts," Verg. *A.* 7.518), a line that follows Allecto's sounding of the pastoral war horn.[33] This is the moment in the *Aeneid* at which the pact between two factions claiming rule over Latium—Aeneas and Latinus, Trojans and Latins—is shattered, and war becomes inevitable. Although part of a passage describing the situation *before* the deal between Atreus and Thyestes, this allusion to a broken pact, following closely upon the sealing of a power-sharing deal on stage, casts an intertextual doubt upon the durability of that deal within the play.[34] It also helps Seneca to emphasize once again how dangerously close the action in this tragedy of fraternal strife comes to actual civil war.

---

30 Lowrie 2016, 351.
31 Tarrant 1985, *ad* Sen. *Thy.* 549–59 and *passim* on this passage, for parallels with Atreus's first speech. See also P. Davis 1989, 430.
32 Picone 1984, 87; Tarrant 1985, *ad loc.* For further discussion of the allusion, see Trinacty 2014, 55–57, and Lowrie 2016, 342–43.
33 Parallel observed by Picone 1984, 87; Tarrant 1985, *ad loc.*
34 Cf. Trinacty 2014, 55: "... a sense of foreboding (enhanced by intertextual nods to the *Eclogues*) undercuts the song's optimism."

2 Unfinished Business in the *Phoenissae*

A tale in which fraternal strife does indeed turn into war, a tale, moreover, in which tragedy and epic already co-exist, is of course the conflict between the brothers Eteocles and Polynices over the throne of Thebes.[35] This conflict traditionally ends with both brothers killing each other on the field of battle. However, in Seneca's tragedy *Phoenissae*, this outcome is never realized. Rather, the fear of *bellum ciuile* that the chorus of the *Thyestes* had expressed is raised to fever pitch in the *Phoenissae*. Just as the chorus of *Thyestes* was haunted by fears of disorder and conflict within the soul, the city, and the cosmos,[36] so Jocasta imagines the horrors of civil war that Polynices and Eteocles may inflict on her city and her body.[37] Seneca's treatment of the civil war looming over Thebes contains several allusions to moments of crisis and strife in Vergil's *Aeneid*. In this way, Seneca offers an invitation to epic poets to turn his Theban tragedy into a full-fledged epic of civil war.

This intertextual challenge is most clearly presented in the middle of the play, when both Oedipus and Jocasta are informed of the rapidly approaching conflict between Polynices and Eteocles. First, Oedipus is urged by a messenger to stop the approaching war between his sons (Sen. *Phoen.* 320–27); in return, Oedipus expresses his wish for something greater than a *ciuile bellum* (Sen. *Phoen.* 354–55).[38] Following Oedipus's angry response to this messenger, the scene shifts to the city walls, and we find a *satelles* addressing Queen Jocasta, impressing upon her that the war between her sons is now imminent (Sen. *Phoen.* 388–93). Only Jocasta's intervention can halt or at least delay the war, as both the *satelles* and Antigone point out: *impia arma matris oppositu impedi* ("check this unnatural warfare by interposing as a mother," Sen. *Phoen.* 402), the *satelles* says; *aut solue bellum ... aut prima excipe* ("Either break up the fighting ... or be first to suffer it," Sen. *Phoen.* 406), Antigone advises her mother. Jocasta decides to intervene: *ibo, ibo et armis obuium opponam caput, | stabo inter arma* ("I shall go and interpose my body against their weapons, take my stand between their weapons," Sen. *Phoen.* 407–8).

---

[35] On the opportunity for a poet to fuse epic and tragedy when dealing with the conflict between Eteocles and Polynices, cf. Bessone 2011, 75–79, with references.
[36] Lowrie 2016.
[37] Ginsberg 2018, 70–74.
[38] Petrone 1997, 67, points out that Oedipus falls short here of the example set by Anchises, who in the *Aeneid* urged his descendant Caesar not to begin a civil war (Verg. *A.* 6.834–35). On the importance to the *Phoenissae* of this passage from the *Aeneid*, see also Bessone in this volume.

The word *arma* is prominently present in this short scene featuring Jocasta, the *satelles*, and Antigone. Moreover, once Jocasta has rushed down from the city walls to the expected site of battle, she addresses her sons with the following words: *in me arma et ignes uertite* ("Turn against me your weapons and your fires," Sen. *Phoen.* 443). Seneca's emphasis on *arma* here is no accident. As so often in Latin poetry, his use of the word *arma* here suggests to the reader that the poet is engaged in an intertextual dialogue with Vergil's *Aeneid*.[39] An even more pointed use of the word may be found in Oedipus's encouragement to his sons, *ferte arma* (Sen. *Phoen.* 340), words that could easily be translated as "Bring on your *Aeneid*!" Seneca is clearly emphasizing his response Vergil's epic here.[40]

The purpose of Seneca's emphasis on his response to the *Aeneid* becomes clearer in the *satelles*' description of Jocasta's flight from the city walls down to the battlefield (Sen. *Phoen.* 427–34), as his allusions begin to concentrate on the disturbing second half of Vergil's epic. Barchiesi notes that this frenzied intervention of a woman in the masculine public sphere is very similar to that of Amata in the *Aeneid*.[41] Paradoxically, Jocasta's attempt at preventing war and *nefas* is reminiscent of the madness of Amata, a queen herself responsible for a *maius nefas* (Verg. *A.* 7.386) as she spirits Lavinia away.[42]

But Seneca goes even further than this. The *satelles* compares Jocasta to a Parthian arrow: *sagitta qualis Parthica uelox manu | excussa fertur* ("As an arrow flies swiftly when shot from a Parthian's hand," Sen. *Phoen.* 428–29). Both Hirschberg and Frank have compared the *satelles*' words to Vergil's comparison of the flight of the Dira to a Parthian or Cydonian arrow (Verg. *A.* 12.856–60). In other words, the intervention that should put an end to the Theban civil war is compared to the intervention that had removed Juturna, the last instrument that Juno had used to delay Turnus's doom, and finally brought about the duel between Aeneas and Turnus. Jocasta, who calls herself *belli moram* (Sen. *Phoen.* 458), is compared to the Dira that put an end to all *belli mora*.[43] More generally, we should note that for Seneca the disturbing events of both *Aeneid* 7 and *Aeneid* 12 are at

---

39 Cf. Fowler 1997, 20: "... the word '*arma*' would I think now be seen as always in post-Augustan Latin verse significantly intertextual with the opening of the *Aeneid*, to a greater or lesser extent."
40 In addition to Seneca's emphasis on the word *arma*, it is worth observing that Barchiesi, Hirschberg, and Petrone in their commentaries have all discerned Vergilian coloring in the language used by the *satelles* (Sen. *Phoen.* 387–402). Furthermore, as Ruurd Nauta points out to me, because Oedipus is encouraging his sons to destroy their own city, we can also read this line as an invitation to a Lucanean epic of civil war.
41 Barchiesi 1988, *ad* Sen. *Phoen.* 427.
42 Compare Schiesaro 2003, 35, on the importance of Amata's *maius nefas* to Seneca's *Thyestes*.
43 On Seneca's use of *belli mora* here see Barchiesi 1988, *ad loc.*

stake. When considered together, these allusions strongly suggest that, as in the *Thyestes*, Seneca is preparing us for a poetry of *nefas* in which this tragic poet— in spite of Jocasta's attempts at delay—will further develop the horrors that can already be found in the second half of Vergil's epic *Aeneid*.

Not just on an intertextual level is Jocasta's intervention a highly problematic event. Jocasta, the mother of children born from incest, is herself too much a part of Theban madness and criminality to exercise unqualified maternal authority to bring about peace between the brothers.[44] The problem of Jocasta's complicity in Theban criminality has been most extensively explored by Lauren Donovan Ginsberg.[45] Ginsberg observes that Jocasta's invitation to penetrate her body with swords and make her the first victim of the war (Sen. *Phoen*. 443–50), as well as her invitation of Polynices to a motherly embrace (Sen. *Phoen*. 467–77), carry disturbing sexual overtones, precisely through the emphasis on the body of a mother to incestuous children. Like his father, Polynices returns to Thebes and to his mother's embrace, but he may well outdo his father, violating both his mother and his city.[46] In Senecan Thebes, the crime of incest and the figure of Jocasta literally embody the boundary dissolution and disorder characteristic of Roman civil war.[47]

Highly problematic though the figure of Jocasta is, a few scholars have offered a more optimistic interpretation of her intervention. They do so by arguing that Polynices gives up his claim to the throne at the very end of the play, and that the *Phoenissae* actually ends the way it has come down to us, rather than being unfinished. In Zwierlein's edition, the play stops in the middle of a debate on kingship and exile between Eteocles and Jocasta, which ends with the following lines (Sen. *Phoen*. 660–64):[48]

> Ioc: inuisa numquam imperia retinentur diu.   660
> Et: praecepta melius imperi reges dabunt;
> exilia tu compone. pro regno uelim—
> Ioc: patriam penates coniugem flammis dare?
> Et: imperia pretio quolibet constant bene.

---

44 See Li Causi 2009, 285–88, who points to Jocasta's awareness of her "complicitness" in Theban criminality by giving birth to Eteocles and Polynices (Sen. *Phoen*. 367–69).
45 Ginsberg 2018.
46 Ginsberg 2018, 68–70.
47 Ginsberg 2018. On the female body as a *locus* of civil war, see Keith in this volume.
48 With Zwierlein, I consider Jocasta and Eteocles the speakers of these lines. Fitch, whose translation I follow, considers Polynices and Eteocles the speakers. I have altered the speakers' names in the translation to match Zwierlein's text.

> Joc: Hated power is never held for long.
> Et: Kings will give better advice about power; you should organize your exile. For kingship I would be willing—
> Joc: To give fatherland, house gods, wife to the flames?
> Et: Power is well purchased at any price.

This open-ended stopping point is fitting of a play that may very well be the last one that Seneca has written. But it is also fitting of Senecan tragedy in general. Richard Tarrant—who makes the case for a finished *Phoenissae*—has argued that the fact that the conflict remains unresolved is characteristic of Senecan tragedy, and that this need not imply that the play is unfinished. He adduces the endings of *Medea*, *Agamemnon* and *Thyestes* as parallels.[49]

Frank rightly responds to this that there is a difference between fundamental unresolvedness and the threat of a continuation of violence uttered at the end of a play.[50] Nevertheless, the idea that the *Phoenissae* is a finished tragedy has remained attractive. Gottfried Mader keeps the possibility of completeness open and offers the intriguing suggestion that Eteocles' unqualified acceptance of absolute power in Thebes and the self-destruction that it brings with it is in itself a fitting fulfillment of Oedipus's wishes.[51] Some scholars, opting for a more radical approach and following in the footsteps of Grotius, have chosen to assign the words *regna, dummodo inuisus tuis* (Sen. *Phoen.* 653) to Polynices rather than Jocasta, which would imply that Polynices surrenders the crown to Eteocles and in this way ends their fraternal strife.[52] According to Umberto Moricca, this supposed radical transformation of the myth was inspired by Livy's story of Coriolanus, in which Coriolanus's mother Veturia convinced her son not to attack Rome (Liv. 2.39–40).[53]

---

[49] Tarrant 1978, 229–30 with n. 88.
[50] Frank 1995, 11. On the open-ended nature of Senecan tragedy see, e.g., Schiesaro 2003.
[51] Mader 2010, 310. As my editors point out, the fact that this line belongs to Polynices in the manuscript tradition (Grotius was the first to attribute it to Eteocles, and his reading has found favor) is problematic for this interpretation. Petrone 1997, 8 and 18–19, argues that the play is finished, apart from the missing choral odes, because it reaches its thematic climax here. Mazzoli 2002, 158–59, too, considers the play virtually complete. For a parallel discussion of an "open" ending, see Penwill in this volume on the ending of Valerius's *Argonautica*.
[52] Moricca 1917, 481–93. Paul 1953, 68–75, also assigns this line to Polynices but does not consider the play complete.
[53] Moricca 1917, 491–93. See also, *contra*, Frank 1995, 11, and Li Causi 2009, 285–88. See, however, La Penna 1994 and Ginsberg 2018, 68–70, on the connections between Jocasta's and Veturia's intervention, which is probably more relevant to the Senecan passage than Frank allows.

There are good reasons to assign *Phoen.* 653 to Jocasta, especially given the improbability of so radical a divergence from the legend on Seneca's part;[54] the line also fits Jocasta's line of argument very well.[55] The constant references to the approaching battle between Eteocles and Polynices are so dominant that this battle would form the only logical dramatic climax of the play.[56] But the fact remains that the play stops, finished or not, before we have reached this point. Theoretically, it is still possible that Jocasta will succeed and that Polynices will indeed turn around and go back to Argos.

3 Jocasta's Intervention in Statius's *Thebaid*

In the end then, Seneca's *Thyestes* and *Phoenissae* leave the reader with an intriguing paradox. The civil war at which both plays so often hint always eludes them: even in the *Phoenissae*, which could have been Seneca's tragedy about civil war *par excellence*, the actual poetic treatment of civil war remains outside Seneca's grasp, although for a brief moment it seems that Seneca's civil war has indeed arrived. As we have seen, the attendant narrates how the armies are already storming at each other (Sen. *Phoen.* 387–402) and how only the arrival of Jocasta halts the war (Sen. *Phoen.* 433–42). Moreover, the disorder that civil war brings is omnipresent in other ways as well: through the themes of fraternal strife and cosmic disorder and through the problematic figure of Jocasta herself.

In writing his own epic of fraternal strife, Statius responds to this tension within Seneca's two presumably final tragedies. Statius knows that Polynices' march against Thebes must eventually result in a war between brothers, and unlike Seneca he is able to actually reach this point in his narrative. Moreover, for Statius, the civil war that Seneca had feared in his mythological poetry of *Thyestes* and *Phoenissae* had become a Roman reality in the events of 69 CE. Statius leads Senecan poetry out of the nominally civil war-free Julio-Claudian age into the Flavian age, in which civil war is a lived-through memory. But Statius does not force this move from feared civil war to actual civil war upon Seneca's plays. We have seen that Statius presents his epic as a continuation of Senecan tragedy, and this is no less true in Book 7 of his epic—in which he reworks the second half of the *Phoenissae* (Stat. *Theb.* 7.470–563)—than it was in Book 1. Statius offers a

---

[54] Frank 1995, 11–12 and *ad loc.*
[55] Barchiesi 1988, *ad* Sen. *Phoen.* 651–64.
[56] Frank 1995, 12. See Opelt 1972, 284, and Frank 1995, 12, for possible endings.

careful reading of Senecan tragedy and its engagement with Latin epic, using Seneca's own texts to finally bring the civil war that his predecessor had dreaded about.[57] On the conceptual level, Statius's ability to move beyond Seneca also results in a surpassing of Seneca's civil war metaphors.[58]

To fully appreciate Statius's response to Senecan tragedy in this scene, we have to begin our analysis a little earlier than the actual Jocasta-scene, at the moment when news of the Argive army's approach reaches Thebes (Stat. *Theb.* 7.227–42). This news is reported to king Eteocles by a messenger. Eteocles calls his troops to arms, and the women and children of Thebes mount the walls to look at the Theban army standing on the future battlefield. In this scene, Statius combines allusions to epic and tragedy, thereby continuing the dialogue between genres present in Senecan tragedy.

The messenger's report to Eteocles of the enemy's approach is not without epic precedent: we may compare the messenger report breaking up the Latin war council upon Aeneas's approach (Verg. *A.* 11.447–50) and Iris telling the Trojans of the approach of the Achaeans (Hom. *Il.* 2.786–89).[59] But the sudden appearance of a *nuntius* reporting that Thebes is on the brink of war also calls to mind the sudden arrival of the *nuntius* in Seneca's *Phoenissae*. First of all, there is a structural parallel. The arrival of Statius's messenger marks the end of the conversation on Olympus between a father (Jupiter) planning the destruction of Thebes and a son (Bacchus) attempting to avert it; the arrival of Seneca's messenger abruptly cuts short the exchange between Oedipus and Antigone that had been going on for more than 300 lines. In this dialogue between father and daughter, Antigone had desperately tried to keep Oedipus from self-destruction and suggested that his intervention might put a stop to the destruction that fraternal warfare would bring to Thebes (Sen. *Phoen.* 288–94). In addition to this, both messengers emphasize that the conflict between brothers is not far off: Statius's *nuntius* reports that *Graios | ire duces, nec iam Aoniis procul afore campis* ("Grecian leaders are marching in lengthy column and will soon be no great distance from Aonian fields," Stat. *Theb.* 7.228–29); Seneca's warns that *iam propius*

---

57 There are other intertexts at work in Statius's treatment of Jocasta and the seventh book in general that I cannot discuss here. On the Lucanean tension between Statius's attempt at delaying the war and the irresistible drive of the poem towards *nefas* in the catalogue and river-crossing scenes, see McNelis 2007, 97–123. On Statius's Lucanean plot, see also Ganiban 2011. See Smolenaars 1994, *ad locc.*, for an overview of the parallels with Seneca and other intertexts such as Euripides' *Phoinissai* and Liv. 2.40. On the Coriolanus intertext, to which I will briefly return, see Soubiran 1969. For further literature, see below.
58 McAuley 2016, 297–344. See below.
59 Smolenaars 1994, *ad* Stat. *Theb.* 7.227–42.

accessit malum ("the evil has come closer," Sen. *Phoen.* 323). Finally, the sudden shift from the divine to the human level, marked by Statius through the use of the word *nuntius* at the beginning of the line following Jupiter's and Bacchus's scene on Olympus, can be read as a metapoetic sign that we are moving from epic to tragedy: no more divine councils, but messengers reporting bad news to kings.[60]

The messenger scene forms the beginning of Statius's response to the "civil war on the horizon" theme that had featured so prominently in *Thyestes* and *Phoenissae*. It is also a first indication that, just as at the beginning of the *Thebaid*, Statius is responding to the *Thyestes* and the *Phoenissae* here in tandem. This response is continued in the Argive women's mounting of the walls of Thebes: *nondum hostes contra, trepido tamen agmine matres | conscendunt muros, inde arma nitentia natis | et formidandos monstrant sub casside patres* ("The enemy does not yet face them, but mothers mount the walls in an anxious throng and thence show their children the shining armor and their fathers, figures of fear under their helms," *Theb.* 7.240–42). This scene has antecedents in Latin epic, but it also calls to mind Andromache's climbing the walls with Astyanax to watch the fighting (Hom. *Il.* 6.386–87) and Astyanax's fear at the sight of his father's helmet (Hom. *Il.* 6.467–70).[61] The epithet *trepido* is derived from Vergil's *et trepidae matres pressere ad pectora natos* (Verg. *A.* 7.518),[62] a line which—as we have seen—had been reworked by Seneca in his *pallidae natos tenuere matres* (Sen. *Thy.* 563). Seneca had followed this line with *uxor armato timuit marito* ("wives feared for their husbands in arms"). In Statius we find the same combination of children, frightened mothers, and terrifying armed husbands[63] in a city on the brink of war.[64]

Following a catalogue of the Theban army and the description of the arrival of the Argive host, Statius focuses in greater detail on the Thebans' psychological response to the arrival of the enemy (Stat. *Theb.* 7.452–69). The connection with the previous description of the situation at Thebes is emphasized through Statius's use of the word *attonitas* at the beginning of both passages (Stat. *Theb.* 7.227

---

60 I agree with Soerink 2014, 183, who argues that the word *nuntius* in Stat. *Theb.* 5.717 alludes to the messenger in Euripides' *Hypsipyle*, thereby activating—and signalling Statius's departure from—the major tragic intertext there.
61 Smolenaars 1994, *ad locc.*
62 Smolenaars 1994, *ad* Stat. *Theb.* 7.240–41.
63 The *patres* could very well be *formidandos* not only to their children, but also to their wives.
64 Smolenaars 1994, *ad* Stat. *Theb.* 7.240–41, does not refer to this passage in *Thyestes*, but he does refer to a similar line in another tragedy (Sen. *Ag.* 622). Jörn Soerink suggests to me that Leucothea pressing Palaemon close upon hearing Tisiphone's hisses earlier in the epic (Stat. *Theb.* 1.121–22) also forms part of this intertextual network of terrified mothers.

and 452, of Eteocles' ears and Thebes itself respectively).[65] Likewise, Statius's account of the panic seizing Thebes upon the Argive army's arrival (Stat. *Theb.* 7.452–69) is followed by four lines placing the general panic in a divine framework (Stat. *Theb.* 7.466–69):

> it geminum excutiens anguem et bacchatur utrisque
> Tisiphone castris; fratrem huic, fratrem ingerit illi,
> aut utrique patrem: procul ille penatibus imis
> excitus implorat Furias oculosque reposcit.

> Tisiphone shakes her twin serpents and runs riot in both armies. She thrusts his brother upon one and his brother upon the other, or their father on both. He afar in the depths of the palace is roused and invokes the Furies and reclaims his eyes.

These lines continue the dialogue between epic and tragic predecessors. Tisiphone wields her snakes in both camps, just as she had against Ino and Athamas earlier in Theban history, and just as Allecto had against Turnus.[66] The verb *bacchatur* refers the reader back to two Vergilian moments of madness: *concussam bacchatur Fama per urbem* ("Rumor runs riot through the shocked city [i.e., Carthage]," Verg. *A.* 4.666) and *Allecto medias Italum bacchata per urbes* ("Allecto running riot through the cities of Italy," Verg. *A.* 10.41).[67] Moreover, Tisiphone pits brother against brother in a way that is reminiscent of Allecto (*tu potes unanimos armare in proelia fratres | atque odiis uersare domos*, "you can arm like-minded brothers against each other and overturn houses with hate," Verg. *A.* 7.335–36) and is an allusion to the opening of *Thyestes*, which opens with a Fury summoning the shade of Tantalus from the Underworld in order to infest his descendants' house with terrible fraternal strife (Sen. *Thy.* 1–121). This fraternal strife will eventually cover the world in (civil) war (Sen. *Thy.* 40–46).[68] Vergil's Allecto is likewise the most important model for Seneca's Fury.[69] As Alessandro Schiesaro has argued, Seneca summons the troubling civil war aspects of Vergil's *Aeneid* here, as it was Allecto who incited a war between Latins and Trojans— peoples destined to be united into one—and who is characterized by Juno as

---

[65] The account of panic in the city is concluded through repetition of the word *attonitis* (Stat. *Theb.* 7.465), as Smolenaars 1994, *ad* Stat. *Theb.* 7.464–65, observes.
[66] Smolenaars 1994, *ad* Stat. *Theb.* 7.466.
[67] Smolenaars 1994, *ad* Stat. *Theb.* 7.466–67.
[68] On the convergence of fraternal strife and civil war in these lines, see Petrone 1996, 163, and Korneeva 2011, 37.
[69] See, e.g., Tarrant 1985, *ad locc.*, and Schiesaro 2003, 32–36.

uniquely fit to incite fraternal strife (Verg. *A.* 7.335).[70] Statius alludes to this Fury here, who could implicate the father in this cycle of violence as well: *fratrem expauescat frater et gnatum parens | gnatusque patrem* ("Let brother be afraid of brother, parent of son, son of father," Sen. *Thy.* 40–41).[71] The section concludes with a reminder and repetition of Oedipus's summoning of the Furies at the beginning of the *Thebaid*.[72]

In short, all the intertextual pieces are set to finally drive Argos and Thebes, Polynices and Eteocles, to destruction. In addition to this, we should note that these infernal causes provide a supernatural backdrop to Statius's reworking of Seneca's civil war moments. These moments, already present in the background in the scene that we just discussed, will shortly occupy center stage in the *Thebaid*. Moreover, Statius's emphasis on the role of Tisiphone just before the entrance of Jocasta is significant. He is about to rework the second half of Seneca's *Phoenissae* but has attached to it a brief Thyestean prologue.

As Ilona Opelt has argued, central to the structure of Seneca's *Phoenissae* is the contrast between Oedipus's encouragement of the war between his sons and Jocasta's attempt to put a stop to this war.[73] Jocasta's intervention in the seventh book of the *Thebaid* can be opposed to Oedipus's curse in the first.[74] Statius, then, has chosen to organize his poem along Senecan lines, and the "civil war" within his epic between the need to sing of *fraternas acies* and the desire to avoid or delay is not just Lucanean, but also very Senecan.[75] It should be observed that this tension between the spread and the delay of (poetic) *nefas* is not only present

---

70 Schiesaro 2003, 35.
71 Smolenaars 1994, *ad* Stat. *Theb.* 7.466–69.
72 Smolenaars 1994, *ad* Stat. *Theb.* 7.469. See also Ganiban 2007, 114, on the association between Oedipus and the Furies in this passage. Still more depth can be added to the inter-generic dialogue in this passage: Harm-Jan van Dam suggests to me that the lines *fratrem huic, fratrem ingerit illi, | aut utrique patrem* (*Theb.* 7.467–68) also allude to Seneca's *ingesta orbitas | in ora patris* (*Thy.* 282–83, where Atreus imagines his revenge on his brother), which would be another example of Statius combining Theban and Thyestean notions.
73 Opelt 1972. This contrast is relevant to the dynamics of Statius's simultaneous reworking of the *Thyestes* and *Phoenissae* in response to tensions already present in the Senecan corpus. Gilder 1997, 97–98, has argued that Oedipus assumes the role of Fury, Jocasta that of anti-Fury, thereby drawing the *Phoenissae* closer to the *Thyestes*. Opelt 1972, 276; Barchiesi 1988, 24–25, and Mader 2010, 308, compare Oedipus to the shade of Tantalus in the *Thyestes* or that of Thyestes in Seneca's *Agamemnon*.
74 See, e.g., Bernstein 2008, 88.
75 McNelis 2007; on Statius's poetics of *nefas* see also Ganiban 2007; Bessone 2011; Ganiban 2011; Walter 2014, 112–239. Ganiban and particularly Bessone emphasize the importance of Seneca, in addition to Lucan, for Statius in developing his poetics of *nefas*.

in the "struggle" between Oedipus and Jocasta in *Phoenissae*, but also in that between the Fury and Tantalus in *Thyestes*.[76] In the *Thebaid*, Jocasta is up against both Oedipus and a very Thyestean Fury. By pitting these Senecan forces against each other, Statius stages a civil war within the Senecan tragic corpus.

As we have seen above, Seneca's Jocasta was inevitably implicated in the cycle of Theban crime, specifically through the crime of incest. Statius continues this Senecan emphasis on incest as the supreme Theban crime and Jocasta as its embodiment.[77] In the intervention scene in the seventh book, Jocasta's problematic nature is emphasized several times in ways that are reminiscent of Seneca: she is compared to a Fury (Stat. *Theb*. 7.474–78); she calls herself *impia belli | mater* ("The impious mother of the war," Stat. *Theb*. 7.483–84), and she states *nupsi equidem peperique nefas* ("I married and gave birth to sin," Stat. *Theb*. 7.514).[78] In the *Thebaid*, too, Jocasta tries to stop the impending civil war between her sons through an appeal to her authority as their mother, an authority that collapses under the weight of civil war and Theban crime.[79]

On the level of the narrative, Jocasta still functions as a force of delay, especially because her early morning intervention cuts short Tisiphone's encouragement of war in both camps during the preceding night.[80] Her anger at her son is most strongly indebted to Livy's Veturia.[81] On the other hand, much of the sense of urgency that her actual proposal to Polynices (Stat. *Theb*. 7.504–27) carries is

---

[76] Schiesaro 2003, 36–45, with comparisons to similar dynamics in Lucan. Ganiban 2007, 33–38, argues that Statius inserts his *Thebaid* into this tradition. Gilder 1997, 146–54, also discusses the struggle between Tisiphone and "Anti-Fury" Jocasta and argues that Statius is thereby further developing Seneca's opposition between Oedipus and Jocasta in the *Phoenissae* (Gilder 1997, 101).

[77] McAuley 2016, 333–34, establishes the connection between Seneca and Statius in this respect.

[78] On Jocasta's Fury-like nature and/or morally ambiguous status, see, e.g., Hershkowitz 1998a, 280–82; Keith 2000, 96; Markus 2004, 118–20; Ganiban 2007, 110–12 (emphasizing continuity between the rhetoric of Seneca's and Statius's Jocasta at 111 n. 56); Bernstein 2008, 88–94; Augoustakis 2010a, 62–68; Korneeva 2011, 205–6, who also mentions Seneca as a predecessor in presenting Jocasta as a Fury; McAuley 2016, 321–44, on whose arguments I have drawn here. See also Bessone and Keith in this volume on Jocasta's complex and problematic rhetoric. See also Frings 1991, 106–19.

[79] McAuley 2016, 331: "The ambiguous representation of Jocasta coheres with a general pessimism in the *Thebaid* towards relations between kin (to be expected in an Oedipod epic): even those familial relationships characterized in the Oedipus myth by care rather than enmity, such as mother and sons, can no longer remain functional under civil war, whose sheer *nefas* drowns out the moral authority of maternal *pietas*." McAuley inserts Jocasta in a long tradition of reflection on Roman motherhood, including Cornelia, mother of the Gracchi, and Vergil's Amata.

[80] Fantham 1997, 206; Keith 2000, 96. Dietrich 2015, 308, also emphasizes Jocasta's role as a force of delay and as opposed to Tisiphone, in spite of her own Fury-like appearance.

[81] Smolenaars 1994, *ad Theb*. 7.497–527a.

derived from Seneca's *Phoenissae*. Statius picks up on some of the more troubling aspects of Seneca's Jocasta here. In both poems, Jocasta makes a frenzied entry, which is brought out by implicit and/or explicit comparisons to Furies or similar creatures. Both Seneca and Statius describe Jocasta as *attonita* (Sen. *Phoen.* 433; Stat. *Theb.* 7.492–93).[82] As she proposes that her son come to Thebes to talk with his brother, she invites him to pay *patriosque deos arsuraque* ... | *tecta* ("your country's gods and the dwellings about to burn," Stat. *Theb.* 7.507–8) a visit. As Hans Smolenaars points out in his commentary, this is an allusion to the motif of Thebes' impending destruction which figures prominently in *Phoenissae*, which was discussed above.[83]

Having addressed Polynices, Jocasta turns to the Argive host as a whole (Stat. *Theb.* 7.519–27). The soldiers are moved (Stat. *Theb.* 7.528–33), and so is their leader, who is ready to go to Thebes and start negotiations (Stat. *Theb.* 7.534–38). Due to Jocasta's intervention, *ferrique auidus mansueuerat ardor* ("their eager passion for battle grew milder," Stat. *Theb.* 7.533). For the moment, Jocasta's intervention seems to have succeeded.[84] Statius retains a balance here between the problematic aspects of Seneca's Jocasta on the one hand and the unfinished nature of the *Phoenissae* on the other, which left the ultimate outcome of the parley between Eteocles and Polynices hanging in the balance.[85]

It should be noted that the scene that Statius presents to us is not yet the actual parley. Smolenaars observes that Statius, in his response to the various accounts of Jocasta's intervention, "has transposed elements of the celebrated scenes of tragedy to a moment which Euripides merely indicated in passing and which Seneca, for the sake of dramatic tension, did not differentiate from the actual meeting: Jocasta's suggestion to Polynices of a truce during which the matter can be discussed."[86] In Euripides' play, this role is performed by a pedagogue; in the *Thebaid*, it is performed by Jocasta; but the parley itself never actually takes place in Statius's epic.[87] Whether the actual parley would have succeeded,

---

[82] Smolenaars 1994, *ad loc.*
[83] Smolenaars 1994, *ad locc.*, adduces the following passages from the *Phoenissae:* Sen. *Phoen.* 322, 540–41, 547–48, 555–57, 565–66.
[84] Cf. e.g., Vessey 1973, 274–75, and Gilder 1997, 151: "Because of the *Eumenidum antiquissima* that is Iocasta, Iocasta in the role of traditional Fury, the war is on the verge of not happening."
[85] McNelis 2007, 146, hints at a similar idea when discussing Polynices' hesitation shortly before the final duel (Stat. *Theb.* 11.382–87): "Particularly in light of the fact that the extant version of Seneca's *Phoenissae* does not relate the conclusive battle between the brothers, Polynices' hesitation raises the possibility that the war will be put off yet again."
[86] Smolenaars 1994, *ad* Stat. *Theb.* 7.470–563.
[87] Smolenaars 1994, *ad* Stat. *Theb.* 7.470–563. See also Marinis 2015, 356–57.

Statius's readers will never know, just as the situation in Seneca's *Phoenissae* had remained unresolved.

But there is more still to Statius's reworking of the second half of Seneca's *Phoenissae*. Statius has split up Jocasta's attempt to stop Polynices and Eteocles, making her intervene both at the Argive camp and in Thebes, when Eteocles goes out to fight his brother (Stat. *Theb*. 11.315–53).[88] In dividing Jocasta's intervention between the two brothers, Statius is responding to the fact that most of the second half of Seneca's play is concerned with Jocasta's attempt to persuade Polynices to give up his claim to the throne, whereas Eteocles only joins the conversation just before the play as we have it breaks off. We may even consider the fact that Polynices is temporarily persuaded by Jocasta to go on with the parley as a Statian prefiguration of those 20th century interpretations of Seneca's play that claim that Polynices does give up his claim to the throne.[89] In either case, the open-ended nature of Jocasta's intervention in Statius's epic—Tydeus's speech does change the mood to general war lust again (Stat. *Theb*. 7.559–62), but nothing is decided yet at this point[90]—matches the unfinished nature of Seneca's play.

We have seen that Statius has inserted this Phoenissan scene within a wider Thyestean cosmic framework, involving real Furies. Statius uses this Thyestean framework here to finally move the story beyond Seneca's stalemate. Of course, Tydeus's speech changes the mood, but it is the Fury Tisiphone who seizes this opportunity to decisively tip the balance towards war and madness:[91] *arma iterum furiaeque placent; fera tempus Erinys | arripit et primae molitur semina pugnae* ("Once again arms and madness are in favor. The fierce Erinys seizes her moment and sets in place the seeds of battle's beginning," Stat. *Theb*. 7.562–63).

In starting armed conflict through the maddening of Bacchus's tigresses (Stat. *Theb*. 7.564–607), Tisiphone will succeed in seizing control over the poem in a way that other characters, such as Bacchus and Jupiter, had not, exploiting the Junonian subplot of Vergil's *Aeneid*.[92] Although the maddening of Bacchus's

---

88 Cf. e.g., Vessey 1973, 273–74.
89 See the discussion on the (in)completeness of Seneca's *Phoenissae* above.
90 Cf. Vessey 1973, 275: "Tydeus's opposing viewpoint, however powerfully expressed, was an insufficient reason for Polynices to reject the offer of arbitration."
91 Vessey 1973, 275, rightly observes that Tisiphone maddens the tigresses "to counteract Jocasta's influence." See also Frings 1991, 119, and Dietrich 2015, 308. Smolenaars 1994, *ad* Stat. *Theb*. 7.470–627: "Jocasta's attempt at mediation is frustrated by intervention on both the human and divine level." Mader 2010, 309, mentions the *Phoenissae's* lack of a cosmic framework in contrast with the *Thyestes*.
92 Ganiban 2007, 112–16. See especially 115, at the end of his discussion of the interventions of Bacchus, Jupiter, Mars and Pavor, Jocasta, and finally Tisiphone in *Thebaid* 4 and 7: "The scenes

tigresses is mostly indebted to the killing of Silvia's stag in the *Aeneid*,[93] Statius also makes clear that Tisiphone's intervention is a very Senecan one. The Fury drives the tigresses mad with a snake-scourge (*uipereo ... flagello,* Stat. *Theb.* 7.579). This snake-scourge can also be found in Seneca's *Medea* (Sen. *Med.* 961–62) and—more relevant for our purposes—his *Hercules Furens* (Sen. *Her. F.* 87–88).[94] As soon as Juno has decided that the only way to bring Hercules down is to turn him against himself, she calls upon the Furies (Sen. *Her. F.* 86–88). Even more significantly, Juno calls upon these Furies to bring about a civil war within Hercules himself (Sen. *Her. F.* 85): *bella iam secum gerat* ("Now he must war with himself").[95] Statius now invokes this metaphorical civil war in order to bring about a real one.

Tisiphone's success is immediate: Jocasta flees (Stat. *Theb.* 7.608–11), and the Argives and Thebans rush to meet each other in battle (Stat. *Theb.* 7.615–27). There is no way back now: the impious war that both Seneca's tragedies and the first half of Statius's epic had anxiously awaited has now finally arrived. Having toyed with the idea of Senecan open-endedness for a while, Statius's epic moves beyond the incompleteness of Seneca's tragic *Phoenissae*. The central conflict governing the *Phoenissae*, between the onset of Oedipus's madness and Jocasta's attempt to prevent or at least delay it, is finally resolved in Oedipus's favor by Seneca's epic successor through the use of a Fury that is both Junonian and Thyestean. In this way, Statius finally brings about Seneca's long-awaited civil war. From this point onwards, the *Thebaid* is firmly set on a Senecan trajectory as it barrels towards the terrible duel between the brothers, a dreadful criminal climax that fundamentally undermines epic's traditional function of the commemoration of heroic deeds.[96] When this climax, the duel between both brothers, finally takes place, Statius calls the duel the *unius ingens | bellum uteri* ("the mighty

---

I have examined, like many others in the *Thebaid*, involve a struggle among the gods to commandeer, as it were, the power of Virgil's Juno, and in particular her actions in *Aeneid* 7. This episode provides a poetic foundation for three of the most important moments of the epic's plot: Oedipus' prayer to Tisiphone (book 1), Dis' injunction to Tisiphone (book 8), and Tisiphone's exhortation to Megaera (book 11). Indeed *Aeneid* 7 represents the most effective model for action in the *Thebaid*, but it is one that Statius' *superi* cannot exploit fully."

93 A point often observed. See Smolenaars 1994, *ad* Stat. *Theb.* 7.564–607, and on shorter passages or individual lines for the parallels, and Ganiban 2007, 113 n. 62, for bibliography.
94 Smolenaars 1994, *ad loc.*
95 On the very Roman preoccupations to which Seneca connects Hercules' madness here, see Petrone 1996, 162.
96 See especially Bessone 2011, 75–101, on this Senecan trajectory and its generic tensions and implications; also Walter 2014, 112–239, on the problems that singing of the *nefas* of fratricide presents to Statius's epic voice.

battle of a single womb," Stat. *Theb.* 11.407–8). With these words, the battle between the brothers and the womb that is their incestuous origin merge, and Polynices and Eteocles are "suck[ed] back into a place where all difference, all meaning collapses."[97] In this way Statius brings the notion of civil war as the ultimate dissolution of categories to its Theban climax.[98]

---

97 McAuley 2016, 341.
98 See McAuley 2016, 297–344, on the *Thebaid* as a devastating inversion of the Roman narrative of historical progress through male descent, which is undone through endless returns to the mother, be it the Theban earth or Jocasta's womb. On the climactic nature of this passage in the Roman discourse on civil war, its emphasis on incest and self-destruction, and its undermining of epic discourse, see also Bessone in this volume.

Part III: **Leadership and Exemplarity**

Alice König
Reading Civil War in Frontinus's *Strategemata*: A Case-Study for Flavian Literary Studies

> To avoid having to touch upon the detestable memory of the civil wars (*ac ne ... ad ciuilium bellorum detestandam memoriam progredi cogar*) by looking at too many home-grown examples of this sort, I will confine myself to just two Roman examples which reflect well on some very illustrious families without evoking public sorrow (*ita nullum publicum maerorem continent*).
>
> (V. Max. 3.3.2)[1]

Part way through his collection of *Memorable Deeds and Sayings*, Valerius Maximus famously stops short, just as his section on *patientia* (endurance) is getting going. Most sections of the text boast a healthy number of Roman *exempla*, followed by a smaller number of foreign tales. This section tells just two Roman stories (compared with seven foreign ones) before Valerius decides that enough is enough: additional Roman *exempla* on this topic might test the *patientia* of author and reader because they would lead to detestable recollections of Rome's civil wars. As Valerius presents it here, civil war is both a distinctively Roman problem and a taboo subject, although one never far away from the Roman consciousness: a festering historical wound, not to be casually uncovered in the quest for exemplary anecdotes.[2]

Frontinus's *Strategemata* takes a different approach. This collection of specifically military *exempla* is first and foremost a didactic handbook, part of a well-established military writing tradition; but it draws also on historiography and the *exempla* tradition, and on Valerius's text in particular. Indeed, it is in some senses

---

[1] All translations in this chapter are my own. I am grateful to Lauren Donovan Ginsberg and Darcy Krasne not only for including me in their stimulating Celtic Classics Panel in 2014 but also for their feedback and patience during the drafting of this chapter. My thinking on civil war in the Flavian era has been greatly enhanced by the conversations I continue to enjoy with Emma Buckley and Tommaso Spinelli on this and many related topics.

[2] On this passage and Valerius's distaste for the civil wars throughout the work, see Gowing 2005, 55–56, and Gowing 2010, who notes (250–51) that amongst other Tiberian authors "the civil wars were a very, very hot topic" but also points to the example of Cremutius Cordus (Tac. *Ann.* 4.34–35), whose story "is important evidence for the anxiety the memory of the civil wars could produce." Cf. Suet. *Cl.* 41 (and Osgood 2006, 1, on this passage), where Suetonius tells us that Claudius, on the overbearing advice of his mother and grandmother, omitted everything after Caesar's assassination in a history he wrote, picking up his narrative again with the "civil peace" that followed those years of conflict, because writing frankly and honestly about the civil wars was impossible.

https://doi.org/10.1515/9783110585841-008

an enormous expansion of just one section of *Memorable Deeds and Sayings* (V. Max. 7.4, dedicated to *strategemata*—stratagems), and some conspicuous echoes of Valerius's opening preface in the introduction to Frontinus's first book positively invite comparison.[3] Frontinus was writing a couple of generations later, when a recent bout of civil wars—the factional fighting that caused so much upheaval at Rome and abroad in 68–70 CE—arguably made civil strife an even more sensitive topic than it was for Valerius and his contemporaries, even well into Domitian's reign.[4] Rather than recoil from it, however, Frontinus regularly transports his readers to episodes from different civil wars, and clusters of civil war *exempla* even dominate some sections of his treatise. But whereas Josephus in his *Bellum Judaicum* and Tacitus in his *Histories* both confront readers with the details/horrors of near-contemporary campaigns,[5] Frontinus, in contrast, generally steers clear of recent events, perhaps an overlap of sorts with Valerius Maximus after all.[6] However, in a way that might be comparable with the interest shown by Statius, Valerius Flaccus, Silius Italicus, and other contemporaries in *past* episodes of internal sedition and civil strife, Frontinus returns repeatedly to the conflicts that accompanied the collapse of the Republic and the rise to power of a series of increasingly autocratic individuals: precisely the conflicts from which Valerius Maximus averts his/our eyes.

This chapter considers how we might read Frontinus's treatment of civil strife both within the *Strategemata* as a whole and in relation to the text's wider Flavian context. How eye-catching—or inconspicuous—are the civil war anecdotes that Frontinus incorporates into his collection? Do particular narrative threads build up between them, or is the civil nature of their conflicts submerged by other

---

[3] On these parallels, and the competitive edge to Frontinus's engagement with Valerius, see especially Gallia 2012, 192.
[4] As Tuck 2016, 112, notes, while Vespasian and Titus's success in the Jewish-Roman war enabled them to divert some attention from their role in the civil war of 68–69 CE, Domitian could not exploit it in the same way, having taken no part in it: "One way in which Domitian created continuity with Vespasian and Titus was by emphasizing his role during the civil war, in which he had figured more directly." Domitian may himself have written an epic on civil war (Hardie 2003, 140). Woolf 1993 brings out particularly clearly the fragile veneer of Vespasian's emphasis on foreign campaigning, and the inevitable evocation of civil—not just foreign—war in the Flavian *pax Romana*. But see below for further reflection on the possible fading of anxiety (if not of memory) under Domitian, and Ginsberg 2017, 190–93, for a nuanced account of the evolution of responses to civil war in the immediate aftermath of 68–69.
[5] See Ash 2010, however, on Tacitus's parallel interest in Republican civil wars as a kind of route map to the civil wars of his own generation (and beyond).
[6] Like Valerius, Frontinus includes very few *exempla* from the Imperial period (Turner 2007, 431–32; Gallia 2012, 203–4; Malloch 2015).

themes and agenda? Does the *Strategemata* reflect on or engage with specifically contemporary concerns about civil strife? Was it even influenced by—might it perhaps have influenced—contemporary literary treatments of this topic? How much is this a text about war generally (or generals generally), a universalizing survey of timelessly successful stratagems that transcends specific temporal and cultural coordinates; and how much is it a distinctively Flavian meditation on war and generalship—*imperator*-ship, even? Indeed, how might a reading which foregrounds the *Strategemata*'s treatment of civil war and discusses its possible Flavian dimensions not just depend upon but contribute to the study of its Flavian context, both literary and historical?

Beyond those questions lie some deeper ones, about the methodological and interpretative trends that currently dominate Flavian literary studies. The last couple of decades have produced a profusion of highly contextualized and interconnected readings of various Flavian texts. A welcome turnaround after years of neglect, this intense focus on the surviving literary corpus and its very "Flavianness" often entails a degree of circularity, as such an approach does in literary studies of many other periods too: literary leitmotifs that appear to dominate the works of both Statius and Valerius Flaccus (for instance) get adduced to testify to apparently defining features of the wider context against which those (now quintessentially) Flavian texts are then read. This circularity is not just inevitable, it is also productive—up to a point. The advantages of highly contextualized readings vastly outweigh the disadvantages. However, it can sometimes take on a self-fulfilling momentum, whereby what we piece together of "the Flavian context" can grow legs and run away with us, obscuring details and difference in individual texts and skewing our picture of whole bodies of literature and entire periods.

My own reading of Frontinus's *Strategemata* will frequently gravitate towards some of the contextual super-themes that have come to dominate Flavian literary studies;[7] but it will also make a point of stepping back from them to consider other possibilities, as a way of reflecting on the pitfalls and challenges inherent in relating the content of a so-called Flavian text to its Flavian context. A central aim of the chapter is to put the *Strategemata* firmly on the Flavian map, to integrate this overlooked treatise into Flavian literary studies. Its late inclusion in these studies makes it a good case study for thinking afresh about a recurring "Flavian" theme (civil war) and for scrutinizing our interpretative habits when it comes to reading the "Flavian-ness" of that theme and the texts that discuss it. In bringing Frontinus's treatise into dialogue with the other material examined in this volume, I thus hope to address an issue that is central to all of our discussions.

---

7 Bernstein 2016 offers a handy overview.

1 "Civil War": A Theme or a Construct?

A word on "civil war" itself, before we delve into the details of the *Strategemata*. We often talk and write sweepingly of civil war, as if it is a stable and easily definable concept. Our ancient sources—and many modern studies—indicate the opposite. The historian Appian (for instance) might argue for a clear-cut caesura in 88 BCE, when Sulla marched on Rome and when decades of infighting (*stasis*) finally broke out into "proper" civil war (*polemos*);[8] modern historians might introduce studies of civil war with a working (and inevitably subjective) definition of what they are prepared to include in that category;[9] but the variation between approaches and ideas, ancient and modern, reveals a spectrum, not a binary, between civil war and other kinds of conflict (as other chapters in this volume discuss). It was in Augustus's interests, of course, both to demarcate civil war as trauma in the past (e.g., *RG* 34.1) and to blur distinctions between the civil and non-civil aspects of the conflicts that brought him to power; but it was not only his influence that caused near-contemporary authors to hesitate over the definition and to explore and exploit the slippage between the two. In different ways, Cicero, Sallust, Caesar, Livy, and Vergil all reveal ongoing ambiguity about what counts as (and how readers might be expected to respond to) "civil" war.[10] In our period, Josephus's *Bellum Judaicum* foregrounded internal sedition (Roman and Jewish) as a recurring theme[11] and also fudged distinctions between civil and foreign conflicts.[12] Shortly afterwards, Tacitus famously characterized the Flavian era as one that saw *trina bella ciuilia, plura externa ac plerumque permixta* ("three civil wars, more foreign ones, and several that were hybrid versions of the two,"

---

[8] App. *BC* 1.7.58, on which see Osgood 2006, 5; Price 2015; Börm 2016, 19. Cf., e.g., Cic. *Rep.* 1.31 and Tac. *Hist.* 2.38 for different takes on when/how factional in-fighting evolved into civil war.

[9] E.g. Flower 2010, following Appian; Börm 2016; also Lange 2016, 20–27, who offers a useful outline of different perspectives and whose volume as a whole nicely illustrates the blurred edges around definitions of civil war. See also the opening chapters of Armitage 2017a and the introduction to this volume.

[10] On the slippage between civil and foreign war in Caesar's *De Bello Ciuili*, for example, see Batstone/Damon 2006, 117; on the intertwined nature of civil and non-civil war in Vergil, see (amongst many others) Quint 2010.

[11] Mason 2009, 326–30; also Mason's chapter in this volume.

[12] On this see, e.g., Edmondson 2005, 8, and (for a different take) Mason 2005a. On the slippage between *bellum iustum* and *bellum ciuile* (and optimism/pessimism about the Flavian dynasty and its rise to power) in Valerius Flaccus's *Argonautica*, see Buckley 2010.

Hist. 1.2).[13] "Civil war" was an imprecise and malleable concept, perhaps more so after the events of 68–69 CE than earlier in the Principate.

In their introduction to *Citizens of Discord*, Breed, Damon, and Rossi write that "the burden of civil war on Roman minds would be hard to overestimate. Civil wars, more than other wars, sear themselves into the memory of societies that suffer them."[14] While I agree that civil war was a recurring *topos* and, as such (as they suggest), an ever-present "intertext" against which other events might always be read, it does not necessarily follow that it evoked the same levels of emotion all the time. Lucan is perhaps more responsible than any other Imperial author for the fetishization of civil strife as a distinctive and horrifying trauma, an extension of—but also apart from and much worse than—other kinds of war.[15] Lucan influenced the Flavian epicists in all sorts of ways,[16] but it is my hypothesis in what follows that he may have influenced us scholars even more on this particular issue. Building on Alain Gowing's arguments about gaps in treatment and the gradual forgetting or exhaustion of civil war as a topic of interest from Tiberius to Lucan,[17] I explore the possibility that civil war was not only a more ambiguous phenomenon but also a less conspicuous and troubling part of cultural discourse in the later Flavian period than many modern studies recognize, and I argue (as some evidence for that) that Frontinus's *Strategemata* reveals an ambivalent rather than super-anxious attitude to it.

In fact, Frontinus's treatise blurs the boundaries between civil and non civil conflict in ways that might get readers asking (not for the first time, but perhaps with growing uncertainty) "what IS civil war?" as well as "how much do we Romans really need to worry about it?" A quick read-through of the text will reveal that Frontinus uses the phrase *bellum ciuile* in just a smattering of anecdotes (Fron. *Str.* 1.3.2, 1.5.9, 1.10.4, 2.1.11, 2.5.40, 3.14.1, 4.2.1, 4.5.2), almost exclusively

---

13 On Tacitus's blurring of boundaries in the *Histories*, see especially O'Gorman 1995.
14 Breed *et al.* 2010b, 4.
15 For a particularly penetrating analysis, see Henderson 1987, recapitulated in 1998, 168–70.
16 On this, see especially Stover 2012, 3, and Ginsberg 2017, 193 (with further references n. 65). See also O'Gorman 1995 for Lucan's possible influence on Tacitus's *Histories*. Arguably, Lucan and Tacitus between them not only bookend but distort our readings of the Flavian texts they sandwich, with their memorably pessimistic characterizations of different bouts of civil strife.
17 See especially Gowing 2010, 257, on the urge to remember civil war sometimes colliding with the urge to forget. While noting the "cultural imperative" to write about civil war as a way of working through "national traumas," he underlines the lack of writing on civil war from Tiberius to Nero (when it was reignited as a literary topic by Lucan), pointing out that the subject of civil war may at times become exhausted, as well as being potentially dangerous or "simply unpleasant" to dredge up.

in connection with the fighting between Caesar and Pompey.[18] One might conclude that this conflict figures as THE Civil War in his book—the archetype, or perhaps the only conflict that truly deserves such a name.[19] For the speed-reader, in other words, civil war might appear to be packaged neatly, discretely, as a relatively isolated phenomenon. As we will see, however, these episodes are surrounded by a huge variety of other *exempla* from a bewildering range of foreign, civil, and less-easy-to-define conflicts. Accounts of foreign campaigns, internal sedition, revolts amongst allies, and strife between Roman leaders sit alongside each other and invite comparison. Frontinus offers little commentary of his own, and his civil war anecdotes do not prompt us to particular outrage or horror by evoking *topoi* such as the *furor* or madness of civil strife.[20] That said, the text as a whole (as I have argued in König 2017) foregrounds above all the chaos and unpredictability of war, a supertheme that often dominates narratives of civil strife, and it sets the military capability of powerful individuals (far more than nations) in direct competition with each other.[21] The reader might read the *Strategemata* in more than one way, in other words, and what emerges depends very much on our viewpoint. Frontinus puts hundreds of different narratives into dialogue with each other and leaves readers to make what they will of the connections and interplay that build up between them.[22] That makes it an excellent laboratory for

---

18 There are just a couple of exceptions: at Fron. *Str.* 4.2.1, where the *exemplum* refers to the civil war that followed Caesar's assassination; and at Fron. *Str.* 1.10.4, which is hard to date (Laederich 1999, *ad loc.*) but may relate to events around or just after the Battle of Actium.
19 When he opens some of his anecdotes with the phrase *Caesar bello ciuili*, Frontinus is not referring to Caesar's commentaries on the civil war, of course, but to Caesar's activities during this conflict; but see below, n. 48, where I note a couple of *exempla* that directly evoke Caesar's text. As I explain the next section, reading the *Strategemata* is an inevitably intertextual experience, so readers might well think of Caesar's *Civil War* as well as Caesar's civil war when Frontinus uses such phrasing. We might even be prompted to reflect on the role that writing (Caesar's and others') played in crystalizing his conflict with Pompey as *the* defining civil war.
20 On these *topoi* among others, see, e.g., Breed *et al.* 2010b, 4–5; also Tac. *Hist.* 2.38 for a near-contemporary collection (*deum ira, rabies, scelus*); O'Gorman 1995 on the language of civil war in Lucan and Tacitus; and Federica Bessone's chapter in this volume on the emergence of a civil war "koine."
21 As Börm 2016, 20, notes, "the issue underlying all Roman civil wars from the time of Augustus at the latest was, ultimately, to procure or preserve monarchy." While Frontinus's *exempla* take us to many different Roman and non-Roman contexts, where confrontations between individual commanders are clearly part of much greater clashes between whole nations, there is no getting away from the emphasis the text places on the agency and power of individual *imperatores*, which might prompt reflection on the rise and fall of *Imperatores* as I discuss further below.
22 I draw here on research I am conducting jointly with Nicolas Wiater on interplay between battle narratives in antiquity: https://arts.st-andrews.ac.uk/visualising-war/.

exploring the interpretative role that we play in constructing (or deconstructing) "civil war" as a (particularly Flavian?) theme.

2 Frontinus's *Strategemata*

It is still often the case that when people talk of "Flavian literature," they mean "Flavian epic." That said, literary studies of the period are increasingly inclusive, welcoming not just Martial but also outliers like Quintilian and Josephus, alongside Pliny the Elder and—at a push—Tacitus and Suetonius (whose inclusion somewhat distorts the "Flavian" lens, of course).[23] And yet Frontinus, an enormously prominent statesman and the author of two if not three Flavian-era texts, continues to languish in the footnotes of most Flavian studies—and sometimes not even there.[24] The latest major overview of Flavian Rome is a case in point: Frédéric Hurlet's survey of Flavian "sources" towards the start of the 2016 Wiley-Blackwell *Companion to the Flavian Age of Imperial Rome* does not even consider Frontinus as an author "worthy of passing mention" (how it describes Quintilian),[25] and Frontinus barely gets a look-in anywhere else in that volume—or, indeed, in Boyle and Dominik's monumental *Flavian Rome*, let alone in more specialist readings of Flavian literature.[26] There are obvious—if unsound—reasons why his texts have not been much read alongside other Flavian works. His Flavian-era treatises do not flag their "Flavian-ness" particularly conspicuously. Frontinus does not foreground the emperor's centrality to his text with an opening invocation/dedication, for instance, unlike Valerius Flaccus's *Argonautica*

---

23 For the present volume's understanding of "Flavian" literature, see the introduction.
24 On Frontinus's career, see Eck 1982, 47–52; Rodgers 2004, 1–5. Tac. *Ag.* 17.2 comments on his great achievements as governor of Britain under Vespasian; Aelianus Tacticus attests to his military and literary reputation (Ael. *Tact.* pr. 3); cf. also Plin. *Ep.* 5.1, where the Flavian Frontinus is described as one of the most highly regarded men of his day. In addition to the *Strategemata*, Frontinus wrote an earlier "Science of Warfare," a treatise on land surveying, and (under Nerva and Trajan) an account of Rome's aqueduct network. It is difficult to date his land surveying treatise in particular, but this and his military works are most likely of Flavian date, with the *Strategemata* at least being clearly Domitianic.
25 Zissos 2016; quotation at Hurlet 2016, 21.
26 See also Frontinus's omission from Edmondson's survey of the "period of great literary creativity under the Flavians" (2005, 12–13). In Boyle/Dominik 2003, Frontinus features just once in a footnote (43 n. 136) concerning Domitian's military activities, where the *Strategemata* is not mentioned for its own sake but as evidence of something else; his absence from Evans 2003 seems particularly perverse.

(1.7–21) or Statius's *Thebaid* (1.16–33). More generally, compare the *Strategemata*'s few passing mentions of Flavian-period exploits with the more sustained engagement in, say, Statius's *Siluae* and many of Martial's *Epigrams*.[27] His works also tend to be pigeon-holed or written off as (merely) "technical" treatises, not "proper" literature, hence the lack of engagement with them in discussions of other, more obviously "literary" or wide-ranging texts. And yet the *Strategemata* is about very much more than successful generalship and military stratagems, and it flags its embeddedness in a range of Greek and Roman literary traditions right from the start.

It markets itself first and foremost as a didactic endeavor: one that distills the hands-on experience of former generals into a handy handbook to which future or aspiring generals might turn in search of inspiration or reassurance about the stratagems they are trying to come up with (Fron. *Str.* 1.pr.1):

> Since I, alone amongst those studying it, have attempted to draw up a science of military matters, and since I seem to have achieved my objective, as far as my efforts could manage, I feel that the project I have begun still requires me to collect together in a serviceable handbook (*expeditis amplectar commentariis*) the clever deeds of generals (*sollertia ducum facta*) which the Greeks have gathered together under the one name *strategemata*. For in this way, future generals will be surrounded by examples of wisdom and foresight, and through them their own ability to think up and execute similar deeds will be nourished. A further benefit will be that a commander able to compare his stratagem with tried and tested experiments need not worry about the outcome of his own ingenuity.[28]

Real military engagements are at the heart of the *Strategemata*, then, as both its substance and its ultimate end-goal—at least for readers who were militarily active themselves.[29] Frontinus himself had an impressive military career behind him: as well as conquering parts of Wales during his stint as governor of Britain, he was clearly involved in some of Domitian's campaigns in Germany (as, e.g., Fron. *Str.* 1.3.10 and 2.11.7 suggest). His strategic experience is perhaps in evidence in the military metaphors he uses to talk about his strategic arrangement of the *exempla* into different books and subsections that correspond to different stages and features of battle—something that enhances the practical feel of the text, for it enables readers (or so Frontinus claims) to consult the work for answers to specific questions (Fron. *Str.* 1.pr.2):

---

27 On the *Strategemata*'s limited engagement with its Flavian context, see especially Turner 2007.
28 On the *Strategemata*'s preface, see Santini 1992; Gallia 2012, 193–94.
29 See below, n. 32, on the wider range of Frontinus's readers.

Reading Civil War in Frontinus's *Strategemata* — 153

> My effort centers around the challenge of setting out precisely whichever example is required, in any given circumstance, as if in response to questions. For, having surveyed the categories, I have prepared a set of suitable examples as one might prepare a plan of campaign (*praeparaui opportuna exemplorum ueluti consilia*).

The list of subheadings which Frontinus includes at the start of each book, outlining the different topics under which different *exempla* have been collected, reinforces this sense that one might dip in and out of the treatise on the hunt for useful know-how.[30]

What follows in the main body of the text is a roll-call of famous and not-so-famous generals, a vast collection of over 500 examples of successful strategic ploys, almost all of them beginning with the triumphant general's name—in a manner perhaps faintly reminiscent of the *Fasti Triumphales* (the list of Rome's triumphant generals which Augustus had inscribed on marble and set up in the Roman forum).[31] Frontinus's emphasis on the commander at the start of each anecdote particularly focuses attention on these figures as *the* agents of success. If we take one lesson away from the *Strategemata*, it is that a commander's quick-wittedness, cunning, and decisiveness repeatedly win the day (a point we will return to). Frontinus's formulaic presentation of these hundreds of anecdotes, all stripped down to easily digestible essentials, maintains the impression given in his prefaces that what the text offers us is a series of simple military lessons, all drawn directly from real history. On the surface at least, the *Strategemata* appears to function just as it presents itself, as an instructive conduit between past deeds and present and future action—indeed, between past victors and present/future commanders. Real military events are textualized here, Frontinus suggests, with a view to nourishing future military episodes that may one day be (written down as?) history.

But of course the *Strategemata* is not just a catalogue of instructive military deeds for future replication; it is also a miscellany of anecdotes, harvested from the vast swirl of cultural memory and from many different literary works for the entertainment as well as instruction of a range of readers.[32] As Frontinus tells us,

---

[30] Modern readers must not be misled by our familiarity with modern (codex) reference manuals, of course, into thinking that these "contents pages" functioned quite as ours do; on this point in relation to Pliny's *Natural History*, see Doody 2001, and on a range of Latin "contents pages" (but not Frontinus's), Riggsby 2007.
[31] Cf. Gallia's suggestion (2012, 200) that Frontinus's roll-call of famous faces might be compared to the gallery of statues of *summi uiri* in the *Forum Augustum*.
[32] On the mixed readership of military handbooks in general (and their parallels with as well as differences from historiography) see Campbell 1987, esp. 27. While some readers may have

he has trawled through the huge body of historiography (not just history) so that we do not have to, transferring all useful nuggets into his own work. In the main body of the text we read about Hannibal, Scipio, Alcibiades, Coriolanus, Spartacus, Xerxes, Pyrrhus, and Fabius Maximus (among many others), but along the way we will also recognize the hand of Livy, Nepos, Julius Caesar, Polybius and plenty more such authors. And usually there is a twist: Frontinus's excerpting technique is often a distorting one, which extracts, distills and re-spins episodes we are vaguely familiar with from other sources. The stories may be stripped down to their instructive essentials, but they still get the reader recognizing and thinking comparatively about other texts. As Rebecca Langlands has emphasized in relation to Valerius Maximus, *exempla* collections are inherently intertextual.[33]

The preface to Book 1 specifically invites reflection on whole genres and writing traditions, and on the *Strategemata*'s relationship to them. In its opening sentence Frontinus flags his own (potentially innovative) contribution to the field of military writing, and his gloss of *sollertia ducum facta* as "what the Greeks have grouped together under the term *strategemata*" (*quae a Graecis una* στρατηγημάτων *appellatione comprehensa sunt*, Fron. *Str.* 1.pr.1) arguably draws attention to the Latin take-over of that Greek tradition by sandwiching the Greek contribution with more recent Latin terminology and authorial activity. If more evidence were needed that Frontinus was interested in the evolution of a specifically Latin tradition of military writing, one might look at the very first *exemplum* of the collection, which depicts Cato, an exemplary general but also the man credited with founding the Latin military writing tradition,[34] *writing* (Fron. *Str.* 1.1.1). Frontinus also engages competitively with less "technical" literary traditions: the *exempla* tradition (which he claims leaves readers "befuddled" by "a great heap of material") and historiography more generally. Far from being merely a "technical" treatise, Frontinus's *Strategemata* thus draws on and oscillates between a number of different genres and clearly anticipates a readership that will do likewise. Understanding this is crucial to understanding the text's internal dynamics.

As well as engaging with literary issues, the *Strategemata* also prompts reflection on cultural and political topics of immense contemporary interest, from the nature and foundations of Roman *imperium* to models of leadership and

---

turned to the *Strategemata* for pragmatic guidance, many would have been reading with more leisurely intellectual agendas.

33 My reading of the internal dynamics of Frontinus's *Strategemata* has much in common with Langlands's analysis of the didactic dynamics of Valerius and other *exempla* collections, particularly the active role they make readers play in comparing different *exempla* with each other; on this, see especially Langlands 2008; see also Langlands 2011 and Langlands *forthcoming*.
34 Veg. *Mil.* 2.3.

Domitian himself (the text is full of *imperatores* who were or wanted to be kings, dictators, even emperors). Frontinus organizes his material strictly according to military themes. The chronological or teleological narratives that we are familiar with from other texts are thus broken up, as *exempla* from lots of different times and places are brought together in a series of very different configurations, under headings like "Finding out the enemies' plans," "Escaping from difficult places," and "Choosing a time for battle." As the text jumps backwards and forwards across time and space, a collection of recurring and seemingly universal strategic leitmotifs begins to build up, over and above the specific lessons contained within individual sections: the enduring importance of surprise, the value of discretion, the perennial need for firmness with one's troops, and so on. Macro battle narratives emerge, in other words, through the collation of lots of micro battle narratives.

However, readers might also recognize some more widely recurring rhetorical or literary (not just militarily instructive) leitmotifs, or recurring *topoi* in ethical and political debate (stories of self-denial, the role played by chance, the distrust and dissimulation that often characterizes powerful leaders, for instance). As Frontinus's *exempla* mount up, in other words, and as the reader notes (or makes) all sorts of connections between them, the patterns and interpretative threads that emerge not only feed off but also point the reader back out to wider discourses beyond the military sphere. The *Strategemata* is a text which offers readers a (potentially bewildering) multitude of answers to a series of simple strategic questions; and its disorientating re-presentation of hundreds of historical anecdotes (out of their historical contexts) entails a lot of proactive reading on the part of the reader, lots of critical comparison and piecing together, which invites reflection on many broader topics and brings the treatise into dialogue with many other texts.[35] Indeed, it demands that we read it more proactively ourselves alongside the whole range of works and discourses with which Frontinus's readership might have been familiar, especially near-contemporary ones, and not simply as an isolated/narrow technical treatise.

It is not just that we *can* read Frontinus's *Strategemata* alongside other Flavian texts, in other words, but that we must do so, if we are to read it on its own terms. And when we do, its civil war anecdotes not only coalesce into an intriguing narrative strand (perhaps of our own making) but also prompt wider reflection on the treatment of civil strife in contemporary literary culture.

---

[35] For a fuller discussion of this, see König 2017.

3 *Str.* 1.1: "On Concealing One's Plans"

The first section of the *Strategemata* (*Str.* 1.1: *De occultandis consiliis*) offers a good flavor of the internal dynamics of the whole work and a good opportunity for outlining the difficulties of reading its treatment of civil strife.[36] Straight after his opening anecdote about Cato the Elder (who outwitted a group of enemy commanders by writing letters to them all at once), Frontinus moves us back in time at *Str.* 1.1.2 to an episode from the start of the fourth century BCE, when Himilco (a Carthaginian general) was embarking on an ultimately doomed campaign in Sicily, against Dionysius of Syracuse. There is no Roman in sight here; but Sicily, the site of Rome's first skirmishes with Carthage and the first overseas territory that Rome acquired, might make readers think forward to the Punic Wars and to Rome's eventual victory over other doomed Carthaginian generals—not least after Frontinus's mention of Cato at *Str.* 1.1.1 (he of *Carthago delenda est* fame[37]). The third *exemplum* (Fron. *Str.* 1.1.3) then transports us to those very wars: specifically, to an episode from the Second Punic War when the Roman commander Gaius Laelius came up with a cunning ruse in Syphax's Carthaginian camp.[38] On the one hand, we jump backwards and forwards in time and space, to three quite separate conflicts and three distinctive stratagems devised by three unconnected commanders; on the other hand, the juxtaposition of these three *exempla* and the narrative threads that build up between them get us thinking, right from the start of the treatise, not just about military stratagems but about Roman military history, Roman *imperium*, and Rome's rise to power.

Strategemata 1.1.4 then takes us back in time again, to the period when Rome was ruled by (some rather unappealing) kings. That, in turn, is followed by more time-travel, as we fast-forward once again to three episodes from the late first century BCE, all concerning Roman commanders who conducted successful campaigns abroad (here we see Caesar in Egypt, Ventidius in Parthia, and Pompey being outmaneuvered in the Third Mithridatic War) but whose campaigns were

---

[36] It might be going too far to suggest that "concealment of plans" becomes a metatextual as well as strategic lesson in the *Strategemata*'s opening section, but Cato's deceptive writing to multiple (but unwitting) audiences in the text's very first anecdote may at least alert readers to the dangers of reading things only at face value and in isolation from other narratives and readers.
[37] Liv. fr. 49; Plin. *Nat.* 15.20; Plu. *Cat. Ma.* 26–27.
[38] Syphax, of course, had previously supported the Romans against the Carthaginians, but changed sides shortly before this episode; the deception that Laelius deploys is thus set against a wider backdrop of deception and betrayal, prefiguring the to-and-fro between allies and enemies that recurs throughout the *Strategemata*.

also mixed up with the civil wars that led eventually to the establishment of the Principate. And then comes Domitian, practicing concealment *en route* to Germany (like all the commanders in this section, "On Concealing One's Plans"), and acting, Frontinus stresses, for the good of the empire as a whole (Fron. *Str.* 1.1.8):

> The Emperor Caesar Domitianus Augustus Germanicus, wanting to crush the Germans who had risen up in arms and aware that they would begin the battle better prepared if they had got wind of the arrival of so great a general, used a census of the Gauls as the cover story for his journey; launching an unexpected campaign through this ruse, he crushed the ferocity of these savage tribes and in so doing served the wider interests of the provinces.

Domitian is followed by another Punic War *exemplum* (Fron. *Str.* 1.1.9: a Roman commander outwitting Hasdrubal and Hannibal, "the shrewdest Carthaginian generals"[39]); then we look at an encounter between the Athenian Themistocles and his Spartan foes (Fron. *Str.* 1.1.10), before ending with three more Romans (Fron. *Str.* 1.1.11–13, if 1.1.11 is not a later interpolation). The penultimate example concerns an episode from the Sertorian War—perhaps more a rebellion than a full-blown civil war (I discuss this further below), but whichever way one looks at it, a conflict that saw Roman statesmen fighting each other. The section ends with another Roman general and statesman from the same era, Marcus Licinius Crassus, one-time ally of both Caesar and Pompey.

The connecting factor uniting all the *exempla* in this section is the strategic lesson that is to be gleaned from them: the value of keeping one's plans to oneself, with illustrations of the many different military contexts and ways in which that might be effected. As in other sections, the text's to-and-fro across time and space supports that didactic focus; indeed, in papering over chronological, cultural, social and political differences, it may even keep distracting cultural and political subtexts at bay. We learn (*inter alia*) that concealment of plans has always been (*is* always) useful, in lots of different situations, and that it is not a skill or technique that has been practiced by one nation, era, or general more than any other. We learn to exchange narrow, particularizing perspectives (revolving around, e.g., particular kinds of "heroism" or particular historical periods) for the bigger picture: to see Romans and Carthaginians, long-dead kings and more recent *imperatores*, in much the same light as each other, on a strategic continuum that largely overrides partisan narratives. Frontinus's economical and homogenizing narrative style contributes to that, affording no room for the contextual specifics or cultural contrasts which Livy and Valerius Maximus (for instance) like to draw to our attention.

---

[39] Cf. V. Max. 7.4.4 and Liv. 27.43–49.

Alongside that universalizing message, however, we might pick out other currents, some of which at least are hinted at by the text. For instance, Roman *exempla* bookend the section and dominate it numerically: Rome *does* end up taking center stage, as a long-lived military power whose commanders have been thinking up successful stratagems from the time of Rome's highly mythicized monarchy to the present day.[40] In terms of leadership models, on the other hand, we move from the elder Cato—a figure famous both for great military successes and for his integrity (verging on severity) in private and public life—to the more controversial Crassus, who led Roman forces to one of Rome's heaviest defeats in the battle of Carrhae and whose accumulation of wealth and political alliances made him an ambiguous political figure in the late Republic. What, if anything, might we make of that textual trajectory, especially if we factor in the little cluster of *exempla* at *Strategemata* 1.1.5–7, which revolve around the campaigning that accompanied the dying days of the Republic, followed in *Strategemata* 1.1.12 by Metellus Pius fighting Sertorius in Spain (at an earlier date, perhaps even prefiguring those later conflicts)? On his own, Ventidius could stand as a fine exemplar, a general whose successful Parthian campaigns earned him a triumph, no less. With Caesar and Pompey flanking him, however, and indirectly at loggerheads (in Caesar's *exemplum*, he has just finished Pompey's forces off, although Frontinus makes no explicit mention of that), our thoughts might turn to the wider context and the disturbing messiness of it all, which saw great Roman generals repeatedly embroiled in conflict with each other.[41] We do not *have* to read anything significant into this cluster of *exempla*, but if we have been reading (say) Caesar's own account of his activities in Egypt (esp. *Ciu.* 3.107–12), Lucan's *Bellum Ciuile*, or Josephus's *Bellum Judaicum* recently, we might make some connections. We might feel reminded right at the start of the *Strategemata* that internal discord/civil war was (is?) as significant a part of Rome's history as foreign (particularly Punic) campaigns, perhaps even that civil strife sometimes masqueraded as or blurred into foreign conflicts, and vice versa (a standout theme at the start of Tacitus's *Histories*, as I noted above, but a phenomenon observable in many other texts). We might also notice the role played by powerful individuals in that, something which Flavian epic clearly thematizes, and an issue foregrounded also

---

40 With Cato leading off as a model of both military action and military writing, we might even be tempted to pull together a subtext about the superiority of Roman military "science," not just practice.

41 Also in the background to the episode narrated at Fron. *Str.* 1.1.5, of course, is the Egyptian civil war in which Caesar was embroiled. For a wider discussion of the post-69 CE resonances of Egypt in the Flavian text of Pliny the Elder, see Manolaraki in this volume.

by Josephus and Tacitus in different ways.[42] There are no minor figures in Frontinus's opening section: almost all of the commanders were powerful politicians in their own spheres, and several were kings... or (aspiring) *principes*.

This brings us to a perennial problem dogging all Flavian studies: what to do with Domitian, whose inclusion must mean that Frontinus wants us to think about him and, by extension, about the Flavian present, not just the Republican and pre-Republican past. He keeps excellent strategic company here and, on some level, benefits hugely from the comparison. Frontinus rarely makes authorial interventions in the *Strategemata*; his pointed praise of Domitian at 1.1.8 is an exception to his general rule.[43] But does this *tantus dux* (a phrase which demands some measuring up against the others in the section) really deserve more admiration than his fellow commanders, either for this stratagem in particular or for his campaigns more generally?[44] We might read Frontinus's treatment of Domitian as a genuine or at least as a conventional tribute to his emperor; but we might also bear in mind that this is a section which (for all its universalizing momentum) prompts reflection on the history of Rome and on the trajectory of Cato to Crassus, perhaps even the trajectory of Tarquin the Proud to Domitian, for those two exemplars sandwich the cluster of Caesar, Ventidius, and Pompey at *Strategemata* 1.1.5–7, perhaps suggestively so.

However one reads Frontinus's treatment of Domitian (and we will come back to this question towards the end of my chapter), the *Strategemata*'s opening section as a whole presents us with a series of impressively resourceful generals from all around the Mediterranean world, exemplars who can teach the reader useful and indeed universal strategic lessons. This is how almost every section of the *Strategemata* works, offering a wide range of models which prompt both micro and macro reflections on the conduct of different aspects of battle. There is, however, no getting away from the fact that certain clusters of *exempla* at *Strategemata* 1.1 foreground particularly powerful individuals whose maneuverings ultimately brought war upon Rome itself.

Frontinus's presentation of Caesar in Egypt, Ventidius in Parthia, and Pompey being outwitted by Mithridates may in fact smother the whiff of civil war that

---

[42] See especially Mason 2009 on Josephus's interest in succession as well as monarchy; and Ash 1999 on Tacitus's reflections on leadership models in the *Histories*.
[43] Turner 2007, 427; Malloch 2015, 90, who discusses Frontinus's other positive mentions of Domitian.
[44] How does Domitian's stratagem match up, for example, against the momentous events of the following narrative (Fron. *Str.* 1.1.9), which Frontinus flags as an almost iconic victory of Roman *consilium* (he had used the verb *consulo* to characterize Domitian's thinking at Fron. *Str.* 1.1.8) over Rome's greatest enemy?

these characters carry with them, by foregrounding their campaigns on foreign soil.⁴⁵ The *Strategemata* may even neutralize the trauma of civil war here and elsewhere by presenting it as something which many great leaders had been intermittently involved with down the ages, and as something not so very different— indeed, strategically indistinguishable—from other kinds of campaign. Frontinus does not make heavy weather of civil conflicts as CIVIL conflicts here, and his readers might conceivably have been reassured to see civil strife contextualized and almost disarmed in this way, made part of a series of *exempla* from which future generals might glean useful military lessons. The text may even reflect a wider recovery from the trauma of civil war that was already underway. Perhaps Frontinus's inclusive, almost flattening treatment of civil conflict is evidence that the subject was not quite so sensitive as some readings of Statius, Valerius Flaccus, and Silius have suggested.⁴⁶

The text might work in the other direction too, however, by (incautiously? deliberately? even provocatively?) exposing the festering sore that Valerius Maximus suggested should be kept out of sight. Indeed, as well as bringing historical civil conflicts into the frame, Frontinus's opening section might even faintly evoke the civil-war origins of Domitian's own dynasty through its juxtaposition of the emperor with that series of *exempla* at *Strategemata* 1.1.5–7. That is what a reader familiar with other Flavian texts (and with Flavian literary scholarship) might be tempted to suggest, at any rate; interpretation is so often a matter of perspective. But how does the rest of the *Strategemata* pan out? To what extent does civil strife rear its head in the rest of the treatise, and with what effects?

---

45 Cf. Gowing 2005, 60–61, on the way in which Valerius Maximus smothers the civil war dimension of Pompey's activities at V. Max. 6.2.6, "softening some of its potentially risky meanings." While Frontinus does something similar in many individual *exempla*, the collocation of connected anecdotes might in fact work against that, as I discuss below.
46 Cf. Fucecchi's chapter in this volume on the possibility that some Flavian epic may in fact be part of a recovery or "inoculation" too, "metabolizing" the nightmare of civil war inherited from Lucan.

4 Isolated Episodes or a Recurring Theme?

Book 3 of the *Strategemata* contains relatively few examples of civil war stratagems, perhaps unsurprising for a book focused on sieges.[47] Book 4, which has a different feel from the other three books, being structured around ethical concepts (*disciplina*, *continentia*, *iustitia*, and so on) rather than more pragmatic "how-to" topics, contains a similarly small number: five from the conflicts that accompanied Caesar's rise and fall,[48] plus an *exemplum* featuring Sertorius's reflections on how best to vanquish the whole Roman army, bit by bit (Fron. *Str.* 4.7.6).[49] There is also the anecdote at *Strategemata* 4.3.14, narrating a Domitianic success during the Batavian revolt, which I discuss in the final section of this chapter. In both of these books, the small smattering of civil war anecdotes blend in yet also stick out a bit from the other anecdotes in their sections. Civil war is not a dominant theme, but it rears its head from time to time, in ways that point (unnervingly, perhaps) to continuity with other kinds of conflict. Generals of all types

---

[47] There are just six *exempla* from civil war conflicts in *Strategemata* 3: 3.13.7 and 3.13.8 (detailing the ways in which Hirtius and Brutus stayed in touch while Brutus was under siege at Mutina), 3.14.1 (where one of Pompey's soldiers outwits Caesar's troops), 3.14.3 (where Hirtius gets supplies of salt past Antony's blockades at Mutina), 3.14.4 (a follow-on *exemplum* again featuring Hirtius), and 3.17.4 (where Caesar is ambushed by Pompey while trying to besiege some of his troops). In addition, *Strategemata* 3.17.8 details an episode involving Pompeius Strabo (father of Pompey the Great) during the Social War.

[48] Fron. *Str.* 4.2.1, featuring Brutus and Cassius; *Str.* 4.5.2, where "amid the tumult of civil war" (*in tumultu ciuilium armorum*) Caesar deals brutally with sedition amongst his troops; and *Str.* 4.7.32, which shows us the armies of Caesar and Pompey physically fighting each other. In addition, *Str.* 4.7.14 narrates an episode that readers might recognize from Caesar's *De Bello Ciuili* (Caes. *Ciu.* 3.101); and while Frontinus's "Caesar used to say" (*C. Caesar dicebat*) at *Str.* 4.7.1 depicts him speaking rather than writing, perceptive readers might again recognize a nudge to Caes. *Ciu.* 1.72, where Caesar himself expands on the principle of starving the enemy to spare his own troops a fight.

[49] Frontinus's phrasing sets Sertorius up in opposition to the whole Roman army from the start, and the climax of the *exemplum* visualizes Sertorius tearing it to pieces (*lacerabit et carpet*). This *exemplum* is also narrated at Fron. *Str.* 1.10.1. The penultimate anecdote of Book 4 (Fron. *Str.* 4.7.41) takes us back to the Social War. The final *exemplum* (commentators assume) refers to Quintus Caecilius Metellus Macedonius's activities in Hispania in 143 BCE, not a conflict which pitched Romans against Romans; however, Frontinus names its "hero" only as Q. Metellus, and given the volume of *exempla* across the text which touch on Sertorius's activities in Spain, readers might be forgiven if their thoughts fly also to Metellus Pius's activities in Spain (which are detailed at Fron. *Str.* 1.1.12, 2.1.2, 2.1.3, 2.3.5, and 2.13.3). The thrust of this final *exemplum* is that generals must always be prepared for the unexpected, a recurring theme of the *Strategemata* which helps to characterize war generally as a chaotic and unpredictable business.

behave in similar ways to each other within each section; indeed, as elsewhere in the treatise, we see Pompey, Caesar, and co. applying the same strategic nous in civil and non-civil contexts and being promoted as strategic models regardless of the context. These parallels teach useful strategic lessons but may also lead to some uncomfortable reflections—for example, about how easily strategic skill can be deployed in the wrong directions. In Book 4, which contains a higher proportion of Roman (and indeed Imperial-era) anecdotes than the rest of the treatise, a reader might be reassured to see so few civil war anecdotes; the statistics establish Rome's conflicts with Carthage as the defining feature of her past, with civil conflict only intermittently disruptive. On the other hand, the sudden sight of Sertorius plotting to destroy the whole Roman army or Caesar's troops having to shield their faces from Pompey's swordsmen might remind us, not least through the element of narrative surprise, that Roman military activity (and Rome's leading military commanders) can turn dangerously and unexpectedly inwards.

In Books 1 and 2, civil conflict crops up more frequently, albeit (as for Books 3 and 4) rather unevenly: some sub-sections contain no such anecdotes, while others feel more dominated by them. Take *Strategemata* 1.5, for instance, where several of the *exempla* on the theme "Escaping from Difficult Locations" take us to the conflicts between Caesar and Pompey and to Sertorius's Spanish campaigns, with one of Sulla's successes in the Social War also thrown in.[50] Like Sertorius's rebellion, the Social War was not a civil war as such, but a conflict which saw Rome and its Italian allies fighting each other and a prelude to some "proper" civil war, in which Sulla would play a leading role.[51] Frontinus's juxtaposition of full-blown civil war with more nebulous types of conflict arguably blurs the boundaries between the two in ways which might soften the impact/lessen the extraordinariness of particularly iconic civil war episodes, but which might also make civil war feel like a pervasive, even invasive phenomenon.

Consider next *Strategemata* 1.7, a short section on "How to disguise the absence of things which we lack or to find substitutes for them." It begins with a renowned Roman commander finding a clever way of getting elephants across a river during the First Punic War and then offers us a parallel story in which

---

[50] Fron. *Str.* 1.5.1, 5, 8, 9, 17; a different kind of internal rebellion crops up at Fron. *Str.* 1.5.20–22 where Spartacus features as the hero of a small cluster of *exempla*. On Spartacus's revolt as indicative of the wider disruption within Italy at the time, see, e.g., Steele 2013, 116.

[51] On the Social War and Sulla's campaigns as watershed events in the history of Roman civil war (arguably, the first "real" civil wars of the Republic, which triggered everything that followed) see Flower 2010, 78–79; Lange 2016, 25.

Hannibal came up with a similar ruse during the Second Punic War.⁵² The next *exemplum* also showcases Carthaginian cunning, but these opening anecdotes are followed by a brief reference to Julius Caesar's siege of Massilia (Fron. *Str.* 1.7.4) and then an equally fleeting visit to the aftermath of Mutina (that civil war milestone where Octavian emerged as a force to be reckoned with), where we see Mark Antony—in conflict with his own countrymen—deploying similar ingenuity and resourcefulness as the commanders in the preceding and subsequent *exempla*. The brevity of the narratives at *Strategemata* 1.7.4 and 5 (in fact also at *Str.* 1.7.6) is perhaps significant; Frontinus does not dwell on details or context. We turn next to an episode from the Third Servile War (Fron. *Str.* 1.7.6) and have Spartacus held up as an *exemplum* to emulate alongside Alexander the Great, the subject of the next and final *exemplum*—that famous story in which he denied himself a measure of water rather than drink when his men could not.⁵³

The whole section at *Strategemata* 1.7 thus juxtaposes Roman, Carthaginian, and a variety of other commanders, with civil war coming into focus only briefly. Nonetheless, by crossing back and forth between these different kinds of *exempla* and by drawing attention to their similarities as well as their differences (above all to the similarities in leadership), this section underlines parallels or irons out distinctions between external and internal conflicts, as if they are on a par or are part of the same phenomenon; indeed, as if the likes of Spartacus are as admirable or inspiring as the great Alexander himself. Internal strife is blended with more conventionally impressive or less controversial campaigning, in a way that perhaps submerges the civil war dimension; but—equally possible—those juxtapositions and parallelisms may also jar with the Roman reader. As I have noted, Frontinus generally refrains from passing judgment on the episodes he narrates, preferring didactic concision over *enargeia*; as a result, each anecdote individually tends to have a detached, unemotional feel. Read in juxtaposition with other contrasting ones, however, they (and the lack of ethical commentary or moral/political/social differentiation) may become more shocking and may prompt readers to think afresh about the differences between *bella ciuilia/externa/permixta* (to use Tacitus's categories) and possible leadership models.⁵⁴ Interplay between Frontinus's narratives elicits a different emotional response—or,

---

52 On Roman/Carthaginian parallelism, see also below (pp. 167–68).
53 Variations of this story are found in Plu. *Alex.* 42.4–6; Polyaen. 4.3.25; and Curt. 7.5.9–12.
54 I am indebted to both Daniel Chiritoiu (Cambridge, 2017) and Matthew Myers (Nottingham, 2018), whose PhD theses, which I was privileged to examine, have helped to advance my own thinking on *enargeia* in military narratives.

to put it another way, teaches different lessons—from the individual *exempla* themselves.

Strategemata 1.8 offers further illustration of this. It begins with Coriolanus and his attempts to sow internal discord and "wear down the unanimity of the Romans" (*consensus Romanorum distringeret,* a rare moment in the treatise where Frontinus's language becomes almost judgmental). It then goes on to juxtapose various Punic *exempla* with *exempla* in which Italian states formed alliances against Rome or Rome ravaged the land of other Italians, throwing in an episode from Caesar's civil wars along the way (Fron. *Str.* 1.8.9). Revolt, deception and shifting loyalties are standout themes in this section, with commanders of all backgrounds deploying similarly cunning ruses against each other. Strategic success passes backwards and forwards between groups and nations, with a particularly vivid demonstration in the run of anecdotes from *Strategemata* 1.8.5–9 of how rapidly allies might become enemies and how often trust is abused.[55] There is no moralizing commentary: just the same neutral presentation for all *exempla*, which (as at *Str.* 1.7) are juxtaposed in both flattening and contrasting ways. In anecdote *Strategemata* 1.8.2, for instance, Hannibal behaves rather like Coriolanus in *Strategemata* 1.8.1, trying to sow division and distrust amongst the Romans. As individuals, Coriolanus and Hannibal are both presented here as potentially inspiring models of a particular kind of strategic leadership. In juxtaposition, the contrasting contexts and the very different impact of their similar ruses (Coriolanus disrupting the harmony of the Roman state, Hannibal failing to undermine the noble reputation of his Roman counterpart) might lead readers to reflect on the differences between types of commander and conflict and on Rome's patchy record in both regards. Meanwhile, the placement of that Caesarian civil war narrative at *Strategemata* 1.8.9, after a series of anecdotes in which the difference between ally and enemy becomes increasingly blurred, might appear to gloss over the "civil" nature of Caesar's campaign (by presenting it on a continuum with other kinds of conflict), but it might also invite readers to read the preceding anecdotes as all on a spectrum with civil war.

Section 1.9 pursues the theme of desertion and rebellion within the Roman empire by presenting four *exempla* in which generals devised ways of quelling mutinies amongst their own troops. All four *exempla* depict Roman generals having to wage a campaign, almost, against their subordinates (internal sedition thus emerges as a particularly Roman problem). And the final example transports us to the heart of Julius Caesar's camp during the civil war, so that we get a picture

---

[55] Woolf 1993, 189, underlines the topicality of this after 68–69 CE, when inter-city rivalries flared up into armed conflicts, "and provincials allied with barbarians against other provincials."

of internal sedition within the context of wider internal strife.[56] The following section (*Str.* 1.10, on "How to restrain an intemperate demand for battle"—another theme that throws up conflict between generals and their troops) continues in the same vein. *Strategemata* 1.10.1, for example, depicts Sertorius dealing with dissent among his own men, who are all too eager to engage in battle against their fellow Romans: more internal tension, within the wider context of inter-Roman antagonism.[57] In *exemplum* 1.10.4, a foreign general hammers home (to his presumably impatient troops in the first instance, but also to us as readers) the self-defeating impact of "the divisions caused by Rome's civil wars" (*dissociatum armis ciuilibus populum Romanum*): he refuses to engage in battle with the Romans for fear of bringing their warring parties together, and he vividly illustrates that principle by setting two dogs on each other before introducing a lone wolf, against whom the dogs unite.[58]

There are many other kinds of anecdotes around and about the ones I have highlighted here (e.g., Jugurtha in Africa, Agesilaus in Lydia and Thebes), but Frontinus's occasional clustering of *exempla* that revolve around civil conflict and internal strife suggest that he himself saw civil war as a significant theme while composing the *Strategemata*: one civil war story made him think of another, even as he arranged his material according to stratagem-types. It also intermittently flags that theme for the reader, from the first book onwards, so that it becomes a recurring topic for those who read the treatise all the way through. Readers cherry-picking answers to specific strategic questions might miss this; but those who scroll from section to section, enjoying the variety, build-up, and interaction between different anecdotes, might end up seeing civil war as a prominent, even perennial, Roman phenomenon, and Rome itself as a state bristling with soldiers and generals periodically intent on each other's destruction.

That is perhaps nowhere more apparent than at *Strategemata* 2.5.31–40. This part of the treatise ("On Ambushes") begins with an anecdote showcasing Romulus (*Str.* 2.5.1): another moment in the text where we recognize that, for all the universalizing messages about generalship which the treatise teaches, Rome and Romanness is under the microscope. The bulk of the section narrates anecdotes

---

[56] Additionally, *Str.* 1.9.2 and 3 both concern events and commanders connected with different civil wars. As Ash 1999 illustrates, relations between commanders and subordinates are a revealing *topos* in many civil war narratives (Caesar, Appian, Cassius Dio) and one that becomes particularly politicized in Tacitus's *Histories*.
[57] As I noted above, this *exemplum* crops up again in Book 4.
[58] While the wolf represents the Dacian general and his army, at first glance at least, readers conscious of the Romulus and Remus myth might be prompted by it to read Roman in-fighting and self-destruction back in time to the city's very foundations.

from lots of different foreign conflicts (Roman and non-Roman), but a sequence of *exempla* towards the end puts the spotlight firmly on internal strife/civil war; and at *Strategemata* 2.5.40, Frontinus uses that very phrase—*bello ciuili*—in case we had not noticed. This sequence begins with a particularly lengthy account of Sertorius's persistence in ambushing Pompey's troops during the Sertorian War (Fron. *Str.* 2.5.31), which climaxes with Pompey suffering a double catastrophe (*duplex damnum*) and having no other option but to stand by and watch as disaster falls upon his men. Sertorius's "cleverness" is strategically impressive (something we might emulate), but the narrative also becomes uncharacteristically emotive for the *Strategemata*, thanks not least to the unusual level of detail which Frontinus goes into. He then concludes the *exemplum* by reminding us that this was the first of many encounters between Sertorius and Pompey and by noting that Livy put the death toll on Pompey's side at ten thousand men (plus the whole baggage train): such Roman-on-Roman conflict was costly as well as repetitive.

The next *exemplum* (Fron. *Str.* 2.5.32) takes us to the closing stages of the Sertorian conflict, as Pompey outmaneuvers Perperna, who had just assassinated Sertorius: there are Romans turning on each other in between Frontinus's *exempla*, not just within them. And just as that conflict is settled (temporarily, at least; Frontinus's narrative comes back to it several more times as if it is never quite over),[59] we turn our attention first to an *exemplum* from Pompey's Mithridatic campaigns before heading back to the year after Perperna's assassination (72 BCE), to an episode from the slave rebellion led by Spartacus.[60] All the famous civil war faces of the first century BCE then turn up, including those we met in the *Strategemata*'s opening section: Ventidius (Fron. *Str.* 2.5.36–37), Julius Caesar, Afranius (Fron. *Str.* 2.5.38), Mark Antony, and Pansa (Fron. *Str.* 2.5.39), among others. We move roughly chronologically through their various campaigns, climaxing with the struggles between Pompey's and Caesar's factions into which King Juba I of Numidia, among others, was drawn (Fron. *Str.* 2.5.40).[61] In tracing this temporally short but geographically far-reaching trajectory, the text not only makes civil war the defining feature of that particular era; it also gets us to look at Rome's different civil wars (indeed, at the whole spectrum of "civil war," from

---

[59] See Fron. *Str.* 2.7.5, 2.12.2, 2.13.3, and 4.7.6.

[60] As at Fron. *Str.* 2.5.31, Frontinus underlines the (staggering) loss of life, again with reference to Livy: "Livy recounts that thirty-five thousand soldiers were killed, along with their commanders." However, Frontinus also identifies Spartacus's troops here as "barbarians" and Crassus's troops as Romans, reducing the internal-strife dimension of the episode.

[61] Chronological organization of *exempla* is not a standard feature of the *Strategemata*; this section therefore stands out in that respect.

rebellions to outright conflict) from a variety of angles, even to ask "what counts as 'civil war'?" given its many different faces.

Arguably, the striking concentration of civil war *exempla* at *Strategemata* 2.5.31–40, together with Frontinus's emphasis on continuity (perhaps even amounting to a domino-effect from one conflict to another) and loss of life, foregrounds internal strife not just as a significant theme but as a potentially sensitive subject—all the more so if we read these anecdotes in dialogue with other Latin texts, as Frontinus's references to Livy and allusions to other works (in particular, Caesar's *commentarii* and Valerius Maximus's *exempla* collection) occasionally encourage us to do. When Frontinus notes at *Strategemata* 2.5.31 that Livy put the death toll so high, for example, he reminds readers of the existence of other, more detailed accounts, which do not simply flesh out but often complicate or put a different spin on the stories that Frontinus tells so briefly. Rather than (or as well as) saving readers the bother of reading Livy *et al.* (as Frontinus claims in the preface to Book 1), those allusions to other texts invite readers to map what they read in the *Strategemata* against a broader network of narratives, and the resulting intertextuality often activates more emotive *topoi* and discourses than the *Strategemata* itself goes in for. Intertextual interplay between narratives enriches—and complicates—both the micro and macro stories that Frontinus's treatise tells.

5 Carthaginian Conflicts and Civil War at *Strategemata* 2.3

At *Strategemata* 2.3 (to look at one final illustrative section), we might be particularly tempted to read Frontinus's work in dialogue with epic as well as historiography, and with Flavian as well as pre-Flavian texts. There are some loose parallels, for instance, between Frontinus's treatise and Silius Italicus's (possibly later) *Punica*.[62] Punic *exempla* recur again and again in the *Strategemata*, and Hannibal crops up more often than any other general. Throughout the text, in fact, we see Roman stratagems and triumphs repeatedly followed (indeed,

---

[62] Gallia 2012 is currently the only study to offer some sustained comparison of these two texts; other recent readings of the *Punica* (e.g., McGuire 1997, 88–146; Dominik 2003; Marks 2005b; Touahri 2009; Tipping 2010; Stocks 2014) overlook the potentially illuminating overlaps between Silius and Frontinus. Stocks's chapter in this volume on the politics of (decisive) individualism and brotherhood in the *Punica* points to some obvious opportunities for comparative analysis.

frequently matched) by Carthaginian ones—and vice versa—in a seemingly endless to-and-fro. At *Strategemata* 2.3, for example, we begin with a couple of Roman successes (*Str.* 2.3.1 and 4) involving two different Scipios; but they are swiftly followed by Carthaginian triumphs, not least at Cannae (Fron. *Str.* 2.3.7), and then on different fronts at *Strategemata* 2.3.9 and 10 (with *Str.* 2.3.8—a Roman success—thrown in between them). In these oscillating *exempla*, Roman and Carthaginian generals behave in similar ways to each other, adopting variations of each other's tactics, like the Roman-Carthaginian parallelism at *Strategemata* 1.7.1–2 and 1.8.1–2, mentioned above. Strategically, there is little to choose between them; sometimes one has the upper hand, sometimes the other. The ongoing to-and-fro between these two nations and the commanders who represent them hammers home the repetitive, unpredictable nature of these Punic conflicts, and of military conflict generally. Victories are invariably followed by defeats, and successful strategists are always only one episode away from being outmaneuvered themselves in turn[63]—a lesson that perhaps contextualizes (normalizes—or brings into sharper relief?) the to-and-fro we see between Roman commanders in the civil war context.[64]

Civil war keeps a relatively low profile in *Strategemata* 2.3, but episodes from civil conflicts are intermittently juxtaposed with Punic and other *exempla*, as in other sections, as if they are on a continuum with each other. At *Strategemata* 2.3.5, for instance, we move straight from an *exemplum* in which Scipio Africanus outwits Hasdrubal to an *exemplum* in which Metellus Pius adopts a similar stratagem (and formation of troops) to defeat a fellow Roman, Hirtuleius, in the Sertorian War. At *Strategemata* 2.3.11, we are told that "Sertorius employed the same tactics in Spain [as Xanthippus in the first Punic War] in his campaign against Pompey." Pompey himself crops up in a non-civil campaign, at *Strategemata* 2.3.14; similarly, Sulla, Mark Antony, and Caesar also appear—fighting Macedonians, Parthians, and Gauls—alongside *exempla* which gesture towards their involvement in episodes of civil strife. Sulla was involved in aspects of the Sertorian conflict, for example, and as we will see, we soon come to an *exemplum* in which

---

[63] Cf. Lovatt 2016, 370–74 (following Beard 2003 on the double-edged nature of triumph in Josephus), who argues that scenes of triumph in Flavian epic inevitably evoke the potential for future defeat.

[64] For Sallust, of course, it was Rome's victory over Carthage that triggered the beginning of her moral and political decline, leading ultimately to the kind of intra-state violence epitomized by Catiline (Sal. *Cat.* 10–13; *Jug.* 41); Silius would later suggest something similar (Sil. 8.243–57, on which see Dominik 2003, 492; Sil. 10.657–58, on which see McGuire 1997, 57). This *topos* is worth bearing in mind given the recurring juxtaposition of Punic and civil war anecdotes across the *Strategemata*.

Caesar and Pompey confront each other at Pharsalus (Fron. *Str.* 2.3.22). The text oscillates between images of Romans fighting foreign forces and images of them fighting each other, in other words, in ways that continue to underline the slippage between the two—and indeed the ways in which foreign and civil wars in Roman history tended to generate each other.

Frontinus also weaves numerous different nations into the picture that builds up of Punic conflicts, as he does in his presentation of civil war *exempla*. At *Strategemata* 2.3.1, for instance, the Roman commander Gnaeus Scipio is in Spain, contending not only with *Afri* but also *Hispani*. At *Strategemata* 2.3.10, the Carthaginian forces are led by a Spartan mercenary (as at Fron. *Str.* 2.2.11); and at *Strategemata* 2.3.16, Hannibal masses auxiliary troops of Italians, Gauls, Ligurians, Balearians, Moors and Macedonians, along with his Carthaginian troops, against the Romans.[65] In view of the fact that in some surrounding *exempla* these different nationalities fight on different fronts against a variety of other enemies,[66] this mix of nationalities in Punic *exempla* takes on an extra significance, for it exposes the ephemerality of shifting alliances between different peoples across history, a theme that recurs, as I have noted, in *Strategemata* 2.5. In juxtaposing Punic and non-Punic *exempla* in which overlapping sets of peoples, allies and enemies, repeatedly engage with (and betray) each other in different variations, the *Strategemata* presents all history (not just Roman-Carthaginian history, or indeed civil war history) as an endless succession of spats and alliances, of conquests and desertions, between a revolving cast of characters who team up with and confront each other *ad infinitum*.

Far from helping readers to distinguish between friends and foes, then, or offering us a story of enduring domination or imperial progress (or decline), the *Strategemata* breaks such predictable narratives down and rearranges history into a much more panoramic and disconcerting miscellany of episodes, which *en masse* emphasize how short-lived victory can be, how unpredictable war is, and how difficult it has always been to know who is on whose side or who will be in the future. In Silius's epic there is an element of conflation between Hannibal and Scipio, between Rome and her nemesis, and indeed between different allies and enemies; but the trajectory of the text shifts the momentum inexorably away from Hannibal and Carthage and towards the Romans and the success of their empire, in the end, via one particularly inspiring (and autocratic) leader, Scipio. That does not happen in the *Strategemata*. There are leaders (even autocrats) a-plenty;

---

[65] We are told, too, that he cannot rely on all of them equally (he distrusts the Italians' loyalty and indifference, having dragged most of them from Italy against their will).
[66] E.g., Spartans against Lucanians and Persians at Fron. *Str.* 2.3.12 and 13.

remember the text's emphasis on the decisiveness and cunning of individual leaders as the key to success. But there is no steady build-up to one decisive individual or national triumph. Instead, the different leaders pull the momentum of the many different conflicts in different directions, back and forth, and we watch the repetitive rise and fall of Mediterranean history in the process.

What, if anything, do we—as readers of Josephus, Statius, Silius, and Tacitus (as well as of Livy, Caesar, Valerius Maximus, *et al.*)—do with this? Do we simply read in it some universal lessons about the chaos of war and the enormous challenges involved in being consistently successful as a general? (The importance of quick thinking, and the ability to capitalize on chances when you get them, for example.) The text is aimed primarily at contemporary and future generals, after all, by an author who had himself recently campaigned at the outer edges of Rome's empire, in places (the German borders especially) where to and fro between victory and setback were the norm, under Domitian no less than other emperors. Is the treatise as straightforwardly or universally didactic as that? Certainly Frontinus has excerpted and organized all of his material strictly according to military time (battle-order), not according to any teleological chronology, precisely in order to focus on and bring out some timeless strategic lessons. But is that all that readers would have got out of it? Is it all that they would have looked for in it?

Or might they (or we) read some particularly Roman, even particularly Flavian, flavors here, as elsewhere? Is my emphasis on chaos and unpredictability, on the continuity of fighting, the sense that there is fighting on all fronts, the blurring of allies and enemies, and the destabilizing effects of all of that in fact a product of that very temptation, to find contemporary Roman narratives beneath the surface? And if it is, does that set me apart from Frontinus's original readers— is it primarily those who are caught up in current trends of Flavian scholarship who are likely to make that maneuver, or might others including Frontinus's near-contemporaries have been acutely sensitive to these themes, too? If we want, we can extrapolate from the immediate Flavian context and from other Flavian-era texts to build up a dossier of both external and internal evidence arguing that the *Strategemata* presents us with images of war and generalship that are particularly destabilizing in the light of ongoing border disputes and rebellions in Frontinus's day—and, above all, against the backdrop of the Flavians' rise to power and Domitian's increasingly autocratic tendencies. Images that not only reflect contemporary phenomena and concerns but potentially offer some oblique commentary on them, perhaps even challenging the presentation (in other texts, art, official rhetoric, and other media) of Vespasian and his sons as deliverers of peace and stability.⁶⁷ The roll-call of *imperatores* outwitting each other on seemingly endless repeat might vaguely trouble a readership still "in recovery" from the civil wars of 68–70 CE, or might (especially if one has been reading Tacitus's *Agricola* lately) foreground differences between the relative independence of former generals and those who serve under Imperial (especially late Flavian) regimes. We might even feed some of that back (in a circular way) into the wider study of Flavian war and Flavian war-literature, seeing in Frontinus's *Strategemata* parallels or even prequels to features of (say) Silius's, Tacitus's, and Josephus's texts. We could plausibly argue that, rather than being retrospectively over-interpreted or misread along (e.g.) anachronistically Tacitean lines,⁶⁸ Frontinus's *Strategemata* in fact reflects and articulates a Zeitgeist which Tacitus himself goes on to pick up on and discuss far more explicitly, until it becomes a distinctively Tacitean tale.⁶⁹

We might also be tempered in that endeavor, however, by the recognition that many a military text down the ages has underlined the chaos and unpredictability of war, just as many a history has explored the overlapping nature of allies and enemies, of exemplary and less exemplary models. In the context of Punic and civil war *exempla*, in particular, we would also do well to remember that reading parallels (and indeed a pessimistic trajectory) between Carthaginian and later civil conflicts was a habit of late Republican authors long before the likes of Silius and Frontinus put the two into implicit juxtaposition; and therefore, Frontinus's presentation of both Punic and civil strife might owe more to his familiarity with those earlier writers than it does to any particularly Flavian discourses. Without heavy-handed guidance from the treatise itself (as I have noted, Frontinus's authorial absence is particularly striking in contrast to Valerius Maximus's more interventionist approach), we find ourselves attempting to sift historical,

---

67 *Fortuna* (for instance) was an imperial virtue found on Domitianic coins as well as the coinage of Vespasian and Titus (Fears 1981, 901), with *Fortuna Redux* particularly suggesting analogies with Augustus and the restoration of peace (Boyle 2003, 7); but (as Osgood 2006, 5, notes) Fortune could also be spun as a more capricious, disruptive force in the context and aftermath of civil war. In that light, Frontinus's emphasis on unpredictability in the *Strategemata* might work against Flavian attempts to appropriate *Fortuna* as a symbol of restored stability.
68 As, e.g., Malloch 2015, 84 n. 37, argues.
69 On this possibility, see Buckley 2018, who (drawing particularly on Joseph 2012) explores the likelihood that the "Tacitean" feel of Valerius Flaccus's *Argonautica* is not simply down to our retrospective reading lenses but "is evidence of a much broader, distinctly post-Julio-Claudian and obviously shared cultural discourse in these texts" (Buckley 2018, 88) that crossed between the Flavian and post-Flavian eras that Tacitus's writings tried so hard to separate.

enduring, even timeless *topoi* from context-specific ones (and vice versa), universals from Flavian particularities.

6 Factoring Domitian In

That said, the second half of *Strategemata* 2.3 picks up an unusually pro-Roman momentum. While the *Strategemata* generally frustrates attempts to identify subtexts about Roman superiority or imperial destiny, here we get a series of *exempla* in which a foreign stratagem is immediately answered by a successful Roman counter-stratagem, and Frontinus intrudes to offer some rare approbation of Roman commanders. Hannibal's formation of his (very mixed) troops at *Strategemata* 2.3.16 is bettered by Scipio's shrewd (*prudens*) organization of Roman forces, for instance, in what readers will identify as the Battle of Zama, the decisive final victory that brought the Second Punic War to an end. Sulla's clever thinking (*ratio*) at *Strategemata* 2.3.17 outclasses Archelaus's battle dispositions and results in a Roman victory over the Macedonian forces. Romans triumph at *Strategemata* 2.3.18 and 20; and Roman consuls counter Pyrrhus's battle arrangements very judiciously (*aptissime*, Fron. *Str.* 2.3.21) with a different arrangement of their own, which (while not resulting in a Roman victory) limited Roman losses while inflicting far greater losses on the enemy.[70]

At this point, however, as we draw towards the climax of this particular subsection of the treatise, we are plunged suddenly into one of the most famous civil war battles of all, the decisive encounter between Caesar and Pompey at Pharsalus (Fron. *Str.* 2.3.22):

> Cn. Pompeius aduersus C. Caesarem Palaepharsali triplicem instruxit aciem[.] ... aduersus hanc ordinationem C. Caesar et ipse triplici acie dispositis in fronte legionibus sinistrum latus, ne circumiri posset, admouit paludibus. in dextro cornu equitem posuit, ... sex deinde cohortes in subsidio retinuit[.] ... nec ulla res eo die plus ad uictoriam Caesari contulit: effusum namque Pompei equitatum inopinato excursu auerterunt caedendumque tradiderunt.
>
> Gnaeus Pompey, facing Caesar at Pharsalus, drew up three lines of battle. ... To meet this formation, Caesar also arranged his legions in three lines at the front and placed his left wing on the marshes to avoid being surrounded. On the right flank he positioned his

---

[70] This is the same Pyrrhus whose writings on generalship/warfare Frontinus cites at *Str.* 2.6.10. He was an authority of the subject, which makes the Roman (partial) success here perhaps the more impressive.

cavalry. ... Finally, he held back six cohorts in reserve. ... And on the day nothing contributed more to his victory; for when Pompey's cavalry poured forward, these legions routed them with an unexpected sortie and handed them over for slaughter.

Frontinus's account agrees in very basic terms with what Caesar himself tells us about troop dispositions in the *De Bello Ciuili*,[71] although it is heavily compressed and simplified. The final phrase of the *exemplum*, however, feels more Lucanesque. In the other *exempla* of *Strategemata* 2.3, we see commanders and armies surrounding each other and routing each other, but only occasionally killing each other.[72] At the end of *Strategemata* 2.3.22, the vocabulary and imagery step up a notch, for the *exemplum* ends both with a Roman victory (which offers a distorted parallel of the Roman victories celebrated at the ends of Fron. *Str*. 2.3.16 and 17) and also with the ambush and slaughter of Roman cavalry units by their countrymen, who are handed over to be killed (*caedendumque tradiderunt*) in a macabre inversion of the celebration at the end of *Strategemata* 2.3.21 of relatively light Roman losses (2.3.22 might thus be read as another "pyrrhic victory" of sorts, but for Romans this time).[73] There is no explicit authorial approbation or condemnation here, but this *exemplum* has a certain shock-factor to it, not least because of the contrast it offers after the unusual build-up we have had of images of Roman superiority/success. For much of *Strategemata* 2.3, Roman commanders triumph splendidly over a series of foreign enemies—but as the section comes to a close, they also keep turning on each other in bursts of increasingly brutal self-destruction.

Is it mere coincidence that *exemplum* 2.3.22—in which the man who effectively established Rome's first imperial dynasty triumphs over a fellow contender towards the end of a long period of chaotic and destructive civil war—is immediately followed by an *exemplum* in which *Imperator Caesar Augustus Germanicus* (i.e., Domitian) pops up (just as the cluster of civil-war-ish *exempla* at *Str*. 1.1.5, 6, and 7 are followed by Domitian right at the start of the treatise)?[74] It could be. The spread of *exempla* from *Strategemata* 2.3.22–24 (the close of the section) takes us from Pharsalus in the 40s BCE to the forests of the Chatti in 83 CE to the great naval Battle of Mylae during the First Punic War, showcasing the effectiveness of different battle formations in very different contexts across more than three centuries of history. Variety—indeed, contrast—between *exempla* is part of the point

---

71 Caes. *Ciu*. 3.88–89.
72 At Fron. *Str*. 2.3.6, 7, and 14.
73 Cf. Caes. *Ciu*. 3.98, on Caesar's *clementia* towards those who surrendered; also *Ciu*. 3.99 on Pompey's heavy losses compared to Caesar's lighter ones.
74 See pp. 158–60, above.

here: the text's pro-Roman momentum (Domitian and Gaius Duellius win further victories for the fatherland in their own *exempla*) is enhanced by the differences as well as the similarities between all these successful Roman stratagems. Domitian's appearance at *Strategemata* 2.3.23 thus weaves him into a section which celebrates the diversity of Roman strategic cleverness, indeed of Roman models of *imperator*-ship. Nonetheless, he is still positioned alongside two Roman *imperatores* (one of them, a proto-*Imperator*) with Roman blood on their hands. For all that his stratagem against the Chatti differs significantly from Pompey and Caesar's complex, even textbook, maneuverings at Pharsalus, Domitian enters the stage in this section in the wake of civil slaughter.

Domitian's final appearance in the text also carries with it the faint odor of (more recent) civil war (Fron. *Str.* 4.3.14):

> auspiciis Imperatoris Caesaris Domitiani Augusti Germanici eo bello, quod Iulius Ciuilis in Gallia mouerat, Lingonum opulentissima ciuitas, quae ad Ciuilem desciuerat, cum adueniente exercitu Caesaris populationem timeret, quod contra exspectationem inuiolata nihil ex rebus suis amiserat, ad obsequium redacta septuaginta milia armatorum tradidit mihi.

> Under the auspices of the Emperor Caesar Domitianus Augustus Germanicus, in the war which Julius Civilis had initiated in Gaul, the extremely wealthy city of the Lingones—which had revolted to Civilis, and then begun to fear for its people as Caesar's army advanced—on discovering against expectation that nothing was plundered and no one lost any of his possessions, returned to their former obedience and handed seventy thousand of their soldiers over to me.

As I noted above, Book 4 is a little different from the other three books of the *Strategemata*.[75] In particular, it contains a higher percentage of Roman *exempla* than the rest of the treatise and a higher number also of Imperial-period *exempla*. Thus, with its sudden turn to ethics, it prompts readers to reflect a little more closely on what it means to be a successful Roman *imperator* NOW, in the Flavian present, not just the distant past. This particular *exemplum* is a good example of that, not least because Frontinus himself turns up at the end as the real hero of the tale, although initially Domitian gets all the credit.[76]

---

[75] So much so that some have suggested it was not authored by Frontinus: the authorship of *Str.* 4 was questioned in the nineteenth century (Wachsmuth 1860; Wölfflin 1875), but Bendz 1938 argued in favor of identifying Frontinus as its author and has since been followed by the majority of commentators (e.g., Goodyear 1982; Campbell 1987, 15; Wheeler 1988, 20; Campbell/Purcell 1996, 785; Turner 2007, 432; Gallia 2012, 204; Malloch 2015).

[76] On *Str.* 4.3.14 and what we might read more generally into the smattering (but ongoing paucity) of Imperial-era *exempla* in the *Strategemata* (particularly *exempla* involving generals from outside the Imperial family), see Turner 2007 and Gallia 2012, 204–13, who argues that "[t]he

The episode under discussion took place during the Batavian revolt led by Julius Civilis—a "mixed" conflict if there ever was one, in which former Roman allies rose up against Rome and exploited/involved themselves in the civil strife of 69–70 CE, siding vaguely with Vitellius along the way.[77] Frontinus's narrative thus obliquely invokes some of the recurring themes of the text: shifting loyalties, broken alliances, desertion and rebellion, and blurred distinctions between foreign and civil conflict. It also plunges us specifically into the period following Vitellius's death, before Vespasian had consolidated his claims to power—and so into the closing stages of the civil wars that brought the Flavians to power. (Given that, there is perhaps some irony—not just deferential courtesy—in Frontinus's anachronistic use of all of Domitian's imperial titles at the start of the story.) Frontinus's narration of Domitian's involvement in this stratagem (which in fact Frontinus himself oversaw, as the final word of the *exemplum* reveals by surprise: the Lingones handed their soldiers over *mihi*, "to me") might be read positively: "under Domitian's auspices" clemency prevailed, allies were brought back on side, and order was restored. Given what readers know of the wider context, however, this anecdote might set off more negative trains of thought.[78] It is possible, indeed, to read it as something of a climax in a long, slow build-up of autocratic and civil war threads that began in the *Strategemata*'s opening section and takes readers right through the text and up to the present day. That might not be "right," just as it cannot simply be "wrong"; rather, it is one of the interpretative options that opens up when we read the *Strategemata* in dialogue with the discourses that emerge from other Flavian-era texts and Flavian scholarship.[79]

People have been pulling different stories out of the *Strategemata* for centuries. It enjoyed great popularity in the Middle Ages and the Renaissance, when it was incorporated into crusading manuals and many different works of political

---

Stratagems ... offers very little in the way of tangible proof of the continued vitality of the art of Roman generalship under the emperors" (Gallia 2012, 204).

[77] As Joseph 2012, 35, notes, Josephus characterizes the Batavian revolt as a foreign war, a German attack on Rome; Tacitus, by contrast, emphasized its civil aspects (*Hist*. 4–5) and states its "mixed" nature (*Hist*. 4.22.2: *mixta belli ciuilis externique facie*). O'Gorman 1995, 124–25, notes the narrative to-and-fro/hybridity at this point in Tacitus's text, when attention shifts from *bellum ciuile* to *bellum Ciuilis*: "the transition from civil to external conflict, the period of mingling, reaches back into the sphere of civil war as well as forward into 'straightforward' war." On Silius's treatment of the Batavian revolt, see Tipping 2010, 47–48.

[78] Tacitus would later suggest that the Batavian revolt triggered seeds of sedition within the Flavian imperial family and set Domitian on his tyrannical course (*Hist*. 4.85–86).

[79] This is something that Malloch 2015 underestimates in his refutation of Turner 2007.

philosophy.[80] In 1417 one Jean Gerson, tutor to the then Dauphin of France, listed the *Strategemata* alongside the Bible, other Christian texts, and works by Aristotle, Sallust, Livy, Valerius Maximus, Seneca, Vegetius, and Augustine (*inter alia*), as a kind of literary "Ark of the Covenant" that the young prince should absorb and carry metaphorically about with him "through the desert of this world."[81] It was translated time and again, sometimes supplemented by appendices of more up-to-date stratagems. In 1539, for instance, an Englishman called Richard Morysine addressed a translation of it to Henry VIII, promising that it would aid that "moste high, excellente, and myghtye Prynce" by inspiring and instructing his military captains who "have oft declared that they lytell nede any instructions, any bokes."[82] Most recently, a pair of Greek students undergoing compulsory military service in the Greek army managed to persuade their commanding officer that the best use of their time (rather than the normal drills and exercises) was to produce a modern Greek translation of the *Strategemata*; it was published in 2015.[83] The *Strategemata* was—is—universalizing enough, in other words, to prove ongoingly instructive in many different military and political contexts; it has transcended its immediate Flavian context in many ways and has been read over and over again (like many other ancient texts) for the lessons it can offer to other times and places.

I have also tried to show what we might learn by reading the *Strategemata* as a specifically Flavian text, however, alongside and in dialogue with other Flavian literature, not least because that exercise in itself can prompt fruitful reflection on the process and challenges of connecting text to context and vice versa. Indeed, in some ways the *Strategemata* might be thought of as a useful metaphor for that very process: for in the *Strategemata* we have a collection of narratives (extensive, but not comprehensive) which we as readers end up juxtaposing and comparing with each other to make meaning from their interconnections, just as we do with the wider body of texts, artifacts, and traces of discourse that survive from the period. As we pick through the *Strategemata* (and that wider body of material), we end up accumulating an increasingly complex array of lessons and

---

80 E.g., John of Salisbury's *Policraticus* (Keats-Rohan 1993); Marino Sanudo Torsello's *Book of the Secrets of the Faithful of the Cross* (Lock 2011); and Christine de Pizan's *Book of Deeds of Arms and Chivalry* (Willard 1995; Forhan 2002, 150–57; le Saux 2004). Machiavelli, too, clearly drew on it (Wood 1967).

81 Gerson, *Au précepteur du Dauphin, Constance, vers Juin 1417* (Glorieux 1960, 203–15; cf. Thomas 1930, 30–55, who dates the letter rather to 1408–10 CE; also Mazour-Matusevich/Bejczy 2007).

82 See also d'Assigny's 1686 translation, to which he appended a further collection of *exempla* from antiquity to his present day, plus a short essay on engines of war.

83 Pappas/Theotokis 2015.

narrative threads—and far from getting one clear picture of civil war, or leadership, or military history, or the Flavian present, we see how organic and evolving our vision of such things necessarily is and how torn we and all of those narrative threads are between context-specific and more timeless, boundary-crossing dimensions.

The *Strategemata* reminds us—reassures us, perhaps—that war, civil strife, and autocratic leaders were not just a Flavian phenomenon, but issues of perennial concern and significance the world over, going right back in time. Its blurry, non-committal treatment of civil war might even indicate that this supposedly traumatic phenomenon was not quite the stand-out source of anxiety under Domitian that some studies have suggested: remember the progressive disappearance of civil war as the treatise goes on, and note, too, that my discussion has inevitably foregrounded the *Strategemata*'s civil war *exempla* disproportionately. That said, Frontinus did not write civil war out of his treatise, nor did he write it out of the Flavian present, as Gowing suggests Velleius Paterculus and Valerius Maximus did for their own era, in deference to/praise of the emperor Tiberius.[84] Indeed, Frontinus's frequent returns to the subject and his suggestive juxtapositions of *exempla* might have fed off of and into other, even more sensitized, Flavian treatments of the topic. The difficulty we face as readers lies not so much in identifying or constructing (or even in choosing between different) Flavian readings of civil war in the *Strategemata*; it is more in measuring those particularizing strands up against the text's wider-ranging dimensions.

---

[84] Gowing 2010.

Neil W. Bernstein
Inuitas maculant cognato sanguine dextras: Civil War Themes in Silius's Saguntum Episode

The Roman exemplary tradition long remembered the conflict that sparked the Second Punic War, the siege of the Spanish city of Saguntum by Hannibal's forces. The Saguntines elected to remain loyal to their Roman allies in the face of an overwhelming invasion rather than surrender to Hannibal. They patiently waited for the Romans to send troops to their rescue and then began to succumb to plague and starvation as the result of a prolonged siege. At that point, they constructed a communal pyre and sacrificed themselves. According to Livy, only some of the wealthier Saguntines did so; others remained to resist Hannibal and were executed when Hannibal's forces took the city.[1] In the view of the Roman moralists, however, the mass suicide was universal and performed in the name of *fides*, or loyalty. Valerius Maximus describes the fall of the city in the chapter *De Fide Publica*, "On Loyalty Publicly Demonstrated" (Val. Max. 6.6.ext.1):

> post duorum in Hispania Scipionum totidemque Romani sanguinis exercituum miserabilem stragem Saguntini uictricibus Hannibalis armis intra moenia urbis suae conpulsi, cum uim Punicam ulterius nequirent arcere, collatis in forum quae unicuique erant carissima atque undique circumdatis accensisque ignis nutrimentis, ne a societate nostra desisterent, publico et communi rogo semet ipsi superiecerunt. crediderim tunc ipsam Fidem humana negotia speculantem maestum gessisse uultum, perseuerantissimum sui cultum iniquae Fortunae iudicio tam acerbo exitu damnatum cernentem.

> After the pitiable slaughter of the two Scipios in Spain and as many armies of Roman race, the Saguntines were driven by Hannibal's victorious arms inside the walls of their city. Unable to fend off the Punic power any longer, they collected into their forum all that each

---

Thanks to Lauren Donovan Ginsberg and Darcy Krasne for inviting me to the Celtic Conference, and to all the participants in the "After 69 CE" panel for a stimulating and productive exchange in the idyllic surroundings of the Confucius Institute, Edinburgh. This paper is partly based on my Oxford commentary on *Punica* 2 (Bernstein 2017). I am grateful also to Neil Coffee and Kyle Gervais for many helpful comments and suggestions. Translations, where not otherwise specified, are my own.

1 In Livy, a group of leading citizens throw themselves and their wealth on a pyre. Meanwhile, others remain alive to continue the resistance to the Carthaginians, thereby compelling Hannibal to order the adult males to be put to death (Liv. 21.14.1–4). See Hulls in this volume for discussion of the Livian and Polybian tradition of the Saguntine siege and comparison to motifs in Josephus's *Bellum Judaicum*.

one of them held dearest and set inflammable substances around and ignited them. Then, rather than defect from our alliance, they threw themselves on top of the public and communal pyre. I could believe that Faith herself on that occasion watching the affairs of men wore a face of sorrow as she saw her most persevering cult condemned by judgment of unkind Fortune in so bitter an outcome. (transl. Shackleton Bailey)

Valerius Maximus makes a slight error in chronology: the siege of Saguntum occurred at the beginning of the war, not after the major military actions in Spain. What is more relevant to Roman literary history is the personification of Fides, who looks down in sorrow on the suffering that the Saguntines endure in her name.[2] This narrative motif, which is likely much older than Valerius Maximus, proves formative for representations of the event by authors throughout the rest of the first century, especially Lucan and Silius Italicus.[3]

The *Punica* of Silius Italicus traces the whole course of the Second Punic War in seventeen books of epic, from the commencement of hostilities in Spain to the triumph of Scipio Africanus. The epic opens with two books devoted to the siege and capture of Saguntum that have been praised even by Silius's most vocal detractors. Clarence Mendell, for example, observed in the 1920s that "the first two books by sheer narrative force sustain the interest with scarcely a break and had Silius had the good fortune to die before writing more, he might have been hailed as another of those incomparable geniuses lost to the world through a premature death."[4] Book 2 of the *Punica* concludes with the mass suicide of the Saguntines (Sil. 2.457–707). Since they do so under the influence of the Fury and slaughter their own relatives, this deed has long been read as a representation of civil war.

Reception horizon, narrative position, and scale of narration each partly condition the interpretation of Silius's version of civil war.[5] As a former Neronian courtier, Silius looked back on the aesthetic sensibilities of the period that created Lucan's epic-length *Bellum Ciuile*, Petronius's parodic *Bellum Ciuile*, and Seneca's *Phoenissae*. But unlike these other courtiers, Silius lived to see the actual civil war that broke out upon the suicide of Nero and participated in a significant role as one of this emperor's last consuls. As Marks has persuasively argued, Silius left to his Flavian contemporaries the task of addressing recent

---

2 For the personification of divine qualities, see Clark 2007.
3 See also Petr. 141 and Plin. *Nat.* 3.20.
4 Mendell 1924, 99.
5 McGuire 1997, 207, has described the Saguntine suicide as "a representation in miniature of the strife associated with civil war." See also Hulls in this volume.

history through the vehicle of mythological epic.[6] He instead employed the epic genre to fulfill the retired consul's traditional task of writing Roman history, while reimagining the distant past of the Second Punic War to provide moral lessons for the Flavian era.

The suicide is the culmination of the Saguntines' suffering on both political and divine levels, as the Romans abandon their allies to the besieging Carthaginians and the Fury drives innocent victims to suicide. The episode responds to similar instances of civil and intrafamilial violence in prior epic, including the Massilian episode of Lucan's *Bellum Ciuile*, the Lemnian massacre in Valerius Flaccus's *Argonautica* and Statius's *Thebaid*, and the brothers' duel in Book 11 of Statius's *Thebaid*.[7] This paper argues that the episode's political, moral, theological, and intertextual narratives all challenge simple assessments of the Saguntines' fate, as Silius emphasizes the compromised exemplarity of the Saguntine suicide and the Romans' failure to meet their political obligations. The *Punica* enters into dialogue with the earlier epic tradition's treatments of civil war and focuses it on the experience of a Flavian audience, who as survivors of a very recent civil war were likely skeptical of appeals either to *fides* or to exemplarity.

1 Political Narrative

Silius's narrator presents Saguntum as a sacrificial stand-in for Rome and its capture as the prelude to Hannibal's assault on Rome.[8] In the same manner as the general's ancient biographers, he characteristically views every element of Hannibal's prior career as leading toward its acme, the victory at Cannae and the subsequent abortive attempt to attack Rome. A similar tradition can be found in Livy, where the Roman Senate reacts to the capture of Saguntum "as if the enemy were already at the gates" (*uelut si iam ad portas hostis esset*, Liv. 21.16.2). In Silius, the motif is widespread. Carthaginians and Romans alike see the capture of Saguntum as the first step toward the capture of Rome. The narrator describes Hannibal as "striking at the Capitol from the edge of the world" (*extremis pulsat Capitolia terris*, Sil. 1.270). As Hannibal later crosses the Alps *en route* to Italy, Venus reprises her Vergilian counterpart's fearful supplication of Jupiter and tells

---

6 Marks 2010b.
7 For Silius's use of Lucan, see Marks 2010a and Marks 2010c. For interactions with Statius's *Thebaid*, see Marks 2013; Walter 2013; Marks 2014.
8 See Hardie 1993a on sacrificial stand-ins in Roman epic. For Saguntum as a sacrificial substitute for Rome, see Dominik 2003, 474–80.

the supreme god that "Rome already fears the fall of Saguntum" (*casus metuit iam Roma Sagunti*, Sil. 3.564).[9] The Saguntine defender Murrus even taunts a Carthaginian invader, as he kills him, with failing to ascend the Capitoline Hill (*certe Capitolia primus | scandebas uictor*, Sil. 1.384–85), as if both combatants had fully identified the Spanish city with the Roman capital. Yet as they prepare for suicide, the Saguntines express a contrary view. They symbolically destroy their ties with Rome by burning their *arma* and *penates* on a communal pyre.[10] The Penates are their link with one side of their mythical origins, to an Ardea strongly identified with Vergil's Turnus (Sil. 1.665–69). Though Romans and Carthaginians will attempt to represent the Saguntines as dying for Rome, they choose to die in a state of deracination.

Epic narratives of other doomed Roman allies offer clear contrasts to this extraordinary means of resistance. Lucan's loyal Massilians promise to die resisting the invader Caesar and committing suicide if need be. Their spokesman sets their resolution of defiance in the tradition of the Saguntine resistance to Hannibal (Luc. 3.340–42, 349–55):

> et post translatas exustae Phocidos arces   340
> moenibus exiguis alieno in litore tuti,
> inlustrat quos sola fides …
>
> …
> nec pauet hic populus pro libertate subire
> obsessum Poeno gessit quae Marte Saguntum.   350
> pectoribus rapti matrum frustraque trahentes
> ubera sicca fame medios mittentur in ignis
> uxor et a caro poscet sibi fata marito,
> uolnera miscebunt fratres bellumque coacti
> hoc potius ciuile gerent.   355

Driven from the ancient seat of our nation, when Phocis was burnt down and her towers were removed, we dwell on a foreign shore and owe our safety to narrow walls; and our only glory is our fidelity. … In defence of freedom we do not shrink from sufferings that were bravely borne by Saguntum when beset by the army of Carthage. Our infants, torn from their mothers' arms and tugging in vain at breasts dry with famine, shall be hurled into the midst of the

---

9 This scene is modeled on Verg. *A.* 1.229–53; for the type scene in Latin epic, see Hershkowitz 1997.
10 As Augoustakis 2010a, 135, observes, "the Saguntines themselves strive to erase their ties with Rome. The obliteration of Roman identity becomes an absence at all levels, absence of strategy and common policy, absence of virtue and pity. As Book 2 comes to a close, there is no distinction between the always cunning Carthaginians and the Romans: their mutual lack of *fides* proves destructive for the Iberian city."

flames; wives shall seek death at the hands of loved husbands; brother shall exchange wounds with brother, and shall choose, if driven to it, that form of civil war. (transl. Duff)

As Lucan's epic does not feature intervention by gods or personifications, the Massilians' decision to die resisting Caesar's invasion is made with full consciousness and responsibility. They have neither been inspired by a personification of virtue nor driven mad by a Fury. The Massilians also identify mass suicide to evade capture as one possible form of a civil war in which they have been compelled to participate (*bellumque coacti | hoc potius ciuile gerent*, Luc. 3.354–55). Silius develops themes that Lucan left abbreviated in the Massilian ambassador's speech. Like the Massilians, the Saguntines also view themselves as descendants of Greek emigrants, and they oppose Hannibal, a figure whom Silius aligns with Lucan's Caesar.[11] Even when dying from plague and famine, they respond to Fides' call to resistance in order to demonstrate the *fides* for which the exemplary tradition will remember them (Sil. 2.513–25). Almost immediately afterwards, however, Tisiphone's intervention maddens them and turns them to mass suicide motivated by *furor* not *fides*, in which parents kill children, husbands kill wives, and brothers kill one another. Silius imposes the consequences of the Massilians' threat on his Saguntines in order to connect this episode to the tradition of Lucan's civil war epic.

Silius's reader meets a different type of *fides*-narrative in the Capua episode and so looks back to Saguntum as a contrasting exemplification of the virtue. The southern Italian city has been divided between its oligarchic leaders, who treacherously hand it over to the Carthaginians, and Decius the loyalist, who risks death to urge his fellow citizens to stand by their promises to Rome.[12] The Capuan traitors commit suicide as the Romans retake the city in *Punica* 13. A small group of aristocrats gather in a private house to drink poison rather than throw themselves on a mass pyre in the public square. For their part, the Romans are in the grip of fury and are about to massacre their former allies. The god Pan then intervenes to calm their spirits. His entry into their minds causes them to spare and reintegrate a populace clearly divided in its response to their leaders' treachery (Sil. 13.314–20):

---

11 See Marks in this volume for discussion of Marcellus's capture of Syracuse as a further contrast to Lucan's battle at Massilia (p. 61): "Silius's program of allusion to *Bellum Ciuile* 3 in the sea battle of *Punica* 14, therefore, not only sets Syracuse's *perfidia* in contrast to Massilia's *fides* but reinforces the Massilians' likeness to Silius's faithful Saguntines." For the identification between Silius's Hannibal and Lucan's Caesar, see Kißel 1979, 108–12, and Stocks 2014, 61–70.
12 See Littlewood 2014.

atque ea dum miles miratur inertia facta
exspectatque ferox sternendi moenia signum,   315
ecce repens tacito percurrit pectora sensu
religio et saeuas componit numine mentes,
ne flammam taedasque uelint, ne templa sub uno
in cinerem traxisse rogo. subit intima corda
perlabens sensim mitis deus.   320

> While the soldiers looked with wonder at such weakness, and waited eagerly for the command to raze the walls, a sudden awe, felt but not expressed, came over them, and some divine power tamed their ferocity, making them loath to hurl their fire-brands and reduce all the temples of Capua to ashes in a single conflagration. A merciful god made his way by slow degrees into their inmost hearts ... (transl. Duff)

Pan's gentle entry into the Roman soldiers' minds contrasts with Fides' invasion (*inuadit*) of the Saguntines and encirclement (*implicat*) of their marrows (Sil. 2.515–17):

inuadit mentes et pectora nota pererrat   515
immittitque animis numen. tum fusa medullis
implicat atque sui flagrantem inspirat amorem.

> She invades minds and traverses breasts that know her well and sends her divine power into their spirits. Then spread within their marrows, she embraces them and inspires them with burning love of herself.

The language of Fides' entry into the Saguntines suggests violent rather than benign effects. A triple run of verbs compounded with *in-* at the beginning of each line (*inuadit, immittit, implicat*) emphasizes Fides' invasion of the Saguntines' bodies and minds. The passage's intertexts also signal divine infiltration. *Implicat* evokes the encirclement of Vergil's Amata by Allecto's snakes (*pertemptat sensus atque ossibus implicat ignem*, Verg. *A.* 7.355), while the clausula of Sil. 2.517 (*inspirat amorem*) recalls Valerius Flaccus's scene of Venus maddening Medea with her kiss (*oscula permixtumque odiis inspirat amorem*, V. Fl. 7.255). Both scenes lead to civil war and/or family violence. Amata's Bacchic revolt in Vergil is one of the causes of the war in Latium, while Medea's madness in Valerius ultimately leads to her betrayal of her father and murder of her brother. Silius accordingly invites the reader to contrast the political outcome of the Fides and Pan scenes in terms of their divine framing.

Flavian readers would have evaluated the Saguntine and Capuan suicides against the conventions of exemplary aristocratic suicide.[13] As one of the consuls of the year 68 CE, Silius likely knew something about the staging of the suicides of Nero's courtiers Seneca, Lucan, and Petronius only a few years before,[14] and the conclusion of the Capua episode (Sil. 13.261–98) shows how Silius translated such an exemplary narrative into epic.[15] The Capuan leaders retreat to a private house and prepare philosophically for the soul's departure from the body's prison. Their leader Virrius "expels concern for living from his breast" (*pulsis uiuendi e pectore curis*, Sil. 13.263) and appeals to liberty as the goal of suicide (Sil. 13.271–72). Rather than disfigure themselves through stabbing one another in a maddened frenzy, the Capuan traitors embrace before drinking poison. Fides and the Fury here work in concert rather than in opposition as they did at Saguntum. The fact that they now can apparently be collaborators creates a further opportunity to question the *bona fides* of the personification Fides at Saguntum. At Capua, the personified virtue lectures the traitors on keeping their word, while the demon from hell hands out the poison. The scene features the same Republican-themed appeals to liberty as in Valerius Flaccus's scene of Jason's parents' suicide at the conclusion of *Argonautica* 1,[16] although Silius has made the suicide of the Capuan leaders appear even more tranquil. Unlike Pelias's sudden attempt to arrest Jason's parents, the threats that lead to their death are no surprise but are visible throughout the long siege. The Roman forces have not yet invaded their houses, and so there is no clash of arms to disturb their procession to the underworld. It is as if a circle of Neronian aristocrats had gathered to commit suicide on the decorous pattern set by Seneca and Lucan. Silius links the events of the middle Republic to the concerns of the Flavian era through the consciously anachronistic style of the Capuan conspirators' death.[17]

---

[13] See Hill 2004. For Silius, see McGuire 1997, 207–19.
[14] For the suicides of Lucan and Seneca, see Fantham 2011 and Ker 2009 respectively. On staging suicide as a spectacle, see Edwards 2007.
[15] See Burck 1984b.
[16] See, recently, Zissos 2009, 357–66, with additional bibliography.
[17] For the sympotic behavior of the Capuans, see Schenk 1989. Wilson 2013 claims that Silius's poetics reflect the emphasis on historical epic in the Neronian era; Marks 2010b argues that Silius's choice to write a historical epic represents a deliberate aesthetic contrast with the mythological epics of his Flavian contemporaries.

By contrast, the Saguntines' mass suicide involves every inhabitant and does not discriminate among social classes.[18] Famine has destroyed the Saguntines' bodies, and so the Carthaginian invaders will not be able to admire the beauty of their corpses. The Fury shrouds the city in smoke (Sil. 2.609–11) so the gods cannot watch to certify the deed's exemplary value. Most significantly, there is none of the conscious psychological framing that Roman suicides viewed as essential to participation in an exemplary tradition.[19] The Saguntines are unwilling killers who hesitate to strike and must be compelled by the Fury: "they stain their unwilling hands with their relatives' blood" (*inuitas maculant cognato sanguine dextras*, Sil. 2.617). The opening molossus *inuītās* prompts the reader to linger over the evaluation of the Saguntines' mental state. Silius thereby calls attention to the difference between the Saguntines and the other mass killers of kin in first-century epic, such as Ovid's *terrigenae,* Lucan's Opitergian soldiers on Vulteius's raft, and the Lemnian women of Valerius's and Statius's epics (episodes that I briefly examine in what follows). Through its emphasis on compulsion by the Fury rather than self-motivated choice, the Saguntum episode deliberately reverses the decorous quasi-philosophical aristocratic suicide, as later exemplified at Capua. I accordingly turn to consideration of Silius's complex divine framing of the earlier suicide at Saguntum.

2 Divine Narrative

Divine framing further complicates the moral problems already introduced in the political narrative. A single divine intervention typically ignites epic civil or intrafamilial conflict, as in Allecto's sparking of the war in Italy in Vergil *Aeneid* 7 or Venus's instigation of the Lemnian massacre in Valerius *Argonautica* 2. Silius, however, stages the Saguntine massacre as the outcome of a contest between Hercules and Fides on one side and Juno and Tisiphone on the other.[20] Hercules, Saguntum's patron god, pleads with Fides as he views the plague and famine resulting from the prolonged Carthaginian siege to allow the Saguntines to save themselves.[21] Fides' response in Silius echoes the Vergilian Jupiter's response to

---

18 See, for example, Sil. 2.681–82: *semiambusta iacet nullo discrimine passim | infelix obitus permixto funere turba* ("Unhappy in their death, half-consumed by the fire, without distinction or order, the bodies of the people lay pell-mell, one upon another," transl. Duff).
19 See Hill 2004 and Edwards 2007.
20 See Ripoll 1998.
21 See Asso 2010b and Tipping 2010.

Hercules' tears at the prospect of Pallas's death. She modifies the famous sententia *stat sua cuique dies* ("his day stands for each man," Verg. *A.* 10.467–68) to refer to "the day of vengeance" that awaits Hannibal: "Indeed I see this. Not for nothing are my treaties broken, and the day that avenges such dire ambitions stands fixed long since" (*cerno equidem, nec pro nihilo est mihi foedera rumpi,* | *statque dies ausis olim tam tristibus ultor*, Sil. 2.494–95). This day comes much sooner for Vergil's Turnus than it does for Hannibal, who escapes Roman capture and does not die until decades after the fall of Saguntum. In the meantime, Fides' wish is that the Saguntines die fighting to demonstrate their loyalty to Rome so they can inscribe themselves in the exemplary tradition. The effect of the adaptation is to emphasize the difference between human and divine time scales. The gods know that vengeance will come eventually, but in the short term the Saguntines perceive only the destruction of their city.

Where the Vergilian Jupiter merely averts his gaze from Pallas's death, Silius's personified Fides intervenes on behalf of the Saguntines. Fides' descent to Saguntum actualizes the metaphor of the city's loyalty to Rome into a narrated interaction between human and divine agents.[22] The attribution of a personality to the divine quality Fides further evokes her cult worship in the world outside the text.[23] As discussed above, the Saguntine commitment to Rome even unto death was already one of the *memorabilia facta*, the kind of behavior that exemplifies the action of Fides herself. Yet Silius immediately complicates the simple equation of the Saguntines with a single virtue both by creating an ambiguous portrait of Fides and by introducing a second divine agent, the Fury Tisiphone, as her opponent.[24]

Fides is an ambivalent ally, and following her is no straightforward path to virtue. She inspires the besieged Saguntines to take up arms against the Carthaginian invaders—but must immediately restrain them from engaging in cannibalism (Sil. 2.513–25). As in the later Capua scene, where Silius's Pan guides the Romans to exact a limited form of retribution upon their treacherous former allies while keeping them from acquiring a reputation for brutality,[25] Silius's apparently benevolent gods attempt to keep violence within proper boundaries, and they do so in the context of idealized interstate relations. Here, Fides endeavors to guide the Saguntines to exemplary death through heroic resistance

---

[22] The examples of Pietas and Virtus as "actants" in Statius's text are broadly comparable. See Franchet d'Espèrey 1996.
[23] See Clark 2007, 167–70.
[24] Contrast Feeney 1991, 301–12.
[25] See Bernstein 2009.

and so restrains their initial impulse to act like beasts (*saeuasque ferarum | attemptare dapes*, Sil. 2.522–23). As Petronius sardonically hinted, cannibalism is hard to reconcile with moral exemplarity.[26] Juno then observes Fides' work and attributes it to "the virgin's madness that stirs up war" (*uirgineum increpitat miscentem bella furorem*, Sil. 2.528). Through Juno's comment, Silius draws attention to the association between virgin Fides' actions, virgin Tisiphone's *furor*, and the *furor* that epic generically associates with civil war.[27] The phrase *miscentem bella* especially evokes the appeal of Lucan's Massilians to their *fides* that pairs them with the Saguntines (Luc. 3.354–55, quoted above).[28]

Fides' ambivalent support of her devotees also recapitulates the ambivalence of Hercules' support for Silius's Saguntines. Hannibal's attack on Saguntum puts two versions of the Hercules myth into conflict. In the Saguntine version, Hercules serves as patron and guardian of the city through his connection to the mythical founder Zacynthus. In the Carthaginian version, Hercules should stand by Hannibal as a hero who similarly crosses the Alps and who plans to destroy the Roman descendants of the Trojans, just as Hercules once sacked Laomedon's Troy.[29] Moreover, the evocation of the Vergilian Jupiter's words to the *Aeneid*'s Hercules on the death of Pallas (Verg. *A.* 10.467) should call into question any faith in Hercules' ability to help the Saguntines (Sil. 2.494–95, quoted above). Throughout the Saguntum episode, the limited power and ambivalent identities of the exemplary figures Fides and Hercules are repeatedly on display.[30]

---

[26] *quod si exemplis quoque uis probari consilium, Saguntini obsessi ab Hannibale humanas edere carnes nec hereditatem expectabant. Petelini idem fecerunt in ultima fame, nec quicquam aliud in hac epulatione captabant nisi tantum ne esurirent* ("But if you also wish the plan to be supported by precedents, the people of Saguntum, when Hannibal besieged them, ate human flesh without any legacy in prospect. The people of Petelia did likewise in the extremities of famine, and gained nothing by the diet, except of course that they were no longer hungry," Petr. 141.9, transl. Heseltine and Rouse).

[27] For Fides, see Sil. 2.493, 513, 520; for Tisiphone, see Verg. *A.* 7.331 *uirgo sata Nocte* with Horsfall's note (Horsfall 2000). On *furor* as a key civil war term, see this volume's introduction and Bessone in this volume (pp. 90–92).

[28] See also the Bacchant's description of Roman civil war as *furor*: *quis furor hic, o Phoebe, doce, quo tela manusque | Romanae miscent acies bellumque sine hoste est* ("say, Phoebus, what madness is this that drives Romans to fight Romans; what war is this without a foe?," Luc. 1.681–82, transl. Duff).

[29] See Ripoll 1998, 112–32. "In his destruction of a city dear to Hercules [Saguntum], how can Hannibal hope for the god's help?" (Asso 2010b, 183).

[30] See Tipping 2010. We must also remember that the tradition frequently insists on Hercules as the murderer of his own family, a story dramatized by an important Flavian precursor, Seneca the Younger, and before him by Euripides.

After the ambiguous presentation of Fides' intervention, Tisiphone's assault quickly supersedes its effect,[31] and Silius's presentation of the Saguntine suicide as the result of a double divine intervention evokes a series of acts of familial violence in prior epic. Tisiphone bursts into a gathering (Sil. 2.558–79) and addresses the Saguntines in disguise as Tiburna, widow of the Saguntine champion Murrus. This disguise recalls Vergil's Iris, who disguised as the Trojan Beroë incites her fellow Trojan women to burn the ships (*A.* 5.604–40); Tisiphone disguised as Tiburna incites the Saguntines to burn *themselves*. There is also a recollection of Valerius's angry Venus, who similarly incites the Lemnian women to commit mass murder in disguise as Dryope (V. Fl. 2.174–85).[32] The assimilation of family violence to civil war recalls Ovid's *terrigenae*, who spring up from the earth after Cadmus sows the dragon's teeth. As they are all brothers born at the same moment, they identify their warfare as civil war in ordering Cadmus "not to involve" himself in it (*nec te ciuilibus insere bellis*, Ov. *Met.* 3.117). In Silius's Saguntum, however, there can be no innocent bystanders: the Carthaginians burst into an empty city where all of the noncombatants have been murdered by their relatives.

The next extant example of family violence in the epic tradition is the suicide of Lucan's Opitergians, Caesarian troops led by Vulteius. As mentioned above, they undertake their mass suicide without divine intervention when their raft is cut off and surrounded by the Pompeians.[33] Lucan's Vulteius describes the suicide as an act of *fides* and *amor* for Caesar, the complement to his opponents the Massilians' eagerness to die resisting his commander.[34] As a pragmatic leader, he is aware that suicide likely offers little practical benefit to Caesar and so must serve as a demonstration of their *amor* for their general. Immediately afterward,

---

[31] See Küppers 1986, 164–70.
[32] See Elm von der Osten 2007 and Fucecchi 2014. See also Keith in this volume for discussion of "the displacement of responsibility for civil war and kin murder onto a series of 'women out of control,'" which "reflects a potent enabling fiction of the warmongers, who are thereby absolved of responsibility for the dissolution of familial and community bonds in civil war" (quotations taken from p. 320).
[33] On Lucan's Opitergians, see Eldred 2002.
[34] *nescio quod nostris magnum et memorabile fatis | exemplum, Fortuna, paras. quaecumque per aeuum | exhibuit monimenta fides seruataque ferro | militiae pietas, transisset nostra iuuentus. | namque suis pro te gladiis incumbere, Caesar, | esse parum scimus; sed non maiora supersunt | obsessis tanti quae pignora demus amoris* ("By our death Fortune designs some mighty and memorable example for posterity. Our company would have surpassed all records that time has preserved of loyalty and military devotion, maintained by the sword. For we know that it is not enough for Caesar's men to fall upon their swords in his defence; but hemmed in as we are, we have no greater pledge to give of our deep devotion," Luc. 4.496–502, transl. Duff).

however, Vulteius redefines his actions as the result of *furor:* "I have thrown away my life, comrades, and the excitement of my upcoming death drives me completely. This is madness!" (*proieci uitam, comites, totusque futurae | mortis agor stimulis: furor est*, Luc. 4.516–17). Lucan's narrator then characterizes the mass suicide as an example of *ardua uirtus* (Luc. 4.576) in his coda to the episode.[35]

Silius's Saguntines recapitulate each of these motifs introduced in Lucan's Opitergian episode: a desperate siege, *fides*, exemplary behavior, murderous madness, and *ardua uirtus*. The deceptive speech that Silius assigns to his disguised Fury ironizes the scene on Vulteius's raft. Immediately after an intervention by Fides, Tisiphone appeals to the besieged Saguntines to murder one another in order to escape from enslavement by the Carthaginians: "use your hands to take your mothers away from slavery" (*uestris seruitio manibus subducite matres*, Sil. 2.577). The Fury characterizes the young men's action of killing their mothers not as the crime that she characteristically punishes with madness, but as a step along the arduous path to virtue (*ardua uirtutem profert uia*, Sil. 2.578). As Lucan's Vulteius could not clearly distinguish between *fides* and *furor*, neither can Silius's Saguntines. Unlike Vulteius, who confidently boasts of the role of his troops in the subsequent exemplary tradition, these desperate civilians do not seem aware that posterity will remember them. Such reassurances come in the voice of the narrator and are essential for assigning the verdict of exemplarity. Nevertheless, viewing the murders of either episode as exemplary requires considerable credulity on the observer's part, as these putative manifestations of *ardua uirtus* appear to be gruesome acts of madness.

The fall of Saguntum, the climactic scene of the *Punica*'s opening set-piece, also enters into an extensive intertextual dialogue with the personifications who attend the long-deferred anticlimax of the *Thebaid*, the duel of Eteocles and Polynices. Fides' actions recapitulate the failed attempt of Pietas to oppose Tisiphone and halt the brothers' duel in Statius *Thebaid* 11. The contest between the Fury and a personified virtue sets the episode in dialogue with the brothers' duel in Statius. The following discussion sets out some of the more important correspondences briefly and schematically. These are: (a) the role of the attendant divinities; (b) the marveling human observers; (c) the narrator's envoi to the principals; and (d) the narrator's appeal to commemoration.[36]

---

[35] *non tamen ignauae post haec exempla uirorum | percipient gentes, quam sit non <u>ardua uirtus</u> | seruitium fugisse manu* ("Yet even after the example set by these heroes, cowardly nations will not understand how simple a feat it is to escape slavery by suicide," Luc. 4.575–77, transl. Duff).
[36] Further contextualization and detail may be found in Bernstein 2017.

a. The role of the attendant divinities

As Hercules looks down from Olympus and observes the Saguntines' suffering, he accuses Fides of culpable indifference: "Goddess, can you witness unmoved the city suffering so many punishments for you?" (*et tot pendentem pro te, dea, cernere poenas | urbem lenta potes?*, Sil. 2.488–89). The accusation of indifference aimed at a divinity putatively allied in concern recalls Tisiphone's remarks to her sister Megaera just before she instigates the brothers' duel in the *Thebaid* (Stat. *Theb*. 11.97–101):

> non solitas acies nec Martia bella paramus,
> sed fratrum (licet alma Fides Pietasque repugnent,
> uincentur), fratrum stringendi comminus enses.
> grande opus! ipsae odiis, ipsae discordibus armis   100
> aptemur. quid lenta uenis?

> No customary battle, no Martian war do we prepare, but the swords of brothers (though kindly Faith and Piety resist, they will be vanquished), brothers, I say, must be drawn in conflict. A mighty work! Let us ourselves fasten onto their hate and quarrelling arms. Why do you dawdle? (transl. Shackleton Bailey)

The brothers' duel forms a preliminary climax integral to Statius's narrative, but the interventions of Fides and the Fury are only part of a local episode in *Punica* 2. Tisiphone's remark regarding the potential objections of personified Fides and Pietas is suggestive in this regard. Personified Fides plays no role in Statius and so has no reason motivated by the text to object to the brothers' duel. She is, however, a major figure in Silius's *Punica* 2. This is the strongest intertextual clue that Silius's Saguntine episode may come first. As Ganiban observes, "by grouping them together in this line, Tisiphone acknowledges their interconnectedness not only in the cultural tradition of Rome but perhaps also in the literary tradition, since she will go on to rout Pietas in the *Thebaid* as she also had already overpowered Fides in the *Punica*."[37] Marks suspects "bidirectional influence": "the number of parallels is not inconsiderable, and one would expect that as the number of parallels between the epics increases, so does the probability of bidirectional influence."[38]

In Statius, Tisiphone's reference to the "mighty work" (*grande opus*) of the Furies forms part of a traditional Roman epic discourse about the contents of its genre, as in the comment of Vergil's narrator as he previews the latter half of the

---

[37] Ganiban 2007, 174.
[38] Marks 2014, 137.

Aeneid: "I set a greater work in motion" (*maius opus moueo*, Verg. *A.* 7.45). Aeneas eventually triumphs in Latium and gives rise to a future dynasty. In the *Thebaid*, by contrast, Statius's Fury assists in the extinction of one of the Labdacid dynastic lines. Silius's narrator similarly describes the Saguntine suicide as a remarkable *opus*: "Then the Saguntines embark on a noble deed which unfortunate glory preserves eternally for unconquered people throughout the whole world" (*inde opus aggressi, toto quod nobile mundo | aeternum inuictis infelix gloria seruat*, Sil. 2.612–13). The context of mutual suicide also recalls the challenge that Seneca's Hercules gives himself as he resolves to commit suicide after killing his family in a maddened rage, like the Saguntines: "Come, my right hand, endeavor to embark on a mighty work, greater than the twelfth Labor" (*agedum, dextra, conare aggredi | ingens opus, labore bis seno amplius*, Sen. *Her. F.* 1281–82). The Saguntine suicide both evokes the attempted suicide of their patron hero Hercules and may, in turn, be recalled in the mutual slaughter of the Theban brothers.

b. The marveling human observers

Climactic duels in epic are often attended by amazed observers.[39] This tradition begins for Roman epic with Vergil's king Latinus, who marvels as he surveys the champions Aeneas and Turnus (Verg. *A.* 12.707–9):

> stupet ipse Latinus
> ingentis, genitos diuersis partibus orbis,
> inter se coiisse uiros et cernere ferro.

> Latinus himself marvels that such mighty men, born in different parts of the world, have come together to decide their fate with the steel.

What stuns the king is the unlikelihood that such different combatants should have come from such distant shores to kill one another. The Saguntines instead marvel as they kill the people closest to home, who are the most similar to themselves (Sil. 2.617–19):[40]

> inuitas maculant cognato sanguine dextras
> miranturque nefas auersa mente peractum
> et facto sceleri inlacrimant.

---

[39] See Bernstein 2004 on the tradition of viewing duels in Roman epic.
[40] For discussion of a similar inversion of this *Aeneid* passage in Statius's *Thebaid*, see Bessone in this volume (pp. 101–2).

> They are stunned by the unspeakable deed, perpetrated with minds averse, and they weep at the committed crime.

The subsequent narrative will emphasize similarity, not Vergilian difference, as parents kill children and identical twin brothers kill one another. The motif of amazement, however, creates another connection to the brothers' duel in Statius. The Furies marvel as Polynices and Eteocles begin to fight one another without further need for their instigation (Stat. *Theb.* 11.535–38):

>   necdum letalia miscent   535
> uulnera, sed coeptus sanguis, facinusque peractum est.
> nec iam opus est Furiis; tantum mirantur et astant
> laudantes, hominumque dolent plus posse furores.

> Not yet do they mingle death-dealing strokes, but bloodshed has begun and the evil deed is done. There is no more need of the Furies; they only marvel and stand by applauding, chagrined that men's madness is mightier than their own. (transl. Shackleton Bailey)

The overlaps in phrasing noted by the underlines again suggest a dialogue between the two poets.

c. The narrator's envoi to the principals

Silius's narrator endeavors to assign exemplarity to the Saguntine suicide victims in the envoi to *Punica* 2 (Sil. 2.696–98):

> at uos, sidereae, quas nulla aequauerit aetas,
> ite, decus terrarum, animae, uenerabile uulgus.
> Elysium et castas sedes decorate piorum.

> But you, starry souls, whom no age will equal, glory of the world, praiseworthy crowd, go to Elysium and bring honor to the virtuous dwellings of the dutiful.

Statius's narrator similarly exhorts the souls of the Theban brothers to go from this world to the next. But here the emphasis is the opposite: the malevolent brothers can look forward to a afterlife of torture in Tartarus rather than reward in Elysium: "Go, fierce souls, pollute grisly Tartarus with your death and exhaust all the pains of Erebus!" (*ite, truces animae funestaque Tartara leto | polluite et cunctas Erebi consumite poenas!*, Stat. *Theb.* 11.574–75).

The shared phrase *ite … animae* evokes the burial of the war dead in Vergil's *Aeneid*. Aeneas orders his men to perform appropriate rituals for the Trojan and allied fighters who have fallen in the previous days' combats (Verg. *A.* 11.24–26):

> "ite" ait, "egregias animas, quae sanguine nobis
> hanc patriam peperere suo, decorate supremis   25
> muneribus."

> "Go now," he says, "honor with final rituals those outstanding souls, who have obtained this homeland for us with their blood."

These three passages demonstrate Flavian epic's characteristic method of reprising Vergilian heroic motifs in a context that undermines their heroism. Statius's Theban brothers act against the benefit of the Thebans: they eliminate the legitimate line of succession to the throne and leave Thebes vulnerable to Theseus's invasion. Silius's Saguntines may act praiseworthily, but they lose rather than gain their homeland and leave no descendants to benefit from their sacrifice.

d. The narrator's appeal to commemoration

Silius's narrator exhorts the world never to forget the Saguntines' heroic adherence to *fides*: "Hear, o peoples, and do not break peace treaties nor put loyalty second to rule!" (*audite, o gentes, neu rumpite foedera pacis | nec regnis postferte fidem!,* Sil. 2.700–1). Statius's narrator, by contrast, attempts to reverse the epic genre's conventional goal of commemorating for all time the deeds that it relates (Stat. *Theb.* 11.577–79):

> omnibus in terris scelus hoc omnique sub aeuo
> uiderit una dies, monstrumque infame futuris
> excidat, et soli memorent haec proelia reges.
>
> In all lands and every age let one day only have seen such a crime. Let the monstrous infamy be forgotten by future generations and only kings remember this duel. (transl. Shackleton Bailey)

There is no linguistic replay between Silius and Statius in the appeal to commemoration found at the conclusion of both scenes. The point of connection is the rather thematic contrast between Silius's appeal for commemoration and Statius's appeal for amnesia. As Walter observes: "What is problematic here is not so much the fact that the traditional language of epic has totally disappeared, but that it has become so hard to tell the glorious and the reprehensible apart."[41]

---

[41] Walter 2013, 317.

Taken collectively, these passages constitute a clear example of poetic interplay, epic interaction, or bidirectional influence between two contemporary writers of epic, a phenomenon now well studied in the Flavian epics.[42] The question of priority of composition is ultimately undecidable because many of the arguments are reversible. The proposition that Silius composed the fall of Saguntum either before or concurrently with Statius's duel rests mainly on the reference to the Fury in Statius's description of the fall of Saguntum (Stat. *Silu.* 4.6.82–84):[43]

> praecipue cum sacrilega face miscuit arces
> ipsius immeritaeque domos ac templa Sagunti
> polluit et populis Furias immisit honestas.
>
> ... above all when Hannibal with sacrilegious torch mangled the god's own towers, defiling the houses and temples of innocent Saguntum and filling her people with a noble frenzy. (transl. Shackleton Bailey)

Inclusion of Tisiphone appears to be Silius's innovation in a lengthy exemplary tradition. There is no reference to any Fury in Valerius Maximus, Lucan, Petronius, or the Elder Pliny. As Statius's *Siluae* dates to the early 90s, it is plausible that Statius could look back to work Silius had disseminated in the mid- to late-80s, eliminating the potential for positive exemplarity in Silius's scene as he elaborates its grim motifs. If, instead, bidirectional influence is the most likely model for interaction, then both passages mutually reinforce the extreme madness of the characters. The Saguntine suicide recalls the horror of the Theban fratricide, and vice versa.

3 Civil War and the Exemplary Narrative of Suicide

Romans aristocrats could view suicide as an exemplary deed that ennobled its perpetrator, if correctly justified and presented in an appropriately moralized narrative.[44] The Capuan leaders' decorous suicide by poison is in this tradition. By contrast, the Saguntum episode's deforming famine, disgusting wounds, hesitant homicides, and unrecognized victims are all deliberate contrasts to the exemplary suicide narrative. The episode's descriptions of violence allude

---

42 See Lovatt 2010, Marks 2013, Walter 2013.
43 See Coleman 1988 and Littlewood 2011, lix.
44 See Hill 2004.

instead to the slaughters at Massilia and on Vulteius's raft in Lucan's *Bellum Ciuile*. References to the Saguntines' fate recur throughout the *Punica*, tempering the narrative of the Romans' struggle against Hannibal with programmatic reminders of their earlier abandonment of their allies. The heroism of Scipio and other Roman leaders does not fully ameliorate the poem's criticism of the Romans, Hercules, or Fides in the Saguntum episode.[45]

Silius emplots the well-known story of the Saguntine suicide in the context of divine competition. The struggle between Hercules and Fides on one side, and Juno and Tisiphone on the other, to control the events and their reception by posterity mirrors the ambivalence found elsewhere in the tradition of writing about civil war. Silius's narrative literalizes the metaphor found in Valerius Maximus of Fides gazing down upon the besieged town by making her an agent in the text who attempts to lead the Saguntines in armed resistance. The Fury instead turns the violence of the victims against themselves by maddening them and instigating a massacre. This complex framing enables Silius to address one of the major political issues of his own day, the recovery from civil war promised by the Flavian imperial dynasty. Silius's participation as consular in peace negotiations between the Vitellians and the Flavians (Tac. *Hist.* 3.65.2) gave him a perspective not shared by any other epic poet on the role of *fides* in wartime politics, though it should go without saying that we cannot determine how the *Punica* specifically expresses such a perspective.

Silius's account of the Saguntines' loyalty unto death and Tisiphone's partial corruption of their exemplary deed suggests the spectrum of views that a reader of the 90s may have adopted toward contemporary talk of *fides*. The Saguntines received indirect rewards for their loyalty in the form of eventual vengeance by the Romans and a secure place in the exemplary tradition. Were these enough to compensate parents for filicide and brothers for fratricide? Silius creates a contradiction of a type familiar from Lucan's *Bellum Ciuile*, where political context compromises the exemplarity of individual characters' actions. Just as there can be no praiseworthy victory in a civil war, so there can be no praiseworthy mass suicide by perpetrators who have not been allowed to choose their actions. The repeated references to the Saguntines' fate throughout the epic instead create a narrative of negative exemplarity within the *Punica* itself. Characters in the *Punica* remember the Saguntines more frequently for the extremity and unfairness of their suffering than for their *fides*.[46]

---

45 See Dominik 2003; *contra*, Pomeroy 2010.
46 Examples include *non aequo superum genitore euersa Sagunti* (Sil. 3.2), *casus metuit iam Roma Sagunti* (Sil. 3.564), *passamque infanda Saguntum* (Sil. 5.160), *arta fames poenas miserae*

Such implicit criticisms of Roman *fides* during the Punic wars also reflect upon the Romans of the Flavian era.[47] Memories of the recent civil war likely precluded any naïve belief in an immediate reward for the virtue of *fides*. We find similar concerns expressed in a different context in Tacitus's account of the war's outbreak in the *Histories*. The historian introduces the advent of the Flavian era with one story after another of loyalty betrayed and fraud rewarded, from the assassinations of Galba and Piso to the revolt of the German legions.[48] In a telling early example, Piso attempts to convince the soldiers that "your loyalty and reputation remain undamaged to this day. And Nero even deserted you, not you Nero" (*uestra fides famaque inlaesa ad hunc diem mansit. et Nero quoque uos destituit, non uos Neronem*, Tac. *Hist.* 1.30.7–8). The soldiers soon kill Piso and sell his head to his widow (*Hist.* 1.47.2), demonstrating thereby that *fides* means far less to them than cash. As Haynes observes, "the frankness of Piso's statement about the 'empty names' of 'Republic,' 'Senate,' and 'people' is misguided because he has nothing strong enough to offer in their place."[49] The story of the Saguntines' compromised heroism accordingly reflects aspects of the experience of the senatorial class in the Flavian era. The accounts of the transition to the Flavian era show the senatorial class caught up in a clash of forces beyond its control, engaged in a war frequently compared to family violence, and slowly coming to terms with the fact that the pursuit of short-term interest has compromised the traditional evaluation of moral behavior.

---

exactura Sagunti (Sil. 7.280), *captae stimulatus caede Sagunti | Amphitryoniades* (Sil. 9.292), *claro deletum est Marte Saguntum* (Sil. 17.328). Saguntum is recalled in the context of *fides* only at Sil. 12.431–32: *Petilia ... | infelix fidei miseraeque secunda Sagunto*.
47 See Dominik 2003; Dominik 2006.
48 See Ash 1999; Haynes 2003.
49 Haynes 2003, 60.

Steve Mason
Vespasian's Rise from Civil War in Josephus's *Bellum Judaicum*

scriptores temporum, qui potiente rerum Flauia domo monimenta belli huiusce composuerunt, curam pacis et amorem rei publicae, corruptas in adulationem causas, tradidere. nobis ... aemulatione etiam inuidiaque, ne ab aliis apud Vitellium anteirentur, peruertisse ipsum Vitellium uidentur.

Writers of the times, who composed their accounts of this war while the Flavian house was in power, have handed down the motives—perverted on account of obsequiousness—of "concern for peace" and "love of the republic." But in our view ... it was from rivalry and a jealous fear that they would be outdone by others in Vitellius's favor that they overthrew Vitellius himself.

Tac. *Hist.* 2.101.1

With Josephus's *Bellum Judaicum* we are probably getting as close as we ever can to the "official version" (or one of the "official versions") of the Flavian accession.

Beard 2003, 556

Between these two reflections, by an ancient and a modern historian of the early Empire, we have the germ of a problem worth exploring: To what extent did Titus Flavius Josephus promote the Flavian myth of origins disdained by Tacitus? As it happens, his *Judaean War* and *Antiquities* are the only surviving histories from Flavian Rome, and *War* was more or less ready for presentation to Vespasian before his death in June of 79 CE.[1] For that reason alone we might assume that Tacitus, who implies that historians could not avoid flattery before Nerva and Trajan (Tac. *Ag.* 2–3; *Hist.* 1.2), included Josephus in the group. Josephus was undeniably a Flavian protégé, having arrived as a new citizen alongside Titus in 71 CE, after the latter's destruction of his home *polis*, Jerusalem. It is even possible, though not widely agreed upon, that Tacitus knew Josephus's *War*.[2]

---

[1] J. *Vit.* 361; *Ap.* 1.50–53. Scholars have often proposed that at least *BJ* 7 came under Titus or Domitian, but the recent trend is to accept Josephus's plain statements: Jones 2002; Brighton 2009, 33–41; Siggelkow-Berner 2011, 25–33. A neglected point is that *BJ* 1.8 and 1.16 seem to assume that Vespasian and Titus are both alive as Josephus writes.
[2] So Rajak 1983, 193. This possibility is doubted because Tac. *Hist.* 5.1–9 (on Judaean origins) differs markedly from Josephus. But ancient historians were never bound to follow a given source, and Tac. *Hist.* 5.10–13 has conspicuous overlaps with *BJ* 5–6; compare especially *Hist.* 5.13 with *BJ* 6.287–315. Tacitus's friend Suetonius (*Ves.* 4.5–6; 5.6) knew of Josephus. Why not Tacitus?

Although Josephus's thirty surviving volumes deal mainly with Judaean history, scholars have tended to regard the seven-volume *Judaean War*, which includes much material on Vespasian and Titus, as the work of their *Gefolgsmann*. The idea is that Josephus was lifted from destroyed Judaea because of his skills in dissimulation and a willingness to concoct omens for rulers who had staked their claim to power on events in his patch.[3] How could he, given his circumstances, have been anything other than a court historian? Beard's effort to make lemonade from this lemon—"if we want to understand how any political regime wants itself to be seen, where better to go than to the writings of one of its lackeys?"—would be a sensible way of using Josephus's works if this picture were valid.[4] But how valid is it?

Our question is about the extent to which this lone surviving Flavian historian, whose fealty has become a byword, lives up to Tacitus's description of a Flavian press corps, so to speak. The jaded senator's own account of Vespasian's motives goes in a different direction. Using his customary palette, Tacitus depicts a tragic psychological drama, a struggle in Vespasian's very soul between his desire for power and his fear of its dangers. Between the regime's image of a heroic rise propelled by love of country and Tacitus's deep skepticism and humanism, where does Josephus's portrait of the conflict between Vespasian and Vitellius fall? The outcome of such an investigation may affect our understanding of both the nature of Josephus's writing (how sophisticated was it?) and the literary life of Flavian Rome in its varied social layers and two languages. After a brief consideration of Josephus's *Judaean War* and Vespasian's place in it overall, we shall explore the account in Book 4 of the civil war that brought Vespasian to power.

1 Josephus's *Judaean War*: Aims and Interests

Characterization of Josephus's *Judaean War* as Flavian propaganda was nearly universal from the early twentieth century until the 1970s or 80s. In those decades Josephus's works were studied chiefly for what lay beneath the text: events, data, and sources, the last of which many hoped to recover bodily. His works were not yet read as coherent compositions, in the way that the "linguistic turn" following

---

[3] Cf. Künzl 1988, 9 (he stood "auf der Seite der Römer und nicht mehr auf der seines Volkes"); Beard 2003, 558 ("besotted with the Flavians"); Itgenshorst 2005, 28–29 (a member of the *Kaiserhaus*); Curran 2007, 77 ("His depiction of Vespasian is adulatory and that of Titus little short of sycophantic").

[4] Beard 2003, 543.

the Hippie era would recommend. The decisive *data* for understanding Josephus seemed to be: the circumstances in which he wrote, under the gaze of his Flavian masters; his assumed incompetence in Greek learning, hence dependence on regime-supplied literary assistants; a few mildly flattering notices about Vespasian and Titus in the latter half of *Judaean War*; and mention in its proem of an Aramaic precursor to the Greek work, which Josephus claims to have sent to locales in the Parthian empire (J. *BJ* 1.3, 6). This lost forerunner was then vividly imagined as commissioned propaganda, written from Rome at Flavian direction to warn the Parthians against making trouble—given Jerusalem's fate as an example. If the Greek *War* was more or less a *translation* of this effort, made by the assistants provided, it needed little further explanation: it was simply a translation of the same regime propaganda.[5]

The gradual crumbling of this picture over the past generation and more, in specialist circles, has been due to three factors: re-examination of the supposed data on which it rested, a new interest in Josephus's Greek *Judaean War* as a composition worth trying to understand, and a parallel concern to make sense of its place in the corpus. Scrutiny of external conditions has rendered it unlikely that Parthia was a threat in the 70s; that it would, in any case, have been dissuaded by the fate of provincial Jerusalem; or that the Flavians would have commissioned an Aramaic history for Parthian rulers well versed in Greek, to make such an obvious (after Corbulo) and lapidary point.[6]

Compositional study of Josephus's *Judaean War* has fed these doubts. It turns out to be a rich contribution to Greek literature, saturated with classical allusions. It devotes its first and only double-length volume to a tragic history of King Herod, a century before the war or the Flavians. It cannot be the translation of an Aramaic narrative, something Josephus seems to forget about in later accounts of his writing process (*Vit.* 364–67; *Ap.* 1.50–51)—and so that formerly crucial precursor has nearly disappeared from recent research. The Greek work claims instead to be motivated by Josephus's immediate concerns in Flavian Rome and the need to restore Judaea's post-war reputation (*BJ* 1.1–16). His distinctive portraits of Vespasian and Titus, late in the work, are hard to read even as boosterism for the regime, let alone as some kind of deterrent for Parthia.[7]

---

[5] Fundamental were Laqueur 1920, 245–78; Weber 1921, 246 ("prophet of the new Caesar"), 283–84; Thackeray 1929, 3, 15–16, 37–39, 42, 52–53.
[6] Rajak 1983, 174–84.
[7] Lindner 1972; Rajak 1983; Bilde 1988; Mason 1991; Mason 1994; Rajak 1998; Mason 2003; Mason 2005b; McLaren 2005; Eberhardt 2005, 274–75, 277; Goodman 2007, 445, 452; den Hollander 2014 esp. 188–99.

Finally, a *Judaean War* written in Flavian service would not explain how Josephus turned so abruptly to writing the *Judaean Antiquities* and its sequel *Against Apion*, which extol the laws and constitution of his ancient *ethnos*. They have nothing Flavian about them, even though the *magnum opus* was completed under Domitian (*AJ* 20.267; *Vit.* 429). Josephus claims that he had prepared this material for *Judaean War* but thought better of including it there (*AJ* 1.6–7). Whatever we make of that reflection, research has exposed marked continuities of theme and language from his first work to his last, as well as gaps between Josephus's *War* and Flavian claims.[8] Certainly early Christian readers considered Josephus's *Judaean War* a thoroughly Jewish work.[9] Taken together, these kinds of considerations now incline specialists in Josephus to regard his work as part of a coherent literary program from a Judaean perspective, rather than as commissioned propaganda.

What were Josephus's aims and themes, then? Given the limited space available here, a glance at the structure and most prominent motifs of his *Judaean War*, then at the work's proem, must suffice as context for our passage. As for structure, the passage describing the bloody Roman civil war that brought Vespasian to power (*BJ* 4.491–663) comes just past the half-way point of the work. I have argued elsewhere that *Judaean War*'s dramatic plot, which obviously reaches a climax with Jerusalem's destruction in Book 6, is interwoven with a different sort of aesthetic structure, which we might call periodic, concentric, or ring-compositional.[10] That is, the narrative coils itself toward the middle of the work as events tragically align in Jerusalem, and the spindle occupies the middle of the middle volume (*BJ* 4.314–44). There, Jerusalem's revered aristocratic leaders, the chief priests Ananus II and Jesus, are brutally murdered by politically uncouth, power-seeking interlopers ("tyrants") who have overrun Jerusalem from regions north and south. With the loss of the city's virtuous and public-spirited aristocrats, things quickly unravel into the *stasis oikeia* and tyranny anticipated in the preface (*BJ* 1.10). These moves by the "freedom"-spouting men of violence will lead to Jerusalem's tragic fall.

In that dense middle section, Josephus juxtaposes Rome's own would-be tyrants after Nero's death and Galba's murder—Otho and Vitellius—with the Judaean strong men. It is worth noting again that the Flavians do not appear in this

---

[8] Bilde 1988, 121–22; Rajak 1998.
[9] Theoph. *Ad Autol.* 3.23; Tert. *Apol.* 19.6 ("champion/vindicator of the Judaeans' antiquities"); Min. Fel. *Oct.* 33; Clem.Al. *Strom.* 1.21; Origenes, *in Ev.Matt.* 10.17; *Cels.* 1.47; 2.13; Eus. *Hist. eccl.* 3.9.2; Heges. *praef.*
[10] Mason 2016, 94–100.

profoundly Judaean account until near the halfway point (by word count), in Book 3, where they serve first as foils to Josephus's remarkable generalship, the dominant subject of that volume.

Judaean War's unifying themes, running from the preface through the end of Book 7, likewise serve Josephus's interests and do not overlap noticeably with imaginable Flavian concerns. Different readers would cluster these currents differently, but I reckon that four can be distinguished, though they often mingle and mix.[11] The first stream, flagged in Josephus's promise to counter the humiliation of Judaeans, concerns the character of his people, which is embodied in himself. This interest prompts his frequent references to Judaean masculine virtue, martial prowess, dogged endurance, resourcefulness, cheerfulness in adversity, and contempt for death. Second is a large array of themes, familiar to any cultured reader, having to do with *polis* management and its challenges: keeping the populace quiescent in the face of outside threats and internal demagoguery, relations between the mother-*polis* and compatriots on the *chōra*, and those between *polis* leaders and unreliable partners in imperial administration. Third, interwoven with these are themes of a markedly tragic hue, as abrupt reversals of fortune bring *tyrannoi* and overweening ambition into play, and the atmosphere becomes heavy with pity, fear, lament, and the language of classical tragedy. Equally inseparable but still distinguishable are, fourth, potent themes related to the holy temple of Jerusalem, its pollution by compatriot bloodshed, and the necessary purgation. The Flavians, their legions, and supporting forces play assigned roles, certainly, but this is hardly a regime product.

Finally, the proem. Our supposed *Römling* opens his *War* with a frontal attack on the jingoistic histories of the conflict currently being composed in the capital. He knows their substance, perhaps by hearing parts of them recited,[12] and implies that his own efforts have already faced harsh criticism, again suggesting the give and take of an oral literary culture (*BJ* 1.1–8, 13–16). Josephus's characterization of those one-sided Roman accounts, by authors who either lacked first-hand knowledge of the Judaean conflict or were willing to suppress the truth for political advantage, suggests that they propounded the simple Flavian messaging we know from the triumph, coins, and monuments. Namely, under Vespasian and Titus Rome's brave legions justly conquered a hostile nation (*gens*). Josephus charges (*BJ* 1.7):[13]

---

11 For elaboration of what follows, with references, see Mason 2016, 101–21.
12 Cf. Lucianus, *Hist.Conscr.* 5–6, 14–15, 19, 23, 24, 29.
13 Hart 1952; Mason 2016, 3–59.

> They dare to entitle those books "histories," in which there is nothing sound. … Although they want to portray the Romans as great, they are always putting down and humiliating the Judaean side (καταβάλλουσιν δὲ ἀεὶ τὰ Ἰουδαίων καὶ ταπεινοῦσιν).

Although those other accounts are lost, the scene he describes is plausible enough, partly because it reflects human experience across the ages (cf. Allied portraits of a supposedly contemptible Japanese army in World War II) and partly because we have a near-contemporary parallel in the Syrian Lucian's attack on the ill-informed, regime-flattering nonsense making the rounds in connection with Lucius Verus's eastern war of the 160s (Lucianus, *Hist.Conscr.* 2, 7, 13, 24). Josephus counters anti-Judaean misinformation in part by punctuating his narrative with stories of Judaean courage and contempt for death, often at the expense of the storied legionaries.[14] What, then, does he have to say about Vespasian's accession?

The old image of a Flavian apparatchik has yielded, as one might expect in the course of scholarly development, to something much more textured. Josephus emerges as a proud Judaean spokesman, seeking above all to enhance his own status as a master historian and public moralist, whose identity is all tied up with a correct understanding of his ancient *ethnos*. To explore the implications of this for Josephus's position in relation to the Flavians, scholars have invoked post-colonial theory, Frederick Ahl's "safe criticism,"[15] double-speak, and irony.[16] A survey of Vespasian's whole presence in Josephus's *Judaean War* will show why these approaches commend themselves. It is not the paean one would expect from the traditional billing.[17]

2 Vespasian in Josephus's *Judaean War*

Vespasian does not appear in *Judaean War* until Book 3, and by the end of Book 4 he is leaving for Berytus, Antioch, and Alexandria before finally crossing to Rome (*BJ* 4.620, 630, 656). Whatever we make of his character, then, it hardly dominates the story. The basic narrative of Book 3 is that, upon Vespasian's arrival at the coastal Roman colony of Ptolemais, just west of Galilee (Nero having dispatched

---

[14] Mason 2016, 101–6.
[15] Ahl 1984a.
[16] Spilsbury 2003; Barclay 2005; Mason 2005a; Mason 2005b; Barclay 2006. For the often complex positions of proud Greek writers under Roman rule, see Swain 1996.
[17] For the other Flavians see Mason 2016, 121–30.

him from Greece), the region's *polis* leaders rush to welcome him and the Judaean King Agrippa II, even before Titus has reached him with the Fifteenth Legion from the south (*BJ* 3.1–8, 65). The northern Judaean capital Sepphoris is prominent in the welcoming committee, and it requests a Roman garrison to supplement the small one left by Cestius Gallus (*BJ* 3.29–30). Even before the Flavians advance into Galilee, therefore, the region has demonstrated a tranquil posture. And as soon as the Flavians move their menacing 60,000-strong army into the area, the army that Josephus claims to have trained for protection of the Galileans instantly vanishes. Vespasian immediately enjoys theater dominance, while Josephus—who has reportedly always known that war with Rome was hopeless, but has done his duty regardless—makes a beeline for King Agrippa's lakeside resort of Tiberias, far from danger, as he says (*BJ* 3.29–34, 59–69, 127–34).

Josephus is able to make himself the star of his Book 3 only because of Vespasian's massive army. In Tiberias he hears that the small town of Iotapata, where he has friends, is in the sights of Vespasian and his marauding soldiers, after their vicious destruction of nearby Gabara in retaliation for the event that had triggered the war: the Judaean ambush of Cestius's legion as it left the Jerusalem area. Josephus rushes to join the endangered central-Galilean town, apparently in the hope of mediating terms (*BJ* 3.132–34, 141–43). After all, he has recently led a successful diplomatic mission to Nero's court in Rome (*Vit.* 13–16). But when his efforts in Iotapata prove fruitless, he finds himself trapped and unable to flee. Book 3 will now become the story of a contest between two giant generals: Josephus, with nothing but raw resourcefulness, must face down the mighty Vespasian at the head of the world's finest army. Vespasian needs no aggrandizement; everyone in Rome knows of his power. The narrative serves rather to enhance Josephus's image in having the sheer courage and skill to confront him.

The elaborate story of Josephus's surrender to Vespasian continues the battle of wits. In the ways that matter most to his image, Josephus wins—under divine protection. When the legions finally overrun Iotapata, Vespasian sends two tribunes to pledge safety if he will leave his cave (*BJ* 3.344). Certain that this is a lie aimed at exposing him for death, Josephus refuses (*BJ* 3.345). Frustrated that he will not take the bait, Vespasian tries again with the tribune Nicanor, who somehow knows Josephus. Nicanor expatiates on the Romans' innate kindness, while insisting that Vespasian is a huge fan of Josephus's work and can hardly wait to meet him. As he thus lies through his teeth, it is all Nicanor can do to restrain his soldiers from burning the cave with Josephus in it (*BJ* 3.346–51). Josephus, who is obviously right not to trust Vespasian's ploys, still refuses to budge (*BJ* 3.350).

When he finally does move it is not because he thinks that Vespasian will spare him but because God has promised him protection (*BJ* 3.351–54). When he arrives in the Roman camp, his assumptions about Vespasian's intentions are validated. The Roman commander has not the slightest interest in him, while the enraged legionaries want to lynch the man who has kept them outside Iotapata for over a month. Only a sudden change of heart on the part of Titus inspires others to take pity on the young Judaean: "Indeed, he [Titus] became the greatest factor with his father in his preservation" (πλείστη δ' αὐτῷ καὶ παρὰ τῷ πατρὶ μοῖρα σωτηρίας ἐγένετο, *BJ* 3.397).

The surrender story confirms the *Judaean War*'s picture of Vespasian as a wily and tough commander—and congenital dissembler. This last may be no bad thing for a general, whose success depends on deceit,[18] and in his autobiography, Josephus happily recounts his own tricks, lies, and deceptions.[19] But such concessions to military necessity do not constitute flattery, especially when it comes to casually violating pledges of safety, as Vespasian expects to do at Iotapata. Later in Book 3, Vespasian promises anti-Agrippa rebels in lakeside Taricheae that he will spare their lives if they leave town unarmed. Believing him, they put down their weapons. They are then directed through a cordon of soldiers along the road southward, an hour's walk to the stadium of Tiberias. There Vespasian orders many of them killed, others sent to Nero for hard labor, in violation of his pledge (*BJ* 3.532–42). Josephus blames Vespasian's advisors, who in a nod to Thucydides insist that he choose advantage over propriety (λέγοντες καὶ χρῆναι τὸ συμφέρον αἱρεῖσθαι πρὸ τοῦ πρέποντος, *BJ* 3.536). Given that Vespasian elsewhere overrules his advisors with commanding wisdom (e.g., *BJ* 4.366–77), this apparent mitigation may make things worse for the impression made by Josephus's Vespasian.

Episodes involving Vespasian in Book 4 do nothing to lighten these dark hues. First, he leads his soldiers to "unprecedented disaster" in a rash assault on nature's fortress-town, Gamala, a situation that Titus must salvage after the loss of many legionaries (*BJ* 4.20–53, 39, 70). Later, on a trip to the famed Dead Sea (Lake Asphaltites), Vespasian orders certain men who cannot swim to be dropped in its deepest part, with their hands cuffed, to test the lake's reputed buoyancy (*BJ* 4.476–77). They float, happily, although the reader has the feeling that Vespasian would have enjoyed himself as much either way. The story of his bid for imperial power, our focus below, concludes this volume and marks his departure from the Judaean theater.

---

18 Cf. the Flavian work on *Stratagems* by Frontinus, with König in this volume.
19 E.g., *Vit.* 22, 39, 71, 128–30, 141, 148, 163, 168–69, 175–76, 263, 273–74, 282, 287–91, 377–80.

Vespasian is thus used to enhance the image of Josephus and the Judaeans. This becomes clear in *BJ* 4.87–91, as Vespasian sends his legions to winter quarters for several months, between subduing Galilee and invading Judaea. He recognizes the need for intensive athletic training because "He reckoned the high spirits and daring of the [Judaean] men difficult to overcome even without the walls [of Jerusalem]" (*BJ* 4.91). Second, after deciding to bid for imperial power and moving up to Berytus, Vespasian finally releases his prisoner Josephus from chains (*BJ* 4.622–29). Our man has been manacled for two years because Vespasian had spared him only at Titus's insistence and never trusted him, as Josephus repeats (*BJ* 4.625). Now that Vespasian is planning to seize power, however, he sees the wisdom in rewarding all his omen-producers and so decides to release Josephus. Josephus makes it clear that this is only a long-delayed recognition of Josephus's courage (in giving Vespasian such a hard time outside Iotapata, then predicting his rise while Nero was still emperor), his "trustworthy knowledge of things to come," and his status as "minister of the voice of God." The passage is about the virtues of Josephus, not Vespasian.

Vespasian will appear again in the *Judaean War*, as emperor but still displaying his familiar character traits. He will decline the separate triumph offered him by the Senate in order to take first position in Titus's event for the destruction of Jerusalem. This is a more spectacular achievement than anything Vespasian accomplished in southern Syria, and their joint parade (as Domitian's later Arch of Titus) will feature the temple furnishings as the war's foreign spoils. These too, from Titus's victory, Vespasian covets. After the triumph, he will divide them between his palace and, after 75 CE, the new Flavian Forum and Temple to Pax (*BJ* 7.121, 148, 152, 158, 161–62).

Josephus thus presents Vespasian overall as a tough, shrewd, and usually effective general. His odder behavior passes without overt criticism, any potential for censure being left between the lines. It is nevertheless difficult to find anything approaching adulation. Vespasian looks realistically human and unique: certainly a great man favored by fortune, but hardly the object of panegyric.

3 Josephus on the Civil War and Vespasian's Rise

As we turn now to Josephus's account of Vespasian's rise, my proposal *in nuce* is that Josephus's account is much closer to Tacitus's cool analysis than to a regime-coddling historiography. Although not hostile to Vespasian, of course, Josephus's narrative serves his interests. Why the Flavians found Josephus's *Judaean War* valuable is a question worth exploring elsewhere, but the reason cannot be that he disseminated their self-image.[20] I wish to highlight Josephus's independence from the Flavian program by considering four aspects of his account: its possible implication that Vespasian's victory in civil war—one initiated by him—was his decisive military achievement; Josephus's assimilation of Vespasian's story to the civil strife among Judaean tyrants; his redating of crucial events in the Flavian calendar; and, coming full circle, his analysis of Vespasian's motives for initiating the war with Vitellius.

3.1 Vespasian as Initiator of—and Victor in—*Bellum Ciuile*

The mere fact that Josephus includes the pre-Flavian civil war, while downplaying any threat to Rome from Judaea, seems an index of his independence. Classical literature everywhere laments the blight of civil or compatriot discord.[21] This is the principle adduced by Dionysius to justify his preference for Herodotus as master historian over the lauded Thucydides: Thucydides, he grumbles, chose shameful inner-Greek warfare as his subject (D.H. *Pomp.* 3).

In Rome, everyone knew that civil strife had plagued the late Republic and early Empire, but the public preferred to hear about victories over foreigners.[22] Carsten Lange has effectively challenged the perception that Romans programmatically excluded hints of civil strife from memorializations of successful wars.[23] But he does not deny the odium that attached to initiating a civil war, as distinct from ending one, or the general desirability of harnessing civil strife to a nobler foreign conflict.[24] Near the end of his life Augustus mentioned his suppression of domestic conflicts to illustrate his justice and clemency, albeit in oblique terms

---

20 See Mason 2016, 129–30.
21 On στάσις οἰκεία see Pl. *R.* 5.470c–d; similar phrases are in App. *Mith.* 83.4; *BC* 4.3.14; D.C. 53.8.2. The classic narrative is Th. 3.82–84 (at Corcyra), but the theme is also prominent in Herodotus (Hdt. 1.59.3, 60.2, 150.1; 3.82.3; 5.28.1; 6.109.5); Isoc. *Paneg.* 4.79, 114, 174; Pl. *Lg.* 1.628c, 629c–d; Arist. *Ath.* 5.2–3, 13.1; *Pol.* 1265b; D.S. 9.11.1; 11.72.2, 76.6, 86.3, 87.5; Plu. *Mor.* 16.813a, 32.823f–825b; D.Chr. 1.82; Paus. 3.2.7; 4.18.3. Salient literature includes Lintott 1982; Keitel 1984; Gehrke 1985; Henderson 1998; Price 2001; and on Josephus's usage, Rajak 1983, 91–94; Feldman 1998, 140–48; Mader 2000, 55–103; Mason 2012.
22 See the previous note and Lange 2009, 73–93.
23 Lange 2009, 73, 79, 93.
24 Lange 2009, 68. Note the careful formulation (my emphasis) concerning Octavian's war, 49: "There can be no doubt that the war, when it finally came, *was represented as a foreign war*; Octavian successfully avoided starting a civil war. But looking at the chronology and the context of events from 36–32 BC, even if there was an *official stress on Cleopatra as the formal enemy*, this did not conceal that Actium was *at the same time a civil war*."

except concerning the murderers of his father Julius Caesar (*RG* 2–3.1, 34.1). His tone in recounting his many salutations as *imperator*, triumphs, and additions of territories to Rome's *imperium*, symbolized by foreign kings humbled before him in triumph, was different altogether (*RG* 4, 15, 21.2–3, 26–33).

The political benefits of using a foreign conflict to distract from suffering at home are obvious. Concerning Octavian's behavior on returning to Rome after defeating Antony and Cleopatra, Cassius Dio says that with all the money he splashed around, "the Romans forgot all their conflicts and viewed his triumph with pleasure—as though the defeated were foreigners all" (ὡς καὶ ἀλλοφύλων ἁπάντων τῶν ἡττηθέντων ὄντων εἶδον, D.C. 51.21.4). Claudius used his invasion of Britain and ensuing triumph (44 CE) to expunge memories of the crisis that had led to Gaius Caligula's recent murder, which had potentially dire implications for his own rule: the remaining consul of 41 CE, Cn. Sentius Saturninus, had demanded a change in the form of government (e.g., Suet. *Cl.* 11). According to Eutropius, Claudius's British campaign allowed him to give Sentius high honors from an easy foreign conquest (Eutr. 7.13.2).

The Flavian situation was clear in this respect. The really devastating war(s) for Romans had begun with the revolts of the ex-consuls Julius Vindex and Sulpicius Galba, early in 68 CE, with the citizen armies under their command. The former was violently blocked by the legions under Verginius Rufus, legate in Germania Superior. Galba succeeded, but his victory attracted the ire of two other senators commanding citizen armies: Vitellius and Otho. The toll of those internal conflicts was so devastating that ancient writers attributed Otho's suicide, following the Battle of Bedriacum, not to irrecoverable defeat but to his refusal to countenance the deaths of more Roman soldiers—more than the alleged 80,000 already taken.[25] The six-month struggle that would ensue between Vitellius and Vespasian claimed many thousands more. This internecine war reached the streets of Rome itself, finally setting ablaze the ancient temple to Jupiter Optimus Maximus. The civil wars that brought Vespasian to power obviously mattered more immediately to Romans than whatever was happening in southern Syria.

As everyone knows, nevertheless, the Flavians managed to take their suppression of unrest in the 130-year-old province of Syria, which had dubious claims to meriting a triumph at all,[26] and represent it as one of the greatest foreign

---

[25] Suet. *Otho* 9.3; D.C. 64.10.2–3.
[26] Judaea had been conquered by Pompey in 64/63 BCE and been under continuous Roman administration since. Even if the period of the revolt (66–70 CE) marked a notional interval of independence, that could hold only for walled Jerusalem. The rest of the region, including all Judaean centers in Galilee and Peraea, had welcomed Vespasian's arrival and sought peace.

conquests ever, over the whole Eastern Menace.[27] The triumph, the Flavians' ambitious building program, and their empire-wide production of celebratory coins grounded their ruling legitimacy in alleged conquest of a foreign *gens*.

What was our Judaean author up to, then, pulling the skeletons of civil war out of the Flavian closet, during the high season of this jubilation over foreign victory in the seventies? The question is all the more interesting when we recall that Josephus structures his work such that Book 1 gives full attention to Judaea's real Roman conquest by Pompey, in 64–63 BCE. The great general had refrained from seizing temple furnishings, in contrast to the Flavians, who depended on them. Moreover, Pompey's conquest had laid the foundation for 130 years of successful Roman administration, which Josephus's *Judaean War* describes over successive generations. If I am correct in proposing that Josephus's account of the Flavian triumph has an ironic tone, since the author cannot take seriously the claim that Vespasian and Titus conquered Judaea,[28] we must be curious about his handling of Vespasian's conflict with Vitellius in Book 4.

This question becomes yet more interesting if Josephus portrays Vespasian as initiating a civil war against Vitellius. Modern historians tend to think of one civil war after Nero, running continuously from the revolt in spring 68 CE, which Vespasian finally ended. But could we be falling into the classic historian's fallacy of hindsight (or teleological) compression? One problem is how to know when a civil war is truly over. A foreign war is clearly finished when a Carthage, Corinth, or Jerusalem is reduced to rubble and ash, foreign fighters are dead or enslaved, and their leaders have been killed or captured for display. Such definitive endings are not possible in internal conflicts. The homeland cannot be destroyed, and killing some number of internal opponents might only energize those who have been quietly sympathetic. The insidious nature of civil war helps to explain why it is considered such a curse.

That said, Vitellius had good reasons to consider Rome's civil war over, after Otho took his own life on 16 April 69 CE, or at least when the Senate recognized him as sole ruler days later. Vitellius had set out to topple Galba and then the new rival Otho. Since he had prevailed in April 69 and there were no giants left to slay,

---

Exceptions were smaller sites endangered by Vespasian's marauders that showed resistance (Iotapata and Iapha) or towns recently given to King Agrippa II that opposed him (Tiberias, Taricheae, hence Gamala). The Flavians had encircled Jerusalem by the spring of 68 CE (Vespasian was able to ride up to its walls, even after Simon's forces had entered, in spring 69 CE: *BJ* 4.550–55), though Titus would not besiege the city until after a nearly two-year suspension of the campaign, in 70 CE. See Mason 2016, 292–93.

27 See Mason 2016, 4–43.
28 See Mason 2017.

he had every reason to think it finished. He could begin the task of uniting the empire's legions and their commanders under his leadership. That is what his beautiful coins proclaim: "the concord of the Roman People," "the consensus of all the armies," and even—taking presumptive ownership of Vespasian's campaign—"victory" in the east.[29] The tales of his lewd conduct after Otho's demise, whatever their historical merits, incidentally confirm that he no longer considered his army at war. During the three months it took him to reach Rome, he must have believed Rome's internal wars to be over.

He was wrong, of course. Soon after his arrival in Rome he learned of Vespasian's challenge, with the sole support of the eastern armies. But what does this challenge mean? Tacitus describes the period in his *Histories*, beginning from Galba, as including three civil wars (*trina bella ciuilia*), with more external conflicts and most sharing elements of both (*Hist*. 1.2). The first two civil wars appear to be those of Vitellius against Otho and Vespasian against Vitellius. He portrays Vespasian weighing up the prospects of initiating a *bellum* against Vitellius (*Hist*. 2.74), which can mean nothing other than civil war. Suetonius likewise remarks with insouciance that Vespasian, "initiating a civil war" (*suscepto ... ciuili bello, Ves*. 7.1), sent commanders and armies to Italy as he seized control of Alexandria. But those authors wrote a generation after the events. More surprising is that it seems impossible to read Josephus's account, composed while Vespasian ruled, any differently. Josephus does not pretend that Vespasian thought there was an existing civil war, in which he should intervene to end. Rather, the upsetting news that Vitellius has risen to supreme power leads him to ponder whether to use his knowledge of how to be governed or of how to govern (καίπερ ἄρχεσθαι καθάπερ ἄρχειν καλῶς ἐπιστάμενον, *BJ* 4.589). Unable to accept Vitellius as master, he launches a civil war against a ruler with no other rivals, duly recognized by the Senate.

It seems no great leap to imagine that Vespasian and Titus maintained such a disciplined focus on Jerusalem for a decade and more, as we see in their constructions and coins, precisely because it was so obvious that Vespasian had come to power by initiating a *bellum ciuile*. Blackening the character of Vitellius, as our sources unanimously do, could only go so far. The safer way to get past the stigma of civil war was to change the conversation, redirecting attention to Vespasian's other role as commander of a proper war against foreigners, in which he personally faced hazards and personal injury on behalf of all Romans.

---

29 Respectively, from British Museum examples: BM R.6585 (aureus), BM 2011,4133.1 (silver), and BM 1872,0709.466, 1950,1006.972, 1964,0401.4, R.10275 (bronzes).

Interest in Rome's internal power struggles turns out to be characteristic of Josephus. As a matter of principle he favors government by hereditary aristocracy and views monarchy as latent tyranny, even if a given king rules justly, because of the inevitable succession problem.[30] Further, the *Judaean War*'s opening sentence highlights the disease of Roman domestic strife that followed Nero's demise. It refers explicitly to civil war, which induced "many" to contend for monarchical rule (πολλοὺς μὲν βασιλειᾶν ὁ καιρὸς ἀνέπειθεν), even as soldiers were looking to maximize their profits (*BJ* 1.4–5). The only occurrence of βασιλειάω ("contend for sovereignty") outside of this prologue passage is in *BJ* 4.546, describing Vitellius's war against Otho. So we have a programmatic entrée to the civil war after Nero as a matrix for power-seeking among strong men in both Rome and Judaea. *War*'s long first volume arrays the powerful men of the late Republic—Pompey, Crassus, Caesar, Cassius, Mark Antony, Octavian—as they cross the Judaean stage in turn, each enjoying his moment in the sun before the next one topples him. Judaea's leaders, notably the wily Antipater and his son King Herod, constantly adapt to this unstable Roman background.

Book 2 devotes a surprising amount of space, in a work on Judaean history, to affairs in Rome following Gaius's assassination (*BJ* 2.204–14). The standoff between the Praetorian Guard, supporting their chosen monarch Claudius, and the Senate, who demand a return to aristocratic rule, anticipates the volume Josephus will devote to this crisis in *Antiquities* (*AJ* 19). But the *Judaean War*'s language already shows that he includes this material with thoughtful purpose, as part of the Rome-Jerusalem dialectic. For he remarks that the Senate, led by the consuls, intended either to re-establish their aristocratic government or to choose a worthy *princeps*. Either way, they "voted to make war on Claudius," though the force at their disposal was negligible (*BJ* 2.204). Claudius replies from the Praetorian camp (*BJ* 2.210):

> An area must be pre-arranged outside the *polis* for the *polemos*, for it would not be holy for the sacred precincts of our native land to be polluted by compatriot murder—on account of their bad decision (οὐ γὰρ ὅσιον διὰ τὴν αὐτῶν κακοβουλίαν ὁμοφύλῳ φόνῳ μιαίνεσθαι τὰ τεμένη τῆς πατρίδος).

Since compatriot slaughter and the pollution of sacred precincts are central themes of Josephus's Judaean story,[31] this is no mere filler, nor is its diction arbitrary. An important effect of this dialectic is to puncture the popular post-war

---

30 Mason 2012.
31 Mason 2016, 101–21.

image of the Judaeans as primitives congenitally opposed to Rome.[32] Rather, the Judaeans have capable leaders who have long worked with Roman partners, but both nations have faced the scourge of civil conflict.

Near the end of the work, Josephus concludes this thread with his final remark on the triumph, an event ostentatiously about a foreign war. He calmly intrudes on this picture with his reflection: "For on this day the city of Rome held a festival for the victory of its army over [foreign] enemies, the cessation of its internal ills (πέρας δὲ τῶν ἐμφυλίων κακῶν), and the beginning of hopes for happiness" (*BJ* 7.157).

Josephus's *Judaean War* thus maintains a dialectic between Roman and Jerusalemite internal conflict. Each side has its public-spirited leaders, fickle masses, and self-serving strong men. In place of the Flavian portrait of a rebellious (even previously unconquered) *gens* in the East receiving its just deserts, Josephus presents a complex account of productive amity between the two great nations, tried and tested since the days of Pompey, Augustus, and Herod. In ways understandable to anyone familiar with the sweep of Greek literature, however, our statesman-author charts the tragic internal conflicts that arose in Nero's last days, when established government collapsed and fateful collisions put tyrants at the helm in both centers.

3.2 Judaean and Roman Civil War—and Their Tyrants

The narrative of particular interest to us, concerning the civil war that brought Vespasian to power, is part of this thematic dialectic. Table 1 shows the constant movement between Rome and Jerusalem. This is not merely for a change of scene. Explicit connectors and transitional passages compel Josephus's audience to bring the two locations into conversation.

---

32 E.g., "This man, in the bloom of youth, will put an end to fierce war with the nation of Palestine (*fera gentis* | *bella Palaestinae*)" (Sil. 3.605–6).

Tab. 1: *BJ* 4.492–663. Josephus Interweaves Judaean and Roman Civil War

Rome	Rome/Judaea fused	Judaea
4.492–96: surveys ἐμφύλιος πόλεμος from Nero's death to defeat of Vitellius's legions		
	4.497–501: Vespasian's concern for *Rome's* civil war; abortive mission of Titus to Galba; Judaean campaign suspended	
		4.502–44: non-Flavian war in Judaea; rise of Simon bar Giora—at Masada, Judaean hills, opposition to John and Disciples, devastates Acrabatene and Idumaea, rescues wife from kidnap by Disciples, threatens Jerusalem
4.544–49: *stasis* and civil war in Rome: struggle between Othonian and Vitellian forces; Otho's suicide; Vitellius enters Rome in force (μετὰ τῆς δυνάμεως)		
		4.550–84: "Meanwhile" Vespasian consolidates hold on Judaea. Simon returns to Jerusalem's walls. Idumaeans mutiny from John's army and join surviving elite, invite Simon, who enters in April 69 CE.
4.585–87: "At about this very time heavy sufferings engulfed Rome." Galba arrives and turns the capital into an armed camp. His soldiers plunder and kill from unchecked avarice.		
	4.588–629: Vespasian wants to attack wretched Vitellius but is aware of the perils;	

Rome	Rome/Judaea fused	Judaea
	arguments of soldiers; Vespasian feels entitled but balks at risks; is forced by soldiers with swords drawn. Writes to Tiberius Julius Alexander, who secures Alexandria's legions. In Berytus Vespasian frees Josephus.	
4.630–55: Flavian forces in Italy defeat Vitellians; defection of Aelius Caecina; murder of Vespasian's brother; elevation of his son Titus.		
		4.656–63: Vespasian, in Alexandria, dispatches Titus to Judaea "to take out/destroy Jerusalem" (ἐξαιρήσοντα τὰ Ἱεροσόλυμα).

In the large block *BJ* 4.502–44, for example, Josephus connects Roman and Judaean events both chronologically and thematically. At the beginning, he says of Vespasian and Titus (*BJ* 4.502–3):

> Being in suspense about the larger events, as Rome's *imperium* was shaken to the core, they looked away from the campaign against Judaeans. Given their fear for their homeland, they considered it the wrong moment for an assault on foreign peoples. But *another war* loomed over Jerusalem. There was a certain Simon son of Giora, a Gerasene by origin: a young man unequal to John (who already controlled the city) in craftiness, but surpassing him in strength of body and audacity.

After elaborating this conflict in Jerusalem between "the tyrants" John and Simon, he opens the next block (in Table 1) with a bridge back to sedition and tyranny in Rome. Whether or not Josephus's audience should have noticed parallels between the older-and-shrewd Galba and more vigorous Otho, on the Roman side, and older-but-cunning John and younger Simon in Judaea, Josephus connects the two conflicts with language such as this (*BJ* 4.545–46):

> *Stasis* and civil war were not only in Judaea but had also come upon Italy. For Galba had been done away with in the middle of the Roman Forum, and as Otho was designated *imperator* he was at war with Vitellius, who was contending for royal power, for the legions in Germany had elevated him.

Josephus does not spell out the chronology that supports his narrative moves, though the Roman side was presumably fresh in his audience's mind. After describing the contest between Otho and Vitellius (January–April 69 CE), he gives the lunar month of Xanthicus (March/April) of 69 CE as the time of Simon bar Giora's entry into Jerusalem and the onset of extreme violence there. Greek-speaking audiences might have noticed that this coincided with the victory of Vitellius and his nervous-making approach to Rome.[33] In each capital, the arrival of the usurper with unruly forces from elsewhere brings turmoil and pollution to the sacred *polis*.

I am not suggesting that Josephus matches the two sides, person for person, in any precise or allegorical way. It is a matter of atmosphere and evocation: such tyrants all share certain traits and behaviors. Most striking are their indulgence, lack of masculine self-control, and effeminacy.[34] For example, Vitellius attracts the only two occurrences of the noun λαγνεία in Josephus, a graphic word ("semen") used metonymically here for power-lust (*BJ* 4.596, 652). Josephus remarks of this Roman: "If he had survived to a full life-span, I reckon that the Empire itself would have failed to satisfy his λαγνεία" (*BJ* 4.652). Consider also these passages:

BJ 4.586–87:

> Vitellius was now present from Germany, dragging along with his army a different sort of vast rabble. Being unable to accommodate them in the area marked off for soldiers, he made the whole of Rome into a military camp and filled every house with armed fighters. Seeing the wealth of the Romans with such impressionable eyes, with silver and gold glittering everywhere they looked, these fellows could hardly restrain their desires (τὰς ἐπιθυμίας μόλις κατεῖχον). The result was that they could not be turned from plunder, while they did away with all those who obstructed them.

BJ 4.592–93 [Vespasian's men in Judaea talk amongst themselves]:

> Those soldiers in Rome, who are <u>indulging themselves</u> and unable to bear even <u>hearing a rumor of war</u> (τρυφῶντες καὶ μηδ' ἀκούειν πολέμου φήμην ὑπομένοντες), are voting in those whom they want in power and appointing emperors in the hope of profits, whereas <u>we</u>, who have come through so many hardships and are ageing under these helmets, yield

---

33 Morgan 2006, 139, 152–53.
34 Cf. Tac. *Hist.* 2.73.1: "Both he himself [Vitellius] and the army, as if they had no rival to fear, with savagery, lust, and rapine indulged fully in foreign behaviors (*saeuitia libidine raptu in externos mores proruperant*)."

this authority to those guys. And we do this even though we have someone here among us who is much more worthy of ruling!

BJ 4.651:

Then Vitellius comes out of the palace, drunk and stuffed, having gorged himself from a table for the doomed, as happens in extreme circumstances.

Or compare these remarks about Vitellius and the wild Rhine army with Josephus's picture of John of Gischala and his rustic fighters, newly arrived from Galilee in Jerusalem (BJ 4.560–63):

Their longing for plunder was indefatigable, as was their searching of rich people's homes; murder of men and violation of women was their sport. They washed down what they had robbed with blood, and when full they insolently behaved like women: styling their hair and putting on women's clothes, soaking themselves in perfumes and, for a fetching look, applying eyeliner. It was not only the makeup they imitated, however, but also women's passions. With extraordinary wantonness they dreamed up illicit sexual modes. They wallowed about the *polis* as though in a brothel and polluted everything with their impure actions. But while feminizing their faces, they murdered with their right hands. Adopting an unmanly gait, they fell upon men suddenly and became warriors. Bringing out swords from their fancy dyed gowns, they ran through the fellow they happened to meet.

What unites the two civil wars most conspicuously, of course, is that the Flavians end both—Vespasian defeating Vitellius, Titus handling John and Simon.

Gwyn Morgan highlights a chronological problem with Josephus's BJ 4.586–87, which is quoted above: namely, Josephus makes the reported actions of Vitellius and his soldiers *in Rome* the cause of Vespasian's decision to enter the fray. But Vitellius could not have reached Rome before Vespasian's acclamation on 1 July 69 CE, which means that Vespasian and his supporters could not have been inspired by reports about Vitellius's behavior in Rome.[35]

Plainly, Josephus has fused Vespasian's disgust for Vitellius with the man's alleged later behavior in the capital itself. But it is still plausible that Vespasian made his bid for power because of his hatred for Vitellius, in power from mid-April, influenced by reports about him. Vitellius was recognized by the Senate as soon as word of Otho's death in mid-April reached Rome (Tac. *Hist.* 2.50–55). Tacitus claims that his forces, once relieved of war against Otho, began behaving atrociously toward local populations throughout Italy: "robbing and plundering and polluting with violence and lust," they "plunged with foreign manners into cruelty, sexual crime, and plunder" (*Hist.* 2.56, 73). In Tacitus, this reported

---

35 Morgan 2006, 182.

behavior frames Vespasian's consideration of his options (*Hist.* 2.74–79) well before Vitellius arrives in Rome (*Hist.* 2.89). Josephus's claim that Vespasian is enraged when he "hears about the troubles in Rome *and* that Vitellius was emperor" (*BJ* 4.588) is not very different, in spite of the chronological error. His audience in Flavian Rome would presumably have overlooked such a compression, although indeed Vespasian's actual motives (now lost to us) may have sprung from older and colder political calculations.

3.3 When and How Did Things Begin?

A different sort of chronological problem is much more consequential. Not only does Josephus inconveniently portray Judaea as a longstanding ally of Rome, against the simple claims of the triumph, and not only does he draw attention to Vespasian's initiation of civil war against Vitellius. Even the basic sequence of events he provides for Vespasian's acclamation differs awkwardly from the authorized version. The Flavians and their pliant Senate antedated Vespasian's *dies imperii* to the calends of July 69 CE, because that was the day on which Egypt's Prefect, Tiberius Julius Alexander, led his two legions in an oath of allegiance to Vespasian, nearly six months before the issue with Vitellius was actually settled in Rome (Suet. *Ves.* 6.3). As always in political fights, early support is remembered and treasured. As Tacitus puts it (*Hist.* 2.79):

> initium ferendi ad Vespasianum imperii Alexandriae coeptum, festinante Tiberio Alexandro, qui kalendis Iuliis sacramento eius legiones adegit.

> The first step in transferring the *imperium* to Vespasian occurred in Alexandria, where Tiberius Alexander moved quickly and administered the oath of allegiance to his legions on the calends of July.

The official story cherished the Egyptian Prefect's independence of political judgement. Suetonius claims that he was influenced by a straw poll taken among a large detachment of Moesia's legionaries (Suet. *Ves.* 6.3). Looking for a strong leader of consular rank after Otho's death, that force had chosen Vespasian over Vitellius, in turn influenced by comrades who had come from Syria. Tiberius Alexander saw which way the wind was blowing and made the first open declaration for Vespasian, with some confidence of broader legionary support in the East against Vitellius's forces from the West.

However he came to his decision, it was important that Tiberius Alexander be understood to have acted independently, setting off a chain reaction that strengthened Vespasian to confront Vitellius. The convergence of his decision with the support of Syria's legate Mucianus, the Danubian provinces, and soon Vespasian's own three legions in Judaea,[36] distinguished this bid for power from a *coup d'état*. The need for action against Vitellius was supposedly recognized by many independent commanders and senators with armies, and Vespasian humbly accepted the duty thrust upon him. That story would be more or less wrecked if people thought that Vespasian's plan sprang from his personal desires and a conspiracy among his intimates in Judaea.

Enter Josephus. Most inconveniently, his story has Vespasian first acclaimed by the commanders and troops around him in Caesarea (*BJ* 4.588).[37] They act from mixed motives, among which their indignation and hopes for personal status and power figure largely (*BJ* 4.602–4, 616–21). This greatly complicates the Flavian story, even as it anticipates the Judaean author's later assertions about mysterious ancient oracles that had predicted all this even though most of his people did not see it.[38] In those later passages, he connects Vespasian's rise with ambiguous ancient scriptures which no scholar has been able to identify, predicting that "someone from their [Judaean] land would come to rule the inhabited earth" (ἀπὸ τῆς χώρας αὐτῶν τις ἄρξει τῆς οἰκουμένης, *BJ* 6.312–13; cf. 3.352–53).

The alleged prediction is ambiguous indeed. Does it mean that someone from their land will rule or that, from their land, someone will begin his rule? With the great advantage that the oracle does not exist now and perhaps did not then, Josephus insists on the latter reading, "he received the imperium in Judaea" (ἀποδειχθέντος ἐπὶ Ἰουδαίας αὐτοκράτορος, *BJ* 6.313). Although mysterious oracles play no role in the accession story itself, it is reasonable to imagine that, in

---

36 The legions of Judaea acclaimed Vespasian on 11 July according to Suetonius (*Ves.* 6.3) and on 3 July according to Tacitus (*Hist.* 2.79).
37 Morgan 2006, 178, 182, places Vespasian on Mt. Carmel in May–June of 69 CE, apparently assuming Tacitus's support, for Mucianus's speech and the fateful decision. Tacitus only mentions Carmel, however, in the paragraph following Mucianus's speech, as Vespasian recalls omens in his favor, including one on Mt. Carmel. Tacitus does have them disperse from their meeting place, Mucianus to Antioch and Vespasian to Caesarea (*Hist.* 2.79), but since he does not say where they were, the colony of Berytus (cf. *Hist.* 2.81) seems a more likely meeting place for Vespasian and Mucianus; indeed, that is where Josephus has them meet shortly after Vespasian's acclamation in Caesarea (*BJ* 4.620–21).
38 Nicols 1978, 72–73, with most others who considered Josephus a Flavian mouthpiece, did not explain this departure from crucial Flavian chronology. Weber 1921, 168–69 n. 1, consigned it to a lengthy footnote, suggesting that there was no real problem if one considered the complexity of events in both Caesarea and Alexandria, which must have overlapped. His interest was in the underlying realities and sources rather than in what the text implies, though he conceded that foregrounding the Caesarean acclamation suited Josephus's narrative. Lindner 1972, 65, may have been the first to highlight this important index of Josephus's independence from the Flavians.

having Vespasian acclaimed first in territory the vicinity of Judaea, Josephus was laying the ground for the scriptural link—if he was not also declaring a reality he knew, in spite of Flavian claims.

Whatever Josephus's precise train of thought was, he shatters the official scheme completely when he adds that Vespasian, once he reluctantly yielded to his soldiers' demand that he accept power, immediately understood the strategic importance of Egypt and therefore wrote to Tiberius Alexander to solicit his support, explaining that his army's zeal had forced him to assume the burden of power (*BJ* 4.616–19). When Alexander duly administers the oath of allegiance to Vespasian, therefore, in Josephus's account he does so as the obliging equestrian prefect of a province neighboring the province of a senator who commanded a large army. Any independence of mind or originality has vanished. Vespasian has conscripted him, making him an offer he cannot easily refuse.

3.4 Personal Animus as Motive

The motives that Josephus attributes to Vespasian, finally, suit his dramatic tendencies and "realistic" portrait of the Roman better than does the reported Flavian story of simple virtue saving the Republic from civil war. After Nero's death, Josephus and Tacitus agree, Vespasian and Titus had no reservations about serving the septuagenarian blueblood Galba (*Hist.* 1.10).[39] When Galba was murdered in mid-January of 69 CE, however, Vitellius (one cause of his demise) and brash young Otho seemed to the Flavians equally repugnant successors.[40] Both historians describe Titus's immediate termination of his journey to greet Galba, somewhere around Corinth, when he learned of Galba's lynching; but only Tacitus mentions a popular rumor that Titus had actually been going to Rome in the hope of being adopted by Galba, and only he discloses Titus's internal dialogue on hearing that Galba was dead (*Hist.* 2.1). The young Flavian weighs the

---

39 Morgan 2006, 177–79, plausibly suggests that Vespasian became unsettled by the lack of communication from Galba, including fear for his position as Nero's man, and that his dispatch of Titus in late 68 CE was calculated to settle the matter. Then again, since Galba only reached Rome in October and Vespasian had to hear that news and respond, Titus's trip (with King Agrippa II, for which see below) is sufficiently explained without deep speculation about Vespasian's worries until then.

40 All classes united in thinking that *utrasque impias preces, utraque detestanda uota inter duos, quorum bello solum id scires, deteriorem fore qui uicisset* ("prayers for either would be ungodly, vows for either of these two abominable; in their war, you knew only that the winner would be the worse one," Tac. *Hist.* 1.50.3).

pros and cons of continuing to greet the new man (who would not thank him for honors he had intended for Galba, and who might turn hostile) or instead turning back (risking offense to the new man, but secure with his father in Caesarea). And although Tacitus mentions that Vespasian had dutifully administered oaths of loyalty in Judaea to Otho and Vitellius, in turn (*Hist*. 1.76; 2.6, 73), in his account Vespasian begins weighing his prospects already from the time of Galba's murder (15 January 69 CE). Titus's decision to return rather than meet Otho or Vitellius, which opens Book 2 of the *Histories*, is a turning point in these calculations, which creates its own momentum (*Hist*. 2.1–7).

Josephus agrees on the basic story. He, however, in having Titus accompanied by the key Flavian ally King Agrippa II, strengthens the impression that their shared purpose was to honor old Galba and receive his orders for Judaea (*BJ* 4.498). The Judaean king's presence, unmentioned by Tacitus, would undermine popular speculation about Titus's hidden purpose (*Hist*. 2.1). When the pair hear the news of Galba's death, according to Josephus, Agrippa realizes that he must continue to Rome in any case, for he can be nothing other than a loyal allied king, whoever should take power, whereas Titus abruptly turns back to confer with his father (*BJ* 4.501–2). Josephus attributes Titus's decision to an "otherworldly impulse" (κατὰ δαιμόνιον ὁρμὴν), the cause of many fateful developments in this work.[41] Their different choices, and Josephus's notice that both Flavians were "in suspense" given the empire's instability, show that Titus and his father are in a position to influence events, whereas Agrippa is not. Even in Josephus, the Flavians are players in high Roman politics long before Vespasian hears of Vitellius's offensive behavior.

Once Vitellius emerges victorious from the struggle with Otho, however, both historians portray Vespasian as deeply conflicted. According to Tacitus, Vespasian was "at one moment buoyed by hope, at the next pondering the consequences of failure"—death for himself and his two sons, if a bid for power should fail (*Hist*. 2.74). Josephus explores a similar psychological drama, which is all the more vivid here because it is driven by potent personal animosity. He uses a variety of terms to make Vespasian's outrage palpable: the indignation (ἀγανάκτησις, *BJ* 4.589), the overwhelming distress and unbearable torment (περιαλγήσας δὲ τῷ πάθει καρτερεῖν τὴν βάσανον, *BJ* 4.590), the anger (θυμός, *BJ* 4.591), the rage (ὀργή, *BJ* 4.591) he experienced in thinking about Vitellius as emperor. Although he would like nothing more than to cross the sea and deal

---

[41] Aside from our passage (*BJ* 4.501), see *BJ* 1.69, 82, 84, 331, 347, 370, 373, 376, 613; 2.455, 457; 3.341, 485; 4.34, 76, 217, 622, 649; 5.377, 502; 6.59, 252, 296, 303, 429; 7.82, 120, 159, 185, 318. Underlined references are other turning points attributed to uncanny (δαιμόνιος) forces.

with the impudent wretch Vitellius, however, Josephus's Vespasian is paralyzed by three considerations: the distance involved, the supposed winter weather, and the unpredictability of fortune (*BJ* 4.591). These are enough to immobilize him, boiling though his rage is.

Of all the models of the great commander one could imagine, from Achilles to Alexander, Hadrian, or Marcus Aurelius, it would be difficult to find a place for what we today might label a passive-aggressive, tortured soul who rages so impotently, constrained by manifold fears—and practical inconvenience. It is difficult to spot in Josephus's account any hint of transcendent justice, virtue, or self-sacrificing courage for the good of the Republic among Vespasian's motives.

The winter-travel problem is conspicuous because Vespasian could not have heard of Vitellius's April accession before May, after which winter travel was not an issue. He would have sailed and his army would have marched in the most favorable season possible. As for fortune, Josephus's model Polybius had made it a central theme of his work that Rome succeeded because its great leaders were never cowed by fortune's reversals. Virtue and discipline, embodied in the Roman constitution and army, had enabled Romans to overcome fortune's reversals.[42] Why, then, does Josephus portray Vespasian as such a worry-wart?

Josephus turns his audience's attention to Vespasian's officers and soldiers. They have plans of their own, which serve their interests. They base their claim as much on *their* superiority to Vitellius's Rhine legions as on their commander's advantages over Vitellius. To be sure, they contrast Vespasian's virtue with Vitellius's notorious character, but they quickly turn to practical matters and political calculations. It seems that they think more strategically than their commander. Whereas Vitellius is childless, they reason, Vespasian has both an heir and a spare. His older brother, Flavius Sabinus, is an ex-consul well positioned in Rome, and Vespasian's younger son, Domitian, is on the scene also. If Vespasian does not delay, he will surely swing the many eastern legions, including those in Egypt under Tiberius Alexander (still to act), behind him.

With such considerations, Vespasian's officers convince themselves that they are objectively the best ones to secure imperial rule, under this commander, and that the Senate and people will agree (*BJ* 4.592–600). Without bothering to hear Vespasian's views, right there in Caesarea they proclaim him emperor and demand that he save the endangered empire (καὶ σώζειν τὴν κινδυνεύουσαν ἡγεμονίαν παρεκάλουν, *BJ* 4.601). There are echoes here of the Praetorian Guard's earlier choice of the terrified Claudius, irrespective of his wishes (*BJ* 2.204; *AJ* 19.216–20).

---

42 Plb. 1.1.2, 35.2, 63.9, 64.2; 2.7.1–2, 20.7–8; 3.2.6; 6.2.5–8; 16.28.1; 18.28.4–5; 38.2.1–2.

Tacitus pictures Vespasian calculating his chances and expressing doubts, but the sharp edge of personal animosity toward Vitellius is missing.[43] There Vespasian is more calculating. He counts on the support of Mucianus and Syria, the Danubian legions, and Tiberius Alexander, already declared, but still he vacillates between hope and fear because he realizes that failure would be terminal (*Hist.* 2.74). In Tacitus's account, Mucianus speaks for the officers in persuading Vespasian that his prominence and eastern support have already made him a target for Vitellius and so his only option is to try for supreme power (*Hist.* 2.76.2):

> torpere ultra et polluendam perdendamque rem publicam relinquere sopor et ignauia uideretur, etiam si tibi quam inhonesta, tam tuta seruitus esset. abiit iam et transuectum est tempus quo posses uideri non cupisse: confugiendum est ad imperium.

> Remaining sluggish to the end and abandoning the Republic to violation and ruin seems like laziness and timidity, even if slavery [i.e., submission to Vitellius] could protect you—at the cost of disgrace. The time has already passed when you could still be seen as lacking ambition: *imperium* is your only refuge now.

This is not a million miles from Josephus's treatment of the same events, but the Judaean historian brings Vespasian's interests into sharper conflict with those of his soldiers. Josephus has Mucianus speak only later, after the decisive event (*BJ* 4.605, 621), which goes as follows (*BJ* 4.602–4):

> His [Vespasian's] mind had certainly been on general affairs for a long time, though definitely without intending that he himself should rule. Although he certainly considered himself worthy by virtue of his accomplishments, he preferred the security that comes with private life to the dangers that attend eminence (προκρίνων δὲ τῶν ἐν λαμπρότητι κινδύνων τὴν ἐν ἰδιώταις ἀσφάλειαν). But when he refused, the commanders became all the more insistent, and the soldiers, sword in hand, threatened to do away with him if he should not be willing to live in a worthy manner (ἀναιρεῖν αὐτὸν ἠπείλουν, εἰ μὴ βούλοιτο ζῆν ἀξίως). After expounding to them the many reasons why he was resisting the rule, finally, as he could not persuade them, he yields to the titles.

Josephus's Vespasian is confident that he *deserves* supreme power, then. He is in every way a better man than Vitellius. His reasons for eschewing the throne have little to do with modesty and everything to do with fear. Given the fate of recent holders of supreme power, he unashamedly prefers personal safety. In the end, only his more immediate fear of the blades next to his face makes him abandon

---

43 Morgan 2006, 182: "There is not one word about the excesses of Vitellius." That is literally true, but surely *polluendam perdendamque* in *Hist.* 2.76.2 glosses Vitellius's regime, while 2.74.1 has Vespasian counting on the eastern army's revulsion at Vitellius's insolent troops.

his preferred inertia. "Forced to shoulder the burden of empire" (*BJ* 4.616), Josephus's Vespasian might seem like a noble Cincinnatus-like Roman, drafted into public service—an admiring trope. But the accompanying details, supplied by Josephus, of a deeply frustrated, angry man, steaming against Vitellius and yet crippled by fear, do not straightforwardly support the noble image.

Josephus's audience could not but recall, from near the end of the preceding volume in *War*, a strikingly similar scene. There, it is the author's own character, as Judaean general in Galilee, who has been opposing and embarrassing Vespasian and who faces the existential question. At Iotapata, after heroically exhausting all possible avenues of defense for the poor townsfolk, Josephus resolves to surrender, now confident of divine support for his admittedly unheroic finale (*BJ* 3.350–54).[44] His officers, however, draw their swords and demand that he do what is right, alongside them, which by their lights means collective suicide. He can join them voluntarily or their blades will take the decision out of his hands: "they brandished their swords at him and threatened to do away with him, if he should give himself up to the Romans" (*BJ* 3.360). But Josephus's resolve, unlike Vespasian's, never wavers. Utterly confident of his purpose, he remains master of the situation and prevails: first by bamboozling them with a philosophical disquisition against suicide (*BJ* 3.361–82), then by using the sheer force of his personality to unman his assailants (*BJ* 3.383–86), and in the last extremity by a cunning deception—"ἐπίνοια did not abandon him" (*BJ* 3.387)—involving the casting of lots to determine the order of death.[45]

I am not suggesting that Josephus intends an overt contrast between himself and Vespasian, to the latter's detriment. A volume separates the incidents, and one could conceivably justify both men by supposing that in Josephus's case the soldiers wanted something bad (even if they saw it as virtue), which he rightly refused, whereas Vespasian's men wanted something virtuous, which he nobly came to accept. Still, Josephus's account of Vespasian's decision is not one of undiluted virtue and courage. Vespasian's hatred of Vitellius is the furnace of rage, but he overcomes his debilitating fear only with the more proximate fear of his officers' blades. The regime's image of Vespasian as a supremely tough and fortune-blessed conqueror, motivated solely by heroic love of country and a desire for

---

44 On the episode at Iotapata, see also Hulls in this volume.
45 How he rigged this has come down to modern mathematicians as the Josephus Problem (http://mathworld.wolfram.com/JosephusProblem.html). Given a circle of 41 persons (*BJ* 3.342) and the rule that every *n*th must die, where should one stand to be among the last two? Josephus's description gives no such order, however. One must imagine rather some sleight of hand with the lots (if not actual divine protection).

peace, is at least greatly nuanced by the realistic human portrait painted by their client Josephus.

4 Conclusion

As an external control on the question of how closely Josephus's account of Vespasian's rise to power reflects Flavian interests, I have asked how well it matches Tacitus's characterization of the Flavian historians he knew who had treated the subject. My conclusion is that Josephus's account of this crucial episode in the Flavian story, though obviously different from that of the senator Tacitus in scope and level of detail, resembles it to a surprising degree—surprising, if we consider their very different backgrounds and circumstances, and given that Josephus wrote while Vespasian still lived rather than in the post-Flavian safety enjoyed by Tacitus. Neither of these canny political historians explains Vespasian's bid as motivated by simple love of peace and country. Both write as worldly-wise statesmen, thoroughly familiar with the grubbier hopes and fears that always attend power. Both accounts are skeptical, deeply human, psychologically oriented, and plausible-seeming. Both are therefore quite at odds with the simple images disseminated in the Flavian triumph, coins, and monuments, and the flood of pseudo-historical literature that both writers decry.

Leo Landrey
Embroidered Histories: Lemnos and Rome in Valerius Flaccus's *Argonautica*

Valerius Flaccus recasts the traditional Lemnian disaster as a sprawling account of civil war (V. Fl. 2.82–310), a striking shift of emphasis that far surpasses the tidy backstory provided in Apollonius Rhodius's *Argonautika*.[1] Valerius's flashback narrative serves to introduce the theme of large-scale social conflict into his poem and offers details about Hypsipyle's actions unexampled in the prior, extant tradition.[2] Civil war, which, in the Lemnian myth, comprises the murder of husbands, fathers, and sons by wives, daughters, and mothers, becomes a horrifying backdrop for the narrator but also a defining context for his pious heroine.[3] The *Argonautica*'s simultaneous treatment of Lemnos as a social nightmare and a cultural achievement, combined with the story's novel shape, emphasizes the episode's importance for understanding Roman responses to the renewed outbreak of civil war—the murder of citizens by other citizens in the service of a political faction—during 69 CE.[4]

This is especially true when we consider the allusive relationship between Valerius's new Lemnian disaster and contemporary Roman traumas. If Valerius wrote his epic during the reign of Vespasian, he would have composed his violent and original episode shortly after Rome witnessed the long year 69 CE, which culminated in the destruction of the temple of Jupiter Optimus Maximus on the Capitoline Hill during factional fighting between Vitellian and Flavian forces. Regardless of the *Argonautica*'s exact date of composition, however, this rift in Rome's social fabric would have lingered in the minds of its readers; this paper, accordingly, examines the similarities between Valerius's prominently remodeled

---

[1] Garson 1964, 272; Vessey 1985, 336. Apollonius Rhodius's account of the Lemnian disaster occupies only thirty lines of his first book (A.R. 1.609–39), making Valerius's narrative of the same events almost eight times longer.
[2] I presume that Hypsipyle's story in Statius's *Thebaid*, which contains numerous resemblances to Valerius's Lemnian narrative, postdates the *Argonautica*. Stover 2012, 7–27, argued most recently that Valerius began writing during Vespasian's principate and did not likely compose much after 79 CE. For Statius's status as a follower after Valerius (which is not to say a follower *of* Valerius!) see Kozák 2013; Parkes 2014b; Finkmann 2015; Lovatt 2015.
[3] For the contrast between crime (*scelus*) and piety (*pietas*) in this episode see Adamietz 1976, 33–34.
[4] For recent studies of civil war in Valerius Flaccus, see Buckley 2010; Bernstein 2014; Seal 2014; Heerink 2016.

https://doi.org/10.1515/9783110585841-011

Lemnian narrative and the events of 19 December 69 CE.[5] Understanding how Hypsipyle's radical piety amidst civil strife relates to his readership's experiences of the same will, I propose, offer important insight into how Valerius Flaccus synthesized the social and political crisis of 69 CE in his *Argonautica*.

I begin by exploring how the first half of Valerius's Lemnian episode deploys a recognizably Roman discourse of civil war, before next considering how the poem's narrator sets his account of Hypsipyle's actions within a real-world, Roman context. After revealing himself to be personally traumatized by the facts of his story (V. Fl. 2.216–19), the narrator turns to praise Hypsipyle's traditionally distinguishing efforts to save her father (V. Fl. 2.242–46). I argue that both of these brief interruptions in the narrative draw firm connections between the epic's mythological subject matter and Roman treatments of historical civil war. Moreover, the terms in which Valerius couches his praise of Hypsipyle specifically signal his engagement with the destruction of the Capitoline temple to Jupiter Optimus Maximus.

I turn next to consider the novel path Hypsipyle takes to save her father. As many scholars have remarked, her course of action is unusual within the extant Argonautic tradition.[6] Valerius Flaccus, I will argue, remodels Thoas's flight from Lemnos to closely resemble Domitian's escape from Vitellian soldiers on 19 December. This remarkable flight sequence engages intertextually with the historical event itself, an interaction we can witness through later historical treatments of the Capitolium's destruction.[7] Although it is possible to read Domitian's disguised flight as a source of shame and mockery for the future emperor, we do not need to read either encomiastic or snickering implications into *Argonautica* 2. Instead, the narrative resists debating the role of the *gens Flauia* in this event, preferring to display Hypsipyle as an *exemplum uirtutis* ("exemplar of virtue").[8] By hewing to traditional Roman *mores*, abstaining from participation in civil war,

---

[5] Connections between Hypsipyle's pious rescue of her father Thoas and Domitian's escape from the burning Capitolium have been recognized but not analyzed at any length. Clauss 2014, 109–11, has done the most to excavate these connections, noting that "one has to wonder if Valerius's decision to describe Thoas's salvation by way of disguise was inspired by Domitian's similar escape during the last days of Vitellius's attempt to defeat the supporters of Vespasian in Rome" (110). Poortvliet 1991a, 159, aligns Hypsipyle's actions with "similar tricks," including Domitian's escape. Burkert 1970, 7 n. 4, remarks only that "Domitian had made a very similar escape from the troops of Vitellius." I believe that these connections deserve more sustained exploration.

[6] See Garson 1964; Burkert 1970; Vessey 1985; Aricò 1991; McGuire 1997, 104–5; Frings 1998.

[7] For history as an intertext, see Damon 2010.

[8] It is not a new claim to view Hypsipyle as a model heroine; see, e.g., Hershkowitz 1998b, 136.

and seeking to preserve the life of her kin, the heroine emerges as a unique object of poetic praise within the *Argonautica*.

Finally, I will consider the implications of Hypsipyle's actions for the poem's audiences. Although Jason remains unaware of Hypsipyle's piety, her gift of her father's sword and a cloak embroidered with scenes from her father's escape (V. Fl. 2.408–25) situates Jason as a model reader within Valerius's narrative. As a miniature, hand-crafted version of the Lemnian episode itself, the cloak offers Jason the same challenge of interpretation that the narrative proper (V. Fl. 2.82–310) poses to Valerius's readers. Yet Jason does not read Hypsipyle's cloak, and he fails to comprehend the relevance of her *exemplum* for his own behavior.[9] Ignoring her model, he engages blindly in a civil war with Cyzicus and burns her cloak in the aftermath. Whether the *Argonautica*'s audience read these embroidered histories of civil war more perspicaciously than Jason remains an open question, but the epic's subtext suggests its expectation of a pessimistic answer.

1 *Clades Lemnia, Clades Romana*

The Lemnian massacre was not a civil war in its Greek incarnations, but rather an example of *stasis* (sedition), something slightly different.[10] By Valerius's day, however, the emergence of the concept of civil war made it easy to innovatively rework the traditional story into a microcosm of just such a conflict. Valerius's Lemnos meets the criteria for civil war specified in Armitage's recent study of the concept: the butchery involved "swords ... drawn in public," the upsetting of "the delicate balance ... between the spheres of civil life and military discipline," and

---

[9] Walter 2014, 37–42, extensively discusses Hypsipyle's gift of a cloak to Jason at his departure. She similarly argues that his destruction of her cloak bears negative implications for the narrator's efforts, concluding that "the narrator, as this episode makes clear, will not be able to bring his epic to its goal" (42). Where Walter approaches this episode from a narratological perspective, the present paper seeks to demonstrate that, for Valerius, the continual Roman relapse into civil war, most recently in 69 CE, arises from a failure to read correctly that is exemplified within the narrative by Jason's preference for sword rather than cloak. In her discussion of the Lemnian narrative, Walter 2014 cites a working version of this essay. Happily, the current version has been able to incorporate and build on her arguments.

[10] For the difference between *stasis* and *bellum ciuile*, and the emergence of the concept of civil war at Rome, see Armitage 2017a, 3–58, and the Introduction to this volume.

"a war by the people against the people."[11] In his treatment of the initial fighting, Valerius Flaccus pitches the violence at the level of warfare, as when the men mistake the massed women for "a battle-line of Furies" (*uelut agmina cernant | Eumenidum*, V. Fl. 2.227–28).[12] The text equates the women to the island's former foreign enemies (*hostes*) when it declares that they kill men "whom the gigantic Bessi could not lay low, nor Getic hands" (*inmanes quos sternere Bessi | nec Geticae potuere manus*, V. Fl. 2.231–32). When Valerius states that some husbands are unable to flee their burning homes because "a hard wife besieges the threshold" (*dura in limine coniunx | obsidet*, V. Fl. 2.237–38), the link between familial strife and civil war is complete.

Prior to the Flavian era, Latin literature had established diverse networks of association between Roman history, mythological narrative, and civil war. Through these links, internecine violence from long ago (whether outwardly mythological or quasi-historical; whether intra-familial or intra-communal) could directly inform contemporary iterations of civil war.[13] As the inheritor of this long tradition, Valerius Flaccus extends to the mythological violence on Lemnos several features of this civil war discourse while suppressing overt references to the battles and wars of history, a feature of the tradition that would mark it out as specifically "Roman." Thus, where Vergil adumbrates Actium on Aeneas's shield through explicit references to Augustus and Antony (Verg. *A.* 8.678–81 and 8.685–88, respectively),[14] Valerius's practice is to draw upon the structures and vocabulary of his Latin predecessors without name-dropping historical figures.[15]

The *Argonautica* deploys several notable civil war *topoi* in the first half of its Lemnian episode (V. Fl. 2.82–241). Most obviously, the contest of wife against

---

11 Armitage 2017a, 49–50. For Valerius's Lemnian narrative as an example of Roman civil war discourse, see Walter 2014, 30, and Keith in this volume. See also Newlands 2012, 43, on Statius's debt to Valerius's Lemnos in this regard.
12 All translations are my own. The text for the *Argonautica* is Liberman 1997.
13 For an Augustan example that, unlike the Flavian examples discussed here, is typically centered on Rome, see Horace's 7th *Epode*. On *Epode* 7 and Augustan civil war discourse, see further the introduction and the chapters of Keith and Bessone in this volume.
14 The text of Vergil's *Aeneid* is Mynors 1969.
15 After his opening dedication to Vespasian (V. Fl. 1.1–21), Valerius Flaccus never mentions another Roman historical figure, and his Jupiter conspicuously avoids mentioning Rome when he reveals his *Weltenplan* to Sol (V. Fl. 1.542–60). Still, his address to Vespasian forges a tight bond between myth and history, and his epic is stuffed with overt references to Rome and its culture: his ostensibly Greek heroes work within a fully Romanized universe. See Zissos 2009, 351–52 n. 2 with bibliography; Stover 2012, 46–50; Bernstein 2014. For Valerius's imperial dedication, see Penwill in this volume.

husband and mother against son constitutes the very stuff of a civil war story.[16] But in Roman civil war literature it was also common to attribute intra-community conflict to divine anger, and Tacitus blames the violence of 69 CE on the anger and vengeance of the gods (*deis ... ultionem*, Tac. *Hist.* 1.3.2; *deum ira*, *Hist.* 2.38.2; *propitiis, si per mores nostros liceret, deis*, *Hist.* 3.72.1).[17] Taking her place in a long line of angry divinities, Valerius's Venus provides the match that ignites Lemnos into social warfare.[18]

The *Argonautica*'s narrator peppers his account with a negatively-valued vocabulary of discord, madness, and destruction—all the poet's usual armaments for (re)telling a *bellum ciuile*.[19] Venus resembles nothing so much as a Fury (V. Fl. 2.106), and she earns the title "Mars's wife" (*Mauortia coniunx*, V. Fl. 2.208).[20] At the outset Venus "heaps up crimes," "moves maddened ruin" (*struit illa nefas* ... | *exitium furiale mouet*, V. Fl. 2.101–2), and spreads her frenzy to the Lemnians. Each "raving" wife (*furens*, V. Fl. 2.191) is compared to Tisiphone (V. Fl. 2.192–95), and later the narrator identifies the Thracian captives as the nominal "cause of their madness" (*causam furorum*, V. Fl. 2.239).[21]

The Roman discourse of civil dissolution is thus already in full effect by the time the reader reaches the narrator's first apostrophe, where the poet's personal connection to his subject matter casts the episode as a trauma ripped from the recent past (V. Fl. 2.216–19):

> unde ego tot scelerum facies, tot fata iacentum
> exsequar? heu uatem monstris quibus intulit ordo,
> quae se aperit series! o qui me uera canentem
> sistat et hac nostras exsoluat imagine noctes!

> Where do I begin describing so many forms of crimes, so many fates of the slain? O! Upon what *monstra* does the sequence of the story cast the poet! What a chain of events reveals itself! O it stops me short as I sing real events, and with this specter it undoes my nights!

---

16 For similar civil war *topoi* in Lucan, see Fantham 2010.
17 Joseph 2012, 67–70, explores Tacitus's use of *ira deum* to create civil conflicts modeled on the epics of Vergil and Lucan. See further Bernstein 2016, 400–1, for the *ira deum* theme in Tacitus and Valerius Flaccus.
18 See Hershkowitz 1998b, 177–82.
19 McGuire 1997, 106, likewise notes that "our perception of this episode depends to a significant degree on the language and rhetoric drawn from Roman civil war literature."
20 For Venus as a Fury in the *Argonautica*, see Hershkowitz 1998b, 178–79 (with further bibliography at n. 285); Elm 1998 and Elm von der Osten 2007.
21 For the role of *furor* as part of Roman civil war discourse, see Jal 1963, 417–25.

This apostrophe invites the reader to consider the poet choking on his own utterances and lying awake at night, tormented by his own visions, and its emphatically first-person sentence breaks from the third-person epic narrative. Valerius's narrator appears as the object of his poem's affliction, persecuted by his own subject matter by the mere act of following his plot. The eye-witness atmosphere suggested by his phrasing rhetorically collapses the distance of space and time standing between the Flavian poet and Heroic Age Lemnos.[22] Unlike the *Thebaid*'s narrator, who selects his subject matter from a wide array of Theban crimes ("a long series"; *longa ... series*, Stat. *Theb.* 1.7), the "sequence of the story" in Valerius's plot (*series*, V. Fl. 2.218) thrusts him into personally traumatic territory.[23]

The poet asserts that his song consists of real events (*uera*, V. Fl. 2.218),[24] thereby leaping past the long-porous boundary between myth and history and bringing the mythic *clades Lemnia* into the realm of the historical.[25] Valerius also engages intertextually with Lucan's *Bellum Ciuile*, the only extant historical epic among his models. At *Bellum Ciuile* 7.552–55, Lucan's narrator issues an apostrophe disparaging his own poetic activity as he approaches the decisive moment at the Battle of Pharsalus, a rhetorical outburst that aligns the narrator with the characters who function as "tragic messengers."[26] By using a historical epic on

---

22 Valerius draws on two important intertexts for 2.216–19, Aeneas's despair at relating Troy's destruction (Verg. *A.* 2.361–62) and the despairing apostrophe of Lucan's narrator before the Battle of Pharsalus (Luc. 7.552–55), for which see below. For Valerius's use of Luc. 7.552–55, see Walter 2014, 29–32. For Valerius's use of *A.* 2.361–62, see Davis 2015, 165–66, and Clare 2004, 133–34; Clare further argues (134–36) for two Apollonian intertexts.
23 However, see Stover in this volume for a potential connection between the two *series*.
24 Feeney 1991, 250–69, surveys fundamental features of the ancient discussion of myth's relationship to history; according to Feeney, *uera*, "real events," align with *historia* and not *fabula* (myth). Analyzing Cicero's discussion of myth and history in the *De Legibus*, Feeney concludes that his use of *ueritas* refers not to "truth," but to "the concepts of verisimilitude that were taken as normative for history writing: the yardstick for history is first and foremost 'real life,' and the probabilities of real life, and only secondarily whether something happened or not" (259). In asserting that he sings *uera*, therefore, Valerius insists that the Lemnian episode is historical and like real life, even if it didn't exactly happen.
25 *Argonautica* 2.216–19 contain a number of Vergilian reminiscences, and Valerius's presentation of the massacre as the sack of a city by hostile forces certainly points ahead, mythologically, to the sack of Troy and backwards, intertextually, to the *Aeneid*. In addition to the intertext noted above, n. 22, Valerius's *ordo* recalls Vergil's *maior rerum mihi nascitur ordo* (Verg. *A.* 7.44), which introduces the Italian civil war. For Lemnos as Vergil's Troy, see further Garson 1964, 273; Poortvliet 1991a, 136–37. For Hypsipyle's similarities to Aeneas, see Poortvliet 1991a, 152; Hershkowitz 1998b, 137–38.
26 One such character is the old man whose lengthy monologue begins Lucan's second book (Luc. 2.67–233). Ambühl 2010, 29–37, argues that the old man's gloomy narration functions as a

Roman civil war as a model while labeling his own civil war "real" and "historical" (*uera*), the *Argonautica*'s narrator forges a tight chain between the mythological past and Rome's imperial present.[27]

The narrator's use of *cano* to present his own poetic activity (*canentem*, V. Fl. 2.218) further aligns the Lemnian narrative with the Roman world. Valerius uses *cano* to describe his own activities at programmatic moments, such as during his *incipit* and medial proem (V. Fl. 1.1, 1.11–12, and 5.224). Just as Valerius connected Vespasian's career in Britain to his theme, the opening of the seas, at the beginning of the epic, so in Book 2 the link between his subject matter and his own personal trauma brings the past into the present.[28] As a direct witness to the real events that his reader sees him "singing" of (*canentem*), the poet establishes a bond between himself and any readers who witnessed the civil disturbances of 69 CE: they have glimpsed the same terrifying sights.

The apostrophe suggests that the poet knowingly inflicts on his readership a narrative that ought to traumatize them, since it has apparently traumatized him. This element of his storytelling offers a wider glimpse into how repetition marks his poetics of civil war.[29] The use of present-tense verbs (*aperit; sistat*, V. Fl. 2.218–19) freezes the poet in the process of viewing and re-viewing reiterated nightmares. The horrified poet compels his readers, already traumatized by their own encounters with history, to discover their civil war experiences in his mythology. By breaking down the dividing line between poetic subject matter and personal experience, Valerius draws the reader into the story's collective wound. And when sequences of divinely-inspired civil wars recur later, in *Argonautica* 3 and 6, the poet triggers his readers all over again.

Valerius Flaccus did not have to dwell at length on this episode, and he alone within the extant Argonautic tradition chose to do so.[30] At *Argonautica* 2.216–19

---

tragic messenger speech that "turns intertextual memory into character memory" and "mirror[s] the process of transforming history into poetry" (37). I would suggest that the same process is at work in Valerius; Walter 2014, 31, observes that "no particular further information needs to be conveyed to the narrator, but even without the help of the Muses, he already sings the truth."

27 As Buckley 2010 has argued about the Colchian civil war, Valerius Flaccus is also writing Lemnos into "the form of originary *bellum ciuile*, a proto-civil war epic providing a model for all later versions of war" (442), including the war treated in Lucan's epic.

28 For the creation of an "Argonautic moment" at Rome by way of the link between Vespasian's career and the Argonautic story, see Stover 2012, 27–77.

29 For Valerius's poetics of civil war, see Buckley 2010. For the repetition of civil war within the *Argonautica*, see Schenk 1999 and Clauss 2014; within Tacitus's *Historiae*, see Joseph 2012, esp. 1–28. For typological repetition in Valerius generally, see Mitousi 2014.

30 Indeed, some examples of the tradition are masterpieces of poetic selection. Pindar, in his magisterial Fourth *Pythian* ode, only arrives at Lemnos for three lines (Pi. P. 4.251–53), and

the narrator calls attention to his choice to include details we might otherwise consider unusual in an Argonautic story. What does he invite his reader to see? Crimes, corpses, atrocities, real events (*scelerum, fata iacentum, monstris, uera*), rhetorical buzzwords that pique the reader's interest. The "Table of Contents" that Tacitus attaches to his *Historiae* shows another imperial text pursuing a similar strategy to entice readers by advertising such grisly topics as "Italy afflicted with fresh disasters" (*Italia nouis cladibus ... adflicta*, Tac. *Hist.* 1.2.2). As in Valerius's Lucanean apostrophe, Tacitus conveys a sense of total state disaster. His *clades* are natural and social, and the destruction extends to urban spaces and human lives.

2 The Capitol and the Palatine

Valerius deploys a second apostrophe amidst the ruins of Lemnian society, this time addressing Hypsipyle, whose fame he pins to prominent features of Rome.[31] Yet even as he praises her, Valerius interweaves his apostrophe with competing Vergilian, Horatian, and Lucanean intertexts. His use of Vergil and Horace constructs positive models for Rome's longevity, yet he deletes their mention of Rome's most prominent Republican symbol, Jupiter's Capitoline temple.[32] His Lucanean allusion, to the speech of an imminently-suicidal Cato in *Bellum Ciuile* 9, builds on the Capitol's deletion, limiting the uplifting effects of the Vergilian-Horatian intertexts by underlining the perishability of Rome's institutions. The text thus reenacts the Republic's death at the same time as it promises immortality according to new, purely imperial standards: *palatia*, not *Capitolia*.

Aeschylus uses scarcely more lines to summarize the event (*Ch.* 631–38). Apollonius gives the massacre less airtime (A.R. 1.609–26) than Valerius. Euripides' *Medea*, Catullus, Seneca, and Diodorus Siculus (and therefore Dionysius Scytobrachion?) omit Lemnos entirely from their treatments of the Argo's voyage. Hypsipyle's account of Lemnos in Statius's *Thebaid* (5.335–85) proves the exception, but Statius was presumably responding to Valerius's earlier account. For Statius's status as a follower after Valerius, see above, n. 2.

31 This second apostrophe follows only thirty lines after the first, yet aside from an appeal to the Muses in Book 3 (V. Fl. 3.14–18), these are the only extended passages issued in the poet's voice between his *incipit* (V. Fl. 1.1–21) and medial proem (V. Fl. 5.217–25).

32 For the temple as a Republican monument, see its obituary in *Historiae* 3.72.2: *sed gloria operis libertati reseruata: pulsis regibus Horatius Puluillus iterum consul dedicauit* ("But the glory of the work was held back until *libertas* came: when the kings had been expelled from the state, Horatius Pulvillus dedicated it in his second consulship").

In order to break down this complex web of intertexts we will begin with the positive model created by the poet's engagement with Horace and Vergil (V. Fl. 2.242–46):

> sed tibi nunc quae digna tuis ingentibus ausis
> orsa feram, decus et patriae laus una ruentis,
> Hypsipyle? non ulla meo te carmine dictam
> abstulerint, durent Latiis modo saecula fastis   245
> Iliacique lares tantique palatia regni.

But how now to make a start worthy of your huge daring, Hypsipyle, adornment and sole boast of your faltering fatherland? No ages will bear you off now you've been named in my poem, if only the Latin *fasti*, the Trojan *lares*, the palaces of so great a kingdom endure.

Valerius links Hypsipyle's literary immortality to Rome's continued endurance, reflecting a promise Vergil makes Nisus and Euryalus (Verg. *A.* 9.446–49) and a boast Horace makes about himself (Hor. *Carm.* 3.30.6–9).[33] In Valerius's hands, *non ulla ... saecula* evokes Vergil's *nulla dies umquam* ("no day ... ever," Verg. *A.* 9.447) and Horace's *non omnis moriar* ("not all of me shall die," Hor. *Carm.* 3.30.6). The *Argonautica*'s *meo ... carmine* riffs on Vergil's *mea carmina* ("my poems" Verg. *A.* 9.446), an idea that is also implicit in Horace's metapoetic ode. The *Argonautica*'s praise of Hypsipyle culminates in "the palaces of so great a kingdom," an allusion to the Palatine where the emperor lived that invokes Vergil's "Roman emperor [holding] command" (*imperiumque pater Romanus habebit*, Verg. *A.* 9.449). Valerius Flaccus amplifies the assertions of his poem's longevity by citing similar passages from his influential predecessors, insinuating his poetic efforts into their tradition and extending to a new generation of poetic subjects a confidence in Rome's endurance.

But Valerius removes one specific measure of Rome's continued existence that is conspicuous in his source texts. Both Horace and Vergil mention the Capitolium as a key guarantor of Roman longevity. Vergil calls it "the Capitoline's immovable stone" (*Capitoli immobile saxum*, Verg. *A.* 9.448), and Horace swears that his work will endure "so long as the priest climbs the Capitolium" (*dum Capitolium | scandet ... pontifex*, Hor. *Carm.* 3.30.8–9). Valerius removes the

---

[33] For these intertexts see Poortvliet 1991a, 148–50; Clare 2004, 136–37; Walter 2014, 32–36. Note also a reminiscence and inversion, in *non ulla ... te ... | abstulerint ... saecula* (V. Fl. 2.244–45), of the Lucanean apostrophe discussed above, *nullaque ... discat ... | aetas* (Luc. 7.553–54). Walter 2014, 32–33, discusses Valerius's *Latiis ... fastis* and *Iliaci ... lares* and demonstrates that the latter further obscures the presence of the Capitolium in this passage. For a further allusion to Vergil's Nisus and Euryalus episode, see Clare 2004, 132–33.

Capitolium from *Roma aeterna* entirely. Its absence must have registered with Flavian readers familiar with Vergil and Horace, allowing the tradition Valerius ostentatiously evokes to create for the Capitol an absent presence. It constitutes a ghost beneath the text that pulls on its readers' minds, perhaps giving them a painful jolt as they recognize its literary removal and reflect on the shrine's parallel, historical absence.

The Capitolium's deletion in the *Argonautica* is especially remarkable when we consider that the temple's historical destruction otherwise receives frequent mention in Flavian poetry. In his *recusatio* at the beginning of the *Thebaid* Statius demurs from singing "the wars of Jupiter, won when you were hardly yet a teenager" (*aut defensa prius uix pubescentibus annis | bella Iouis*, Stat. *Theb.* 1.21–22), a specific allusion to the Capitoline fighting on 19 December and, by extension, to the entire year's worth of civil war. Silius Italicus's Jupiter does not fail to mention Domitian's survival in his prophecy, claiming that "the fires of the Tarpeian height will not terrify" the future emperor (*nec te terruerint Tarpei culminis ignes*, Sil. 3.609). We also know of two poems written about the event directly, although they do not survive. Martial suggests that Domitian wrote a poem on the fire, which he favorably advertises as "the heavenly poem of the Capitoline war" (*Capitolini caelestia carmina belli*, Mart. 5.5.7); and Statius's father evidently composed a commemoration of the conflagration shortly after the event, as well.[34]

While these Domitianic authors mention the flames of 19 December ostentatiously, if perhaps only ostensibly, to complement their emperor, the Jovian temple also served as a site for numerous political meanings during 69 CE and its aftermath. Suetonius reports that Galba legitimized his claim to the throne in part by highlighting his connection to Quintus Catulus Capitolinus, the temple's most recent Republican dedicator.[35] The temple precinct, of course, became the last major iconic battlefield in the year 69 CE. Its rebuilding offered a killing field for the resistance to Vespasian's authority, as senatorial leaders looking to reassert the political significance of their order fought, and failed, to secure Senatorial responsibility for the temple's rededication.[36] The Flavian dynasty not only arose (in part) from the Capitolium's flames, it also solidified Vespasian's power (in part) through a dispute over the temple's next iteration.

The *Argonautica*'s omission of this prominent edifice therefore leaps off the page. Instead of the Republican temple, its review of everlasting Roman cultural markers ends with the Palatine, seat of *regnum*. Poortvliet notes that *palatia*

---

[34] Stat. *Silu.* 5.3.195–202. See further Dewar 2016, 475; Galimberti 2016, 94.
[35] Suet. *Gal.* 2.
[36] Wardle 1996; Dézspa 2016, 171–73.

"came to mean 'imperial residence, palace', first, it would seem, in [this] passage, and then in Statius (*Silv.* 1.1.34, 4.1.8)."[37] Valerius replaces the Republican Capitoline with no less than imperial literature's first (surviving) instance of *Palatium* to mean "imperial residence." Framed within a larger narrative of civil war, the absent presence of the *Capitolium* summons those smoking temple ruins to the reader's mind right before Valerius tells a story that, as we shall see, strongly resembles a tale from the night of its destruction in a civil war waged for the imperial throne. Roman flames and Lemnian flames begin to merge as one night anticipates the other.

An intertext with Lucan deepens this reading. Within the narrator's second apostrophe, Valerius Flaccus acclaims Hypsipyle an "adornment and sole boast of [her] faltering fatherland" (*decus et patriae laus una ruentis*, V. Fl. 2.243). This construction alludes to Cato's speech in *Bellum Ciuile* 9 (Luc. 9.379–81, 385):[38]

> o quibus <u>una salus</u> placuit mea castra secutis
> indomita ceruice mori, componite mentes   380
> ad magnum uirtutis opus summosque labores.
> ...
> durum iter ad leges <u>patriae</u>que <u>ruentis</u> amorem.   385

> O followers of my camp, whose sole pleasing welfare is to die with necks unyoked, steel your minds to a masterpiece of bravery and your final toils ... it's a hard road to law and love of a faltering fatherland.

The *uirtus* to which Cato exhorts his troops, their *una salus*, stands as the model for Hypsipyle's pious actions through which she becomes her community's *laus una*. In its proper context, the *Argonautica*'s "faltering fatherland" (*patriae ... ruentis*, V. Fl. 2.243) stands clearly enough for Lemnos, but through Lucan's mediating text, Hypsipyle's fatherland takes on a second identity as Rome floundering in civil strife. *Laus una* ("sole boast" V. Fl. 2.243) carries a double meaning as well: on the surface it acclaims Hypsipyle for her pious actions, but to the extent that it evokes Cato's *una salus* ("sole welfare" Luc. 9.379), it shoulders his self-destructive impulse (which he also imagines for his soldiers) to die free. Most

---

[37] Poortvliet 1991a, 150.
[38] The text for Lucan is Shackleton Bailey 1988. For the role allusion to Lucan plays in Valerius, see Zissos 2004a; Buckley 2010; Stover 2012; Stover 2014; Heerink 2016. See also Fucecchi and Penwill in this volume. *Patria* also appears linked to the participle of *ruere* at Sen. *Oed.* 73 and *Ag.* 611, however Valerius does not otherwise echo those passages. For the influence of Seneca's *Agamemnon* on Valerius's Lemnos episode, however, see Antoniadis 2015. For Statius and Senecan tragedy, see van der Schuur in this volume.

importantly, this intertext deflates the predominantly Vergilian material that follows by prefacing assurances of poetic longevity and Roman immortality with a reference to the fact that, for Lucan, the Republic had long ceased to exist.[39] Lucan's anti-Caesarist Cato simmers beneath the surface of the apostrophe, undercutting its straightforward sincerity. The reminder of Lucan's *patriae ruentis* reinforces Valerius's construction of an imperial Rome shorn of its Republican heritage.

Comparison with Statius's *Siluae* confirms the exceptional nature of Valerius's razed Capitolium. Thrusting himself into the same Vergilian-Horatian tradition as Valerius, Statius takes the opportunity to assure Domitian that his generosity will not be forgotten so long as his poetry is read (Stat. *Silu.* 1.6.98–102):[40]

> quos ibit procul hic dies per annos?
> quam nullo sacer exolescet aeuo,
> dum montes Latii paterque Thybris,   100
> dum stabit tua Roma dumque terris
> quod reddis Capitolium manebit!

> Through how many years will this day go? Holy, it will vanish no sooner than never, so long as the Latin hills and Father Tiber, so long as your Rome will stand, so long as the Capitolium that you returned to earth will remain.

Like many before him, Statius ties the survival of his poetry to Rome's topography, but in the *Siluae* the climax of this sequence is the Capitoline, not Valerius's Palatine. It is not only the Capitolium, but Domitian's shrine to Jupiter Optimus Maximus, restored by the emperor himself after a fire in 80 CE.[41] If Valerius Flaccus was writing *Argonautica* 2 during one of two windows of time when the temple lay in ruins, it is possible that the Capitolium's historical absence lined up with its literary deletion.[42] No matter when Valerius's period of composition,

---

[39] For the use of Lucanean material to ironize other allusive material, see Zissos 2004a.

[40] The text for the *Siluae* is Shackleton Bailey/Parrot 2015. I understand *Siluae* 1 to have been written later than the *Argonautica*'s second book, regardless of when Valerius likely began his poem. For the relative chronology of Statius and Valerius, see above, n. 2.

[41] For the Domitianic temple, see Darwall-Smith 1996, 105–10. Heinemann 2016, 209–11, discusses the commemoration of Domitian's temple to Jupiter Optimus Maximus in Martial, Silius Italicus, and Statius, including this passage. Statius's poetry mentions the Capitolium's historical destruction, and Domitian's survival therein, rather often. Statius mentions Domitian's mid-80s restoration a second time at *Silu.* 4.3.16.

[42] Darwall-Smith 1996, 41–47, 96–97, and 105–7, identifies two windows when the Capitolium would have been absent from the Roman skyline. These are 19 December 69 CE until the early or

though, for a poet of his age the Capitolium's longevity may have seemed a poor yardstick for codifying poetry's power to preserve.[43]

Valerius's deletion of the Capitoline temple may have cut against the line of Flavian propaganda, as well. By replacing *Capitolia* with *palatia*, the *Argonautica* reenacts the death of the Roman Republic and its replacement by a reinvigorated Principate. Yet Heinemann has seen the Flavian occupation of the Capitoline on 19 December as "an act of symbolic communication that is [so] exceptionally rich in its appeals to the republican past" that it was possibly premeditated by Sabinus.[44] If the Flavians sought to tar the Vitellian faction by baiting it into destroying Rome's most venerable temple, Valerius's engagement with Vergil, Horace, and Lucan shows that its razing is hardly a restoration of republican norms.[45] By acknowledging the destruction of the Republic's central shrine, the poet's claim to poetic immortality emerges damaged. He will be read only so long as "the palaces of so great a kingdom endure" (*durent ... modo ... tantique palatia regni*, V. Fl. 2.245–46), yet physical buildings can fall, as his deleted Capitolium shows. The imperial refoundation of the Temple of Jupiter erased its traditional association with Republican *libertas* and rebranded it as a token of Flavian dynastic rule, but a precarious one.[46] If the poet lacked freedom of speech under this new world order, his poetic immortality became that much more contingent.[47]

---

mid-70s, and 7 December 80 CE until the mid-80s. Its rebuilding was a care for all three Flavian emperors.

43 Heinemann 2016, 211, makes a similar observation regarding *Siluae* 1.6.102.

44 Heinemann 2016, 222.

45 After its destruction, the Capitoline temple continued to be a flashpoint for appeals to Republican government and assertions of imperial authority as Rome debated who would be in charge of its reconstruction and dedication. Helvidius Priscus, who led the charge for the Republican faction, lost the debate and lost his life. See Wardle 1996; Heinemann 2016, 192–93.

46 See, e.g., Gallia 2012, 73.

47 Río Torres-Murciano 2009, 301–5, analyzing Valerius's use of the Vergilian "*fortunati ambo*" *topos*, sees in the changed terms of the protasis an unbalancing of the "Virgilian reciprocity between the literary fortune of *epos* and the historical *aeternitas* of *imperium*" (303) that leads him to conclude that Valerius's "epic poetry retains its aspirations for immortality ... but does not recognize the guarantee of its own survival in the stability of the empire" (305). In a similar, if more general, vein, Roman 2014, 263–339, argues that, compared to the Augustan poets, Flavian poets exhibit a diminished reliance on poetic autonomy and a heightened acknowledgement of their disposable materiality. Many have rightly detected a sense of precariousness elsewhere in the *Argonautica*, and especially in Jupiter's *Weltenplan* (V. Fl. 1.531–67), where the king of gods and men refuses to bestow Vergilian *imperium sine fine* (Verg. *A.* 1.279) on Rome, and even to name Rome entirely. Instead, he simply promises to favor the Greeks and "soon other races" (*gentesque fouebo | mox alias*, V. Fl. 1.555–56). See further Criado 2013 and Ganiban 2014. For the

The narrator's dual apostrophes set up Hypsipyle's efforts to save her father as split narratives. By addressing a mythological heroine, the narrator identifies the ostensible story as distant from Rome in both space and time. Simultaneously, he couches his Greek story in the language of Roman civil strife and likens it to "real events" (*uera*). The narrator inflicts his own trauma on his Roman readers, possibly calling to mind their private experiences. A network of intertexts woven throughout the narrator's praise of Hypsipyle establishes the Capitolium's absence in the text, evoking its recent destruction. Hypsipyle's *audax pietas* amidst the Lemnian civil war mirrors Cato's extreme devotion to Rome, even after the Republic became a lost cause at Pharsalus. Put together, these resonances suggest that Hypsipyle's actions occur in two parallel dimensions, amid the mythological ruins of Lemnos and during the culminating conflagration of 69 CE.[48]

3 Hypsipyle as *Exemplum Virtutis*

A comparison of Hypsipyle's exploits and the Capitol fire will show the degree to which the *Argonautica* reflects and reacts to Rome's recent civil wars. At the height of the crisis, Hypsipyle finds her father, Thoas, to alert him to the true nature of the conflict. The language of her appeal to him bears all the hallmarks of a civil war narrative (V. Fl. 2.249–51):

> illa pias armata manus "fuge protinus urbem
> meque, pater! non hostis," ait "non moenia laesi   250
> Thraces habent; nostrum hoc facinus. ne quaere, quis auctor!"

> Hypsipyle, having armed her pious hands, said, "Flee the city right away, and me, too, father! No enemy, not the wounded Thracians hold the walls: this crime is ours. Don't seek who its author is!"

Hypsipyle hesitates to name the slaughter's perpetrators before finally confessing to the crime's civil origins. Instead of advising Thoas to flee the island altogether, at first she focuses on the city as the site of the civil disturbance. These elements condemn the shame of the situation and also convey its character as

---

instability and ephemerality of the Flavian poet's constructed world, see also Chomse and Krasne in this volume.

48 The claim made by Wiseman 2010, 41, that "the Romans' own explanations of civil war not only invoke the two-headed state but also exemplify it," resonates here: Valerius's Lemnos narrative is indeed two-headed.

civil strife localized to Lemnos's urban area. Hypsipyle's rhetorical response to the Lemnian disaster shapes it into an event similar in nature to the burning of the Capitoline temple. Both are chaotic urban conflicts and permanent blots on their communities' histories, crimes committed by *ciues* (citizens), not *hostes* (foreign enemies).[49]

If similar contexts of disgraceful, urban, civil conflict form a unified backdrop, the parallels between Lemnos and Rome continue in the foreground. Valerius has Hypsipyle implement an unprecedented rescue, a stark intervention in the mythographical tradition and a bold marker of his originality.[50] Grabbing her father, Hypsipyle takes him to the temple of Bacchus, where they pass the night before escaping the next morning in disguise. Although it is unclear exactly where the temple is located, Hypsipyle's escape route through the city to the sea (*rapiturque per urbem*, V. Fl. 2.273) suggests a location near, if not in, the city center.[51] She passes crowds of women hostile towards her actions before hiding her father in the woods, "far removed from the savage city" (*saeua procul urbe remotum*, V. Fl. 2.279). The overall itinerary of the escape is therefore clear: from the temple of Bacchus, through the city, past would-be opponents, and out into hiding beyond the walls.

This narrative pattern overlaps substantially with what is known about Domitian's escape from the Capitolium.[52] In Tacitus's account, Domitian, assisted by

---

49 Tacitus's obituary of the temple, *Hist.* 3.72, itself recycles a number of the same tropes of civil war: the Capitolium's destruction is a crime (*facinus*) committed "by no foreign enemy" (*nullo externo hoste*). Yet Tacitus's sources for the destruction of the Capitoline temple include Vergil's fall of Troy, demonstrating how permeable the boundary between myth and history had become. For the intertextual debt of *Hist.* 3.72–85 to Vergil, see Joseph 2012, 106–12.
50 According to Vessey 1985, 337, this rescue plan "cannot be said ... to possess verisimilitude." As Garson 1964, 275, and Poortvliet 1991a, 159, point out, the pattern of Hypsipyle's actions fits the plot of both Euripides' *Iphigenia in Tauris* and Ovid's tale of Procne and Philomela. There is strong evidence that Valerius was thinking of both passages, and I do not see the presence of these models as disrupting the Capitolium's resonance in this episode, as they contribute to the poem's appeal to unbreakable patterns of interfamilial strife in barbaric landscapes. For Valerius Flaccus and Euripides, see further Frings 1998.
51 Hypsipyle's actions possibly allude to a prophet of civil war, Lucan's *matrona*, who appears at the end of *Bellum Ciuile* 1 "rush[ing] through the thunderstruck city" (*et attonitam rapitur matrona per urbem*, Luc. 1.676). Poortvliet 1991a, 164, sees an allusion to Amata at Verg. *A.* 7.384. Hypsipyle, though, counters her models by resisting the madness of civil war. Statius's Hypsipyle likewise has to escape the city, and Bacchus specifically instructs her to avoid the gate where Venus has taken charge of the violence (Stat. *Theb.* 5.280–83). See further Gibson 2004, 158–59, and Ganiban 2007, 78–86.
52 For competing reconstructions of Domitian's escape and the events of 19 December generally, see Wiseman 1978 and Wellesley 1981. Although Heinemann 2016, 208–9, recognizes that

a clever freedman, first hides at an *aedituus*'s house, then escapes to a client's near the Velabrum, before finally sneaking out of the city in the midst of a religious procession, concealed in Isiac vestments (Tac. *Hist.* 3.74).[53] Suetonius offers a slightly different version, claiming that the future emperor secretly spent the night at the *aedituus*'s before escaping across the Tiber in the morning, disguised as a priest of Isis and accompanied by a single companion (Suet. *Dom.* 1). Both sources agree that Domitian overnighted on or near the burnt-out Capitol, probably close to the temple of Jupiter, before making his escape the next day in disguise. In our epic and historical narratives, then, a member of the ruling family passes the night in or near a religious shrine before hiding in sacred garb and escaping with the help of a single assistant. Thoas received favorable signs from his father Bacchus (V. Fl. 2.259–60), and as soon as his own father gained power, Domitian is said to have thanked Jupiter for saving him by dedicating a shrine to *Iuppiter Conseruator* at the location of his hideout, complete with an altar depicting his ordeal.[54] Because of this prominent, physical commemoration the story of Domitian's escape would have probably been well known to Valerius's immediate Roman readership.

Reading Valerius's Lemnos as Rome on 19 December 69 CE aligns Thoas with Domitian, but the episode's emphasis remains on Hypsipyle's assistance. The *Argonautica*'s narrator relegates the character of Thoas to the margins of the episode and focuses exclusively on his daughter, who acts relentlessly. In one sequence she "speaks to," "lifts," "hides," "snatches," "speaks to," and "sets down" her father (*ait, excipit, obnubit, rapit, ait, locauit*, V. Fl. 2.249–58) before he becomes the subject ("he hides," *latet ille*, V. Fl. 2.258). But Hypsipyle soon reclaims the spotlight, and between his departure from the city and his exit from the story aboard ship (V. Fl. 2.261–300), Thoas is the grammatical subject only

---

the accounts handed down by Tacitus and Suetonius form part of the "anti-Domitianic tradition," he nonetheless concludes that other evidence, including commemorative coinage, Domitian's *bellum Capitolinum*, and mentions in literature, points to the Capitoline siege as an event celebrated, at the time, as "Domitian's finest hour" (209).

53 See Wellesley 1956, 211–14. Josephus merely records that Domitian "escaped miraculously" (δαιμονιώτερον διασώζεται, *BJ* 4.649). For the narrative centrality of Josephus's account of the Flavian rise to power through civil war, see Mason in this volume.

54 *ac potiente rerum patre, disiecto aeditui contubernio, modicum sacellum Ioui Conseruatori aramque posuit casus suos in marmore expressam; mox imperium adeptus Ioui Custodi templum ingens seque in sinu dei sacrauit* (Tac. *Hist.* 3.74.1). Based on numismatic evidence, Heinemann 2016, 204–8, argues that Tacitus erroneously flipped the names of the *modicum sacellum* and the *templum ingens*, and that a modest chapel was dedicated to *Iuppiter Custos* under Vespasian while the huge shrine to *Iuppiter Conseruator* was Domitianic in date. See also Darwall-Smith 1996, 110–12.

once, in a subordinate clause (V. Fl. 2.270–71). Although Hypsipyle addresses a little more than fifteen lines of dialogue at her father on three separate occasions, he never speaks or replies.

The poet's attention remains focused on Hypsipyle because of the example she provides amid the flames of communal strife. Where Flavian commemorations of 19 December tended to bolster their dynastic claims, Hypsipyle's example shows how Roman elites can act commendably even under the communally destructive conditions introduced by civil war. Her lesson is to hew close to traditional morals at all hazards. Simultaneously, the fact that Hypsipyle hides her deviant piety seems to betray how dangerous it had become at Rome to recognize traditional *uirtus*.[55] Still, the mechanisms for glory are not all smashed: Valerius's poetic activity renders Hypsipyle's praise visible to his readers even as it pays tribute to those who bore no arms throughout 69 CE.[56]

Hypsipyle's actions suggest a way out of the cycle of divine anger, human neglect, decaying community *mores*, and collective madness. Valerius's tale emerges from this analysis as a carefully crafted antidote to all of civil war's ills.[57] Since he remodels his Lemnos to reflect conflicts from Rome's recent history, Valerius Flaccus's Hypsipyle becomes an *exemplum uirtutis* for those watching her from outside the poem, who alone can access the detailed account of her piety that she hides from her peers within the text. The main social ills that her example remedies are the same cancers that Romans diagnosed within their own body politic, as we have seen. Valerius's Hypsipyle supplies a solution to the crisis that the Capitolium's destruction symbolized.[58] She shows that all Roman elites need to do amid civil war is abstain from violence and stay true to their traditional values. Either the gods will protect them, or their peers will recognize their worth

---

55 For a related reading of Pollux's boxing match in *Argonautica* 4, see Zissos 2003.
56 See Fucecchi in this volume.
57 Statius, in his own reworking of this heroine, may have disputed the efficacy of Valerius's Hypsipyle as such a model. Newlands 2012, 43, argues that "Statius' poem suggests that the piety of Hypsipyle ... was necessarily but terribly compromised by events largely outside her control. She does not instigate violence, but she is involved in it on Lemnos and is its hapless cause in Nemea. She thus is far from the ideal of womanhood lauded by Valerius as *decus et patriae laus* (the honour and glory of your country, V.Fl. 2.243)." Ganiban 2007, 90–91, also argues that Statius downplays and complicates Hypsipyle's virtuous agency in contrast to Valerius's treatment.
58 A crisis to which Tacitus gave voice in his *Historiae*. Yet Hypsipyle's solution to Rome's cultural crisis—to remain true to traditional values—also resembles a solution to the same crisis proposed by Tacitus in his laudatory biography of his father-in-law, *Agricola*. For the *Agricola* as a response to an aristocratic culture crisis, see Sailor 2008, 51–118; for Valerius's *Argonautica* and Tacitus's *Agricola*, see Davis 2015, 167–69.

and—clandestinely, artistically, perhaps posthumously—acclaim them *patriae laus*, "the pride of their fatherland" (V. Fl. 2.243).

4 Jason as a Model Reader

Although Hypsipyle's glory must remain a secret within the poem, she does try to communicate a narrative of her exploits to Jason at his departure. Rather than speak her story aloud, she weaves her rescue of Thoas into one half of a cloak that she gives, along with her father's sword, to her departing lover (V. Fl. 2.408–25). Yet the medium of needlework remains perhaps less than fully communicative, and Valerius does not say how Jason reacts or even if he understands what the scenes stitched into the cloak mean. Instead of communicating Hypsipyle's *exemplum uirtutis* in civil war, the cloak's narrative appears to make no impact on Jason. Instead, he learns the wrong lessons from Hypsipyle's gifts, drawing her father's sword in civil war and deploying her *chlamys* as a death shroud for Cyzicus, the host he murdered.

Valerius describes Hypsipyle's handiwork briefly, retelling through ekphrasis the story of Thoas's escape. Although half of the cloak is devoted to Jupiter's abduction of Ganymede, a potentially unrelated scene,[59] in the first half of his cloak ekphrasis the poet once again attributes Hypsipyle's greatness to her radical piety (V. Fl. 2.410–13):

> illic seruati genetoris conscia sacra   410
> pressit acu currusque pios: stant saeua pauentum
> agmina dantque locum; uiridi circum horrida tela
> silua tremit; mediis refugit pater anxius umbris.

---

[59] For connections between the two stories on the cloak, or lack thereof, see Shey 1968; Frank 1974; Poortvliet 1991a, 226–27; Hershkowitz 1998b, 142 n. 143; Ripoll 2000a; Newlands 2012, 78–79; Harrison 2013, 219–20; Walter 2014, 38. There might be a connection between Domitian's escape and the Ganymede story: Tacitus says that he dedicated an altar in his *sacellum* to *Iuppiter Conseruator* that "told of his ordeal" (*aramque posuit casus suos in marmore expressam*, Tac. *Hist*. 3.74.1), and a later shrine to *Iuppiter Custos* erected during his own principate featured "himself in the lap of the god" (*seque in sinu dei*, Tac. *Hist*. 3.74.1), presumably as a part of the cult statue. Perhaps either of these statue groups included a depiction of Jupiter physically snatching Domitian from his enemies, or perhaps decorative paintings associated the event with Jupiter's abduction of Ganymede. Although this must remain speculation, Domitian's placement in Jupiter's lap (*in sinu dei*) opens up an interpretation linking the emperor to Ganymede.

On this side she embroidered the temple, her accomplice in saving her father, and her pious chariot: the savage battle columns of frightened women, formerly closing in, give way; the forest primeval trembles all around in a green web; her nervous father escapes through the surrounding darkness.

The ekphrasis's first sentence labels her chariot "pious" and with *conscia sacra* recalls the complicit temples of the earlier narrative (*ad conscia Bacchi | templa rapit*, V. Fl. 2.254–55), underscoring Hypsipyle's claim to fame.[60] The contrast between the Lemnian women, formerly threatening but now frightened by Hypsipyle's ruse, adds to the atmosphere of contrasts between piety and impiety, right and wrong, flight and violence. Brief though it is, the first half of the cloak ekphrasis telegraphs everything Jason needs to know about the actions that earned Hypsipyle the poet's praise.

As a weaver attempting to communicate her glorious account to Jason, the Lemnian queen resembles the poet, who had earlier communicated her *laus* to his readership.[61] As a soon-to-be civil warrior, Jason might learn how to behave in the flames of communal strife by carefully reading Hypsipyle's cloak, and a reading in which the narrative of Thoas's rescue also resembles Domitian's historical escape raises the stakes for Jason's interpretation of the garment. Jason constitutes an internal reader, interpreting the work of a weaver who uses a constructed, indirect account of civil war to promote a moral model. Both internal and external readerships—the hero soon to be embroiled in civil violence and the survivors of 69 CE—can gain insight into their own situations by contemplating each carefully constructed narrative.

Hypsipyle's woven gift thus resembles the entire earlier Lemnian narrative, both because it summarizes the earlier event (V. Fl. 2.82–310) and because its relationship to the narration of those events mirrors the relationship of that narrative to the night of 19 December 69 CE. Each is a mimetic account of an earlier event created through artistic craft. The Lemnian flashback constructs a nightmarish narrative out of the ruins of Rome's greatest temple while the cloak (V. Fl. 2.410–13) weaves a story in miniature from the flashback itself (V. Fl. 2.82–

---

60 For the gift as a mark of characteristic piety, see Garson 1964, 273 and 276.
61 Walter 2014, 38, observes that Valerius's "Hypsipyle and the epic narrator try in equal measure to impart longevity to this quietly accomplished heroic feat." Dietrich 1999, Gibson 2004, Newlands 2012, 40–44, and Soerink 2014, 184–86, see Statius's Hypsipyle as an epic poet and regard her Valerian cloak as a mimetic emblem of poetic narrative, a rough, minaturized equivalent to the story she tells in the *Thebaid*. Ganiban 2007, 91 n. 74, suggests that Hypsipyle's gift in Valerius "might also have suggested to Statius the potential of having Hypsipyle herself narrate the Lemnian massacre." See further Stover in this volume.

310). This abbreviated narrative has the ability to instruct Jason, just as the story it summarizes can instruct the poem's readers.[62]

Yet if Jason can function as an internal reader whose reactions might model those of the *Argonautica*'s immediate Roman audience, he soon proves a dull pupil: he does not react to the gifts at all and simply sails away.[63] Hypsipyle herself mixes her messages when she gives Jason her father's sword (V. Fl. 2.418–21), contradicting the cloak's theme of divine rescue while refraining from impious war. It is possible that her description of Thoas's "sword, ... the flaming gifts of the Aetnean god that [her] father bore" (*ensem, ... | Aetnaei genitor quae flammea gessit | dona dei*, V. Fl. 2.418, 420–21), recalls the poem's first ekphrasis, in which Jason's father, Aeson, appears "raging with a sword" (*ense furens*, V. Fl. 1.144). The fiery, uncontrolled aspect of Thoas's weapon (*flammea*, V. Fl. 2.420) recalls Aeson's raging *furor* and the conflagrations of that night on Lemnos, undercutting Hypsipyle's carefully composed images of piety, nonviolence, and succor.[64]

Jason never takes the time to learn the cloak's signal lessons, preferring to treat it instead as a disposable prestige object. In its next appearance, Jason consigns it to the same fire that will consume the corpse of his former host (V. Fl. 3.340–42).[65]

---

[62] Mitousi 2014 has argued that the *Argonautica* works as a didactic "epic à thèse" where "the narrated story entails its own specific meaning and interpretation to which the reader is led by the narrative hypersystem of the text" (154). I disagree. Instead, I argue that the *Argonautica*'s omniscient narrator has the potential, even the desire, to dictate "not only the story but its interpretation too" (154), as seen here by his dramatic refashioning of the Lemnian narrative to reflect in specific ways the destruction of the Capitoline temple on 19 December 69 CE. But although he may *want* to communicate an important message about proper behavior in civil war to his Roman readership, Valerius Flaccus envisions his message falling on deaf ears. He models this failure through Jason's disinterest in reading Hypsipyle's cloak.

[63] As Clare 2004, 143–45, points out, the text parallels Dido and Aeneas with Hypsipyle and Jason, yet Jason is silent where Aeneas attempts to explain himself to Dido (Verg. *A.* 4.333–61). Similarly, Valerius Flaccus does not narrate Jason's reaction to Hypsipyle's cloak where Vergil had narrated Aeneas's reaction to several ekphrases, including the Temple of Juno (Verg. *A.* 1.459–63) and the shield (Verg. *A.* 8.729–31). For Dido and Hypsipyle, see further Hershkowitz 1998b, 138–46.

[64] Adamietz 1976, 36, however, suggests that "her father's sword should probably recall her failure to murder him." Still, since he has further shown (35–36) that Hypsipyle's gifts prove her to be purposefully constructed as an anti-Medea, we may still suppose that Jason's neglect of her cloak and of her example forms a part of the larger failings that lead Jason to throw in his lot with the woman who will bear, and murder, his children. Hershkowitz 1998b, 143, sees the sword-gift as a sign that Hypsipyle "will not follow the same path as Dido." See further Manuwald 1999, 236.

[65] It is possible that the cloak Jason gives to Cyzicus's pyre is a different cloak than the one described at *Argonautica* 2.410–13, since the narrator does not specify that it is the exact same

In the brief space of time between his departure from Lemnos and his murder of Cyzicus, Jason is never seen contemplating the cloak's stories. In contrast to the image of a thoughtfully crafted work presented by the cloak ekphrasis, in Book 3 the narrator describes it as a garment "that rushed Hypsipyle grabbed from the loom" (*quas rapuit telis festina*, V. Fl. 3.341). Far from achieving immortality as an object to be passed down over the generations, Hypsipyle's cloak is almost immediately destroyed.[66]

It is evident that Jason has not succeeded in absorbing the weight of his lover's example.[67] Pitched headlong into a civil conflict at the start of *Argonautica* 3, Jason makes all the mistakes Hypsipyle avoided. Like the Lemnian conflict, divine wrath instigates the Argonauts' fight with the Doliones, which takes place at night (V. Fl. 3.14–248). Unlike Hypsipyle, though, Jason gets caught up in the conflict and even leads the charge. In a pre-battle exhortation, Jason dedicates his first fight to his father and misleads his men by suggesting that they face the Colchians, a foreign enemy (V. Fl. 3.81–82). Where Hypsipyle was able to accurately identify the civil nature of the conflict and save her father, Jason's ignorance of his true foe leads him to kill his former host (V. Fl. 3.239–42). Indeed, Jason becomes in this conflict the image of his own father, "raging with a sword" (*ense furens*, V. Fl. 1.144).[68] The cloak's second appearance suggests that Jason appreciates Thoas's blazing weapon (*flammea ... dona*, V. Fl. 2.420) more than Hypsipyle's cloak, which hits the pyre "burning with crimson dye" (*ardentes murice*, V. Fl. 3.340). Hypsipyle's *exemplum uirtutis*, as communicated to Jason by her cloak, receives no reprise. The theme of civil war, however, will thread its way throughout the poem without reprieve.

---

cloak. However, Valerius's readers only witness Hypsipyle giving Jason a single cloak. Walter 2014, 39–40, and Manuwald 2015, 155, have suggested that it is reasonable to assume that both cloaks are the same; Hershkowitz 1998b, 143, points out that Jason's use of the cloak for Cyzicus's funeral echoes Aeneas's donation of Dido's cloak to Pallas's funeral (Verg. *A*. 11.72–77).

66 Walter 2014, 41–42, suggests that the cloak's metapoetical destruction indicates that "the *Argonautica*'s narrator and the protagonists of his work seem to have different ideas about what should be immortalized in this epic."

67 In his disregard of Hypsipyle's pious actions, I would suggest that Jason confirms a negative reading of his fight in *Argonautica* 3. As Heerink 2016, 523, concludes of that episode, the epic "reveals a disappointed attitude concerning the Principate and shows that an *Aeneid* in the Flavian age is not possible anymore." See, *contra*, Stover 2012, 113–50.

68 In an added irony, Jason's abduction of Pelias's son Acastus led directly to his own father's suicide (V. Fl. 1.700–850). Jason had feared this outcome (V. Fl. 1.693–99), but Juno, "lest blazing Jason turn around in the middle of his voyage" (*mediis ardens ne flectat ab undis*, V. Fl. 2.3), made him blithely sail on, "ignorant" (*ignarus*, V. Fl. 2.1). For the echoes of Roman history in Aeson's death, see Franchet D'Espèrey 1988; McGuire 1997, 189–97; Dietrich 2009.

5 Conclusions

Valerius Flaccus substantially reshapes the Lemnian narrative he received from the extant Argonautic tradition, updating the story to resonate with a contemporary readership and designing his *clades Lemnia*, and specifically Hypsipyle's role therein, to reflect a recent *clades Romana*, the destruction of the Capitoline temple. The poet crafts a heroine who adheres to traditional Roman virtues amidst a recurring Roman horror, civil war, which he aligns with historical realities through standard *topoi*, two apostrophes, rhetorical buzzwords, and a conspicuously innovative escape narrative. Hypsipyle, meanwhile, perhaps like the poet himself, uses an artfully created object to attempt to convey key lessons about the importance of traditional morality in the midst of trauma and social unraveling. Yet she fails to steer Jason away from civil war, and Jason's failure to read the cloak raises troubling questions about the epic's ability to reach its author's Roman audience.

The *Argonautica* emerges from this analysis as a text woven from the flames of 69 CE. Despite the narrator's ringing endorsement of Hypsipyle's actions, her example goes unheeded. The cloak ekphrasis conveys to Jason an important summary of her exemplary behavior in the same way that, I have argued, the Lemnian narrative itself synthesizes recent Roman history to counter dynastic claims of legitimacy while promoting traditional elite behavior. But Jason expresses no interest in the cloak and prizes it only for the conspicuous richness that makes it a suitable funeral shroud. When Hypsipyle presents her gift to Jason, she hopes it "will remain wrapped tight around the dear leader" (*haesuraque caro | dona duci promit*, V. Fl. 2.408–9). Instead, the cloak is about to burn, like the crown Medea wears at her wedding to Hypsipyle's man (*arsuras alia cum uirgine gemmas*, V. Fl. 8.236). These two acts of arson—one enacted in Book 3, the other portended in the incomplete epic's final book—center on the dissolution of community and family bonds, the central ruptures of the *clades Lemnia* to which Hypsipyle responds so heroically. Despite her efforts to compose an alternative narrative both through her own actions and through her weaving, Hypsipyle's embroidered histories unravel.

Similarly, the *Argonautica* can hold up its heroine's unique morals to an audience scarred by civil war, but it cannot avert the outbreak of communal violence. Like the poet, Hypsipyle can only react to the horror around her, and her virtue results in only a single life saved. Thereafter she must rule a society of criminals, disguising her singular *pietas* to escape conviction by her guilty subjects. Hers is a precarious sort of heroism, necessarily private, fundamentally ironic, and contingent on finding an astute readership. Valerius himself is skeptical that she does, or will, find such an audience.

Although the Capitolium's destruction crowns the wars of 69 CE, the Lemnian conflict that resembles it instead initiates long cycles of civil war within the *Argonautica*. Just as violence continues to break out after, and despite, Hypsipyle's actions, so too does the *Argonautica* anticipate renewed cycles of Roman strife. The poet presents a world in which the power of example makes little difference. Although Valerius Flaccus perhaps hopes to grab his readers' attention by calling out the nightmares of civil war and the quality of Hypsipyle's piety, his Jason shrugs off the cloak that emblematizes the episode, consigning it to flames lit by his own blind *furor*. Like Hypsipyle, the poet does what he can to govern a criminal cast of characters, including readers like Jason. This meagre victory is the best possible reality in a universe where the Republic's guarantor of *libertas*, the temple of Jupiter Optimus Maximus, has been wiped from the face of the earth and where, consequently, all physical guarantors of power and fame can go up in smoke.

Part IV: **Family, Society, and Self**

Claire Stocks
Band of Brothers: Fraternal Instability and Civil Strife in Silius Italicus's *Punica*

> But we in it shall be remembered—
> We few, we happy few, we band of brothers;
> For he to-day that sheds his blood with me
> Shall be my brother; ...
>
> Shakespeare, *Henry V* (Act IV, Scene 3)

> Within Easy Company they had made the best friends they had ever had, or would ever have. They were prepared to die for each other; more important, they were prepared to kill for each other.
>
> Stephen E. Ambrose, Band of Brothers:
E Company, 506th Regiment, 101st Airborne
from Normandy to Hitler's Eagle's Nest

Comradeship in battle has been consistently styled by authors from ancient times onwards as a form of brotherhood. Roman authors were no exception to this rule, and the motif of the brothers-in-arms who would fight—and die—together was prevalent in texts from the Republic and Principate. Just as Shakespeare's *Henry V*, along with Ambrose's *Band of Brothers*, popularized by the Emmy award-winning drama of the same name,[1] depicted warriors whose shared experiences in battle created a pseudo-fraternal bond between them, so Roman texts offered their readers warriors whose friendship was portrayed as fraternal (e.g., Polynices and Tydeus, Stat. *Theb.* 9.53).[2] Yet when it came to "brotherhood," it

---

I would like to thank the editors of this volume for their comments, as well as the audience at the Celtic Conference in Edinburgh 2014 for their feedback on this paper in its original form.

1 *Band of Brothers*, HBO mini-series (2001). http://www.imdb.com/title/tt0185906/ (sourced 07/25/15).
2 Polynices mourns for the dead Tydeus: *melior mihi frater ademptus* (Stat. *Theb.* 9.53). On the fraternal bond between Polynices and Eteocles in this scene, see especially Bannon 1997, 185. While Polynices and Tydeus are not blood-brothers, Statius places constant stress upon "blood" and "fraternity" in relation to these two men (e.g., *exultat fratris credens hunc ille cruorem*, *Theb.* 11.515). Not only will Polynices strike the fatal blow against his own blood-brother Eteocles (*Theb.* 11.539–43), but Tydeus too is presented as a killer of brothers (e.g., *fraterni sanguinis illum | conscius horror agit*, *Theb.* 1.402–3; *pollutus ... fraterno sanguine Tydeus*, *Theb.* 2.113); see Henderson 1993, 176. Ironically, Statius draws attention to Tydeus's fraternal "blood-guilt" (*Theb.* 2.113) at the point at which he first stresses the eternal bond of comradeship between Polynices and Tydeus: *dant animos socer augurio fatalis Adrastus | dotalesque Argi, nec non in foedera uitae | pollutus placuit fraterno sanguine Tydeus* (*Theb.* 2.111–13).

https://doi.org/10.1515/9783110585841-012

was the bond of blood-brothers-in-arms that appears to have fascinated Roman authors the most.

Rome was built, so our ancient sources would have us believe, on the spirit—and blood—of brotherhood. From Romulus and Remus, the legendary twins who fought to found a city, to the Scipios of the Punic wars, the Gracchi, and the fraternal pairs of the Julio-Claudians and Flavians, Rome was defined by its brothers and often found itself negotiating a difficult path between two extremes. On the one hand, it heralded the ideal of brotherhood through the brothers who fought and died for Rome; on the other, it bemoaned its perversion, epitomized through the negative image of Rome's legendary founder Romulus being responsible for the death of his brother Remus, an event continually cited by ancient authors, including Horace (*Epod.* 7.17–20) and Lucan (1.95), as a sign of Rome's inherent civil-war tendencies.[3] This paper takes as its focus the dual-faceted nature of Roman brotherhood and considers the implications and repercussions of its portrayal in Silius Italicus's *Punica*, an epic that is dominated by powerful fraternal partnerships, notably those between the Scipios and the Barcids. In his portrayal of the relationship between Scipio Africanus and his brother Lucius, as well as that between Hannibal and his brothers Mago and Hasdrubal, Silius appears to defy expectations.

The Scipio brothers should come in pairs, the twin lightning bolts of war (Cic. *Balb.* 34; Lucr. 3.1034; Verg. *A.* 6.842), and while the pairing of Lucius and Cornelius Scipio is not as celebrated as that of their father, Publius Cornelius Scipio, and his elder brother Gnaeus Cornelius Scipio Calvus (who both fought and died [211 BCE] during the Second Punic War), Livy, at least, still devotes some lines to showing the brotherly bond between Africanus and his sibling.[4] Yet this situation does not play out in the *Punica*. While stress is placed upon the image of brotherhood presented by the two elder Scipios, especially once they have died, the relationship of the two younger Scipios is downplayed to the extent that there is only one fleeting reference to Lucius; the reader could even be forgiven, therefore, for thinking that young Africanus was in fact an only child. Conversely, the relationship between Hannibal and his brothers receives singular attention, with both Hasdrubal and Mago assuming roles beyond those assigned to them by Livy.

This paper suggests that Silius's decision to use Carthage as the focal point for his exploration of the fraternal bonds between individuals who hold positions of power is intended to show that fraternity and the tension that can arise

---

[3] On civil war as a repeated and evolving theme for Rome's authors, see the introduction to this volume.

[4] See below.

between equally matched brothers have the potential to jeopardize the stability of a nation. In so doing, Silius's "fraternal bonds" serve as a warning for (Flavian) Rome of the complications involved in the combination of family and state, with a nod to Rome's imperial brothers (notably the Julio-Claudians) and to one of the most complex fraternal pairings of them all—that of Titus and Domitian: two brothers who offer an image of fraternal harmony and dynastic continuity but whose relationship was portrayed by later sources as one of bitter discontent.

1 Brotherhood and the *Punica*

Romulus and Remus: the twin brothers whose legendary quarrel ensured that Rome's foundation was a bloody business. While myths involving the twins featured in early Republican literature, it was not until the late Republic and early Principate that references to them became increasingly politicized.[5] With the exception of some of the Augustan poets, who tried to deflect attention away from the more unsavory aspects of their story,[6] Romulus and Remus's tale of brotherhood-gone-bad was used as proof by authors that Rome's lapses into civil conflict were due as much to its foundation through fraternal bloodshed[7] as to its military

---

[5] The first Roman writer to give an extended account of Romulus and Remus was Fabius Pictor (see Ogilvie 1965, 53); part of the story, at least, also featured in Ennius's *Annales* (Enn. *Ann.* 46–47 [Skutsch]). For an overview of the development of the Romulus and Remus myth as a model for civil war, see Keith in this volume.

[6] Bannon 1997, 158: "Augustan poets, with the exception of Ovid, deflect attention from the fratricide, and focus on reconciliation, as if putting the civil war aside to move forward under Augustus's peace." The Ovidian exception to which Bannon refers is most probably *Fast.* 2.127–44, where Romulus is presented as a thug. Ovid's treatment of Romulus in the *Fasti* is not only controversial, it is contradictory: at *Fast.* 4.807ff. he ignores the established version of the fratricide (alluded to in *Fasti* Book 2) and presents an alternative version of Remus's death; on this controversy and its implications, see especially Boyle/Woodard 2004, xxxix–xliv. Romulus was an important model for Augustus, despite his contradictory status as both fratricide and *conditor* (see Ogilvie 1965, 54). The tension inherent in Romulus as a model is evident in Suetonius (*Aug.* 7.2) and Cassius Dio (53.16.7–8), who both depict Octavian considering, and then dismissing, the name Romulus for his new identity as *princeps*.

[7] See Horace (*Epod.* 7.17–20) and Lucan (1.95), although Keith (in this volume) observes that Horace later rehabilitated Romulus once Augustus's control over the empire was secure. On Rome's perception of the fratricidal conflict between Romulus and Remus as a cause for Rome's history of civil war, see, for example, Hardie 1993a, 6 and 10. Livy's account (1.6.3–1.7.3) muddies the fratricidal waters by offering two versions of the death of Remus. At first he cites the "abominable quarrel" (*foedum certamen,* Liv. 1.6.4), between them, but then states that Remus was

supremacy in the Mediterranean, which had left it, as Livy's Hannibal so omnisciently states (Liv. 30.44.8), without an external enemy left to fight.[8]

But while these images of fratricide and civil conflict offered negative readings of Roman brotherhood, they were offset by the positive image that Rome sought to portray of those brothers who fought—and often died—together, such as Bitias and Pandarus in the *Aeneid* (Verg. *A.* 9.672–716, 722–54, 11.396) and Publius and Gnaeus Scipio in the *Punica*.[9] The *Punica* offers ample opportunity for viewing both the best and worst that Rome had to offer in terms of its fraternal relationships, and allusions to Romulus are frequent throughout the epic, suggestive both of Rome's foundation and the fraternal nature of that foundation.[10] These fraternal pairings have received detailed attention from scholars in the past,[11] but it is worth (re)considering some of those pairings that offer an insight into the dual nature of Roman brotherhood.

At Saguntum, for example, Silius simultaneously shows the destructive and exemplary nature of brotherhood in the tale of twin brothers who die together

---

killed (assailant unnamed) in the tumult following the augury contest between the two brothers (1.7.2). He then leaves the matter open for debate by writing that "the more common report" (*uulgatior fama*) was that Remus was killed by Romulus after he had jumped over the latter's walls. Tipping 2010, 23–24, observes that "Romulus's... reference to 'my walls' (*mea moenia*) marks him as a proto-imperial master, not a republican servant, of nascent Rome." On Livy's Romulus, see Alfonsi 1983 and Stem 2007.

8 See Stocks 2014, 45–46 and 132 n. 74. In addition to Livy, ancient writers who perceived the Hannibalic war as a turning point for Rome include Plb. 6.2.5–7, 11.1, and Sil. 10.657–58. Despite nominally dealing with the subject matter of the Second Punic War (Rome vs. Carthage), allusions to Rome's civil wars are rife throughout Silius Italicus's *Punica*: see, for example, Tipping 2010, esp. 35–44; see, too, Marks in this volume, who argues that Silius uses the theme of civil war (in *Punica* 14) "to point to positive developments in Rome's story." Conversely, Lucan's epic on the civil war between Caesar and Pompey uses Carthage as a means of exploring the horror of Rome's civil strife by depicting Caesar as being worse than Hannibal (e.g., Luc. 7.799–801).

9 Rome's history is marked by a number of notable fraternal pairings, including Tiberius and Gaius Gracchus (2nd c. BCE); Cicero and his brother Quintus (1st c. BCE); and the Julio-Claudian pairings of Gaius and Lucius Caesar, Tiberius and Drusus, and even the adoptive pairing of Nero and Britannicus (see n. 49). The association between brotherhood and civil strife at Rome is a topic frequently referred to by ancient authors. For example, Dionysius of Halicarnassus (2.11.2–3) and Appian (*BC* 1.1.1, 1.2.4–5), among others, write that despite many conflicts between the Roman people in the years following Rome's foundation by Romulus, it was not until the murder of Tiberius Gracchus, in light of the Gracchi brothers' attempted reforms, that Rome's citizens violently turned against each other (see especially Wiseman 2010, 25–29).

10 On the *Punica*'s allusions to Romulus, see especially Tipping 2010, 22–26.
11 See McGuire 1997, 213–14; Augoustakis 2010a, 132–34; Hulls 2011.

during the siege, as brothers should, but do so within the context of a Lucan-inspired kin-killing spree (Sil. 2.636–49):[12]

> uos etiam primo gemini cecidistis in aeuo,
> Eurymedon fratrem et fratrem mentite Lycorma,
> cuncta pares, dulcisque labor sua nomina natis
> reddere et in uultu genetrici stare suorum.
> iam fixus iugulo culpa te soluerat ensis,   640
> Eurymedon, inter miserae lamenta senectae,
> dumque malis turbata parens deceptaque uisis
> "quo ruis? huc ferrum" clamat "conuerte, Lycorma,"
> ecce simul iugulum perfoderat ense Lycormas.
> sed magno "quinam, Eurymedon, furor iste?" sonabat   645
> cum planctu geminaeque notis decepta figurae
> funera mutato reuocabat nomine mater,
> donec transacto tremebunda per ubera ferro
> tunc etiam ambiguos cecidit super inscia natos.

You, too, twins, fell in the prime of life, Eurymedon and Lycormas, brother imitating brother, alike in every respect. And it was a sweet struggle for a mother to ascribe the right names to her sons and to be sure of the features of each of her own. Now fixed in your throat, the sword has absolved you from blame, Eurymedon, amidst the grieving of your wretch old mother, and meanwhile the parent, troubled by this evil and deceived in what she has seen shouts "Where are you hurrying? Turn your sword here, Lycormas." Look! At the same time Lycormas pierces his throat with the sword. But with a great groan she wailed "What madness, Eurymedon, is this?" and deceived by the marks of the twins' features the mother kept calling back the dead with alternating names, until, with a sword driven through her trembling breasts she, ignorant, then fell upon her indistinguishable sons.

Here the stress is less upon the violence of these brothers' deaths than upon their likeness to one another. These are identical twins (*gemini*, 2.637),[13] indistinguishable from one another, even in the eyes of their mother, and as such their darkly Lucanean act of suicide becomes simultaneously a form of kin-killing, since their identities are ambiguous (*ambiguos*, 2.649), and in a constant state of flux

---

[12] All translations are my own. The text used for *Punica* is Delz 1987.
[13] Calderini (Muecke/Dunston 2011), *ad loc.*, sees a parallel between this line and *Aeneid* 10 where the twin sons of Daucus, Larides and Thymber, who are so similar that their parents cannot tell them apart (*Daucia, Laride Thymberque, simillima proles, | indiscreta suis gratusque parentibus error*, Verg. *A.* 10.391–92), are killed by Pallas. The brutality in the death of Vergil's twins (*A.* 10.394–98), is matched in Silius's account, but whereas Pallas's different modes of dispatch leave the dead twins with physical differences to distinguish them in death (Hardie's "fatal discrimination" [1993b, 62]), Silius's twins remain indistinguishable: rather, their perpetual similarity serves to reiterate the act of "kin-killing" that has taken place.

(*mutato reuocabat nomine*, 2.647). Thus this scene is not only a reminder of Lucan's Rome, which through its civil conflict turned a sword upon itself (Luc. 1.2–4); it is a reminder of those twin-pairings that have ended in kin-conflict/civil strife (notably Romulus and Remus and Eteocles and Polynices[14]), and it ensures that the deaths of these twins is entrenched within an epic cycle of bloodshed and the breakdown of civil and familial bonds.[15]

So too in Book 9, in a scene which scholars have noted "points backwards and forwards to Lucan's epic and Roman civil war,"[16] the Italian Solimus ends up mortally wounding his father and then committing suicide, all because he attempts to live up to his responsibilities as brother to the dead Mancinus. The reason cited for his nighttime escapade is that he is searching for the body of his brother (*fratrisque petebat | Mancini ... corpus*, Sil. 9.93–94); he sees the moonlight reflected off the fraternal shield (*fraternus ... umbo*, Sil. 9.108–9) and refers to himself as a *frater* at line 112. When the Romans later come upon Solimus's corpse, their previous grief for Mancinus is described as being renewed by this new fraternal death (*fraterna ... morte*, Sil. 9.258). Yet the stress is not only upon the fraternal aspect of the act but also upon the aspect of mistaken identity. For Solimus commits suicide after he fails to recognize his father Satricus as *his* father, just as Satricus failed to recognize the dead Mancinus as his son. Hardie offers a detailed reading of the "recognition and misrecognition" in this scene, observing that mistaken identity, in this instance, leads also to a switching of roles.[17] For when Satricus unwittingly dons the armor of his dead son Mancinus, he also assumes his identity: "father does not know son, but unwittingly

---

14 On Eteocles and Polynices' brotherhood, see Cowan 2003; Coffee 2006; Bernstein 2008, esp. 64–104. Like the twins in this episode, as well as Vergil's Larides and Thymber (see n. 13), Statius's Polynices and Eteocles are famously difficult to tell apart. O'Gorman 2005, 32, explores the tension created in Statius's epic by the identical nature of Oedipus's twin sons, especially when dealing with the issue of primacy; Hardie 1993b, 62, goes a step further, noting that "in Statius the problem of telling brothers apart becomes programmatic."
15 On the "intra-familial conflict" of this scene, see also Hulls in this volume. Bernstein, in this volume, who deals more broadly with the suicides at Saguntum, also draws attention to this familial violence and its connection to civil war.
16 Tipping 2010, 37; see also, in particular, Dominik 2006, 124–25; Marks 2010a, 137. Marks 2010a, 137, observes that "this tale evokes civil war not only because of the confusion between friend and foe or, rather, father and foe, but because the details of familial killing and suicide are common analogues of civil strife and the story as a whole is modeled after double-death tales associated with Rome's own history of civil war." Tipping 2010, 37 n. 82, however, notes that "although Satricus is involved in a scenario suggestive of civil war, his speech at Sil. *Pun.* 9. 124–43 is, as Lundström (1971: 101) observes, deeply patriotic."
17 Hardie 1993b, 68.

impersonates son."[18] Yet Solimus, catching sight of his brother's armor in the moonlight, recognizes the arms, but not the man: he sees neither his father nor his "brother"; rather he mistakes Satricus for the enemy, Carthage.[19] Kin-killing appears excusable by virtue of this mistaken identity, and yet… Solimus may have "seen" the enemy, but he also recognized the familiar arms. In killing his foe, therefore, he simultaneously—and knowingly—killed his brother's "double." Thus this scene of mistaken identities highlights the air of civil strife that underpins Silius's narrative as all boundaries are broken down. Not only is friend mistaken for foe, but that foe is still dressed as kin; so, too, Solimus commits patricide out of *pietas* for his brother, while his father momentarily usurps the position of his son, so overturning the natural order of succession. By overturning expected norms, Silius reiterates the perverted nature of Rome's civil conflicts.

Such scenes, therefore, place stress upon the association between kin-killing and the fraternal pairing, but even those scenes which supposedly depict positive images of brothers-(dying)-in-arms make us pause for thought. In one of the most detailed accounts of brotherly action in the *Punica*, the three brothers Xanthippus, Eumachus, and Critias (sons of the Spartan Xanthippus and Carthaginian Barce) face off in the battle of the Ticinus against three Italian brothers, Virbius, Capys, and Albanus (Sil. 4.392–400).

> Xanthippus gladio, rigida cadit Eumachus hasta,
> et tandem aequatae geminato funere pugnae.
> inde alterna uiris transegit pectora mucro,
> inque uicem erepta posuerunt proelia uita. 395
> felices leti, pietas quos addidit umbris!
> optabunt similes uenientia saecula fratres,
> aeternumque decus memori celebrabitur aeuo,
> si modo ferre diem serosque uidere nepotes
> carmina nostra ualent, nec famam inuidit Apollo. 400

Xanthippus was killed by the sword, Eumachus by the unyielding spear. And at last, after this twin-slaughter, the fight was even. Then each drove his sword through the other's chest, and with their lives snatched away, mutually they put an end to the battle. Fortunate in death were those, whom *pietas* added to the shades! Future ages will wish for brothers like these, and their eternal glory will be celebrated forever, if only my poetry has the strength to endure and to behold subsequent generations, and if Apollo does not envy my fame.

---

18 Hardie 1993b, 68.
19 Hardie 1993b, 68, notes that Satricus uses this case of mistaken identity as justification for exonerating his son from the guilt of patricide: "[he] exonerates him for the wound already delivered; 'when you threw your spear at me, I was a Carthaginian (*Poenus eram*)'. (129–30)."

After they have killed one another, the poet interrupts his narrative to praise these "brothers" (*fratres*, Sil. 4.397) whose *pietas* is responsible for sending them to the shades (*umbris*, Sil. 4.396).[20] But while the poet claims that future generations will long to have brothers just like these—brothers who fight and die beside you—the question of what these brothers have actually achieved remains. This scene, which Jean-Michel Hulls has explored in some detail,[21] bears echoes of the famous battle between the Horatii and the Curiatii in Livy's *Ab Urbe Condita*, but unlike the outcome of Livy's fraternal conflict, both sets of Silius's brothers die. The emphasis on kin-killing and fraternal, "twin" pairings is evident through the "twin slaughter" (*geminato funere*, Sil. 4.393) of the brothers Xanthippus and Eumachus. So too the last two brothers standing (Virbius and Critias), although they are not brothers in blood, through their mutual slaughter of one another bear a resemblance to the twins Eteocles and Polynices in their final battle to the death.[22]

At first glance, these examples of brothers-in-arms may appear to offer little more than nuance to Silius's portrayal of brotherhood in the *Punica*, and yet this recurrent aspect of what we may term "twin-dom" has repercussions for how we should view the fraternal bonds between those brothers whose actions can be said to impact upon the fate of a state or nation—namely our Barcids and Scipios. Bannon notes that "if brothers could differ, Romans measured their differences against a belief that brothers were innately similar, identical in a way even when they weren't twins."[23] It is this notion of twin-dom in brotherhood that is, I believe, key to our understanding of when a brother can or cannot be deemed to present a threat to his sibling's authority in the *Punica*. For in being his brother's equal—in being twin-like—a brother can fight as a kindred spirit beside, but also has the potential to supplant, his sibling. And if that brother should also happen to be a leading figure in the state, then that potential may have devastating repercussions.

---

20 See Bessone in this volume, who argues that values such as *pietas* are redefined in Flavian literature as a "celebration" of kin-slaughter.
21 Hulls 2011.
22 See Cowan 2007, 17.
23 Bannon 1997, 62.

2 Scipios come in pairs?

The family of the Scipios held a prominent place within Rome's cultural memory. The stars of all three Punic wars, they were remembered for their lightning-bolt speed and tenacity and cited as *exempla* by, among others, Valerius Maximus and Cicero.[24] Not only were the Scipios lauded for their protection of Rome during all three of these conflicts, but the fact that they almost invariably came in fraternal pairs proved appealing to Rome's authors who viewed this as an *exemplum* of fraternal piety for the sake of Rome.[25]

In the *Punica*, the most notable Scipiad pairing is that of Publius and Gnaeus in the first half of the war. While it is clear from the outset that Publius, at least, views himself as being one of a pair (e.g., he prays in Book 4 that he might have a death his brother would approve of: *liceat bellanti accersere mortem, | quam patriae fratrique probem*, Sil. 4.674–75), there is little sense of—or opportunity for—rivalry between them. Both fight separately, and both die separately. It is notable that the idea of them being paired is only stressed when they are already dead: at the start of Book 15, for example, the poet refers to the twin Scipios who have been killed in battle (*geminus iacet hoste superbo | Scipio, belligeri, Mauortia pectora, fratres*, Sil. 15.3–4). And prior to this, in Book 13, during the younger Scipio's trip to the underworld, they are described as being of one mind (*succedunt simulacra uirum concordia, patris | unanimique simul patrui*, Sil. 13.650–51), wandering together around the *loca amoena* of the pious (*loca amoena piorum*, Sil. 13.703). They even appear together on Africanus's shield, an image of fraternal piety (Sil. 17.396–98).[26]

This positive fraternal dynamic—albeit one that is only stressed in death—stands in contrast to that of Scipio Africanus with his brother Lucius, who makes

---

[24] Scipio Africanus was the favorite *exemplum* of Valerius Maximus (see Bloomer 1992, 150; Tipping 2010, 53). Cicero was particularly fond of Scipio Aemilianus as an *exemplum*; see, for example, the famed "dream of Scipio," where the younger Scipio is visited in a dream by his dead grandfather, Africanus (Cic. *Rep.* 6.12). This scene has caused some controversy over how best to interpret its function in Cicero's text; cf., e.g., Stevenson 2005.

[25] Tipping 2010, 169, observes that while Scipio regards his and his brother's death as "nobly Roman" (Sil. 13.663–95), he also views them as resulting from "a lack of caution." His advice to his son, therefore, is to employ caution in battle.

[26] Although presenting an image of fraternal piety, the images on this shield are described as "dread" (*dira | effigies*, Sil. 17.397–98); they are "effigies associated with the dead and dark practices" (Stocks 2014, 89 n. 29). *dira effigies* parallels the description of the images on Scaevola's shield (*cui dirae caelatur laudis honora | effigie clipeus*, Sil. 8.384–85).

little more than a fleeting appearance at the funeral games held by his brother in Book 16 (Sil. 16.575–82):

> quos postquam clamor plaususque probauit honores,   575
> germanus ducis atque effulgens Laelius ostro
> nomina magna uocant laeti manesque iacentum
> atque hastas simul effundunt. celebrare iuuabat
> sacratos cineres atque hoc decus addere ludis.
> ipse etiam mentis testatus gaudia uultu   580
> ductor, ut aequauit meritis pia pectora donis
> et frater thoraca tulit multiplicis auri.

> After a shout and applause approved these honors, the brother of Scipio, and Laelius shining in purple, joyfully summoned the great names and shades of the dead, and at the same time hurled their spears. They delighted in honoring the sacred ashes and in adding glory to the games by this act. The leader himself also, with an expression that bore witness to the joy of his spirit, he matched his faithful friends to the gifts they had earned, and his brother received a corselet woven with gold.

Lucius is not named by the poet but rather is called *germanus ducis* (16.576) and *frater* (16.582). Compare this with Livy's account of this fraternal pairing, and the contrast is striking. Lucius may not match his brother in terms of his achievements, but Africanus still wishes to compare his brother's deeds to his own, stating that Lucius's sacking of Orongis was equal to his own victory over New Carthage (*Scipio conlaudato fratre cum quanto poterat uerborum honore Carthagini ab se captae captam ab eo Orongin aequasset*, Liv. 28.4.2). Again the stress is upon the equality of this relationship—the "twin" nature of their victories, at least in the mind of Scipio Africanus. And yet, while Livy's portrayal of this fraternal pairing is one of harmony, he too shows the danger that brotherhood can pose to the state when, after the Second Punic War, he describes Scipio Africanus's reaction to his brother's prosecution for allegedly misappropriating revenues from his victory over Antiochus. Livy tells us that Africanus snatched his brother forcibly away from the tribunes who had come to arrest him, and in doing so, he placed brotherly loyalty above civic duty (Liv. 38.56.8–9):[27]

---

[27] Seneca also offers an account of this story in the *ad Polybium*, observing that Scipio's impatience for the law was as much on display as his *pietas* for his brother (*et quam impatiens iuris aequi pietas Africani fuerit, cunctis apparuit*, Sen. *Dial.* 11.14.4). Briscoe 2008, *ad* 38.56.9 notes that "in the principate emperors often tried to behave as if they were ordinary citizens." His words draw attention to the position held by Scipio here—a figure of preeminence (a pseudo *princeps*) who does not perform the role he should—namely, acting as an ordinary citizen and respecting the position of the *elected* tribunes.

> et illi auctores sequendi sunt, qui, cum L. Scipio et accusatus et damnatus sit pecuniae captae ab rege legatum in Etruria fuisse Africanum tradunt; qua post famam de casu fratris adlatam relicta legatione cucurrisse eum Romam et, cum a porta recta ad forum se contulisset, quod in uincla duci fratrem dictum erat, reppulisse a corpore eius uiatorem, et tribunis retinentibus magis pie quam ciuiliter uim fecisse.
>
> And one should follow those writers who say that, when Lucius Scipio was both accused and condemned of accepting money from the king, Africanus was an ambassador in Etruria; that after he had received the report about his brother's downfall, he had left his post as legate and had hurried to Rome; and that when he'd made his way directly from the gate to the forum because it was said that his brother was being led in chains, he had pushed the messenger away from his person and had attacked the tribunes as they tried to hold him back, acting more in accordance with familial loyalty than as a citizen.

Ironically, it is brotherly loyalty that is a danger to the State, rather than an act of kin-killing, and yet even this loyalty is depicted as a perversion of the ideal fraternal bond. For brotherhood is shown as a dangerous concept when taken to the extreme, be that extreme competition and hence a model for civil strife, or as with Scipio here, an extreme case of *pietas*. Both extremities are destabilizing; both are detrimental to the state, revealing the conflict that can exist between state and family obligations.[28]

Perhaps, then, it should come as no surprise that Silius should choose to depict Scipio as a solo figure, a model of one-man rule—and a model, as Marks has observed,[29] for Domitian. But we would also do well to remember that the *Punica*'s Scipio is still an individual who takes *pietas* to the extreme:[30] he is the boy who initially attempts to commit suicide when he sees his father on the verge of death in battle in Book 4 and is only prevented by the god Mars (Sil. 4.457–59), and he is the young man who states that he will avenge his father and uncle (*uobis ultor ego*, Sil. 15.205) with blood-shed, even after Jupiter has been revealed as Scipio's real father (Sil. 13.615–49). (Jupiter's paternity, a "fact" in the epic that is merely a rumor at Liv. 26.19.6–9,[31] might not have diminished Scipio's loyalty to his family, but it surely drives a wedge between him and Lucius [now revealed as his half-brother], and it shows that perhaps we should not expect Africanus to be one of a fraternal pair, given that he is not really a Scipio at all....)[32]

---

[28] On the conflict between family and state, especially in relation to the *Punica*, see Bernstein 2010.
[29] Marks 2005b, 218–44.
[30] On the young Scipio's less-than-heroic motivation in this scene, see for example Tipping 2010, 147–48.
[31] Levene 2010, 119–20, discusses the possible parallels that may be implied between Scipio and Alexander the Great in this scene from Livy. He notes (119 n. 87) that a similar story was told about Augustus.
[32] On Scipio's paternity in the *Punica* see Marks 2005b, 187–206; and Bernstein 2008, 150–56. Bernstein 2010, 386–87, notes that Scipio's true paternity remains concealed from most of the

3 Carthaginian Brotherhood: Hannibal and Hasdrubal and Mago

The complexity of Scipio's family relations stand in contrast to the portrayal of Hannibal and his two brothers: Mago and Hasdrubal, whose position as brothers is never cast in doubt and who are at times shown to be his equal in combat.[33] Augoustakis has previously noted that 12 of the 54 references to *frater* in the *Punica* occur in Book 15 emphasizing Hasdrubal's clear attachment to his brother.[34] A similar case can be seen for Mago in Book 5, where 6 out of 7 references apply to the brotherly bond between the Barcid boys during the battle of Lake Trasimene. Here Mago is wounded, and as a result Hannibal is unable to focus on the battle (he is described as *amens*, Sil. 5.347) until he knows that his brother (*fratrem*, Sil. 5.347) is safe. Mago, in turn, is seen trying to comfort Hannibal's "brotherly cares" (*fraternas ... curas*, Sil. 5.370). That we should think of Mago as a brother equal to—and as such perhaps rival to—Hannibal is suggested by his first appearance in the Punica, where he is described as "breathing" like his brother in battle, literally his brother-in-arms (*fratrem spirat in armis*), and dressed, like him, in purple (Sil. 3.238–40):

> his rector fulgens ostro super altior omnes
> germanus nitet Hannibalis gratoque tumultu
> Mago quatit currus et fratrem spirat in armis.   240

> Their leader, gleaming in purple, shining above them all, the brother of Hannibal, Mago, rejoicing in the tumult, drove his chariot and breathed as his brother-in-arms.

The depiction of Mago as the brother upon whom Hannibal relies is an accentuation of his role in Livy. A case in point is Silius's depiction of events after Cannae,

---

characters in the epic. Although Marks 2005b, 187–88, perceives the references to Scipio's divine and mortal fathers as creating "mixed signals" (187) that reflect the contradictions in the received tradition on Scipio's parentage, the continued prominence of Scipio's mortal father after Book 13 ensures that Silius's Scipio maintains his association with other sons of Jupiter (notably Alexander and Hercules) and yet also continues to demonstrate filial *pietas*. The "double-edge" to Scipio's paternity is also evident in the manner in which Scipio's mother, Pomponia, reveals the story of his conception. Despite having been raped by Jupiter, she succeeds in presenting this event as necessary for Rome's salvation: "thus, she becomes the carrier of divine will, without at the same time damaging her chastity and reputation as *univira*" (Augoustakis 2008, 68).
33 On Hannibal's relationship with his brothers (as well as brotherhood in the *Punica* in general), see recently Stocks 2014, 167–81.
34 Augoustakis 2003, 111 n. 3.

where he shows Mago encouraging his brother to continue his march to Rome, a role that in Livy (Liv. 22.51.2–4) is played by Hannibal's cavalry commander, Maharbal, but here is shifted to maintain Silius's fraternal focus (Sil. 10.382–87):[35]

> "tanta mole" inquit "non Roma, ut creditur, ipsa,
> sed Varro est uictus. quonam tam prospera Martis
> munera destituis fato patriamque moraris?
> mecum exsultet eques; iuro hoc caput, accipe muros   385
> Iliacos portasque tibi sine Marte patentes."
> dumque ea Mago fremit cauto non credita fratri.

> "By so great an effort," he said, "not Roma herself, as is believed, but Varro has been conquered. Because of what fate do you toss aside the oh so desirable gifts of Mars and keep your country waiting? Let the cavalry charge forth with me; I swear on my life, accept the 'Trojan' walls and the gates lying open to you without war." And while Mago fumed thus, his cautious brother did not believe him.

Here Hannibal not only appears as the inferior of the two brothers, at least in terms of martial spirit, but he also displays a worrying lack of trust. *Non credita* (10.387), translated by Duff as "refused to believe," could equally refer to a lack of trust between the brothers. While there is no overt suggestion that Hannibal is anything other than troubled by the nightmare sent to him by *Somnus* at the bidding of Juno (Sil. 10.343–71),[36] there is still a hint of (the potential for) friction in the fraternal bond, a suggestion that the trust between brothers—such trust as is required to prevent a fraternal pairing turning bad—is now lacking.

Furthermore, while Silius often depicts Mago as the more decisive of the two brothers, Livy highlights the indecisiveness of Mago as a contributing factor to the stagnation of Hannibal's campaign in Italy (*nihil usquam spei, nihil auxilii esse. nec Magonem ex Gallia mouere tumultus quicquam nec coniungere sese Hannibali, et Hannibalem ipsum iam et fama senescere et uiribus*, Liv. 29.3.15). And it is not just Livy whom Silius deviates from. Although the ruse which Hannibal employs to evade Fabius in Book 7, in which Mago plays a vital role, is also

---

[35] See Spaltenstein 1990, *ad* 10.382. The attribution of this comment to Maharbal is evident in sources prior to Livy (see Calderini [Muecke/Dunston 2011], *ad* 10.375; Chaplin 2000, 56 n. 22); these include Cato *hist.* 86–87 and Coel. *hist.* 25. Valerius Maximus also records the tale (V. Max. 9.5.ext.3).

[36] There is a certain irony in Juno's choice to use *Somnus* to relay her message to Hannibal. At the introduction to this scene (Sil. 10.343–71), Silius notes that Juno had often used Sleep to close Jupiter's eyes (her brother) against his will: *quo saepe ministro | edomita inuiti componit lumina fratris* (Sil. 10.341–42). Just as *Somnus* has previously been used to cause friction between siblings, now he will do the same between Hannibal and Mago.

referred to by Polybius (3.92.3–3.94), here there is no mention of Mago: Hannibal is assisted instead by a certain Hasdrubal, an officer in command of the service corps.

Silius's elevation of Mago's role in the *Punica* is not, I believe, something that we should dismiss simply as epic license. For in stressing the relationship that existed between Hannibal and Mago, Silius offers a brotherly pairing that simultaneously highlights the positive and negative aspects of Rome's attitude to brotherhood. For Mago is Hannibal's brother-in-arms, who fights beside him, even if he does not die beside him. But he is also someone who through his decisiveness and his parity with his brother, has the potential,—even if it is not realized,—to replicate and hence threaten Hannibal's position as leader. While it might be counterintuitive to engage too deeply in a case of counterfactual narrative—i.e., what might have happened had Mago not died on his way back from Gaul, had Carthage won the war, etc.—the potential that the little brother has to supplant his elder sibling offers an intriguing parallel for contemporary Rome, where Domitian was the little brother who did survive and who did, to all intents and purposes, supplant his brother.

But Hannibal has not just one little brother, but two; and Hasdrubal, the little brother who never fights alongside Hannibal in the epic, appears to revel in his deeds. Unlike Mago, who breathes as Hannibal's brother in arms, Hasdrubal "breathes" the deeds of his brother (*fratris spirans ingentia facta*, Sil. 15.411). But while Hasdrubal shows due deference to his brother, Rome perceives him as a "substitute"[37]—or rather, "twin"—Hannibal and recognizes the potential that these "twins" have for fraternal strife as her collective populace imagines the pair competing to destroy the city (*uenisse, superbo | qui fratri certet, cui maxima Gloria cedat | urbis deletae*, Sil. 15.585–87). Is Rome, then, incapable of recognizing harmony in brotherhood when the greatest prize—mastery of Rome—is at stake? Through the use of *certet*, and the sense of competition implied therein, there is a hint that Rome has paid the price too many times, at least in epic terms (e.g., Lucan's Caesar and Pompey; Statius's Eteocles and Polynices), to believe that kinship at the top can lead to anything other than civil conflict.

---

37 See Augoustakis 2003, 119: "Silius has already prepared the reader to consider Hasdrubal as a substitute for Hannibal."

4 Domitian and Titus

Thus this depiction of Carthaginian brotherhood, where Hannibal's brothers remain loyal to him but Rome nevertheless sees the potential for rivalry, stands juxtaposed with the solo Scipio Africanus, an almost brotherless figure who becomes a model for one-man rule. This is not to suggest that this model is unproblematic: Scipio is still an individual driven by bloodlust and still an individual who, in his wearing of the purple, is akin to the Carthaginian he is fighting (Sil. 15.205, 17.395).[38] But by removing that threat of brotherly rivalry, we do have an image of a man who offers stability for Rome, even if that stability will come at a price (the eventual loss of the Republic). In this way Scipio fits in with a Flavian model that sought to promote a return to Augustanism and, after the damaging effect of civil war, a return to peace.[39]

This idea of peace featured heavily on the coinage from Vespasian's reign, and even though Titus and Domitian subsequently introduced new themes on their coinage, peace remained the valuable commodity that the Flavians offered Rome's *populus*.[40] Yet the Flavians' return to Augustanism aimed at more than promoting the image of peace and stability through the depiction of *Pax*. For Vespasian, in presenting his imperial family to the world, depicted his two sons as the heirs apparent: a pair of brothers, united to secure the future of the empire, who shared the title *principes iuuentutis* on his coinage.[41] This stylization recalled the fraternal pairings of the Julio-Claudians: Gaius and Lucius Caesar, as well as Tiberius and Drusus, and Drusus *minor* and Germanicus (among others) thereafter, who also received (or shared) the title of *princeps iuuentutis*. In the case of the Julio-Claudian pairings, and maybe even our Flavians, the image of fraternal harmony was further cemented through their association via imperial imagery with

---

38 On Scipio's desire to wear purple at Sil. 15.205, see Marks 2005b, 92 n. 80, and Stocks 2014, 192 and 211. On Sil. 17.395, Hardie 1993a, 25, writes: "both ... wear purple – the Punic colour!"
39 See, for example, Noreña 2003, 28 (who focuses in particular on Vespasian's *Templum Pacis* and its link to Augustus's *Ara Pacis*).
40 See especially Carradice/Buttrey 2007 (=*RIC* II²), who offer an overview of the themes central to Flavian coinage. The Flavians' coinage indicates a desire to look back to Augustan ideals, especially in their use of the legends *Pax*, *Pietas*, and *Fides*. See, too, Liebeschuetz 1979, 167–82, as well as Bernstein 2008, 156, and Bernstein 2010, 389, who notes that Domitian stopped producing *Pietas* types in 83CE and started issuing *Fides Publica* types in 84 CE.
41 On the significance of this depiction of Titus and Domitian on Vespasian's coinage, see especially Wood 2016, 131–32.

the mythic twins Castor and Pollux, who offered an *exemplum* of brotherly concord.[42] "Twin-dom" once more, but this time with a positive face.

Yet offset against these images of familial harmony and the young *princeps* Domitian venerating his father and elder brother after their deaths[43] is the image offered by later literary sources, of an embittered young man trying to usurp the position of his brother Titus.[44] Much has been made by Rome's authors of Domitian's supposed plots against his brother (e.g., Suet. *Tit.* 9.3, *Dom.* 2.3),[45] but in the *Punica* (Sil. 3.571–629), Silius's Domitian is shown to supplant, and surpass, his brother legitimately, for when he joins the gods, Jupiter tells us, he will no longer be the second son but shall take Romulus's throne, and his father and brother shall sit either side of him (*tarda senectam | hospitia excipient caeli, solioque Quirinus | concedet, mediumque parens fraterque locabunt*, Sil. 3.626–28). Neither Vespasian nor Titus is mentioned by name in this digression; Vespasian is *pater/parens* (Sil. 3.597, 628) and Titus *iuuenis/frater* (Sil. 3.603, 628). Domitian, by contrast, is referred to as *Germanicus*, alluding to his "triumph" over the Chatti

---

[42] On the application of the title *princeps* (or *principes*) *iuuentutis* to the Julio-Claudian brothers, as well as to Titus and Domitian, see especially Krasne 2011, 156–57, esp. n. 732. Krasne also notes the importance of the Dioscuri as "the traditional *exemplum* for fraternal *pietas* between imperial heirs in the Julio-Claudian period" (156). She suggests that the association between the Dioscuri and the imperial fraternal heirs could be extended to Titus and Domitian, an association that Wood 2016, 132, asserts as a fact.

[43] See, for example, Tuck 2016, 123, who notes, in reference to the Arch of Titus, that Domitian's addition of the image depicting the apotheosis of Titus following his brother's death was "a posthumous statement … promoting the Flavian Dynasty."

[44] Hardie 1993a, 10, observes the prominence given to fraternal pairings in the early Principate by Rome's authors: "Brothers, harmonious or discordant, continue to be a theme in the history of the first-century imperial household: Tiberius and Drusus, Gaius and Lucius, Nero and Britannicus, Titus and Domitian." On Silius's relationship with Domitian and the Flavian emperors, see Dominik 2010, esp. 430–31 and 444–45.

[45] The accounts of Suetonius and Tacitus concerning Domitian's hatred towards his brother will most certainly have been influenced by the reception of Domitian after his death (on this see Flower 2006, 234–75). Wilson 2003, 529, however, argues against reading these sources simply as "implementing official policy [*damnatio memoriae*] through literary means." Levick 1999, 188–89, suggests that any bitterness on the part of Domitian towards his brother Titus may have been due to Vespasian and Titus's refusal to allow him any serious advancement during their lifetime. This suggestion is supported by the Flavian coinage after 71 CE, which indicates the implementation of a hierarchal scheme by Vespasian that placed Domitian in a distinctly inferior position to his brother Titus (see Hurlet 2016, 32). Despite the depiction of Titus and Domitian as *principes iuuentutis*, therefore, there appears to have been a clear distinction made between the two brothers during Vespasian's reign. On the rivalry between Titus and Domitian, see also Jones 1992, 20–21, and Gering 2012, 95–99.

in 83 CE.[46] Both Pliny (*Pan.* 16.3, 20.24) and Tacitus (*Ag.* 39) show contempt for Domitian's Germanic triumph, but Silius suggests that it is precisely this victory that allows Domitian to surpass the achievements of his brother and father: *at tu transcendes, Germanice, facta tuorum* ("but you, Germanicus, will surpass the deeds of your family," Sil. 3.607).[47] But this is still panegyric with an edge. Domitian may surpass his brother and show himself as Rome's second founder by taking Quirinus's seat, but in showing him assuming the seat of a god closely associated with Romulus,[48] this scene also serves as a reminder of the cost in brotherly blood for that foundation: a reminder that two brothers, however harmonious their pairing, cannot rule an empire.[49]

---

46 See Augoustakis 2010c, 7.

47 McDermott/Orentzel 1977, 27, note that "by addressing the emperor as Germanicus Silius compliments Domitian on his victory in the war with the Chatti, and by his phrase *facta tuorum* marks it as more important than the Judaic victory of Vespasian and Titus." The portrayal of Domitian surpassing his father and brother may also be a nod to Ovid's *Metamorphoses* (15.850–51), where Caesar rejoices in his "son" Augustus surpassing him in *bene facta* (*Met.* 15.850), thus couching Domitian as a new Augustus and Silius, by extension, as a new Ovid. The name *Germanicus* suggests a further parallel with Scipio (as well as the Julio-Claudians, e.g., Claudius's son "Britannicus"), who through his title Africanus was the first be given a title associated with the people whom he had conquered (Liv. 30.45.6–7). See Tipping 2010, 45.

48 The god Quirinus was frequently identified with the deified Romulus (see, for example, Cic. *Leg.* 1.3; Verg. *A.* 1.292–93; Liv. 1.20.2). This reference to Quirinus may in fact be a reference to Augustus, since similar praise is employed by Vergil (*G.* 1.24–42, 4.560–62; *A.* 6.791–805, 8.714–16) and Ovid (*Met.* 15.868–70) for Augustus and his deification (see Spaltenstein 1986, *ad* 3.627). If true, this would show Domitian assuming an Augustan role as a (re)founder of the *res publica*. Yet the reference to Quirinus, even if it should be an indirect reference to Augustus, cannot be disassociated from its ties to Romulus. The reference thus maintains a "fraternal edge" especially since it features in a passage where Domitian is shown to surpass the achievements of his brother (and father). Tipping 2010, 22 n. 31, observes that Scipio is also associated with Quirinus in the *Punica* (Sil. 15.82–83), further cementing the parallels between Scipio, Domitian, and Romulus.

49 The Julio-Claudians may have presented sets of harmonious brother-heirs (see pp. 267–68 above), but at least one member of all of these pairs conveniently died before the issue of succession ever became an issue. The exception to this rule was the adoptive pairing of Nero and Britannicus; this, too, ended in death, with Nero, so our sources would have us believe, securing his succession through the murder of his "brother" and rival. Tacitus, on the death of Britannicus, records the following anecdote from his funeral, noting the supposed ancient discord between "brothers" and the belief that it was impossible for a kingdom to be shared: *in campo tamen Martis sepultus est, adeo turbidis imbribus, ut uulgus iram deum portendi crediderit aduersus facinus, cui plerique etiam hominum ignoscebant, <u>antiquas fratrum discordias et insociabile regnum</u> aestimantes* (Tac. *Ann.* 13.17.1).

5 Conclusion: The One-man Band (of Brothers)

What, then, does this mean for the *Punica*'s attitude towards brotherhood? It is clear that both the positive and negative facets of brotherhood are present within the *Punica*. So, too, it is clear that any tension that exists in the fraternal pairings of our power-figures never reaches fruition. Scipio Africanus's brother Lucius may be defined by his role as *frater*, but through only a fleeting appearance, he is utterly forgettable. Hannibal's relationship with his siblings is given far greater prominence, but these little brothers never actually threaten to usurp his position, and both die before the end of the epic. In both cases, then, we have younger brothers whose potential for power is never realized. This is in contrast to Domitian, the little brother who does outlive his elder brother and who, in the *Punica* at least, is depicted as surpassing him. He is presented as a man who is part of a lineage, who honors his family, but who works better alone. His achievements as the brother who does *not* share "twin-ship" with Titus are shown to be better for Rome, just as the solo achievements of Scipio (whose little brother is inconsequential) surpass those of his "twin" predecessors, Publius and Gnaeus. Fraternal instability—or the potential for that instability—in the *Punica* is thus shown to be something that primarily affects the substitutes for Rome: notably Carthage and the Barcid brothers, but also Saguntum and Rome's Italian allies. These substitutes allow us to view the dual-faceted nature of Roman brotherhood (fraternal/civil conflict vs. exemplary *pietas*) at a safe enough distance from Rome that Silius is able to allude—as he frequently does—to Rome's civil-war future without descending into the Lucanean, or even Statian, darkness and pessimism of that civil conflict. Civil strife and fraternal instability remain tangible, yet distant qualities, with Domitian and Scipio illustrating, at least superficially, that it is possible to still be a brother and to govern at the top, provided that you govern alone, as a "one-man band" (of brothers).

William J. Dominik
Civil War, Parricide, and the Sword in Silius Italicus's *Punica*

Silius Italicus's account of the Second Punic War (218–201 BCE) in the *Punica* reveals a preoccupation with civil war and strife, including historical episodes of civil war (e.g., Sil. 13.852–67), literary representations of civil war and its constituent scenes (e.g., Sil. 2.614–91), the metaphorical *topoi* and imagery of civil war (e.g., Sil. 2.654–55), and the manifestations of civil strife at different levels and in various sectors of society (e.g., Sil. 2.243–47).[1] In this regard, he is a paradigmatic Roman author; civil war is one of the topics that characterizes Roman writers and puts them very much in contact with their own society. Constituting no mere rhetorical artifice or declaimer's characterization, their works speak directly to the Romans of their day, as the subject of civil war was central to the Roman mindset and reflected the political climate of the late Republican and early Imperial periods.

Silius himself had a particularly close connection with the effects of civil war, since the tumultuous events of 69 CE took place only one year after the poet's consulship. It therefore stands to reason that his personal experience of civil war as a political figure would inform his explorations, in the *Punica*, of issues concerning power, dynastic struggle, and the political and social consequences of civil strife. In particular, despite the dramatic action of the *Punica* being removed by almost three hundred years from the time of Silius, a contemporary application of the epic would appear to explain the manipulation of the plots and treatment of themes and characters.[2] Similarly, Lucan discusses events that occur before his own time in the *Bellum Ciuile* as a way of commenting upon his own age, while Statius praises Lucan for having composed the quintessential Roman epic (*Silu.* 2.7.48–53, esp. 52–53). For his part, Silius includes just enough obviously

---

I thank the editors Darcy Krasne (Columbia) and Lauren Donovan Ginsberg (Cincinnati) for their many perceptive critical remarks on earlier drafts and their numerous helpful suggestions. In addition, I express my gratitude to Kyle Gervais (Western Ontario) for his astute comments on an earlier draft and to my sister Jane K. Dominik (San Joaquin Delta College) for her remarks on my writing. I also thank the anonymous reviewer for her/his comments and suggestions for improvement. Finally, in composing this chapter I gratefully acknowledge the financial assistance of CAPES (Coordenação de Aperfeiçoamento de Pessoal de Nível Superior), Brazil.

1 This chapter builds further upon the ideas of Dominik 2003 and Dominik 2006.
2 On recent scholarly trends concerning Silius's relationship with the Principate and political discourse in the *Punica*, see Dominik 2010, 444–45.

historical material—along with inserting frequent intertextual references to various Republican and Imperial works—to suggest the relevance of his themes and subject matter to contemporary circumstances. Through his poetic account of a long bygone war of Rome's past, Silius suggests the relevance of the theme of civil discord to Rome's political system during both the Republican and Imperial periods.

Silius is not alone in looking to the long-distant Punic Wars as a historical context for his own time. Lucan's historical epic also reaches backward toward the Second Punic War, while the mythological epics of Statius and Valerius Flaccus—like that of Vergil—point generally forward toward the time of the war and Rome's subsequent hegemony. Despite their different perspectives, all these epics help to define the national consciousness of Rome and therefore to provide illuminating contexts for reading Silius's epic.[3] The *Punica*, like Vergil's *Aeneid*, narrates a story moving from military annihilation to geo-political hegemony; like Lucan's *Bellum Ciuile*, an account of political dissolution arising from military victory; and like Statius's *Thebaid*, a story of the abuse of power leading to social disintegration.[4] Furthermore, like Valerius's *Argonautica*, it suggests the pervasiveness of civil war through various accounts of (actual or threatened) civil conflict or the use of associated *topoi*.[5] Accordingly, though it has been argued that Silius's model is "not a grim episode of civil war,"[6] much of the *Punica* speaks directly to the political issues of the first century CE, including civil strife.

In establishing parallels between his mytho-historical narrative of the Second Punic War and later periods in Roman history, including the periods of civil war from which contemporary Rome emerged, Silius engages in a strategy that can be described as "historical distancing," in contrast to his contemporaries Valerius Flaccus and Statius, who instead engage in "mythological distancing" by using versions of the Argonautic expedition and the Seven against Thebes, respectively, to touch upon the theme of civil war.[7] In addition, Silius engages in a

---

[3] On this idea see Dominik 2003, 488–89; Dominik 2006, 113.
[4] On the theme of power in Statius's *Thebaid*, see Dominik 1994b.
[5] For allusions to civil war in the *Argonautica*, see n. 7; McGuire 1997, 31, 47–50, 58–60, 92, 103–13; and the chapters of Fucecchi, Keith, Krasne, Landrey, Penwill, and Stover in this volume with their attendant bibliographies.
[6] Santini 1991, 1.
[7] Valerius, for example, engages with the theme of civil discord (or potential civil conflict) at Iolcus (V. Fl. 1.71–73, 1.761), Lemnos (V. Fl. 2.107–310), Cyzicus (V. Fl. 3.15–332), and Colchis (V. Fl. 6.1–760), while Statius does so through his accounts of the internecine struggle between the brothers Eteocles and Polynices over the throne of Thebes (cf., e.g., Stat. *Theb.* 1.1, 33–37, 11.524–40, 12.429–35) and of the Lemnian women's crazed massacre of their husbands (*Theb.* 5.190–240). See Marks 2010b on Silius's choice to write historical rather than mythological epic

strategy of "geographical distancing," as discussed below, whereby he identifies various foreign and Italian cities with Rome to comment upon Roman actions, circumstances and values.[8] Silius complements his use of these "distancing" strategies through the employment of a number of other narrative strategies that keep the theme of civil discord vividly before the reader in the *Punica*. The main focus of this chapter is three of these strategies that have not hitherto been combined into a single discussion: the close connection established between parricide[9] and civil war; the association made between civil strife and the *sceptrum/ensis* ("scepter"/"sword"), an emblem of *imperium* associated with kingship, inheritance, and dynasty; and the mention of events from Roman history and scenes from mythology that are suggestive of civil strife, not only from the *Punica* but also in the works of other Imperial writers such as Lucan, Statius, and Tacitus.[10]

1 Saguntum

"[C]ivil war ... spills the blood of their fathers, sons, brethren, friends and countrymen, and makes a total destruction and dissolution."

Margaret Cavendish

1.1 Saguntum as a Distant Rome

In 219 BCE, Hannibal broke camp at New Carthage and proceeded to lay siege to Saguntum, a small city on Spain's south coast, inaugurating the Second Punic War. In mytho-literary terms, the origins of the conflict lay in Aeneas's betrayal

---

and the long timespan between Silius and his subject matter. See also the chapters of Bessone, Fucecchi, Keith, Krasne, Landrey, Penwill, Stover, and van der Schuur in this volume, which deal with direct and indirect civil war in Valerius Flaccus and Statius.

8 See also Bernstein and Marks in this volume on the identification of foreign cities with Rome.
9 In this chapter I use the word "parricide" when making reference to the slaying of one's father, mother, or other close relative; this usage is to be distinguished from "suicide," which of course refers to the killing of oneself.
10 Cf. Bernstein in this volume, p. 181, who in his discussion of the Saguntum episode identifies the main narratives as "political," "divine," and "exemplary" in the process of arguing that the episode's "political, moral, theological, and intertextual narratives all challenge simple assessments of the Saguntines' fate." See also Dominik 2003, who argues that the episode's commentary on the Rome of the Flavian Principate is not especially flattering, and Dominik 2006, who further maintains that this episode (along with the Cannae episode) undercuts Rome's ideal image of itself as an active moral force; for an opposing view, see Marks in this volume.

of Dido in *Aeneid* 4 (Verg. *A.* 4.296–629, esp. 4.586–629). This aetiology is repeatedly evoked in the *Punica*: in *Punica* 2, the Spanish tribes present Hannibal with a gift of armor (Sil. 2.395–456) that includes depictions of Aeneas's desertion of Dido (Sil. 2.420–25), while in *Punica* 8 Anna relates her own version of the betrayal and its aftermath (Sil. 8.50–201). In historical terms as well as within the *Punica's* dramatic action, the siege of Saguntum marks the beginning of renewed hostilities between Rome and Carthage. While the conflict ends with Rome's victory over Carthage (Sil. 17.618–24), Silius casts this victory as the beginning of Rome's decline into civil war and anarchy (cf. Sil. 13.853–69),[11] thus continuing unbroken the trajectory from Dido's death to Rome's recent and present-day misfortunes.

Within eight months of the Carthaginian siege, Saguntum was sacked (Sil. 2.659–95), but not before its citizens committed parricide and suicide *en masse* (Sil. 2.614–707). This collective parricide-suicide, which is the most important scene in the programmatic Saguntum episode, contributes much to the explanation of the city's prominence in the *Punica*;[12] moreover, the attention that Silius devotes to this scene pertains especially to the issue of civil war. Although this parricide-suicide of the Saguntines, who appear paradoxically to embody traditional Roman qualities from an earlier period of Rome's history,[13] occurs as the result of a war with a foreign power, it tropes similar motifs and exemplary events of civil war from Republican and Imperial literature, thereby obfuscating the boundaries between foreign conflict and civil strife. Before examining the epic's poetics of parricide as civil war, the critical nexus of historical and literary themes that envelop the Saguntum episode and its collective parricide-suicide should be considered.

Although, according to Michael von Albrecht, Silius's Saguntum is another Troy, while Silius's Rome is a Troy or an anti-Troy,[14] Rome in fact abounds in alteregos of her own throughout the epic: in addition to Troy (cf., e.g., Sil. 1.42–44, esp. 43), she becomes another Ardea (cf., e.g., 2.603),[15] Capua (cf., e.g., 11.44–

---

11 Cf. Häußler 1978, 208; McGuire 1985, 9; Ahl *et al.* 1986, 2502; Feeney 1991, 302 n. 2; Dominik 2003, 491.
12 On the programmatic aspects of the Saguntum episode, see Dominik 2003.
13 See Dominik 2003, 474–77.
14 Von Albrecht 1964, 172–83; cf. Hardie 1993a, 81–82.
15 Cf. Dominik 2003, 493; cf. 477.

50),[16] Syracuse (cf., e.g., 14.676–78),[17] and Carthage (cf., e.g., 17.618–24).[18] These identifications form part of Silius's aforementioned narrative strategy of "geographical distancing," whereby he projects Rome onto foreign cities and their inhabitants to comment upon historical events and political circumstances at Rome.[19] But the most significant identification of Roman with non-Roman occurs between Saguntum and Rome.[20] The Saguntines suffer a fate similar to the one that besets Rome in the civil wars mentioned by Silius in *Punica* 13, in which the Sibyl prophesies the civil wars of the 80s and 40s BCE featuring the antagonists Marius and Sulla and then Pompey and Caesar (Sil. 13.853–67):[21]

> hic Marius: nec multa dies iam restat ituro
> aetheriam in lucem. ueniet tibi origine parua
> in longum imperium consul. nec Sulla morari   855
> iussa potest, aut amne diu potare soporo:
> lux uocat et nulli diuum mutabile fatum.
> imperium hic primus rapiet, sed gloria culpae,
> quod reddet solus, nec tanto in nomine quisquam
> exsistet, Sullae qui se uelit esse secundum.   860
> ille, hirta cui subrigitur coma fronte, decorum
> et gratum terris Magnus caput: ille deum gens,
> stelligerum attollens apicem, Troianus Iulo
> Caesar auo. quantas moles, cum sede reclusa

---

16 While Capua is represented by Fulvius Flaccus as a second Carthage to Rome (Sil. 13.99–103), a link between Capua and Rome is made generally through references to their shared Trojan ancestry (cf., e.g., Sil. 11.292–97 and 1.40–44 respectively). But even more significant is the connection that Silius makes between the cities through a specific allusion to civil and political strife at Capua in a passage replete with Roman cultural furniture (Sil. 11.44–50; cf. 33–43, 41–54), with Capua being represented as a second Rome through a description (Sil. 11.44–45) of the *patres* ("senators") oppressing the *populus* ("people") and the *plebes* ("plebeians") despising the *senatus* ("Senate"), while the reference to ignoble men who hungered after power (Sil. 11.48–50) recalls the passage featuring the demagogue Varro (Sil. 8.243–57, esp. 247–49, 253–56), discussed below.
17 Marcellus responds to the slaying of Archimedes as if he were one of his own countrymen he had lost in battle (*tu quoque ductoris lacrimas, memorande, tulisti*, Sil. 14.676). For a discussion of civil war in the Syracuse episode in *Punica* 14, see Marks in this volume.
18 Cf. Dominik 2003, 493.
19 On this idea see Dominik 2003, 475–77, 490–94; Dominik 2006, 122. Cf. Marks in this volume, esp. pp. 60–67.
20 Dominik 2003, *passim*.
21 The text used of Silius Italicus's *Punica* in this chapter is that of Delz 1987, with some minor changes in capitalization and punctuation. All other ancient texts and references are from the Teubner editions (also with some minor changes in capitalization and punctuation). All translations are mine.

>   hac tandem erumpent, terraque marique mouebunt!   865
>   heu miseri, quotiens toto pugnabitis orbe!
>   nec leuiora lues quam uictus crimina, uictor.

> Here is Marius: it is not long before he will ascend to the upper world. From humble origins he will become consul for a long period of rule. Nor is Sulla able to delay following the orders or to drink long from the river of forgetfulness. Life calls him and the fate that none of the gods can change. This man will be the first to seize supreme command, but guilty though he is, he alone will resign it. Nor will any man who attains such power be willing to follow Sulla's lead. That handsome head pleasing to the world is that of Magnus, with its shaggy hair rising from the forehead. The other, whose head bears a starry crown, is Trojan Caesar, the offspring of gods and ancestor of Iulus. When they break forth at last, freed from their underworld seclusion, they will shake hard the earth and sea! Ah, wretched men, how often you will fight throughout the whole world! Nor will you, victor, pay less lightly for crimes than the vanquished.

It has been argued that Silius does not relate the Sibyl's vision of the future to Scipio Africanus's present.[22] The Sibyl's pointed remark, *nec leuiora lues quam uictus crimina, uictor*, however, seems at least somewhat applicable as a warning to the Romans of Scipio's day, as discussed below. Other scholars, meanwhile, have maintained there is nothing in the Sibyl's vision to take the reader into the Imperial period,[23] but her vision is reflected in other representations of Rome by Imperial writers such as Vergil (e.g., *Ecl.* 1.65–73, 9.2–6; cf. *Ecl.* 1.11–12; *G.* 1.463–514; *A.* 8.675–713), Lucan (*passim*), and Tacitus (e.g., *Hist.* 1–3 *passim*, 4.1–3; *Ann.* 3.27–28; cf. *Ann.* 1.1–10), who mention or discuss civil war and moral decline at Rome during the Late Republic and Early Empire.[24]

Through the recurrent image of civil war exemplified in these pairs of Roman adversaries, Silius seems to suggest that history never changes: it merely repeats itself in cyclical fashion. Time present and time future are contained in time past.[25] The cyclicality of Roman civil war, starting from the very foundation of Rome, is a *topos*.[26] The political and military antagonists involved—for example, Marius versus Sulla, Pompey versus Caesar—come and go; only the names change. Like the figures involved in these civil wars, the cities they represent come and go; again, only the names change: Troy, Alba Longa, Ardea, Saguntum, Capua, Syracuse, Carthage, and then Rome, since in her descent into civil war

---

22 Horsfall 1995, 291.
23 Ahl *et al.* 1986, 2552–53.
24 Cf. Dominik 2003, 494–95; Dominik 2006, 122.
25 Dominik 2003, 494; Dominik 2006, 122. On the unending cyclicality destined for Roman civil war in Flavian epic, see also Krasne and Penwill in this volume.
26 See also the introduction to this volume.

and anarchy, Rome is to suffer a fate similar to these other cities. As Fabius himself observes, *non ulla perenni | amplexu Fortuna fouet* ("Fortune never embraces anyone forever," Sil. 7.244–45), while in Petronius's *Satyricon*, Eumolpus recites a mini-epic on the civil war of 49–45 CE between Caesar and Pompey (Petr. 119–24) in which Fortune decrees and ensures that an arrogant, corrupted Rome has her day of reckoning on the blood-drenched fields of civil war in the Republic (Petr. 120–24).

According to Cicero in *De Officiis*, the seeds of civil war during the Republic are situated in the abandonment of Rome's policy and custom of waging war in the interest of her allies, in her oppression of and triumph over the same nations that had once helped Rome to defeat enemies outside Italy, and in her failure to punish the crimes of powerful individuals who had abused their political and military powers (*Off.* 2.8.26–29). It could be said that these were some of the same seeds that led to the development of Rome's empire too. Mithridates in Sallust's *Historiae* (*Hist.* 4.69.5–9, 17, 21) and Ariovistus in Caesar's *Bellum Gallicum* (*Gal.* 1.36, 44; cf. 35, 40, 43) comment variously on the Roman practice of destroying allies and dictating the terms of friendship. Given that Rome's failure to defend Saguntum militarily is represented primarily as an act of self-preservation (cf. Sil. 1.679–89), the origins of the civil wars and attendant moral decline in the *Punica* would appear to lie not so much in Rome's abandonment of her ally as in the Roman envoys' belligerent demands to the Carthaginian Senate (cf. Sil. 2.11–14, 44–51, 368–71, 383–86), Fabius's manifest eagerness for war after his demands are rejected (Sil. 2.387–89), the self-interest (cf. Sil. 1.679–89) and inaction of Rome evident as a whole in the Saguntum episode, and the apparent lack of any compassion on the part of the Romans after news of Saguntum's fall reaches Rome.[27]

At the time Silius was writing the *Punica*, Carthage had long been a part of the Roman empire. Indeed, there is a sense from all three of the episodes discussed in this chapter, which come from the beginning, middle, and end of the *Punica*, that the war Rome will wage with Carthage is not just a struggle with a foreign power but also a harbinger of civil conflict. From the moment of the Saguntines' *Selbstvernichtung* in Book 2 through the period leading up to the Roman defeat at Cannae in Book 10 until the triumph of Scipio Africanus at the end of Book 17, Silius turns his gaze ahead to the time of Lucan's *Bellum Ciuile* and to the several eras of Roman civil war.[28] He suggests that in fighting Hannibal and

---

[27] Dominik 2003, 495–96.
[28] A discussion of the suicide of several citizens at Capua (Sil. 13.256–98, esp. 294–98; 13.369–80, esp. 369–76) is not included here because it is not strictly a parricide (and because of issues

removing the last real political obstacle to Mediterranean domination, Rome, with an accompanying loss of Roman *mores*, set herself on a downward course into unending civil war.

1.2 Writing Parricide as Civil War

In suggesting a connection between parricide and civil war and elaborating upon its various manifestations in a number of different scenes, Silius follows in a long line of Roman writers for whom parricide has an innate predisposition to metastasize and turn into civil war. The episodes in which parricide plays a role not only reflect Silius's concern with the political uncertainties of his age but also come to serve as an illustration of one of the worst consequences of civil war—the intentional or unintentional killing of close relatives. The major episodes include the parricide-suicide of the Saguntines (Sil. 2.614–707, esp. 614–49, 655–80), who are situated at the western edge of the Roman empire, and the parricide of Satricus at Cannae (Sil. 9.66–177, esp. 102–77), a village almost 500 kilometers from Rome. These episodes featuring parricide help to draw attention to the leitmotif of civil war in the epic.[29]

In addition to directly incorporating episodes of civil war and its analogues, Imperial epics frequently accentuate the theme of civil and political conflict through intertextual references. The internecine reality of the mass parricide-suicide of the Saguntines specifically recalls both Lucan's *Bellum Ciuile*, as the opposing figures Pompey and Caesar were related by marriage (cf. *cognatas acies*, "familial strife," Luc. 1.3), and Statius's *Thebaid*, a mythological poem with the theme of *fraternas acies* ("fraternal strife," Stat. *Theb.* 1.1), in which the main antagonists Eteocles and Polynices are related by birth.[30] Despite the different perspectives and contexts of the *Bellum Ciuile* and the *Thebaid*, as well as the *Argonautica* and the *Aeneid*, the victims of the wars described in them endure a fate similar to the Saguntines in the *Punica*. Their fates are also similar to the victims of the civil wars of the Republic and Empire recounted in various historical or biographical accounts by Cicero (e.g., *Catil.* 3.10), Sallust (e.g., *Cat.* 61.8–9), Livy

---

of length); however, see McGuire 1995, 219–27, and Bernstein in this volume, as well as Hulls in this volume on suicide in the *Punica* more generally.

29 For discussions of civil war in the *Punica*, see especially Ahl *et al.* 1986, 2518; McGuire 1997, 88–146, esp. 126–44; Dominik 2003, 488, 492–96; Marks 2005b, 245–88 and *passim*; Dominik 2006, 113, 119–27; Tipping 2010, 35–44. See also the chapters of Bernstein, Fucecchi, Hulls, Marks, and Stocks in this volume with their attendant bibliographies.

30 For further exploration of these intertexts in the Saguntum episode, see Bernstein in this volume.

(e.g., *Per.* 79), Tacitus (e.g., *Hist.* 3.33–34, 51, 83–85), Valerius Maximus (e.g., 5.5.4), Velleius Paterculus (e.g., 2.67.3), and Plutarch (*Mar.* 39). Among the aforementioned writers, Cicero is the earliest to associate *parricidium* ("parricide") specifically with civil war (e.g., *Catil.* 1.7, *Sul.* 2), but the connection between civil strife and parricide, especially fratricide, as well as suicide, is emphasized by all of them.

Elsewhere in Roman literature civil war is often represented as parricide in the form of fratricide alongside suicide. The mass parricide-suicide of the Saguntines (Sil. 2.612–707, esp. 614–91) is particularly reminiscent of scenes in Lucan's *Bellum Ciuile* (2.148–59;[31] 4.474–581, esp. 541–71; 7.617–31), Josephus's *Bellum Judaicum* (3.387–91; 7.389–406),[32] Statius's *Thebaid* (5.207–61), and Valerius Flaccus's *Argonautica* (2.184–241) in respect of the gruesome nature of the crimes committed and the innominate scrambled corpses that litter the city, but it is also similar to the first-mentioned scene in the *Bellum Ciuile*, where the conquered attempt to steal deaths from their conquerors (Luc. 2.156–57; cf. Sil. 2.632–35).[33] Notwithstanding the similarity of the Saguntine parricide to other scenes in Greek and Roman Imperial literature, it is my contention that it surpasses all other literary parricides in terms of the variety of its manifestations of parricide and suicide, even in the *Bellum Ciuile*, *Bellum Judaicum*, *Thebaid*, and *Argonautica*, which feature fratricide (e.g., Luc. 7.626–27; Stat. *Theb.* 11.552–73), patricide (e.g., Luc. 2.149–51; Stat. *Theb.* 5.236–38), filicide (e.g., J. *BJ* 7.391–93; V. Fl. 2.184–85), uxoricide (e.g., J. *BJ* 7.391–93; Luc. 1.377–78), and mariticide (e.g., Stat. *Theb.* 5.207–17; V. Fl. 2.229–31), as well as suicide (e.g., J. *BJ* 3.397; Stat. *Theb.* 2.640–41; V. Fl. 1.767–826). In addition to the aforementioned forms of parricide that appear in the Saguntine episode, there is matricide and geminicide, as well as suicides by a son, mother, and wife (Sil. 2.614–49, 655–80).

Just as Lucan's account of civil war looms especially large in the background of the *Punica*, his narration of the siege of Massilia lies behind Silius's description of the Saguntum episode.[34] In fact, in his narrative of the lengthy siege of Massilia (Luc. 3.372–508), which eventually falls in the first battle of the *Bellum Ciuile* (Luc. 3.509–762), Lucan specifically mentions the siege of Saguntum and its inhabitants' parricide (Luc. 3.349–55). Silius can be seen as transforming Lucan's first battle into his own (Sil. 1.296–2.692), with the result that his Saguntum

---

[31] Cf. McGuire 1985, 72–73; McGuire 1990, 38–39; McGuire 1997, 213–14; Dominik 2006, 125.
[32] For a discussion of suicide and civil war as tropes in both the *Punica* and *Bellum Judaicum*, see Hulls in this volume.
[33] Cf. Dominik 2003, 487–89; Dominik 2006, 125.
[34] Cf. Marks in this volume, pp. 61–62.

becomes an epitome of Lucan's Massilia. Under the possession of Tisiphone, the Saguntines commit parricide against their will (Sil. 2.617–19). In this scene fathers slay sons, sons fathers, sons mothers, husbands wives, wives husbands, twins twins (brothers brothers), and men and women themselves (Sil. 2.614–49, 655–80). The carnage is noteworthy especially for the muddled identities of the victims: *semambusta iacet nullo discrimine passim | infelix obitus permixto funere turba* ("The corpses, wretched in death, lie half-burned everywhere without distinction in a mass grave," Sil. 2.681–82). The parricide-suicide reflects the confusion that results from civil disorder.[35]

2 Cannae

> "Toutes les guerres sont civiles; car c'est toujours l'homme contre l'homme qui répand son propre sang, qui déchire ses propres entrailles."
>
> François Fénelon

2.1 Further Sowing the Seeds of Civil War

The Cannae episode (Sil. 8.25–10.658) of Silius Italicus's *Punica* takes up and elaborates upon the epic's opening episode, which introduced the major themes, images, and figures of the epic.[36] Like the Saguntum episode, the Cannae episode, which is positioned at the halfway point of the epic, suggests that the origins of the Roman propensity for civil strife lay in the events of the Second Punic War through its framing by two significant passages connoting this unflattering commentary on Flavian Rome: the election of Varro to the consulship (Sil. 8.243–57), which is portrayed by Silius as the representation and precursor of civil discord, and Silius's apostrophe of the fallen Carthage after his description of the defeat of the Roman army at Cannae (Sil. 10.657–58). This narrative framing of Rome's greatest military defeat stresses the link between Rome's eventual victory over Carthage and her descent into civil and moral anarchy;[37] moreover, Silius also

---

35 Cf. Dominik 2006, 125.
36 On the link between the Saguntum and Cannae episodes, see Dominik 2006.
37 Dominik 2006, 114–15. Scipio Africanus's victory over Hannibal at Zama was the final first step on this path of decline, as Scipio himself predicts: *restare haec ordine duro | lamentor rebus Latiis* ("I lament the grim future ahead for the Roman nation," Sil. 13.868–69).

suggests that the *populus Romanus* was already a fertile field for receiving such seeds of moral turpitude.

Once Hannibal, Rome's arch enemy, is defeated and dies, Rome begins a slow decline that eventually leads to civil strife (cf. Sil. 10.657–58; cf. 3.588–90), but the potential for civil war is evident already in the calamitous defeat at Cannae made possible in the first place through the emergence of the demagogue Varro (Sil. 8.243–57), whose own mind is afflicted with *discordia* ("discord," Sil. 8.648), a word long associated with violence and civil strife in Republican and Imperial literature.[38] While such violence is inevitably infectious,[39] Silius implies that the real crime was Varro's very election, which elevated him to the same political rank as the Fabii, the Scipios, and Marcellus (Sil. 8.243–57).

In the eyes of his colleague Paulus, Varro is a gift to Carthage and more ruthless in his designs on Rome than even a Carthaginian senator (cf. Sil. 8.332–36). But the citizens of Rome are just as responsible as their leaders for the moral corruption that leads to civil strife, for they are bribed and vote blindly for Varro (Sil. 8.253–57):

> hunc Fabios inter sacrataque nomina Marti
> Scipiadas interque Ioui spolia alta ferentem
> Marcellum fastis labem suffragia caeca   255
> addiderant, Cannasque malum exitiale fouebat
> ambitus et Graio funestior aequore Campus.

> Blind voters had given him, that disaster for the Fasti, a place among the Fabii and the Scipios, whose names are sacred to Mars, and Marcellus, who gave his lofty spoils to Jove. Bribery and the Campus Martius, more deadly than the battlefield of Cannae, caused its ruinous disaster.

Subsequently, Silius emphasizes the theme of civil discord by comparing Varro leading the army from Rome to an inexperienced charioteer losing control of the reins out of the starting gate (Sil. 8.278–83), which specifically recalls Vergil's simile comparing the civil wars of the 40s BCE to a chariot out of control (Verg. G. 1.512–14).[40] This reminiscence constitutes a clear indictment of Varro's leadership, but there is a further layer of intertextual ramification.

Read in conjunction with the aforementioned passage about the moral taint of Rome's citizens that led to Varro's disastrous consulship (Sil. 8.253–57),

---
[38] Cf. Gee 2013, 49–55, 122.
[39] As shown in the *Punica* when even the gods are drawn into the conflict on the human level at Cannae and fight among themselves (Sil. 9.287–303).
[40] Cf. McGuire 1997, 131–32; Dominik 2006, 121.

Silius's notable apostrophe of Carthage after the defeat of the Roman army at Cannae suggests that Rome's national character, already suspect at the time of her war with Carthage, would experience a further decline in the aftermath of her victory over her arch foe:[41] *post te cui uertere mores | si stabat fatis, potius, Carthago, maneres* ("if fate was fixed that our nature should change after you fell, Carthage, would that you still remained," Sil. 10.657–58; cf. 3.588–90). This simultaneously proleptic and analeptic lament inverts Lucan's praise of Nero (whether given verily or ironically) at the beginning of the *Bellum Ciuile*, where he remarks that the horrors of the civil war were worth the cost if they were necessary for the advent of Nero (Luc. 1.33–45), an assertion paralleled by the last line of Seneca's *Phoenissae*, which asserts that the acquisition of power is worth any cost (*imperia pretio quolibet constant bene*, 664). Lucan's immediately subsequent image of Nero mounting the *flammigeros Phoebi ... currus* (Luc. 1.48) to ascend to the heavens alludes to the same out-of-control Vergilian charioteer that Silius appropriated for Varro at the beginning of the Cannae episode.[42] In morphing these Lucanean and Senecan sentiments to intimate that the victory over Carthage was *not* worth the cost of the subsequent decline in Roman moral fiber, Silius brings the Varronian disaster at Cannae full circle with an indirect allusion to the same charioteer motif with which it opened and to the incendiary cosmic blaze that accrues to that motif in all its incarnations.[43]

2.2 Brothers at Arms

Although Silius looks forward to the Late Republic as inspiration for the Varro episode, the theme of civil strife goes back, as suggested by Silius himself (Sil. 1.95), to the founding of Rome and to Romulus's slaying of Remus, which seemed to later Romans to foredoom her to eternal civil strife.[44] But the Varro episode also looks forward to the Rome of Silius's day, where the theme of fraternal strife in the Imperial house was a political *locus communis* for civil discord in the first century CE. The Flavian epicists' preoccupation with fraternal discord echoes the socio-political environment of Flavian Rome, notably the uneasy

---

[41] Cf. Dominik 2003, 492–93; Dominik 2006, 114–15, 119–21.
[42] Nelis 2011.
[43] Hinds 1987 points to the implicit presence of Ovid's Phaethon episode behind Lucan's Nero; more recently, see Nelis 2011, 258–59, for a summary of subsequent scholarship illuminating the intertextual triangle between Lucan's Nero, the *Georgics*' charioteer, and Ovid's Phaethon.
[44] Cf. Hor. *Epod.* 7.17–20; Verg. *G.* 2.495–96; Liv. 1.6.4–2.7.3; Luc. 1.95.

relationship between Domitian and Titus recounted in Suetonius.[45] Accordingly, one particular brand of fraternal discord—that arising from putatively shared power—informs the dissensions of the *Punica* more thoroughly than others.[46]

In the *Thebaid*, Statius provides the classic mythical example of two brothers (Eteocles and Polynices) whose agreement to alternate power breaks down (Stat. *Theb.* 1.138–43; cf. 2.415–41). While there are several traditional counterexamples, including another Theban myth (Amphion and Zethus), the exemplary myth for the potentially shared power of the Imperial household was that of Castor and Pollux. This "political" compromise has Republican, Augustan, and Julio-Claudian precedents that extend well into the Flavian period and beyond.[47] In the *Punica*, however, the Dioscuri's model rarely obtains: most of the opportunities for fraternal harmony have less than desirable outcomes.[48]

Silius tellingly does not depict Lucius Scipio (cf. *germanus ducis*, "the brother of the general," Sil. 16.576), the younger brother of Scipio Africanus, as a rival for military or political leadership in the *Punica*, which leaves Scipio unchallenged as a superhuman figure by the end of the epic (Sil. 17.625–54).[49] But Silius picks up on the theme of discord not only between Roman power-brokers but also the Carthaginian leaders. The epicist describes the conflict (or potential for conflict) through his paired depictions of senators such as Lentulus and Fabius (cf. Sil. 1.767–86), generals like Fabius and Minucius (cf. Sil. 7.380–408), and consuls such as Varro and Paulus (cf. Sil. 8.243–350). When Fabius is compelled to share his dictatorial power and army with Minucius (Sil. 7.494–516), Silius comments upon the situation with a Lucanean phrase reminiscent of civil war: *diuiditur miles* ("the army is divided," Sil. 7.515; cf. Luc. 1.109: *diuiditur ferro regnum*, "the empire was divided by the sword").[50] The divided camps of Varro and Paulus are described in similar terms with another Lucanean phrase: *diuersa* …

---

[45] E.g., Suet. *Dom.* 2.3; *Tit.* 9.3; cf. *Tit.* 10.2; D.C. 66.26. On the relationship between Titus and Domitian, see, e.g., Stocks in this volume, pp. 267–69, with further references; Dominik 1994b, 148–80 *passim*; Stocks 2014, 168–69.

[46] Cf. Tacitus, who asserts that Romans condoned Nero's murder of Britannicus because of the ancient examples of fraternal strife and the infeasibility of dividing the throne (*Ann.* 13.17).

[47] E.g., Mart. 1.36, 5.38, 9.51; Plu. *Mor.* 486B; cf. V. Fl. 3.186–89. See Bannon 1997, 5, 11, 41, 59, 174–88.

[48] This may be programmatically intimated by an explicit mention of the Dioscuri's arrangement (*alternusque animae mutato Castore Pollux*, Sil. 9.295) at the midpoint of the passage about the theomachy (Sil. 9.290–99) halfway through the Cannae episode at the heart of the epic (see Dominik 2006 on the centrality of Cannae).

[49] See below on Scipio Africanus's superhuman status at the end of the *Punica*; on the representation of various pairs of brothers in the *Punica*, including the Scipios, see Stocks in this volume and Stocks 2014, 167–81.

[50] Cf. Sil. 7.738–39.

castra petebant ("they set out for the divided camps," Sil. 8.349–50; cf. Luc. 2.43: *diuersaque castra petentes*, "setting out for the divided camps").[51] At least in the case of Fabius and Minucius, however, Silius seems to provide a solution to the fraught Roman custom of power-sharing, for when Minucius and his forces are rescued by Fabius in an ensuing battle at Gerunium (Sil. 13.705–35), Minucius gratefully returns command of his half of the army to Fabius (Sil. 13.737–45).[52]

On the Carthaginian side, the division between the leading generals is even more pointed since it involves fraternal conflict. Silius stresses the dissension between Hannibal and his brother Mago in the aftermath of Cannae when they argue vehemently about the latter's desire to march on Rome and the extent of the Roman defeat (Sil. 10.373–87).[53] This discord between the Carthaginian brothers lies in stark contrast to the harmony that existed between Scipio's father and his uncle (cf. Sil. 13.650–51).

At Cannae, however, an unintended intrafamilial conflict also epitomizes the odd foreign/civil hybridity of the *Punica*'s thematized parricide. On the eve of the battle of Cannae, a young Italian soldier, Mancinus, dies during a clash (Sil. 9.12–14). Satricus, Mancinus's father, who is attempting to escape from the Carthaginian camp, comes upon the corpse of his son (cf. Sil. 9.86). Unaware of its identity, Satricus strips the body of its armor and weapons (Sil. 9.85–89). At the same time, Solimus, Satricus's other son, leaves the Roman camp to search for his brother's corpse (Sil. 9.90–95). Solimus sees the figure of his father *nocturno ... lumine* ("in the nocturnal light," Sil. 9.170) and, not recognizing him, hurls his spear and fatally wounds him (Sil. 9.96–105; cf. 9.120, 166–67). The phrase *nocturno ... lumine* casts a Senecan shadow over the setting since it repeats the words used in the *Thyestes* when Thyestes devours his sons (*nocturna ... lumina*, 795),[54] thus tainting the Silian scene through an intertextual allusion to a particularly sickening act.[55] As Satricus is dying, he identifies himself to his son but then says, *iaceres in me cum feruidus hastam, | Poenus eram* ("When you hurled your frenzied spear at me, I was a Carthaginian," Sil. 9.129–30). After this, Solimus commits suicide (Sil. 9.173–74).[56]

---

51 Cf. Littlewood 2011, xxvii, l–li, lxxx, 196–97, 245.
52 Dominik 2003, 493; Dominik 2006, 121.
53 On Hannibal and his brothers Hasdrubal and Mago in the *Punica*, see Stocks in this volume, pp. 264–67; Stocks 2014, 167–81.
54 Spaltenstein 1990, *ad* Sil. 9.169.
55 On civil war more generally in the *Thyestes*, see Schiesaro 2003, 35, 72, 146; on the *Thyestes*' use in Flavian civil war literature, see van der Schuur in this volume.
56 For the ramifications of the *ensis* (Sil. 9.173) with which Solimus takes his life, see pp. 286–88 below.

Although the vignette featuring Solimus and Satricus is mainly military in nature rather than civil, by contrast with the *Selbstvernichtung* of the Saguntines, the theme of parricide connects the two scenes. The consequences of these obscured or blurred identities in the scene featuring Satricus and Solimus recalls on a micro-level the collective parricide and suicide of innominate victims graphically described in the Saguntum episode (cf. Sil. 2.614–49, 655–80): son kills father, son commits suicide. As in the Saguntum scene, the parricide reflects the confusion that results from the sense of disorder caused by the Carthaginian threat—but on the field of battle rather than within the confines of the city. The magnitude of the confusion and disorder emblematized by the unintentional parricide of Satricus is heightened further by the post-parricide suicide of Solimus.

The story of Satricus and Solimus recalls most vividly the parricide of Julius Mansuetus, especially as recorded by Tacitus, during the civil war of of 68–69 CE.[57] In *Historiae* 3.25 Tacitus relates how Mansuetus mortally wounds his father before recognizing him. Tacitus describes the scene in words equating the scene to a parricide emblematic of civil strife (Tac. *Hist.* 3.25.2–3):

> ... et exanguem amplexus, uoce flebili precabatur placatos patris manis, neue se ut parricidam auersarentur: publicum id facinus; et unum militem quotam ciuilium armorum partem? simul attollere corpus, aperire humum, supremo erga parentem officio fungi. aduertere proximi, deinde plures: hinc per omnem aciem miraculum et questus et saeuissimi belli execratio. nec eo segnius propinquos adfinis fratres trucidant spoliant: factum esse scelus loquuntur faciuntque.

> Embracing the expiring man, in a plaintive voice he entreated the shade of his father to be appeased and not to turn against him as a parricide. That crime was public, he said; how much was a single soldier a part of these civil wars? At the same time he lifted the body up, dug a grave, and performed the last rites for his father. Those nearby noticed first, then many others followed: astonishment, complaints, and curses against this most brutal war pervaded the entire army. Yet no less feverishly did they kill and despoil the bodies of their neighbors, relatives, and brothers: they speak of a crime having been done and commit it themselves.

The close association established by Tacitus between the *facinus/scelus* ("crime") of parricide and civil war in this scene stresses the consequences of moral corruption and the breakdown of civic order. While the parricide of Solimus parallels that of Mansuetus in that it is unintentional and a single incident, it is also emblematic of civil war, as suggested in the Tacitean passage where Mansuetus's parricide is repeatedly referred to as a crime that is equated with the *scelus* of

---

57 Dominik 2006, 124. Fucecchi 1999, 316–22, mentions two epigrams of Seneca from Riese's *Anthologia Latina* (462, 463) as another possible source for this story; Marks *forthcoming* notes various reminiscences of Ovid's *Fasti* in Silius's account of the tale of Satricus and Solimus.

parricide on a large scale in the form of civil war. As discussed above, this is indicative of the tendency in Roman literature for parricide to metastasize and become civil war, a leitmotif that Silius most frequently associates with possession of the *sceptrum* ("scepter") and the *ensis* ("sword").

3 Wielders Of The Scepter and Sword

"[I]l est plus glorieux de mériter un sceptre que de le porter."

Napoléon Bonaparte

3.1 The Parricidal Sword and Flame

On a general level, the *sceptrum* and *ensis* are interchangeable tropes for the *imperium* (power/command) that is associated with kingship and inheritance. As do other poets of the Republican and Imperial literature (e.g., Lucr. 5.1293; Verg. *G.* 2.540; Stat. *Theb.* 1.34; Sen. *Phoen.* 555–56),[58] Silius Italicus links the *sceptrum*/*ensis* with civil discord and internecine conflict. When Fides informs Hercules, who appeals to her to intercede on the Saguntines' behalf (Sil. 2.484–92), that she has fled the earth because of the depravity of the human race (Sil. 2.496–506),[59] the goddess emphasizes the tyranny of its rulers and the violence of its nations (Sil. 2.498–505):

> impia liqui
> et, quantum terrent, tantum metuentia regna
> ac furias auri nec uilia praemia fraudum   500
> et super haec ritu horrificos ac more ferarum
> uiuentes rapto populos luxuque solutum
> omne decus multaque oppressum nocte pudorem.
> uis colitur, iurisque locum sibi uindicat ensis,
> et probris cessit uirtus.   505

I fled from evil reigns that fear as much as they terrify, the madness for gold, the cheap rewards of deceit, and moreover reigns hateful in their customs and that live in the manner

---

58 Cf. Gee 2013, 50–53, 56.
59 Darcy Krasne has pointed out to me that Silius's description of Fides is a "nod to the Aratean Dike/Iustitia/Pietas figure" and thus is in more extensive dialogue with the broader thematization of *ensis* as a term of civil war and parricide in Roman literature (as discussed by Gee 2013, 39–53).

of wild beasts, where honor is weakened by luxury and where shame is buried in the darkest night. Force is cultivated and the sword takes the place of justice, and virtue has given place to shameful acts.

Here *ensis* is in the last metrical position of line 504, a position of emphasis that draws attention to its significance as an emblem of power and civil conflict, a positioning that reminds us of other passages in Roman literature in which *ensis* appears at line-end (Lucr. 5.1293; Verg. *G.* 1.508, 2.540).[60] Later in this programmatic episode, Silius connects the image-symbol of the *ensis* more closely with the theme of parricide. While the gods and the Carthaginians are portrayed as being partly responsible for Saguntum's demise in the *Punica*, the Saguntines also incur blame for their own downfall through their use of the *ensis* (Sil. 2.654–58):

> urbs, habitata diu Fidei caeloque parentem
> murorum repetens, ruit inter perfida gentis   655
> Sidoniae tela atque immania facta suorum,
> iniustis neglecta deis: furit ensis et ignis,
> quique caret flamma, scelerum est locus.

The city, long inhabited by Fides and claiming a divine founder of her walls, falls amid the treacherous arms of the Carthaginian people and the monstrous deeds of her own citizens, neglected by the unjust gods. The sword and fire rage; any place lacking flames is a scene of crime.

Here the parricidal *ensis* becomes closely associated with *ignis* ("fire") and *flamma* ("flames"), both also image-symbols of civil war, with *ignis* now appearing in the emphatic last foot of line 657. The juxtaposition of *ensis*, *ignis*, and *flamma*, together with the reference to *immania facta suorum* ("the monstrous deeds of her citizens," Sil. 2.656) and the representation of the scene as *scelerum locus* ("a scene of crime," 658), combine to tarnish the collective suicide-parricide as a morally ambiguous act. Accordingly, when *ignis* and *flamma* again appear jointly elsewhere in the *Punica*, they retain something of their earlier flavor of civil war and parricide, notably when they jointly occur in reference to the burning of the temple of Jupiter on the Capitoline in the civil war of 68–69 CE (Sil. 3.609–10, esp. *ignes*, 609; *flammas*, 610).

The civil war apparatus imputed to *ignis* by its association with *ensis* is reinforced by the strong resonances between Silius's description of the siege of Saguntum (Sil. 2.614–707) and Tacitus's account of the invasion of Rome by forces loyal to Vespasian and under the command of Antonius Primus (*Hist.* 3.82–86).

---

[60] Cf. Gee 2013, 50–53.

This account, which follows the burning of the Capitoline temple (*Hist.* 3.71–73), features Roman troops slaying their fellow soldiers and inhabitants of the city (*Hist.* 3.83–85, esp. 83). The consequent bloodshed and piles of corpses that littered Rome entailed, according to Tacitus, *quidquid in acerbissima captiuitate scelerum* ("whatever crime could be perpetrated in the most brutal capture," *Hist.* 3.83.2). The scene of devastation at Saguntum also parallels Tacitus's story of the siege and destruction of Cremona, when tens of thousands of Roman soldiers under the command of the same Antonius burst into the town and pillaged it (*Hist.* 3.33.1–2). These Roman troops not only slew their fellow citizens but even their own comrades in arms, with Tacitus remarking that no act was considered unlawful (*nec quicquam inlicitum*, *Hist.* 3.33.2). After pillaging the town, the soldiers set fire to it; in this civil war setting, as in the *Punica*, *ignis* (Tac. *Hist.* 3.33.2) becomes closely associated with the devastation and havoc wrought by civil war.

The images of sword and fire at Saguntum are superimposed upon a scene that for Tacitus was *facinus ... luctuosissimum foedissimumque* ("the most wretched and most shameful crime," *Hist.* 3.72.1) that Rome had suffered since her foundation.[61] As Tacitus observes, it was no foreign foe who had burned the Capitol, but rather Roman citizens arrayed against each other in civil war (Tac. *Hist.* 3.72). Thus when reference is made later in the *Punica* to Hannibal's threatened burning of this temple (*cum ferrem in Capitolia flammas*, "when I brought fire against the Capitol," Sil. 17.266; cf. 15.803–5), it becomes a harbinger of the climactic moment of the civil wars of 69 CE: civil war accomplishes at Rome what Hannibal himself could not achieve.

3.2 The Power-Hungry Scepter

If the *ensis* and its associated conflagration suggest the drive to attain power by any means, including parricide, the *sceptrum* suggests the *desire* for that power—often unmoderated.[62] Indeed, the *sceptrum* in the *Punica* is not just symbolic of

---

[61] For other recollections of the burning of the Capitoline in Flavian epic, see Landrey in this volume.

[62] For instance, an internecine duel occurs between two twin non-Roman brothers for the *sceptrum* (Sil. 16.536) at the funeral games in honor of Scipio Africanus's father and uncle (16.533–48). Silius's main intertext for this scene is the duel between Polynices and Eteocles for the throne of Thebes in Statius's *Thebaid* (11.387–579, esp. 497–573); cf. McGuire 1985, 163 n. 15; Mezzanotte 1995, 361–62; Marks 2005b, 184 and n. 56. Likewise, the *ensis* features memorably in a scene at the battle of the Ticinus (Sil. 4.355–95), where Silius depicts a trio of Carthaginian brothers (Eumachus, Critias, Xanthippus) fighting against a Roman trio of brothers (Virbius,

royal power but crazed, irreverent power (e.g., Sil. 14.33–34, 85–98, esp. 33, 86), seen most notably when the Sibyl explains the penalties that await tyrannical holders of the *sceptrum* (13.601–12):[63]

> has inter formas coniunx Iunonis Auernae
> suggestu residens cognoscit crimina regum.
> stant uincti, seroque piget sub iudice culpae:
> circum errant Furiae Poenarumque omnis imago.
> quam uellent numquam sceptris fulsisse superbis!   605
> insultant duro imperio non digna nec aequa
> ad superos passi manes, quaeque ante profari
> non licitum uiuis, tandem permissa queruntur.
> tunc alius saeuis religatur rupe catenis,
> ast alius subigit saxum contra ardua montis,   610
> uipereo domat hunc aeterna Megaera flagello.
> talia letiferis restant patienda tyrannis.

The husband of Avernian Juno, sitting among these forms and sitting on his throne, examines the crimes of kings; they stand in chains and repent their crimes too late before their judge. Every form of the Furies and of Vengeance wander about. How kings wish they had never held the gleaming scepter of pride! Shades who suffered undue and unjust treatment under harsh rule insult them to higher powers. What they were not allowed to say in life, they have permission at last to complain about. Then one monarch is fastened to a rock with cruel chains; yet another pushes a stone up a steep mountain; and Megaera forever scourges a third with her snakelike whip. Such are the punishments to be endured by deathly tyrants.

The Sibyl's explanation, which suggests the association between *crimen* ("crime"; cf. Sil. 13.602) and *sceptrum* ("scepter"; cf. Sil. 13.605), is particularly reminiscent of references in the *Phoenissae* and *Thebaid* to the punishment that awaits the wielding of the scepter by a cruel monarch (e.g., Sen. *Phoen.* 648–49; cf. [Sen.] *Her. O.* 874; Stat. *Theb.* 11.654–57, 704–5) and of suggestions in the *Thebaid* that the assumption of power foredooms its possessor and disposes him to a lack of compassion and inhumanity (e.g., Stat. *Theb.* 11.654–66, 677–82, 701–5).[64]

Capys, Albanus). Although this scene does not strictly feature brother fighting brother, it likewise encapsulates a particularly graphic image of fraternal strife through its mirror image of triplets fighting triplets (cf. Hardie 1993a, 97) and the image-symbol of the *improbus ensis* ("impious sword," Sil. 4.386); the epithet *improbus* further stresses the internecine aspect of the *ensis*, as it and its synonyms do elsewhere in Roman literature (e.g., Verg. *G.* 1.145–46, cf. Verg. *A.* 6.613; Hor. *Carm.* 3.24.25–26; Luc. 1.238; Sen. *Phoen.* 274–76, 538–94, 599–600; cf. Stat. *Theb.* 1.33–37 with Dominik 1994b, 170).
63 Cf. Tipping 2010, 183–84.
64 On these ideas in the *Thebaid*, see Dominik 1994b, 88–92.

Scipio Africanus's connection with the *sceptrum* not only gives us our most panoptic view of its role and significance in the epic but also casts a clearer light on Scipio's own role. Toward the end of the *Punica*, Scipio is described as *securus sceptri* (Sil. 17.627), an ambiguous reference that could mean he is "unconcerned about the scepter," i.e., not desirous of royal power; "secure in the scepter," i.e., trusting of the power of Rome; "confident in the scepter," i.e., in his own ability to wield its power; or even "assured of the scepter," i.e., of a triumphal scepter because of his victory over the Carthaginians.[65] But *securus* (with the genitive) also has an unfavorable, mainly post-Augustan, sense that could suggest Scipio is "reckless" or "negligent" in his use of the scepter,[66] a suggestion given emphasis not only by the negative connotations of *sceptrum* elsewhere in the *Punica* (e.g., Sil. 13.601–12, esp. 605; 14.33–34, 85–98, esp. 33, 86) but also by Scipio's own reckless conduct in battle. At the battle of the Ticinus, Scipio charges *propere* ("hastily," "recklessly," Sil. 4.217) onto the battlefield (4.217–19), searches for the thickest part of the fray (4.230–31), and *instinctus* ("incited," "enraged," 4.231) by the loss of his own men, slays numerous Carthaginians (4.231–47). The scene is reminiscent of *Aeneid* 10 when Aeneas charges into battle (Verg. *A.* 10.310–13) and, upon hearing about the death of Pallas at the hands of Turnus, completely loses control, raging madly across the battlefield and slaying numerous Italian warriors (*A.* 10.513–604). In the *Punica*, Scipio upbraids his soldiers for holding back and scattering (Sil. 4.401–13, esp. 402–12), then threatens to use the *ensis* (4.416) against himself and his own men if they refuse to fight (4.413–16, esp. 415–16); encircled and severely wounded (4.445–53), Scipio must be rescued from death through the intercession of his son at the behest of Jupiter and with the aid of Mars (4.417–44, 454–71). At the battle of the Trebia the wounded Scipio displays similarly rash conduct, plunging into the river amidst the carnage and slaying countless Carthaginians (4.622–37), and must be saved by Venus and Vulcan from the river god (4.638–99, esp. 667–99). In all these battles Scipio's quasi-Homeric display of heroic behavior seems misguided because it threatens not only the lives of his soldiers but also himself, upon whom his men depend, and ultimately the safety of Rome.

Such a self-centered style of leadership was already foreshadowed by Scipio's argument before the Senate that he should be allowed to lead the Roman forces into Africa (Sil. 16.663–69). There is an obvious suggestion of self-aggrandizement on the part of Scipio since the military expedition led by him will

---

[65] McGuire 1997, 100–1, and Tipping 2010, 184–85, discuss some possible interpretations, including the negative associations of the *sceptrum* in the *Punica*; *contra* Marks 2005b, 113–14, 203–6.
[66] Cf. *OLD*, s.v. "securus," 4.

result in the Roman Senate conferring the honorary title of *Africanus* upon him (Sil. 17.625–26; cf. 16.668). But there is a hint too, in his plea, of the blind ambition of Rome's leaders that leads to civil war and her dismemberment in Lucan's world (cf. Luc. 1.87–89).[67] The mentions of and allusions to other Scipios throughout the epic confirm the potential for hearing problematic echoes in Scipio's behavior; for instance, another Scipio appears in the Cannae narrative (Sil. 8.546) amidst a number of anachronistically named soldiers who proleptically recall the generals, politicians, and emperors of Rome's future civil warscapes.[68]

By the end of the *Punica*, Scipio is portrayed as a divinized figure in the mold foretold by Lucan, who suggests that the environment of civil war is particularly ripe for the emergence of superhuman figures (Luc. 7.457–59):

> bella pares superis facient ciuilia diuos,
> fulminibus manes radiisque ornabit et astris
> inque deum templis iurabit Roma per umbras.

> Civil wars will make deities equal to the gods above; Rome will adorn shades with thunderbolts, haloes, and stars; and in the temples of the gods she will swear by the shadows of men.

Here Lucan refers specifically to the Imperial cult whereby dead emperors were apotheosized, though as he observes, these shades in fact were little more than *manes* (Luc. 7.458) and *umbras* (Luc. 7.459), that is, literally and metaphorically insubstantial. In the final lines of the *Punica* Silius apostrophizes Scipio: *nec uero, cum te memorat de stirpe deorum, | prolem Tarpei mentitur Roma Tonantis* ("Rome surely does not lie when she declares you of divine lineage and the son of the Tarpeian [i.e., Capitoline] Thunderer," Sil. 17.653–54). The final words, *Roma Tonantis*, which are distinctly reminiscent of the last words of *Bellum Ciuile* 8 (*Creta Tonantis*, Luc. 8.872),[69] serve as a closing reminder of the Lucanean pall that overlays much of the *Punica*. Elsewhere in the *Punica*, Scipio is linked to the Jovian thunderbolt (Sil. 15.403–5, esp. 404–5; 16.143–45; cf. 7.106–7), as is Caesar in the *Bellum Ciuile*, where the association is tainted with supreme power and destruction (Luc. 1.143–57, esp. 151–57). Scipio is also associated with the serpent, whose guise Jupiter adopts to rape his mother Pomponia (cf. Sil. 13.637–44, esp. 642–44), which leads to his birth (cf. 13.645–46). As the Romans consider who should

---

[67] Dominik 2006, 126–27.
[68] See the detailed discussions of McGuire 1995; McGuire 1997, 61–62, 136–44; see also Ahl *et al.* 1986, 2542, 2552; Mezzanotte 1995, 383–85; Marks 2005b, 253–54, 275 n. 104; Dominik 2006, 126–27.
[69] Cf. Hardie 1997, 159–60.

be put in charge of the army to be sent to Spain (Sil. 15.1–138, esp. 1–8, 133–37), the god confirms with thunder the portent of a serpent that races through the sky (Sil. 15.139–45), which encourages the Roman people to grant an eager Scipio command (Sil. 15.149–53; cf. 10–11, 122–23, 129–32). While the portent of the serpent is an obvious sign of Jupiter's support for Scipio, the negative associations of the serpent that discharges its poison and slays Zacynthus in the Saguntum episode (2.283–87), the inherent violence of the god's rape (cf. 13.638–39, 643–44), and Pomponia's subsequent death after delivery (13.645–46) mar both the significance of the Jovian omen and the image of snakeborn Scipio.

In the Sibyl's prophecy of the civil wars to afflict Rome (Sil. 13.853–67), Caesar is portrayed as a descendant of the gods through Iulus and wearing a *stelligerum ... apicem* ("starry crown," 13.863) emblematic of his divine pretensions and status (13.862–64). At the close of the *Punica*, Scipio Africanus, like Roman emperors under the Imperial cult, is depicted similarly as a direct descendant of Jupiter and as a prototype of the deified Caesar, who in the accounts of the Roman historians and poets was a key figure and symbol of civil war.[70] In Silius's embedded encomium of Vespasian (Sil. 3.593–606), the *uirtus caelestis* ("godlike excellence") of the emperor "will soar to the stars" (*ad astra / efferet*, 3.594–55),[71] and he will gain divine honors (3.602), much like Caesar who is divinized and wears the *stelliger apex* (13.862–64). Among the Italian troops assembled before the battle of Cannae (Sil. 8.349–621), Silius mentions an Etruscan leader Galba (8.468–71), whose name recalls the Galba who was emperor for seven months during the civil war of 68–69 CE and claimed paternal descent from Jupiter (Suet. *Gal*. 2).[72] Silius's divinization of Scipio at the end of the *Punica* recalls the apotheoses of Caesar and Vespasian and the claim to divine descent from Jupiter of an emperor like Galba under the Imperial cult. While Vespasian emerged victorious from the eighteen months of civil war in 68–69 CE and is favorably treated on the whole by Roman historians and biographers (e.g., Tac. *Hist*. 4; Suet. *Ves*.),[73] both Caesar (e.g., D.C. 37–44; Suet. *Jul*.) and Galba (e.g., D.C. 64; Suet. *Gal*.) were divisive figures whose names became associated with autocracy, tyranny, and civil war at Rome—and who were assassinated, ultimately to become (in the words of Lucan) *manes* (Luc. 7.458) and *umbras* (Luc. 7.459).

---

[70] Dominik 2006, 126–27.
[71] Cf. Sil. 15.100, where Virtus ("Virtue") describes her apotheosis *ad astra* ("to the stars").
[72] Mentioned above in the passage of Tacitus, *Histories* 3.25.
[73] Levick 1999 has a more detached perspective of Vespasian's reign than ancient writers and most modern scholars.

The last lines of the *Punica* therefore suggest that the type of self-aggrandizing leaders that emerged from Rome's war with Carthage would continue into the Principate, as would the seemingly endless civil wars that resulted from the conflict between these strongman figures. Silius suggests that if the general Marcellus, who met his death in battle against Hannibal (Sil. 15.334–96), had lived, he could have rivaled Scipio (cf. 15.341–42). But at the close of the epic, Scipio lacks such a rival for either military or political power. At this point, the contemporary Rome of Silius, ravished in recent memory by civil war and by a succession of five emperors in 68–69 CE (Nero, Galba, Otho, Vitellius, Vespasian) and three emperors (Vespasian, Titus, Domitian) in 79–81 CE, might well recognize the potential danger posed by a figure such as Scipio, with or without a "brother" to check his power.

4 Epilogue

The three main scenes that constitute the foregoing discussion on civil war, parricide, and the scepter/sword in Silius Italicus's *Punica*—the Saguntum parricide-suicide, the programmatic episode in Books 1–2; the Cannae episode in Books 8–10, the narrative centerpiece of the epic; and the rise of Scipio Africanus at the end of Book 17—form part of the vision of political and ideological reality of a poet who experienced the reigns of a dozen emperors from Tiberius to Trajan in the first century CE. The spirit and ambience of the Flavian age is reflected in Silius's reconstruction of the Second Punic War through specific reminiscence of events and figures from the civil wars of the 80s BCE (e.g., Sil. 13.853–60), 40s BCE (e.g., 13.861–67), and the late 60s CE (e.g., 8.468–69). Silius's treatment of civil war also has a distinctly Flavian air through its extensive engagement with the preceding literary tradition of civil war and its historical background. The atmosphere of violence, greed, and fear that pervades Lucan's *Bellum Ciuile*, Statius's *Thebaid*, and the Iron Age passage in Ovid's *Metamorphoses* (1.127–50) stains the Saguntum (e.g., Sil. 2.498–505) and Cannae (e.g., 9.287–89) episodes and is mirrored in the accounts of civil discord by ancient historians and biographers in the first centuries BCE and CE. As is evident not only in references to actual civil war in the *Punica* (e.g., 13.853–67) but also in passages indicative of civil discord more generally (e.g., 2.654–58, 11.44–50), for Silius Italicus civil strife was a real cause for concern.

Alison Keith
Engendering Civil War in Flavian Epic

The Flavian epic poets' recurrent obsession with the theme of civil war has been well documented, especially in connection with the *fraternas acies* that lies at the heart of Statius's *Thebaid*, as well as in the Cyzican and Colchian wars of Valerius's *Argonautica*, and in Silius's Saguntum episode in the *Punica*.[1] Here I wish to reorient discussion of civil war from the masculine, fraternal focus these battles have typically received in order to pursue a recurrent tendency in the Flavian epics to map civil discord onto the gender system. Before broaching these poems, however, it will be salutary to rehearse some of the evidence for a peculiarly Roman fascination with the theme of specifically fratricidal civil war, across a range of literary genres and historical periods, but especially in the genre of epic at Rome. In my prolegomena, I ask when fratricide was gendered, as a preface to the exploration of the gender of civil war in Latin epic after 69 CE.

1 Before 69 CE

Roman obsession with the theme of fratricidal civil war can be discerned as early as mid-Republican Latin epic, where the founding myth of Romulus and Remus received concentrated development in Ennius's *Annales*, not only in the account of Remus's jumping Romulus's wall, thus authorizing fratricide (Enn. *Ann.* 92–95), but also, already, in the augury scene (Enn. *Ann.* 72–91):[2]

My thanks to Lauren Donovan Ginsberg and Darcy Krasne for the invitation to participate on their panel "After 69 CE" at the Edinburgh Celtic Conference in Classics in June 2014 and for their helpful comments on an earlier version of this paper. I am also grateful to the other panel participants for a stimulating exchange of ideas during the course of the conference. They have saved me from numerous errors; those that remain are entirely my responsibility.

1 McGuire 1990; McGuire 1997; Henderson 1998; Baier 2001; Fucecchi 2006a; the essays collected in Dominik *et al.* 2009; Marks 2010a.
2 I cite Ennius from the edition of Skutsch 1985; Horace from Klingner 1959; Valerius Flaccus from Ehlers 1980; Statius's *Thebaid* from Hill 1983; and Silius from Delz 1987. Throughout, translations of Ennius follow Warmington 1956; translations of Horace are adapted from the interlinear translation series of A. Hinds & Co. 1894; translations of Valerius Flaccus and Statius's *Thebaid* are lightly adapted from Mozley 1934 and Mozley 1928, respectively; translations of Silius Italicus are lightly adapted from Duff 1934; and translations of Suetonius are my own.

curantes magna cum cura tum cupientes
regni dant operam simul auspicio augurioque.
in †monte Remus auspicio sedet atque secundam
solus auem seruat. at Romulus pulcer in alto   75
quaerit Auentino, seruat genus altiuolantum.
certabant urbem Romam Remoramne uocarent.
omnibus cura uiris uter esset induperator.
expectant ueluti consul quom mittere signum
uolt, omnes auidi spectant ad carceris oras   80
quam mox emittat pictos e faucibus currus:
sic expectabat populus atque ore timebat
rebus utri magni uictoria sit data regni.
interea sol albus recessit in infera noctis.
exin candida se radiis dedit icta foras lux   85
et simul ex alto longe pulcerrima praepes
laeua uolauit auis. simul aureus exoritur sol
cedunt de caelo ter quattuor corpora sancta
auium, praepetibus sese pulcrisque locis dant.
conspicit inde sibi data Romulus esse propritim   90
auspicio regni stabilita scamna solumque.

Then, careful and with a great care, each in eagerness for royal rule, they are intent on the watching and soothsaying of birds … on a hill. Remus devotes himself to watching and apart looks out for a favourable bird. But handsome Romulus makes his search on high Aventine and so looks out for the soaring breed. Whether they should call the city Roma or Remora— this was their contest. Anxiety filled all the men as to which of the two should be ruler. As, when the consul means to give the signal, all men look eagerly at the barrier's bounds to see how soon he will send the chariots forth from the painted mouths — so they waited. Thus were the people waiting, and held their tongues, wondering to which of the two the victory of right royal rule should be given by the event. Meanwhile the white sun withdrew into depths of night. Then clear shot forth, struck out in rays, a light: just when, winging to the left, there flew from the height a bird, the luckiest far of flying prophets, just then all golden there rose up the sun. Thrice four hallowed forms of birds moved down from the sky, and betook themselves to places lucky and of happy omen. From this saw Romulus that to him, to be his own, were duly given the chair and throne of royalty, established firm by the watching of birds.

An exclusively male interest in the contest is perhaps implied by the augural context in which the brothers compete to name the city, for the augural college was an elite male prerogative in classical Rome.[3] Moreover, Ennius emphasizes the anxiety of the men (*uiris*, Enn. *Ann.* 78) watching the brothers' competition by likening them to greedy spectators at the circus whose masculinity is assumed in

---

3 On augurs and augural law in ancient Rome, see Linderski 1986.

the adjective *auidi* (Enn. *Ann.* 80) and in the collective noun *populus* (Enn. *Ann.* 82).

The fratricidal foundation myth seems to have been reworked with increasing urgency in the century of civil wars between Roman strongmen that followed the publication of the *Annales* towards the end of the first quarter of the second century BCE. Twenty-five years before Octavian came to power, for example, the politician and historian C. Licinius Macer (tribune in 73 BCE) apparently treated the legend as an aetiological myth. T.P. Wiseman has argued that he located the source of the Romans' fatal propensity for political strife and civil war in Romulus's unscrupulous deceit in the augury competition. The ensuing confrontation with his brother Remus resulted not only in fratricide but also in quasi-parricide, when Faustulus was killed too.[4] In the Republican material, much of which is fragmentary, it is not possible to discern an interest in the gender of civil war: arms belong to the man and conflict between brothers is easily expanded to conflict between *patres* and *plebs*. For, as Steele Commager well put it, "What is civil war but expanded fratricide?"[5]

It thus seems to have been in the Augustan period, when Rome's bloodstained history of civil war was also a prominent leitmotif of literary discussion,[6] that a gendered dimension was introduced into the discourse of civil war. Civil war continued to be thematized in this period, as was by then traditional, in connection with the twin founders of the city, especially in the poetry of Vergil and Horace. Indeed the latter explicitly identified Romulus's fratricide as the origin of the seemingly endless cycle of civil bloodshed that deformed the state in his youth and was to culminate in the installation of the Principate after Actium, the battle perhaps envisaged in Horace's seventh *Epode*:

> quo, quo scelesti ruitis? aut cur dexteris
>   aptantur enses conditi?
> parumne campis atque Neptuno super
>   fusum est Latini sanguinis,
> non ut superbas inuidae Karthaginis   5
>   Romanus arces ureret
> intactus aut Britannus ut descenderet
>   sacra catenatus uia,
> sed ut secundum uota Parthorum sua

---

[4] On this version of the myth, see Wiseman 1995, 143–44, with a wealth of references to contemporary primary literature. Cf. also Luc. 1.93–95, which locates in Romulus's fratricide the origins of Rome's endless cycle of fratricidal civil wars.
[5] Commager 1962, 181.
[6] Good discussion in Hardie 1993a, 1–22; Gurval 1995.

urbs haec periret dextera?   10
neque hic lupis mos nec fuit leonibus
    umquam nisi in dispar feris.
furorne caecus an rapit uis acrior
    an culpa? responsum date.
tacent et albus ora pallor inficit   15
    mentesque perculsae stupent.
sic est: acerba fata Romanos agunt
    scelusque fraternae necis,
ut inmerentis fluxit in terram Remi
    sacer nepotibus cruor.   20

Where, oh where, guilty men, are you rushing? Or why are the swords (lately) sheathed again fitted to your right hands? Is there too little Latin blood shed upon land and sea, not that a Roman might burn the proud citadels of envious Carthage or that the (still) unmastered Briton might go down through the sacred way bound in chains, but that, in accordance with the wishes of the Parthians, this city might perish by its own right hands? Neither wolves nor lions have this custom, beasts never fierce except against a different species. Does madness or a more powerful force, or guilt, hurry you on blindly? Give me an answer. They are silent, and a white pallor tinges their faces; and their minds, thus struck, are stupefied. So it is: the cruel fates and the crime of a brother's death drive the Romans; from the time when the blood of innocent Remus flowed upon the earth, bringing a curse on his descendants.

Horace here explicitly names Romulus's fratricidal murder of Remus (*scelusque fraternae necis*, Hor. *Epod.* 7.18) as the bloody origin of the Roman propensity for civil war (Hor. *Epod.* 7.19–20). It is clear, moreover, that he envisages civil war—like the external wars he urges upon Rome with the Carthaginians, Britons, and Parthians—as an all-male affair. For he addresses the Roman male citizen body directly (*scelesti ruitis*, Hor. *Epod.* 7.1; cf. *responsum date*, Hor. *Epod.* 7.14), as the citizenry who constitute Remus's heirs (*nepotibus*, Hor. *Epod.* 7.20) bear the swords that rend the Republic.

But it is the discursive strategies that Horace developed, after Augustus's control over the empire was seemingly secured in the 20s BCE, that repay closer attention, for in this period Horace rehabilitates Romulus (Hor. *Carm.* 2.15.10–12, 3.3, 4.8.22–24) and also re-envisions the nature of the Romans' guilt, in the so-called "Roman Odes." In *Odes* 3.3, for example, Horace depicts Juno at the moment of her reconciliation with the Roman people (a reconciliation also depicted by Vergil, in *Aeneid* 12).[7] The Horatian Juno promotes Romulus's translation to

---

[7] On the Vergilian Juno's reconciliation with Jupiter and his plan for Roman dominion, see Feeney 1984.

heaven by ignoring his association with fratricide (which goes unmentioned in the ode) and by instead articulating a rationale for accepting Roman rule that shifts her hostility from the Romans onto the Trojans (Hor. *Carm.* 3.3.18–68)—a rationale that also animates the Vergilian Juno in *Aeneid* 12 and is already prominent in her initial speech in the epic (Verg. *A*. 1.23–49). In this way, Horace implicitly displaces responsibility for Rome's propensity towards fratricidal war retrospectively, onto the perfidious Trojans. In the final Roman Ode, moreover, Horace develops another highly effective rhetorical strategy of displacement, which we may call "lateral," in that he there shifts the responsibility for Rome's civil wars away from the men who waged them, laterally, onto the women who did not. Thus in *Carmen* 3.6, Horace seems to conceive of the present generation, "fertile in crime," as feminized (Hor. *Carm.* 3.6.17–48):[8]

> fecunda culpae saecula nuptias
> primum inquinauere et genus et domos:
>   hoc fonte deriuata clades
>   in patriam populumque fluxit.   20
>
> motus doceri gaudet Ionicos
> matura uirgo et fingitur artibus
>   iam nunc et incestos amores
>   de tenero meditatur ungui.
>
> mox iuniores quaerit adulteros   25
> inter mariti uina neque eligit
>   cui donet inpermissa raptim
>   gaudia luminibus remotis,
>
> sed iussa coram non sine conscio
> surgit marito, seu uocat institor   30
>   seu nauis Hispanae magister,
>   dedecorum pretiosus emptor.
>
> non his iuuentus orta parentibus
> infecit aequor sanguine Punico
>   Pyrrhumque et ingentem cecidit   35
>   Antiochum Hannibalemque dirum.
>
> sed rusticorum mascula militum
> proles, Sabellis docta ligonibus

---

[8] Cf. "the Spartan adulteress" (*Lacaenae adulterae*, Hor. *Carm.* 3.3.25).

> uersare glaebas et seuerae
> matris ad arbitrium recisos 40
>
> portare fustis, sol ubi montium
> mutaret umbras et iuga demeret
> bubus fatigatis, amicum
> tempus agens abeunte curru.
>
> damnosa quid non inminuit dies? 45
> aetas parentum peior auis tulit
> nos nequiores, mox daturos
> progeniem uitiosiorem.

> Generations fertile in crime first stained marriage, lineage, and homes: derived from this source, disaster flowed into the fatherland and among the populace. The teenage girl enjoys being taught Ionian dances, is instructed in skills, and now even contemplates illicit love affairs wholeheartedly. Soon she seeks younger adulterers at her husband's parties, nor waits to choose the man to whom to give unpermitted joys in secret when the lights have been removed, but openly rises at a man's bidding, in the full knowledge of her husband, whether a shopkeeper invites her, or the captain of a Spanish ship, an expensive buyer of disgrace. The young men born of these parents haven't stained the sea with Carthaginian blood or killed Pyrrhus, huge Antiochus, and dread Hannibal, but the manly offspring of rural soldiers, taught how to turn clods with Sabine hoes and carry logs hewn at their mother's command, when the sun changed the mountains' shadows and stripped the yokes from the tired plough-oxen, driving on with his departing chariot the friendly eventide. What has the damaging present-day not diminished? The time of our parents, worse than that of our grandparents, has borne us, still worse, and soon to produce an even more vicious progeny.

Horace implicitly links the Romans' crimes with their women's fertility (Hor. *Carm.* 3.6.17) and explicitly locates the mark, or "stain" (*inquinauere*, Hor. *Carm.* 3.6.18), of crime in the house (*domos*, Hor. *Carm.* 3.6.18), along with marriage (*nuptias*, Hor. *Carm.* 3.6.17) and generational continuity (*genus*, Hor. *Carm.* 3.6.18). The domestic taint thus seeps out of the home into the populace to contaminate the fatherland (*in patriam populumque fluxit*, Hor. *Carm.* 3.6.20). He therefore focuses our attention on the unchaste women of these households: the seductive teenager, whose enjoyment of Ionian dances leads, apparently ineluctably, to unchastity (Hor. *Carm.* 3.6.21–24); and the lustful married woman who not only conducts her adulterous affairs under her husband's very eyes, but does so at his bidding (Hor. *Carm.* 3.6.25–28). In this way, Horace implicates contemporary "women out of control" in the moral failures of the civil war that authorized Augustan rule.[9]

---

[9] There is an extensive feminist critical literature on these rhetorical strategies in war narratives and imperial propaganda: see, e.g., Rubin 1975; Wittig 1986; Caplan 1987; Elshtain 1987;

Both rhetorical moves—of retrospective and lateral displacement in the historicization and feminization of responsibility for civil war—animate Vergil's contemporary epic, the *Aeneid*, a poem whose action moves from the Greek sack of Troy (*Aeneid* 2) to the quasi-civil war between the Italians and the Trojan exiles in Latium (*Aeneid* 7–12), via a stopover in Carthage that affords an aetiology of the Punic Wars (*Aeneid* 1–4). I have argued elsewhere that "in the symbolic economy of the *Aeneid*"—the code model for so many of the Flavian epics—"the very voice of violence and war is female," connecting the prominence of upper class Roman women in the triumviral politics of the decade between Philippi and Actium, and Octavian's propaganda about such women, with Vergil's representation of social disorder and its causes in the *Aeneid*.[10] The male conquest of the militant female in the *Aeneid* reflects a potent enabling fiction of the early Augustan regime, in which Roman Order is re-established externally through the defeat of Cleopatra[11] and internally through the re-domestication of Roman women. While I do not intend to rehearse this argument here, I do want to recuperate one aspect of my findings, *viz.* that civil discord in particular is frequently mapped onto the gender system in the *Aeneid*.

Georgia Nugent has brilliantly analyzed the episode in *Aeneid* 5 where the Trojan women fire the Trojan ships (Verg. *A*. 5.605–79), one of many passages in the poem that figuratively dramatize the Roman propensity for civil war. She has demonstrated Vergil's inscription of conflict between the sexes at the center of the episode.[12] Similarly, conflict between male and female informs the initial breakdown of Italian order in *Aeneid* 7. The narrative displaces the challenge to the established order in Italy, posed by the arrival of the Trojan exiles, from the external group onto an internal out-group, reinscribing the potential conflict between Trojans and Latins as a challenge to the traditional territorial assignments of gender that rises from within Latin society. The figural evocation of civil discord in Latinus's city (Verg. *A*. 7.376–405) is confirmed by situational echoes of the Trojan women's flight into the woods after the firing of the ships (Verg. *A*. 5.677–78). In both episodes the women's actions are aligned with insurrection. Thus the feminization of responsibility for civil war is what we might call an equal

---

MacDonald *et al.* 1987; Cooper *et al.* 1989; Higonnet 1989; Marcus 1989; Montrose 1991; Bronfen 1992; Hamer 1993. For classical scholarship on these rhetorical strategies in ancient Rome, see Edwards 1993, 34–97; Joshel 1997; Keith 2000, 65–100; Wyke 2002, 195–243; Milnor 2005.
10 Keith 2000, 65–81, quote at 69; cf. Nugent 1992.
11 On Cleopatra in Octavian's propaganda and the writers of the Augustan age, see Hamer 1993; Gurval 1995; Wyke 2002, 195–243. For Cleopatra in the pictorial record, see also Kleiner 1992.
12 Nugent 1992. My discussion in this paragraph rehearses the argument of Keith 2000, 69–70.

opportunity rhetorical strategy in the *Aeneid*—both the Trojans and the Italians are the victims of "women out of control."

The urgency with which the hierarchy of gender informs the structure of civil war in the *Aeneid* reflects the social and political uncertainties of the period in which it was written, uncertainties which were in some measure diffused over the course of Augustus's unpredictably long, stable and stabilizing rule.[13] As the Actian moment receded, however, the filiation of women with conflict in the poem's civil war narratives was familiarized and naturalized through the elevation of the *Aeneid* to a central place in the Roman literary and educational establishments. At the same time, the institutionalization of the Principate resulted in a shift of power from senators to *princeps* and from Senate to *Domus Augusta*, with the concomitant rise in the visibility of the women of the imperial household that is commemorated in the historical and biographical narratives of Tacitus and Suetonius, as well as in the rich dossier of extant epigraphic, numismatic, and iconographic material evidence.[14] Thus the complex network of gender relations that articulates the structure of civil war in the *Aeneid*, and the unresolved tensions that they set in play, invite continual renegotiation in later Latin epic.

Indeed, the unifying framework that the hierarchy of gender lends to the structure of civil war in the *Aeneid* recurs with particular urgency in the epics of the Flavian period.[15] This renewed urgency is undoubtedly related to the collapse of Julio-Claudian rule and the ensuing civil wars that engulfed Rome in the aftermath of Galba's revolt and Nero's suicide at the end of 68 CE. The civil wars ended with the investiture of imperial power, late in 69 or early in 70 CE, in the victorious general Vespasian who, like Augustus, promoted a view of himself as the restorer not only of the state but also of its morals (Suet. *Ves.* 8.1). He even introduced legislation designed to rein in the "licentiousness and extravagance" that was perceived to have "increased without restraint" (*libido atque luxuria coercente nullo inualuerat*, Suet. *Ves.* 11), including a law that reduced a woman who took another's slave as her lover to a slave herself (*auctor senatui fuit decernendi, ut quae se alieno seruo iunxisset, ancilla haberetur*, Suet. *Ves.* 11).[16] A similar fascination with Augustan precedent in every area of imperial governance, including that of morality, has been observed in Domitian,[17] during whose rule (81–

---

13 My discussion in this paragraph rehearses a portion of the argument of Keith 2000, 81.
14 On the political role of women in the Julio-Claudian Principate, see Purcell 1986; Corbier 1995; Perkounig 1995; Winkes 1995; Barrett 1996; Bartman 1999; Wood 1999; Kleiner/Matheson 2000; Barrett 2002; Severy 2003; Milnor 2005; Fantham 2006; Ginsburg 2006; Kunst 2008.
15 My discussion in this paragraph rehearses the argument of Keith 2000, 89–90.
16 On Vespasian and his rise to the principate, see Nicols 1978; Levick 1999; Murison 1999.
17 Jones 1992, 13; cf. D'Ambra 1993, 36–39.

96 CE) the epics of Valerius Flaccus, Statius, and Silius Italicus were first put into circulation (though Valerius's, at least, was probably begun under Vespasian[18]). Domitian assumed the office of censor in perpetuity in 85 CE, and in this capacity he undertook to correct public morals (*suscepta correctione morum*, Suet. *Dom.* 8.3). He is also reported to have revived Augustan moral legislation (Suet. *Dom.* 8.3; D.C. 67.2–3), for which he is praised in contemporary court poetry (Mart. 5.8; 6.2, 4, 7; 9.6). On two separate occasions he even executed Vestal Virgins for sexual misbehavior (*incesta*, Suet. *Dom.* 8.3–4). The Flavian emperors' architectural, religious, military, and legislative programs participate in traditional Roman moralizing discourses designed to legitimate their (seizure of the imperial) power, and it is in this context that we may interpret the renewed attention in Flavian epic to the gendered structure of civil war.

2 After 69 CE

Both Valerius and Statius, for example, treat the battle between the sexes at Lemnos in their epics, inscribing conflict between the sexes at the center of a civil war that has been seen as paradigmatic for both epics.[19] Intra-familial conflict and civil war pervade Valerius's *Argonautica*, which opens with Pelias enjoining upon his nephew Jason the quest for the Golden Fleece because there are no wars in Greece to which he can be sent (V. Fl. 1.33–34; cf. 5.495–97).[20] The shadow of war, and especially civil war, with its domestic counterpart of kin-killing, looms large over the journey of the Argonauts:[21] at Cyzicus they inadvertently do battle with their erstwhile hosts (V. Fl. 3.15–458);[22] in Colchis they find a civil war underway (V. Fl. 3.487–508, 5.265–6.760);[23] internecine conflict erupts among the Sown Men (V. Fl. 7.607–43);[24] the Fleece itself hangs in a grove sacred to the war-god

---

[18] On the dating of Valerius Flaccus's *Argonautica*, see Stover 2012, 7–26.
[19] See, e.g., Hardie 1990; Nugent 1996; Keith 2000, 93–95, 97–98; Augoustakis 2010a, 21–22, 34–61. This paragraph and the next rehearse a portion of the argument of Keith 2000, 93–94.
[20] On kinship and its discontents in Flavian epic, see Hardie 1993a, 88–119; McGuire 1990; McGuire 1997; Bernstein 2008; Cowan 2014.
[21] McGuire 1997, 103–13; Bernstein 2008, 51–54; Stover 2012, 113–50.
[22] On the Cyzicus episode, see Manuwald 1999; Spaltenstein 2004, 10–137; Stover 2012, 113–50; Lovatt 2014, 214–17; Manuwald 2015.
[23] On the war at Colchis, see especially Wijsman 1996; Schenk 1999, 83–142, 188–212, 228–45; Wijsman 2000; Baier 2001; Fucecchi 2006a; Lovatt 2014, 224–27; cf. Cowan 2014, 244–47.
[24] On the episode, see Stadler 1993; Perutelli 1997; Spaltenstein 2005, *ad loc.*

Mars (V. Fl. 1.528–29, 5.228–30);[25] and the Colchians under Absyrtus pursue the Argonauts to try to recover the Fleece (V. Fl. 8.259–467).[26] Paradoxically, the only war in which the Argonauts do not participate is the first fully narrated conflict in the poem, the Lemnian massacre, which occurs just before the Argonauts arrive on the island (V. Fl. 2.101–310).[27]

Precisely because the Argonauts do not participate in the Lemnian conflict of Book 2, however, the episode invites interpretation as a commentary on the economy of civil war in the *Argonautica*. The Lemnian episode shows significant points of contact with the Argonautic project, most obviously in the interconnection of war with sea-travel. The Lemnian men make use of the technology of shipbuilding and seafaring to wage a long war in Thrace (V. Fl. 2.107–14), much as the Argonauts' voyage provides them with the opportunity to engage in wars throughout the Mediterranean and Black Seas. Moreover, the Lemnian men's spoils of war are herds and female slaves (V. Fl. 2.111–14), rewards that resonate symbolically with the twin prizes, the Golden Fleece and Medea, of which Jason will despoil the Colchians. On Lemnos, the absence of the men undermines the social order and results in intra-familial conflict, just as in Thessaly the absence of Jason gives his uncle Pelias the opportunity to kill his parents Aeson and Alcimede. Besides the thematic interconnections between the Lemnians' war in Thrace and the Argonauts' journey, the massacre on Lemnos foreshadows the civil war in which Jason and the Argonauts become embroiled at Colchis and anticipates their night battle at Cyzicus. Finally, Jason's dalliance with Hypsipyle after civil war on Lemnos rehearses his acquisition of a wife after civil war at Colchis. The Lemnian episode thus furnishes an exemplary model of the structure of civil war in the *Argonautica*, and it is notable that this structure is gendered. For the Furies, who elsewhere in the epic summon men into conflict on the Vergilian model of war (V. Fl. 1.817, 3.214, 3.520, 4.13, 6.403),[28] are, on Lemnos, physically embodied in women who instigate the worst kind of insurrection against the political order of the state, a conflict that overturns the natural hierarchy of gender and moves the poet to intervene directly in his narrative to comment on the magnitude of the women's crime (V. Fl. 2.216–19):[29]

> unde ego tot scelerum facies, tot fata iacentum
> exsequar? heu uatem monstris quibus intulit ordo,

---

25 On the Fleece, see Zissos 2008, *ad* V. Fl. 1.528–29; Wijsman 1996, *ad* V. Fl. 5.228–30.
26 On the episode, see Pellucchi 2012 and Spaltenstein 2005, *ad loc.*
27 On the Lemnian massacre, see Harper Smith 1987; Aricò 1991; Poortvliet 1991a; Parkes 2014b.
28 Cf. Hardie 1989.
29 On this apostrophe, see also Landrey in this volume (pp. 231–34).

> quae se aperit series! o qui me uera canentem
> sistat et hac nostras exsoluat imagine noctes!

> How should I record so many scenes of wickedness, so many deaths of the fallen? Alas, to what ghastly deeds has the recital brought the bard, what a long tale of horror opens before me! Oh that someone might check me, though I recite true deeds, and release my nights from this vision!

The Lemnian women's slaughter of their menfolk takes to its (ideo)logical limit the reversal of social order implicit in civil war and reveals at every point the pressure of the gendered structure of civil war at play in the epic.

But this is not the only civil war narrative in Valerius's *Argonautica* in which the gender system is inscribed. It is especially instructive to consider Medea's role in the civil wars that beset Colchis—not only that waged between her father Aeetes and her uncle Perses, but also those fought by the sown men at Colchis and instigated at sea by her brother Absyrtus's pursuit of the Argonauts. For in these conflicts, Valerius merges civil war with intra-familial conflict and returns to the central problematic of fratricide in Roman myth and history, while giving it a decisively gendered structure.

Medea is introduced in Book 5 of the *Argonautica*, after Valerius's second invocation of the Muse (V. Fl. 5.217–21).[30] But the first women who appear in the book are the Amazons, whose shores the Argonauts sail past and whose defeat by Hercules Jason requests the hero's abandoned companions to relate (V. Fl. 5.120–39):[31]

> transit Halys longisque fluens anfractibus Iris   120
> saeuaque Thermodon medio sale murmura uoluens,
> Gradiuo sacer et spoliis ditissimus amnis,
> donat equos, donat uotas cui uirgo secures
> cum redit ingenti per Caspia claustra triumpho
> Massageten Medumque trahens. est uera propago   125
> sanguinis, est ollis genitor deus. hinc magis alta
> Haemonidae petere et monitus non temnere Phinei.
> ipse autem comitum conuersus ad ora nouorum
> 'uos mihi nunc pugnas' ait 'et uictricia' ductor
> 'Herculis arma mei uestrasque in litore Martis   130

---

30 On the invocation, apparently modeled after Vergil's second invocation at the outset of the second half of his epic, see Wijsman 1996, 123–28; Spaltenstein 2004, 442–46.

31 On the passage, see Wijsman 1996, 73–87, and Spaltenstein 2004, 415–21; neither of them is interested in the intrusion of the Amazons into the Argonautic myth or in Valerius's treatment of the archetypal female warriors of myth.

> interea memorate manus.' sic fatus et aegro
> corde silens audit currus bellique labores
> uirginei, exciderit frenis quae prima remissis,
> semianimem patrius quam sanguine uexerit amnis,
> quae pelta latus atque umeros nudata pharetris   135
> fugerit, Herculeae mox uulnere prensa sagittae,
> utque securigeras stimulauerit Ira cateruas
> fleturusque pater, quantus duce terror in ipsa,
> qui furor in signis, quo balteus arserit auro.

Halys goes by, and the long meanderings of Iris' stream, and Thermodon that rolls even in mid-sea his angry tumult, a river sacred to Gradivus and most rich with spoils, for to it the maiden presents horses and promised battle-axes, when in great triumph she returns through the Caspian gates, with Medians and Massagetae at her chariot-wheels. True breed and blood are they, the war-god is their sire. Hence did the Haemonians rather seek the deep, and despised not Phineus' warnings. Jason himself turns to face his new companions, and says, "You, now narrate the battles and victorious affrays of my own Hercules, and your own exploits on the shore of Mars." So he speaks, and silently, with regretful heart, he hears of the pursuits and the labours of the maidens' warfare, which first let go the reins and fell, which one her father's stream bore half-dead with blood, which fled away stripping the shield from her side and the quiver from her shoulder, overtaken soon and pierced by the shaft of Hercules; how Anger and a sire whom tears awaited urged on the axe-wielding companies, what terror the leader herself inspired, what fury drove her on, and how her baldric blazed conspicuous with gold.

The Amazons' conventional characterization as women who fight with men often provides a focal point for gendered war paradigms in classical epic (and other ancient genres).[32] Here, I would suggest, their generalized hostility to men puts programmatic pressure on the poet's introduction of the Colchian princess in their wake. For she is represented as a potential locus of intra-familial conflict even before the Argonauts' arrival, in the warning Phrixus's ghost makes to her father Aeetes from the grave (V. Fl. 5.231–40):[33]

> quondam etiam tacitae uisus per tempora noctis
> effigie uasta, socerumque exterruit ingens
> prodita uox: "<o> qui patria tellure fugatum
> quaerentemque domos his me considere passus
> sedibus, oblata generum mox prole petisti,   235
> tunc tibi regnorum labes luctusque supersunt

---

[32] Keith 2000, 68. On the Amazons in myth and art, see Dubois 1982; Tyrrell 1984; Henderson 1994; Mayor 2014.

[33] On the passage, see Wijsman 1996, 131–34, and Spaltenstein 2004, 448–51. On Medea in Valerius Flaccus's *Argonautica*, see Stover 2003; Zissos 2012; Davis 2014, all with further bibliography.

> rapta soporato fuerint cum uellera luco.
> praeterea infernae quae nunc sacrata Dianae
> fert castos Medea choros, quemcumque procorum
> pacta petat, maneat regnis ne uirgo paternis."   240

Once he even appeared, a huge phantom, at the time of silent night, and a great voice spoke forth and terrified his father-in-law: "O you who suffered me, in exile from my paternal land and seeking a home, to settle in these abodes and, having offered your daughter, sought me for son-in-law—ruin and grief await your kingdom at the time when the fleece shall be stolen from the sleep-drugged grove. Moreover Medea who, now, consecrated to chthonic Diana, leads modest dances—let her seek marriage with any of the leading men, let her not remain a maiden in her father's royal halls."

Aeetes takes Phrixus's warning seriously, praying to Mars to guard the Fleece (V. Fl. 5.250–55) and engaging his daughter to an Albanian prince: *ergo omnes prohibere minas praedictaque Phrixi | inuigilat, plena necdum Medea iuuenta | adnuitur thalamis Albani uirgo tyranni* ("Therefore he is careful to foil all the threats and dangers foretold by Phrixus, and Medea, though not yet of mature age, is plighted to the marriage chamber of the Albanian tyrant," V. Fl. 5.256–58).

We first meet Medea herself in a context that characterizes her as another woman opposed to men—not yet those who are foreign, but definitely those who are familial. Thus, Valerius introduces her just as she wakes from a nightmare that prefigures her murderous career (V. Fl. 5.333–40):[34]

> namque soporatos tacitis in sedibus artus
> dum premit alta quies nullaeque in uirgine curae,
> uisa pauens castis Hecates excedere lucis,   335
> dumque pii petit ora patris, stetit arduus inter
> pontus et ingenti circum stupefacta profundo
> fratre tamen conante sequi. mox stare pauentes
> uiderat intenta pueros nece seque trementem
> spargere caede manus et lumina rumpere fletu.   340

For while deep sleep held her slumbering limbs in silent chambers and no cares troubled her maidenhood, she seemed to leave Hecate's chaste grove in fear, and while she sought her loving father's face, the harsh sea stood between them, and she was terrified at the huge deep around them, though her brother tried to follow. Next, she had seen children stand fearful at the threat of death, and she herself, trembling, sprinkle her hands with their blood, and her eyes burst with weeping.

---

[34] On the passage introducing Medea into the epic (V. Fl. 5.329–454), see Wijsman 1996, 166–218; Spaltenstein 2004, 472–507.

Here Medea is set in opposition to her father, brother, and two sons, with a summary of her progression of kin murders—from fratricide to infanticide—that maps closely onto the Latin epic tradition of the familial devastation of civil war.

The Colchian intra-familial conflicts are mirrored by those on Olympus, where the tutelary divinities of Aeetes and the Argonauts square off along gendered lines, with Mars opposing Pallas Athena and Juno (V. Fl. 5.618–48).[35] Mars complains bitterly to Jupiter about Minerva's meddling in Colchian affairs (V. Fl. 5.624–32):

> quae studiis, rex magne, quies? iam mutua diui
> exitia in solos hominum molimur honores   625
> teque ea cuncta iuuant, rabidam qui Pallada caelo
> non abigis neque femineis ius obicis ausis.
> non queror exstructa quod uexerit ipsa carina
> uellera sacra meis sperantem auertere lucis
> quodque palam tutata uiros. sic cetera pergat,   630
> si ualet. insidiis quid nunc fallacibus ambit,
> nostra ut Phrixeo spolientur templa metallo?

> What respite is there, great king, to these pursuits? Already we gods undertake mutual destruction for the sole glory of mortals, and all these things please you, who neither drive Pallas in her raving from heaven nor oppose law against women's daring. I am not complaining because she herself has constructed a ship and conveyed him who hopes to take away the sacred fleece from my grove and because she openly keeps the men safe. Let her continue the rest so, if she can. Why now does she plot with deceptive tricks to despoil my temple of Phrixus's golden fleece?

This imputation to Pallas of deceptions, while not borne out in the narrative, allows the poet to gesture knowingly towards the proliferation of acts of deception and treachery among both divine and mortal characters. Thus Juno and Venus reprise their Vergilian roles as mutual deceivers, while Aeetes plots to deceive the Argonauts, and Medea (the dupe of both Juno and Venus) goes on, as the literary tradition dictates, to deceive her father.

When the Argonauts reach Colchis, moreover, they find Aeetes embroiled in a civil war with his brother, Perses (because the Colchian tyrant has refused to return the Fleece to Hellas), whom the poet describes as "next in rank to the king, and brother by maternal blood" (*ordine regi | proximus et frater materno sanguine Perses*, V. Fl. 5.265–66). This civil war is thus another of the *fraternas acies* (Stat. *Theb.* 1.1) that Flavian epic poets explore with such intensity after 69 CE. Participants in the Colchian conflict, moreover, repeatedly succumb to the

---

[35] On the scene, see Wijsman 1996, 278–88; Spaltenstein 2004, 546–52.

oppositions that disfigure kin relations and other community standards under the pressure of civil discord. Fighting on Perses' side, for example, we find the Iazyges, a people who traditionally practice euthanasia in the form of parricide, and who are thus well versed already in *paternas acies* (V. Fl. 6.122–28):

> ... et expertes canentis Iazyges aeui.
> namque ubi iam uires gelidae notusque refutat
> arcus et inceptus iam lancea temnit eriles
> magnanimis mos ductus auis haud segnia mortis   125
> iura pati, dextra sed carae occumbere prolis
> ense dato, rumpuntque moras natusque parensque,
> ambo animis, ambo miri tam fortibus actis.

> ... and the Iazyges, unversed in white-haired old age. For when now their strength begins to fail and the well-known bow denies them and the lance despises the efforts of its lord, they have a custom, inherited from great-hearted ancestors of old, not to suffer the slow laws of death but to give a sword to their own dear offspring and die by his right hand; so child and parent burst delays, in courage both, in gallant deed, both admirable.

The poet's approval of this practice notwithstanding, the Iazyges would seem to be expert practitioners of civil war between the generations.[36]

There are also hints of gendered divisions in the civil war fighting at Colchis. Thus, the Amazon Euryale leads a contingent of her sisters on the battlefield in support of Aeetes, and the Colchian tyrant singles her cohort out for special praise when informing Jason of the participants in the war at Colchis (V. Fl. 5.610–14):[37]

> ... ingentes animo iam prospice campos   610
> atque hanc alipedi pulsantem corpora curru
> Euryalen, quibus exultet Mauortia turmis
> et quantum elata ualeat peltata securi,
> cara mihi et ueras inter non ultima natas.

> Now survey in your mind the vast plains and Euryale, trampling bodies with her swift chariot; see with what troops the martial maid exults and how she prevails, armed with lunate shield and uplifted battle-axe—dear to me and not least among my true daughters.

In battle, moreover, Euryale rewards Aeetes' confidence, rescuing the corpse of his ally Canthus from Perses' troops in a passage that maps the battle of the sexes onto the civil war before the walls of Colchis (V. Fl. 6.369–80):

---

[36] See Fucecchi 2006a, *ad loc.*
[37] See Wijsman 1996, 274–77; Spaltenstein 2004, 543–45.

> quem manus a tergo socium rapit atque receptum
> uirginis Euryales curru locat. aduolat ipsa 370
> ac simul Haemonidae Gesandrumque omnis in unum
> it manus. ille nouas acies et uirginis arma
> ut uidet "has etiam contra bellabimus?" inquit
> "heu pudor!" inde Lycen ferit ad confine papillae,
> inde Thoen, qua pelta uacat iamque ibat in Harpen 375
> uixdum prima leui ducentem cornua neruo
> et labentis equi tendentem frena Menippen,
> cum regina grauem nodis auroque securem
> congeminans partem capitis galeaeque ferinae
> dissipat. 380

From behind, his comrades drag Canthus away and set him, once regained, in the maiden Euryale's chariot. She flies forth, and the Haemonidae with her, and the whole band attacks Gesander alone. When he sees the new lines and the maiden's weapons, he cries, "These women, too, are we to fight against? For shame!" Then he strikes Lyce near the breast, and Thoe, where her shield leaves a space, and now he was going against Harpe, who had scarcely first begun to draw the horns of her bow with her light string, and Menippe, who strained the reins of her stumbling horse, when the queen, redoubling the blows of a battle-axe heavy with golden knobs, cleft asunder his head and helmet of wild-beast's hide.

Euryale bears a name that is otherwise unattested of an Amazon but is the feminine form of that belonging to the Vergilian Euryalus, whose indiscriminate slaughter of Rutulians in *Aeneid* 9 takes on the overtones of civil war in the context of the fated union of Trojans and Italians in the *Aeneid*.[38] Elsewhere, interestingly, the name is attested of one of the Gorgons,[39] and Valerius may be thinking of this association here as well, since he follows Gesander's gruesome death with an account of Ariasmenus's assault on the Argonauts and the intervention he provokes from Pallas, who wields the Gorgon-head aegis against him (V. Fl. 6.394–403):

> diluuio tali paribusque Ariasmenus urget
> excidiis nullo rapiens discrimine currus. 395
> aegida tum primum uirgo spiramque Medusae
> ter centum saeuis squalentem sustulit hydris,
> quam soli uidistis, equi. pauor occupat ingens
> excussis in terga uiris diramque retorquent
> in socios non sponte luem. tunc ensibus uncis 400
> implicat et trepidos lacerat discordia currus.

---

38 See Hardie 1994, 18 and *passim*.
39 Hes. *Th.* 276; Pi. *P.* 12.20; Eratosth. *Cat.* 32; Hyg. *Astr.* 2.34; Apollod. 1.25. The name also appears of the mother of Orion: see Spaltenstein 2004, *ad* V. Fl. 5.612; and Baier 2001 and Fucecchi 2006a, both *ad* V. Fl. 6.370.

> Romanas ueluti saeuissima cum legiones
> Tisiphone regesque mouet ...

Such is the deluge and destruction as Ariasmenus hurries his chariots in indiscriminate course. Then first did the Maiden lift her aegis and Medusa's coils all bristling with three hundred savage snakes, which you alone, his horses, saw. Great terror seizes them, their drivers are flung backward to the ground, and they perforce wreak dire destruction on their comrades. Then, with the curved blades, discord entangles and lacerates the panic-stricken cars. As when fierce Tisiphone stirs Roman legions and their princes to war ...

Here, moreover, Valerius brings his epic narrative into particularly close contact with contemporary Roman warfare, in his anachronistic simile of Roman legionary warfare.[40] He thereby implies the relevance of his mythological epic to the most recent episode of Rome's history of civil wars, in the year of four emperors.

The proliferation of civil war contexts in which the Argonauts find themselves embroiled at Colchis allows, as we have seen, for a rich diversity of gendered sites for conflict, and this continues even after the Argonauts' victory on behalf of the Colchian tyrant. For Aeetes subsequently refuses to honor his compact with the Hellenes to surrender the Golden Fleece. Instead, he invites Jason to yoke his fire-breathing bulls and sow the dragon's teeth, which results in a new crop of fratricidal civil warriors. On this occasion, Jason's task is not to join battle with their fratricidal ranks, but rather to avoid it, and in this he is assisted by Medea's magic arts (V. Fl. 7.625–40):[41]

> ergo iter\<um\> ad socias conuertere Colchidos artes   625
> et galeae nexus ac uincula dissipat imae
> cunctaturque tamen totique occurrere bello
> ipse cupit. spes nulla datur, sic undique densant
> terrigenae iam signa duces clamorque tubaeque.
> iamque omnes uidere uirum iamque omnia contra   630
> tela uolant. tum uero amens discrimine tanto
> quam modo Tartareo galeam Medea ueneno
> in medios torsit; conuersae protinus hastae.   634
> qualis ubi atto\<nitos\> maestae Phrygas annua Matris   635
> ira uel exsectos lacerat Bellona comatos,
> haud secus accensas subito Medea cohortes
> implicat et miseros agit in sua proelia fratres.
> omnis ibi Aesoniden sterni putat, omnibus ira
> aequalis ...   640

633] om. Ehlers

---

40 Cf. Fucecchi 2006a, *ad loc.*
41 On the passage, see Stadler 1993 and Perutelli 1997, *ad loc.*

Once more then he has recourse to the Colchian's friendly arts, and disjoins the chain and fastening at his helmet's base; yet he hesitates and nevertheless desires to meet the whole array himself; but no hope offers, so closely throng the banners of the earth-born on every side, so loud their shouts and trumpet calls. And now all caught sight of the man, and at once all the weapons are flying at him. Then mad with fear in such peril, he flung into their midst the helmet which Medea just now had drugged with Hellish poison: immediately, the spears were turned about. And just as the anger of the mournful Mother rends every year the frenzied Phrygians, or as Bellona lacerates the long-haired eunuchs, so Medea suddenly inflames and embroils the cohorts, and drives the doomed brothers to battle with their kin. Each one thinks that it is Jason he is laying low, all alike are fired with similar rage.

Although the Sown men imagine that they do battle with Jason, Valerius Flaccus represents the hero instead as a mere cipher for Medea, whose poisons carry the day. The gendered framework of the contest is underlined by the simile that likens Medea's victory over the Sown Men to those of Cybele over the Phrygians and Bellona over the eunuch Bellonarii (V. Fl. 7.635–36). The popular reputation for effeminacy ascribed to both Phrygians and eunuchs in antiquity further genders the Colchian conflict,[42] undermining the masculinity of the Spartoi and overdetermining the inevitability of their defeat by a woman. After her unheroic

---

[42] The simile comparing Medea's victory over the Spartoi to Cybele's defeat of the Phrygians and Bellona's conquest of the Bellonarii in *Argonautica* 7 pointedly recalls an earlier quasi-civil war in the epic orchestrated by Cybele early in *Argonautica* 3. There the Argonauts are embroiled in a night battle with their friends and erstwhile hosts, the inhabitants of the city of Cyzicus, which anticipates in its structure the gendered framework of the quasi-civil war between the Sown Men (and Medea and Jason) in *Argonautica* 7. At the outset of *Argonautica* 3, the poet invokes the Muse Clio to ask "why hands once joined in friendship should meet in strife" (*quid hospitiis iunctas concurrere dextras?* V. Fl. 3.17), before explaining Cybele's plot to avenge Cyzicus's killing of her sacred lion while he hunted on Mt. Dindymus (V. Fl. 3.19–31) by drawing him and his people into conflict with the Argonauts: *ut socias in nocte manus utque impia bella | conserat et saeuis erroribus implicet urbem* ("how in the night she set allied hands at strife in unnatural war, how she enmeshed the city in cruel error," V. Fl. 3.30–31, transl. Mozley, adapted); cf. V. Fl. 3.235 (*numine diuae*, "as the goddess had willed," transl. Mozley). During the battle, moreover, Cyzicus taunts his fellow-citizens with an effeminate reluctance to enter the manly fray, in contrast with the (self-directed) bloodlust inspired by their devotion to the emasculating goddess Cybele, '*numquamne dolor uirtusue subibit | nil ausas sine rege manus? at barbara buxus | si uocet et motis ululantia Dindyma sacris, | tunc ensis placeatque furor, modo tela sacerdos | porrigat, et iussa sanguis exuberet ulna*' ("Will grief and valor never enter hands that have dared nothing without their king? But if the barbarian box-wood pipe and Mt. Dindymus, re-echoing with revival of the rites, summon you, then sword and battle-lust would please you, provided that the priest provide weapons and the blood stream from your arms at his command," V. Fl. 3.230–34, transl. Mozley, adapted). Thus already at Cyzicus in *Argonautica* 3, Valerius embeds the hierarchy of gender in (quasi-)civil war: see further Manuwald 1999 and Manuwald 2015, *ad loc.*

conquest of the Sown Men and treacherous assistance to Jason, moreover, Medea finds herself embroiled in further communitarian conflict when she flees from Colchis with the Argonauts. For her father's dispatch of Absyrtus in pursuit of the Fleece inaugurates yet another potentially fratricidal war—between brother and sister, Colchians and Argonauts, and even rival suitors for Medea's hand, since her erstwhile fiancé Styrus accompanies Absyrtus in an effort to reclaim her from Jason.

In the extent and coherence of its affiliation of women with civil war, Valerius's unfinished poem moves far beyond Vergil's *Aeneid*, and both Silius and Statius follow Valerius in embedding the hierarchy of gender in the structure of civil war in their epics. Silius follows Valerius's lead by introducing Rome's conflict with Carthage in a passage that pairs foreign war with civil war and, in addition, genders civil war. When the Carthaginians attack the Spanish city of Saguntum, in breach of the treaty with Rome, Hannibal invests Saguntum from without, and Juno sends Tisiphone to undermine the city from within (Sil. 2.526–52).[43] Assuming the form of Tiburna, a Saguntine war-widow, the Fury exhorts the Saguntines to mutual slaughter (Sil. 2.553–79). Prompted by the Fury (*agit addita Erinnys*, Sil. 2.595), they erect a huge funeral pyre and then follow her example in mass carnage (Sil. 2.614–16):

> princeps Tisiphone lentum indignata parentem
> pressit ouans capulum cunctantemque impulit ensem   615
> et dirum insonuit Stygio bis terque flagello.

> First Tisiphone, resenting a father's half-hearted stroke, pushed the hilt forward in triumph and drove in the reluctant sword, and cracked her hellish scourge again and again with hideous noise.

The whole scene resonates with civil war horrors (Sil. 2.617–95) and introduces a note of moral ambivalence concerning the generic affiliation of women with war, for the Saguntines' mass suicide was regarded by the Romans as an exemplary display of the loyalty owed by an ally to Rome. Silius accordingly praises the Saguntines for their fidelity (in contrast to Punic treachery, Sil. 2.654–57) even as he abhors the carnage, with its overtones of civil discord, effectively depicting "the paradoxical nature of the act, at once glorious and repellent, noble and bestial."[44]

---

[43] The rest of this paragraph draws on the argument of Keith 2000, 92–93.
[44] Feeney 1991, 308. On the Saguntines' suicide as a negative *exemplum* within the *Punica*, see Bernstein (pp. 183–86, 195–97) and Hulls (pp. 323–32) in this volume; but *contra*, see Marks in this volume (p. 52 n. 6).

Yet his attribution of praise and blame in this episode also demonstrates a clear-eyed commitment to the "natural" hierarchy of gender in the structure of civil warfare, for the glorious achievement of the Saguntines is inspired by Hercules, who sends Loyalty (Fides) to fortify the citizens out of concern for the city he founded (Sil. 2.475–525), while their un-heroic mutual slaughter is provoked by the Fury Tisiphone (disguised as Tiburna), acting on Juno's instructions.[45]

Statius, too, fully integrates and innovates in his reuse of Vergil's embedding of the gender system in the structure of civil war in the *Thebaid*. Like all Roman epicists after Vergil, he assigns the Furies a central role in his epic war narrative.[46] The poem opens with a description of Oedipus's death-in-life after the discovery of his incestuous marriage and parricide (Stat. *Theb.* 1.46–55). The blind former king lurks in the recesses of the palace and shuns contact with any but the *Dirae*, who have taken up residence in his breast: *illum ... adsiduis circumuolat alis | saeua dies animi, scelerumque in pectore Dirae* ("yet with unwearied wings the fierce daylight of the mind hovers around him, and the Avenging Furies of his crimes assail his heart," Stat. *Theb.* 1.49, 51–52). Under their tutelage he prays to the Fury Tisiphone to accomplish his curse against his sons (Stat. *Theb.* 1.53–88). The Furies are thereby unleashed to instigate fratricidal conflict (*fraternas acies*, Stat. *Theb.* 1.1) and civil war at Thebes, a role they have played many times in Thebes' history, beginning with the civil war among the Spartoi, born from the earth in which Cadmus sowed the teeth of the dead serpent (*quis funera Cadmi | nesciat et totiens excitam a sedibus imis | Eumenidum bellasse aciem*, Stat. *Theb.* 1.227–29). Tisiphone immediately leaves Hades for Thebes, heading directly to the palace where she enmeshes the brothers in conflict (*indomitos praeceps discordia fratres | asperat*, "furious discord enrages the proud brothers," Stat. *Theb.* 1.137–38). Losing Thebes to Eteocles by lot, Polynices travels in exile to Argos, where he acquires a wife, a brother-in-law, and an Argive force he can deploy against Thebes.

In addition to maintaining a central role for the Furies in engendering civil conflict, Statius revives the Vergilian—and Valerian—motif of the wife who destines her husband to civil war.[47] On the day of the double wedding at Argos of Adrastus's daughters Argia and Deipyle to Polynices and Tydeus, respectively,

---

[45] Silius's account of the siege of Saguntum has received a great deal of critical attention; see Augoustakis 2010a, 113 n. 46, for bibliography; and see further Bernstein and Hulls (pp. 323–32) in this volume. On the gendered structure of the siege and the Saguntines' mass suicide, see Keith 2000, 92–93; Augoustakis 2010a, 113–35; and Hulls in this volume (pp. 329–32).

[46] Hardie 1993a, 40–48, 57–87. In this paragraph, I draw on the argument of Keith 2000, 95–96.

[47] The following argument rehearses Keith 2000, 95–98; cf. Bessone 2011, 200–23. On women in Statius's *Thebaid*, see also Augoustakis 2010a, 30–91; Manioti 2012.

Fama announces the marriage to the cities allied with Argos (Stat. *Theb.* 2.201–7) but announces war to Thebes: *hospitia et thalamos et foedera regni | permixtumque genus ... iam bella canit* ("she relates the welcome and the marriage, and the royal covenant, and the union of houses, ... at last she tells of war," Stat. *Theb.* 2.211–13). Part of Argia's trousseau is the necklace of Harmonia (Stat. *Theb.* 2.265–305), a deadly device (*infaustos ... | ornatus ... dirumque monile | Harmoniae. longa est series sed nota malorum*, Stat. *Theb.* 2.265–67) fashioned by the Cyclopes and the Telchines on Vulcan's instructions as a gift for the daughter of his wife Venus by her lover Mars (Stat. *Theb.* 2.269–76), on the occasion of her marriage to the founder of Thebes, Cadmus.[48] On the necklace is engraved a series of ill-omened figures—including the Gorgons, the Hesperides, and Tisiphone— and the whole piece is lavishly smeared with poisons (Stat. *Theb.* 2.277–85). The necklace symbolizes strife itself: *non hoc Pasithea blandarum prima sororum, | non Decor Idaliusque puer, sed Luctus et Irae | et Dolor et tota pressit Discordia dextra* ("Not Pasithea, eldest of the gracious sisters, nor Charm, nor the Idalian youth fashioned it, but Grief, and all the Passions, and Anguish and Discord, with all her right hand's craft," Stat. *Theb.* 2.286–88). By wearing the necklace her husband Polynices gives her, Argia is drawn into the fatal series of intra-familial conflicts that recurs in every generation (and between every generation) in the House of Cadmus. Moreover, the necklace enmeshes another hero in the conflict between Polynices and Eteocles, for when Amphiaraus's wife sees it she determines to acquire it (Stat. *Theb.* 2.299–305) and commits her husband to joining the Argive expedition in return for the necklace (Stat. *Theb.* 4.59–62, 187–213; cf. Stat. *Theb.* 8.104–5, 120–22). By marrying Polynices, Argia also becomes privy to his desire for war with his brother (Stat. *Theb.* 2.319–62), and so it is she who overcomes her father's reluctance to send the Seven to war against Thebes (Stat. *Theb.* 3.678–721).

Throughout the Argive scenes that inaugurate war, Statius exploits Vergil's thematic pairing of conflict between the sexes with civil war, and nowhere more urgently than in his own account of the Lemnian massacre, narrated by Hypsipyle to the Argive leaders in *Thebaid* 5 (5.29–498).[49] As in Valerius's *Argonautica*, to which it may allude, Statius's account of the Lemnian women's slaughter of their male kin invites interpretation as a commentary on the

---

[48] On Harmonia's necklace, see Chinn 2011, with further bibliography, and Stover in this volume.
[49] On the gendered structure of the episode, see Nugent 1996; Keith 2000, 97–98; Augoustakis 2010a, 37–61. On iterative structures in the episode, and the episode's thematic relationship to Polynices' fratricidal war, see O'Gorman 2005.

structure of civil war in the *Thebaid* as a whole.[50] Hypsipyle's account begins with the conventional reference to the central role of the Furies in conflict, and the assurance that the women's rebellion against the hierarchy of gender merits the most severe condemnation: *Furias et Lemnon et artis | arma inserta toris debellatosque pudendo | ense mares; redit ecce nefas et frigida cordi | Eumenis* ("the tale of Lemnos and its Furies and of murder done even in the bed's embrace, and of the shameful sword whereby our manhood perished; ah! the wickedness comes back upon me, the freezing Horror grips my heart!" Stat. *Theb.* 5.30–33). Hypsipyle identifies the instigators of the women's violence as Venus (Stat. *Theb.* 5.58–69, 157–58, 303) and Polyxo (Stat. *Theb.* 5.90–142): Venus provokes the men to prefer war in Thrace to their marriage on Lemnos (Stat. *Theb.* 5.75–89) and, in the absence of the men, Polyxo challenges the Lemnian women to assume the conventionally male prerogatives of militarism and government (Stat. *Theb.* 5.97–103). Similes link Polyxo and the Lemnians to the militant and militaristic women of myth (Maenads, Stat. *Theb.* 5.92–94; Procne, Stat. *Theb.* 5.120–22; Amazons, Stat. *Theb.* 5.144–46). With the convenient return of the Lemnian men, therefore, each woman is prompted by her own Fury (*cuncto sua regnat Erinys | pectore*, Stat. *Theb.* 5.202–3) to embark on a slaughter that pits family member against family member—wife against husband, mother against son, sister against brother, and daughter against father—to overturn the "natural" hierarchy of the sexes (Stat. *Theb.* 5.200–39). The women's violence survives the slaughter of their men and leads them to try to oppose the landing of the Argonauts (Stat. *Theb.* 5.347–60) before Venus cools their battle-lust (Stat. *Theb.* 5.445–46). In the topsy-turvy world of Lemnos, where all order is overwhelmed once the hierarchy of gender has been overturned, Hypsipyle's rescue of her father can only be represented as a crime (Stat. *Theb.* 5.486–92) for which she pays at Nemea with the death of Opheltes (*exsolui tibi, Lemne, nefas*, Stat. *Theb.* 5.628).

Statius delays the war for five books, but when the Argive forces arrive at Thebes, the Fury duly initiates war and accomplishes Oedipus's curse. Tisiphone is at first unable to incite hostilities (Stat. *Theb.* 7.466–69) for Jocasta temporarily succeeds in averting an engagement (Stat. *Theb.* 7.470–534).[51] Her success cannot last, however, as Statius signals in the very comparison that introduces her onto the battlefield, rushing out "like the most ancient of the Furies," with filthy hair, bloody cheeks, and holding in her bruised arms an olive-branch, which should betoken peace but is bound with funereal skeins (*ecce truces oculos sordentibus*

---

50 Cf. Stover in this volume.
51 On Jocasta's role in Statius's *Thebaid*, see Keith 2000, 96; Smolenaars 2008; Augoustakis 2010a, 62–68.

obsita canis | exangues Iocasta genas et bracchia planctu | nigra ferens ramumque oleae cum uelleris atri | nexibus, Eumenidum uelut antiquissima, Stat. *Theb.* 7.474–77; cf. *luctu furiata*, Stat. *Theb.* 7.489). In her speech, Jocasta names herself "impious mother of the war" (*impia belli | mater*, Stat. *Theb.* 7.483–84), a formulation that hardly inspires confidence in her ability to promote a peaceful settlement at this juncture. As she herself recognizes, in fact, her marriage and motherhood align her with the Furies in promoting the conflict (*nupsi equidem peperique nefas*, Stat. *Theb.* 7.514).

At Thebes, the Fury-like Jocasta receives support from an unusually pacific pair of women, her daughters Antigone and Ismene (Stat. *Theb.* 7.534–37; 11.354–82), but as the conflict progresses, Antigone is inexorably drawn into the role of combatant herself when she witnesses the continuing commitment of Eteocles and Polynices to fratricidal enmity even after their deaths, as the flame of their shared pyre is sundered and parts in mutual hostility (Stat. *Theb.* 12.429–46):

> ecce iterum fratres: primos ut contigit artus
> ignis edax, tremuere rogi et nouus aduena busto   430
> pellitur; exundant diuiso uertice flammae
> alternosque apices abrupta luce coruscant.
> pallidus Eumenidum ueluti commiserit ignes
> Orcus, uterque minax globus et conatur uterque
> longius; ipsae etiam commoto pondere paulum   435
> secessere trabes. conclamat territa uirgo:
> 'occidimus, functasque manu stimulauimus iras.
> frater erat: quis enim accessus ferus hospitis umbrae
> pelleret? en clipei fragmen semustaque nosco
> cingula, frater erat! cernisne, ut flamma recedat   440
> concurratque tamen? uiuunt odia improba, uiuunt.
> nil actum bello; miseri, sic, dum arma mouetis
> uicit nempe Creon! nusquam iam regna: quis ardor?
> cui furitis? sedate minas; tuque exsul ubique,
> semper inops aequi, iam cede (hoc nupta precatur,   445
> hoc soror), aut saeuos mediae ueniemus in ignes.'

Look again at the brothers: as soon as the devouring fire touched the body, the pile shook, and the newcomer is driven from the pyre; a flame streams up with double head, each darting tongues of flashing light. As though pale Orcus had set in conflict the torches of the Eumenides, each ball of fire threatens and strives to outreach the other; the very timbers, with all their massive weight, were moved and gave way a space. The maiden cries out in terror: "We are undone; ourselves we have stirred his wrath in death. It was his brother; who else would be so cruel as to spurn the approach of a stranger ghost? Look! I recognize the broken buckler and the charred sword-belt – it was his brother! Do you see how the flame shrinks away and yet rushes to the fight? Alive, yes alive, is that impious hatred. The war was in vain: while thus you strive, wretches, Creon has conquered after all! Gone is your realm, why then such fury? For whom do you rage? Appease your anger. And you, everywhere an exile, ever debarred from justice, yield at last; this is your wife's and your sister's prayer, or else we shall leap into the fierce flame to part you."

In just this way, the fratricides' sister Antigone and Polynices' widow Argia at first oppose one another with mutual suspicion when they meet on the battlefield while searching for Polynices' unburied corpse (Stat. *Theb.* 12.366–72):

> "cuius," ait, "manes, aut quae temeraria quaeris
> nocte mea?" nihil illa diu, sed in ora mariti
> deicit inque suos pariter uelamina uultus,
> capta metu subito paulumque oblita doloris.
> hoc magis increpitans suspecta silentia perstat   370
> Antigone, comitemque premens ipsamque; sed ambo
> deficiunt fixique silent.

"Whose body do you seek in this night that is mine? Who are you, daring woman?" She answered nothing, for a long time, but cast her garments about her husband's face and likewise her own, a prey to sudden fear and forgetful for a while of her sorrow. Antigone, chiding her suspected silence, persists the more, and urges her comrade and herself; but both are lost in utter silence.

Their mutual suspicion is overcome when they discover their shared determination to accomplish the burial of Polynices (Stat. *Theb.* 12.372–91), but their unity does not—indeed, cannot—last in the fratricidal universe of Statius's *Thebaid*. For when they are discovered by Creon's guards, they contest with one another to claim sole responsibility for the crime (Stat. *Theb.* 12.450–63):

> ... ruit ilicet, omnem   450
> prospectum lustrans armata indagine miles.
> illos instantes senior timet unus; at ipsae
> ante rogum saeuique palam spreuisse Creontis
> imperia et furtum claro plangore fatentur
> securae, quippe omne uident fluxisse cadauer.   455
> ambitur saeua de morte animosaque leti
> spes furit: haec fratris rapuisse, haec coniugis artus
> contendunt uicibusque probant: "ego corpus," "ego ignes,"
> "me pietas," "me duxit amor." deposcere saeua
> supplicia et dextras iuuat insertare catenis.   460
> nusquam illa alternis modo quae reuerentia uerbis,
> iram odiumque putes; tantus discordat utrimque
> clamor, et ad regem, qui deprendere trahuntur.

Straightway the watchmen rush forth, and with a ring of arms search the whole countryside. As they draw near, only the old man is afraid; but the women openly before the pyre confess to have spurned fierce Creon's injunctions, and with loud lament they admit their secret deed, careless, for they see that already the whole corpse has been consumed. They are ambitious for cruel destruction, and a spirited hope of death blazes within them; they contend that they stole, the one her husband's, the other her brother's limbs, and prove their case by turns: "I brought the body," "but I the fire," "I was led by affection," "I by love." They delight in demanding cruel punishments and thrusting their arms in the chains. Gone is the reverence that just now was in each one's words; you would think it anger and hatred, so loud on either side rise the cries of discord; they even drag their captors before the king.

As Antigone and Argia succumb to the civil war imperative of dissension between kin, we see the perverse logic of the Roman tradition of fratricidal discord both engulfing and engulfed by the "natural" hierarchy of gender.[52]

The traditional territorial assignments of gender can thus often be discerned, underlying the Flavian poets' civil war narratives, just as the gender system consistently structures the many civil wars they rehearse in their epics. Flavian tastes and appetites for civil war narratives extend to the conjunction of gender and fratricidal conflict, even as the Flavian epicists simultaneously undermine the neat dichotomies they attempt to construct between the opposing sides of each civil war—blurring the divisions between brother and sister, sister and sister-in-law, husband and wife—in the relentless succession of familial and civil conflicts they unleash in their epics. Valerius, Silius, and Statius thus both confirm and critique not only the fatal Roman propensity for civil conflict but also their own aesthetic projects of memorializing their scandalous myths and histories of civil discord.[53]

The Flavian epic poets' aestheticization of civil war, through mythicization and historicization, draws on the twin rhetorical strategies of retrospective and lateral displacement that we traced in the Augustan poets Horace and Vergil, *viz.* historicization and feminization. Such rhetorical strategies may be felt to distance the new Flavian regime from the excesses of the old—the Julio-Claudian propensity for deviant sexuality, kin murder, and civil strife, enthusiastically documented in our historical and biographical sources, which were themselves indebted to the many civil war narratives that proliferated in the Flavian era, after

---

[52] On Antigone and her quasi-sororal relationship with Argia, see Manioti 2012, 83–15; cf. Pollmann 2004, 178 *ad* 12.385–86, on the "remarkable ... omission of names and pronouns that would differentiate the sisters-in-law as they embrace Polynices." On the descent of the sisters-in-law into rivalry, see also Hardie 1993a, 45–46.
[53] Cf. Masters 1992 on Lucan's self-reflexive poetics in the *Bellum Ciuile*.

69 CE, inverting the Julio-Claudian message of *pax et princeps*.[54] In repeatedly rehearsing the tight connection between women and civil war, the Flavian epicists reinforce the Vespasianic family narrative about the disciplined masculinity and old-fashioned Roman morality of the new dynasty. The displacement of responsibility for civil war and kin murder onto a series of "women out of control" reflects a potent enabling fiction of the warmongers, who are thereby absolved of responsibility for the dissolution of familial and community bonds in civil war. Yet the considerable visceral power and aesthetic appeal of the Flavian epics lie in their undifferentiated proliferation of civil strife—to such an extent that both its original audience and all subsequent readers may, in fact, find it difficult to credit the authority of any strongman to check the bloodshed.

---

54 Cf., e.g., the discussion in Ginsberg 2013 of the rhetorical strategies of the pseudo-Senecan *Octavia* in promoting "a new cultural memory of [the Julio-Claudian] dynasty [as] rooted in civil strife" (quotation at 641).

Jean-Michel Hulls
A last act of love? Suicide and civil war as tropes in Silius Italicus's *Punica* and Josephus's *Bellum Judaicum*

After her first major attempt at suicide, Sylvia Plath's first words in hospital to her mother are said to have been, "It was my last act of love." The phrase captures the neat equation between love and death. We glimpse the internally logical yet radically divergent world of the would-be suicide; these words depict an act which is at once egotistical but on its own terms also altruistic.[1] She was unaware of the worry her disappearance caused and the panic that ensued when her mother found an empty bottle of sleeping pills,[2] and the mention of love together with finality instead suggests a rational and compassionate act. We can see that essential quality of paradox that lies behind acts of suicidal self-destruction, the sense that harming oneself is a great benefit.

The nature of suicide in the 1st century CE displays a similar sense of paradox, but the reasons behind it are articulated in rather different terms. The pre-Cartesian sense of self which operates in this period, where individuals are essentially delineated through objective and social constructions,[3] means that suicide is frequently motivated by external and socially-ordered considerations, especially by notions of shame or honor.[4] Modern notions of suicide as an essentially individualistic act predicated upon severe social alienation are often challenged by ancient depictions, especially when these involve the self-destruction of a group. In this chapter we will explore the ethical and literary possibilities afforded by taking the socially-motivated act of self-destruction to the next level—that is, by acts of mass suicide.

Mass suicide is, of course, where a society turns in on itself and destroys or attempts to destroy itself, and we should be more than comfortable by now with the commonplace connection made between civil war and suicide in Roman literature.[5] As individual and society as a whole are both entities which are

---

[1] I deliberately use Durkheim's terms, see Durkheim 1951; Davies/Neal 2000, 36–39; Hill 2004, 5–6.
[2] The disappearance was reported in the *Boston Globe*, 25th August 1953.
[3] On the objective self, see Gill 2006, 341–42.
[4] See Hill 2004, 12–19.
[5] On which, in this volume, see especially the discussion of Hor. *Epod.* 7 in the Introduction (pp. 9–10) and Bessone's chapter (pp. 90–92), who also highlights the way in which paradox informs not only the content, but also the form of Flavian epic poetry.

https://doi.org/10.1515/9783110585841-015

constructed in a similar fashion by objective and social means, then the conceptual leap from individual suicide to civil war depicted as suicide is relatively easy to make; moreover, we should see ancient instances of societal self-destruction in similar ethical terms to individual suicide (which might not be true in modern, post-Cartesian terms).[6]

Suicide as an act of political opposition bleeds back into the discourse of Roman poetry in the Flavian period, most notably in the suicide of Maeon in Statius's *Thebaid*, a classic instance of a Tacitean *ambitiosa mors* (Stat. *Theb.* 3.82–91):[7]

> magnanimus uates, et nunc trucis ora tyranni,
> nunc ferrum aspectans: "numquam tibi sanguinis huius
> ius erit aut magno feries imperdita Tydeo
> pectora; uado equidem exultans ereptaque fata   85
> insequor et comites feror expectatus ad umbras.
> te superis fratrique..." et iam media orsa loquentis
> absciderat plenum capulo latus; ille dolori
> pugnat et ingentem nisu duplicatus in ictum
> corruit, extremisque animae singultibus errans   90
> alternus nunc ore uenit, nunc uulnere sanguis.

> But the great-hearted seer gazing now at the fierce tyrant's visage, now at the steel: "Never shall you hold this blood in your power or strike a breast that great Tydeus left unscathed. I go rejoicing and press upon the doom that was snatched away and am borne to the comrade shades that await my coming. You to the gods and your brother..." and now his side plugged to the hilt cut short his speech midway. He fights the pain and doubles up thrusting against the mighty blow; he falls and with the last sobbing breaths the blood goes this way and that, coming now from the mouth, now from the wound. (transl. Shackleton Bailey)

As blood flows from his mouth instead of words, Maeon articulates his opposition to a tyrannical Eteocles by silencing himself through an act of self-destruction. Suicide's essentially paradoxical nature is made highly visible by its apparent futility. Maeon can no longer see any way in which he can fit into either the heroic, epic landscape as a survivor (*imperdita Tydeo | pectora*, *Theb.* 3.84–85) or within the tyrannical cityscape which Eteocles has constructed (*numquam ... ius erit*, *Theb.* 3.83–84). Yet this fatalistic self-destruction is also paradoxically an act of reintegration into the society of his peers in the underworld (*comites ... ad umbras*, *Theb.* 3.86). In this ancient depiction of suicide, self-killing is the means by

---

[6] We think of all the *ambitiosae mortes* of Tacitus's historical narratives, Seneca's in particular. See Sailor 2008, 11–24; Ker 2009 *passim*, esp. 247–79.
[7] See McGuire 1997, 200–5.

which one maintains one's position in society.⁸ A combined sense of shame (that he has survived the ambush on Tydeus) and honor (that he find a way to oppose Eteocles) demands that he kill himself. His action only makes sense in a world where the self is an objective entity, and indeed his suicide is predicated upon a pretty radically objective notion of self-construction. But Maeon's death is also an act of proto-civil war; he anticipates exactly the kind of societal self-destruction that will consume Thebes throughout the remainder of the poem. We can therefore make the initial observation not simply that both civil war and suicide are important subjects in literary thought at the end of the 1st century CE, but that these two distinct topics become amalgamated and form a bizarre kind of indissoluble whole in literary discourse of the period. Where this amalgamation may be most powerfully visible is where self-destruction literalizes the metaphor of civil war, when whole societies decide that they will kill themselves rather than be shamed or dishonored by defeat, death at the hands of an enemy, or enslavement. In this paper, I examine the applied manifestation of these principles primarily within two narratives, the mass suicide of the Saguntines in Silius Italicus's *Punica* and the mass suicides at Jotapata and Masada in Josephus's *Bellum Judaicum*.

1 Silius Italicus

These principles are most obvious in the opening books of Silius's *Punica* and in the episode which he chooses as a programmatic opening for his poem as a whole,⁹ the siege of Saguntum.¹⁰ As we shall see in a moment, a mass suicide becomes for the Saguntines the honorable escape route from the indignity of conquest by Hannibal and his Carthaginian besiegers, although the ethics of this singular action are made most complicated by the poet. While I would not contend for one second that historicity (at least in the sense in which it is generally

---

8 For the problems of fitting modern models of suicide to ancient evidence, see Hill 2004, 4–11. Durkheim is surprisingly dismissive of such altruistic suicides, seeing them as products of primitive and/or militaristic societies: "it is the same today in those special settings where abnegation and impersonality are essential. Even now, military esprit can only be strong if the individual is self-detached, and such detachment necessarily throws the door open to suicide" (Durkheim 1951, 330–31); see also 175–200. He brushes past mass suicides in two pages (82–83).
9 Dominik 2003, 469. Important bibliography for this episode includes Vessey 1974, 28–36; McGuire 1990, 33–41; McGuire 1997, 207–19; Feeney 1991, 307–8; Hardie 1993a, 81–82; Tipping 2010, 19–20, 70–71.
10 On the Saguntum episode, see also in this volume Bernstein, Dominik (pp. 273–94), Keith (pp. 313–14), and Marks (p. 61).

understood in the 21st century) is a primary concern for Silius, it is nonetheless striking to what extent the mass suicide becomes the defining event of Silius's account of the siege and the opening of the entire war. For Polybius, Saguntum was the flashpoint rather than a genuine *aition*, and indeed he chastises Hannibal for not finding a better excuse to start the war (Plb. 3.15.9):

> καθόλου δ' ἦν πλήρης ἀλογίας καὶ θυμοῦ βιαίου· διὸ καὶ ταῖς μὲν <u>ἀληθιναῖς αἰτίαις</u> οὐκ ἐχρῆτο, κατέφευγε δ' εἰς <u>προφάσεις ἀλόγους</u>· ἅπερ εἰώθασι ποιεῖν οἱ διὰ τὰς προεγκαθημένας αὐτοῖς ὁρμὰς ὀλιγωροῦντες τοῦ καθήκοντος.

> Being wholly under the influence of unreasoning and violent anger, he did not allege <u>the true reasons</u>, but took refuge in <u>groundless pretexts</u>, as men are wont to do who disregard duty because they are prepossessed by passion. (transl. Paton)

Polybius's account of the siege is firmly focused on Hannibal and his motivations and character; the fate of the Saguntines themselves is largely ignored.[11] Furthermore, his brief and bland report of the siege makes no mention of mass suicide among the Saguntines (Plb. 3.17.9–10):[12]

> πᾶσαν δὲ κακοπάθειαν καὶ μέριμναν ὑπομείνας τέλος ἐν ὀκτὼ μησὶ κατὰ κράτος εἷλε τὴν πόλιν. κύριος δὲ γενόμενος χρημάτων πολλῶν καὶ σωμάτων καὶ κατασκευῆς τὰ μὲν χρήματ' εἰς τὰς ἰδίας ἐπιβολὰς παρέθετο κατὰ τὴν ἐξ ἀρχῆς πρόθεσιν, τὰ δὲ σώματα διένειμε κατὰ τὴν ἀξίαν ἑκάστοις τῶν συστρατευομένων, τὴν δὲ κατασκευὴν παραχρῆμα πᾶσαν ἐξέπεμψε τοῖς Καρχηδονίοις.

> At length after eight months of hardship and anxiety he took the city by storm. A great booty of money, slaves, and property fell into his hands. The money, as he had determined, he set aside for his own purposes, the slaves he distributed among his men according to rank, and the miscellaneous property he sent off at once to Carthage. (transl. Paton)

Again, the Saguntines themselves are conspicuous by their absence from Polybius's narrative, and there is certainly nothing as sensational as a mass suicide.

The account given in the *Punica* has a much closer relationship with Livy's account of Saguntum. Here, at least, there are a couple of mentions of suicides in

---

11 Walbank 1957, *ad* 3.17 gives a plausible reason for this focus: "P. clearly follows a pro-Carthaginian source for his account of the siege, probably Silenus." For other accounts of the siege, see D.S. 25.15; App. *Hisp.* 10–12; Zonar. 8.21.

12 The seeds of Silius's account can be found in Polybius 3.15.6–8, with its mention of Romans unjustly killing leading men in a period of civil strife and Carthaginians refusing to overlook a breach of faith, corresponding to the involvement of *Fides* and the mass suicide. For Lucan's Massilia and Vulteius narratives as literary inspiration, see Marks 2010a and, in this volume, Bernstein pp. 182–83, 188–90, 195–96; on Vulteius more generally, see Eldred 2002.

the face of the final Carthaginian assault (although not quite at the level where Saguntum's society can reasonably be said to have destroyed itself). In the first instance, a number of members of the Saguntine Senate fling their precious belongings onto a fire and throw themselves on afterwards (Liv. 21.14.1):

> repente primores secessione facta priusquam responsum daretur argentum aurumque omne ex publico priuatoque in forum conlatum in ignem ad id raptim factum conicientes eodem plerique semet ipsi praecipitauerunt.
>
> Suddenly, however, the leaders of the senate, before an answer could be given, left their places, collected all the precious metal from public buildings and private houses they could find, and flung it into a fire hastily kindled for the purpose in the Forum, and themselves leapt after it into the flames. (transl. De Selincourt)

Then, as the Carthaginians sack the city, some Saguntines fight to the death or prefer to shut themselves in their houses and burn themselves alive rather than be captured. Again, thinking of this episode as mass suicide seems to misrepresent the Saguntines' actions. Yet here, at least, we can see men who would die on their own terms and would rather their families not become slaves (Liv. 21.14.3–4):[13]

> quod imperium crudele, ceterum prope necessarium cognitum ipso euentu est; cui enim parci potuit ex iis qui <u>aut inclusi cum coniugibus ac liberis domos super se ipsos concremauerunt</u> aut armati nullum ante finem pugnae quam morientes fecerunt?
>
> It was a barbarous order, though hardly avoidable, as the event proved; for how was it possible to show mercy to men who in desperation either fought to the death <u>or set fire to their own houses and burned themselves alive together with their wives and children</u>?

Although this may seem like stating the obvious, the siege is, for both historians, a relatively minor moment in a major conflict, and the instances of self-killing are, in Livy, relatively minor details.[14] The centrality of the suicide element in the narrative and the presence of a personified Fides are taken, instead, from the moralist tradition (esp. V. Max. 6.6.ext.1),[15] but Silius maintains a tighter sense of historicity (as well as giving it a powerful programmatic force) by placing the episode at the opening of his Second Punic War narrative.[16] The morality of the

---

13 See Rupprecht 1995, 498.
14 On the relationship with historical authors and the elasticity of time in Silius's Saguntum episode, see Dominik 2003, 471–73.
15 Durkheim 1951, 180, again mentions the Roman historians and moralists in connection with Gallic and Germanic *barbarian* suicides, but avoids the mass suicide of Rome's seemingly less primitive allies.
16 See, in this volume, Bernstein, esp. pp. 179–80, 195–97.

suicide is perhaps also left ambivalent by Livy; is the concern with wealth displayed by the Saguntine *primores* to be condemned, or is it a futile attempt to deny Hannibal the plunder he required following a lengthy siege (cf. Liv. 21.15)? Is the furious final opposition of the besieged prompted by the *imperium crudele* or is it resistance which necessitates a lack of mercy? What is certain is that Silius places the act itself, along with its moral ambiguity, front and center in his own narrative of Saguntum.[17] The descent into mass suicide is a complicated one. After eight months of siege, hunger takes hold in the city, and the quintessential Roman hero-god Hercules, its founder, pities the citizens and sends the personification Fides to instill the Saguntines with new strength to resist (Sil. 2.457–525).[18] The moral ambiguity of the process is already apparent: Fides' possession of the minds of the people is depicted as a kind of mad passion. However, Silius is not done there.

Juno sees Fides and, trumping the act of her step-son, sends Tisiphone to infect the city with another kind of madness (Sil. 2.526–91). Putting on the appearance of a recent widow, Tiburna, Tisiphone gives a speech, recalling or pretending to recall the final words of her dead husband Murrus (Sil. 2.575–79):[19]

> sed uos, o iuuenes, uetuit quos conscia uirtus   575
> posse capi, quis telum ingens contra aspera mors est,
> uestris seruitio manibus subducite matres.
> ardua uirtutem profert uia. pergite primi
> nec facilem populis nec notam inuadere laudem.

> But you, young men, whose conscious valor has denied that you can ever be taken captive, you who have in death a mighty weapon against misfortune, rescue your mothers from slavery with your swords. Steep is the path that makes virtue seen. Hasten to be the first to snatch a glory that few can attain to, a glory unknown till now![20]

Tisiphone then runs to the top of the city and summons a snake from a burial mound built by Hercules (Sil. 2.580–91). Several commentators have explored the comparisons made between Saguntum and Rome, prompted not least by the name Tiburna and in the constant references to Saguntum's Daunian and

---

17 There are clear shifts in emphasis from the Livian version; see Bernstein 2017, xxxiii–xxxvi.
18 For more on Fides in Saguntum and its political implications for the *Punica*, see in this volume Bernstein pp. 183–86.
19 On these personifications, see Dominik 2003, 485–90, and Tipping 2010, 19–20 and n. 25, who rightly asserts (*contra* Kißel 1979, 91) that "pursuit of acclaim through excellence is, or can be, a kind of insanity."
20 Translations of Silius's *Punica* are from Duff 1934.

Rutulian origins.[21] There are obvious Vergilian overtones here, and this passage blends the appearance, in the *Aeneid*, of a snake in Sicily that symbolizes an approving divine spirit, probably that of Anchises (Verg. *A.* 5.84–96), with Allecto's possession of Amata by wrapping a snake around her heart (Verg. *A.* 7.341–56).[22] But while the serpent's appearance in Saguntum certainly has the equivalent impact of Allecto's assault upon Amata, here it impacts the entire population (*tum uero excussae mentes*, "then indeed men's reason tottered," Sil. 2.592). Furthermore, Livy is clearly evoked as the Saguntines build a pyre onto which they throw their most valuable possessions (Sil. 2.600, 605–8):

> in media stetit urbe rogus. ...   600
> ...
> huc, quicquid superest captis, clipeosque simulque   605
> infaustos iaciunt enses et condita bello
> effodiunt penitus terrae gaudentque superbi
> uictoris praedam flammis donare supremis.

> A pyre was erected in the centre of the city. ... They throw on the pile all that the conquered still possess, and their shields too and swords that could not save; and they dig up from the bowels of the earth hoards buried in time of war, and with joy and pride consign the conqueror's booty to the all-devouring flames.

Silius takes the notion of a civil conflict implied by the fighting, in the second half of the *Aeneid*, between Trojan proto-Romans and Rutulian Italians and makes this an explicit fact of the Saguntine mass suicide. Yet this is a peculiar moment in that the Saguntines do the work of the Carthaginians for them; the narrative shows the citizens killing each other but very rarely killing themselves. Silius goes out of his way to reduce this heroic, honorable, community self-killing to a civil conflict in miniature.

Being Flavian epic, the lack of restraint shown by the protagonists is echoed by the text itself (Sil. 2.614–28; 2.632–35):

> princeps Tisiphone <u>lentum</u> indignata <u>parentem</u>
> pressit ouans capulum cunctantemque impulit ensem   615
> et dirum insonuit Stygio bis terque flagello.

---

[21] For a detailed analysis of the connections between Saguntum and Rome, see Dominik 2003, 474–80. On Hercules as a model of *Romanitas* in the Saguntum episode, see Asso 2010b, esp. 180–89. On the ethnic identity of Saguntum, see Bernstein 2010, 390–95. For more on the divine forces at work here and especially on poetic interconnections with *Thebaid* 11, see in this volume Bernstein pp. 186–95.

[22] For further details of Silius's allusive complexity, see Bernstein 2017, *ad loc.*

inuitas maculant <u>cognato sanguine</u> dextras
miranturque nefas auersa mente peractum
et facto sceleri inlacrimant. hic turbidus ira
et rabie cladum perpessaeque ultima uitae   620
obliquos uersat materna per ubera uisus.
hic raptam librans <u>dilectae in colla</u> securim
<u>coniugis</u> increpitat sese mediumque furorem
proiecta damnat stupefactus membra bipenni.
nec tamen euasisse datur; nam uerbera Erinys   625
incutit atque atros insibilat ore tumores.
sic thalami fugit omnis amor, dulcesque marito
<u>effluxere tori</u>, et subiere obliuia taedae.

First Tisiphone, resenting a <u>father's half-hearted stroke</u>, pushed the hilt forward in triumph and drove in the reluctant sword, and cracked her hellish scourge again and again with hideous noise. Against their will men stain their hands <u>with kindred blood</u>; they marvel at the crime they have committed with loathing, and weep over the wickedness they have wrought. One man, distraught with rage and the madness of disaster and extreme suffering, <u>turns a sidelong glance at the breast of his mother</u>. Another, snatching an axe and <u>aiming it at the neck of his loved wife</u>, reproaches himself and curses his unfinished crime, and, as if paralysed, throws his weapon down. Yet he is not suffered to escape; for the Fury repeats her blows, and breathes black passion into him with her hissing mouth. Thus <u>there is an end of all wedded love: the husband has forgotten the joys of his marriage-bed</u>, and remembers his bride no more.

at medios inter coetus pietate sinistra,
infelix Tymbrene, furis, Poenoque <u>parentis</u>
dum properas <u>auferre necem</u>, reddentia formam
ora tuam laceras temerasque simillima membra.   635

Again, in the midst of the crowd, ill-starred Tymbrenus, distraught with love assuming strange disguise, and <u>eager to rob the Carthaginian of his father's death</u>, mutilates the features that resemble his own, and desecrates a body that is the image of himself.

Fathers kill children, sons kill mothers and fathers, husbands wives; here we see the *cognatas acies* and *fraternas acies* of Silius's predecessors writ large. There is an important double step which is taken by Silius here. Firstly we see that a war between a Roman ally and a foreign enemy is condensed into a single instance of communal self-destruction. Secondly we can see that this suicide is itself depicted as a civil and especially an intra-familial conflict: the war with Carthage is transformed into the worst kind of civil conflict.[23] There is a complex play on

---

23 This is further underlined by the intertextual connections between this episode and the conflict between Eteocles and Polynices in Statius's *Thebaid*. See Bernstein in this volume, pp. 186–95.

gender in all this:[24] although the protagonists are all female figures (Fides, Tisiphone, Tiburna), the act of killing family members appears an almost exclusively male activity.[25] The female members of the community only participate to kill themselves and not others[26] and often look masculine in so doing.[27] The identification of Saguntum with Rome in Silius's text means that this foreign war/suicide/civil war axis has huge implications for the Roman imperial audience of his poem.[28]

But for now I want to explore the blurring of suicide and civil war. There is a reflexivity in Tymbrenus's parricide; his looking at his father is like looking into a mirror at himself and so his killing of his father becomes a species of self-murder by the similarity of their features (note the rhyming, interwoven order *reddentia formam | ora tuam*, Sil. 2.634–35), but the futility of this act is suggested by the word-play in the juxtaposition of *furis Poeno* (Sil. 2.633), as the apostrophe *pietate sinistra … furis* ("you rage with perverted piety," Sil. 2.632–33) and the inverted syntax of *Poenoque parentis | dum properas auferre necem* ("while you rush to take your parent's death from the Carthaginian," Sil. 2.633–34) place two words side by side which suggest possession by Tisiphone.[29] The actions of besieger and besieged, of human and Fury, of suicide and civil war become an amorphous whole. The trope of homogeneity is underlined in the vignette which follows. One twin brother kills another, preventing the latter from killing their mother, and she in turn confuses her sons in death (Sil. 2.636–49):

> uos etiam primo gemini cecidistis in aeuo,
> Eurymedon fratrem et fratrem mentite Lycorma,
> cuncta pares; dulcisque labor sua nomina natis
> reddere et in uultu genetrici stare suorum.
> iam fixus iugulo culpa te soluerat ensis,   640
> Eurymedon, inter miserae lamenta senectae,
> dumque malis turbata parens deceptaque uisis
> "quo ruis? huc ferrum" clamat "conuerte, Lycorma,"
> ecce simul iugulum perfoderat ense Lycormas.
> sed magno "quinam, Eurymedon, furor iste?" sonabat   645
> cum planctu geminaeque notis decepta figurae

---

24 For a broader discussion of the intersection of gender and civil war in the Flavian epics, especially the *Thebaid* and *Argonautica*, see Keith in this volume.
25 *hic … hic … marito … ille … Tymbrene … Eurymedon … Lycorma*, "this man … this man … the husband … that man … Tymbrenus … Eurymedon … Lycormas" (Sil. 2.619, 622, 627, 629, 633, 637).
26 See, e.g., the mother of Eurymedon and Lycormas (Sil. 2.648–49).
27 See below on Tiburna's appearance at Sil. 2.665–80.
28 On the (im)morality of Rome's abandonment of Saguntum, see Dominik 2003, 490–97.
29 The Furies are even described as *Poenae* at Sil. 2.551.

> funera mutato reuocabat nomine mater,
> donec transacto tremebunda per ubera ferro
> tunc etiam ambiguos cecidit super inscia natos.

> Twin brethren also, alike in every point, Eurymedon and Lycormas, each an exact likeness of the other, were slain there in their prime. To their mother it had been a sweet perplexity to name her sons aright, and to be uncertain of her own children's features. The sword that pierced the throat of Eurymedon, while the poor old mother lamented, had already cleared him of guilt; and while she, distraught with sorrow and mistaking whom she saw, cried out, "What mean you, madman? Turn your sword against me, Lycormas," lo! Lycormas had already stabbed himself in the throat. But she cried aloud: "Eurymedon, what madness is this?"—and the mother, misled by the likeness of the twins, called back her dead sons by wrong names; at last, driving the steel through her own quivering breast, she sank down over the sons whom even then she could not distinguish.

One brother and the mother do commit suicide here (*culpa te soluerat* acknowledges the difference between this and what has preceded it), but it is the overwhelming sense of confusion and blurring of identities that is important here.[30] The mirroring, chiastic word order in line 637, the ambiguous word *mentite* (Sil. 2.637), and the mother's confusion of names (Sil. 2.647) all point to a greater sense of confusion in the mass suicide.[31]

The mirroring in Silius's language is picked up in the mother's apostrophe to these twin brothers which apes the opening lines of both Horace *Epode* 7 and Lucan's *Bellum Ciuile*.[32] For the mother, *furor* is *not* turning a sword against one's own family. Here Horace's late Republican sentiment is transformed, and the imperative *conuerte* (Sil. 2.643) gives not only the instruction to her son but also the notion that Horace's horror at civil war has been transformed as well. Truly these are *ambigui nati* (Sil. 2.649). Mass suicide as conceived here becomes something impossible to fit into familiar theoretical models; instead we see an event which

---

30 The name Lycormas is that of a river into which a son of Hercules named Evenus fell; see Ps.-Plu. *Fluv.* 8. Is this a very subtle play on self-destruction in a city of Herculean foundation? Eurymedon is a common enough name in mythology, but also the name of a river in Asia Minor. There is a flow to the (il)logic of all this: we might even read the verb *stare* (Sil. 2.639), here meaning "to be indecisive," as a pun on the Greek idea of *stasis*, civil strife (e.g., Th. 3.82).
31 Note the way in which language which suggests confusion and deception is used throughout: *mentite ... decepta ... decepta ... mutate ... transacta ... ambiguos* (Sil. 2.636–49).
32 For more on the *quis furor* trope, see Introduction and Bessone in this volume pp. 90–95.

can only comfortably be explained by Silius with the (both epic and historical) apparatus of civil war narratives.[33]

This idea of the city boldly resisting a foreign invader becoming a mad desire for self-destruction, which becomes in turn a kind of civil war, is echoed in the final episode of the Saguntine story. Tiburna appears again, is compared to a Fury, and commits a spectacular suicide (Sil. 2.665, 671–80):

> ecce inter medios caedum Tiburna furores   665
>
> ...
>
> qualis, ubi inferni dirum tonat aula parentis,
> iraque turbatos exercet regia manes,
> Alecto solium ante dei sedemque tremendam
> Tartareo est operata Ioui poenasque ministrat.
> arma uiri multo nuper defensa cruore   675
> imponit tumulo inlacrimans, manesque precata
> acciperent sese, flagrantem lampada subdit.
> tunc rapiens letum "tibi ego haec" ait "optime coniunx,
> ad manes, en, ipsa fero." sic ense recepto
> arma super ruit et flammas inuadit hiatu.   680

> Lo! In the midst of madness and murder, unhappy Tiburna was seen. ... Such seems Alecto, when the palace of the Infernal Father thunders doom, and the monarch's wrath troubles and vexes the dead; then the Fury, standing before the throne and terrible seat of the god, does service to the Jupiter of Tartarus and deals out punishments. Her husband's armour, lately rescued with much bloodshed, she placed on the mound with tears; then she prayed to the dead to welcome her, and applied her burning torch to the pile. Then, rushing upon death, "Best of husbands," she cried, "see, I myself carry this weapon to you in the shades." And so she stabbed herself and fell down over the armour, meeting the fire with open mouth.

The games that Silius is playing with his audience should be familiar by now. Identity is again at stake; the real-life Tiburna was clearly a good choice for Tisiphone to imitate, and she herself now resembles no one so much as Allecto. Silius juxtaposes *Tiburna* with both *caedum* and *furores* (Sil. 2.665), placing her right in the midst of slaughter and madness; the four-line simile which immediately follows, comparing her to Allecto (Sil. 2.671–74), is undeniably overkill but proves the point with absolute thoroughness. Tiburna also resembles Dido in her moment of suicide in *Aeneid* 4, both stabbing herself with her husband's sword and leaping onto a pyre. The poet cannot resist a further, unsubtle juxtaposition,

---

[33] So Durkheim's essentially sociological notion of suicide as an individual act in relation to society is exploded as an entire society dissolves itself. Ironically, he mentions Sil. 1.225–29 for the tendency to suicide of Saguntum's Spanish Celtic opponents (Durkheim 1951, 176).

arma uiri (Sil. 2.675; cf. Verg. *A.* 4.495), just in case we miss the allusion to Vergil's Carthaginian heroine.[34] Throughout the scene, Tiburna, who wields her husband's sword and wears his armor, has a disconcertingly male aspect; the blurring of identities sewn together with the sword is underlined by the elisions in *tibi ego haec* (Sil. 2.678). All the literary and intellectual baggage that comes with the Furies and with a furious suicidal Dido underlines the point that there is more to this episode of historical epic than heroic suicide. Silius's constant play with and subversion of Vergilian imagery underpins the self-destructive theme of the episode. The language of civil war, self-annihilation, and mass suicide infects the opening episode of this narrative of Rome's finest hour. Only when the civil war in miniature is complete are the real enemy, the Carthaginians, allowed to participate once more (*irrumpunt uacuam Poeni tot cladibus arcem*, "the Carthaginians rushed into the citadel which so many disasters had left undefended," Sil. 2.692).

2 Josephus

Similar themes and considerations are visible, I contend, in a very different text of the same period. Josephus's *Bellum Judaicum* famously deals with two very similar episodes of mass suicide, at Jotapata and Masada, in ways which betray some striking similarities to the Saguntum episode in the *Punica*.[35] Josephus was a commander in the Jewish revolt against Rome in 67 CE when he was caught in the siege at Jotapata by Vespasian (*BJ* 3.340–91). After the town fell, Josephus hid in a pit which connected to a cave with about forty other fighters. Eventually, the Romans found his hiding-place and promised Josephus safe conduct, and the Jewish fighters debated what to do. Josephus himself tells us that he received a message from God instructing him to survive and tell his people's story and that, when the other men decided to kill themselves rather than be enslaved, Josephus tried to persuade them against this in a long, philosophizing speech. This merely angered the others, who attempted to kill him. Eventually Josephus pacified them and organized an elaborate suicide pact from which only he and one other man survived.

---

34 On the *arma uirumque* theme in Silius, see Landrey 2014, esp. 630. Here the repetition encourages the female participants not to be successors of Aeneas but of Dido. Much as Silius exploits the ironies of Carthaginians aping Aeneas, so here we have their opponents imitating their founding queen.

35 On the events at Jotapata, see also Mason in this volume (pp. 205–6).

In his long speech against suicide, Josephus includes the notion that suicide is an offense against God and is regarded by others as a kind of war against the self (J. *BJ* 3.375–79). Yet Josephus's speech proves ineffective, and the other Jews, now utterly set on suicide, try to kill him. Their disagreement centers on the nature and efficacy of suicide as a mode of resistance: most of Josephus's men consider suicide an essentially fatalistic act, while Josephus construes self-killing in the nihilistic terms familiar from Silius's Saguntine narrative. Josephus's story seems almost bizarre at this point; having been unpersuasive to the point that his comrades wish to kill him, he is now able to defend himself by force of personality and rhetoric alone (ὁ δὲ τὸν μὲν ὀνομαστὶ καλῶν, τῷ δὲ στρατηγικώτερον ἐμβλέπων, τοῦ δὲ δρασσόμενος τῆς δεξιᾶς, J. *BJ* 3.385). It is almost as if we can see evidence of his divine protection projected through the power of his personality, especially as the blades of the other men are miraculously turned aside, their arms suddenly grow weak, and they spontaneously drop their swords, so awed are they by the authority of their commander (J. *BJ* 3.385–86):

> ὁ δὲ τὸν μὲν ὀνομαστὶ καλῶν τῷ δὲ στρατηγικώτερον ἐμβλέπων, τοῦ δὲ δρασσόμενος τῆς δεξιᾶς, ὃν δὲ δεήσει δυσωπῶν, καὶ ποικίλοις διαιρούμενος πάθεσιν ἐπὶ τῆς ἀνάγκης εἶργεν ἀπὸ τῆς σφαγῆς πάντων τὸν σίδηρον, ὥσπερ τὰ κυκλωθέντα τῶν θηρίων ἀεὶ πρὸς τὸν καθαπτόμενον ἀντιστρεφόμενος. τῶν δὲ καὶ παρὰ τὰς ἐσχάτας <u>συμφορὰς ἔτι τὸν στρατηγὸν αἰδουμένων</u> παρελύοντο μὲν αἱ δεξιαί, περιωλίσθανεν δὲ τὰ ξίφη, καὶ πολλοὶ τὰς ῥομφαίας ἐπιφέροντες αὐτομάτως παρεῖσαν.

> But he, addressing one by name, fixing his general's eye of command upon another, clasping the hand of a third, shaming a fourth by entreaty, and torn by all manner of emotions at this critical moment, succeeded in warding off from his throat the blades of all, turning like a wild beast surrounded by the hunters to face his successive assailants. <u>Even in his extremity, they still held their general in reverence</u>; their hands were powerless, their swords glanced aside, and many, in the act of thrusting at him, spontaneously dropped their weapons.[36]

Finally compelled to engage in the suicide pact, Josephus manages to survive. Whether this is, as he claims in the Greek version, by virtue of fortune or by the will of God or, as the hostile Slavonic version suggests, because he deliberately engineered the counting of lots so that he would be one of the last two alive, does not matter very much here.[37] What is more interesting from our point of view is that Josephus's account of the suicide at Jotapata contains many of the same

---

[36] Translations of Josephus's *Bellum Judaicum* are from Thackeray 1927.
[37] On this Slavonic version, see Williamson 1959, 470–71; Leeming et al. 2003. For the "Josephus count," see Rajak 1983, 171.

elements of Silius's account at Saguntum. Both narratives exploit a tension between the historical and the fictional (to what extent in Josephus's case is harder to say).[38] Both have an element of divine inspiration: Silius has Fides and Tisiphone driving the emotional responses of the Saguntines, while there is a divine force protecting Josephus from his dangerously unbalanced comrades. Finally, both narratives make explicit connections between mass suicide and civil war. Both the Saguntines and the Jewish rebels are fighting themselves as much as their enemies; Josephus himself says that he has survived both a war with the Romans and one with his own people: ὁ μὲν οὖν οὕτως τόν τε Ῥωμαίων καὶ τὸν οἰκείων διαφυγὼν πόλεμον ἐπὶ Οὐεσπασιανὸν ἤγετο ὑπὸ [τοῦ] Νικάνορος ("having thus survived both the war with the Romans and that with his own friends, Josephus was brought by Nicanor into Vespasian's presence," J. BJ 3.392).

The civil war theme is a salient feature of the final phase of the siege of Jerusalem, especially in Simon's torture and execution of Matthias "as though he were any other enemy" (J. BJ 5.529) and in the behavior of robbers in their treatment of both the dead and the living in the besieged city. In the run-up to his account of the fall of Masada, Josephus laments not the destruction of his world by the Romans, but the appalling and irreligious behavior of the various resistance groups and leaders during the revolt (J. BJ 7.259–75), not least the Sicarii holding Masada.[39]

Similar concerns and narrative structures are present in the Masada episode. At the point when Romans have destroyed the defenses and have retired for the night, the Jewish leader Eleazar makes a short speech advocating mass suicide.[40] The community remains unpersuaded and Eleazar makes a second, improbably long speech (J. BJ 7.341–88), which is so persuasive that he never quite finishes it.[41] The community rapidly destroys itself following a system rather similar to that which Josephus narrated after the siege at Jotapata (J. BJ 7.389–401). The radical difference between the two narratives is that, while one might articulate the mass suicide pact at Jotapata as the altruistic activity of a small group within

---

38 See Rajak 1983, 167–72, on the narrative of events at Jotapata and 219–22 on the *inuentio* of Josephus's Masada narrative; on the archaeological evidence for Masada, see Atkinson 2007, 349–58.
39 Josephus also attacks John of Gischala, the Zealots, and Simon bar Giora in particular. Cf. Rajak 1983, 81–88.
40 Eleazar also asks his people to destroy all their possessions apart from their vast supply of food, so that the Romans will see that they have committed suicide of their own free will, rather than by being to desperation by hunger. The reverse is true at Silius's Saguntum, where the people are weakened by their hunger before divine forces set to work.
41 Cf. Mason 2005a, 271, on irony in this speech and its relationship with Josephus's speech (J. BJ 3.361–82).

a much larger and resistant Jewish community, here we see, as we did at Saguntum, an entire society obliterating itself. The divine element of this kind of narrative is also clearly visible at Masada, as it was at Saguntum and Jotapata: when the Roman siege engines battering the walls are set on fire, a sudden shift in the wind direction causes the flames to undermine the walls further, and the Romans retire for the evening safe in the knowledge that they will be able to enter the fortress at dawn; and both Josephus and Eleazar (J. BJ 7.318–36) acknowledge the divine power at work supporting the Romans in this.[42]

The play on gender which we saw in Silius's Saguntum is also at work here; survival is explicitly portrayed as effeminate or even feminine. When his first speech proves unpersuasive to some of the "softer" men (τοὺς δ' αὐτῶν μαλακωτέρους, J. BJ 7.338), Eleazar is worried that the people have been "unmanned" (συνεκθηλύνωσι, J. BJ 7.339); his initial speech is addressed to the "most manly" (ἀνδρωδεστάτους, J. BJ 7.322)[43] of his men in the fortress, and he accuses any unwilling of killing themselves of being "unmanly" (ἄνανδρος, J. BJ 7.378); the seven survivors are led by a woman whom Josephus describes as greater in wisdom and education than other women (φρονήσει καὶ παιδείᾳ πλείστων γυναικῶν, J. BJ 7.399); and the men compete to be the first to commit suicide, thinking that it will be proof of *andreia* (bravery, J. BJ 7.389) not to be last.

Such an observation makes an interesting counter-point to Josephus's own desire to survive at Jotapata, but we might suggest that his rhetorical tricks and forceful personality *in extremis* also link him to the mass suicide at Saguntum in Silius's poem. Both the Saguntines and Josephus are compared to wild animals driven by extreme circumstances (J. BJ 3.385; Sil. 2.683–88):

… ὥσπερ τὰ κυκλωθέντα τῶν θηρίων ἀεὶ πρὸς τὸν καθαπτόμενον ἀντιστρεφόμενος.

… turning like a wild beast surrounded by the hunters to face his successive assailants.

ceu, stimulante fame, cum uictor ouilia tandem
faucibus inuasit sicci leo, mandit hianti
ore fremens imbelle pecus, patuloque redundat   685

---

[42] Josephus: Ῥωμαῖοι μὲν οὖν τῇ παρὰ τοῦ θεοῦ συμμαχίᾳ κεχρημένοι χαίροντες εἰς τὸ στρατόπεδον ἀπηλλάττοντο ("the Romans, thus blessed by God's aid, returned rejoicing to their camp," J. BJ 7.319); Eleazar: ἀλλὰ καὶ τροφῆς ἀφθονίαν καὶ πλῆθος ὅπλων καὶ τὴν ἄλλην ἔχοντες παρασκευὴν περιττεύουσαν ὑπ' αὐτοῦ περιφανῶς τοῦ θεοῦ τὴν ἐλπίδα τῆς σωτηρίας ἀφῃρήμεθα ("nay, though ample provisions are ours, piles of arms, and a superabundance of every other requisite, yet we have been deprived, manifestly by God Himself, of all hope of deliverance," J. BJ 7.331). See Brighton 2009, 107.
[43] A *hapax legomenon* in Josephus, see Brighton 2009, 110.

> gutture ructatus large cruor; incubat atris
> semesae stragis cumulis, aut murmure anhelo
> infrendens, laceros inter spatiatur aceruos.

> Even so, when a lion, driven by hunger, has at last prevailed and stormed the sheepfold with parched gorge, he roars with gaping jaws and devours the helpless sheep, and streams of blood are vomited forth from his vast gape; he couches down on dark heaps of victims half-devoured, or, gnashing his teeth with panting and roaring, stalks between the piles of mangled carcasses.

Unlike the exhausted, monstrous lion which represents the (now dead!) Saguntines, Josephus uses his wild, natural instincts in a rather different manner: while he is, like the Saguntines, overcome by passion at the key moment in Book 3 (ποικίλοις διαιρούμενος πάθεσιν, "distracted by conflicting emotions," J. *BJ* 3.385), he transcends the gap between animal and divine by channeling his emotion towards an overwhelming desire for continued existence. By contrast, the desire which grips the Sicarii at Masada is very much depicted as something external and outside their control (as were the compelling actions of Fides and Tisiphone at Saguntum). The men are filled with an unstoppable, hasty desire (ἀνεπισχέτου τινὸς ὁρμῆς πεπληρωμένοι, J. *BJ* 7.389), they compete at mass suicide like men possessed (δαιμονῶντες, J. *BJ* 7.389), and a love of slaughter takes hold of them (σφαγῆς ἔρως ἐνέπεσεν, J. *BJ* 7.389; contrast: εἶργεν ἀπὸ τῆς σφαγῆς πάντων τὸν σίδηρον "he succeeded in warding off from his throat the blades of all," J. *BJ* 3.385), which is naturally maintained as the men begin to kill their loved ones (J. *BJ* 7.390). The act is completed "as if by the hands of others" (ὁμοῦ δὲ καθάπερ ἀλλοτρίαις χερσὶν ὑπουργούμενοι, J. *BJ* 7.392). Although the sense in which this mass suicide is a species of civil conflict is perhaps less explicit than the self-destruction at Saguntum, the final disaster at Masada is emphatically not a victory for the Romans but, paradoxically, one for the Jewish resistance.[44]

3 Conclusion

My own juxtaposition of Silius and Josephus is not designed to make any ethical point; the understanding of suicide and particularly mass suicide is a morally complex issue in any period of history and for the Classical world in particular. Josephus's accounts of Jewish suicides (and his own, narrowly-avoided death) may well mark a middle ground between the objectively determined and morally motivated suicides of political and philosophical elites in 1st century CE Rome

---

[44] Eleazar himself makes this point in his speech, *BJ* 7.360. Cf. Mason 2005a, 256.

and the internalized, subjective, Cartesian self on which Durkheim's theories of suicide are based. What is arresting about these two narratives is the way in which suicide dominates the telling: suicide becomes, in fact, the process by which the story is told. Silius gives a highly but thoughtfully fictionalized account of the outbreak of the second Punic war and the fall of Saguntum in which suicide becomes the dominant literary trope of the story; Josephus gives accounts of two historical mass suicides which become highly stylized in their narration. I do not make any claim that these texts are interacting directly with one another, although I would not preclude the possibility that Silius read Josephus or that there exists a more complex literary relationship.[45] However, to advocate too strongly for such a linear interpretation seems to limit the importance of the trope which connects war, civil war and mass suicide. Rather we should say that these texts are products of a socially and ethnically broad Flavian literary culture obsessed with self-killing as a means of accounting for human behavior. They share similar peculiar features: the divine motivation, the strong and paradoxical connection between suicide and civil conflict, the gendering of survival as feminine. Both men had direct experience of the realities of Flavian wars condensing into societal self-destruction, Josephus in Judaea, Silius in Rome at the destruction of the Capitoline by the Vitellians (Tac. *Hist.* 3.65).[46] Better than a narrow, intertextual reading, we might see these mass suicides as symptomatic of the Flavian literary condition, a condition which takes us beyond the caustic, violent *exempla* of the Augustans and Neronians.

In conclusion, therefore, I would like to show one final example of suicide contaminating a narrative. Suetonius's very brief biography of the elder Pliny is unremarkable but for one feature, an alternative account of his death in the eruption of Vesuvius, an assisted suicide at the hands of a slave (Suet. *Vita Plin.*):

> nec aduersantibus uentis remeare posset, ui pulueris ac fauillae oppressus est, uel ut quidam existimant a seruo suo occisus, quem aestu deficiens ut necem sibi maturaret orauerat.

> But being prevented by contrary winds from sailing back, he was suffocated in the dense cloud of dust and ashes. Some, however, think that he was killed by his slave, having implored him to put an end to his sufferings, when he was reduced to the last extremity by the fervent heat. (transl. Rolfe)

---

45 There are, however, many elements of the Masada narrative which are provocatively echoed in Silius's later epic. Rupprecht 1995, 499–500, argues for a direct imitation of Josephus by Silius, so similar are the accounts of Saguntum and Masada.
46 Bernstein 2017, xxxvi makes the connection between the criticism of *fides* in *Punica* 2 and the repeated violations of *fides* in Tacitus's *Histories*. On the looming presence of the Capitoline's invasion and fiery destruction in the Flavian literary imagination, see Landrey in this volume.

It is a surprising alternative account, given the closeness of Suetonius to the younger Pliny, who of course gives us the dominant narrative in *Ep.* 6.16. Suetonius may be reflecting the elder Pliny's own suggestion that suicide is God's greatest gift to mankind (*ne deum quidem posse omnia—namque nec sibi potest mortem consciscere, si uelit, quod homini dedit optimum in tantis uitae poenis*, "not even for God are all things possible—for he cannot, even if he wishes, commit suicide, the supreme boon that he has bestowed on man among all the penalties of life," Plin. *Nat.* 2.27, transl. Rackham), but I would rather read this peculiarity as a further reflection of the way in which suicide comes to dominate the narratives of this period.[47]

Suetonius's alternative rendering of Pliny's death shares with Plath's suicide the sense that self-destruction is of benefit. In Pliny's case, this seems pretty indisputable; he would have died anyway, and the slave's action is merciful. Yet writers in the 1st century can take this sense of suicide as altruistic even further. Maeon's suicide in the *Thebaid* neatly carries with it the sense of paradox so visible in Plath's equation of love and death, yet Maeon's end differs in that he is not removing himself from society or seeing himself as separate from it, as Durkheim's essential model (and the many 20th and 21st-century models which have built upon his foundational sociological work) requires us to believe. Rather, Maeon removes himself from the damaged world of the tyrannical Eteocles and places himself in an alternative martial and heroic society. Maeon's altruism comes more from the exemplary value his suicide provides.

The difficulties with understanding suicide through the relationship of individual and society become much starker when one looks at mass suicide, especially those where entire communities destroy themselves, as at Saguntum and Masada. The strongly individualistic approach to self-killing simply does not fit well with ancient conceptions of selfhood. In a Roman world where all narratives of conquest become narratives of self-destruction, Flavian writers depict wars against foreign enemies as self-destruction through this trope of suicide. For the mass suicides of Silius and Josephus, self-killing is the ultimate act of altruism, a last act of love which transcends their status as bit-part players in a bigger, Roman story. For the authors themselves, the narration of a society nobly destroying itself allows for exploration of the dark underbelly of the Roman empire at its height.

---

47 As a rather more frivolous group of suicides, the Judaean People's Front, say at the end of Monty Python's *Life of Brian*: "That showed them, huh?"

Part V: **Ruination, Restoration, and Empire**

Eleni Hall Manolaraki
Domesticating Egypt in Pliny's *Natural History*

It is a truism that the events culminating in Octavian's triple triumph inscribed Egypt in Roman thought as a *topos* of both *bellum externum* and *bellum ciuile*.[1] A century later, however, Vespasian's Alexandrian *dies imperii* imbued the land of the Nile with new political and moral agency: Cleopatra's kingdom became Vespasian's stronghold, bolstered by Egypt's legions and gods.[2] Throughout the seventies, Vespasian continued to claim kinship with Egypt to style himself as the heir of the Julio-Claudians and their predecessors, the Ptolemies and Alexander. The currency of Egypt as a material and ideological resource for the new dynasty is suggested by the proliferation of Ptolemaic aesthetics in Rome during this period.[3]

Given the circumstances of Vespasian's succession, however, his "new" Egypt unsurprisingly remained a specter of war. During the war with Vitellius, Vespasian had withheld grain in Alexandria, threatening Rome with its inveterate dependence on the Nile. Moreover, his stay in Alexandria from November 69 to September 70 CE exemplified (at least for the culturally literate) the Roman rulers' flirtation with Egyptian absolutism.[4] In sum, the oppositional dynamic between the Vespasianic reinvention of Egypt as a font of imperial legitimacy and its traditionalist casting as Rome's antagonist contested its meaning in post-civil war Rome. Considering the centrality of Egypt in the construction of Roman identity, "the gift of the Nile" could not be ignored in the cultural marketplace of the capital. Since, however, its othering was no longer an apt foundation myth, what would succeed the Augustan paradigm of *Aegypto Capta*?

Many thanks to Darcy Krasne and Lauren Donovan Ginsberg for their invitation to the 2014 conference and to my fellow participants for their feedback on the early version. The text of Pliny is from Jan and Mayhoff's 1875 Teubner edition; translations of the *Natural History* are adapted from Rackham *et al.* 1938. All other translations are mine.

1 On the contested definition of civil (as opposed to foreign) war, see Osgood 2015, 1683–84; Armitage 2017a, 3–27; and the introduction and König's chapter in this volume (esp. pp. 7–8, 148–50).
2 On the so-called *lex de imperio Vespasiani* and the constitutional shift of Vespasian's dating of his reign from his Alexandrian acclamation, see Levick 2009; Venturini 2009; Nicols 2016, 61–62. On his stay in Alexandria and the lore of prophecies and miracles endorsing his rise, see Luke 2010; Capriotti Vittozzi 2014, 240–43.
3 Flavian appropriations of Egypt: Takács 2011; Davies 2011, 367; Pfeiffer 2010b; Bommas 2012; Capriotti Vittozzi 2014; Bülow Clausen 2014.
4 Roman rulers' fascination with Egypt: Luke 2010, 82–83. Vespasian's emulation of Augustus: Levick 1999, 70–71, 79–80, 206–8. See also Rosso 2009.

https://doi.org/10.1515/9783110585841-016

1 Pliny's Flavian Egypt

As a political quantity during the imperial transition, the Elder Pliny offers promising clues to this question.[5] His *Natural History* details Egyptian geography, history, institutions, fauna and flora, and marvelous miscellanea, in segments ranging from brief mentions to multiple chapters.[6] His centerpiece is a lengthy and critical review of Pharaonic monuments (*Nat.* 36.64–89), which has been a valuable source for Egyptologists, archaeologists, historians, art historians, and classicists.[7] Yet because of the attention it has received, Pliny's censure of Egyptian monumentality has reduced his "Egypt" to a foil of barbarian otherness upended by Rome. For instance, his claims that the pyramids are emblems of monarchical arrogance (*Nat.* 36.75), and that the transport of obelisks to Rome is a more impressive feat than the obelisks themselves (*Nat.* 36.68, 36.72), are routinely cited as examples of his narrative imperialism.[8] Yet since these landmarks are not Pliny's only indexes of Egyptian ethnography, they cannot be relied upon exclusively as carriers of its function. Dozens of minor Egyptian articles and details about their acquirement, processing, and usage are also nested in his thirty-seven books. Because these modest items and technologies are typically discussed in the context of Rome's administration of Egypt, it is unclear how they nuance the colossal and historic Egypt concentrated in the penultimate book.[9]

This essay argues that Pliny's quotidian *Aegyptiaca* are driven by a narrative impulse to establish correspondences between Egypt and other regions, especially Italy.[10] Interlaced throughout the work, these analogies repeatedly disarm

---

[5] On Pliny's publication date (probably 77 CE) and his imperial connections, see Beagon 2005, 1–11.
[6] The Packard Humanities Institute database lists *Aegyptus* and its derivatives 349 times in Pliny (the most in any Roman author and 33.11% of its occurrences in all Roman authors). Notable Egyptian marvels and eccentricities in the *Natural History* include an antelope who hails the star Sirius (*Nat.* 2.107), a hippo-centaur (*Nat.* 7.35), an amorous elephant (*Nat.* 8.13), the mongoose (*Nat.* 8.88), and a human with extra eyes on the back (*Nat.* 11.272), as well as drunkenness (*Nat.* 14.149), magic herbs (*Nat.* 25.11), and epidemic diseases (*Nat.* 26.4, 26.8). See also Merrills 2017, 279–97, for Pliny's discussion of the Nile.
[7] Obelisks (*Nat.* 36.64–74), pyramids (*Nat.* 36.75–76, 36.78–82), Sphinx (*Nat.* 36.77), Ptolemaic Pharos (*Nat.* 36.83), labyrinths (*Nat.* 36.84, 86–89). See Carey 2003, 86–91; Davies 2011, 365–66; Capriotti Vittozzi 2014, 243–46, 258–59; Swetnam Burland 2015, 81–93; Merrills 2017, 290–92.
[8] Carey 2003, 87–88; Murphy 2004, 52; Naas 2011, 61–62; Leemreize 2014, 73–74, 77; Swetnam Burland 2015, 90–91; Merrills 2017, 292.
[9] Nicholson/Shaw 2000, 111, 197–99, 231–33, 335, 338, 626, 631, 643.
[10] I borrow *Aegyptiaca* from art history as shorthand for Pliny's Egyptian material (see full definition in Versluys 2015, 136).

and domesticate Egyptian otherness for Pliny's contemporaries: the witnesses of Nero's final years, of the civil war, and of Vespasian's *aduentus* from Egypt. Moreover, Pliny's neutralizing strategies are in dialogue with a larger political project in Vespasianic Rome, the reinscription of Egypt into the post-civil war imagination. The war among provincial legions and ethnically diverse auxiliaries, ending with a usurpation from the East, had confounded the categories of self and other, of *bellum ciuile* and *bellum externum*.[11] Vespasian redressed this fractious experience through textual and pictorial narratives of unification between Italy and the provinces, purporting their mutual enrichment as opposed to the raw domination of the latter by the former.[12] Along the same lines, Pliny's mundane *Aegyptiaca* cast Egypt not as a precariously contained enemy, but as an integrated limb of the newly reconstituted imperial body. Pliny's rhetorical rapprochement with Egypt harnesses this historically and ideologically marked province into the Flavians' synthesizing worldview.[13]

My argument about Pliny's redefinition of Egypt as a *topos* of imperial rhetoric is aligned with one strand of Flavian literature, condensed by the volume editors as "literature that provides strategies of recuperation and healing as it seeks ways of moving beyond Rome's iterative curse of civil war."[14] While not explicitly writing about civil war, the Elder Pliny belongs in a collective discussion on responses to Vespasian (Penwill, Mason), on Flavian "metabolizings" of civil war trauma (Fucecchi, König), on literary configurations of monuments (Chomse), and on analogies between the political and natural orders (Krasne). By fleshing out Pliny's Egypt, this paper links his factual enumeration to his ideological commitments, it nudges the Flavian reception of *bellum ciuile* beyond the primacy of Flavian epic, and it contributes to the discussion on Roman ideations of Egypt in the early empire.

---

11 The disparate ethnicities, citizenship, geography, and leadership of the warring armies in 69 resist the *bellum ciuile* classification (Master 2016, 63–73).
12 On Vespasian's unifying of Italy and the provinces through legislation and public works, see Levick 1999, 170–83; Manolaraki 2013, 122–27; Osgood 2015, 1693; Parker 2016; Pogorzelski 2016; Nicols 2016, 72–73. On the unificatory symbolism of the *Templum Pacis*, see Levick 1999, 126–27; Manolaraki 2015, 649. Beagon 1992, 183–91, links the Romans' expanded concept of the edges of the world during the Flavian period to developments in navigation.
13 Complementarity between Plinian rhetoric and Vespasianic politics: Pollard 2009; Fear 2011; Manolaraki 2015.
14 p. 6.

2 *Pares et in Aegypto*: Egyptian Products and Practices

In her study of Egyptian artifacts in Italy, Swetnam Burland touches on various wares from Egypt featured in the *Natural History*. For Pliny, she argues, "Rome is an emporium in which anything is available, where a good can be found to suit every need; all manners of products from Egypt were deeply entwined in Roman commercial and consumptive life."[15] The Romanocentric gravity of Pliny's Egyptian material is elegantly captured here, but Swetnam Burland's macroscopic view substantiates only a broad inference: since all Egyptian resources belong to Rome, all mentions of Egypt in the *Natural History* are *de facto* assertions of its Roman ownership. A more nuanced picture emerges by breaking down Pliny's hegemonic narrative into itemizations of individual *Aegyptica*.

Before we proceed with specific articles, let us first extricate their narrative ontology from their materiality in Rome. Many Egyptian perishables mentioned in Pliny were never meant to reach the city. They were either common in Italy and therefore not cost-effective for import, or too perishable to make the journey (e.g., radishes, *Nat.* 19.84; leeks, *Nat.* 19.110). Others, such as grain, vinegar, gems, or marble, were so integrated into Roman economy that their Egyptianness was no longer recognizable.[16] Therefore, regardless of its value as buyer information, Pliny's stock of *Aegyptiaca* functions primarily as a supply of knowledge; it constitutes a narrative display, to be appraised as notional merchandise. It is as such that I examine these products, independently of their consumption in Rome.

2.1 Shopping Around

In this vein, Pliny's presentation of Egyptian wheat exemplifies his recurrent relativizing of Egyptian goods in the imperial inventory. Wheat repays attention as Egypt's trademark, especially since the Nile Valley was Rome's largest grain supplier from the time of Augustus to the end of the fourth century. Tacitus's complaint that Romans stake their sustenance on the vagaries of sailing from Africa and Egypt (Tac. *Ann.* 12.43.2) condenses the well-founded notion of Egypt as

---

15 Swetnam Burland 2015, 24. See also 4–25, 74–75, 87–88, 90–97, 102–3, 161–62.
16 Many Egyptian wares not recognized as such in Rome: Swetnam Burland 2015, 63. Pliny's entwining of material economy and knowledge economy: Murphy 2004, 49–76; Lao 2011.

Rome's breadbasket.[17] Closer to Pliny, Vespasian's victory was credited partly to his hold of Egyptian grain during the war with Vitellius.[18] Indeed, under Vespasian, Isis became prominent in Rome as the patron of Rome's grain supply.[19]

Pliny's segment on wheat or *triticum* (*Nat.* 18.63–70) is mediated by these cultural politics. The account opens with the confident assertion that while wheat is produced in many parts of the world, the Italian kind is the best. Imported wheats, Pliny continues, can only be graded against the somewhat lesser wheat of Italy's rugged country (*Nat.* 18.63). Having established the unquestionable inferiority of all imported wheat, he then ranks the Boeotian, the Sicilian, and the African as the top three in weight (*Nat.* 18.63). The third place for weight, concludes this introduction, was once held successively by the Thracian, the Syrian, and the Egyptian (*Thracio, Syrio, deinde et Egyptio, Nat.* 18.63). In discussing the above passage, Doody notices several divergences between Pliny and his main source, Theophrastus. While there are no contenders for the third place in Theophrastus, Pliny adds that category to create a longer hierarchy of wheat in "a narrative of competition and nationalism."[20] Doody does not connect this point to Egypt (her focus is different), but it seems plausible that Pliny's updating of Theophrastus highlights Egypt only to sideline its importance as grain provider.

A few chapters later, Pliny again demotes Egyptian *triticum* by announcing that, although Egypt makes flour from its wheat, it is by no means equal to Italian flour (*Aegyptus similaginem conficit e tritico suo nequaquam Italicae parem, Nat.* 18.82). To the same effect he compares Italian and Egyptian alica, a type of hulled wheat cooked into a gruel of the same name. Predictably, Italy wins "without doubt" for its alica, while its Egyptian counterpart is dismissed as "rather tasteless" (*palma frugum indubitata Italiae contingit. fit sine dubio et in Aegypto, sed admodum spernenda, Nat.* 18.109). Elsewhere, Nilotic fertility is surpassed by

---

17 See, similarly, Tac. *Ann.* 3.54.4 with Woodman/Martin 1996, 396–97, and further on Egyptian grain: Erdkamp 2005, 225–37; Capponi 2005; Pfeiffer 2009; Manolaraki 2013, 30–31; Versluys 2015, 139–44. On other providers of Rome, see Erdkamp 2005, 207–8, 309.
18 According to Tacitus and Suetonius, Vespasian planned to "obtain the keys to Egypt" (*obtinere claustra Aegypti placuit*, Tac. *Hist.* 2.82.3 ~ *ut claustra Aegypti optineret*, Suet. *Ves.* 7.1; cf. J. *BJ* 4.605–6) and to starve the Vitellians into submission (Tac. *Hist.* 3.8.2; cf. *Hist.* 3.48.3). Regardless of Vespasian's actual plans (see speculations in Morgan 2006, 187–89), what remained was the impression of Egypt as a menace. For instance, a delay of grain shipments from Africa in January 70 CE bred fears of a new uprising; the rumors were quelled when Vespasian sent grain from Alexandria (Tac. *Hist.* 4.38.1–2, *Hist.* 4.52.5; cf. D.C. 65.9.2a).
19 Pfeiffer 2010a, 119–20; Bommas 2012, 182–96; Manolaraki 2013, 121–23.
20 See Doody 2016, 251. See also Doody 2010, 23–30, 162–69, on Pliny's hierarchical lists.

that of the Tigris and the Euphrates; these rivers create more abundance (*felicitas maior*, *Nat.* 18.170) because their flow is controlled more efficiently.

Taken together, these remarks on Egyptian grain diffuse its import for Rome's sustenance and, more recently, for Vespasian's victory and urban management. The casual inclusion of Egypt *inter alia* implies that it holds no special consequence or threat, at least no more than Rome's other grain providers. Pliny's admission that wheat grows mostly in Sicily, in Spain, and "above all in Egypt" (*in primis Aegyptus*, *Nat.* 18.95) is his only nod to the millions of *modii* shipped annually from Alexandria to the granaries at Ostia.[21] Relativizing the Nile Valley moderates Egypt with a reassuring plenitude generated in Italy and elsewhere in the empire.

Similarly to wheat, several Egyptian botanicals are disempowered by being ranked beneath their counterparts from other areas: the aromatic lichen sphagnos grows in Egypt, but the top three varieties are found in Cyrene, Cyprus, and Phoenicia (*Nat.* 12.108);[22] a type of sage named maron is better in Lydia than in Egypt (*Nat.* 12.111); the cinnamon-like malobathrum grows in Syria and Egypt, but the Indian kind is the best (*Nat.* 12.129); the Libyan fir is more fragrant than the Egyptian fir (*Nat.* 12.134); Egyptian starch comes third after those from Chios and Crete (*Nat.* 18.77); Egyptian sedge is less efficacious as a disinfectant than those from Libya, Rhodes, and Thera (*Nat.* 21.117). Egyptian flowers are virtually odorless due to the stifling humidity of the Nile (*Nat.* 21.36, 21.69); Egypt produces the most perfumed oils, but Campania outdoes it in rose oil (*Nat.* 13.26).[23] In fact, "the Egyptians have many plants of no repute" (*multas praeterea ignobiles habent*, *Nat.* 21.90). Egyptian linen gets the dubious compliment that it is the most profitable (for the sellers) but also the flimsiest (for consumers, *Nat.* 19.14). And similarly to Egypt's plethora of inferior plants, the stone sinopis is found in Egypt, but Lemnos and Cappadocia provide the best kind (*Nat.* 35.31).

Several *Aegyptiaca* are likewise offset by their doppelgangers elsewhere: a certain sheep wool has the same consistency in Gaul and in Egypt (*similis ... Narbonensis, similis et in Aegypto*, *Nat.* 8.191); Egypt shares two varieties of pomegranates with Samos (*Nat.* 13.113); large scallops are found in Alexandria, Lesbos, Chios, Illyria, Sicily, and northern Italy (*Nat.* 32.150); alabastritis is mined in

---

[21] Le Bonniec/Le Boeuffle 1972, 220, consider "comme fabuleux" Pliny's claim about the wheat production in Sicily.

[22] Identifying ancient plants is notoriously problematic (Doody 2011, 115–18; Hardy/Totelin 2016, 93–113). Bonet 2014, 463–79, provides detailed indexes of plants mentioned in the *Natural History*. For convenience, I follow the names in the Loeb translation.

[23] Egyptian aromatics in Pliny: Manniche 1999 esp. 7–31, 74–75, 77–78.

Egypt and in Syria (*Nat.* 37.143); the Egyptian gemstone phloginos resembles the ochre of Attica (*Nat.* 37.179). Papyrus, Egypt's other brand product next to wheat, is akin to the common reed (*cognata in Aegypto res est harundini papyrum*, *Nat.* 24.88). Moreover, papyrus grows also in Syria, where it is also used for paper (*nascitur et in Syria ... eundem usum habere chartae*, *Nat.* 13.73).

Even in its peculiarities, Egypt is not alone: both Egypt and Gaul are equally immune to earthquakes (*Nat.* 2.195); a provincial governor saw in the Alps the ibis, a bird native to Egypt (*uisam in Alpibus ab se peculiarem Aegypti et ibim*, *Nat.* 10.134);[24] certain Egyptian rodents are bipedal, and they use their front paws as hands as do those in the Alps (*bipedes ambulant ceu Alpini quoque*, *Nat.* 10.186 ~ *pares et in Aegypto*, *Nat.* 8.132);[25] palms grow bifurcated in Egypt and Syria, but in Crete they split into three or even five trunks (*Nat.* 13.38); tapeworms thrive in Egypt, Arabia, Syria, and Cilicia (*Nat.* 27.145); the plant perdicium is introduced with the remark that it is consumed by people other than the Egyptians (*perdicium et aliae gentes quam Aegyptii edunt*, *Nat.* 21.102).

Occasionally, *Aegyptiaca* are proclaimed as the best in their class, but most of these Egyptian prizes are found also in Italy or they are perishable.[26] Their exceptional status is hence countered by the ready availability of (admittedly lesser) alternatives. More importantly, the instances where Egypt does not "win the palm" put its victories into perspective. Egyptian products take their turn in the spotlight, but so do those of Italy, Greece, Arabia, and India. Through his rotation of bests, Pliny strips Egypt of proprietary pride and frames its putative preeminence within the empire's plurality.

2.2 A Rose by Any Other Name

Another means of converting the Egyptian extraordinary into ordinary, and hence establishing parity between Egypt and other areas, is botanical nomenclature. As Doody illustrates, Pliny cites numerous phytonyms and their synonyms

---

[24] On the possible identity of the Alpine ibis, see De Saint-Denis 1961, 139. On the ibis, see pp. 353–56 below.

[25] Pliny probably compares the Alpine marmot to the Egyptian gerboa. Herodotus (4.192) places the gerboa in Libya, not in Egypt. Aristotle (*HA* 6.37, 581a) places it in Egypt but without mentioning an Alpine counterpart.

[26] Egypt excels in aromatic cypros (*Nat.* 12.109), acacia-gum (*Nat.* 13.66, *Nat.* 24.109), medicinal thapsia (*Nat.* 13.126), oregano (*Nat.* 19.165), radishes (*Nat.* 19.84), leeks (*Nat.* 19.110), mustard seed (*Nat.* 19.171), coriander (*Nat.* 20.216), absinthe (*Nat.* 27.53), sori plant (*Nat.* 34.120), alum (*Nat.* 35.184), ochre and white pigments (*Nat.* 35.35–36), azurite (*Nat.* 33.161).

not for practical usage but for their aesthetic properties. His superabundance of names, she argues, suggests his intent to display his botany as a theater of the imagination rather than as a field guide.[27] Applied to Egyptian plants and trees, Pliny's aesthetics of naming again breaches, I believe, the insularity of Egypt as a land of unique exotica.

One aspect of this tactic is providing regional varieties or alternate names for the same plant: while the *ficus Aegyptia* grows only in Egypt (*Nat.* 13.56), it resembles a variety that grows in Crete but is called Cyprian (*quae uocatur Cypria ficus in Creta*, *Nat.* 13.58); elsewhere, the same tree is said to be endemic in Egypt and Cyprus (*in Aegypto et Cypro sui generis*, *Nat.* 23.134).[28] Egyptians call a certain sweet wine Thasian, even though it is native to Egypt (*Thasiam uuam Aegyptus uocat apud se praedulcem*, *Nat.* 14.117).[29] The Egyptian cici tree is also called croton, sibi, or sesamon (*Nat.* 15.25). Sweet marjoram is known in Sicily as amaracum, but in Egypt and Syria as sampsucum (*Nat.* 21.61); the name amaracum also describes a plant known also as parthenium, leucanthes, perdicium, and muralis (*Nat.* 21.176). The purportedly magical herb cynocephalia is called osiritis in Egypt (*Nat.* 30.18). In sum, Egyptian species known by other names and Egyptian synonyms for common plants are notional contact points among disparate geographies. Their contiguity harmonizes Egypt with the imperial herbarium and alchemizes its botanica into concinnity with Rome.

It is fair to object at this juncture that botanical assimilation is not original to Pliny. Indeed, analogizing between things Egyptian and Greek (Roman) is established ethnographic strategy since Herodotus.[30] Closer to botany, both Theophrastus and Pliny's contemporary Dioscorides routinely compare Egyptian trees to Greek ones for clarification.[31] Yet to gloss Pliny's comparisons as a function of tradition is to miss how that tradition is adapted to the ideology of the *Natural History*. Pliny does not blindly follow his sources but rather renders them relevant

---

[27] Doody 2011, 123: "Names can represent, for Pliny, a form of knowledge even when they are names for things that no longer exist or are not identifiable." On the *Natural History* as a notional marketplace, see p. 344 above.
[28] André 1971, 118, untangles Pliny's varieties. Cf. Theophrastus, who mentions the Αἰγυπτία συκάμινος (Thphr. *HP* 1.1.7) but without any comparanda.
[29] Probably wine from the Sebennytes nome; cf. *Sebennytico ... Thasio* (*Nat.* 14.74) with André 1958, 109.
[30] Amigues 1995; Naas 2011, 64.
[31] Bonet 2014, 120–21; Hardy/Totelin 2016, 109–12; Irwin 2016.

for his own audience. The acknowledged similarities between his botany and that of Dioscorides offer an opportunity to test this argument in the context of Egypt.[32]

Consider, for instance, the root vegetable colocasia, a type of taro (*Nat.* 21.87). Dioscorides mentions Egypt as the home of the *kolokasion*, which he identifies with the edible root of the Egyptian bean (*Nelumbo nucifera*). That bean, he says, is named "Egyptian" because of its preeminence in Egypt (ὁ δὲ Αἰγύπτιος κύαμος … πλεῖστος ἐν Αἰγύπτῳ γεννᾶται, Dsc. 2.106.1). The same information is treated differently in the *Natural History*. Pliny introduces the colocasia more discursively as "very famous in Egypt … which the locals harvest out of the Nile" (*in Aegypto nobilissima est colocasia … hanc e Nilo metunt*, *Nat.* 21.87), and he goes on to amplify its morphology as follows (Plin. *Nat.* 21.87):

> foliis latissimis, etiam si arboreis conparentur, ad similitudinem eorum, quae personata in nostris amnibus uocamus, adeoque Nili sui dotibus gaudent, ut inplexis colocasiae foliis in uariam speciem uasorum potare gratissimum habeant. seritur iam haec in Italia.
>
> Even when compared with those of trees, its leaves are very broad, similar to the leaves (of the plant) we call personata in our rivers. So much do the people appreciate the bounty of their Nile that they consider very gratifying to drink from vessels of various shapes plaited from colocasia leaves. The colocasia is now grown in Italy.

These comments invite a cultural response to the colocasia absent from Dioscorides. The introductory superlative *nobilissima* piques curiosity about the significance of the plant for Egyptians, and it foreshadows the use of its leaves for goblets. The actions denoted by *metunt* (the Egyptians) and *uocamus* (the Romans) infuse human agency into the colocasia, molding it into a socialized object. The "we" implicit in *uocamus* and *nostris amnibus* appeals to the national solidarity between Pliny and his readers, and it awakens the latter to the transnational correspondence of the Egyptian colocasia and the Italian personata. The similarity between the two, however, also highlights the Egyptian use of the plant for drinking cups, a practice without an Italian parallel. The Egyptians' enjoyment of their plaited goblets offers a glimpse of native simplicity, in contrast perhaps to the Roman *luxuria* of tableware (*Nat.* 37.17, 37.20).[33] Finally, the assertion that the colocasia is now grown in Italy conclusively denudes this plant of its stigmatized ethnicity. Naturalized in its new home, the once-Egyptian and now Italian colocasia narrows the gap between Italian normalcy and Egyptian idiosyncracy.

---

[32] Resemblances between Pliny and Dioscorides are ascribed to their common use of Sextius Niger (Irwin 2016, 265, 274, 276).
[33] *Luxuria* in Pliny: Manolaraki 2015, esp. 649, 651–53.

Unlike Dioscorides' colocasia, Pliny's exposition of the same exudes his proprietary interest in Egypt.

Another example of Pliny's Egyptian sensibilities is his account of the centunculus, a kind of bindweed. He begins by giving the Latin and Greek names for this plant, centunculus and clematis respectively (*centunculum uocant nostri ... Graeci clematidem*, *Nat.* 24.138), but he opts for the Greek name in the remainder of his account. After reviewing the Greek and Roman varieties of the clematis and their medicinal properties (*Nat.* 24.138–40), he adds "another clematis called also Egyptian, which is called by some daphnoides and by others polygonoides with leaf like that of the bay. ... Egypt especially produces this clematis" (*est alia clematis Aegyptia cognomine, quae ab aliis daphnoides, ab aliis polygonoides uocatur folio lauri ... Aegyptus hanc maxime gignit*, *Nat.* 24.141–42). Dioscorides (4.7.1) includes δαφνοειδές, πολυγονοειδές, and μυρσινοειδές as alternative names of the clematis, but he does not mention Egypt in connection to this plant. An early commentator of Pliny glosses his appellation "Egyptian" (*Aegyptia cognomine*, *Nat.* 24.141) by noting the absence of this name in Dioscorides.[34] Pliny alone adds the Egyptian clematis as a tertium quid to the Greek and Roman varieties. His identification of it with the one known as daphnoides and the detail that it resembles the laurel (*folio lauri*, *Nat.* 21.142) vest the Egyptian bindweed with the prestige of the daphne, the laureate plant of Greek athletics and Roman triumphs.[35]

Pliny's treatment of the chicory (*cichorium*) shows the same assimilative logic. Dioscorides considers the κιχόριον a variety of the plant seris (*Nat.* 2.132), but he omits its place of origin.[36] Pliny, on the other hand, reiterates that the Egyptian *cichorium* is identical to the Italian *intubum*, the wild endive (*intubum, quod in Aegypto cichorium uocant*, *Nat.* 19.129; *erraticum apud nos ... in Aegypto cichorium uocant*, *Nat.* 20.73; *in Aegypto ... cichorio est, quod diximus intubum*, *Nat.* 21.88). His repetition of this point in different books suggests his investment in imparting upon his audience the mutual recognition of Egyptian and Italian. Here too, the figurative incivility of Egyptian wilderness is converted, through shared botany, into political fraternity with Rome.

Although necessarily limited, the above examples indicate that Pliny's negotiation of Egyptian botanica is informed by a concern with the cultural associations of his contemporary Egypt. His presentist instinct is well illustrated by Jones-Lewis in her discussion of poisons in the *Natural History*. As she argues,

---

34 Desfontaines 1830, 450: "*prior Dioscoridis qui hujius cognominis nusquam meminit.*" See also Bonet 2014, 52.
35 Cf. *daphnoides ... siluestris laurus* (*Nat.* 23.158) with André 1971, 125.
36 Dioscorides' κιχόριον: McVaugh/Ogden 1997, 112–13.

while Pliny's sources link magical herbs with Helen and Medea, Pliny relocates this tradition with Cleopatra and Mithridates to a moralizing end. His contemporizing welds the ethnography and politics of poison to venomous historical exempla.[37]

Pliny updates his botanical sources along the same didactic lines, to render Egypt timely and inoffensive for his contemporaries. His conscious and unconscious narrative choices de-individualize Egyptian flora, and by implication challenge the notion of Egypt as a toxic substance in the empire. Devoid of its putative separatism and spread across heterogeneous geographies, Egypt draws near Italy through the recognition of items common and communal across Vespasian's ecumenical empire.[38]

2.3 Monsters and Marvels

The demystification of Egypt in the *Natural History* extends beyond physical goods, into continuities between Egyptian and Italian practices. In one instance, we learn that emmer is fermented in a similar manner to make the soup tragum "in Campania and Egypt at least" (*simili modo e tritici semine tragum fit, in Campania dumtaxat et Aegypto, Nat.* 18.76).[39] While the qualifying *dumtaxat* reserves the possibility that other ethnic groups share that practice, it singles out Italians and Egyptians for the connection. The dominant center and the subdued fringe become conversant through their shared foodways.

A segment on anomalous pregnancies and parturitions in Book 7 (partly dedicated to human physiology, *Nat.* 7.33–52), develops a longer congruence between Egypt and Italy. Pliny's contextualizing of Egypt here merits attention, because traditional mythologies of Egypt depend in part on its prodigious, and even monstrous, fertility. Yet, as we will see, Pliny's investment in the universality of the human species brings Egypt in line with the rest of mankind.[40]

On the topic of multiple births, Pliny argues that while deliveries of twins and triplets are ordinary, quadruplets and above are considered ominous "except in

---

[37] See Jones-Lewis 2012, esp. 52–56, for Egyptian poisons associated (not accidentally) with Nero. For the demonization of Nero in Flavian literature, see Ginsberg 2017, 190–93, with additional bibliography. On the prominence of Egypt in botanical lore, see Hardy/Totelin 2016, 40, 45–46.
[38] Mutuality of power and knowledge in the *Natural History*: Doody 2009, 1–2, 19–21; Guasparri 2013, 352.
[39] Emmer wheat and *tragum*: Dalby 2003, 131–32.
[40] Egyptian monstrosities: Meyboom/Versluys 2007. Pliny on the human condition: Beagon 2005, 44–45.

Egypt, where drinking the Nile causes fecundity" (*praeterquam in Aegypto, ubi fetifer potu Nilus amnis*, *Nat.* 7.33). As evidence for the portentousness of multiple births in Italy he cites the delivery of quadruplets in Ostia at the time of Augustus's death, which "accurately foretold" (*portendit haud dubie*, *Nat.* 7.33) a subsequent food shortage in Rome. In the same passage he then records the birth of four separate sets of quintuplets in the Peloponnese and the birth of septuplets in Egypt, but without any portents attached to either event.

Here, too, the deviance of Egypt is tempered through comparison. Pliny's attribution of compound conception to the Nile is a piece of "scientific" reasoning that normalizes the copious fertility and reduces its sinister connotations. In the same mitigating vein, the multiple birth at Ostia suggests that omen arbitration is circumscribed by its own context and construal: while in Italy the quadruplets foretell famine, the multiple Peloponnesian quintuplets and the Egyptian septuplets come without peril. Pliny expressly states the subjectivity of omens elsewhere (*Nat.* 28.10–17) when he concludes that "their power is in our control, and they have as much power as is ascribed to them" (*ostentorum uires et in nostra potestate esse ac, prout quaeque accepta sint ita ualere*, *Nat.* 28.17).

Finally, the Egyptian births rank below the cumulative Greek delivery of twenty infants, a record that spotlights Peloponnese over Egypt. The story comes from Aristotle, who records that "some woman gave birth to twenty over four labors" (μία δέ τις ἐν τέτταρσι τόκοις ἔτεκεν εἴκοσιν, Arist. *HA* 7.4, 584b). While the location of these births is not specified in the Greek author, Pliny anchors them securely *in Peloponneso* (*Nat.* 7.33). His specificity renders the exotic more familiar and brings it closer to Rome. Clustered with Italy and the Peloponnese under the rubric of birth oddities, Egypt eludes the stigma of outrageous parturitions and reaches toward the intellectual and moral center of the empire.

The same principle guides Pliny's comments on fetal development: "it is common in Egypt to be born even in the eighth month, and indeed in Italy also for such cases to live, contrary to the belief of old times. These vary in more ways also" (*tralaticium in Aegypto est et octauo gigni, iam quidem et in Italia tales partus esse uitales, contra priscorum opiniones. uariant haec pluribus modis*, *Nat.* 7.39). As proof of his claim that pregnancy terms vary beyond the alternatives of the (short) eight or (regular) nine months, Pliny goes on to enumerate seven Italian pregnancies lasting from six to ten months, concluding with a thirteen-month record (*Nat.* 7.39–40).

The remarks on eight-month pregnancies also harken to Hippocratic embryology, in which such gestations result in stillborn or defective babies.[41] Through

---

41 Hp. *Oct.* See Hanson 1987; Parker 1999, 525–26, 528–30; Beagon 2005, 185–89; Nutton 2013, 90.

his distribution of this unusual duration to both Egypt and Italy and his rejection of the Hippocratic theory as outmoded, Pliny challenges the notion of the eight-month pregnancy as abnormal. His list of unusually short (six months) or long (thirteen months) pregnancies in Italy further deflates the eight-month mythology in both lands by situating it within a wider spectrum of possible terms. More importantly, while he follows Aristotle in arguing that eight-month infants are viable, he silences the former's teratological inference about Egypt: "eight-month children around Egypt ... are able to survive, even if they are born monstrous, ... and they are reared" (τὰ δ' ὀκτάμηνα περὶ μὲν Αἴγυπτον ... δύναται ζῆν κἂν τερατώδη γένηται ... καὶ ἐκτρέφεται, *HA* 7.4, 584b).

2.4 Sacred Animals, Vegetables, and Minerals

Pliny's rehabilitation of things Egyptian embraces even theriomorphism, the cult of zoomorphic gods including certain animals. To a classical audience, Egypt's "animal worship" is its most shocking practice, yet this trope is notably absent from Pliny's paradoxographies.[42] His silence on this central institution aims to alleviate its disturbing subtext: Egypt's monster gods against Italy's human ones, a shadow in the Roman imaginary stylized by the Vergilian Actium (Verg. *A.* 8.698–700).

A section in the ornithological Book 10 speaks to the point. Pliny's account of migratory birds (*Nat.* 10.58–75) concludes with a species which opens a door to Egypt (*Nat.* 10.75):

> seleucides aues uocantur quarum aduentum ab Ioue precibus inpetrant Cadmi montis incolae, fruges eorum locustis uastantibus. nec unde ueniant quoue abeant compertum, numquam conspectis nisi cum praesidio earum indigetur. inuocant et Aegyptii ibis suas contra serpentium aduentum, et Elei Myiacoren deum muscarum multitudine pestilentiam adferente, quae protinus intereunt quam litatum est ei deo.

> Those birds are called seleucids, for whose arrival prayers are offered to Jupiter by the inhabitants of Mount Cadmus, when locusts destroy their crops. It is not known where they come from, or where they go when they depart, and they are never seen except when their protection is needed. Also the people of Egypt invoke their ibis to guard against the arrival of snakes, and those of Elis invoke the god Myiacores when a swarm of flies brings plague, the flies dying as soon as a sacrifice to this god has been performed.

---

42 Classical (mis)interpretations of Egyptian religion: Aston 2011, 21–23, 44–49, 226–32; Gruen 2011, 76–114; Manolaraki 2013, 30–31, 34–35; Swetnam Burland 2015, 170. Smelik/Hemelrijk 1984, 1960, appear puzzled that "Pliny the Elder tells surprisingly little about Egyptian animal worship ... while the subject of his work lent itself most readily to an elaborate description."

Pliny digresses from the topic of migration to compare the seleucids of Mt. Cadmus in northern Cilicia to two other pest eradicators, the Egyptian ibises and the Greek Zeus Myiacores.[43] From a modern standpoint these analogies in agricultural folklore appear obvious, yet they should not be taken for granted here given the cultural biases of the *Natural History*. By embedding the ibis into the apotropaic practices of two other Roman provinces, Pliny rationalizes its cult in Egypt.

To trace this process, let us begin with the seleucids' locust killing, mentioned also by Aelian (*NA* 17.19). The second century BCE scholar Eudoxus of Cyzicus is cited by Aelian as his source for these birds, evidence that the story precedes Pliny. While certainly familiar with Pliny's zoology, Aelian omits Jupiter from his story. In his version, as soon as Cilician farmers "pray certain prayers," the seleucids attack the locusts without any divine intermediacy. Jupiter might have been mentioned by Eudoxus as the guide of the birds, but Aelian, at least, chooses to present them as autonomous agents.[44] Pliny, too, had a choice regarding Jupiter's involvement, and he elected to cast him in the leading role. But to what end?

As lord of the seleucids and obviator of locusts, the Cadmeian Jupiter dovetails with the Peloponnesian Zeus Myiacores, "Averter of Flies." Pliny elsewhere mentions this persona of Zeus under the alternative name *Myiodes*. Before the opening of the games at Olympia, a bull is sacrificed to the "deity whom they call Myiodes" (*deo, quem Myioden uocant, Nat.* 29.106). At that moment clouds of flies leave the sacred precinct, "an astounding spectacle" (*mirabilius, Nat.* 29.106). Pausanias tells a similar story: Hercules first prayed to Zeus as *Apomyios* (Ἀπομυίῳ Διί, Paus. 5.14.1) at Olympia, asking him to shield his sacrificial offering from flies. The Arcadian town of Aliphera also sacrifices to a deity whom they call *Myagros*, "Fly Catcher" (Μυάγρῳ προθύουσιν ... τὸν Μύαγρον, Paus. 8.26.7), personas perhaps of Zeus or Hercules (Pausanias does not say). Pliny, too, alludes to Hercules as averter of flies, when he mentions that dogs and flies cannot enter the temple of Hercules in the Forum Boarium (*Nat.* 10.79).[45]

---

[43] Possible identifications of the seleucids: Thompson 1932; De Saint-Denis 1961, 127. On Roman cities of Mt. Cadmus, cf. *Nat.* 5.118 and Thonemann 2011, 203–41.

[44] Aelian says that the seleucids lend an ear (ὑπακούουσι, *NA* 17.19), but if men harm them, they "do not deign to respond again" (οὐκ ἀξιοῦσιν ὑπακοῦσαι, *NA* 17.19). He likewise elides Jupiter probably to emphasize their intellect and morality. On animals in Pliny and Aelian, see Beagon 1992, 137–44; Fögen 2014, 226–27.

[45] On Pausanias, see Frazer 1965, 558–59, with ethnographic comparanda. According to Plutarch, the tale about Hercules and the shunning of dogs from the Forum Boarium traces to Varro (Plu. *Mor.* 285e). On Pliny's claim about the Forum Boarium (*Nat.* 10.79), see De Saint-Denis 1961, 128, and McDonough 1999.

To return to our passage (*Nat.* 10.75), in both his Cadmeian and Elean capacities, Jupiter resembles tutelary aspects of Greek and Italic divinities worshipped as crop patrons. Apollo Parnopius ("Vanquisher of Locusts"; cf. Apollo Smintheus, Sauroctonus, Erythibius, Carneius), Heracles Carnopion ("Captor of Locusts"; cf. Heracles Ipoctonus), Jupiter Pluvius, and various personified *numina* (e.g., Pales, Robigo, Aurruncus, Consus, Tellus, Segetia/Segesta, Bonus Eventus) are well-known defenders of agricultural and pastoral life. Pliny himself mentions the consultation of the Sibylline Books to avert locust infestation (*Nat.* 11.105), as well as Segesta (*Nat.* 18.8), Robigo and Flora (*Nat.* 18.285–86), and statues of Apollo Sauroctonos (*Nat.* 34.70), Bonus Eventus, and Bona Fortuna (*Nat.* 34.77, 36.23).[46] In Pliny, therefore, the Cadmeian Zeus of the seleucids and his associated deities help to obliquely rationalize the ibis cult.

Pliny's homogenizing rhetoric does more than identify analogies between Egyptian, Greek, and Italic religious practice. His choice of the ibis condenses a long discussion of this bird as emblematic of Egyptian theriomorphism.[47] According to Herodotus (2.75), ibises intercept winged snakes attempting to migrate annually from Arabia to Egypt. Both the Arabians and the Egyptians, he claims, agree that the ibis is worshipped in Egypt precisely for this service.[48] Diodorus Siculus proposes multiple explanations for theriomorphism, purportedly given to him by Egyptians, and he lists vermin control among their self-professed reasons. According to Diodorus's informants, the ibis is held sacred because it protects Egyptians from snakes, locusts, and caterpillars (D.S. 1.87.6). The same utilitarian justification for the ibis cult is also proffered by Pomponius Mela (3.82.5) and Cicero (Cic. *N.D.* 1.101 ~ *Tusc.* 5.78).[49]

In casting the Egyptian adoration of ibises in the context of pest extermination, Pliny evidently relies on Classical theories. Yet his geographic association between Cilicia, Egypt, and Greece, the common concerns of their ethnic groups, and the equivalence of the ibis to the Cadmeian and Elean Zeus are his own. The latter gesture is boldly creative, considering the ontological difference between the ibis and Zeus; while the sacred ibis appears zoomorphic or zoocephalic as the manifestation of Thoth, Zeus in his local roles is still very much an anthropomor-

---

[46] Agricultural deities: Secoy/Smith 1977, 3–7; Arias 1986; Scholz 1993; Blaive 1995; McDonough 1999; Bernstein 1997; Zadoks 2007; Aston 2011, 137–40; Kiernan 2014, 604–6; Fratantuono 2014. For the Sibylline Books consulted against epidemics, see Nutton 2013, 162–63, 289.
[47] The ibis in Egyptian religion: Arnott 2007, 73–74; Wyatt 2013; Capriotti Vitozzi 2014, 251–54; Swetnam Burland 2015, 13–14, 148.
[48] See Asheri *et al.* 2007, 290–91.
[49] On the utilitarian argument for Egyptian zoolatry in Diodorus and Plutarch, see Aston 2011, 45–46; Gruen 2011, 92–94; on the same in Cicero, see Dyck 2003, 184–85.

phic god. Additionally, while ibis-Thoth is a major character in the Egyptian pantheon, the pesticide Zeus is a situational deity, "a god conjured for a specific purpose and afterwards subsiding into inexistence."[50] Embedding the ibis within the normative frame of Greek mythology and religion is, to borrow from Rosati in a similar Egyptian context, "a way of normalizing the Other and of assimilating it: a way of taming the monster."[51] Likened to a god no lesser than Jupiter, Pliny's syncretic ibis narrows the gap between theriomorphism and anthropomorphism and the cultures divided by this epistemic and religious binary.[52]

In this vein, some material on medicine and pharmacy in the *Natural History* heightens parallels between Egypt and Italy. When Pliny despairs of traditional remedies against malarial fevers, he proceeds to offer treatments from the sorcerers or *magi* despite his avowed scruples (*Nat.* 30.98–104).[53] To this end, he lists several antifebrile amulets containing ingredients such as dog tooth, eye of lizard, ear of mouse, and human heart (*Nat.* 30.98, 30.99, 30.102). One of these amulets enables a digression into Egypt, as it consists of "the beetle that rolls little pellets. Because of this beetle the greater part of Egypt worships the beetle among its deities. Apion gives a detailed explanation: he gathers that this creature resembles the sun and its revolutions, seeking to find an excuse for the religious customs of his race" (*scarabaeum, qui pilas uoluit. propter hunc Aegypti magna pars scarabaeos inter numina colit, curiosa Apionis interpretatione, qua colligat Solis operum similitudinem huic animali esse, ad excusandos gentis suae ritus, Nat.* 30.99).

Pliny's leap from dung-beetles wrapped into amulets to the scarab cult in Egypt is another narrative byway towards his domestication of Egypt. According to beliefs dating from the Old Kingdom (2500 BCE), the god Khepri rolled the sun daily from east to west and reversed the direction at night. The dung beetle (*Scarabaeus sacer*) pushing its ball was considered an earthly manifestation of this process, and so Khepri came to be depicted as a scarab beetle or with a scarab beetle over his head. With divine potency attributed to it, the scarab was soon

---

[50] See Connor 2006, 124, for this description of Zeus Myacores, and 126–31, 172–74, for ancient attitudes to flies.

[51] Rosati 2009, 276, thus explains Ovid's reference to the Egyptian Ammon as a "horned Jupiter" (Ov. *Met.* 5.327–28).

[52] Comparisons between Egyptian and Greek gods long precede Pliny (von Lieven 2016). The most sustained comparison is Plutarch's *On Isis and Osiris* (Plu. *Mor.* 351d–384c), on which see Griffiths 1970, 554–56, 558–59. More recent discussions include Manolaraki 2013, 252–57, 258–62; Merrills 2017, 180–82.

[53] Pliny's criticism of the *magi*: Ernout 1964; Luke 2016, 298–302. Pliny as a source for understanding malaria in Roman Italy: Sallares 2002, 108–9, 132–34, 177–78, 211.

engraved into amulets, jewelry, and seals. As scarabs became gradually associated with health and good fortune, stone or clay "scarabs" were mass produced and even exported from Egypt.[54]

Plutarch is the first extant author to recognize the religious symbolism of the scarab for Egypt. He mentions beetles alongside asps, weasels, and crocodiles as honored both for their usefulness and because the Egyptians observed in them a distant likeness to the gods (εἰκόνας τινὰς ἐν αὐτοῖς ἀμαυρὰς ... τῆς τῶν θεῶν δυνάμεως κατιδόντες, Plu. *Mor.* 381a). In complementing the utilitarian with the symbolic argument, Plutarch defers to the insider-status of Egyptian authorities. Not so Pliny, who considers the indigenous theory an unconvincing attempt at self-justification, represented by the Hellenized Egyptian Apion.[55] Pliny does not offer a valid (in his opinion) reason for the worship of the scarab, but his motive for his rejection of Apion can be extracted from his magico-medical context. The connection between antifebrile scarab amulets and the Egyptian homage to the scarab may plausibly suggest to Pliny that scarabs are worshiped in Egypt for their healing properties, a rational motive long sublimated into spiritual allegory.

The above argument gains force when we contrast Pliny's rejection of Apion to his touting of medicaments from animal tissue (Books 28–30).[56] There, among remedies such as human flesh found in the stomach of hyena (*Nat.* 28.104) and boar semen before it touches the ground (*Nat.* 28.175), preparations of blister beetle (*cantharis*) are featured as antidote to miscellaneous ailments.[57] We also learn that the stag beetle (*Lucanus cervus*) makes for amulets against childhood diseases in Italy (*Nat.* 11.97, 30.138).[58] From a modern perspective, amulets with Egyptian or Italian beetles might seem equally naïve. Yet magical, popular, and

---

[54] Egyptian scarabs: Griffiths 1970, 555; Ward 1994; Ratcliffe 2006, 86–89; Kitchell 2014, 62. Amulets: Nutton 2013, 17, 204, 210, 274, 276–77.
[55] Apion in Pliny: Bohak 2003, 37; Dillery 2003, 383–86; Damon 2011; Luke 2016, 290–92.
[56] On ancient animal remedies (including Pliny's) see Gordon 2010.
[57] The blister beetle in Pliny: Jones-Lewis 2012, 54–57; Scarborough 1977. Topical emulsions whose active ingredient is the dehydrated flesh of this beetle are deemed useful (*Nat.* 29.93 ~ *Nat.* 29.110). Mixed with lime, it removes skin abscesses (*Nat.* 30.75); with grape, warts (*Nat.* 30.81); with pitch, nail fungus (*Nat.* 30.111); with barley, splinters (*Nat.* 30.122); in a drink, it is an antidote to the poisonous lizard (*Nat.* 29.76); beetle tissue makes good liniments (*Nat.* 29.140 ~ 30.39); the green carapace of beetles rests the eyes and improves vision (*Nat.* 29.132).
[58] The scientific name for the stag beetle, *Lucanus cervus*, originates in Pliny's remark that Nigidius Figulus calls a certain beetle *Lucauus* (or *Lucanus*; see both *lectiones* in Jan/Mayhoff 1875–1906, *ad loc.*). Figulus's appellation has been interpreted as evidence that this particular amulet was common in Lucania (Bradley 2005, 85–90). Generally on medicinal amulets in Italy, see Gaillard-Seux 1998.

"scientific" therapies converged in antiquity, especially to combat the dreaded malaria.[59] By admitting the Egyptian *Scarabaeus sacer* as a possible remedy for malarial fever, Pliny entertains a medicinal (i.e., logical) incentive for the Egyptians' beetle worship. As agricultural anxieties bring together Zeus and ibis, health concerns relate Italic pharmacy to Egyptian devotional.[60]

Pliny's impassive style also sanitizes Egypt's religion. In his book on garden plants, the segment on the onion drily begins, "Egypt swears by garlic and onions among its deities in taking an oath" (*alium cepasque inter deos in iureiurando habet Aegyptus*, *Nat.* 19.101). The remark draws from a body of knowledge about Egyptian dietary habits including injunctions against certain edibles.[61] Onion worship offers an opportunity for reproach or at least humor, but Pliny does not elaborate the point. What follows instead is a list of onion varieties and instructions for their proper storage.

Pliny's rhetorical restraint emerges against Juvenal's famous lampoon of Egyptian superstition (Juv. 15). The satirist rails, "It is blasphemy to desecrate and crunch leeks and onions with a bite. O holy peoples, for whom such divinities spring up in their gardens!" (*porrum et caepe nefas uiolare et frangere morsu | o sanctas gentes, quibus haec nascuntur in hortis | numina*, Juv. 15.9–11). Commentators footnote Juvenal with Pliny as our only sources for the Egyptian worship of the onion, but without noting their disparate mood and tone.[62] Yet even without digressing into the vexed topic of satiric veracity, it is evident that the subject has a diverting potential embraced by Juvenal and eschewed by Pliny.

Pliny's reluctance to inveigh against Egyptian beliefs is foregrounded in an early discussion on human perceptions of the divine (*Nat.* 2.14–27).[63] Traditional beliefs and practices are censured along Stoic lines for their naivety, including those of "certain nations (*gentes uero quaedam*) who have animals, even some loathsome ones, for gods, and many things still more disgraceful to tell of: swearing by rotten articles of food and other things of that sort" (*Nat.* 2.16). The "certain nations" are obviously the Egyptians, but Pliny does not single them out by name. Instead, their sacrilegious nonsense is preceded by another instance of "human idiocy" (*imbecillitatis humanae*, *Nat.* 2.14), which hits closer to home: assuming multiple gods and assigning human forms and personalities to them (*Nat.* 2.14–15).

---

59 Gaillard-Seux 1994; Lane 1999; Bonet 2003; Crippa 2010; Nutton 2013, 12–17, 280–98; Harris 2016.
60 On Pliny's rationalizing habit, see Luke 2016 and Murphy 2016.
61 Griffiths 1970, 280–81, collects the sources for Egyptian attitudes to onions, which range from religious abhorrence to voracious consumption, depending on the region.
62 Griffiths 1970, 280; Courtney 1980, 526.
63 Pliny's religious thought is broadly (and not dogmatically) Stoic: Dumont 1986; Beagon 1992, 26–36.

Pliny makes his criticism of Greco-Roman anthropomorphism even more explicit by chastising a specifically Roman practice. City residents, he protests, have raised shrines to personified calamities in order to placate their diseases and hardships. The shrine of Fever on the Palatine, of Bereavement on the Via Sacra, and of Misfortune on the Esquiline (*Febris fanum ... Orbonae ... Malae Fortunae*, *Nat.* 2.16) are evidence of this pious nonsense.[64] Theriomorphism and swearing by rotten vegetables, which appear immediately after these follies, are hence proleptically attenuated by association to the superstitious worship of human vagaries in Rome. Here too, geographical and qualitative dispersions of Egypt among corresponding practices mitigate its distinctiveness as a wellspring of absurdity.

Pliny's reserved treatment of Egyptian religion reinforces his comparative discussions of materials and practices outlined above. To deride theriomorphism is to retrace ethnographic constructions of Roman civilized selfhood through the reverse mirroring of barbarian otherness. Yet in the political climate of the seventies, such an intellectual position might be neither historically realistic nor ideologically tenable. A century after Actium, Egyptian religious signifiers were ubiquitous in the capital, authorized by an emperor who made no secret of his Egyptian patronage and his interest in Eastern religions.[65] Vespasian's Nile statue in the *Templum Pacis* (*Nat.* 36.58) literally grounded Egypt in the aspirational unification of the empire as advertised by that temple.[66] Given the Vespasianic reconstruction of Egypt as a marker of imperial self-representation and provincial unity, Pliny conditions its divergence in ways that corroborate Flavian rhetoric.[67]

---

[64] Pliny's disapproval of these shrines echoes a similar complaint in Cic. *N.D.* 3.63 and *Leg.* 2.28 (Sallares 2002, 53–54; Beagon 2005, 381).
[65] Levick 1999, 69–70; Luke 2010, 82. Further on Vespasian's character, see Mason in this volume.
[66] Merrills 2017, 95–98, summarizes recent discussions of this statue. Taraporewalla 2010, 156–57, makes the stimulating argument that the statue alluded to the Egyptian miracles associated with Vespasian's rise.
[67] Note also the political ramifications of Pliny's story of Germanicus and the Apis bull (*Nat.* 8.184, with Manolaraki 2013, 130–31).

3 Conclusion: Domesticating Egypt

In discussing building projects in the *Natural History*, Beagon remarks that Pliny "endorses the utilitarian restructuring of nature undertaken by some Roman leaders, including his own patron, Vespasian."[68] I have argued here that Pliny likewise molds his Egyptian material to Vespasian's "utilitarian restructuring" of that land in the aftermath of the civil war. The additions, omissions, and connections which guide his *Aegyptiaca* build kinships with other imperial constituencies, and primarily with Italy. These narrative choices shore up the prosaic aspects of Egypt and preemptively counter its Pharaonic monumentality contained in (and by) Book 36. Egyptian particulars, ordinary and analogous to other parts of the *oikoumene*, build momentum for dismantling Egypt *qua topos* of *bellum externum* and *bellum ciuile*. In place of Egypt the coerced adversary, Pliny offers an Egypt synchronized with his contemporary Rome and set within a network of pacified Roman landscapes. This circumscribed and cooperative land resembles Italy more than it does exotic and more recent frontiers in the *Natural History*, notably India. In retrospect, Pliny's Pharaonic Egypt in Book 36 is an echo of past glories (*Aegyptus ... antiquitatis gloriam*, *Nat.* 5.60), distant from both his quotidian Egypt and from post-69 Rome.[69] As such, the Plinian Egypt enriches imperial efforts for the material and moral restoration of Rome after 69.

Finally, the argument about Pliny's neutralizing of Egyptian exoticism fits with the conceptual mutability of Egypt in ancient thought. From Herodotus onward, the "gift of the Nile" accommodates a range of variances and similarities with the classical world and consequently plays across a wide spectrum of political ethics. The semantic malleability of Egypt is palpable in Augustan literature and art, where reproof of its Cleopatran monstrosity coexists with respect for its ancestral wisdom and fascination with its Nilotic utopias. Recent scholarship has illustrated the adaptation of Egypt to the expanding Roman self-identity, and this work has significantly nuanced the positive/negative reductionism of the Otherness model.[70] The Flavian period, whose birth as a provincial revolt blurred boundaries between ethnic categories, exposes the heuristic limitations of the self vs. other dichotomy and, in turn, opens new ways of thinking about Roman

---

[68] Beagon 2013, 101.
[69] On new frontiers, see *Nat.* 6.21–80 (India); *Nat.* 6.81–90 (Sri Lanka); *Nat.* 7.21–32 (*monstra* in India and Ethiopia); Parker 2008, 78–79, 218–19, 303. On the instability and ruination of monuments, cf. Chomse in this volume.
[70] Versluys 2010; Davies 2011; Gruen 2011, 76–114; Versluys 2012; Manolaraki 2013, 31–36; Leemreize 2014, 56–82; Versluys 2015; Merrills 2017, 234–39.

identity and alterity. In this light, Pliny's domestication of Egypt suggests one way in which Flavian authors gained purchase on evolving concepts of Roman selfhood, provincial foreignness, and borderland discovery after 69.

Darcy A. Krasne
Valerius Flaccus's Collapsible Universe: Patterns of Cosmic Disintegration in the *Argonautica*

The Argonauts' voyage from Greece to Colchis and back has frequently been viewed as a world-shaping voyage.[1] Their precise impact on the world, however, depends on its prior construction—namely, what particular structures have (or have not) already been fashioned by divine and natural forces. Whereas the Greeks seem typically to have understood the Argonauts as a positive force aiding in the completion of cosmic order, in Roman renditions of the voyage, where the Argo is often the first ship, the Argonauts' impact on the already-completed world and its divinely-predetermined organization is more often portrayed as transgressive, an event inherently bound up with the fall from divine grace that accompanies the end of the Golden Age and launches the strife-ridden Iron Age.[2]

From Catullus through Ovid, this connection between the advent of seafaring and the end of the Golden Age takes the spotlight. In the most recent iterations of the myth prior to Valerius Flaccus's *Argonautica*, however—specifically, the choruses of Seneca's *Medea* and a few brief allusions to the myth in Lucan's *Bellum Ciuile*—the shift from Golden Age to Iron Age is deemphasized, and the Argo's transgression of natural boundaries instead becomes the primary focus.[3] Here Nature herself, a Stoic parallel for Zeus, is responsible for the world's structure, and accordingly, the cosmic repercussions inherent in these late Julio-Claudian[4] reformulations of the myth far surpass the basic downward progression and disintegration of human morality which we find in earlier poets: the Argo's voyage

---

[1] Williams 1991, 22, 143–45, 185–210; Hunter 1993a, 162–69; Clare 2002; Barnes 2003; Thalmann 2011; Klooster 2014; etc. While this idea is not stated explicitly in ancient literature, the cited scholarship makes it clear that the implications are there. See Krasne 2014b on Valerius's response to Apollonius's aetiological construction of the cosmos.
[2] Recent and particularly pertinent studies include M. Davis 1989; Zissos 2006; Feeney 2007, 118–31; Fabre-Serris 2008, 17–93; Ripoll 2014; Seal 2014; Slaney 2014, 434–37. Clauss 2000 sees Apollonius's *Argonautica*, too, as more in line with these negative receptions of the Argo.
[3] See especially Sen. *Med.* 335–39, 373–79; Luc. 3.193–97, 6.400–1. On Valerius and Seneca's *Medea*, see in particular Grewe 1998 and Buckley 2014. Biondi 1984 analyzes the Argonautic choral odes of Seneca's *Medea*.
[4] Boyle 2014, xix, takes the play as "late Claudian or early Neronian," acknowledging that composition under an earlier *princeps* is conceivable but unlikely.

https://doi.org/10.1515/9783110585841-017

causes the very bindings of the cosmos to collapse, turning the constituent parts of the world against each other in a sort of cosmic civil war.[5]

In what follows, I examine Valerius's construction of the Argonautic cosmos in light of these Senecan and Lucanean precedents. I focus in particular on three major loci of cosmic instability or disarray in the epic, demonstrating how Valerius crafts his universe as inherently unstable, even prior to the Argo's boundary-transgressing voyage, and how his Jupiter controls and manipulates the instability of the cosmos to his own ends. While there are images of cosmic instability, fragmentation, and collapse sown throughout the epic,[6] in this paper, I primarily address innate and ongoing features of (or flaws in) the cosmic architecture and events of long duration. I also demonstrate that by incorporating suggestions of civil war into these same passages—either directly or intertextually—Valerius heightens the notion of cosmic fragmentation and instability, effectively reversing the direction of Lucan's pervasive analogy between civil war, boundary transgression, and cosmic dissolution. Here, the threatened integrity of the cosmos serves as the narrative baseline, on top of which glimpses of civil war refract and reinforce the concepts. In neither direction is the motif strictly Lucanean, however; civil war and cosmic dissolution are closely analogous in many ancient authors, as two levels of what Lowrie calls a "discursive progression of metaphorical homologies across spheres."[7] In Valerius, metaphor is further layered upon metaphor, as the pervasiveness of cosmic dissolution and the threat of its peren-

---

[5] Fyfe 1983, 86–91; Fabre-Serris 2008, 193–204. There are, of course, hints of this sentiment in earlier literature; cf. e.g., Feeney 2007, 123, on the "atmosphere of … chaotic instability" in Catullus 64 caused by the poem's multiplicity of "violated boundaries." In Lucan, moreover, this confluence of the ethical, the geographical, and the cosmic forms part of a broader program of analogizing cosmic dissolution to civil war, a project which furnished subsequent generations of poets with a rich stock of words and images to exploit in a similar vein (Masters 1992; Henderson 1998; Dinter 2012; Hardie 2013); Bessone in this volume (ch. 5) explores Statius's stylistic and rhetorical development of this Lucanean inheritance. On Gee's 2013 reading, Lucretius's fragmented use of Cicero's *Aratea* to polemically illustrate the cosmos's perpetual clash of atoms is another analogy between cosmic dissolution and civil strife.

[6] Valerius's overall construction of his cosmos is heavily indebted to the cosmic framework of the *Aeneid* that is so well revealed by Hardie 1986.

[7] Lowrie 2016, 334. Gee 2013, 110–47, explores the link in Roman literature between perversions of celestial nature and civil war. Throughout the tradition, standard depictions of cosmic dissolution and disarray largely boil down to the collapsing of permanent order into disorder. Two particularly pervasive tropes are the disarray of stars and constellations and the remixing of disparate elements (fire, water, earth, and air); such images represent a paradoxical alteration of the fixed *lex mundi* and a reversion to primordial chaos (see, e.g., Lapidge 1979, 368). Loupiac 1998, 28–35, gives a relatively extensive accounting of these images in the context of Lucan, and Hardie 1986 is seminal on Vergil.

nial recurrence, embellished by hints of civil war, in turn become a means of speaking implicitly to civil war's similar effects and inevitability.

Within the broader tradition, cosmic dissolution does not always automatically pose an unmitigated crisis. In particular, Stoic theory, which is highly influential for Valerius,[8] treats cosmic collapse as regular and divinely mandated: a periodic overbalancing of other elements by fire, called *ekpyrosis*, leads directly to *palingenesis*, the rebirth of the cosmos.[9] Thus, for the Stoics, the destruction of the cosmos is cyclic and occurs in normal order, allowing cleansing and regeneration,[10] and within the natural order of things is a largely positive occurrence. But Seneca's *Medea* and Lucan's *Bellum Ciuile*, Valerius's two most immediate sources for the Argonautic legend, both disrupt the expected Stoic system to indicate a cosmos in crisis. In these works, Stoic-seeming images of cosmic collapse are not positive and evidently do not automatically lead to regeneration, and the perverted Stoic imagery of both works, along with that of other Senecan tragedies, had a significant impact on Valerius's *Argonautica*.[11] Accordingly, while we

---

[8] Monaghan 2002 reads Valerius as straightforwardly Stoic; more recent scholarship, however, in line with current tendencies to recognize the multivalency of works and ideas, sees Valerius as engaging with but problematizing Stoic ideas (Ferenczi 2014; Zissos 2014; Krasne *forthcoming*), demonstrating that despite a sustained engagement with Stoic images and ideas, Valerius's Stoicism is anything but properly functioning. See Lapidge 1979 and Lapidge 1989 for a coherent study of Stoic cosmological language in Latin literature.

[9] For an overview and discussion of the theory (or theories), see Long 2006, 256–82, and Salles 2009; on the pre-Stoic background, see Hahm 1977, 185–99; on Zeus's role in *ekpyrosis* and *palingenesis*, see Bénatouïl 2009.

[10] The Empedoclean cosmogony is also cyclic (Inwood 2001, 42ff.), although differently (and uncertainly) so, shifting between the two poles of Love and Strife; however, while Empedoclean doctrine is also important for Valerius and his approach to cosmic dissolution (as I will argue in the larger project from which this chapter is developed), I omit it from this current study.

[11] See n. 8. I argue in Krasne 2014b that Valerius in fact constructs his Argonautic universe specifically to pave the way for the post-Argonautic cosmos of Seneca's *Medea*; Slaney 2009, 13–17, demonstrates how Valerius reshapes the late Julio-Claudian colonial and commercial anxieties of Lucan's and Seneca's narratives into a Flavian response. Loupiac 1998, 34, and Roche 2005 both observe that not once does Lucan suggest any sort of *palingenesis* that will result from the repeated images of *ekpyrosis* throughout his epic, whereas normal Stoic writing almost always mentions the effect hand-in-hand with the cause. Studies of the imagery of a deranged cosmos in Seneca's tragedies include the book-length, corpus-wide studies of Henry/Henry 1985, Rosenmeyer 1989, Schmitz 1993, and Gunderson 2015, as well as numerous shorter pieces and studies of individual plays. We can contrast the doctrine of *ekpyrosis* put into the mouth of the character Seneca in the anonymous drama *Octavia*; there, while *palingenesis* is explicitly the teleological thrust, the parallel it establishes with Nero's gross reconstruction of Rome in the form of his *domus aurea* following Rome's own ekpyrotic conflagration make rebirth just as problematic as a final destruction (cf. Van Noorden 2015, 268–82).

can assume that what appear to be Stoic underpinnings of Valerius's cosmos are likely to be precisely that, we should nonetheless not expect a straightforward Stoic worldview.

As I observed previously, while Roman authors tended to proactively align the Argo's voyage with the enactment of the shift from Golden Age to Iron Age, Seneca and Lucan had deemphasized that shift and instead focused on the Argo's penetration and erasure of boundaries, reversing the earlier actions of Nature and the divine. But while Valerius follows Seneca and Lucan in their reformulation of the Argo's crime, he also makes a significant alteration. Rather than simply turning the focus of the myth away from the Golden Age/Iron Age dichotomy, Valerius explicitly positions the Argo's voyage after the inception of the Iron Age, which appears to be in full swing long before the advent of seafaring.[12] To demonstrate the timeframe of his epic, he emphasizes various tropes of the Iron Age found in earlier poetry, including the advent of agriculture (V. Fl. 1.22–25, 1.67–70),[13] the departure of Astraea (V. Fl. 2.361–64),[14] the Gigantomachy (V. Fl. 2.16–

---

12 See also Seal 2014, 120–23, although cf. n. 17 (below). The parallels with other ancient literature in the next few footnotes are *exempli gratia*; for a complete catalogue of *loci* of Golden Age themes in ancient literature, see the *Conspectus rerum* in Gatz 1967, 229–32.

13 Cf. Catul. 64.397; Ov. *Met.* 1.123–24, 1.141. Agriculture straddles the line between positive and negative; see Feeney 2007, 114–15, on agriculture's inherent contradictions. Aratus allowed for agriculture in his Golden Age (see Gee 2013, 25, 40, 247 n. 17), and the old vision of the industrious Italian farmer falls into the Golden Age (Verg. *G.* 2.458–540), but the plow's imposition of order and divisions on the land (antithetical to the Golden Age's general communism and a symptom of mankind's domination of nature) is a hallmark of the Iron Age (e.g., Verg. *G.* 1.125–28, Verg. *Ecl.* 4.33, Ov. *Met.* 1.135–36 [on divisions of land and property in general]; cf. Stat. *Silu.* 4.3.40–41, with Newlands 2002, 284–325, on the ambiguities of the poem). Valerius, by using the verb *imbuit* (V. Fl. 1.70), analogizes Triptolemus's assault on the land to Catullus's formulation of the Argo's assault on the sea (*illa rudem cursu prima imbuit Amphitriten*, Catul. 64.11).

14 Cf. Ov. *Met.* 1.149–50; Verg. *Ecl.* 4.6; *G.* 2.458–74. Tim Stover has drawn my attention (*viva voce*) to the analogy that Valerius establishes between his Medea and Ovid's Astraea, through the anagrammatic phrase *caede madens* (V. Fl. 1.224–25, 5.453–54; also [not of Medea] V. Fl. 2.274–75, 6.415; cf. Ov. *Met.* 1.149–50). (See also now Houghton 2017 on this anagram.) As Ovid positions Astraea's departure at the end of the Iron Age (*Met.* 1.149–50), this if anything increases Valerius's emphasis on the Argo's belatedness, as it is sailing *so* late that we have had time to once more reach the end of the Hesiodic cycle on which Catullus focuses at the end of Catul. 64. This analogy may motivate Valerius's use of *uirgo altera* to describe Medea at the end of the epic (V. Fl. 8.463); see, e.g., Baldini Moscadi 2005, 95–96, 126–34, on the Senecan Medea as a lurid, Iron Age parallel for the Golden Age's *Virgo-Dike*. Gee 2013 argues for a Roman appropriation of the Aratean myth of Dike (which, unlike Hesiod's version, is cyclical) into a context of Rome's own myth and reality of an unceasing cycle of civil war; the multiple ways in which Valerius potentially engages with this tradition are vaster than the scope of this paper allows.

18),[15] humankind's neglect of the gods (V. Fl. 2.98–99),[16] and even internecine strife (intentions at V. Fl. 1.71–73, actuality at 2.220–30).[17] For Valerius, all of these occur prior to the construction of the Argo, and thus her voyage, rather than inaugurating the Iron Age, simply ties it off with a neat little bow.[18] In Valerius's Flavian epic, the first ship and first sea-voyage are so belated that human morality has begun to collapse long before the Argo can take the blame.[19]

This should not be taken to imply that the Argo's voyage is no longer a sinful affair for Valerius; she simply is not responsible for initiating humanity's moral decline. On the cosmic level, her voyage does still have seemingly negative repercussions, as she, like the traditional Roman Argo, travels through a carefully-structured world where seafaring was never meant to happen,[20] removing boundaries imposed by nature and the gods (e.g., V. Fl. 2.613–20), allowing disparate elements and peoples to mingle (V. Fl. 4.711–13), and enabling both *commercia* and foreign wars (V. Fl. 1.245–47, 1.544–46, 1.556–57). But there is, all the same, a significant change from the Roman tradition, in that the Argo's voyage now occurs under the auspices of Jupiter. Thus Valerius's Argo becomes something that she has not been since the Greek Argonautic tradition: the instrument of Jupiter's will.

---

15 Cf. Ov. *Met.* 1.151–55.
16 Cf. Hes. *Op.* 135–36 (on the Silver Age); see Gee 2013, 21–29, and Van Noorden 2015 on the Aratean collapse of the Hesiodic system of ages which becomes so influential for the Roman poets' "bipartite gold and then-everything-else pattern" (Gee 2013, 25).
17 Cf. Catul. 64.399–404; Ov. *Met.* 1.141–48. The passages I cite are those that, temporally speaking, occur prior to the Argo's launch. Here I reach a different conclusion from Seal 2014, 122–26, who proposes that "close examination of Valerius' poem ... shows that he follows these models in connecting navigation with the advent of violence between kin and friends, against a background in which other forms of violence are already common" (122); apart from this, however, I am largely sympathetic to his arguments.
18 This is in clear contradistinction to, for instance, the prelapsarian sailing of the Argo at Sen. *Med.* 309–39; *contra* Feeney 1991, 330, who asserts that the *Argonautica* "enacts the inauguration of Jupiter's own Iron Age with the sailing of the first ship."
19 See Seal 2014 for a salutary reminder that Valerius nowhere unquestionably designates the Argo as the first ship, although I am less skeptical than he that various references to the Argo's primacy ought to be taken at face value; and it is undeniable that we are at least meant to think of this tradition, only for it to be later complicated by the Lemnians' history of sailing and the Colchians' readily-deployable navy (see Thomas 1982 and O'Hara 2007, 33–44, among others, for the trope of bringing to light mutually-incompatible Argonautic traditions).
20 At least not according to Neptune and the Winds: V. Fl. 1.211–17, 598–607, 641–50 (with Zissos 2006). See Ganiban 2014 on the recalibration of Jupiter's dominant, post-Vergilian concerns within the epic, and see Krasne 2014b on Jupiter and Neptune's fundamentally incompatible views concerning the state of the world's completion.

It is paradoxical that Jupiter, a Stoic reflex of Nature and the god who ought to be the most concerned with maintaining cosmic order, who did in fact impose cosmic order when he came to power,[21] actually approves of and even sponsors the Argo's destabilizing voyage. But this is a Jupiter who is tired of the Golden Age's *otia* and rejoices at the coming of universal war and constant change (V. Fl. 1.498–560);[22] he boasts of his intentions to set the world spinning, entrenching the cosmos in a state of perpetual flux. Jupiter has, apparently, organized the cosmos simply to disorganize it according to his desires and his rules, and the visible traces of this process are what we shall examine in what follows.

1 The Sky is Falling

The first indication we receive of the cosmos's eternal instability comes at the very end of the epic's first book, as Valerius describes the organization of the infernal realms (V. Fl. 1.827–31):

> cardine sub nostro rebusque abscisa supernis
> Tartarei sedet aula patris, non illa ruenti
> accessura polo, uictam si uoluere molem
> [Iupiter et primae uelit omnia reddere massae   829b]
> ingenti iacet ore Chaos, quod pondere fessam   830
> materiem lapsumque queat consumere mundum.

829 uoluere ω] soluere *Heinsius (Liberman)* ‖ 829b C] om. γ ‖ 830 iacet γ] placet *Ehlers* iuuet *Sudhaus*

> Beneath our cardinal, and cut off from the things above, sits the palace of the Tartarean father. It would not come near the downward-rushing sky, even if … sent the conquered mass tumbling [and Jupiter should wish to return all things to their primordial stew]. Chaos

---

21 For instance, Jupiter puts a stop to the Winds' old habit of rendering sea and sky indistinct by appointing them a king (V. Fl. 1.586–93). Now, they can only cause temporary chaos within the strictures of Jupiter's rule.

22 He is not very different, in fact, from the Jupiter of Ovid's *Metamorphoses*—a Jupiter who is not a force of stability and order and who does not have the best interests of mankind at heart, but is rather a chaotic force of perpetual change (see Rhorer 1980, 304–5; Tarrant 2002; O'Hara 2007, 108–14). It is, however, possible that change (and all that goes along with it) is neither an evil nor a good for Valerius's Jupiter; rather, it just *is*. I explore below some ramifications of Jupiter's attitude; see Río Torres-Murciano 2010 and Ganiban 2014 for further assessment of Jupiter's priorities.

lies there with his huge mouth, which could engulf matter grown weary from its weight, and the collapsed cosmos.[23]

This entire passage is a notorious textual crux,[24] but no matter how we emend the text, Valerius significantly allows for the possibility that the entire cosmos (*mundus*)[25] could, at any moment, collapse and be subsumed by Chaos; he rephrases the concept three times in quick succession, with *ruenti polo* (V. Fl. 1.828–29), *uictam molem* (V. Fl. 1.829), and *lapsum mundum* (V. Fl. 1.831). This notion that the *mundus* could come tumbling down around our ears, back into the Chaos from which it arose, smacks of *ekpyrosis*, where the framework of the universe grows weaker and weaker as its bonds senesce until all things rush into ruin; in Valerius's text, the *fessa materies* of the *mundus* is particularly suggestive of this Stoic cosmic collapse. An additional line found in Carrio's manuscript (V. Fl. 1.829b) only adds to the same notion: Jupiter could decide on a whim to return the universe to its primordial stew, the *massa* from which—as Ovid tells us—all things arose.[26] The focus here narrows toward the moment of collapse, which Valerius recapitulates two or three times in the space of as many lines.[27] An array of intertexts heightens the notion of cosmic instability inherent in this short description of Chaos; in particular, the image of a collapsed cosmos rushing towards chaos finds precedent in Lucan's description of Rome's rush towards civil war and ruin (Luc. 1.67–81) and the *Octavia*-poet's vision of *ekpyrosis* prior to *palingenesis* ([Sen.] *Oct.* 391–94), the former underscored by the specific verbal echo of *sub pondere lapsus* (Luc. 1.71) in *pondere fessam | materiem lapsumque* ...

---

[23] All translations are my own. For the text of Valerius, I follow Liberman, except as noted; critical apparatus and sigla, where relevant, are adapted and simplified from Liberman.
[24] See Poortvliet 1991b, 38–40; Liberman 1997, 176–77 n. 164; Kleywegt 2005, *ad loc.*; Zissos 2008, *ad loc.* Emendations of various words have been proposed, while Schenkl 1871, 13, and Poortvliet detect a double recension, with 827–29 and 830–31 as alternate versions; for extended (and relatively balanced) discussions, see Kleywegt 1991, 152–55, and Zissos 2008, 413–14. Whatever the infelicities of the lines as they stand, I do not think that the parallelism of the two couplets need be a mark in their disfavor.
[25] See Puhvel 1976 on the semantic connections between *mundus* and κόσμος, as well as the application of *mundus* to the nether realm.
[26] *inque nouas abiit massa soluta domos* ("and the primordial stew, separated, went into new abodes," Ov. *Fast.* 1.108).
[27] This seeming redundancy may look to Lucan's repetitive tendencies (Mayer 1981, 13; Asso 2010a, 29; Dinter 2012, 138–39); the apparent paradox between *non illa ruenti | accessura polo* (V. Fl. 1.828–29) and *Chaos ... lapsum ... queat consumere mundum* (V. Fl. 1.830–31) only increases the feeling of instability. The idea of cosmic sublimity shading into cosmic collapse, in a post-Lucanean world, is well illustrated by Siobhan Chomse's chapter in this volume (ch. 18).

mundum (V. Fl. 1.830–31).[28] Accordingly, Valerius's description of cosmic collapse simultaneously evokes Rome's inexorable progression into civil war, as the *mundus*, like Lucan's Rome, comes tumbling down under its own weary *pondus*.[29]

This brief and striking glimpse of unmitigated apocalypse is all we get before Valerius shifts away from this hypothetical future to a brief geography of the underworld, including the twin gates through which dead souls pass into the realm of Hades (V. Fl. 1.832–35):

> hic geminae aeternum portae quarum altera dura
> semper lege patens populos regesque receptat;
> ast aliam temptare nefas et tendere contra:
> rara et sponte patet.   835

> Here there are, eternally, twin Gates, one of which, always lying open by harsh law, receives peoples and kings; but it is unspeakably wrong to try the other and strain against it. It opens rarely and of its own accord.

While this passage and its continuation at 1.846–50 have an undeniable debt to Vergil's descriptions of the exit from and entrance to the Underworld (Verg. *A.* 6.548–81, 893–96), its intertextual ancestry is more complex than that, and the

---

28 These passages are, in turn, indebted in particular to Lucr. 1.1052–113 (as a counterexample, since Lucretius distinguishes between the indestructible cosmos and the destructible world), Ov. *Met.* 2.295–300, and Sen. *Dial.* 6.26.5–6. It is likely that Valerius had these passages in mind, as well. The trajectory of downward collapse reverses the cosmogonic motion of separation visible in, for instance, Ov. *Fast.* 1.103–20 and Ov. *Met.* 1.7–56, to which the passages from Lucan and the *Octavia* also make allusion (in particular through the phrases *antiquum chaos* [Luc. 1.74] and *caecum chaos* [[Sen.] *Oct.* 391], as well as in their shared reference to the moon as Phoebe [Luc. 1.77, [Sen.] *Oct.* 389; cf. Ov. *Met.* 1.11]). Man. 1.125–70 is additionally a significant antecedent for Valerius, with a curious contrary parallel in Man. 1.168–70, where the poet affirms that due to the equal centripetal *cadendum* of the cosmos, its *medium et imum* cannot fall. (Hosius 1893, 393, notes Lucan's debt to these lines of Manilius at Luc. 9.469–71, in his description of the African sandstorm.) If we read *soluere molem* at V. Fl. 1.829, it echoes Man. 1.718, a hypothetical image of the Milky Way as revealing cracks in the universe; even without this reading, however, Manilius's entire discussion of the Milky Way stands behind this passage, as I plan to discuss elsewhere.

29 Further supported by Pluto's address to Fortune in Petronius's spoof of Lucan: *ecquid Romano sentis te pondere uictam, | nec posse ulterius perituram extollere molem?* ("Do you feel that you've been defeated by Rome's weight and that you're no longer able to lift off her soon-to-perish mass?" Petr. 120.82–83) On the traditional equation between civil war and societal bodies collapsing under their excessive weight, see especially Woodman 1988, 128–34. Rome and civil war are also implicit in the *Octavia* passage, where the image of *ekpyrosis* hints at Rome's own conflagration in both the literal flames of 64 CE (see Williams 1994, 190–91) and the metaphorical flames of civil war (Ginsberg 2017, 87); cf. n. 11.

parallels hint at not just cosmic collapse, but civil war. When Valerius describes his own subterranean *mundus*, here and elsewhere,[30] it clearly draws on not just his more immediate Vergilian model but also the Hesiodic original (Hes. *Th.* 721–814), not least through Valerius's allusion to the implicit Hesiodic etymology of χάος from χάσκω (gape, yawn) with <u>*ingenti* iacet *ore Chaos*</u> (V. Fl. 1.830).[31] Furthermore, the *geminae aeternum portae* which sit next to Chaos, one gate open and one gate shut, allude not only to Vergil's famous *gemi-nae Somni portae* (Verg. *A.* 6.893) but to his *geminae Belli portae* (Verg. *A.* 7.607)—the gates of the Temple of Janus (Verg. *A.* 7.610), the god formerly known as Chaos (Ov. *Fast.* 1.103–12). By collapsing the two sets of twin gates into one, Valerius problematizes their open/shut duality; the ever-open nature of the infernal *ge-minae portae* is a *topos*, but the ever-open nature of Janus's *geminae portae* is traditionally a problem.[32] At Verg. *A.* 7.620–22, moreover, Juno had burst open the gates of war, starting the quasi-civil war between Trojans and Latins and taking on the role of Ennius's Discordia (Enn. *Ann.* 225–26 Sk.), a goddess who, being generally associated with strife both civil and elemental, was not dissimilar to the post-Hesiodic Chaos (cf. Enn. *Ann.* 220–21 Sk.).[33] By doubling the referent of his *geminae portae* allusion, therefore, Valerius suggestively imports multiple versions of strife into his Underworld.

This connection between civil strife and Chaos is augmented just a hundred lines later (V. Fl. 2.82–91):

> tempore quo primum fremitus insurgere opertos
> caelicolum et regni sensit nouitate tumentes
> Iuppiter aetheriae nec stare silentia pacis,
> Iunonem uolucri primam suspendit Olympo,   85
> <u>horrendum chaos</u> ostendens <u>poenasque barathri</u>.

---

30 Most clearly in a simile at V. Fl. 3.224–28.
31 See West 1966, 192–93 *ad* Hes. *Th.* 116, on the etymology. Zissos 2008, *ad loc.*, sees Valerius's use of the term *Chaos* here as indebted to Ovid's metonymic use of *Chaos* for *infera* at *Met.* 10.30, but I would defend a more literal and Hesiodic interpretation of Chaos. Also relevant is Ovid's connection of Chaos with Janus, who professes to have charge over the *mundus* and the *ius cardinis* (Ov. *Fast.* 1.119–20); this could explain the somewhat unusual use of *cardo* at V. Fl. 1.827, although the discussion of the four *cardines* at Man. 2.778ff. may also be pertinent (see Kleywegt 1991, 151, and Zissos 2008, *ad loc.*, on the uncertainty of Valerius's precise meaning). Sen. *Her. F.* 662–79 may be an additional source for the description of the Underworld, here.
32 See Nelis 2014, ¶¶14–22, on further layers of intertextuality that accrue to this passage up through Lucan, noting the tradition that the gates "are either opened or closed."
33 For Chaos as a state of elemental confusion and strife, see Ov. *Met.* 1.5–21 and *Fast.* 1.103–14, among others, with recent discussion at Ham 2013, 223–36; Ham 2013, 453–56, also re-assesses the association between Ennius's Discordia and Empedocles' Neikos.

> mox etiam pauidae temptantem uincula matris
> soluere praerupti Vulcanum uertice caeli
> deuoluit; ruit ille polo noctemque diemque
> turbinis in morem, Lemni cum litore tandem   90
> insonuit.

> When Jupiter first sensed the hidden rumblings of the sky-dwellers emerging, and their rage at the newness of his rule, and that the silence of ethereal peace was not staying put, he hung Juno first from swift Olympus, showing her <u>horrible chaos and the punishments of the abyss</u>. Soon, also, he hurled Vulcan, trying to loosen the chains of his fearful mother, from the sheer peak of the sky. He rushed down from the pole, night and day, in the fashion of a whirlwind, when at last he thudded onto the shore of Lemnos.

Here Valerius recalls the Homeric tale of Jupiter dangling Juno from Olympus (*Il.* 15.18–30), but rather than making it a punishment for her persecution of Hercules, he connects it with an insurrection of the gods;[34] and indeed, the specific language and situation also recall an earlier passage of the *Iliad* (8.5–27), where Zeus threatens to send into Tartaros any god who disobeys him. There, Zeus also briefly sketches out the organization of the cosmos, with Tartaros as the deep βέρεθρον far below the earth (Hom. *Il.* 8.13–16):

> ἤ μιν ἑλὼν ῥίψω <u>ἐς Τάρταρον ἠερόεντα</u>
> τῆλε μάλ', ἧχι βάθιστον ὑπὸ χθονός ἐστι <u>βέρεθρον</u>,
> ἔνθα σιδήρειαί τε πύλαι καὶ χάλκεος οὐδός,   15
> τόσσον ἔνερθ' Ἀΐδεω ὅσον οὐρανός ἐστ' ἀπὸ γαίης·

> Or having taken him, I shall cast him <u>into misty Tartaros</u>, very far off, where there is the deepest <u>abyss</u> below the earth, and there are iron gates there, and a bronze threshold, so far below Hades as the sky is from the earth.

Valerius's *barathri* (V. Fl. 2.86) picks up on the Homeric βέρεθρον; it seems that Chaos, which could be synonymous with Tartaros for Roman poets,[35] is the place where divine civil strife is punished. Feeney also argues convincingly for allegory in the Valerius passage, applying to it the Stoic reading of Hera's suspension in the *Iliad*, where Jupiter was the lofty *aether* and Juno the *aer* suspended below

---

34 Yasumura 2011, 39–57, suggests an original connection between the *Iliad*'s mention of Hera's persecution of Heracles and a hypothesized lost tradition in which she sided with the Giants in the Gigantomachy in an effort to overthrow Zeus. Even without accepting the existence of such a version, the connection between the Homeric chaining of Hera, the fall of Hephaestus, and an insurrection of the gods is demonstrated by Lang 1983, 147–55, and developed in Yasumura 2011.
35 Tarrant 2002, 359–60; Zissos 2008, 413.

it;[36] and I propose that this scene can additionally be interpreted with a view to an additional aspect of the allegory's cosmology, which took Homer's unbreakable chain (δεσμὸν ... ἄρρηκτον, *Il.* 15.19–20) as the force that binds the universe. In particular, *uincula soluere* (V. Fl. 2.87–88) is strongly Stoic language when understood in a cosmological context, *uinculum* translating the Greek Stoic terms δεσμός and πνεῦμα,[37] while *soluere* translates Greek λύω, namely what happens to these binding forces at *ekpyrosis*, resulting in cosmic dissolution.[38] Thus Jupiter, effectively, punishes Vulcan for attempting to destroy cosmic order by loosing the cosmic bindings.[39] However, given that Jupiter, who champions the Argonauts' voyage, apparently has no compunctions about causing other cosmic dislocations, it seems as though Vulcan's real crime is either the inappropriate timing of his attempt or that he, rather than Jupiter, was the one attempting to call the shots. Jupiter appears to be less concerned here about preserving cosmic stability than about preserving his own stability as ruler, an impression which only grows as the epic proceeds.

2 Perpetual Motion Machine

Let us turn now to the Clashing Rocks episode, a second major section of the epic which I see as providing evidence of the cosmos's underlying instability. Our first encounter with the Clashing Rocks comes in the form of a prophecy, when Phineus describes the danger awaiting the Argonauts in terms that combine programmatic civil war terminology with equally clear images of cosmic dissolution (V. Fl. 4.561–66, 574–76, 582–83):

---

[36] Feeney 1991, 329; on the Homeric allegory, see Buffière 1956, 115–17. I address other aspects of allegory visible here and in the following episodes in the larger project out of which this chapter arises.

[37] See Lapidge 1979, *passim*; for other Latin translations of Stoic terminology, see Lapidge 1979 and Lapidge 1989.

[38] Lapidge 1979, 357: "if this binding force were released, the universe would dissolve." Additional places in Valerius's epic where the language of loosened, shaken, and broken chains holds the potential for resonant Stoic undertones are as follows: *uincla Iouis fractoque trahens adamante catenas* (V. Fl. 3.225), *uincula soluere* (V. Fl. 3.435), *uitalia ... uincula ... soluit* (V. Fl. 4.309–11), *uincula mundi ima labant* (V. Fl. 4.564–65), *cunctaeque tremunt ... catenae* (V. Fl. 7.370), *ruperunt uincula* (V. Fl. 7.569), *nexus ac uincula dissipat* (V. Fl. 7.626).

[39] Vulcan's role here may also be relevant to his metonymic existence as the element of fire—namely the very element that will, in the event of *ekpyrosis*, separate out from the moist and overwhelm the cosmic substance.

> hinc iter ad Ponti caput errantesque per altum
> Cyaneas. <u>furor</u> his medio <u>concurrere</u> ponto
> necdum ullas uidere rates; <u>sua</u> comminus actae
> saxa premunt cautesque <u>suas</u>. cum uincula mundi
> ima labant, tremere ecce solum, tremere ipsa repente
> tecta uides: illae redeunt, illae aequore <u>certant</u>.   566
> ...
> uix repetunt primae celeres confinia terrae
> iamque alio clamore ruunt omnisque tenetur   575
> pontus et <u>infestis</u> anceps cum montibus errat.
> ...
>   ... 'Pontum penetrauerit ulla
> cum ratis et <u>rabidi</u> steterint in gurgite montes ...'

564 cum ... labant ω] ceu ... labent *Heinsius (Liberman)* || 566 certant ω] ructant *Taylor-Briggs*

From here, your journey is to the head of the Black Sea and the Cyanean Rocks, wandering across the deep. Their <u>madness</u> is <u>to run together</u> over the midst of the sea, and not yet have they seen any ships: driven to close quarters, they press <u>their own</u> rocks and <u>their own</u> cliffs, when the chains of the cosmos quake at their depths; lo, you see the earth tremble, you see the very firmament[40] suddenly tremble. They return, <u>they fight</u> over the water. ... Scarcely do they swiftly return to the outermost edge of the land when they rush back with another clamor, and the whole sea is held fast and heaves to and fro with the <u>hostile</u> mountains. ... [A voice foretold to me:] "When any ship will have penetrated the Black Sea and the <u>maddened</u> mountains stand fast in the tide ..."

The first word of Phineus's description of the Rocks is *furor*, a key term of civil war from Horace onwards.[41] Like its equivalents *rabies* and *insania*, *furor* is not synonymous with civil war but equates rather with the madness that leads to it;[42]

---

[40] While the standard interpretation of *tecta* is "houses," understanding *tecta* here as a reference to the celestial firmament (i.e., the "roof" of the cosmos) parallels *solum* much better. Although this meaning of *tectum* is largely unparalleled, it is a logical extension of the usual meaning, and a few precedents may be found (Lucr. 2.1110–11; Hor. *S.* 1.5.103; Ov. *Met.* 2.136; Man. 2.118). This is not to deny the very relevant influence on Valerius here of several descriptions in natural philosophical writings of houses (*tecta*) shaking during earthquakes, for which see below, but the potential cosmic dimension cannot be ignored, and *tecta* can serve a double function.

[41] Hor. *Epod.* 7.13; on the pervasive linguistic codification and influence of Horace's *Epode* 7 in Flavian literature, see the introduction to this volume (p. 9). *Furor* also can be excluded from a more generally bellicose interpretation (cf. Jal 1963, 421 n. 9: "Il est rare de voir le mot appliqué à la guerre étrangère").

[42] On the equivalency between *furor*, *rabies*, and *insania*, see Jal 1963, 421–24; see also Horsfall 2000, 310, on Verg. *A.* 7.461.

in the *Aeneid*, Vergil imprisons *Furor* as symbolic of the notion that Augustus had brought civil war to an end, while Lucan makes *furor* a catchword of civil war's criminality.

Here, *furor* compels the Rocks to *concurrere*, a verb often used of combatants in civil war,[43] and when they meet, the repeated reflexive adjectives *sua* and *suas* insist on the self-directed nature of their aggression.[44] Subsequently, their perpetual motion is elevated to explicit strife with *certant*, another arguably programmatic term of Lucanean civil war,[45] and they are also generally hostile (*infestis*), as well as *rabidi*. Later, when the Argonauts actually approach the Rocks, the Rocks are *insana* (V. Fl. 4.641), which like *rabidi* reiterates the madness that drives civil war.[46] Two more key-words of civil war, *nefas* (V. Fl. 4.692)[47] and *ruina* (V. Fl. 4.695),[48] accompany the Clashing Rocks' final closure on the tip of the Argo's stern.[49]

Additional imagery of cosmic disarray and dissolution in this extended sequence parallels and reinforces the Rocks' civil war. When the Argonauts first see the Rocks, they appear to be a part of the starry pole fallen into the sea (*saxa neque illa uiris, sed praecipitata profundo | siderei pars uisa poli*, V. Fl. 4.642–43), which echoes Lucan's image of the stars falling into the sea (*ignea pontum | astra*

---

[43] Cf. Luc. 7.196: *inpia concurrunt Pompei et Caesaris arma* ("The impious weapons of Pompey and Caesar clash"). The verb is often used of attacking armies, whether civil or foreign, and of gladiators (see Coleman 2006, 226, on Mart. *Sp.* 31.5), which scholars have seen as a prime thematic image of Lucan's *Bellum Ciuile* (e.g., Ahl 1976, 82–115; Martindale 1981, 74, 79 n. 16); see also Masters 1992, 34–42. Lyne 1974, 60, observes that the only two occurrences of *concurrere* in the *Georgics* refer to the strife of the Winds and to civil war; Vergil's description of the Battle of Actium on Aeneas's shield likens the massive warships to *montis concurrere montibus altos* ("tall mountains clash[ing] with mountains," Verg. *A.* 8.692), already implicitly suggestive of civil war and perhaps also meant to evoke the Symplegades (cf. Masters 1992, 39). Valerius uses *concurrere* three other times of the Clashing Rocks' motion, at V. Fl. 1.59, 1.630, and 8.196.
[44] See Krasne 2014a on other ways in which the Rocks embody civil strife and self-directed aggression.
[45] *certatum* appears in Lucan's proem (Luc. 1.5). Taylor-Briggs 1995 proposes emending *certant* to *ructant*, however.
[46] Perhaps tellingly, the wind Boreas had earlier applied *insana* to the Argo herself, for her rash temerity in breaching the waters (V. Fl. 1.605).
[47] Ganiban 2007, 34: "During the Triumviral period and the beginning of the Augustan age, *nefas* and the related word *scelus* become important synonyms for civil war."
[48] Masters 1992, 157: "a favourite civil-war word to describe various grades of catastrophe."
[49] In Krasne 2014a, I argue that the Rocks' partial destruction of the Argo's stern is an event parallel to civil war and that the Argo's eventual catasterism, which is inverted, also implicitly embodies stellar disarray, a typical sign of cosmic disorder.

petent, Luc. 1.75–76) and suggests cosmic collapse.[50] It also rearranges the cosmos on a more fundamental level, by inverting the expected arrangement wherein the sky and stars are above the ocean, not in it.[51] This picks up on two tropes of cosmic disarray, the displacement of the stars and the mixing of elements.[52]

Furthermore, Phineus's description of the Rocks' concussions (V. Fl. 4.563–66), quoted previously, makes clear their threat to cosmic order, as he employs explicit Stoic terminology similar to that with which Lucan had depicted cosmic dissolution and Rome's collapse (Luc. 1.79–81). One phrase in particular, *uincula mundi ima labant* (V. Fl. 4.564–65), is loaded with cosmological import; as we have seen, *uinculum* is an important Stoic term, and *mundus* is parallel to κόσμος.[53] Every time that the Clashing Rocks clash together, therefore, cosmic dissolution is threatened, as the foundations of the *uincula mundi* totter and set off seismic tremors that pick up on Lucretius's, Seneca's, and the *Aetna*-poet's natural-philosophical descriptions of cosmos-threatening earthquakes:[54]

Lucr. 6.546–49, 568–74:

quippe cadunt toti montes magnoque repente
concussu late disserpunt inde tremores.
et merito, quoniam plaustris concussa tremescunt
tecta uiam propter non magno pondere tota,

...

quod nisi respirent uenti, uis nulla refrenet
res neque ab exitio possit reprehendere euntis.
nunc quia respirant alternis inque grauescunt   570
et quasi collecti redeunt ceduntque repulsi,
saepius hanc ob rem minitatur terra ruinas
quam facit; inclinatur enim retroque recellit
et recipit prolapsa suas in pondera sedis.

Indeed, whole mountains fall, and therefrom tremors suddenly ripple far and wide at the great concussion. And rightly so, since entire houses next to a road tremble, shaken by wagons of no great weight. ... But if the winds were not to pause for breath, no force would rein

---

[50] Gee 2013, 127, sees Lucan's image as one of all the stars becoming disorderly planets, on an Aratean model; this may be underscored by my reading (Krasne 2014a, 43–44) of the sunken stars as recalling Aratus's epic.
[51] See also Slaney 2014, 445.
[52] See n. 7.
[53] See n. 25.
[54] See also the sources on earthquakes collected by Seewald 2008, 262–63 *ad* Luc. 9.466–71.

things back, nor could it keep things in motion back from destruction; now, because in alternation they pause for breath and increase in force, and they make a sally as if marshalled and withdraw as if driven back, on account of this the earth threatens collapse more frequently than it actually happens; for it tilts in and recoils backwards and, having swayed forward, recovers a stable and solid position.

Sen. *Nat.* 6.1.4–5:[55]

> quid enim cuiquam satis tutum uideri potest, si mundus ipse concutitur et partes eius solidissimae labant? si quod unum immobile est in illo fixumque, ut cuncta in se intenta sustineat, fluctuatur; si quod proprium habet terra perdidit, stare, ubi tandem resident metus nostri? … consternatio omnium est, ubi tecta crepuerunt et ruina signum dedit. … quam latebram prospicimus, quod auxilium, si orbis ipse ruinas agitat, si hoc quod nos tuetur ac sustinet, supra quod urbes sitae sunt, quod fundamentum quidam mundi esse dixerunt, discedit ac titubat?

> For what is able to seem secure enough to anyone, if the cosmos itself is shaken and its most solid parts quake? If that part of it which is unified, immovable, and fixed, so that it holds steady all things directed towards itself, should waver; if the earth has lost that which it holds as its core property—standing still—when at last will our fears subside? … There is consternation for all, when houses have rattled and collapse has been heralded. … What hiding place do we see, what aid, if the world itself sets collapse in motion, if that which protects and supports us, above which cities have been placed, that which some have called the foundation of the cosmos, separates and totters?

Aetna 171–74:

> hinc uenti rabies, hinc saeuo quassa citatu
> fundamenta soli trepidant urbesque caducae.
> inde, neque est aliud, si fas est credere, mundo
> uenturam antiqui faciem, ueracius omen.

> Hence the wind's madness, hence the foundations of the earth, shaken by the savage onslaught, tremble, as do collapsible cities. Then there is no other truer omen, if it is right to believe it, that the world will regain its ancient appearance.

All three authors transition rapidly between the earthquake itself and the closely-related potential for universal destruction;[56] their precise language describing the shaking and the imminent collapse is clearly influential for Valerius. But Seneca and Lucretius in particular demonstrate that instability is not itself an automatic cause for concern, Seneca observing a few paragraphs later that nature conceived

---

[55] Cf. also Sen. *Nat.* 6.22.
[56] Lucretius loosely distinguishes between the *mundus*, which is destructible, and the *summa summarum*, which is not; on the complexities of his terminology in this matter, see Fowler 2002, 154–56.

of nothing as unmovable (*nihil ita ut immobile esset natura concepit*, *Nat.* 6.1.12), and Lucretius noting that the earth threatens to collapse more frequently than it actually does so (Lucr. 6.572–73). However, Seneca also acknowledges here that a characteristic property of the earth is *stare*, to stand still (Sen. *Nat.* 6.1.4). Normally, therefore, the cosmos weakens and dissolves only periodically,[57] since otherwise the so-called cosmos would be merely a temporary departure from chaos; the Rocks' perpetual and unceasing threat of dissolution is, therefore, troubling. Alternatively, a different view of the problem is provided by the Lucretian passage, where he conversely emphasizes the *security* provided by the constant motion, which is caused by the alternating "breathing" of winds (Lucr. 6.568–74).[58] On this model, it is the Rocks' eventual cessation that becomes problematic, albeit differently so, as it is the winds' continued alternating inhalations and exhalations that allow the cosmos to persist: were motion to stop (whether the motion of the winds or the motion of atoms), all would come tumbling down.

In Valerius's epic, the interminable civil-war-like conflict of the Clashing Rocks is part of the divinely-decreed construction of the completed cosmos, being all that divides East from West; but it is Jupiter who oversees its cessation. Therefore, paradoxically, this perpetual (rather than occasional) threat of cosmic disorder (on a Senecan reading) is itself a part of cosmic order,[59] suggesting that Valerius's Argonautic cosmos resembles what Gee describes as "a universe [that is] ethically and cosmologically defective under the pressure of civil war."[60] The paradox grows: the Argonauts, in the mode of their Greek counterparts, help to impose stability on the cosmos by passing through the Clashing Rocks and putting a stop to their eternal civil war, but they simultaneously impose disorder on the cosmos by bursting through the most famously impenetrable *discrimen* of all, allowing East and West to mix (and, on a Lucretian reading, increasing the

---

[57] The rest of the time it "remains stable and secure" (Lapidge 1989, 1396). Even earthquakes follow the same periodic law. Earthquakes are one sign of *ekpyrosis* at Sen. *Dial.* 6.26.6.
[58] O'Brien 1969, 124–26, argues for a world breath as part of Empedocles' cosmic cycle; if correct, that concept may stand behind Lucretius's image here.
[59] The cosmic import is more or less the same regardless of whether we follow the MSS reading of *cum* or adopt Heinsius's generally accepted emendation of *ceu*, although *cum* makes the tottering of the *uincula mundi* less notional and more concrete (appropriate in a Stoic context); however, Murgatroyd accepts the grammatical argument of Taylor-Briggs 1995 for retaining *cum* as a *cum inversum*.
[60] Gee 2013, 145.

likelihood of collapse),[61] as instability and fixity become inverted. The destruction of *discrimina* and the resultant cosmic disarray are, moreover, the precise crime that Seneca and Lucan had laid at the Argo's feet:[62] Valerius is pre-writing the worlds of his predecessors.[63]

3 Sing Down the Moon

The third major threat to cosmic order that exists in the epic is the sorcery of Medea. As is standard for witches, Medea's powers threaten the ordinary workings of the universe, destabilizing the very features which traditionally mark out order, such as the stars and sun (V. Fl. 6.439–48):[64]

>   sola animo Medea subit, mens omnis in una
>   uirgine, <u>nocturnis qua nulla potentior aris</u>.   440
>   illius ad †fremitus† sparsosque per aera sucos
>   <u>sidera fixa pauent</u> et <u>aui stupet orbita Solis</u>.
>   <u>mutat agros fluuiumque uias</u>, †suus† alligat ignis
>   †cuncta soport recolit fessos aetate parentes
>   datque alias <u>sine lege</u> colus. hanc maxima Circe   445
>   terrificis mirata modis, hanc aduena Phrixus
>   quamuis Atracio lunam spumare ueneno
>   sciret et <u>Haemoniis agitari cantibus umbras</u>.

439 mens ω] spes *Bury (Liberman)* || 441 ad fremitus *C*] ad fretus *L (Liberman)* alia alii || 443 ignis *L*] igni *C* illi *Zinzerling (Liberman)*

Medea alone enters [Juno's] thoughts, all her mind is on the one virgin, <u>than whom none is more powerful at the nocturnal altars</u>. At her †roars†[65] and juices sprinkled through the air, <u>the fixed stars grow pale</u>, and <u>the orbit of her grandfather Sun is dumbfounded</u>. <u>She transforms fields and rivers' courses</u>. †Her† fire binds †all things; sleep† tends to parents, wearied

---

[61] See Krasne 2014b, 561–62, on the opposite Greek and Roman implications of the Argonauts' stilling of the Clashing Rocks. For an alternative contemporary perspective, that the ocean was an invading force disrupting the land's (now lands') unity, cf. Plin. *Nat.* 6.1–2.
[62] See n. 3.
[63] See n. 11.
[64] Cf. Man. 2.46–52 and Luc. 6.461–506, esp. 6.499–500. See, e.g., Lapidge 1979, 368–69, and Gordon 1987 on the connections between witches' activity and cosmic disarray.
[65] Liberman prints the reading of *L* for want of a better alternative but notes that the archetype might have "less probably" had Carrio's *fremitus*. If *fremitus* is correct, Medea's powers of cosmic disarray can be linked with the chaos of the pre-Jovian Winds, who characteristically roar (see, e.g., Barchiesi 2005, 186–87; Hardie 2012, 70, 100, 161).

with age, and grants additional spindles <u>without law</u>. Greatest Circe of the terrifying tunes marveled at her; so did the foreigner Phrixus, though he knew the moon to foam with Atracian poison[66] and shades to be disturbed by Haemonian incantations.

Regardless of any difficulties of interpretation due to textual uncertainties,[67] it is clear that Medea's sorcerous activities are described exclusively and comprehensively in these terms: she disturbs celestial nature (*sidera*; *orbita Solis*), she alters terrestrial nature (*agros fluuiumque*), and she interferes with human nature (*sine lege colus*).[68] The phrase *sine lege*, in particular, underscores the acosmia of her magic.[69] Additionally, Valerius's Medea is not just any witch—she is the most powerful witch in the world (*nocturnis qua nulla potentior aris*, 6.440). Even her aunt Circe is in awe of her,[70] as was Phrixus, who came from Thessaly and

---

66 There are three possible ways to understand *Atracio ... spumare ueneno* (see n. 72 for the wider significance of the ambiguity): either the moon foams *because of* Atracian poison (taking *ueneno* as a causal ablative; this is the preference of Fucecchi 1997, 99; cf. also Spaltenstein 2005, 133); or the foam of the moon is *itself* a poison used in Thessaly (taking *ueneno* as an almost pleonastic ablative of specification; this is suggested by the standard interpretation of Luc. 6.669, for which see n. 72, and is the preference of Baier 2001, 207, who still connects the foaming with "Zaubersprüchen," and Bicknell 1984, 68); or moon-foam is just one ingredient in a compounded Atracian poison (taking *ueneno* as a dative; for this cf. Vulcan's use of moon-foam as an ingredient in his "witch's brew" necklace at Stat. *Theb.* 2.284).
67 Although the text of *suus ... recolit* (V. Fl. 6.443–44) is inscrutable and numerous emendations have been proposed, the phrase *alligat ignis* is pleasing for its pertinence to Stoic ideas (or its reversal of them, if *ignis* is accusative or even genitive, as in the comparable ἀκαμάτοιο πυρὸς μειλίσσετ' ἀυτμήν ["she soothes the blast of weariless fire," A.R. 3.531]; Carrio's manuscript has *igni*, however). I find none of the numerous proposed emendations particularly convincing; accordingly I obelize it, *pace* Liberman. See also Schimann 1997, 121–22 n. 65, for consideration of various readings and their implications.
68 Valerius also emphasizes Medea's tripartite control over the celestial, terrestrial, and infernal regions at V. Fl. 7.329–30. Several of the activities that Valerius attributes to Medea find parallels in future events from her own story: Seneca has her bring a number of constellations down from the sky in order to poison Glauce's gift (*Med.* 694–770), and she famously restores Aeson (and others) to youth and tricks Pelias's daughters into murdering him with the same promise (Ov. *Met.* 7.179–349). Fucecchi 2006a, *ad loc.*, also draws a parallel between *mutat agros fluuiumque uias* and Hypsipyle's description of Medea's powers at Ov. *Ep.* 6.87–88. While there is a good deal of overlap too with A.R. 3.531–33 in how Medea's powers are described, as well as with Ov. *Met.* 7.199–209 (of which this passage reads as a distorted summary), Medea's actions in Valerius seem even more sinister. Unlike the Medea of most accounts, Valerius's Medea needs no instigation from Jason to act like her future self.
69 Davis 1980, 77, usefully compares the *certa ... lege* (Man. 1.26) of Manilius's song (and, we might add, his stars).
70 Paradoxically, Circe is called *maxima* (V. Fl. 6.445), although some commentators see *terrificis modis* (V. Fl. 6.446) as an ablative of limitation.

therefore should have been perfectly *au fait* with sorcery. I propose that such an emphasis on Medea's extraordinary power, together with the two specific types of Thessalian magic mentioned at V. Fl. 6.447–48, is meant to help draw Lucan's characterization of his super-witch Erictho into the text here.[71]

While Thessalian witches share many powers throughout the tradition, Lucan is our first source for two elements that are subsequently incorporated into the *topos*: the collection of "moon foam" after drawing down the moon (Luc. 6.500–5)[72] and the use of actual corpses in necromantic ritual (Luc. 6.619–825).[73] The former is characterized as a typical activity of witches which Erictho eschews (Luc. 6.506–9), while the latter is her way of outdoing the standard practice of merely summoning incorporeal shades (Luc. 6.621–23); in both cases, the extraordinary nature of Erictho's character and power can be defined by her rejection of the norm as not wicked enough (*hos scelerum ritus ... damnarat nimiae pietatis Erichtho | inque nouos ritus pollutam duxerat artem*, "Erichtho had disparaged these criminal rituals as too pious and had directed her polluted art to unprecedented rituals," Luc. 6.506–8).[74] Valerius's Medea, in surpassing these same

---

[71] On Medea's larger debt to Erictho, see especially Baldini Moscadi 2005, 135–62.

[72] It has been variously assumed, in the absence of certainty (cf. Tupet 1976, 101), that the moon's production of foam (*spuma*) is simply a reference to the moon as the source of dew (e.g., Roscher 1890, 86; Fahz 1904, 47; similarly, Spaltenstein 2005, 133, tentatively draws a connection with the moon's inherent moisture); that the *spuma* is a poison or other substance naturally produced by the moon (e.g., Hill 1973, 236; Bicknell 1984, 68; Ogden 2002, 197; Baldini Moscadi 2005, 254); or that the moon's foaming is the result of magical activity (see n. 66). Elsewhere, the foam is explicitly mentioned as such only at Stat. *Theb.* 2.284 and Apul. *Met.* 1.3, as well as in Servius Danielis's note on Verg. *A.* 4.513, where he cites Lucan's *despumet in herbas* (Luc. 6.506); Ovid may refer to Medea gathering frost from the moon (*Met.* 7.268; however, see Baldini Moscadi 2005, 252–58), while Valerius's Medea collects an unspecified substance (V. Fl. 7.330). Lucan's reference to *uirus lunare* at Luc. 6.669 is often assumed to refer to the same substance (e.g., Tupet 1976, 101; Gordon 1987, 239; Ogden 2002, 237; Phillips 2002, 383; Baldini Moscadi 2005, 254–55), an assumption that seems first to occur in medieval commentaries on Lucan that derive from the sixth-century work of Vacca (see *TLL* 7.2.1838.29–33), although the gloss was undoubtedly influenced by Statius's combinatorial *spumis lunaribus* (*Theb.* 2.284).

[73] Lucan, although heavily indebted to earlier necromantic episodes such as Hor. *S.* 1.8 and Sen. *Oed.* 548–658, significantly amplifies the necromantic *topos*, in which shades were evoked with a libation of blood and a chant (see Vessey 1973, 242). Erictho's gruesome and hands-on reanimation of a corpse stands out so vividly against earlier scenes of blood-in-a-ditch-style necromancy that it irrevocably alters the trope of necromantic activity. For the tradition, see Ogden 2002, 123–25, 179–209.

[74] Gordon 1987, 238–40, notes that "in Lucan's representation, 'ordinary' magic consists of three types of intervention, each improper"—the erotic, the meteorological, and the drawing down of the moon—whereas Erictho is exclusively "centred upon death and corpses." Ambühl

"ordinary" Thessalian skills, both of which seem to point explicitly back to Lucan,[75] is thus suggestive of the trailblazing Erictho.

The recollection of Erictho throws open the windows of allusion, showing us the Thessalian center of Lucan's world of unremitting strife, where witchcraft and civil war feed each other's frenzy and hasten cosmic ruin, regardless of the gods' desires. In fact, according to Lucan, even "ordinary" witches have more power over the workings of the cosmos than Jupiter does (Luc. 6.462–67):

> ... legi non paruit aether,
> torpuit et praeceps audito carmine mundus,
> axibus et rapidis inpulsos Iuppiter urguens
> miratur non ire polos. nunc omnia conplent   465
> imbribus et calido praeducunt nubila Phoebo,
> et tonat ignaro caelum Ioue.

> The aether did not obey its law; the forward-rushing cosmos, too, grew sluggish as it heard [the witches'] song, and Jupiter, pushing on the poles impelled on the swift axles, marvels that they are not moving. Now they fill all things with rain and bring clouds in front of fiery Phoebus, and the sky thunders unbeknownst to Jupiter.

The perversions of natural law exercised here by Lucan's witches erase the fine line between the sublime and cosmic catastrophe.[76] While the precise balance of power between Medea's magic and Jupiter's cosmic regency is, by contrast, left ambiguous within the *Argonautica*,[77] in looking back at Erictho, we glimpse not only her vertiginous sublimity, but also the sorceress who in turn stands behind Erictho:[78] Medea's own future self, the all-powerful sorceress of Senecan (and perhaps Ovidian) tragedy, likewise a catastrophic force of natural perversions.[79]

2016, 307, likewise observes that the already-extraordinary capabilities of Lucan's witches serve to throw Erictho's even greater talents into stark relief.

75 In addition, so soon after Lucan's epic, *Haemoniis ... cantibus* (V. Fl. 6.448) must evoke thoughts of Erictho, who closes her necromantic procedure *cantu ... Haemonio* (Luc. 6.693–94); Fucecchi 1997, 99 *ad* V. Fl. 6.448 draws attention to Valerius's unique echo of Lucan here. More generally, Vessey 1973, 248, notes in connection with Valerius's first necromantic scene (V. Fl. 1.774–817) that "the presence of the Thessalian witch reminds a reader of Lucan"; cf. Dinter 2009, 559.

76 See Day 2013, 102–4, on the sublimity of Lucan's witches.

77 V. Fl. 8.72–73 may give Medea the upper hand; here, Medea claims to have previously subdued *freta, nubila, fulmina*, and *toto quicquid micat aethere*, a cosmos-encompassing list of *terrena, sublimia*, and *caelestia* (see Sen. *Nat.* 2.1.1) that includes Jupiter's own weapons and domain.

78 E.g., Paratore 1974; Baldini Moscadi 2005, 91–100.

79 Cf. especially Sen. *Med.* 739–70. Lucan inscribes Medea into Thessaly's prehistory at 6.440–42, but he may simultaneously implicitly reject a tradition, preserved by the scholia on Ar. *Nu.* 749, that Thessaly's poisonous pharmacopia originated with Medea's own collection (see

Medea will ultimately, by the end of Seneca's play, be the most powerful being in the universe (just like Erictho),[80] leaving Jason with the belief that *nullos esse deos* (Sen. *Med.* 1027). And that "future" Medea is herself representative of Lucanean-style civil war: parent turned against child, symbolically attacking her own flesh, even promising that she will probe her own womb with a sword to discover and expel any unborn fetus (Sen. *Med.* 1012–13).[81] There is, furthermore, an immediate element of kin-strife inherent in Medea's sorcery even as Valerius constructs it: one victim of her magic is her own grandfather, the Sun, a kinship explicitly emphasized by *aui* ("grandfather," V. Fl. 6.442).[82]

In part, this collection of intertexts serves simply to enhance the ongoing structural destabilization of Valerius's Argonautic cosmos. But for all her power, Medea is, throughout the Argonautic tradition, ultimately the tool of the gods.[83] She is Juno's tool to take revenge on Pelias.[84] She is Venus's tool to continue her revenge against the descendants of Helios.[85] And in Valerius's *Argonautica*, as it turns out, she also becomes Jupiter's tool, as he takes this Lucanean and Senecan generator of cosmic disruption and kin-strife and releases her into the West. Jupiter's express plan is to have Jason bring Medea back to Greece, setting into motion a Herodotean domino-effect of foreign wars and toppling empires (V. Fl. 1.542–51, 558–60):[86]

> adcelerat sed summa dies Asiamque labantem
> linquimus et poscunt iam me sua tempora Grai.
> inde meae quercus tripodesque animaeque parentum
> hanc pelago misere manum. uia facta per undas   545
> perque hiemes, Bellona, tibi. nec uellera tantum
> indignanda manent <u>propiorque ex uirgine rapta
> ille dolor</u>, sed – nulla magis sententia menti
> fixa meae – ueniet Phrygia iam pastor ab Ida
> qui gemitus irasque pares et mutua Grais   550
> dona ferat. ...

Phillips 2002, 379–80). Alternatively, Medea's ability to arrive before her own arrival can be seen as part of the temporal instability of Lucan's Thessaly (see Ambühl 2016, 307) or as a metaliterary conceit.

80 Although Erictho claims that Fortune has more power (*plus Fortuna potest*, Luc. 6.615).
81 Lucan may recall this oath at Luc. 6.558–59, his *extrahitur* echoing Seneca's *extraham*. On Medea as a *locus* for embodying tropes of civil war, see Keith in this volume (pp. 306–8).
82 The change from moon (μήνης) to sun (*Solis*) is one of Valerius's few overt alterations from A.R. 3.531–33.
83 Cf. Zissos 2012, 106–14 (with additional bibliography), on Valerius's Medea specifically.
84 E.g., A.R. 4.241–43.
85 E.g., V. Fl. 6.467–69.
86 Cf. also V. Fl. 4.13–14.

>   ...
> arbiter ipse locos terrenaque summa mouendo
> experiar, quaenam populis longissima cunctis
> regna uelim linquamque datas ubi certus habenas.   560

> But the last day hastens and we have abandoned tottering Asia, and now the Greeks demand of me their time to shine. Accordingly my oaks and tripods and the spirits of their parents have dispatched this band over the sea. A path is being made for you through the waves and through storms, Bellona. Nor does only the fleece remain a cause for indignation, <u>and next, that grief from the snatched maid</u>, but—my mind has no opinion more fixed—a shepherd will soon come from Phrygian Ida, to bring to the Greeks groans and equal angers and reciprocal gifts. ... I myself, by moving locations and terrestrial power, shall test as a judge which kingdoms I would like to exist the longest for all people, and where I shall reliably leave the granted reins of power.

Medea's own translocation to Greece, a piece of the East brought into the West, is no less analogous to cosmic disarray than the stars falling out of the sky, just as Seneca's chorus laments (Sen. *Med.* 361–79).[87] Even if Medea may have spent years wreaking havoc with cosmic order in seeming violation of divine decree, it is only a matter of time before she, like the Winds and the Argo herself, becomes another tool in Jupiter's personal arsenal for controlling the destruction of the cosmos and the onset of civil war;[88] rather than abolishing the threat, he merely harnesses her destructive power to his own ends.[89]

4 Conclusion

And so, in a world where self-aggression and the potential for dissolution are worked into the very fabric of the cosmos, the Argo, which carries Medea back to Greece, is ultimately responsible for triggering the dislocation of natural order that is a necessary part of Jupiter's plan. His plan is to set the world in motion with commerce, wars, and *translatio imperii*, and his strategy is to use the Argo as a catalyst, removing the barriers to forward progress and moving Medea from

---

[87] On Seneca's approach, see also Slaney 2014, 435; for Medea as the transmundial bearer of *nefas*, cf. Baldini Moscadi 2005, 94–96.
[88] See n. 65 for Medea's potential synergies with the Winds.
[89] Seneca's Medea continues to reshape nature after her arrival in Greece, promising to burn into oblivion the Corinthian Isthmus (*Med.* 35–36).

East to West, developing the latent implications of Seneca's and Lucan's indictments of the Argo's voyage.[90]

Jupiter's plan leads directly, if distantly, to Rome's civil wars and their interminability.[91] Rome will be the prophesied empire which holds the reins of power, but rather than ultimately falling to another empire, Rome will only repeatedly fall to herself;[92] Vergil's *imperium sine fine*, it turns out, comes with a price. But whereas the Argo's voyage does provoke the succession of empires that ultimately culminates in *imperium et bellum ciuile sine fine*, the Argo's voyage does not cause the ever-attendant civil war; it is foreign wars that she drags in her wake, newly enabled thanks to the now-open sea (V. Fl. 1.545–46).[93] Just as the cosmos has always had the potential to return to chaos, humankind has, it seems, always had the potential to devolve into civil war, but civil war becomes so much worse once there is a non-self-destructive alternative.[94] Valerius does not, unlike so many Romans before him, try to tease out and label the origins of civil war. Instead, he suggests that civil war has no discrete origin, just as there seems to be no extrinsic cause for the perpetual self-aggression of the Clashing Rocks. Whereas foreign wars are the result of *commercia* and greed and the Argo's own voyage,[95] civil wars need no motivation. Dissolution is inherent in the structure of the cosmos and plans of the gods, and civil wars are inherent in humankind.

---

90 See n. 3.
91 Cf. Feeney 2007, 132–33, and Buckley 2010, 433; see also Penwill in this volume (ch. 4), with a much more thorough discussion of the Lucanean influence and allusions.
92 Just as, in the short term, Medea will repeatedly turn her hand against her own flesh in a standard *topos* of civil war (see p. 383 above), so in the long term Rome's citizens will turn their swords against each other time and again, caught in an endless cycle of internal strife; for the trope of Rome's unending civil strife, see most recently Armitage 2017a, 83–84, as well as König in this volume (ch. 8). These near and distant futures are both relegated to prophetic visions and similes in the epic. Mopsus sees Medea's murder of her children twice, and it is also depicted on the door of the Temple of the Sun at Colchis; Roman civil war serves as the vehicle of a simile in the midst of the real civil war at Colchis. Absyrtus's murder does not occur within the extant portion of the epic.
93 Quoted above. Cf. Luc. 3.193–94.
94 Cf. the Augustan poetic trope of pleading for war against the Parthians in lieu of war against Rome's citizens; Lowrie 2016, 350, notes that "imperial expansion [is] the conventional antidote to civil war." We may contrast the evidently "lawful" kin-murder of Valerius's Iazyges (V.Fl. 6.122–28), which Gesander touts as a preferable alternative to foreign wars (V. Fl. 6.323–39); for the paradox of this, see Buckley 2010, 447–50. For Lucan, because Rome's *urbs* is analogous to the *orbis*, foreign war—enabled by the Argo—becomes another manifestation of civil war.
95 Valerius's Arimaspoi seem still to live in the Golden Age of innocence, before their discovery of gold: *et qui tua iugera nondum / eruis, ignotis insons Arimaspe metallis* (V. Fl. 6.130–31). However, ironically, they are already participating in a civil war, contrary to the suggestion of Ovid and others that the discovery of precious metals caused civil war (e.g., Ov. *Met.* 1.140–50; cf. Slaney 2014, 434, on the connection between seafaring, *auaritia*, and civil war).

Siobhan Chomse
Instability and the Sublime in Martial's *Liber Spectaculorum*

Martial's epigrams are a curious blend of the ephemeral and the eternal: a paradox. Thanks to its original association with the inscription,[1] epigram has a monumental quality, and yet its quotidian subject-matter and the working fiction of its off-the-cuff composition mean that epigram is also fodder for quick consumption and disposal.[2] Martial's seemingly ephemeral light verse has been, then, perversely long-lived;[3] but in the world of epigram all is not what it seems, and the reality of Roman life—or the life in Rome—that Martial represents is as carefully constructed as his poetry. Each is subject to revisions, or renovations.[4] I stress the metaphor of construction here because monumentality is central to Martial's poetry:[5] both the physical, architectural substance of the city of Rome itself and the many little bricks that are Martial's epigrams, piled up to make one great *monumentum*.[6] It is entirely appropriate (and not entirely coincidental) that Martial should be building up his own *monumentum* just as the Flavians were engaged in a program of massive monumental revision at Rome:[7] a transformation of Rome not from a city of bricks into one of marble, but from a Julio-Claudian

---

My thanks to Darcy Krasne and Lauren Donovan Ginsberg for their patience, encouragement and advice throughout the many stages of this chapter's renovation. I am also grateful to Victoria Rimell for reading an earlier draft and for the transformative comments she offered. Needless to say, any cracks that remain in this chapter are of my own making.

---

1 See, e.g., Sullivan 1991, 78–114.
2 Cf. Rimell 2008, 57. Rimell's sense that Martial "reinvents as well as parodies monumentality" in the *Liber spectaculorum* (Rimell 2008, 63) is crucial to what follows.
3 The Younger Pliny would be delighted: *at non erunt aeterna quae scripsit: non erunt fortasse, ille tamen scripsit tamquam essent futura* ("so the things he has written will not be immortal: perhaps not, but he wrote them as though they would be," *Ep.* 3.21.6).
4 Famously, of course, Book 10. On the political nature of this renovated collection, see Fearnley 2003, 613–35, after (and *contra*) Sullivan 1991, 48. Fearnley's sense that the Roman reader was an "*inter*-textual reader; he read both literary text against literary text, but also literary text against physical monument against political act" (Fearnley 2003, 616), is implicit in my argument to follow. For a recent extension of this idea, see Roller 2013 on the "intersignification" of Roman monuments.
5 See recently Rimell 2008, 51–93; Roman 2010.
6 Cf. Roman 2010, 113.
7 See esp. Sullivan 1991, 147–55; Dyson/Prior 1995; Roman 2010. On the Flavian building program, see Fredrick 2003, 199–227; Packer 2003, 167–98.

city into a Flavian city, fit for a new dynasty and a new age of Principate. In the *Liber Spectaculorum*, Martial hails the inauguration of the Colosseum, the greatest monument of this architectural reclamation of Rome, a city stamped with a flourish with the mark of Nero and wrecked by the civil war of 69 CE.[8] This chapter explores how the epigrammatist reads and re-writes civil war through the Neronian age, its architecture and its poetry. Martial's ephemeral epigram is poetry of and for the moment, but in the *Liber Spectaculorum* this is a moment that trembles with the instability of the recent past. To call the Colosseum a sublime monument is perhaps to state the obvious; but Martial's Colosseum is charged with a sublimity that lays a specific claim to the thrill of the unstable.[9]

1 Up Next…

Vespasian's most pressing task upon returning to Rome in 70 CE, Suetonius tells us, was "first stabilizing the ruined and tottering state, and then embellishing it" (*per totum imperii tempus nihil habuit antiquius quam prope afflictam nutantemque rem publicam stabilire primo, deinde et ornare*, Suet. *Ves.* 8.1).[10] In practical terms, the great fire of 64 CE had destroyed huge portions of the city,[11] and the civil blaze of 69 CE on the Capitoline Hill that raged as Flavian and Vitellian forces fought had destroyed the Temple of Jupiter Optimus Maximus.[12]

---

[8] I use Lindsay's Oxford Classical Text throughout; translations of all texts are my own.
[9] On the sublime, see below.
[10] Cf. *deformis urbs ueteribus incendiis ac ruinis erat* ("the city was disfigured by past fires and ruins," Suet. *Ves.* 8.5); see also *incertum diu et quasi uagum imperium suscepit firmauitque tandem gens Flauia* ("for a long time uncertain and as if set adrift, at last the empire was taken on and shored up by the Flavian family," Suet. *Ves.* 1.1).
[11] See Tacitus *Ann.* 15.38–43. On the Neronian fire and the power of ruins see esp. Edwards 2011. Note that in Tacitus's account, Italy and the provinces too are laid waste not by the fire but by Nero, who plundered their resources for his restoration or remodelling of Rome (*conferendis pecuniis peruastata Italia, prouinciae euersae sociique populi et quae ciuitatium liberae uocantur*, "Italy was laid waste for the collection of funds, the provinces were ruined, so too the allied peoples and the so-called the free states," Tac. *Ann.* 15.45.1).
[12] Tacitus describes the destruction of the temple (Tac. *Hist.* 3.71–72) with epic force, alluding powerfully to Vergil's account of the fall of Troy in *Aeneid* 2 (see recently Joseph 2012, 103–6). On Vespasian's restoration of the temple, see Wardle 1996. The inauguration of its reconstruction is recorded by Tacitus at *Hist.* 4.53, on which see Sailor 2008, 218ff. This temple (as Tacitus, of course, knew) was itself destroyed by a fire in 80 CE, so that in the *Histories* Vespasian is always already building a ruin. On Domitian's replacement, the "glittering Capitoline [that] was a ready symbol of tyrannical abuse and moral decay," see Fredrick 2003, 200 (citing Plu. *Publ.* 15.5).

Metaphorically speaking, the "ruin" of Rome was visible in the charred remains of this temple,[13] but also in the unfinished remnants of Nero's *Domus aurea*:[14] a vast monument to excess that was now an embarrassing hangover to be wiped from the face of Rome, its land and accoutrements reappropriated by the amphitheater celebrated in Martial's *Liber Spectaculorum*.[15] In this notoriously slippery collection, probably written for the emperor Titus to mark the amphitheater's inauguration in 80 CE,[16] the Colosseum strives, or so it seems, to transform the city of Rome from the vast palace of the emperor into the cosmic palace of the people.[17]

And yet arguably this is precisely what Nero himself had offered in building his *Domus aurea*; old perceptions of the tyrannical self-indulgence of his building program have been revised to incorporate the idea of the importance of public access—a party to which everyone was invited.[18] The Flavians, insecure newcomers looking back at decades of Julio-Claudian succession, denigrated the last regime of this dynasty in order to bolster their own legitimacy. This was a highly selective process: while Nero was decidedly "Bad," for the Flavians to sever themselves entirely from Rome's first imperial family was neither possible nor desirable. There was some "Good" to be gleaned here, and so the Flavians fostered connections with, in particular, Augustus, not least in their magnificent building program—it is perhaps not entirely coincidental that Augustus was known to have had unfulfilled ambitions to build an amphitheater of this own.[19] Flavian propaganda cast Nero in the role of the extravagant tyrant: the artist-

---

[13] Packer 2003, 167 observes that the temple's "blackened ruins ... not only disgraced the symbolic heart of the Roman world but also visually symbolized the temporary collapse of the imperial system." See also Edwards 1996, 78–82; Woodman 1997, 96; Ash 2007a; Sailor 2008, 205–18. On the symbolic significance of the (now demonstrably unstable) Capitolium in Flavian poetry, see Leo Landrey's chapter in this volume, pp. 234–40.

[14] Packer 2003, 167–68. It is broadly accepted that Nero did not see the *Domus aurea* finished: see *LTUR* 2.49, 61. Our evidence from Suetonius on this point is contradictory: although at *Nero* 31.2 he notes the *Domus aurea*'s completion and dedication, at *Otho* 7.1 he states that Otho signed a substantial grant for the completion of the building complex. Cf. Bradley 1978, *ad* Suet. *Nero* 31.2.

[15] The Colosseum was constructed where Nero's lake had once been (cf. Mart. *Sp.* 2.5–6): see Packer 2003, 168–69.

[16] See Coleman 2006, xxv–xxviii (on the title) and xlv–lxiv (on the identity of *Caesar*—alternatively Domitian, or even the Flavian Emperor as idealized abstraction).

[17] Cf. Tac. *Ann.* 15.37.1 on Nero, whose prodigious partying makes the whole city his palace (*totaque urbe quasi domo uti*).

[18] See, e.g., Ripoll 1999; Flower 2006; Rosso 2008.

[19] Suet. *Ves.* 9.1; see esp. Gunderson 2003, 642–43. For suggestions about what caused Augustus to abandon the project, see Coleman 2000, 228, 249 n. 118; Welch 2007, 133.

emperor and prodigious builder who wrested the city from the people after the fire of 64 CE to raise a private pleasure palace that transgressed the boundaries of propriety in both moral and topographical terms.[20] Martial, of course, must be included in this roster of sources for his lurking picture of the *Domus aurea* in *Sp.* 2, where he locates the new Colosseum emphatically on the site of Nero's palace. While the *Domus aurea* was built on the ruins of the nation,[21] the Colosseum was built on the ruins of this palace and on the rubble of a city razed by civil war. The conflict of 69 CE was a recent memory at which the Flavian dynasty was still smarting; an uncomfortable victory that could not be celebrated.[22] Nero served as a convenient scapegoat: in Flavian propaganda, *bellum ciuile* blurs backwards into *bellum Neronis* as the Neronian principate is cast as a war upon the people precisely by (among other things) portraying Nero's building program as an aggressive occupation of the city of Rome.[23]

Our sources describe the *Domus aurea* as a complex of such extraordinary luxury and bewildering dimension that the idea of the sublime is readily evoked.[24] The sublime is a sensation at once fascinating and terrifying, inspired by an encounter with an object that exceeds normal comprehension. This experience causes the mind, almost simultaneously, to contract in terror and expand in awe.[25] Sublime experience is thus a paradoxical or ambivalent sensation; what Edmund Burke, in his 1757 treatise *A Philosophical Enquiry into the Origin of our Ideas of the Sublime and Beautiful*, described as the feeling of a

---

[20] On the topographical transgression of bringing *rus in urbem*, see Elsner 1994, 121–22; cf. Tac. *Ann.* 15.42.

[21] Tacitus tells us: *Nero usus est patriae ruinis exstruxitque domum* ("Nero made use of the ruins of our country and built a house," Tac. *Ann.* 15.42.1).

[22] See Dewar 2008, 68–69, for the argument that the Flavian building project, funded by the spoils of the Judean wars, was meant to celebrate not only this foreign triumph but—more quietly—victory in the civil wars, bringing peace to Rome after the chaotic demise of the Julio-Claudian dynasty.

[23] On the *bellum Neronis*, see Shotter 1975; Daly 1975. On Tacitus's characterisation of the Principate as a kind of civil war waged against the Roman people, with Nero and Tiberius as principal aggressors, see Keitel 1984; Marshall 2010 expands Keitel's thesis, examining Tacitus's engagement with Lucan as part of this endeavor; see also Joseph 2012 esp. 33–37, 169–89.

[24] See, e.g., Etlin 2012 and discussion below.

[25] The sublime has a long and complex history, both ancient and modern. For a recent overview, see Shaw 2017; on the ancient sublime see Porter 2016. Work on the sublime in the literature of the ancient world is gaining momentum. Of several recent and important works, Porter 2001, Hardie 2009, Porter 2011, and Day 2013 are especially pertinent to the ideas and argument presented in this chapter.

"delight" that "turns on pain."[26] The sense of a mingled delight and terror fits the *Domus aurea* well, particularly as it was reincarnated in our post-Neronian sources as the extravagant, land-grabbing palace of a tyrant. Martial's Colosseum receives the sublime legacy of the *Domus aurea* and counters its antecedent by replacing but not entirely rejecting its attributes. Here is a new and spectacular palace for the people, a gift of cosmic dimensions (as we shall see) offered by the emperor.

The sublimity of the *Liber Spectaculorum* lies in Martial's capacity to take on and transform the difficult past; after all, in the new Flavian era, the past could not (and should not) be entirely forgotten. Martial accepts this and recognizes that the past can provide a destabilizing thrill that makes the present all the more sublime—a delight that turns on pain. The cheap and often not-so-cheerful nature of epigram is perhaps at odds with the idea of the sublime, but sublimity relies on a tension of opposites and this is something that epigram can offer— particularly in the *Liber Spectaculorum* where the vast sublimity of the Colosseum and, above all, of the emperor are described and contained in a poetic form that would seem to contradict their grandeur. Martial has read the Roman tradition that sees the sublime in cosmic phenomena extending from Lucretius's *De Rerum Natura*; as an echo of Roman *imperium* in the *Aeneid*; and unleashed to rail against the Principate and lament the trauma of civil war in Lucan's *Bellum Ciuile*.[27] In each of these texts, instability (physical or metaphorical) is a source of the sublime: amongst a host of examples, think of Lucretius's earthquakes, Vergil's toppling Troy, Lucan's Rome collapsing under its own weight.[28] In the *Liber Spectaculorum*, Martial converts this instability into an epigrammatic sublime suited to the Flavian age as it emerged from a period radically destabilized by the end of the Julio-Claudian dynasty and the chaos of civil war.

Much has been written about the way in which Martial engages with and rewrites the tropes of poetic monumentality familiar from the Augustan age, along with their attendant anxieties about impermanence.[29] In the turbulent years of Nero's decline and the subsequent civil war, impermanence had become

---

[26] Burke 2008, 47.
[27] On Lucretius and the sublime, see Porter 2007 and Hardie 2009; on Vergil, Hardie 2009 again; and Day 2013 on Lucan.
[28] Lucr. 6.535–607; Verg. *A*. 2.624–33; Luc. 1.70–82. My doctoral thesis (Chomse 2015) examines images of architectural instability and their depiction in terms of the sublime in Vergil's *Aeneid*, Lucan's *Bellum Ciuile*, and the historical works of Tacitus.
[29] See esp. Rimell 2008, 51–93.

a fact of life:[30] to be merely monumental in Flavian Rome was not enough. Epigrammatic ephemerality offers a new kind of transcendence, as well as a new lens with which to look at the past: now you see it, now you don't. Like epigram, like the games in the Colosseum that Martial commemorates, the past both endures and crashes out of time. The presence of the past in the *Liber Spectaculorum* destabilizes the present in a way that need not be seen as strictly negative. In creative terms, to destabilize can be to charge with new energy. Martial's Colosseum, like Martial's epigrammatic *opus* (Mart. *Sp.* 1.8), absorbs the thrilling charge of the past to present a Rome sublimed anew for the Flavian age.

2 The Architectural Sublime

Central to this chapter is the idea of the "architectural sublime,"[31] of which we can think, I suggest, in the Kantian terms of mathematical and dynamical sublimity. In his 1790 treatise, *The Critique of Judgement*, Immanuel Kant divides the idea of the sublime into two categories: the mathematical sublime—that is, the sublime in terms of scale or quantity, that which is "*absolutely great*"[32]—and the dynamical sublime, which is concerned primarily with the sublimity of nature's power in her mighty phenomena: great storms, raging seas, volcanic eruptions.[33] The sublime in both categories is connected with an impression of the infinite: infinite space or infinite power. In each case the idea of the infinite is essentially incomprehensible and potentially overwhelming, so the experiencing subject is confronted not only with her physical inadequacy but with the limits of her powers of comprehension: she is able to appreciate only a part of the infinite whole represented by the sublime object.[34] In this moment, the mind shrinks in confrontation with its own inadequacy, but almost simultaneously, the very recognition of this inadequacy prompts an awareness of a "supersensible" capacity for comprehension that gives access to sublime experience.[35] Kant is chiefly concerned with the sublimity of the natural world; so too Edmund Burke

---

30 Cf. Darcy Krasne's chapter in this volume on the relationship between civil war and cosmic instability in the universe of Valerius Flaccus.
31 For a recent discussion of the architectural sublime, see Etlin 2012 (discussed below).
32 Kant 2007, 78: original italics.
33 Kant 2007, 91.
34 Kant 2007, 88, cf. 83.
35 Kant 2007, 81.

in his *Enquiry*. But, as Burke argues, the "artificial infinite"[36] can be created in architectural form when magnitude in building is properly deployed and this impression of the infinite "has a tendency to fill the mind with a sort of delightful horror, which is the most genuine effect, and truest test of the sublime."[37] Kant locates architectural sublimity in the category of the mathematical sublime for its impression of absolute spatial magnitude, offering the examples of St Peter's basilica and the pyramids of Egypt.[38] Burke's artificial infinite can similarly be conceived of in mathematical terms, based on the "succession and uniformity of parts."[39] Indeed, according to Burke, this sense of the artificial infinite is precisely the source of the sublimity of the circular building: "For in a rotund ... you can nowhere fix a boundary; turn which way you will, the same object still seems to continue, and the imagination has no rest."[40] The Colosseum, then, with its ordered facade[41] and vast tiered banks of seats within, offers an impression of infinitude that meets Burke's definition of the architectural sublime exactly.

For sublime dynamism in architecture, we might think immediately of the frozen motion of buildings that soar skywards above us, though the soaring movement of the slender skyscraper offers sublime dynamism of a different kind to that of the Colosseum.[42] From the outside, the amphitheater's massive bulk seems both to drive down into the earth and to surge up out of it.[43] These dynamics would alter radically, of course, for the spectator who, passing into the Colosseum, toils up myriad passages and flights of steps to reach a beetling vantage point from which to peer down at the spectacles below, at the crowds all around and at the colossal structure that contains them.[44] Seating arrangements inside the Colosseum were rigorously structured, with the "cheap seats" perched at the very top of the amphitheater and the Emperor and other luminaries closest

---

[36] Burke 2008, 67–70, 126–27.
[37] Burke 2008, 67.
[38] Kant 2007, 82–83.
[39] Burke 2008, 68–69. The succession of a series of continuous points impress upon the mind "by their frequent impulses" the "idea of their progress beyond their actual limits"; but the points must be uniform, since any change enforces a check upon the imagination which impedes the impression of infinite progress.
[40] Burke 2008, 68.
[41] On the facade, see, e.g., Welch 2007, 134–41.
[42] On the soaring sublimity of the skyscraper, see Nye 1994, 77–108.
[43] For this perspective, consider the tiny figures who stand beneath the great mass of masonry depicted in Piranesi's "Foundations of the Mausoleum of Hadrian or Castel Sant'Angelo" from his 1756 collection, *Antichità Romane*.
[44] On crowd control in the Colosseum (the movement and seating of the audience), see Rose 2005.

to the action down below.[45] Stratified seating thus imposed some order upon the 50,000-strong crowd, transforming it from a thronging mob into the sublime massed ranks[46] of the *populus Romanus* or even, as Martial describes them, the peoples of the world (Mart. *Sp.* 3), held within the miraculous shell of the Colosseum. The spatial dynamics of the amphitheater produce a particularly intense and disorienting relationship between enclosure and openness, height and depth, the static and the moving or unstable. The massive structure of the Colosseum is dedicated to the violent disorder of death marshalled into spectacular form; but spectacle relies on the presence of the crowd, their living bodies also contained within the amphitheater. Living and dying in these most extreme forms meet in the Colosseum to produce a sublime paradox that Martial captures in the *Liber Spectaculorum*. Poised between life and death, in Martial's Colosseum architecture has a peculiar relationship with time: monumentality is an exterior quality for the amphitheater; once inside, the spectacle takes charge, and permanence is called into question. So the sublimity of Martial's Colosseum lies not only in its impression of infinite magnitude but in the tension between its magnitude and its paradoxical instability.

3 Sublimity Rising

In *Liber Spectaculorum* 2, the Colosseum surges into view in a topographical tour of the heart of Rome that makes the amphitheater the supreme monument amongst a host of structures drawn up on a sublime scale (Mart. *Sp.* 2):

---

45 See Rose 2005 and Welch 2007, 159–60.
46 On the ordered, wondering crowd as part of the collective experience of the sublime see Nye 1994, 276, discussing the "American technological sublime" experienced in the display of national technological power and prowess, such as at the centennial of the Statue of Liberty in 1986: "Participation in an immense crowd had apparently become a precondition for the American technological sublime. The very size of the audience had become an important part of the meaning of the event. Just as important, this crowd was not violent, agitated or demanding. ... Rather, at these public moments, another kind of public community briefly becomes visible." On the importance of collective experience in the Colosseum and the overpowering sensation of being a part of the massive crowd assembled there in the presence of the emperor himself, see Zanker 2010 (esp. 70). Note particularly Zanker's observation that "the coins ... struck on the occasion of the games held on the 'grand opening' of the Colosseum in AD 80 give some impression of this 'aestheticisation' of the masses" (Zanker 2010, 70, with the sestertius pictured at fig. 2.19 on 72).

hic ubi sidereus propius uidet astra colossus
　　et crescunt media pegmata celsa uia,
inuidiosa feri radiabant atria regis
　　unaque iam tota stabat in urbe domus.
hic ubi conspicui uenerabilis Amphitheatri　　　　　5
　　erigitur moles, stagna Neronis erant.
hic ubi miramur uelocia munera thermas,
　　abstulerat miseris tecta superbus ager.
Claudia diffusas ubi porticus explicat umbras,
　　ultima pars aulae deficientis erat.　　　　　　10
reddita Roma sibi est et sunt te praeside, Caesar,
　　deliciae populi, quae fuerant domini.

Here where the starry colossus looks at nearby constellations and lofty scaffolding grows up in the middle of the road, the hateful halls of a feral king used to shine out, and a single house stood in all the city. Here where the august mass of the amphitheater is raised up for all to see, was once Nero's lake. Here where we marvel at the speedy gift of the baths, an arrogant estate had stolen the homes of the poor. Where the Claudian portico unfolds its far-flung shade, there was the very edge of the palace finally coming to an end. Rome has been returned to herself, and with you watching over us, Caesar, there are delights for the people which had belonged to the master.

The poem celebrates the monumental requisition by the Flavian *gens* of the vast space once occupied by Nero's *Domus aurea*.[47] Where once a single, gargantuan palace stood (*unaque iam tota stabat in urbe domus*, Mart. *Sp.* 2.4; discussion below), now we find an array of monuments described in language that emphasizes sublime categories including height or expansiveness (*celsa, diffusas ... umbras*), visual wonder (*conspicui, miramur*), and marvellous growth or creative energy (*crescunt, erigitur, uelocia, explicat*); note, too, the cosmic imagery at *Sp.* 2.1.

Martial's emphasis here is on works in motion. Even the completed Baths of Titus remember the rapid movement of their construction (*uelocia munera*, Mart. *Sp.* 2.7), while the Colosseum itself continues to rise (*erigitur*, Mart. *Sp.* 2.6) at the center of this poetic map,[48] and beneath the starry colossus[49] that peers at neighboring constellations, a work-in-progress surges up: *crescunt media pegmata celsa uia* (Mart. *Sp.* 2.2). The identity of these lofty *pegmata* has been the source of much debate, which divides into two camps: one reads stage machinery here,

---

[47] For the area covered (with maps), see Coleman 2006, 14–17.
[48] vv.5–6 of a 12-line epigram. On Martial's poetic maps, see Roman 2010 (esp. 93ff. on Mart. *Sp.* 2).
[49] Cf. Plin. *Nat.* 34.45–46; Suet. *Nero* 31, *Ves.* 18. Housed in the atrium of the *Domus aurea*, a colossal portrait of Nero remodelled under Vespasian into a statue of Helios, or already a depiction of the god when requisitioned by the Flavians. For a concise summary of the debate, see Flower 2006, 229.

the other scaffolding,⁵⁰ and the latter group splinters again when it comes to naming the building that the scaffolding denotes.⁵¹ I take *pegmata* as scaffolding, but if we retain something of the mechanistic sense of the alternative reading, then the building beneath the boards becomes a marvellous spectacle worthy of the amphitheater, swept up to the heavens.⁵² And however we identify the monument underneath the scaffolding, Martial's inclusion of this structure stresses clearly the aesthetic value of the process of construction, keying into a wider Roman sense that the act and fact of construction remembered enhance the merit of a completed work.⁵³ Indeed, the endeavor of construction (as well as the technology required to perform this feat) can be considered a sublime thing in itself.⁵⁴ Martial seems to remind us of this in preserving the scaffolded structure in motion as it grows (*crescunt*), anticipating the upward thrust of the Colosseum itself: *conspicui uenerabilis Amphitheatri | erigitur moles* (Mart. *Sp.* 2.5–6). The rising momentum of the buildings in this epigram, which begins on an astral plane (*hic ubi sidereus propius uidet astra colossus*, Mart. *Sp.* 2.1), instills this topographical scene with a sense of instability as a positive, energizing drive; each monument is as if caught in the moment of its construction. Martial thus captures the optimism and vigor of the Flavian building program (managing to celebrate the complete structures as well as hinting at the impressive process of

---

50 Cf. *TLL* s.v. 1.b.
51 Suggestions include modifications to the *uestibulum* of the *Domus aurea*, and the Arch of Titus. For a succint summary of the debate, see Coleman 2006, *ad Sp.* 2.2, who concludes in favor of the Arch of Titus (see also Coleman 1998, 19–20). Cf. Platner/Ashby 1929, 167; Boëthius 1952, 136.
52 Cf. Coleman's 2006 discussion *ad Sp.* 18 on the "flying machines" of the Roman stage, denoted by *pegma*: "*Pegmata* on the stage included structures that rose into the air and could be let down again by removing the counterweights," citing *pegmata per se surgentia* (Sen. *Ep.* 88.22). On Martial's sky-scraping spectacles, see Rimell 2008, 60–65 (discussed below).
53 Reitz 2012, 317: "Roman viewers were ... frequently encouraged to include awareness of the process of creating a building into their assessment of its merit." Reitz discusses, for example, the Haterii relief, where the inclusion of an image of a crane in the picture of the completed tomb celebrates the fact of its construction. For a possible contemporary image of the Colosseum under construction note the Flavian relief on a marble slab found at the tomb of Aulus Hirtius in the Campus Martius (Palazzo della Cancelleria) that depicts the upper part of a large circular building surrounded by layers of scaffolding. The relief has been associated with Martial's *pegmata* problem: see Rodriguez-Almeida 1994, 211–17, and Thomas 2007, 26. For the idea that the act of construction of a public work could become part of the dialogue between the emperor and the people of Rome, see Zanker 2010, 79.
54 Cf. Burke 2008, 71 on the idea of the "immense force" involved in the construction of Stonehenge as a source of sublimity. On the "technological sublime" in post-Industrial America, see Nye 1994. I argue elsewhere (Chomse 2015) that this form of sublimity can be detected in Roman attitudes to *machinae*, as expressed, e.g., at Luc. 3.455–62.

their construction) and in doing so charges these works with an instability that resonates with the remnants of the recent past.[55]

4 The Sublime, Renovated

Of course, the Colosseum received a sublime legacy on the site of the *Domus aurea*. The sheer scale of the palace building as described by Suetonius (its *uestibulum* large enough to house the colossal statue of Nero; its colonnade a mile long, Suet. *Nero* 31.1), as well as the opulence of its fittings (e.g., *cuncta auro lita, distincta gemmis unionumque conchis erat*, "all was overlain with gold, adorned with gems and mother of pearl," Suet. *Nero* 31.1), mark the *Domus aurea* as "sublime" under the most facile definition. That the Colosseum should be a sublime building was thus not only inevitable but necessary: in the propagandistic fight-back against the newly reconstructed tyrant Nero, the crowning glory of the Flavian building program had to be a monument that could offer a new sublimity to counter and to match that of its predecessor. In the *Liber Spectaculorum*, the sheer expanse of the Colosseum (a great *moles* at Mart. *Sp.* 2.6) and the extravagance of its varied spectacles described throughout the collection presents a sublimity that, even at the most superficial level, can be seen to take on the *Domus aurea* and the spectacular emperor who built it.[56] Martial tells us in *Sp.* 1 that *reddita Roma sibi est*: not just "given back," as William Fitzgerald points out, but "reflected."[57]

The *Domus aurea* is discussed at length by the architectural historian Richard Etlin as a key example of what he defines as Roman architectural sublimity, with a heavy emphasis upon the cosmic symbolism of the domed ceiling.[58] Etlin cites Suetonius's description of the palace (*Nero* 31) and focuses upon the much-debated revolving ceiling (*praecipua cenationum rotunda, quae perpetuo diebus ac noctibus uice mundi circumageretur*, "the most important part of the dining hall

---

[55] Cf. Rosso 2008, 45 who points out that the appeal of the *nouitas* of Nero's reign lay not just in his redevelopment of the city center after 64 CE but in the sense of revival he offered.
[56] Nero built a wooden amphitheater in 57 CE (Suet. *Nero* 12; Tac. *Ann.* 13.31), described by Tacitus as a *molem amphitheatri* (Tac. *Ann.* 13.31.1; cf. *amphitheatri ... moles*, Mart. *Sp.* 2.5–6). If we take Calpurnius Siculus's *Eclogues* to be Neronian, then we find an account of the games that took place there that sings with the sublime (Calp. *Ecl.* 7.23–72). On Calpurnius's *Eclogues* as a "proto-Martialian" source for the *Liber Spectaculorum* (esp. Mart. *Sp.* 24.5), see Hinds 2007, 150.
[57] Fitzgerald 2007, 39.
[58] Etlin 2012, 239–43.

was circular and ceaselessly, night and day, it revolved like the firmament," Suet. *Nero* 31.2),[59] following scholarly postulations on the dome's possible astral and solar decorative scheme and Nero's divine associations (with Jupiter and Apollo-Sol) in order to attach a particular cosmic-sublime resonance to the *Domus aurea*.[60] But there is no sense of this kind of cosmic architectural sublimity in Tacitus's account (Tac. *Ann*. 15.42), nor the Elder Pliny's (Plin. *Nat*. 36.111), nor really in Suetonius's.[61] In these accounts, what most struck Roman viewers of the *Domus aurea* was neither its (possible) status as a declaration of cosmic power[62] nor the palace's luxurious prodigality, which Tacitus dismisses as old news (Tac. *Ann*. 15.42.1). Perhaps these qualities were marvelled at by the lost Martials and Statiuses of the Neronian age. But in the later accounts that survive, what most shocked Roman viewers was what is depicted as the aggressive requisition of vast tracts of the urban landscape of central Rome for the *Domus aurea* and the unnatural transformation of this space into *rus in urbe*.[63]

This idea of the construction of the *Domus aurea* as a tyrannical, transgressive land-grab by Nero in the aftermath of the fire of 64 CE is the most striking unifying feature of our sources, which make the palace a symbol of the emperor's totalizing ambitions.[64] As Rosso notes, the bringing of *rus in urbem* combines with the sense that the *Domus aurea* is a palace of endless expanse, spreading out through Rome, to produce the idea that the Golden House is in fact "un véritable monde dans la Ville."[65] The sublime, then, lies in this mind-boggling act of deception, in which the space contained within the palace's grounds seems so limitless as to suggest the containment of an entire world.[66]

---

[59] Suetonius seems to suggest here that the whole room revolves, but he is imprecise and *uice mundi* is generally taken to imply that it is just the domed ceiling that revolved. Cf. Bradley 1978, *ad loc*. See also Ward Perkins 1956, 211; Boëthius 1960, 117.

[60] Etlin 2012, 239–43. On the *Domus aurea* see Ball 2003; Boëthius 1960; Ward Perkins 1956. For the cosmic symbolism of the dome, see L'Orange 1953, esp. 28–31; on the *Domus aurea*, see Lehmann 1945, esp. 12ff. For Nero's solar-divine associations, see Champlin 2003, 116ff., 209.

[61] For architectural sublimity with a cosmic reach, contrast Mart. 8.36 and Stat. *Silu*. 4.2.18–37 on the palace of Domitian.

[62] After a Hellenistic model, according to L'Orange 1953, 28f.; criticized by Boëthius 1960, 119–20, with n. 37; Ward Perkins 1956, 210–12.

[63] Ward Perkins 1956, 212. See also Elsner 1994, esp. 121, on the *Domus aurea* perceived as transgressive.

[64] Cf. Rosso 2008, 52.

[65] Rosso 2008, 52–53.

[66] See especially Tacitus's description (*Ann*. 15.42.1) for an evocation of the deceptive art of *rus in urbe* at the *Domus aurea*. Burke 2008, 70, in his discussion of "Magnitude in Building," tells

And as such it is met with verve in Martial's Colosseum, a structure so vast it holds all the peoples of the world, boiled down into spectator-delegates: *quae tam seposita est, quae gens tam barbara, Caesar, | ex qua spectator non sit in urbe tua?* ("what people is so remote, so barbarous, Caesar, that a spectator from it is not in your city?" Mart. *Sp.* 3.1–2). Martial plays a numbers game in the *Liber Spectaculorum*, explored by Fitzgerald and particularly by Rimell, that finds the multiple and the singular—one for all, all for one, all or nothing—inverted, compressed, and expanded.[67] In this mathematical play we find a suggestion of the sublime in the idea of vast multiplicity contained within the monumentally singular: not only in the amphitheater's global crowd described in *Sp.* 3, but—to return to Nero—in the urban sprawl of the *Domus aurea* (*unaque iam tota stabat in urbe*, Mart. *Sp.* 2.4), or the *Domus aurea* as palatial world, and in the impossible structure of its architectural heir, the Colosseum.

In the first epigram, the Colosseum has monumental ambitions on a gigantic global scale, encompassing and superseding any comparable architectural wonders that might stand in its way (Mart. *Sp.* 1):

> barbara pyramidum sileat miracula Memphis,
>   Assyrius iactet nec Babylona labor;
> nec Triuiae templo molles laudentur Iones,
>   dissimulet Delon cornibus ara frequens;
> aere nec uacuo pendentia Mausolea   5
>   laudibus inmodicis Cares in astra ferant.
> omnis Caesareo cedit labor Amphitheatro,
>   unum pro cunctis fama loquetur opus.

> Let barbarous Memphis keep silent on the miracle of the pyramids, nor let Assyrian labor boast of Babylon; the soft Ionians may not sing the praises of Trivia's temple, let the altar crowded with horns ignore Delos; nor may the Carians bear up to the stars with their immoderate honors the Mausoleum hanging in empty air. All labor yields to Caesar's amphitheater, Fame will speak of a single work in place of all.

We are taken on a whistle-stop tour of the world's monumental marvels, finding that they all yield (*cedit*) to Caesar's great amphitheater—<u>unum</u> pro <u>cunctis</u> ... <u>opus</u>.[68] As Fitzgerald notes, the phrase can mean not just "one instead of all others" but also "one on behalf of all others," so that the Colosseum not only supersedes but also represents, by encompassing, all other sources of architec-

---

us that sublime art must deceive: "No work of art can be great, but as it deceives; to be otherwise is the prerogative of nature only."
67 See Fitzgerald 2007, 37–43, and Rimell 2008, 112–22.
68 More on this below.

tural amazement.[69] We find these same dynamics of one-versus-many in the second epigram, remembering the *Domus aurea*: <u>unaque</u> iam <u>tota</u> stabat in urbe domus (Mart. *Sp.* 2.4). As Rimell suggests, this single *domus* in place of many is both a public boon ("one for the sake of all") and sends us back to think again about the ambiguous *unum pro cunctis* of *Sp.* 1.8 so that, as she argues, "we end up reading Neronian tyranny back into the imperial and literary ambition/eulogy of *unum pro cunctis*."[70]

This is the aporia of the Colosseum: it seeks to drown out its Neronian inheritance but is simultaneously the true heir to the *Domus aurea*; in replacing that *una ... domus*, it also imitates it (*unum pro cunctis*). The Colosseum does not swallow up Rome (to the exclusion of the people) like Nero's tyrannical *Domus aurea* but sucks it all in, an impossible containment.[71] Of course, one movement recalls the other and we remember that the ambivalent sublime, with which both structures are endowed, can express both jubilant liberty (one for the sake of many) and irresistible tyranny (one in place of many).[72] Such is the pulling power of Martial's amphitheater that the Rome it contains is global—cosmic, in fact, as we see in *Liber Spectaculorum* 3, where the poet picks out from amongst the crowd a parade of the Colosseum's farthest-flung visitors. After all, Martial asks: *quae tam seposita est, quae gens tam barbara, Caesar, | ex qua <u>spectator non sit in urbe tua</u>?* ("what people is so remote, so barbarous, Caesar, that a spectator from it is not in your city?" Mart. *Sp.* 3.1–2).[73] Here city and amphitheater are elided (*in urbe tua*, Mart. *Sp.* 3.2), so that each contains (like the *Domus aurea*, already city-sized at Mart. *Sp.* 2.4) a world. Both are *urbes* and both *orbes*—and now all the world's an arena.[74]

---

69 Fitzgerald 2007, 38.
70 Rimell 2008, 118.
71 My thanks to Victoria Rimell for this image (*per litteras*).
72 On liberty, tyranny, and the sublime see Day 2013, 63–71 and *passim*.
73 As Hinds 2007, 152, has shown, in this poem Martial alludes to Augustus's cosmic triple triumph as depicted by Vergil on the shield of Aeneas, esp. Verg. *A.* 8.705–6 (cf. Mart. *Sp.* 3.7) and Verg. *A.* 8.720–23 (cf. Mart. *Sp.* 3.11): a game of imperial one-upmanship for both emperor and poet.
74 See Gunderson 2003.

5 War Games

This confounding manipulation of the one and the many plays upon the "one versus all" or "one for all" numbers game of Roman epic; a game that Martial co-opts and distorts in the *Liber Spectaculorum*,[75] where it can proclaim new-found liberty but also whisper about tyranny and civil war. The Neronian age and the civil war it precipitated are intertwined in the physical and imaginary space that Martial's renovated Rome occupies; indeed, through Flavian eyes, Nero's aggressive occupation of public space is an act of civil war in itself. There is a civil-war ring about the single house that occupies the whole city (Mart. *Sp.* 2.4), but so too about the cannibalizing mission of the Colosseum that gobbles up Rome's monumental past in *Liber Spectaculorum* 2, after warring down the world's architectural wonders in *Sp.* 1 (cf. *cedit*, "to give ground," Mart. *Sp.* 1.7).[76] The global crowd contained in poem 3, as we saw above, is an example of this totalizing numerical play. Rimell has shown that this epigram can be read as an anticipatory catalogue that condenses the gory spectacles to come: the Rhodopeian farmer from Orphic Haemus (Mart. *Sp.* 3.3), for example, recalled in *Liber Spectaculorum* 21 where the prisoner Orpheus is mauled by a bear in a Metamorphic remake (*quidquid in Orpheo Rhodope spectasse theatro | dicitur, exhibuit, Caesar, harena tibi*, "whatever Rhodope is said to have seen in Orpheus's theater, the arena has presented, Caesar, for you," Mart. *Sp.* 21.1–2; cf. Ov. *Met.* 11.1–66).[77] *Sp.* 3 reveals, as Rimell argues, "a oneness that risks going *too far*" by imposing an uncomfortable, tyrannical unity that blurs the lines between spectators and spectated, making the audience part of the bloody games that break down the boundaries between "spectators and victims, men and beasts."[78] Remember the spatial elision at *Liber Spectaculorum* 3.2: we know that we are in the Colosseum here, but what Martial tells us is that we are in Caesar's city (*in urbe tua*). The last fighting that took place in Rome was the violence of civil war in 69 CE. If we are in Rome in *Sp.* 3, then the spectacles that these audience members anticipate (and thus participate in?) are not just any battles, they are civil-war games. There is a kind of Lucanean logic at work here, according to which civil war made the whole world into citizens of Rome (*nam post ciuilia bella | hic populus Romanus erit*, "for after civil war this will be the Roman

---

75 Rimell 2008, 115–16, cf. Hardie 1993a, 3–10.
76 *TLL* s.v. II.A.
77 Rimell 2008, 119–21, analyses each crowd member and their bloody associations individually; on "Orpheus" cf. Hinds 2007, 148ff.
78 Rimell 2008, 119, 120.

people," Luc. 7.542–43), and its violence is the spectacular slaughter of the amphitheater.[79]

Indeed, once the games begin we find that some of Lucan's beasts are out to play. In *Sp.* 18 a tigress displays unnatural ferocity when she mauls a wild lion (Mart. *Sp.* 18):

> <u>lambere</u> securi dextram <u>consueta</u> magistri
> > <u>tigris</u>, ab Hyrcano gloria rara iugo,
> saeua ferum *rabido* lacerauit *dente* leonem:
> > res noua, non ullis cognita temporibus.
> ausa est tale nihil, siluis dum uixit in altis: 5
> > postquam inter nos est, plus feritatis habet.

> Accustomed to lick the hand of her confident master, the tigress, rare glory from the Hyrcanian mountain, ferociously mauled a wild lion with her rabid teeth: this was a new act, unknown before in any time. She never dared such things while she lived in lofty forests: after living amongst us, she is a more savage beast.

This tiger's tongue is that of the bloodthirsty Pompey, described in Caesar's tigresses simile in *Bellum Ciuile* 1 that has him licking the sword of his master Sulla (Luc. 1.327–31):

> utque ferae *tigres* numquam posuere furorem
> quas nemore Hyrcano, matrum dum lustra secuntur,
> altus caesorum pauit cruor armentorum,
> sic et <u>Sullanum solito tibi lambere ferrum</u>   330
> durat, Magne, sitis.

> Just as wild tigers have never put aside their rage that lived once in the Hyrcanian forest, while they ranged over the haunts of their mothers and drank deep of the blood of slaughtered herds, thus you, Magnus, accustomed to lick the sword of Sulla, are thirsty still.

While the message of Lucan's simile seems to be that a tiger cannot change its stripes, Martial has shown us otherwise, and while his epic beast (*Hyrcano iugo*, Mart. *Sp.* 18.2; cf. *nemore Hyrcano*, Luc. 1.328)[80] may resemble Pompey, her teeth belong to Caesar, the caged beast in Egypt: *sic fremit in paruis fera nobilis abdita claustris | et frangit <u>rabidos</u> praemorso carcere <u>dentes</u>* ("just so the noble beast roars shut up in its small prison and breaks its rabid teeth in biting the bars," Luc. 10.445–46). This is a self-destructive gesture, since the beast breaks (*frangit*)

---

[79] Leigh 1997, 234–91. Cf. Fitzgerald 2007, 35–36, on the problem of the "spectacle".
[80] Cf. Roche 2009, *ad* Luc. 1.328: "the only place for an epic tiger to be since Verg. *A.* 4.367."

its own ravening teeth on the bars.[81] In Martial's spliced re-make, the tiger turns this violence outward to attack an enemy never before dared.

Caesar's feral frenzy is revealed in isolation, but Martial's tiger learns her new savagery in human company: *postquam inter nos est, plus feritatis habet* (Mart. *Sp.* 18.6). Is this "in the company of mankind" or "here in (civilised) Rome?" Coleman asks.[82] Transplanted into the amphitheater that is also the city (*in urbe tua*, Mart. *Sp.* 3.2), a new kind of ferocity, a new *furor*, is required. In *Sp.* 22 the sluggish anger of a rhinoceros leads to fears that there will be no show today until—at last—his *furor* returns (Mart. *Sp.* 22.1–4):[83]

> sollicitant pauidi dum rhinocerota magistri
>   seque diu magnae colligit ira ferae,
> desperabantur promissi proelia Martis;
>   sed tandem rediit cognitus ante furor.
>
> While nervous trainers worried about the rhinoceros and the anger of the great beast took a long time to gather itself, the crowd were giving up hope on the battles of the promised conflict; but at last the anger known before returned.

To whom is this *furor* already known? This is not the natural *furor* of the wild animal but the spectacular *furor* of the tamed beast, unleashed now for display. Towards the end of this epigram,[84] a lion flees the now-raging rhinoceros in an alternative death-leap: *hunc leo cum fugeret praeceps in tela cucurrit* ("the lion as it fled ran headlong into the spears," Mart. *Sp.* 22.11). This suicidal lion seems to recall another (Luc. 1.205–12):

>   sicut squalentibus aruis   205
> aestiferae Libyes uiso leo comminus hoste
> subsedit dubius, totam dum colligit iram;
> mox, ubi se saeuae stimulauit uerbere caudae
> erexitque iubam et uasto graue murmur hiatu
> infremuit, tum torta leuis si lancea Mauri   210

---

81 Cf. the caged beasts that reassert their natural ferocity at the first taste of blood in the simile at Luc. 4.237–42.
82 Coleman 2006, *ad loc.* Her answer compares Tac. *Ag.* 21.2, but strikes a note of caution: "Tacitean cynicism and social criticism do not seem to cohere with Martial's sycophantic jingoism, but the sentiment is common[,] ... and the witty paradox may have taken precedence over the implication that contemporary Rome exercized a corrupting influence on the animal kingdom."
83 On *furor*'s association with civil war in the Roman literary imagination, see Jal 1963, 421–25.
84 See Jal 1963, 187–88, on the problem of the cohesion of this epigram. Note that Mart. 8.53.11 uses elements of this simile (esp. Luc. 1.211) in describing the death of a prodigious lion in the arena.

> haereat aut latum subeant uenabula pectus,
> per ferrum tanti securus uulneris exit.

Like the lion in the barren fields of torrid Libya that, seeing its enemy close at hand, crouches down in hesitation while gathering the whole force of its rage; next, when it has roused itself with the cruel lash of its tail, raised up its mane, and bellowed out a roar from its great gaping jaws, then if the hurled javelin of the light-armed Moor should cling to him or hunting spears should pierce his broad breast, he carries on along the blade, careless of so great a wound.

This, of course, is the simile (with formidable epic credentials)[85] that compares Caesar—as he crosses the Rubicon and unleashes civil war—to a Libyan lion. In poem 22, Martial has divided the elements of this lion simile between the aggressor (the rhinoceros) and its victim (the lion).[86] This division reflects the structure of Lucan's simile, where the lion's gathering madness culminates (*totam ... colligit iram*; cf. *se ... colligit ira*, Mart. *Sp.* 22.2) in self-destruction that anticipates Caesar's own eventual demise and pinpoints suicidal civil war at its root.[87] To return to *Sp.* 18, the tiger's killing of the lion can be read as an ironic reversal of states for Lucan's civil-war adversaries: Caesar the suicidal lion is mauled to death by the tiger Pompey in an act of vengeance that sees civil war's traditional loser not only live up to Caesar's characterisation (the blood-thirsty tigresses simile at Luc. 1.327–31) but employ Caesar's own self-destructive force against him (*rabido ... dente*, 18.3; *rabidos ... dentes*, Luc. 10.446).

With these allusions Martial literalizes what for Lucan was a metaphor, transforming the spectacular beasts (and spectacular violence) of the *Bellum Ciuile* into a series of mashed-up amphitheatrical scene-stealers.[88] The animal sublime, as Burke tells us, relies upon the sense of terror attendant upon the experience of power or strength that far exceeds one's own, and it is the indomitable nature of the wild beast that is the source of its sublimity.[89] In Martial's Colosseum, the sublimity of these bestial spectacles derives precisely

---

[85] See Roche 2009, *ad loc.*
[86] Before we reach the lion, the rhinoceros tosses or spears a bear, two deer, a buffalo, and a bison (Mart. *Sp.* 22.5–6, 9–10).
[87] Masters 1992, 2 n. 5: "the effects of the civil war are that Caesar obscurely destroys himself." Note also that Martial's lion is *praeceps* (Mart. *Sp.* 22.11) in its suicidal flight: a distinctly Caesarean movement, for one who is *in omnia praeceps* ("headlong in everything," Luc. 2.656).
[88] On the amphitheatricality of Lucan's violence, see Leigh 1997 (esp. 234–91); on its sublimity, see Day 2013, 16–17, 63–105.
[89] Burke 2008, 60–61. For an analysis of Lucan's Libyan lion as a sublime object, see Day 2013, 125–28; Day draws on Lucretius's extraordinary description of animals unleashed in battle at Lucr. 5.1310–29 (with Conte 1994a, 26).

from the fact of their astonishing containment: even when an animal reverts to (or perhaps exceeds) its natural, wild ferocity, these thrilling slips are spectacles that augment the sublimity of the emperor.[90] Sublimity is attributed, then, not so much to the animals but to the poet and—above all—to the *princeps*. Martial has destabilized the rules of Lucan's epic civil war, has rewritten (literary) history: Caesar and Pompey, winner and loser, are spliced together or torn apart into the Frankensteined bodies of these marvellous beasts that defy expectation in performance. While this reversal risks a slip into the ridiculous, the sublimity of the animals is not trivialized, it is simply that the object of our sublime astonishment has shifted: it is the emperor we marvel at, who has demanded (and received) a new *ingenium* for man and beast (*quos decet esse hominum tali sub principe mores, | qui iubet ingenium mitius esse feris*, "what manners are fitting for men under such an emperor, who demands a gentler nature for wild beasts?" Mart. *Sp*. 10.5–6).[91] In Flavian Rome the rules of engagement have been destabilized and rewritten: as the Colosseum itself cannibalizes the *Domus aurea* as a symbol of Nero's tyrannical war upon the people, inside the amphitheater with Lucan as intertext Martial takes on another civil-war legacy of the Neronian age as a kind of deconstructed remake. Civil war is not forgotten but is refigured as sublime entertainment.[92]

6 Sublime Instability

We saw earlier that the monuments in the *Liber Spectaculorum* are charged with a kind of unstable energy, seeming to surge up in poem 2 in a representation of the building program that, as we know, was necessitated—or facilitated—by the fact of Rome's ruinous state when the Flavians first came to power under Vespasian. *Liber Spectaculorum* 2 presents an emphatic double vision of monumental Rome, in which the rising structures of the present are held in tension with the buildings they have replaced. Tenses slide in this epigram between present, imperfect, perfect, and pluperfect, but Martial conjures both

---

[90] Cf. Coleman 2006, 112–13, on Mart. *Sp*. 10 (12) and *ad Sp*. 18.6 (21.6).
[91] In this epigram a lion bites the hand of its trainer and is killed on the order of the *princeps*, who thus asserts his power even over resurgent nature; cf. Mart. 2.75, for the lion who mauls two slave-boys in the arena with a *feritate reuersa* that exceeds its natural savagery.
[92] Cf. Marco Fucecchi's chapter in this volume on efforts in Flavian epic to "metabolize" civil war after Lucan. The memory (poetic or historical) of civil war is not "neutralized" by Martial's engagement with the *Bellum Ciuile*, but it is given new, spectacular form in the present.

present and past monuments with equal vividness, so that we seem to see Rome's architectural layers built up in palimpsestic fashion.[93] The ruins of the recent past have an almost palpable presence in *Sp.* 2 that destabilizes the new monuments, drawing attention to the age-old dilemma of their fundamental fragility. For James Porter, writing on the intrinsic sublimity of this dilemma, "monuments are ... spectacles of their own ruin,"[94] structures that always already anticipate their own collapse. He notes the inherent irony of the monument that strives for permanence[95] but that in doing so acknowledges and is thus testament to the potential for future loss.[96] The monument expresses, then, "a tension between permanence and loss," and it is from this tension that the sublime emerges.[97] The amphitheater, a monument dedicated to death but teeming with the living bodies of the crowd, heightens and complicates this tension. Its monumentality is, as we saw earlier, a kind of shell, within which the notions of permanence and loss are easily confused; moreover, once inside the Colosseum, the idea of monumentality becomes part of the performance. Take, for example, the monumental lion of *Sp.* 15 (*ignota spectandum mole leonem*, "a spectacular lion of unbelievable bulk," Mart. *Sp.* 15.5) that recalls the "rising mass" of the Colosseum itself (*erigitur moles*, Mart. *Sp.* 2.6).[98] Note also the bear that, caught in a sticky trap, hangs in empty air (*deprendat uacuo uenator in aere praedam*, "let the hunter catch his prey in empty air," Mart. *Sp.* 11.5) like the sublime mausoleum of *Sp.* 1 (*aere ... uacuo pendentia Mausolea*, Mart. *Sp.* 1.5).[99] As Rimell argues, the epitaphic origins of epigram mean that Martial's poetic sketches serve to rapidly monumentalize the spectacles in the amphitheater as if casting them in quick-dry concrete,[100] so that these fighting and flying beasts become ephemeral little monuments themselves that mimic and recall the massive sublime structures of the first three epigrams.

---

[93] Rimell 2008, 18: "the image of what lies beneath the foundations of the Colosseum stays with us, and it is difficult to erase the idea ... of monument ... as palimpsest, each new structure in some way absorbing as well as covering up and cancelling out the old."
[94] Porter 2011, 686.
[95] Note the memorial function of the Latin *monumentum*, deriving from *moneo*, "to advise" or "warn;" cf. Porter 2011, 685.
[96] Porter 2011, 685–86.
[97] Porter 2011, 685–87.
[98] These are the only two places in which *moles* occurs in Martial's corpus; with Mart. *Sp.* 15.5, cf. Ov. *Met.* 9.197 (*TLL* 2.A.β.II).
[99] *mausolea* recalls not just the mausoleum at Halicarnassus (cf. Coleman 2006, *ad loc.*) but the mausoleum of Augustus. See Rimell 2008, 62; Roman 2010, 113. On the 'empty air' image, cf. Coleman 2006, *ad* Mart. *Sp.* 13.5: "almost a cliché," comparing Hor. *Carm.* 1.3.34 and Verg. *G.* 3.108–9.
[100] Rimell 2008, 51–63, esp. 62–63.

Even the Colosseum itself is a less stable presence than we might imagine. Coleman points out that the physical structure of the Colosseum features much less prominently in the *Liber Spectaculorum* than its "radically innovative" nature would seem to justify.[101] Instead, our image of the Colosseum is built up from its fleeting spectacles, and in the two opening epigrams in which the amphitheater is mentioned, the precise nature of its physical structure remains evasive. The immense *moles* (Mart. *Sp.* 2.6) of the Colosseum is thus strangely insubstantial: we presume its monumental massiveness but Martial refuses to offer confirmation. *moles* does varied duty in Latin, retaining the sense of a large and weighty mass or bulk in both its physical (*TLL* s.v. II.A) and metaphorical (*TLL* s.v. I.A–C) applications, but connoting in the latter group a great responsibility, a burden, exertion or effort, force or might. *moles*, combining expansive reach in its sense of scale with the implication of collapse under the burden of its weight[102] in a single, ponderous word, thus captures both the mathematical (scale) and the dynamical (force) sublime. We see this at work at *Liber Spectaculorum* 2: *hic ubi conspicui uenerabilis Amphitheatri | erigitur moles* (Mart. *Sp.* 2.5–6). The immediate sense here is of dynamic motion, as the great mass of the Colosseum is raised before our very eyes, but the ambivalent thrill of the sublime in this image emerges from the implicit precariousness of the vertiginous rise of this *moles*, which asserts the threat of collapse. In *Sp.* 1, though, the amphitheater is the singular substitution for a host of architectural wonders that are already suspended in a vacuum (*aere ... uacuo pendentia Mausolea*, Mart. *Sp.* 1.5) and that collapse beneath (*cedit*, Mart. *Sp.* 1.7) the Colosseum's indefinite weight. Or rather, their *labor* yields or collapses (Mart. *Sp.* 1.7): just as the scaffolding of *Sp.* 2.2 hints at the (sublime) value of construction,[103] this last collective *labor* has a similar effect. As metonymy for the finished works,[104] *labor* has a flavor of *moles* here, in the sense of effort expended (*TLL* s.v. *moles* I.B), but it is also a final evasion that stresses the paradoxical intangibility of these monumental marvels. They are all sublime structures, and Caesar's amphitheater—unfathomably *unum pro cunctis ... opus* (Mart. *Sp.* 1.8)— is the sublimest of them all.

---

101 Coleman 1998, 15.
102 *TLL* s.v. I.A.2 (*de ui et pondere ruinae ... et ictus*), cf. Hor. *Carm.* 3.4.65 *uis consili expers mole ruit sua*; for natural and cosmic usages, *TLL* s.v. II.A.1.II.
103 See above.
104 Coleman 2006, *ad loc.*

7 Conclusion

This is not only Caesar's multiply singular *opus*, of course, but Martial's.[105] His evasive Colosseum is an unstable monument built on unstable ground ruptured by the remnants of dual civil conflict, one war waged by the emperor upon his people and another by the people upon themselves. This was a past that could not be forgotten but that could be remodelled: looking through the lens of epigram, civil war becomes a Neronian affair—a tyrannical building project and a Lucanean trick. Martial destabilizes and repossesses both: the Colosseum replaces without erasing the *Domus aurea*; once the games begin, we recognize civil war—or rather, *Civil War*—but not as we know it. And all the while, we are celebrating another edifice—the renovated emperor: post-Julio-Claudian, post-civil war, enigmatic, and sublime.[106] Epigram is unstable by nature, a throwaway monument to the moment but one that obsesses perversely about its own (im)permanence. Rimell has shown the ways in which Martial picks off and recasts Augustan tropes of poetic monumentality to reveal that one cannot survive whole, but only in fragments.[107] While Martial's foregrounding and celebration of Flavian architecture has been read as a subversion of Augustan poetic monumentality that hands over endurance to the emperors,[108] we have seen that what is remarkable about this celebration is the way in which Martial emphasizes instability—a quality shared with epigram, though, in fact, instability is always already a part of monumentality.[109] Martial's is a monumentality for the Flavian age, unstable and spectacular: survival is not static but shifting, and Martial shapes the Colosseum into an unstable and dynamic edifice in this image. In re-writing the rules of monumentality, Martial

---

105 For Martial's interest in the poetic *topos* of the architectural *opus*, see, for example, Coleman 2006, *ad* Mart. *Sp.* 1.1, on the catalogue of architectural wonders in this epigram, citing Weinreich 1928 for the possibility that the pyramids' placement first is "because of their prominent exemplary function in Horace's claim to literary immortality." In his reading of Mart. 8.36 (an epigram about another sublime monument charged with instability, the palace of Domitian), Roman 2010, 113, again finds an allusion to Horace in its opening two lines (*regia pyramidum, Caesar, miracula ride! | iam tacet Eoum barbara Memphis opus*, "Laugh, Caesar, at the regal wonders of the pyramids! Now barbarous Memphis keeps silent about her Eastern work," cf. Hor. *Carm.* 3.30.1–2); but these lines clearly recall Mart. *Sp.* 1.1, where Horace's *monumentum* seems to be lurking too.
106 Fitting, perhaps, that the identity of *Caesar* remains uncertain; see n. 16 above.
107 Rimell 2008, 51–93, esp. 71.
108 Roman 2010, 112–13.
109 Fowler 2000, 211: "the essence of the monument is paradoxically its lack of monumental stability;" cf. Porter 2011.

also stakes his claim on sublime transcendence;[110] locating it in the unstable and insecure, he finds astonishment in the rise and a thrill in the threat of the fall.

---

[110] Cf., e.g., Hardie 2009, 123, 184 on sublimity in Hor. *Carm.* 3.30.

Bibliography

Adamietz, J. (1976), *Zur Komposition der Argonautica des Valerius Flaccus*, Munich (Zetemata 67).
Ahl, F. (1976), *Lucan. An Introduction*, Ithaca (NY).
Ahl, F. (1984a), "The Art of Safe Criticism in Greece and Rome," *AJPh* 105, 174–208.
Ahl, F. (1984b), "The Rider and the Horse: Politics and Power in Roman Poetry from Horace to Statius," *ANRW* II.32.1, 40–110.
Ahl, F. (1986), "Statius' *Thebaid*: A Reconsideration," *ANRW* II.32.5, 2803–912.
Ahl, F. (trans.) (2007), *Virgil*: Aeneid, Oxford.
Ahl, F./Davis, M.A./Pomeroy, A. (1986), "Silius Italicus," *ANRW* II.32.4, 2492–561.
Alfonsi, L. (1983), "La figura di Romolo all'inizio delle storie di Livio," in: E. Burck/E. Lefèvre/E. Olshausen (eds.), *Livius, Werk und Rezeption. Festschrift für Erich Burck zum 80. Geburtstag*, Munich, 99–106.
Ambühl, A. (2010), "Lucan's 'Ilioupersis' – Narrative Patterns from the Fall of Troy in Book 2 of the *Bellum civile*," in: N. Hömke/C. Reitz (eds.), *Lucan's Bellum Civile. Between Epic Tradition and Aesthetic Innovation*, Berlin/New York (BzA 282), 17–38.
Ambühl, A. (2015), *Krieg und Bürgerkrieg bei Lucan und in der griechischen Literatur. Studien zur Rezeption der attischen Tragödie und der hellenistischen Dichtung im Bellum civile*, Berlin/Munich/Boston (BzA 225).
Ambühl, A. (2016), "Thessaly as an Intertextual Landscape of Civil War in Latin Poetry," in: J. McInerney/I. Sluiter (eds.), *Valuing Landscape in Classical Antiquity: Natural Environment and Cultural Imagination*, Leiden/Boston (Mnemosyne Suppl. 393), 297–322.
Amigues, S. (1995), "Les plantes d'Égypte vues par les naturalistes grecs," in: J. Leclant (ed.), *Entre Égypte et Grèce. Actes du 5ème colloque de la Villa Kérylos à Beaulieu-sur-Mer du 6 au 9 octobre 1994*, Paris (Cahiers de la Villa "Kérylos" 5), 51–67.
André, J. (1958), *Pline l'Ancien. Histoire naturelle. Livre XIV. Des Arbres fruitiers: la vigne*, Paris.
André, J. (1971), *Pline l'Ancien. Histoire naturelle. Livre XXIII. Remèdes tirés des arbres cultivés*, Paris.
Antoniadis, T. (2015), "Scelus Femineum: Adultery and Revenge in Valerius Flaccus' *Argonautica* Book 2 (98–241) and Seneca's *Agamemnon*," *SO* 89, 60–80.
Arias, P.E. (1986), "Bonus Eventus," *LIMC* III.1, 123–26.
Aricò, G. (1991), "La Vicenda di Lemno in Stazio e Valerio Flacco," in: M. Korn/H.J. Tschiedel (eds.), *Ratis omnia vincet. Untersuchungen zu den Argonautica des Valerius Flaccus*, Hildesheim (Spudasmata 48), 197–210.
Armitage, D. (2017a), *Civil Wars: A History in Ideas*, New York.
Armitage, D. (2017b), "On the Genealogy of Quarrels," *Critical Analysis of Law* 4, 179–89.
Arnott, W.G. (2007), *Birds in the Ancient World from A to Z*, London/New York.
Ash, R. (1999), *Ordering Anarchy: Armies and Leaders in Tacitus' Histories*, London.
Ash, R. (2007a), "Victim and Voyeur: Rome as a Character in Tacitus' *Histories* 3," in: D.H.J. Larmour/D. Spencer (eds.), *The Sites of Rome: Time, Space, Memory*, Oxford, 211–37.
Ash, R. (ed.) (2007b), *Tacitus:* Histories Book II, Cambridge.
Ash, R. (2010), "*Tarda Moles Civilis Belli*: The Weight of the Past in Tacitus' Histories," in: B.W. Breed/C. Damon/A. Rossi (eds.), *Citizens of Discord: Rome and Its Civil Wars*, Oxford, 119–31.
Asheri, D./Lloyd, A.B./Corcella, A./Murray, O./Moreno, A. (2007), *A Commentary on Herodotus. Books I–IV*, Oxford.

Asso, P. (2010a), *A Commentary on Lucan*, De Bello Civili *IV: Introduction, Edition, and Translation*, Berlin (Texte und Kommentare 33).
Asso, P. (2010b), "Hercules as a Paradigm for Roman Heroism," in: A. Augoustakis (ed.), *Brill's Companion to Silius Italicus*, Leiden, 241–76.
Aston, E. (2011), *Mixanthrôpoi: Animal-human Hybrid Deities in Greek Religion*, Liège (Kernos Suppl. 25).
Atkinson, K. (2007), "Noble Deaths at Gamla and Masada? A Critical Assessment of Josephus' Accounts of Jewish Resistance in Light of Archaeological Discoveries," in: Z. Rodgers (ed.), *Making History: Josephus and Historical Method*, Leiden (*JSJ* Suppl. 110), 349–71.
Augoustakis, A. (2003), "*Rapit infidum uictor caput*: Ekphrasis and Gender-Role reversal in Silius Italicus' *Punica*," in: P. Thibodeau/H. Haskell (eds.), *Being There Together: Essays in Honor of Michael C. J. Putnam on the Occasion of his Seventieth Birthday*, Afton (MN), 110–27.
Augoustakis, A. (2008), "The Other as Same: Non-Roman Mothers in Silius Italicus' *Punica*," *CPh* 103, 55–76.
Augoustakis, A. (2010a), *Motherhood and the Other: Fashioning Female Power in Flavian Epic*, Oxford.
Augoustakis, A. (ed.) (2010b), *Brill's Companion to Silius Italicus*, Leiden.
Augoustakis, A. (2010c), "Silius Italicus, A Flavian Poet," in: A. Augoustakis (ed.), *Brill's Companion to Silius Italicus*, Leiden, 3–23.
Augoustakis, A. (2012), "Daphnis' *deductum nomen/carmen* in Silius' Sicilian Pastoral (*Pun.* 14.462–76)," *TiC* 4, 132–52.
Augoustakis, A. (2015), "Statius in Senecan drama," in: W.J. Dominik/C.E. Newlands/K. Gervais (eds.), *Brill's Companion to Statius*, Leiden, 377–92.
Augoustakis, A. (ed.) (2016), *Statius*, Thebaid *8. Edited with an Introduction, Translation, and Commentary*, Oxford.
Baier, T. (2001), *Valerius Flaccus:* Argonautica *Buch VI. Einleitung und Kommentar*, Munich (Zetemata 112).
Baldini Moscadi, L. (1993), "Caratteri paradigmatici e modelli letterari: Manilio e i *paranatellonta* dell'*Aquarius*," in: D. Liuzzi (ed.), *Manilio tra poesia e scienza*, Galatina, 79–94.
Baldini Moscadi, L. (2005), *Magica Musa. La Magia dei Poeti Latini. Figure e Funzione*, Bologna.
Ball, L.F. (2003), *The Domus Aurea and the Roman Architectural Revolution*, Cambridge.
Bannon, C.J. (1997), *The Brothers of Romulus: Fraternal Pietas in Roman Law, Literature, and Society*, Princeton.
Barchiesi, A. (1988), *Seneca. Le Fenicie (Phoenissae)*, Venezia (Letteratura universale Marsilio. Il Convivio).
Barchiesi, A. (2001), "Genealogie letterarie nell'epica imperiale. Fondamentalismo e ironia," in: E.A. Schmidt (ed.), *L'histoire littéraire immanente dans la poésie latine*, Vandoeuvres-Genève (Entretiens sur l'antiquité classique 47), 315–54.
Barchiesi, A. (ed.) (2005), *Ovidio: Metamorfosi, vol. I (Libri I–II)*, Milan.
Barchiesi, A./Rosati, G. (eds.) (2007), *Ovidio: Metamorfosi, vol. II (Libri III–IV)*, Milan.
Barclay, J. (2005), "The Empire Writes Back: Josephan Rhetoric in Flavian Rome," in: J. Edmondson/S. Mason/J. Rives (eds.), *Flavius Josephus and Flavian Rome*, Oxford, 315–32.
Barclay, J. (2006), *Flavius Josephus: Translation and Commentary. Vol. 10: Against Apion*, ed. S. Mason, Leiden.
Barnes, M.H. (2003), *Inscribed* Kleos: *Aetiological Contexts in Apollonius of Rhodes*, PhD diss., University of Missouri.
Barrett, A.A. (1996), *Agrippina: Sex, Power, and Politics in the Early Empire*, New Haven (CT).

Barrett, A.A. (2002), *Livia: First Lady of Imperial Rome*, New Haven (CT).
Bartman, E. (1999), *Portraits of Livia: Imaging the Imperial Woman in Augustan Rome*, Cambridge.
Batstone, W.W./Damon, C. (2006), *Caesar's Civil War*, Oxford (Oxford Approaches to Classical Literature).
Beagon, M. (1992), *Roman Nature. The Thought of Pliny the Elder*, Oxford.
Beagon, M. (2005), *The Elder Pliny on the Human Animal:* Natural History Book 7, Oxford.
Beagon, M. (2013), "*Labores pro bono publico*: the burdensome mission of Pliny's *Natural History*," in: J. König/G. Woolf (eds.), *Encyclopaedism from Antiquity to the Renaissance*, Cambridge, 84–107.
Beard, M. (2003), "The Triumph of Flavius Josephus," in: A.J. Boyle/W.J. Dominik (eds.), *Flavian Rome: Culture, Image, Text*, Leiden, 543–58.
Bénatouïl, T. (2009), "How Industrious can Zeus be? The Extent and Objects of Divine Activity," in: R. Salles (ed.), *God and Cosmos in Stoicism*, Oxford, 23–45.
Bendz, G. (1938), *Die Echtheitsfrage des vierten Buches der Frontinschen Strategemata*, Lund/Leipzig (Lunds Universitets Årsskrift n.f. avd. 1, 34.4).
Bernstein, F. (1997), "Verständnis- und Entwicklungsstufen der archaischen *Consualia*. Römisches Substrat und griechische Überlagerung," *Hermes* 125, 413–46.
Bernstein, N.W. (2004), "*Auferte oculos*: Modes of Spectatorship in Statius *Thebaid* 11," *Phoenix* 58, 62–85.
Bernstein, N.W. (2008), *In the Image of the Ancestors: Narratives of Kinship in Flavian Epic*, Toronto (Phoenix Suppl. 48).
Bernstein, N.W. (2009), "The white doe of Capua (Silius Italicus, *Punica* 13.115–137)," *Scholia* 18, 89–106.
Bernstein, N.W. (2010), "Family and State in the *Punica*," in: A. Augoustakis (ed.), *Brill's Companion to Silius Italicus*, Leiden, 377–97.
Bernstein, N.W. (2014), "*Romanas veluti saevissima cum legiones Tisiphone regesque movet*: Valerius Flaccus' *Argonautica* and the Flavian Era," in: M. Heerink/G. Manuwald (eds.), *Brill's Companion to Valerius Flaccus*, Leiden, 154–69.
Bernstein, N.W. (2016), "Epic Poetry: Historicizing the Flavian Epics," in: A. Zissos (ed.), *A Companion to the Flavian Age of Imperial Rome*, Chichester/Oxford/Malden (MA), 395–411.
Bernstein, N.W. (2017), *Silius Italicus*, Punica 2. Oxford.
Berti, E. (2007), *Scholasticorum Studia. Seneca il Vecchio e la cultura retorica e letteraria della prima età imperiale*, Pisa (*MD* Bibl. 20).
Bessone, F. (2011), *La* Tebaide *di Stazio. Epica e potere*, Pisa/Roma (*MD* Bibl. 24).
Bessone, F. (2015), "Sondaggi di stile. A proposito di uno studio sulla *Tebaide* di Stazio," *RFIC* 143, 183–93.
Bessone, F. (forthcoming), "Allusive (Im-)pertinence in Statius' Epic," in: N. Coffee/C. Forstall/L. Galli Milić/D.P. Nelis (eds.), *Intertextuality in Flavian Epic Poetry*, Berlin (*TiC* Suppl. 64).
Bexley, E. (2014), "Lucan's Catalogues and the Landscape of War," in: M. Skempis/I. Ziogas (eds.), *Geography, Topography, Landscape: Configurations of Space in Greek and Roman Epic*, Berlin (*TiC* Suppl. 22), 373–403.
Bicknell, P.J. (1984), "The Dark Side of the Moon," in: A. Moffatt (ed.), *Maistor: Classical, Byzantine and Renaissance Studies for Robert Browning*, Canberra (Byzantina Australiensia 5), 67–75.
Bilde, P. (1988), *Flavius Josephus between Jerusalem and Rome. His Life, his Works and their Importance*, Sheffield (Journal for the Study of Pseudepigrapha Suppl. 2).

Biondi, G.G. (1984), *Il nefas argonautico:* Mythos e logos *nella* Medea *di Seneca*, Bologna (Edizioni e saggi universitari di filologia classica 33).

Blaive, F. (1995), "Le rituel romain des *Robigalia* et le sacrifice du chien dans le monde indo-européen," *Latomus* 54, 279–89.

Bloomer, W.M. (1992), *Valerius Maximus and the Rhetoric of the New Nobility*, Chapel Hill (NC).

Boëthius, A. (1952), "*Et crescunt media pegmata celsa via* (Martial's De spectaculis 2,2)," *Eranos* 50, 129–37.

Boëthius, A. (1960), *The Golden House of Nero: Some Aspects of Roman Architecture*, Ann Arbor (MI).

Bohak, G. (2003), "The Ibis and the Jewish Question," in: M. Mor/A. Oppenheimer/J. Pastor/D.R. Schwartz (eds.), *Jews and Gentiles in the Holy Land in the Days of the Second Temple, the Mishnah and the Talmud: A collection of articles*, Jerusalem, 27–43.

Bommas, M. (2012), "The Iseum Campense as a Memory Site," in: M. Bommas/J. Harrisson/P. Roy (eds.), *Memory and Urban Religion in the Ancient World*, London/New York, 177–212.

Bonet, V. (2003), "Le traitement de la douleur: quand l'irrationnel vient au secours du rationnel," in: N. Palmieri (ed.), *Rationnel et irrationnel dans la médecine ancienne et médiévale. Aspects historiques, scientifiques et culturels*, Saint-Étienne (Mémoires 26), 145–62.

Bonet, V. (2014), *La pharmacopée végétale d'Occident dans l'œuvre de Pline l'Ancien*, Brussels (Collection Latomus 346).

Börm, H. (2016), "Introduction," in: H. Börm/M. Mattheis/J. Weinand (eds.), *Civil War in Ancient Greece and Rome. Contexts of Disintegration and Reintegration*, Stuttgart (Heidelberger althistorische Beiträge und epigraphische Studien 58), 1–26.

Börm, H./Mattheis, M./Wienand, J. (eds.) (2016), *Civil War in Ancient Greece and Rome. Contexts of Disintegration and Reintegration*, Stuttgart (Heidelberger althistorische Beiträge und epigraphische Studien 58).

Boyle, A.J. (2003), "Introduction: Reading Flavian Rome," in: A.J. Boyle/W.J. Dominik (eds.), *Flavian Rome: Culture, Image, Text*, Leiden, 1–68.

Boyle, A.J. (ed. and trans.) (2011), *Seneca:* Oedipus, Oxford.

Boyle, A.J. (ed. and trans.) (2014), *Seneca:* Medea, Oxford.

Boyle, A.J./Dominik, W.J. (eds.) (2003), *Flavian Rome: Culture, Image, Text*, Leiden.

Boyle, A.J./Woodard, R.D. (2004), *Ovid: Fasti*, London.

Bradley, K.R. (1978), *Suetonius'* Life of Nero: *An Historical Commentary*, Brussels (Collection Latomus 157).

Bradley, K.R. (2005), "The Roman Child in Sickness and in Health," in: M. George (ed.), *The Roman Family in the Empire: Rome, Italy, and Beyond*, Oxford, 67–92.

Breed, B.W./Damon, C./Rossi, A. (eds.) (2010a), *Citizens of Discord: Rome and Its Civil Wars*, Oxford.

Breed, B.W./Damon, C./Rossi, A. (2010b), "Introduction," in: B.W. Breed/C. Damon/A. Rossi (eds.), *Citizens of Discord: Rome and its Civil Wars*, Oxford, 3–22.

Brighton, M.A. (2009), *The Sicarii in Josephus's* Judean War. *Rhetorical Analysis and Historical Observations*, Atlanta (GA) (SBL Early Judaism and Its Literature 27).

Briguglio, S. (2017), Fraternas acies. *Saggio di commento a Stazio*, Tebaide, *1, 1–389*, Alessandria (Millennium 9).

Briscoe, J. (2008), *A Commentary on Livy: Books 38–40*, Oxford.

Bronfen, E. (1992), *Over her Dead Body: Death, femininity and the aesthetic*, Manchester.

Brouwers, J.H. (1982), "Zur Lucan-Imitation bei Silius Italicus," in: J. den Boeft/A.H.M. Kessels (eds.), *Actus: Studies in Honour of H.L.W. Nelson*, Utrecht, 73–87.

Brunner, O./Conze, W./Koselleck, R. (eds.) (1984), *Geschichtliche Grundbegriffe*, vol. 5, Stuttgart.

Buckley, E. (2010), "War-epic for a new era: Valerius Flaccus' *Argonautica*," in: N. Kramer/C. Reitz (eds.), *Tradition und Erneuerung. Mediale Strategien in der Zeit der Flavier*, Berlin/New York (BzA 285), 431–55.

Buckley, E. (2014), "Valerius Flaccus and Seneca's Tragedies," in: M. Heerink/G. Manuwald (eds.), *Brill's Companion to Valerius Flaccus*, Leiden, 307–25.

Buckley, E. (2018), "Flavian Epic and Trajanic Historiography: Speaking into the Silence," in: A. König/C. Whitton (eds.), *Roman Literature under Nerva, Trajan and Hadrian: Literary Interactions, AD 96–138*, Cambridge, 86–107.

Buffière, F. (1956), *Les mythes d'Homère et la pensée grecque*, Paris.

Bülow Clausen, K. (2014), *The Flavian Isea in Beneventum and Rome. The Appropriation of Egyptian and Egyptianising Art in Imperial Beneventum and Rome*, PhD diss., University of Copenhagen.

Burck, E. (1984a), *Historische und epische Tradition bei Silius Italicus*, Munich (Zetemata 80).

Burck, E. (1984b), *Silius Italicus. Hannibal in Capua und die Rückeroberung der Stadt durch die Römer*, Mainz/Wiesbaden/Stuttgart (AAWM 13).

Burke, E. (2008), *A Philosophical Enquiry into the Origin of Our Ideas of the Sublime and the Beautiful*, Oxford.

Burkert, W. (1970), "Jason, Hypsipyle, and New Fire at Lemnos: A Study in Myth and Ritual," *CQ* 20, 1–16.

Campbell, B. (1987), "Teach Yourself How to be a General," *JRS* 77, 13–29.

Campbell, B./Purcell, N. (1996), "Iulius Frontinus, Sextus," in: S. Hornblower/A. Spawforth (eds.), *The Oxford Classical Dictionary*, 3rd ed., Oxford, 785.

Cannizzaro, F. (2016), "Un compendio valeriano in Stazio. L'approdo degli Argonauti a Lemno (Stat. *Theb.* V.335-444): *Teichoskopia*, Cizico, Simplegadi," *Sileno* 42, 39–59.

Cannizzaro, F. (2017), "Elementi argonautici nel monile di Armonia (Stat. *Theb.* II 269-305)," *Maia* 69, 524–36.

Caplan, P. (1987), *The Cultural Construction of Sexuality*, London/New York.

Capponi, L. (2005), *Augustan Egypt: The Creation of a Roman Province*, London/New York (Studies in Classics 13).

Capriotti Vittozzi, G. (2014), "The Flavians: Pharaonic Kingship between Egypt and Rome," in: L. Bricault/M.J. Versluys (eds.), *Power, Politics and the Cults of Isis. Proceedings of the Vth International Conference of Isis Studies, Boulogne-sur-Mer, October 13–15, 2011*, Leiden/Boston (Religions in the Greco-Roman World 180) 237–59.

Carey, S. (2003), *Pliny's Catalogue of Culture: Art and Empire in the Natural History*, Oxford (Oxford Studies in Ancient Culture and Representation).

Carradice, I.A./Buttrey, T.V. (2007), *The Roman Imperial Coinage* II.1, 2nd ed, London.

Casali, S. (ed.) (2017), *Virgilio, Eneide 2*, Pisa (Syllabus 1).

Champlin, E. (2003), *Nero*, Cambridge (MA).

Chaplin, J.D. (2000), *Livy's Exemplary History*, Oxford.

Chinn, C.M. (2011), "Statius, Orpheus, and Callimachus: *Thebaid* 2.269–96," *Helios* 38, 79–101.

Chiritoiu, D.A. (2018), *Commanding Texts: Knowledge-ordering, Identity Construction and Ethics in 'Military Manuals' of the Roman Empire*, PhD diss., University of Cambridge.

Chomse, S.M. (2015), *Sublime Structures: Architecture, Instability and Ruins in Virgil, Lucan and Tacitus*, PhD diss., University of Cambridge.

Cizek, E. (1972), *L'Époque de Néron et ses controverses idéologiques*, Leiden (Roma aeterna 4).

Clare, R.J. (2002), *The Path of the Argo*, Cambridge.

Clare, R.J. (2004), "Tradition and Originality: Allusion in Valerius Flaccus' Lemnian Episode," in: M. Gale (ed.), *Latin Epic and Didactic Poetry*, Swansea, 125–47.
Clark, A. (2007), *Divine Qualities: Cult and Community in Republican Rome*, Oxford.
Clauss, J.J. (1993), *The Best of the Argonauts: The Redefinition of the Epic Hero in Book One of Apollonius'* Argonautica, Berkeley.
Clauss, J.J. (2000), "Cosmos without Imperium: The Argonautic Journey through Time," in: M.A. Harder/R.F. Regtuit/G.C. Wakker (eds.), *Apollonius Rhodius*, Leuven (Hellenistica Groningana 4), 11–32.
Clauss, J.J. (2014), "Myth and Mythopoesis on Valerius Flaccus' *Argonautica*," in: M. Heerink/G. Manuwald (eds.), *Brill's Companion to Valerius Flaccus*, Leiden, 99–114.
Coffee, N. (2006), "Eteocles, Polynices, and the Economics of Violence in Statius' *Thebaid*," *AJPh* 127, 415–52.
Colacicco, A. (2014), *Ubi iura deique? Saggio di commento a Stat. Theb. 11, 315–519*, PhD diss., Università di Salerno.
Coleman, K.M. (1988), *Statius: Silvae IV*, Oxford.
Coleman, K.M. (1998), "The *liber spectaculorum*: perpetuating the ephemeral," in: F. Grewing (ed.), *Toto Notus in Orbe: Perspektiven der Martial-Interpretation*, Stuttgart (Palingenesia 65), 15–36.
Coleman, K.M. (2000), "Entertaining Rome," in: J. Coulston/H. Dodge (eds.), *Ancient Rome: the Archaeology of the Eternal City*, Oxford, 205–52.
Coleman, K.M. (2006), *Martial: Liber Spectaculorum*, Oxford.
Commager, S. (1962), *The Odes of Horace: A Critical Study*, New Haven (CT).
Connor, S. (2006), *Fly*, London.
Conte, G.B. (1994a), *Genres and Readers: Lucretius, Love Elegy and Pliny's Encyclopedia*, Baltimore (MD).
Conte, G.B. (1994b), *Latin Literature. A History*, Baltimore (MD)/London.
Conte, G.B. (2007a), *Virgilio. L'epica del sentimento*, 2nd ed, Torino.
Conte, G.B. (2007b), *The Poetry of Pathos. Studies in Virgilian Epic*, ed. S.J. Harrison, Oxford.
Cooper, H.M./Munich, A.A./Squier, S.M. (eds.) (1989), *Arms and the Woman: war, gender and literary representation*, Chapel Hill.
Corbier, M. (1995), "Male Power and Legitimacy through Women: the *domus Augusta* under the Julio-Claudians," in: R. Hawley/B. Levick (eds.), *Women in Antiquity: New Assessments*, London/New York, 178–93.
Costa, C.D.N. (1973), *Seneca: Medea*, Oxford.
Courtney, E. (1980), *A Commentary on the Satires of Juvenal*, London.
Cowan, R. (2003), *"In my Beginning is my End": Origins, Cities and Foundations in Flavian Epic*, PhD diss., University of Oxford.
Cowan, R. (2007), *The Headless City: The Decline and Fall of Capua in Silius Italicus'* Punica, ORA 1542, https://ora.ox.ac.uk/objects/uuid:dceb6b5a-980c-46ca-ac9e-088615e7fbea.
Cowan, R. (2014), "My Family and Other Enemies: Argonautic Antagonists and Valerian Villains," in: M. Heerink/G. Manuwald (eds.), *Brill's Companion to Valerius Flaccus*, Leiden, 229–48.
Criado, C. (2000), *La teología de la* Tebaida *Estaciana. El anti-virgilianismo de un clasicista*, Hildesheim (Spudasmata 75).
Criado, C. (2013), "The contradictions of Valerius' and Statius' Jupiter: Power and weakness of the supreme god in the epic and tragic tradition," in: G. Manuwald/A. Voigt (eds.), *Flavian Epic Interactions*, Berlin (*TiC* Suppl. 21), 195–214.

Crippa, S. (2010), "Magic and Rationality in Pliny. Transmission of Knowledge: The Medical–Magical Pharmacopoeia," *Palamedes* 5, 115–25.

Curran, J.R. (2007), "The Jewish War: Some Neglected Regional Factors," *CW* 101, 75–91.

D'Ambra, E. (1993), *Private Lives, Imperial Virtues: The Frieze of the Forum Transitorium in Rome*, Princeton (NJ).

d'Assigny, M. (1686), *The stratagems of war, or, A collection of the most celebrated practices and wise sayings of the great generals in former ages written by Sextus Julius Frontinus, one of the Roman consuls; now English'd* (Eebo Editions, Proquest, 2010).

Dalby, A. (2003), *Food in the Ancient World, from A to Z*, London.

Daly, L.J. (1975), "Verginius at Vesontio: The Incongruity of the *Bellum Neronis*," *Historia* 24, 75–100.

Damon, C. (ed.) (2003), *Tacitus: Histories I*, Cambridge.

Damon, C. (2010), "Déjà vu or déjà lu? History as Intertext," in: F. Cairns/M. Griffin (eds.), *PLLS 14: Health and Sickness in Ancient Rome. Greek and Roman Poetry and Historiography*, Cambridge (ARCA 50), 375–88.

Damon. C. (2011), "Pliny on Apion," in: R.K. Gibson/R. Morello (eds.), *Pliny the Elder: Themes and Contexts*, Leiden (Mnemosyne Suppl. 329), 131–45.

Darwall-Smith, R.H. (1996), *Emperors and Architecture: A Study of Flavian Rome*, Brussels (Collection Latomus 231).

Davies, C./Neal, M. (2000), "Durkheim's Altruistic and Fatalistic Suicide," in: W.S.F. Pickering/G. Walford (eds.) *Durkheim's Suicide: A century of research and debate*, London/New York (Routledge Studies in Social and Political Thought 28), 36–52.

Davies, P.J.E. (2011), "*Aegyptiaca* in Rome: *Adventus* and *Romanitas*," in: E.S. Gruen (ed.), *Cultural Identity in the Ancient Mediterranean*, Los Angeles (Issues & Debates), 354–70.

Davis, M.A. (1980), *Flight Beyond Time and Change: A New Reading of the* Argonautica *of Valerius Flaccus*, PhD diss., Cornell University.

Davis, M.A. (1989), "*Ratis audax*: Valerius Flaccus' Bold Ship," *Ramus* 18, 46–73.

Davis, P.J. (1989), "The Chorus in Seneca's *Thyestes*," *CQ* 39, 421–35.

Davis, P.J. (1999), "'Since My Part Has Been Well Played': Conflicting Evaluations of Augustus," *Ramus* 28, 1–15.

Davis, P.J. (2010), "Jason at Colchis: Technology and Human Progress in Valerius Flaccus," *Ramus* 39, 1–13.

Davis, P.J. (2014), "Medea: From Epic to Tragedy," in: M. Heerink/G. Manuwald, *Brill's Companion to Valerius Flaccus*, Leiden, 192–210.

Davis, P.J. (2015), "Argo's Flavian Politics: The Workings of Power in Valerius Flaccus," in: H. Baltusten/P.J. Davis (eds.), *The Art of Veiled Speech*, Philadelphia, 157–75.

Davis, P.J. (2016), "Senecan tragedy and the politics of Flavian literature," in: E. Dodson-Robinson (ed.), *Brill's Companion to the Reception of Senecan Tragedy*, Leiden (Brill's Companions to Classical Reception 5), 57–74.

Day, H.J.M. (2013), *Lucan and the Sublime: Power, Representation and Aesthetic Experience*, Cambridge.

de Pizan, C. (1999), *The Book of Deeds of Arms and of Chivalry*, trans. S. Willard/ed. C.C. Willard, University Park (PA).

De Saint-Denis, E. (1961), *Pline l'Ancien. Histoire Naturelle. Livre X. Des Animaux ailés*, Paris.

Degl'Innocenti Pierini, R. (2007),"*Pallidus Nero* (Stat. *silv.* 2,7,118 s.): il 'personaggio' Nerone negli scrittori dell'età flavia," in: A. Bonadeo/E. Romano, eds., *Dialogando con il passato:*

Permanenze e innovazioni nella cultura latina di età flavia, Florence (Lingue e Letterature), 136–59.
Delarue, F. (2000), *Stace, poète épique. Originalité et coherence*, Leuven/Paris (Bibliothèque d'Études Classiques 20).
Delz, J. (ed.) (1987), *Sili Italici Punica*, Stuttgart.
den Hollander, W. (2014), *Josephus, the Emperors, and the City of Rome: From Hostage to Historian*, Leiden (Ancient Judaism and Early Christianity 86).
Desfontaines, L. (1830), *Caii Plinii Secundi Historiæ naturalis. Libri XXXVII. Pars quarta continens rem herbariam*, Paris.
Dewar, M. (ed.) (1991), *Statius*, Thebaid *IX, Edited with an English Translation and Commentary*, Oxford.
Dewar, M. (2008), "The Equine Cuckoo: Statius' *Ecus Maximus Domitiani Imperatoris* and the Flavian Forum," in: J.J.L. Smolenaars/H.-J. van Dam/R.R. Nauta (eds.), *The Poetry of Statius*, Leiden/Boston (Mnemosyne Suppl. 306), 65–84.
Dewar, M. (2016), "Lost Literature," in: A. Zissos (ed.), *A Companion to the Flavian Age of Imperial Rome*, Chichester/Oxford/Malden (MA), 469–83.
Dézspa, L. (2016), "The Flavians and the Senate," in: A. Zissos (ed.), *A Companion to the Flavian Age of Imperial Rome*, Chichester/Oxford/Malden (MA), 166–85.
Dietrich, J. (1999), "*Thebaid*'s Feminine Ending," *Ramus* 28, 40–53.
Dietrich, J. (2009), "Death Becomes Her: Female Suicide in Flavian Epic," *Ramus* 38, 187–202.
Dietrich, J.S. (2015), "Dead woman walking. Jocasta in the *Thebaid*," in: W.J. Dominik/C.E. Newlands/K. Gervais (eds.), *Brill's Companion to Statius*, Leiden, 307–21.
Dillery, J. (2003), "Putting Him Back Together Again: Apion Historian, Apion *Grammatikos*," *CPh* 98, 383–90.
Dingel, J. (2009), *Die relative Datierung der Tragödien Senecas*, Berlin (BzA 271).
Dinter, M.T. (2009), "Epic from Epigram: The Poetics of Valerius Flaccus' *Argonautica*," *AJPh* 130, 533–66.
Dinter, M.T. (2012), *Anatomizing Civil War: Studies in Lucan's Epic Technique*, Ann Arbor.
Dominik, W.J. (1994a), *Speech and Rhetoric in Statius'* Thebaid, Hildesheim (Altertumswissenschaftliche Texte und Studien 27).
Dominik, W.J. (1994b), *The Mythic Voice of Statius: Power and Politics in the Thebaid of Statius*, Leiden (Mnemosyne Suppl. 136).
Dominik, W.J. (2003), "Hannibal at the Gates: programmatising Rome and *Romanitas* in Silius Italicus' *Punica* 1 and 2," in: A.J. Boyle & W.J. Dominik (eds.), *Flavian Rome: Culture, Image, Text*, Leiden, 469–97.
Dominik, W.J. (2006), "Rome then and now: Linking the Saguntum and Cannae episodes in Silius Italicus' *Punica*," in: R.R. Nauta/H.-J. van Dam/J.J.L. Smolenaars (eds.), *Flavian Poetry*, Leiden (Mnemosyne Suppl. 270), 113–27.
Dominik, W.J. (2010), "The Reception of Silius Italicus in Modern Scholarship," in: A. Augoustakis (ed.), *Brill's Companion to Silius Italicus*, Leiden, 425–47.
Dominik, W.J./Garthwaite, J./Roche, P.A. (eds.) (2009), *Writing Politics in Imperial Rome*, Leiden.
Dominik, W.J./Newlands, C.E./Gervais, K. (eds.) (2015), *Brill's Companion to Statius*, Leiden/Boston.
Doody, A. (2001), "Finding facts in Pliny's encyclopaedia; the *summarium* of the *Natural History*," *Ramus* 30, 1–22.
Doody, A. (2009), "Pliny's *Natural History*: *Enkuklios Paideia* and the Ancient Encyclopedia," *JHI* 70, 1–21.

Doody, A. (2010), *Pliny's Encyclopedia. The Reception of the* Natural History, Cambridge.
Doody, A. (2011), "The Science and Aesthetics of Names in the *Natural History*," in: R.K. Gibson/R. Morello (eds.), *Pliny the Elder: Themes and Contexts,* Leiden (Mnemosyne Suppl. 329), 113–29.
Doody, A. (2016), "The Authority of Greek Poetry in Pliny's *Natural History* 18.63–65," in: F. Cairns/R. Gibson (eds.), *PLLS 16: Greek and Roman Poetry. The Elder Pliny*, Prenton (ARCA 54), 247–68.
DuBois, P. (1982), *Centaurs and Amazons: Women and the Pre-History of the Great Chain of Being*, Ann Arbor (MI).
Duff, J.D. (trans.) (1928), *Lucan. The Civil War*, Cambridge (MA) (LCL).
Duff, J.D. (trans.) (1934), *Silius Italicus. Punica*, Cambridge (MA) (LCL).
Dumont, J.P. (1986), "L'idée de Dieu chez Pline (*HN* 2, 1-5, 1-27)," *Helmantica* 37, 219–37.
Dupont, F. (1995), *Les monstres de Sénèque. Pour une dramaturgie de la tragédie romaine*, Paris.
Durkheim, E. (1951), *Suicide*, trans. J. Spaulding/G. Simpson, New York.
Dyck, A.W. (ed.) (2003), *Cicero:* De natura deorum, *liber I*, Cambridge.
Dyson, S.L./Prior, R.E. (1995), "Horace, Martial, and Rome: Two Poetic Outsiders Read the Ancient City," *Arethusa* 28, 245–63.
Eberhardt, B. (2005), "Wer dient wem? Die Darstellung des flavischen Triumphzuges auf dem Titusbogen und bei Josephus (*B.J.* 7.123–162)," in: J. Sievers/G. Lembi (eds.), *Josephus and Jewish History in Flavian Rome and Beyond*, Leiden (JSJ Suppl. 104), 257–78.
Eck, W. (1982), "Die Gestalt Frontins in ihrer politischen und sozialen Umwelt," in: Frontinus-Gesellschaft (ed.), *Sextus Iulius Frontinus, curator aquarum. Wasserversorgung im antiken Rom*, vol. 1, Munich/Vienna, 47–62.
Edmondson, J. (2005), "Introduction: Flavius Josephus and Flavian Rome," in: J. Edmondson/S. Mason/J. Rives (eds.), *Flavius Josephus and Flavian Rome*, Oxford, 1–33.
Edwards, C. (1993), *The Politics of Immorality in Ancient Rome*, Cambridge.
Edwards, C. (1996), *Writing Rome: Textual Approaches to the City*, Cambridge (Roman Literature and Its Contexts).
Edwards, C. (2007), *Death in Ancient Rome*, New Haven (CT).
Edwards, C. (2011), "Imagining ruins in Ancient Rome," *European Review of History* 18, 645–61.
Ehlers, W.-W. (ed.) (1980), *Gai Valeri Flacci Setini Balbi Argonauticon Libri Octo*, Stuttgart.
Eldred, K.O. (2002), "This Ship of Fools: Epic Vision in Lucan's Vulteius Episode," in: D. Fredrick (ed.), *The Roman Gaze: Vision, Power, and the Body*, Baltimore (MD), 57–85.
Elm, D. (1998), "Venus und die Tradition der Furiendarstellung," in: U. Eigler/E. Lefèvre (eds.), Ratis omnia vincet: *Neue Untersuchungen zu den Argonautica des Valerius Flaccus*, Munich (Zetemata 98), 249–58.
Elm von der Osten, D. (2007), *Liebe als Wahnsinn: die Konzeption der Göttin Venus in den* Argonautica *des Valerius Flaccus*, Stuttgart (PAwB 20).
Elshtain, J.B. (1987), *Women and War*, New York/London.
Elsner, J. (1994), "Constructing decadence: the representation of Nero as imperial builder," in: J. Elsner/J. Masters (eds.), *Reflections of Nero: Culture, History & Representation*, London/Chapel Hill (NC), 112–27.
Erdkamp, P. (2005), *The Grain Market in the Roman Empire: A Social, Political and Economic Study*, Cambridge.
Ernout, A. (1964), "La magie chez Pline l' Ancien," in: M. Renard/R. Schilling (eds.), *Hommages à Jean Bayet*, Paris (Collection Latomus 70), 190–95.

Etlin, R.A. (2012), "Architecture and the Sublime," in: T.M. Costelloe (ed.), *The Sublime: From Antiquity to the Present*, Cambridge, 230–73.
Evans, R. (2003), "Containment and Corruption: The Discourse of Flavian Empire," in: A.J. Boyle/W.J. Dominik (eds.), *Flavian Rome: Culture, Image, Text*, Leiden, 255–76.
Fabre-Serris, J. (2008), *Rome, l'Arcadie et la mer des Argonautes*, Villeneuve d'Ascq.
Fahz, L. (1904), *De poetarum Romanorum doctrina magica: quaestiones selectae*, Giessen.
Fairclough, H.R. (trans.) (1916), *Virgil, Eclogues. Georgics. Aeneid 1–6*, Cambridge (MA) (LCL).
Fantham, E. (1992), *Lucan, De Bello Civili Book II*, Cambridge.
Fantham, E. (1997), "'Envy and fear the begetter of hate': Statius' *Thebaid* and the genesis of hatred," in: S.M. Braund/C. Gill (eds.), *The Passions in Roman Thought and Literature*, Cambridge, 185–212.
Fantham, E. (2006), *Julia Augusti: The Emperor's Daughter*, London/New York.
Fantham, E. (2010), "*Discordia Fratrum*: Aspects of Lucan's Conception of Civil War," in: B.W. Breed/C. Damon/A. Rossi (eds.), *Citizens of Discord: Rome and its Civil Wars*, Oxford, 207–20.
Fantham, E. (2011), "A Controversial Life," in: P. Asso (ed.), *Brill's Companion to Lucan*, Leiden/Boston, 3–20.
Faraone, C.A. (1990), "Aphrodite's κεστός and Apples for Atalanta: Aphrodisiacs in Early Greek Myth and Ritual," *Phoenix* 44, 219–43.
Fear, A. (2011), "The Roman's Burden," in: R. Gibson/R. Morello (eds.), *Pliny the Elder Themes and Contexts*, Leiden (Mnemosyne Suppl. 329), 21–34.
Fearnley, H. (2003), "Reading the Imperial Revolution: Martial, *Epigrams* 10," in: A.J. Boyle/W. Dominik (eds.), *Flavian Rome: Culture, Image, Text*, Leiden, 613–35.
Fears, J.R. (1981), "The Cult of Virtues and Roman Imperial Ideology," *ANRW* II.17.2, 827–948.
Feeney, D.C. (1984), "The Reconciliations of Juno," *CQ* 34, 179–94.
Feeney, D.C. (1991), *The Gods in Epic: Poets and Critics of the Classical Tradition*, Oxford.
Feeney, D.C. (2007), *Caesar's Calendar*, Berkeley.
Feldman, L.H. (1998), *Josephus's Interpretation of the Bible*, Berkeley (Hellenistic Culture and Society 27).
Feraboli, S./Flores, E./Scarcia, R. (eds.) (2001), *Manilio: Il poema degli astri (Astronomica)*. Volume II: Libri III-V, Milan.
Ferenczi, A. (2014), "Philosophical Ideas in Valerius Flaccus' *Argonautica*," in: M. Heerink/G. Manuwald (eds.), *Brill's Companion to Valerius Flaccus*, Leiden, 136–53.
Finkmann, S. (2015), "Polyxo and the Lemnian Episode – an Inter- and Intratextual Study of Apollonius Rhodius, Valerius Flaccus, and Statius," *Dictynna* 12 (http:// dictynna.revues.org /1135).
Fitch, J.G. (1981), "Sense-pauses and relative dating in Seneca, Sophocles and Shakespeare," *AJPh* 102, 289–307.
Fitzgerald, W. (2007), *Martial: The World of the Epigram*, Chicago/London.
Flower, H. (2006), *The Art of Forgetting: Disgrace and Oblivion in Roman Political Culture*, Chapel Hill (NC) (Studies in the History of Greece and Rome).
Flower, H. (2010), "Rome's First Civil War and the Fragility of Republican Political Culture," in: B.W. Breed/C. Damon/A. Rossi (eds.), *Citizens of Discord: Rome and its Civil Wars*, Oxford, 73–86.
Fögen, Th. (2014), "Animal Communication," in: G.L. Campbell (ed.), *The Oxford Handbook of Animals in Classical Thought and Life*, Oxford, 216–32.
Forhan, K. (2002), *The Political Theory of Christine de Pizan*, Burlington (VT).

Fowler, D.P. (1997), "On the Shoulders of Giants. Intertextuality and Classical Studies," *MD* 39, 13–34.

Fowler, D.P. (2000), *Roman Constructions: Readings in Postmodern Latin*, Oxford.

Fowler, D.P. (2002), *Lucretius on Atomic Motion: A Commentary on* De Rerum Natura, *Book 2, Lines 1–332*, Oxford.

Fox, M. (trans.) (2012), *Lucan. Civil War*, New York/London.

Franchet d'Espèrey, S. (1988), "Une étrange descente aux enfers: le suicide d'Éson et Alcimédé (Valerius Flaccus, *Arg.* I 730-851)," in: D. Porte/J.-P. Néraudau (eds.), *Hommage à Henri Le Bonniec. Res Sacrae*, Brussels (Collection Latomus 201), 193–97.

Franchet d'Espèrey, S. (1996), "Pietas, allégorie de la non-violence," in: F. Delarue/S. Georgacopoulou/P. Laurens/A.-M. Taisne (eds.), *Epicedion: Hommage à P. Papinius Statius (96–1996)*, Poitiers (Licorne 38), 83–91.

Franchet d'Espèrey, S. (1998), "L'univers des *Argonautiques* est-il absurd?," in: U. Eigler/E. Lefèvre (eds.), Ratis omnia vincet: *Neue Untersuchungen zu den Argonautica des Valerius Flaccus*, Munich (Zetemata 98), 213–22.

Franchet d'Espèrey, S. (1999), *Conflit, violence et non-violence dans la* Thébaïde *de Stace*, Paris (Coll. Études Anciennes).

Frank, E. (1974), "Works of Art in the Epics of Valerius Flaccus and Silius Italicus," *RIL* 108, 837–44.

Frank, M. (ed.) (1995), *Seneca's* Phoenissae, Leiden/New York.

Fratantuono, L.M. (2014), "Pales," in: R.F. Thomas/J.M. Ziolkowski (eds.), *The Virgil Encyclopedia. Volume II, F–Pe.*, Malden, MA, 958–59.

Frazer, J.G. (1965), *Pausanias's Description of Greece Vol. III. Commentary on Books II–V*, New York.

Fredrick, D. (2003), "Architecture and Surveillance in Flavian Rome," in: A.J. Boyle/W.J. Dominik (eds.), *Flavian Rome: Culture, Image, Text*, Leiden, 199–228.

Frings, I. (1991), *Gespräch und Handlung in der Thebais des Statius*, Stuttgart (BzA 18).

Frings, I. (1992), Odia fraterna *als manieristisches Motiv. Betrachtungen zu Senecas* Thyest *und Statius'* Thebais, Mainz/Stuttgart (AAWM 2).

Frings, I. (1998), "Die Rettung des Thoas," in: U. Eigler/E. Lefèvre (eds.), Ratis omnia vincet: *Neue Untersuchungen zu den Argonautica des Valerius Flaccus*, Munich (Zetemata 98), 261–68.

Fuà, O. (2002), "Echi lucanei nella profezia di Mopso (Val. Fl. 1, 207–26)," *GIF* 54, 105–15.

Fucecchi, M. (1997), *La τειχοσκοπία e l'innamoramento di Medea: Saggio di commento a Valerio Flacco* Argonautiche *6,427-760*, Pisa/Florence (Testi e studi di cultura classica 19).

Fucecchi, M. (1999), "La vigilia di Canne nei *Punica* e un contributo alla storia dei rapporti fra Silio Italico e Lucano," in: P. Esposito/L. Nicastri (eds.), *Interpretare Lucano: Miscellanea di Studi*, Naples (Quaderni del Dipartimento di scienze dell'antichità 22), 305–42.

Fucecchi, M. (2006a), *Una guerra in Colchide: Valerio Flacco*, Argonautiche *6, 1–426*, Pisa.

Fucecchi, M. (2006b), "*Ad finem ventum.* Considerazioni sull'ultimo libro dei *Punica*," *Aevum(ant)* n.s. 6, 311–45.

Fucecchi, M. (2007), "Tematiche e figure 'trasversali' nell'epica flavia," in: A. Bonadeo/E. Romano (eds.), *Dialogando con il passato: permanenze e innovazioni nella cultura Latina di età flavia*, Florence (Lingue e Letterature), 18–37.

Fucecchi, M. (2014), "War and Love in Valerius Flaccus' *Argonautica*," in: M. Heerink/G. Manuwald (eds.), *Brill's Companion to Valerius Flaccus*, Leiden, 115–35.

Fucecchi, M. (2015), "Passato da rimuovere e passato da rivivere: l'incubo della guerra civile (e la sua 'metabolizzazione') nell'epica flavia," in: P. Esposito/C. Walde (eds.), *Letture e lettori di Lucano*, Pisa (Testi e studi di cultura classica 62), 231–53.

Fyfe, H. (1983), "An Analysis of Seneca's Medea," in: A.J. Boyle (ed.), *Seneca Tragicus: Ramus Essays on Senecan Drama*, Bendigo, 77–93.
Gaillard-Seux, P. (1994), *La médecine chez Pline l'Ancien. Ses rapports avec la magie*, PhD diss., Université Paris IV.
Gaillard-Seux, P. (1998), "Les amulettes gynécologiques dans les textes latins médicaux de l' Antiquité," in: C. Deroux (ed.), *Maladie et maladies dans les textes latins antiques, Actes du V*^{e} *Colloque International "Textes médicaux latins"*, Brussels (Collection Latomus 242), 70–84.
Galimberti, A. (2016), "The Emperor Domitian," in: A. Zissos (ed.), *A Companion to the Flavian Age of Imperial Rome*, Chichester/Oxford/Malden (MA), 92–108.
Galli, D. (2007), *Valerii Flacci* Argonautica 1: *Commento*, Berlin/New York (BzA 243).
Gallia, A.B. (2012), *Remembering the Roman Republic. Culture, Politics and History under the Principate*, Cambridge.
Ganiban, R.T. (2007), *Statius and Virgil: The* Thebaid *and the Reinterpretation of the* Aeneid, Cambridge.
Ganiban, R.T. (2011), "Crime in Lucan and Statius," in: P. Asso (ed.), *Brill's Companion to Lucan*, Leiden/Boston, 327–44.
Ganiban, R.T. (2014), "Virgilian Prophecy and the Reign of Jupiter in Valerius Flaccus' *Argonautica*," in: M. Heerink/G. Manuwald (eds.), *Brill's Companion to Valerius Flaccus*, Leiden, 251–68.
Garson, R.W. (1964), "Some Critical Observations on Valerius Flaccus' *Argonautica*. I," *CQ* 14, 267–79.
Gärtner, U. (1994), *Gehalt und Funktion der Gleichnisse bei Valerius Flaccus*, Stuttgart (Hermes Einzelschriften 67).
Gatz, B. (1967), *Weltalter, Goldene Zeit und sinnverwandte Vorstellungen*, Hildesheim (Spudasmata 16).
Gee, E. (2013), *Aratus and the Astronomical Tradition*, Oxford.
Gehrke, H.-J. (1985), *Stasis: Untersuchungen zu den inneren Kriegen in den griechischen Staaten des 5. und 4. Jahrhunderts v. Chr.*, Munich (Vestigia 35).
Georgacopoulou, S. (2005), *Aux frontières du récit épique: l'emploi de l'apostrophe du narrateur dans la* Thébaïde *de Stace*, Brussels (Collection Latomus 289).
Gering, J. (2012), *Domitian, dominus et deus? Herrschafts- und Machtstrukturen in römischen Reich zur Zeit des letzten Flaviers*, Rahden (Osnabrücker Forschungen zu Altertum und Antike-Rezeption 15).
Gervais, K. (ed.) (2017), *Statius,* Thebaid *2*, Oxford.
Gibson, B. (2004), "The Repetitions of Hypsipyle," in: M. Gale (ed.), *Latin Epic and Didactic Poetry*, Swansea, 149–80.
Gibson, R.K. (ed.) (2003), *Ovid,* Ars amatoria, *Book 3*, Cambridge.
Gilder, R. (1997), *Goddesses Unbound. Furies and Furial Imagery in the works of Seneca, Lucan and Statius*, PhD diss., University of Pennsylvania.
Gill, C. (2006), *The Structured Self in Hellenistic and Roman Thought*, Oxford.
Ginsberg, L.D. (2011), "*Ingens* as an Etymological Pun in the *Octavia*," *CPh* 106, 357–60.
Ginsberg, L.D. (2013), "Wars more than Civil: Memories of Pompey and Caesar in the *Octavia*," *AJPh* 134, 637–74.
Ginsberg, L.D. (2017), *Staging Memory, Staging Strife: Empire and Civil War in the* Octavia, Oxford.
Ginsberg, L.D. (2018), "*Vt et hostem amarem*: Jocasta and the Poetics of Civil War in Seneca's *Phoenissae*," *Ramus* 46, 58–74.

Ginsburg, J. (2006), *Representing Agrippina. Constructions of Female Power in the Early Roman Empire*, Oxford.
Giusti, E. (2016), "My Enemy's Enemy is My Enemy: Virgil's Illogical Use of *metus hostilis*," in: P.R. Hardie (ed.), *Augustan Poetry and the Irrational*, Oxford, 37–55.
Glorieux, P. (ed.) (1960), *Œuvres Complètes de Jean Gerson: Vol. 2. L'oeuvre épistolaire*, Paris/New York.
Goodman, M. (2007), *Rome and Jerusalem. The Clash of Ancient Civilizations*, London/New York.
Goodyear, F.R.D. (1982), "Technical Writing," in: E.J. Kenney (ed.), *The Cambridge History of Classical Literature, vol. 2: Latin Literature*, Cambridge, 667–73.
Goold, G.P. (ed. and trans.) (1977), *Manilius, Astronomica*, Cambridge (MA) (LCL).
Gordon, R. (1987), "Lucan's Erictho," in: M. Whitby/P. Hardie/M. Whitby (eds.), *Homo Viator: Classical Essays for John Bramble*, Bristol/Oak Park (IL), 231–41.
Gordon, R. (2010), "Magian Lessons in Natural History: Unique Animals In Graeco–Roman Natural Magic," in: J.H.F. Dijkstra/J.E.A. Kroesen/Y. Kuiper (eds.), *Myths, Martyrs, and Modernity: Studies in the History of Religions in Honour of Jan N. Bremmer*, Brill (Studies in the History of Religions 127), 249–70.
Gowing, A. (2005), *Empire and Memory: The representation of the Roman Republic in Imperial Culture*, Cambridge.
Gowing, A. (2010), "'Caesar grabs my pen': Writing Civil War under Tiberius," in: B.W. Breed/C. Damon/A. Rossi (eds.), *Citizens of Discord: Rome and Its Civil Wars*, Oxford, 249–60.
Grewe, S. (1998), "Der Einfluß von Senecas *Medea* auf die *Argonautica* des Valerius Flaccus," in: U. Eigler/E. Lefèvre (eds.), *Ratis omnia vincet: Neue Untersuchungen zu den Argonautica des Valerius Flaccus*, Munich (Zetemata 98), 173–90.
Griffin, M.T. (1984), *Nero: The End of a Dynasty*, New Haven (CT).
Griffiths, J.G. (1970), *Plutarch's De Iside et Osiride*, Cardiff.
Grillo, L. (2012), *The Art of Caesar's* Bellum Civile: *Literature, Ideology, Community*, Cambridge.
Groß, A. (2003), *Prophezeiungen und Prodigien in den* Argonautica *des Valerius Flaccus*, Munich (Münchner Beiträge zur Sprach- und Literaturwissenschaft).
Gruen, E.S. (2011), *Rethinking the Other in Antiquity*, Oxford.
Guasparri, A. (2013), "Explicit nomenclature and classification in Pliny's *Natural History XXXII*," SHPS 44, 347–53.
Gunderson, E. (2003), "The Flavian Amphitheatre: All the World's a Stage," in: A.J. Boyle/W. Dominik (eds.), *Flavian Rome: Culture, Image, Text*, Leiden, 637–58.
Gunderson, E. (2015), *The Sublime Seneca: Ethics, Literature, Metaphysics*, Cambridge.
Gurval, R.A. (1995), *Actium and Augustus: The Politics and Emotions of Civil War*, Ann Arbor (MI).
Hahm, D.E. (1977), *The Origins of Stoic Cosmology*, Columbus (OH).
Håkanson, L. (1979), "Problems of textual criticism and intepretation in Lucan's *De bello civili*," PCPhS 25, 26–51.
Ham, C.T. (2013), *Empedoclean Elegy: Love, Strife and the Four Elements in Ovid's* Amores, Ars Amatoria *and* Fasti, PhD diss., University of Pennsylvania.
Hamer, M. (1993), *Signs of Cleopatra: History, Politics, Representation*, London/New York.
Hanson, A.E. (1987), "The eight months' child and the etiquette of birth: *obsit omen!*," BHM 61, 589–602.
Hardie, A. (2003), "Poetry and Politics at the Games of Domitian," in: A.J. Boyle/W.J. Dominik (eds.), *Flavian Rome: Culture, Image, Text*, Leiden, 125–47.
Hardie, P.R. (1986), *Virgil's* Aeneid: *Cosmos and Imperium*, Oxford.
Hardie, P.R. (1989), "Flavian epicists on Virgil's epic technique," *Ramus* 18, 3–20.

Hardie, P.R. (1990), "Ovid's Theban history: the first 'anti-*Aeneid*'?," *CQ* 40, 224–35.
Hardie, P.R. (1993a), *The epic successors of Virgil*, Cambridge (Roman Literature and Its Contexts).
Hardie, P.R. (1993b), "Tales of Unity and Division in Imperial Latin Epic," in: J. Molyneux (ed.), *Literary Responses to Civil Discord*, Nottingham (Nottingham Classical Literature Studies 1), 57–71.
Hardie, P.R. (ed.) (1994), *Virgil*, Aeneid *Book IX*, Cambridge.
Hardie, P.R. (1997), "Closure in Latin Epic," in: D.H. Roberts/F.M. Dunn,/D. Fowler (eds.), *Classical Closure: Reading the End in Greek and Latin Literature*, Princeton, 139–62.
Hardie, P.R. (2009), *Lucretian Receptions: History, the Sublime, Knowledge*, Cambridge.
Hardie, P.R. (2012), *Rumour and Renown: Representations of* Fama *in Western Literature*, Cambridge.
Hardie, P.R. (2013), "Lucan's *Bellum Civile*," in: E. Buckley/M.T. Dinter (eds.), *A Companion to the Neronian Age*, Malden (MA), 225–40.
Hardie, P.R. (2016), "Introduction: Augustan Poetry and the Irrational," in: P.R. Hardie (ed.), *Augustan Poetry and the Irrational*, Oxford, 1–33.
Hardy, G./Totelin, L. (2016), *Ancient Botany*, London/New York.
Harper Smith, A. (1987), *A Commentary on Valerius Flaccus'* Argonautica *II*, PhD diss., St. Hilda's College, University of Oxford.
Harris, W.V. (2016), "Popular Medicine in the Classical World," in: W.V. Harris (ed.), *Popular Medicine in Graeco-Roman Antiquity*, Leiden/Boston (Columbia Studies in the Classical Tradition 42), 1–64.
Harrison, S.J. (1991), *Vergil*, Aeneid *10: With Introduction, Translation, and Commentary*, Oxford.
Harrison, S.J. (2013), "Proleptic *Ekphrasis* in Flavian Epic," in: G. Manuwald/A. Voigt (eds.), *Flavian Epic Interactions*, Berlin (*TiC* Suppl. 21), 215–27.
Hart, H. St. J. (1952), "Judaea and Rome: The Official Commentary," *JThS* 3, 172–98.
Häußler, R. (1978), *Das historische Epos von Lucan bis Silius und seine Theorie. Studien zum historischen Epos der Antike. II. Teil: Geschichtliche Epik nach Vergil*, Heidelberg (Bibliothek der klassischen Altertumswissenschaften n.s. 60).
Haynes, H. (2003), *The History of Make-Believe: Tacitus on Imperial Rome*, Berkeley.
Healy, T./Sawday, J. (1990), *Literature and the English Civil War*, Cambridge.
Heerink, M./Manuwald, G. (eds.) (2014), *Brill's Companion to Valerius Flaccus*, Leiden.
Heerink, M. (2016), "Virgil, Lucan, and the Meaning of Civil War in Valerius Flaccus' *Argonautica*," *Mnemosyne* 69, 511–25.
Heinemann, A. (2016), "Jupiter, die Flavier und das Kapitol, oder: wie man einen Bürgerkrieg gewinnt," in: H. Börm/M. Mattheis/J. Wienand (eds.), *Civil War in Ancient Greece and Rome: Contexts of Disintegration and Reintegration*, Stuttgart (Heidelberger althistorische Beiträge und epigraphische Studien 58), 187–235.
Henderson, J. (1987), "Lucan/The Word at War," *Ramus* 16, 122–64.
Henderson, J. (1991), "Statius' *Thebaid*/Form Premade," *PCPhS* 37, 30–79.
Henderson, J. (1993), "Form Re-made/Statius' *Thebaid*," in: A.J. Boyle (ed.), *Roman Epic*, New York, 162–91.
Henderson, J. (1994), "*Danaos* timeo: Amazons in Greek art and poetry," in: S. Goldhill/R. Osborne (eds.), *Art and Text in Ancient Greek Culture*, Cambridge (Cambridge studies in new art history and criticism), 85–137.
Henderson, J. (1998), *Fighting for Rome: Poets and Caesars, History and Civil War*, Cambridge.

Henry, D./Henry, E. (1985), *The Mask of Power: Seneca's Tragedies and Imperial Rome*, Chicago (IL)/Warminster.
Hershkowitz, D. (1997), "*Parce metu, Cytherea*: 'Failed' Intertext Repetition in Statius' *Thebaid*, or, Don't Stop Me If You've Heard This One Before," *MD* 39, 35–52.
Hershkowitz, D. (1998a), *The Madness of Epic. Reading Insanity from Homer to Statius*, Oxford.
Hershkowitz, D. (1998b), *Valerius Flaccus'* Argonautica: *Abbreviated Voyages in Silver Latin Epic*, Oxford.
Heuvel, H. (1932), *Publii Papinii Statii Thebaidos liber primus*, Zutphen.
Higonnet, M.R. (1989), "Civil wars and sexual territories," in: H.M. Cooper/A.A. Munich/S.M. Squier (eds.), *Arms and the Woman: War, Gender and Literary Representation*, Chapel Hill (NC), 80–96.
Hill, D.E. (1973), "The Thessalian Trick," *RhM* 116, 221–38.
Hill, D.E. (ed.) (1983), *P. Papini Stati Thebaidos Libri XII*, Leiden.
Hill, T. (2004), Ambitiosa mors: *suicide and self in Roman thought and literature*, New York/London (Studies in Classics 10).
Hinds, S.E. (1987), "Generalising about Ovid," *Ramus* 16, 4–31.
Hinds, S.E. (1993), "Medea in Ovid: Scenes from the Life of an Intertextual Heroine," *MD* 30, 9–47.
Hinds, S.E. (1998), *Allusion and Intertext: Dynamics of Appropriation in Roman Poetry*, Cambridge (Roman Literature and Its Contexts).
Hinds, S.E. (2007), "Martial's Ovid/Ovid's Martial," *JRS* 97, 113–54.
Hinds, S.E. (2011), "Seneca's Ovidian *Loci*," *SIFC* 9, 5–63.
Hine, H.M. (2000), *Seneca:* Medea, Warminster.
Hirschberg, T. (1989), *Senecas* Phoenissen. *Einleitung und Kommentar*, Berlin (Untersuchungen zur antiken Literatur und Geschichte 31).
Horace (1894), *Classic Interlinear Translations: The Complete Works of Horace*, Harrisburg (PA).
Horsfall, N. (1995), *A Companion to the Study of Virgil*, Leiden/New York (Mnemosyne Suppl. 151).
Horsfall, N. (2000), *Virgil,* Aeneid 7: *A Commentary*, Leiden/Boston (Mnemosyne Suppl. 198).
Hosius, C. (1893), "Lucan und seine Quellen," *RhM* 48, 380–97.
Houghton, L.B.T. (2017), "A Hidden Anagram in Valerius Flaccus?," *CQ* 67, 329–32.
Hübner, W. (ed.) (2010), *Manilius,* Astronomica, *Buch 5, herausgegeben, übersetzt und kommentiert, 2 voll.*, Berlin (Sammlung Wissenschaftliche Commentare).
Hulls, J.-M. (2011), "How the West was Won and Where it got us: Compressing History in Silius Italicus' *Punica*," *Histos* 5, 283–305.
Hunter, R. (1993a), *The* Argonautica *of Apollonius: Literary Studies*, Cambridge.
Hunter, R. (trans.) (1993b), *Apollonius of Rhodes: Jason and the Golden Fleece*, Oxford.
Hurlet, F. (2016), "Sources and Evidence," in: A. Zissos (ed.), *A Companion to the Flavian Age of Imperial Rome*, Chichester/Oxford/Malden (MA), 17–39.
Inwood, B. (2001), *The Poem of Empedocles: A Text and Translation with an Introduction*, Revised Edition, Toronto (Phoenix Suppl. 39).
Irwin, M.E. (2016), "Greek and Roman Botany," in: G. Irby (ed.), *A Companion to Science, Technology, and Medicine in Ancient Greece and Rome*, Malden (MA), 265–80.
Itgenshorst, T. (2005), Tota illa pompa: *Der Triumph in der römischen Republik*, Göttingen (Hypomnemata 161).
Jal, P. (1963), *La guerre civile à Rome. Étude littéraire et morale*, Paris.
Jan, L./Mayhoff, K.F.T (eds.) (1875–1906), *C. Plini Secundi Naturalis historiae libri XXXVII*, Leipzig.
Janan, M.W. (2009), *Reflections in a Serpent's Eye. Thebes in Ovid's* Metamorphoses, Oxford.
Jones, B.W. (1992), *The Emperor Domitian*, London/New York.
Jones, C.P. (2002), "Towards a Chronology of Josephus," *SCI* 21, 113–21.

Jones-Lewis, M.A. (2012), "Poison: Nature's Argument for the Roman Empire in Pliny the Elder's *Naturalis Historia*," *CW* 106, 51–74.
Joseph, T.A. (2012), *Tacitus the Epic Successor. Virgil, Lucan and the Narrative of Civil War in the* Histories, Leiden (Mnemosyne Suppl. 345).
Joshel, S.R. (1997), "Female desire and the discourse of empire: Tacitus's Messalina," in: J.P. Hallett/M.B. Skinner (eds.), *Roman Sexualities*, Princeton (NJ), 221–54.
Kalyvas, S.N. (2006), *The Logic of Violence in Civil War*, Cambridge.
Kant, I. (2007), *Critique of Judgement*, ed. N. Walker/trans. J. Creed Meredith, Oxford.
Keats-Rohan, K.S.B. (ed.) (1993), *Policraticus I–IV. Ioannes Saresberiensis*, Turnhout (Corpus Christianorum Continuatio Medievalis 118).
Keitel, E. (1984), "Principate and Civil War in the *Annals* of Tacitus," *AJPh* 105, 306–25.
Keith, A.M. (1991), "Etymological Play on *ingens* in Ovid, Vergil, and *Octavia*," *AJPh* 112, 73–76.
Keith, A.M. (2000), *Engendering Rome: Women in Latin Epic*, Cambridge (Roman Literature and Its Contexts).
Ker, J. (2009), *The Deaths of Seneca*, Oxford.
Kiernan, P. (2014), "The Bronze Mice of Apollo Smintheus," *AJA* 118, 601–26.
Kißel, W. (1979), *Das Geschichtsbild des Silius Italicus*, Frankfurt am Main (Studien zur klassischen Philologie 2).
Kitchell, K.F. (2014), *Animals in the ancient world from A to Z*, New York.
Klaassen, Y. (2014), *Contested Successions. The Transmission of Imperial Power in Tacitus'* Histories *and* Annals, PhD diss., Radboud Universiteit.
Kleiner, D. (1992), "Politics and Gender in the Pictorial Propaganda of Antony and Octavian," *EMC* 36, 357–67.
Kleiner, D./Matheson, S.B. (2000), *I Claudia: Women in Ancient Rome*, New Haven (CT).
Kleywegt, A.J. (1991), "Praecursoria Valeriana (V)," *Mnemosyne* 44, 137–59.
Kleywegt, A.J. (2005), *Valerius Flaccus, Argonautica, Book I: A Commentary*, Leiden (Mnemosyne Suppl. 262).
Klingner, F. (ed.) (1959), *Q. Horatius Flaccus Opera*, 3rd ed, Leipzig.
Klooster, J. (2014), "Time, space, and ideology in the aetiological narratives of Apollonius Rhodius' *Argonautica*," in: C. Reitz/A. Walter (eds.), *Von Ursachen sprechen. Eine aitiologische Spurensuche/Telling origins. On the lookout for aetiology*, Hildesheim (Spudasmata 162), 519–43.
Knight, V. (1991), "Apollonius, *Argonautica* 4.167–70 and Euripides' *Medea*," *CQ* 41, 248–50.
König, A.R. (2017), "Conflicting Models of Authority and Expertise in Frontinus' *Strategemata*," in: J. König/G. Woolf (eds.), *Authority and Expertise in Ancient Scientific Culture*, Cambridge, 153–81.
Korneeva, T. (2011), Alter et ipse. *Identità e dupicità nel sistema dei personaggi della* Tebaide *di Stazio*, Pisa (Testi e studi di cultura classica 52).
Kozák, D. (2013), "Traces of the Argo: Statius' *Achilleid* 1 and Valerius' *Argonautica* 1–2," in: G. Manuwald/A. Voigt (eds.), *Flavian Epic Interactions*, Berlin (*TiC* Suppl. 21), 247–66.
Krasne, D.A. (2011), *Mythic Recursions: Doubling and Variation in the Mythological Works of Ovid and Valerius Flaccus*, PhD diss., UC Berkeley.
Krasne, D.A. (2014a), "When the Argo Met the Argo: Poetic Destruction in Valerius' *Argonautica*," in: A. Augoustakis (ed.), *Flavian Poetry and Its Greek Past*, Leiden (Mnemosyne Suppl. 366), 33–48.
Krasne, D.A. (2014b), "Where Have All the Aetia Gone?: Aetiological Reassignment in Valerius Flaccus's *Argonautica*," in: C. Reitz/A. Walter (eds.), *Von Ursachen sprechen. Eine*

aitiologische Spurensuche/Telling origins. On the lookout for aetiology, Hildesheim (Spudasmata 162), 545–76.
Krasne, D.A. (forthcoming), "Valerius's Argonauts: A Band of Brothers?," in: L. Fratantuono/C. Stark (eds.), *A Companion to Latin Epic, 14–96 CE*, Malden (MA).
Kunst, C. (2008), *Livia: Macht und Intrigen am Hof des Augustus*, Stuttgart.
Künzl, E. (1988), *Der römische Triumph. Siegesfeiern im antiken Rom*, Munich.
Küppers, J. (1986), Tantarum Causas Irarum: *Untersuchungen zur einleitenden Bücherdyade der* Punica *des Silius Italicus*, Berlin (Untersuchungen zur antiken Literatur und Geschichte 23).
L'Orange, H.P. (1953), *Studies on the Iconography of Cosmic Kingship in the Ancient World*, Oslo/Cambridge (MA).
La Penna, A. (1994), "*Me, me, adsum qui feci, in me convertite ferrum …!* Per la storia di una scena tipica nell'epos e nella tragedia," *Maia* 46, 123–34.
Laederich, P. (1999), *Frontin*, Les Stratagèmes. *Introduction, traduction et commentarie*, Paris.
Landrey, L. (2014), "Skeletons in Armor: Silius Italicus' *Punica* and the *Aeneid*'s Proem," *AJPh* 135, 599–635.
Lane, L.L. (1999), "Malaria: Medicine and Magic in the Roman world," in: D. Soren/N. Soren (eds.), *A Roman Villa and a Late Roman Infant Cemetery. Excavation at Poggio Gramignano, Lugnano in Teverina*, Rome (Bibliotheca archaeologica 23), 633–51.
Lang, M.L. (1983), "Reverberation and Mythology in the *Iliad*," in: C.A. Rubino/C.W. Shelmerdine (eds.), *Approaches to Homer*, Austin (TX), 140–64.
Lange, C.H. (2009), Res Publica Constituta: *Actium, Apollo and the Accomplishment of the Triumviral Assignment*, Leiden.
Lange, C.H. (2016), *Triumphs in the Age of Civil War: The Late Republic and the Adaptability of Triumphal Tradition*, Bloomsbury.
Lange, C.H. (2017), "*Stasis* and *Bellum Civile*: A Difference in Scale?" *Critical Analysis of Law* 4, 129–40.
Lange, C.H./Vervaet, F.J. (forthcoming), *The Historiography of Late Republican Civil War*, Leiden (Historiography of Rome and Its Empire).
Langen, P. (1896–97), *C. Valeri Flacci Setini Balbi Argonauticon Libri Octo*, Berlin.
Langlands, R. (2008), "'Reading for the moral' in Valerius Maximus: The Case of *severitas*," *CCJ* 54, 160–87.
Langlands, R. (2011), "Roman *exempla* and Situation Ethics: Valerius Maximus and Cicero *de Officiis*," *JRS* 101, 100–22.
Langlands, R. (forthcoming), *Exemplary Ethics in Ancient Rome*, Cambridge.
Lanzarone, N. (ed.) (2016), *M. Annaei Lucani Belli civilis liber VII*, Florence (Biblioteca nazionale. Serie dei Classici greci e latini 22).
Lao, E. (2011), "Luxury and the Creation of a Good Consumer," in: R. Gibson/R. Morello (eds.), *Pliny the Elder: Themes and Contexts*, Leiden (Mnemosyne Suppl. 329), 35–56.
Lapidge, M. (1979), "Lucan's Imagery of Cosmic Dissolution," *Hermes* 107, 344–70.
Lapidge, M. (1989), "Stoic Cosmology and Roman Literature, First to Third Centuries A.D," *ANRW* II.36.3, 1379–429.
Laqueur, R. (1920), *Der jüdische Historiker Flavius Josephus: ein biographischer Versuch auf neuer quellenkritischer Grundlage*, Giessen.
Lazzarini, C. (2012), *L'addio di Medea: Valerio Flacco,* Argonautiche *8, 1–287*, Pisa (Testi e studi di cultura classica 55).
Le Bonniec, H./Le Boeuffle, A. (1972), *Pline l' Ancien. Histoire naturelle. Livre XVIII. De l'Agriculture*, Paris.

le Saux, F. (2004), "War and knighthood in Christine de Pizan's *Livre des fait d'armes et de chevallerie*," in: C. Saunders/F. le Saux/N. Thomas (eds.), *Writing War: Medieval Literary Responses to Warfare*, Cambridge, 93–105.

Leeming, H./Leeming, K. (eds.)/Osinkina, L. (trans.) (2003), *Josephus' Jewish War and its Slavonic Version: A Synoptic Comparison of the English Translation by H. St. J. Thackeray with the Critical Edition by N.A. Meščerskij of the Slavonic Version in the Vilna Manuscript*, Brill (Arbeiten zur Geschichte des antiken Judentums und des Urchristentums 46).

Leemreize, M. (2014), "The Egyptian Past in the Roman Present," in: J. Ker/C. Pieper (eds.), *Valuing the Past in the Greco-Roman World: Proceedings from the Penn-Leiden Colloquia on Ancient Values VII*, Leiden (Mnemosyne Suppl. 369), 56–82.

Lehmann, K. (1945), "The Dome of Heaven," *ABull* 27, 1–27.

Leigh, M. (1997), *Lucan: Spectacle and Engagement*, Oxford.

Levene, D.S. (2010), *Livy on the Hannibalic War*, Oxford.

Levick, B. (1999), *Vespasian*, London.

Levick, B. (2009), "The *Lex de imperio Vespasiani*: the Parts and the Whole," in: L. Capogrossi Colognesi/E. Tassi Scandone (eds.), *La Lex de imperio Vespasiani e la Roma dei Flavi (Atti del Convegno, 20-22 novembre 2008)*, Rome (Acta Flaviana 1), 11–22.

Li Causi, P. (2009), "La paternità del male. Caos parentale e guerra civile nelle *Phoenissae* di Seneca," *Annali Online di Ferrara-Teatro* 4, 270–296.

Liberman, G. (1997), *Valerius Flaccus*, Argonautiques *Chants I–IV*, Paris.

Liberman, G. (2002), *Valerius Flaccus*, Argonautiques *Chants V–VIII*, Paris.

Liebeschuetz, J.H.W.G. (1979), *Continuity and Change in Roman Religion*, Oxford.

Linderski, J. (1986), "The Augural Law," *ANRW* II.16.3, 2146–312.

Lindner, H. (1972), *Die Geschichtsauffassung des Flavius Josephus im Bellum Judaicum*, Leiden (Arbeiten zur Geschichte des antiken Judentums und des Urchristentums 12).

Lintott, A.W. (1982), *Violence, Civil Strife and Revolution in the Classical City 750–330 BC*, London.

Littlewood, C.A.J. (2004), *Self-Representation and Illusion in Senecan Tragedy*, Oxford.

Littlewood, R.J. (2011), *A commentary on Silius Italicus'* Punica 7: *edited with introduction and commentary*, Oxford.

Littlewood, R.J. (2014), "Loyalty and the Lyre: Constructions of Fides in Hannibal's Capuan Banquets," in: A. Augoustakis (ed.), *Flavian Poetry and its Greek Past*, Leiden (Mnemosyne Suppl. 366), 267–85.

Lock, P. (trans.) (2011), *Marino Sanudo Torsello, The Book of the Secrets of the Faithful of the Cross. Liber Secretorum Fidelium Crucis*, Ashgate (Crusade Texts in Translation 21).

Long, A.A. (2006), *From Epicurus to Epictetus: Studies in Hellenistic and Roman Philosophy*, Oxford.

Loupiac, A. (1998), *La poétique des éléments dans* La Pharsale *de Lucain*, Brussels (Collection Latomus 241).

Lovatt, H. (2001), "Mad about Winning: Epic, War and Madness in the Games of Statius' *Thebaid*," *MD* 46, 103–20.

Lovatt, H. (2010), "Interplay: Silius and Statius in the games of *Punica* 16," in: A. Augoustakis (ed.), *Brill's Companion to Silius Italicus*, Leiden, 155–76.

Lovatt, H. (2014), "Teamwork, Leadership and Group Dynamics in Valerius Flaccus' *Argonautica*," in: M. Heerink/G. Manuwald (eds.), *Brill's Companion to Valerius Flaccus*, 211–28.

Lovatt, H. (2015), "Following After Valerius: Argonautic Imagery in the *Thebaid*," in: W.J. Dominik/C.E. Newlands/K. Gervais (eds.), *Brill's Companion to Statius*, Leiden, 408–24.

Lovatt, H. (2016), "Flavian Spectacle: Paradox and Wonder," in: A. Zissos (ed.), *A Companion to the Flavian Age of Imperial Rome*, Chichester/Oxford/Malden (MA), 361–75.
Lowrie, M. (2015), "The Egyptian Within: A Roman Figuration of Civil War," in: B. Vinken (ed.), *Translatio Babylonis. Unsere orientalische Moderne*, Paderborn, 13–28.
Lowrie, M. (2016), "Civil War, the Soul, and the Cosmos at Seneca, *Thyestes* 547–622: A Tropology," in: P. Mitsis/I. Ziogas (eds.), *Wordplay and Powerplay in Latin Poetry*, Berlin (*TiC* Suppl. 36), 333–54.
Lowrie, M./Vinken B. (in progress), *Civil War and the Collapse of the Social Bond*.
Luke, T. (2010), "A Healing Touch for Empire: Vespasian's Wonders in Domitianic Rome," *G&R* 57, 77–106.
Luke, T. (2016), "Pliny the Elder on Pythagoras," in: F. Cairns/R. Gibson (eds.), *PLLS* 16: *Greek and Roman Poetry. The Elder Pliny*, Prenton (ARCA 54), 285–313.
Lundström, S. (1971), *"Sprach's" bei Silius Italicus*, Lund (Acta Regiae Societatis Humaniorum Litterarum Lundensis 67).
Lyne, R.O.A.M. (1974), "*Scilicet et tempus veniet...*: Virgil, *Georgics* 1.463–514," in: T. Woodman/D. West (eds.), *Quality and Pleasure in Latin Poetry*, Cambridge, 47–66.
MacDonald, S./Holden, P./Ardener, S. (eds.) (1987), *Images of Women in Peace and War: Cross-Cultural and Historical Perspectives*, London.
Mader, G. (2000), *Josephus and the Politics of Historiography: Apologetic and Impression Management in the Bellum Judaicum*, Leiden (Mnemosyne Suppl. 205).
Mader, G. (2010), "*Regno pectus attonitum furit*: Power, Rhetoric and Self-division in Seneca's *Phoenissae*," in: C. Deroux (ed.), *Studies in Latin Literature and Roman History* XV, Brussels (Collection Latomus 323), 287–310.
Malloch, S.J.V. (2015), "Frontinus and Domitian: the politics of the *Strategemata*," *Chiron* 45, 77–100.
Manioti, N. (2012), *All-female Family Bonds in Latin Epic*, PhD diss., University of Durham.
Mankin, D. (ed.) (1995), *Horace. Epodes*, Cambridge.
Manniche, L. (1999), *Sacred Luxuries. Fragrance, Aromatherapy, and Cosmetics in Ancient Egypt*, Ithaca.
Manolaraki, E. (2013), Noscendi Nilum cupido: *Imagining Egypt from Lucan to Philostratus*, Berlin (*TiC* Suppl. 18).
Manolaraki, E. (2015), "*Hebraei Liquores*: The Balsam of Judaea in Pliny's *Natural History*," *AJPh* 136, 633–67.
Manuwald, G. (1999), *Die Cyzicus-Episode und ihre Funktion in den* Argonautica *des Valerius Flaccus*, Göttingen (Hypomnemata 127).
Manuwald, G. (2009), "What Do Humans Get to Know about the Gods and Their Plans? On Prophecies and Their Deficiencies in Valerius Flaccus' *Argonautica*," *Mnemosyne* 62, 586–608.
Manuwald, G. (2013), "Divine Messages and Human Actions in the *Argonautica*," in: A. Augoustakis (ed.), *Ritual and Religion in Flavian Epic*, Oxford, 33–51.
Manuwald, G. (2015), *Valerius Flaccus:* Argonautica Book 3, Cambridge.
Manuwald, G./Voigt, A. (eds.) (2013), *Flavian Epic Interactions*, Berlin (*TiC* Suppl. 21).
Marcus, J. (1989), "Corpus/corps/corpse: writing the body in/at war," in: H.M. Cooper/A.A. Munich/S.M. Squier (eds.), *Arms and the Woman: War, Gender and Literary Representation*, Chapel Hill (NC), 124–67.
Marinis, A. (2015), "Statius' *Thebaid* and Greek tragedy. The legacy of Thebes," in: W.J. Dominik/C.E. Newlands/K. Gervais (eds.), *Brill's Companion to Statius*, Leiden, 343–61.

Marks, R.D. (2005a), "*Per uulnera regnum*: Self-Destruction, Self-Sacrifice, and *deuotio* in *Punica* 4–10," *Ramus* 34, 127–51.
Marks, R.D. (2005b), *From Republic to Empire. Scipio Africanus in the* Punica *of Silius Italicus*, Frankfurt am Main (Studien zur klassischen Philologie 152).
Marks, R.D. (2008), "Getting Ahead: Decapitation as Political Metaphor in Silius Italicus' *Punica*," *Mnemosyne* 61, 68–88.
Marks, R.D. (2010a), "Silius and Lucan," in: A. Augoustakis (ed.), *Brill's Companion to Silius Italicus*, Leiden, 127–53.
Marks, R.D. (2010b), "The Song and the Sword: Silius's *Punica* and the Crisis of Early Imperial Epic," in: D. Konstan/K.A. Raaflaub (eds.), *Epic and History*, Malden (MA), 185–211.
Marks, R.D. (2010c), "Lucan's Curio in the *Punica*," in: F. Schaffenrath (ed.), *Silius Italicus. Akten der Innsbrucker Tagung vom 19.-21. Juni 2008*, Frankfurt am Main (Studien zur klassischen Philologie 164), 29–46.
Marks, R.D. (2013), "The *Thebaid* and the fall of Saguntum in *Punica* 2," in: G. Manuwald & A. Voigt (eds.), *Flavian Epic Interactions*, Berlin (*TiC* Suppl. 21), 297–310.
Marks, R.D. (2014), "Statio-Silian Relations in the *Thebaid* and *Punica* 1–2," *CPh* 109, 130–39.
Marks, R.D. (forthcoming), "Searching for Ovid at Cannae: A Contribution to the Reception of Ovid in Silius Italicus' *Punica*," in: N. Coffee/C. Forstall/L. Galli Milić/D.P. Nelis (eds.), *Intertextuality in Flavian Epic Poetry*, Berlin (*TiC* Suppl. 64).
Markus, D.D. (2004), "Grim pleasures: Statius's Poetic *Consolationes*," *Arethusa* 37, 105–35.
Marpicati, P. (1999), "Silio 'delatore' di Pompeo (*Pun.* 5, 328 ss.; 10, 305 ss.)," *MD* 43, 191–202.
Marshall, M. (2010), *Tacitus and Lucan on Civil War*, PhD diss., University of Oxford.
Martindale, C. (1981), "Lucan's Hercules: Padding or Paradigm? A Note on *De Bello Civili* 4. 589–660," *SO* 56, 71–80.
Mason, S. (1991), *Flavius Josephus on the Pharisees: A Composition-Critical Study*, Leiden.
Mason, S. (1994), "Josephus, Daniel, and the Flavian House," in: F. Parente/J. Sievers (eds.), *Josephus and the History of the Greco-Roman Period*, Leiden, 161–91.
Mason, S. (2003), "Flavius Josephus in Flavian Rome: Reading on and Between the Lines," in: A.J. Boyle/W.J. Dominik (eds.), *Flavian Rome: Culture, Image, Text*, Leiden, 559–89.
Mason, S. (2005a), "Figured Speech and Irony in the Works of T. Flavius Josephus," in: J. Edmondson/S. Mason/J. Rives (eds.), *Flavius Josephus and Flavian Rome*, Oxford, 243–88.
Mason, S. (2005b), "Of Audience and Meaning: Reading Josephus' *Bellum Iudaicum* in the Context of a Flavian Audience," in: J. Sievers/G. Lembi (eds.), *Josephus and Jewish History in Flavian Rome and Beyond*, Leiden (*JSJ* Suppl. 104), 70–100.
Mason, S. (2009), "Of Despots, Diadems and Diadochoi: Josephus and Flavian Politics," in: W.J. Dominik/J. Garthwaite/P.A. Roche (eds.) *Writing Politics in Imperial Rome*, Leiden, 323–50.
Mason, S. (2012), "The Importance of the Latter Half of Josephus's Judaean Antiquities for his Roman Audience," in: A. Moriya/G. Hata (eds.), *Pentateuchal Traditions in the Late Second Temple Period*, Leiden (*JSJ* Suppl. 158), 129–55.
Mason, S. (2016), *A History of the Jewish War, A. D. 66–74*, Cambridge.
Mason, S. (2017), "Josephus' Portrait of the Flavian Triumph in Historical and Literary Context," in: F. Goldbeck/J. Wienand (eds.), *Der römische Triumph in Prinzipat und Spätantike*, Berlin, 125–76.
Master, J. (2016), *Provincial Soldiers and Imperial Instability in the* Histories *of Tacitus*, Ann Arbor (MI).
Masters, J. (1992), *Poetry and Civil War in Lucan's* Bellum Civile, Cambridge.
Mastronarde, D.J. (1970), "Seneca's *Oedipus*, the Drama in the Word," *TAPhA* 101, 291–315.

Mayer, R. (1981), *Lucan:* Civil War *VIII*, Warminster.
Mayor, A. (2014), *The Amazons: Lives & Legends of Warrior Women Across the Ancient World*, Princeton.
Mazour-Matusevich, Y./Bejczy, I.P. (2007), "Jean Gerson on Virtues and Princely Education," in: I.P. Bejczy/C.J. Nederman (eds.), *Princely Virtues in the Middle Ages 1200–1500*, Turnhout (Disputatio 9), 219–36.
Mazzoli, G. (2002), "Giocasta in prima linea," in: A. Aloni/E. Berardi/G. Besso/S. Cecchin (eds.), *I Sette a Tebe. Dal mito alla letteratura*, Bologna, 155–68.
McAuley, M.T. (2016), *Reproducing Rome. Motherhood in Virgil, Ovid, Seneca and Statius*, Oxford.
McDermott, W.C./Orentzel, A.E. (1977), "Silius Italicus and Domitian," *AJPh* 98, 24–34.
McDonough, C.M. (1999), "Forbidden to Enter the Ara Maxima: Dogs and Flies, or Dogflies?," *Mnemosyne* 52, 464–77.
McGuire, D.T., Jr. (1985), *History as Epic: Silius Italicus and the Second Punic War*, PhD diss., Cornell University.
McGuire, D.T., Jr. (1990), "Textual Strategies and Political Suicide in the Flavian Epics," in: A.J. Boyle (ed.), *The Imperial Muse. Ramus Essays on Roman Literature of the Empire. Flavian Epicist to Claudian*, Bendigo, 21–45.
McGuire, D.T., Jr. (1995), "History Compressed: The Roman Names of Silius' Cannae Episode," *Latomus* 54, 110–18.
McGuire, D.T., Jr. (1997), *Acts of Silence: Civil War, Tyranny, and Suicide in the Flavian Epics*, Hildesheim/New York (Altertumswissenschaftliche Texte und Studien 33).
McLaren, J.S. (2005), "Josephus on Titus: the Vanquished writing about the Victor," in: J. Sievers/G. Lembi (eds.), *Josephus and Jewish History in Flavian Rome and Beyond*, Leiden (JSJ Suppl. 104), 279–96.
McNelis, C. (2007), *Statius'* Thebaid *and the Poetics of Civil War*, Cambridge.
McVaugh, M.R./Ogden, M.S. (1997), *Inventarium sive Chirurgia magna. Volume 2: Commentary*, Leiden (Studies in Ancient Medicine 14/2).
Melville, A.D. (trans.) (1986), *Ovid*, Metamorphoses, Oxford.
Mendell, C.W. (1924), "Silius the Reactionary," *PhQ* 3, 92–106.
Merrills, A. (2017), *Roman Geographies of the Nile*, Cambridge.
Meyboom, P.G.P./Versluys, M.J. (2007), "The Meaning of Dwarfs in Nilotic Scenes," in: L. Bricault/M.J. Versluys/P.G.P. Meyboom (eds.), *Nile into Tiber. Egypt in the Roman World. Proceedings of the IIIrd International Conference of Isis Studies, Leiden, May 11-14 2005*, Leiden/Boston (Religions in the Greco-Roman World 159), 170–208.
Meyer, K. (1924), *Silius und Lucan*, PhD diss., Würzburg.
Mezzanotte, A. (1995), "Echi del mondo contemporaneo in Silio Italico," *RIL* 129, 357–88.
Micozzi, L. (2007), *Il catalogo degli eroi. Saggio di commento a Stazio*, Tebaide *4, 1–344*, Pisa (Testi e commenti 4).
Micozzi, L. (2015), "Statius' epic poetry. A challenge to the literary past," in: W.J. Dominik/C.E. Newlands/K. Gervais (eds.), *Brill's Companion to Statius*, Leiden, 325–42.
Miller, F.J. (trans.) (1929²), *Seneca, Tragedies*, 2 vols, Cambridge (MA) (LCL).
Milnor, K. (2005), *Gender, Domesticity, and the Age of Augustus: Inventing Private Life*, Oxford.
Mitousi, I. (2014), "Valerius' *Argonautica* as an Ideological Epic of the Flavian Era," in: A. Augoustakis (ed.), *Flavian Poetry and its Greek Past*, Leiden (Mnemosyne Suppl. 366), 153–68.
Monaghan, M.E. (2002), *Unfinished Business in the "Argonautica" of Valerius Flaccus*, PhD diss., Stanford University.

Montrose, L. (1991), "The work of gender in the discourse of discovery," *Representations* 33, 1–41.
Moore, M.B. (1988), "Ge," *LIMC* IV.1, 171–77.
Morgan, G. (2006), *69 A. D.: The Year of Four Emperors*, Oxford.
Moricca, U. (1917), "Le *Fenicie* di Seneca," *RFIC* 45, 467–515.
Morysine, R. (1539), *The strategemes, sleyghtes, and policies of warre, gathered together, by S. Julius Frontinus, and translated into Englyshe, by Rycharde Morysine*, London.
Motto, A.L./Clark, J.R. (1974), "*Violenta fata*: The Tenor of Seneca's *Oedipus*," *CB* 50, 81–87.
Mozley, J.H. (ed. and trans.) (1928), *Statius*, 2 vols, Cambridge (MA) (LCL).
Mozley, J.H. (ed. and trans.) (1934), *Valerius Flaccus*, Cambridge (MA) (LCL).
Muecke, F./Dunston, J. (eds.) (2011), *Domizio Calderini/Commentary of Silius Italicus*, Geneva.
Mulder, H.M. (1954), *Publii Papinii Statii Thebaidos liber secundus*, Groningen.
Murison, C.L. (1999), *Rebellion and Reconstruction: Galba to Domitian. An Historical Commentary on Cassius Dio's* Roman History Books 64–67 (A.D. 68–96), Atlanta (GA) (Philological Monographs 37).
Murphy, T. (2004), *Pliny the Elder's* Natural History: *The Empire in the Encyclopedia*, Oxford.
Murphy, T. (2016), "Notes from the Underground: the Curious Katabasis of Dionysodorus," in: F. Cairns/R. Gibson (eds.), *PLLS* 16: *Greek and Roman Poetry. The Elder Pliny*, Prenton (ARCA 54), 269–84.
Myers, M. (2018), *Vision and Space in Tacitus*, PhD diss., University of Nottingham.
Mynors, R.A.B. (1969), *P. Vergili Maronis Opera*, Oxford.
Naas, V. (2011), "Imperialism, *Mirabilia* and Knowledge: Some Paradoxes in the *Naturalis Historia*," in: R.K. Gibson/R. Morello (eds.), *Pliny the Elder: Themes and Contexts*, Leiden (Mnemosyne Suppl. 329), 57–70.
Nappa, C. (2005), *Reading after Actium: Vergil's* Georgics, *Octavian, and Rome*, Ann Arbor (MI).
Narducci, E. (1979), *La provvidenza crudele. Lucano e la distruzione dei miti augustei*, Pisa (Biblioteca di Studi Antichi 17).
Narducci, E. (2002), *Lucano: Un'epica contro l'impero. Interpretazione della* Pharsalia, Roma/Bari (Percorsi 34).
Nelis, D.P. (2011), "Praising Nero (Lucan, *De Bello Civili* 1,33-66)," in: G. Urso (ed.), *Dicere laudes: elogio, comunicazione, creazione del consenso*, Pisa (Convegni della Fondazione Niccolò Canussio 10), 253–64.
Nelis, D.P. (2014), "Empedoclean epic: How far can you go?," *Dictynna* 11 (http://dictynna.revues.org/1057).
Nesselrath, H.-G. (1998), "Jason und Absyrtus—Überlegungen zum Ende von Valerius Flaccus' Argonautica," in: U. Eigler/E. Lefèvre (eds.), Ratis omnia vincet: *Neue Untersuchungen zu den Argonautica des Valerius Flaccus*, Munich (Zetemata 98), 347–54.
Newlands, C.E. (2002), *Statius'* Silvae *and the Poetics of Empire*, Cambridge.
Newlands, C.E. (2012), *Statius, Poet between Rome and Naples*, London.
Nicholson, P.T./Shaw, I. (2000), *Ancient Egyptian Materials and Technology*, Cambridge.
Nicols, J. (1978), *Vespasian and the* Partes Flavianae, Wiesbaden (Historia Einzelschriften 28).
Nicols, J. (2016), "The Emperor Vespasian," in: A. Zissos (ed.) *A Companion to the Flavian Age of Imperial Rome*, Chichester/Oxford/Malden (MA), 60–76.
Nisbet, R.G.M. (1990), "The Dating of Seneca's Tragedies, with Special Reference to *Thyestes*," *PLLS* 6, 95–114.
Nisbet, R.G.M./Rudd, N. (2004), *A Commentary on Horace, Odes, Book III*, Oxford.
Noreña, C.F. (2003), "Medium and Message in Vespasian's Templum Pacis," *MAAR* 48, 25–43.
Nugent, S.G. (1992), "Vergil's 'Voice of the Women' in *Aeneid* V," *Arethusa* 25, 255–92.

Nugent, S.G. (1996), "Statius' Hypsipyle: Following in the Footsteps of the *Aeneid*," *Scholia* 5, 46–71.
Nutton, V. (2013), *Ancient Medicine*, 2nd ed, London/New York.
Nye, D. (1994), *The American Technological Sublime*, Cambridge (MA).
O'Brien, D. (1969), *Empedocles' Cosmic Cycle: A Reconstruction from the Fragments and Secondary Sources*, Cambridge.
O'Gorman, E. (1995), "Shifting Ground: Lucan, Tacitus and the landscape of civil war," *Hermathena* 158, 117–31.
O'Gorman, E. (2005), "Twin Narratives in Statius' *Thebaid*," in: M. Paschalis (ed.), *Roman and Greek Imperial Epic*, Herakleion (Rethymnon Classical Studies 2), 29–45.
O'Hara, J.J. (2007), *Inconsistency in Roman Epic: Studies in Catullus, Lucretius, Vergil, Ovid and Lucan*, Cambridge (Roman Literature and Its Contexts).
Ogden, D. (2002), *Magic, Witchcraft, and Ghosts in the Greek and Roman Worlds: A Sourcebook*, Oxford.
Ogilvie, R.M. (1965), *A Commentary on Livy. Books 1–5*, Oxford.
Osgood, J. (2006), *Caesar's Legacy: Civil War and the Emergence of the Roman Empire*, Cambridge.
Osgood, J. (2014), *Turia. A Roman Woman's Civil War*, Oxford (Women in Antiquity).
Osgood, J. (2015), "Ending Civil War at Rome: Rhetoric and Reality, 88 B.C.E.–197 C.E.," *AHR* 120, 1683–95.
Opelt, I. (1972), "Zu Senecas *Phoenissen*," in: E. Lefèvre (ed.) *Senecas Tragödien*, Darmstadt, 92–128.
Packer, J.E. (2003), "*Plurima et amplissima opera*: Parsing Flavian Rome," in: A.J. Boyle/W.J. Dominik (eds.), *Flavian Rome: Culture, Image, Text*, Leiden, 167–98.
Pappas, V./Theotokis, G. (trans.) (2015), Σέξτου Ιουλίου Φροντίνου ΣΤΡΑΤΗΓΗΜΑΤΑ, Βιβλία I-IV, Athens.
Paratore, E. (1951), *Tacito*, Milan (Biblioteca storica universitaria. Serie II. Monogr. 3).
Paratore, E. (1974), "Seneca e Lucano, Medea ed Erictho," in: *Colloquio italo-spagnolo sul tema Hispania Romana (Roma, 15–16 maggio 1972)*, Rome, 169–79.
Parker, G. (2008), *The Making of Roman India*, Cambridge/New York (Greek Culture in the Roman World).
Parker, G. (2016), "Foreigners and Flavians: Prejudices and Engagements," in: A. Zissos (ed.), *A Companion to the Flavian Age of Imperial Rome*, Chichester/Oxford/Malden (MA), 277–95.
Parker, H.N. (1999), "Greek Embryological Calendars and a Fragment from the Lost Work of Damastes, *On the Care of Pregnant Women and of Infants*," *CQ* 49, 515–34.
Parkes, R. (ed.) (2012), *Statius,* Thebaid 4*: Edited with an Introduction, Translation, and Commentary*, Oxford.
Parkes, R. (2014a), "The Argonautic Expedition of the Argives: Models of Heroism in Statius' *Thebaid*," *CQ* 64, 778–86.
Parkes, R. (2014b), "The Epics of Statius and Valerius Flaccus' *Argonautica*," in: M. Heerink/G. Manuwald (eds.), *Brill's Companion to Valerius Flaccus*, Leiden, 326–39.
Paul, A. (1953), *Untersuchungen zur Eigenart von Senecas* Phoenissen, Bonn (Reihe klassische Philologie 1).
Pellucchi, T. (2012), *Commento al libro VIII delle* Argonautiche *di Valerio Flacco*, Hildesheim (Spudasmata 146).
Penwill, J.L. (2000), "Quintilian, Statius and the Lost Epic of Domitian," *Ramus* 29, 60–83.
Penwill, J.L. (2009), "The Double Visions of Pompey and Caesar," in: L. Watson/P. Watson (eds.), *Roman Byways: Papers from a Conference in Memory of Charles Tesoriero*, Macquarie (*Antichthon* 43), 79–96.

Penwill, J.L. (2013), "Imperial Encomia in Flavian Epic," in: G. Manuwald/A. Voigt (eds.), *Flavian Epic Interactions*, Berlin (TiC Suppl. 21), 29–54.
Perkounig, C.-M. (1995), *Livia Drusilla – Iulia Augusta. Das politische Porträt der ersten Kaiserin Roms*, Vienna.
Perutelli, A. (1997), *C. Valeri Flacci Argonauticon liber VII*, Florence (Biblioteca nazionale. Serie dei classici greci e latini n.s. 5).
Petrone, G. (1996), *Metafora e tragedia. Immagini culturali e modelli tragici nel mondo romano*, Palermo (Nuovo Prisma 4).
Petrone, G. (1997), *Le Fenicie*, Milan (Classici greci e latini).
Pfeiffer, S. (2009), "Octavian-Augustus und Ägypten," in: A. Coşkun/H. Heinen/S. Pfeiffer (eds.), *Identität und Zugehörigkeit im Osten der griechisch-römischen Welt: Aspekte ihrer Repräsentation in Städten, Provinzen und Reichen*, Frankfurt am Main (Inklusion/Exklusion 14), 173–210.
Pfeiffer, S. (2010a), *Der römische Kaiser und das Land am Nil: Kaiserverehrung und Kaiserkult in Alexandria und Ägypten von Augustus bis Caracalla (30 v. Chr. –217 n. Chr.)*, Stuttgart (Historia Einzelschriften 212).
Pfeiffer, S. (2010b), "Ägypten in der Selbstdarstellung der Flavier," in: N. Kramer/C. Reitz (eds.), *Tradition und Erneuerung. Mediale Strategien in der Zeit der Flavier*, Berlin/New York (BzA 285), 273–88.
Phillips, O. (2002), "The Witches' Thessaly," in: P. Mirecki/M. Meyer (eds.), *Magic and Ritual in the Ancient World*, Leiden/Boston (Religions in the Greco-Roman World 141), 378–86.
Picone, G. (1984), *La fabula e il regno. Studi sul Thyestes di Seneca*, Palermo (Letteratura classica 12).
Platner, S.B./Ashby, T. (1929), *A Topographical Dictionary of Ancient Rome*, London.
Pogorzelski, R. (2016), "Centers and Peripheries," in: A. Zissos, (ed.), *A Companion to the Flavian Age of Imperial Rome*, Chichester/Oxford/Malden (MA), 223–39.
Pollard, E.A. (2009), "Pliny's *Natural History* and the Flavian *Templum Pacis*: Botanical Imperialism in First-Century C.E. Rome," *Journal of World History* 20, 309–38.
Pollini, E. (1984), "Il motivo della *visendi cupido* nel Giasone di Valerio Flacco," *Maia* 36, 51–61.
Pollmann, K.F.L. (2004), *Statius, Thebaid 12. Introduction, Text, and Commentary*, Paderborn.
Pomeroy, A.J. (2010), "*Fides* in Silius Italicus' *Punica*," in: F. Schaffenrath (ed.), *Silius Italicus: Akten der Innsbrucker Tagung vom 19.-21. Juni 2008*, Frankfurt am Main (Studien zur klassischen Philologie 164), 59–76.
Poortvliet, H.M. (ed.) (1991a), *C. Valerius Flaccus Argonautica Book II: A commentary*, Amsterdam.
Poortvliet, H.M. (1991b), "Valerius Flaccus and the Last File," in: M. Korn/H.J. Tschiedel (eds.), *Ratis omnia vincet. Untersuchungen zu den Argonautica des Valerius Flaccus*, Hildesheim (Spudasmata 48), 35–43.
Porter, J.I. (2001), "Ideals and Ruins: Pausanias, Longinus, and the Second Sophistic," in: S.E. Alcock/J.F. Cherry/J. Elsner (eds.), *Pausanias: Travel and Memory in Roman Greece*, Oxford, 63–93.
Porter, J.I. (2007), "Lucretius and the Sublime," in: S. Gillespie/P. Hardie (eds.), *The Cambridge Companion to Lucretius*, Cambridge, 167–84.
Porter, J.I. (2011), "Sublime monuments and sublime ruins in ancient aesthetics," *European Review of History* 18, 685–96.
Porter, J.I. (2016), *The Sublime in Antiquity*, Cambridge.
Price, J.J. (2001), *Thucydides and Internal War*, Cambridge.
Price, J.J. (2015), "Thucydidean *stasis* and the Roman Empire in Appian's Interpretation of History," in: K. Welch (ed.), *Appian's Roman History: Empire and Civil War*, Swansea, 45–63.

Puhvel, J. (1976), "The Origins of Greek *Kosmos* and Latin *Mundus*," *AJPh* 97, 154–67.
Purcell, N. (1986), "Livia and the Womanhood of Rome," *PCPhS* 32, 78–105.
Quint, D. (2010), "*Aeacidae Pyrrhi*: Patterns of Myth and History in *Aeneid* 1–6," in: B.W. Breed/C. Damon/A. Rossi (eds.), *Citizens of Discord: Rome and its Civil Wars*, Oxford, 133–44.
Rackham, H./Jones, W.H.S./Eichholz, D.E. (trans.) (1960), *Pliny: Natural History*, Cambridge (MA) (LCL).
Rajak, T. (1983), *Josephus: The Historian and his Society*, London.
Rajak, T. (1998), "The *Against Apion* and the Continuities in Josephus' Political Thought," in: S. Mason (ed.), *Understanding Josephus: Seven Perspectives*, Sheffield (Journal for the Study of Pseudepigrapha Suppl. 32), 222–46.
Ratcliffe, B.C. (2006), "Scarab Beetles in Human Culture," in: M.L. Jameson/B.C. Ratcliffe (eds.), *Scarabaeoidea in the 21st Century: A Festschrift Honoring Henry F. Howden*, Athens (GA) (Coleopterists Society Monographs 5), 85–101.
Reitz, B. (2012), "*Tantae Molis Erat*: On Valuing Roman Imperial Architecture," in: I. Sluiter/R.M. Rosen (eds.), *Aesthetic Value in Classical Antquity*, Leiden (Mnemosyne Suppl. 350), 315–44.
Rhorer, C. (1980), "Ideology, Tripartition and Ovid's Metamorphoses (1.5–451)," *Arethusa* 13, 299–313.
Riese, A/Bücheler, F./Lommatzsch, E. (eds.) (1869–1926), *Anthologia Latina sive Poesis Latinae Supplementum*, Leipzig.
Riggsby, A. (2007), "Guides to the Wor(l)d," in: J. König/T. Whitmarsh (eds.), *Ordering Knowledge in the Roman Empire*, Cambridge, 88–107.
Rimell, V.E. (2008), *Martial's Rome: Empire and the Ideology of Epigram*, Cambridge.
Río Torres-Murciano, A. (2009), "Las secuelas del *fortunati ambo* (Verg., Aen. IX 446-449): Epopeya y imperio," *Emerita* 77, 295–315.
Río Torres-Murciano, A. (2010), "El designio de Júpiter en Valerio Flaco. Providencia, historia y tradición literaria," *CFC* 30, 131–63.
Ripoll, F. (1998), *Le morale héroïque dans les épopées latines d'époque flavienne: Tradition et innovation*, Paris.
Ripoll, F. (1999), "Aspects et fonction de Néron dans la propagande impériale flavienne," in: J.-M. Croisille/R. Martin/Y. Perrin (eds.) *Neronia V. Néron: histoire et légende. Actes du Ve Colloque international de la SIEN (Clermont-Ferrand et Saint-Étienne, 2-6 novembre 1994)*, Brussels (Collection Latomus 247), 137–51.
Ripoll, F. (2000a), "Variations épiques sur un motif d'*ecphrasis*: l'enlèvement de Ganymède," *REA* 102, 479–500.
Ripoll, F. (2000b), "Silius Italicus et Cicéron," *LEC* 68, 147–73.
Ripoll, F. (2008), "Jason au chant VIII des *Argonautiques* de Valérius Flaccus: héros ou anti-héros?" *Pallas* 77, 173–84.
Ripoll, F. (2014), "Le 'tabou de navigation' dans les *Argonautiques* de Valérius Flaccus: invention et liquidation d'une tradition," in: A. Estèves/J. Meyers (eds.), *Tradition et innovation dans l'épopée latine, de l'Antiquité au Moyen-Âge*, Bordeaux (Scripta Receptoria 1), 103–18.
Roche, P.A. (2005), "Righting the Reader: Conflagration and Civil War in Lucan's *De Bello Civili*," *Scholia* 14, 52–71.
Roche, P.A. (ed.) (2009), *Lucan, De bello civili, Book 1*, Oxford.
Roche, P.A. (2015), "Lucan's *De Bello Civili* in the *Thebaid*," in: W.J. Dominik/C.E. Newlands/K. Gervais (eds.), *Brill's Companion to Statius*, Leiden, 393–407.

Rodgers, R.H. (2004), *Frontinus. De Aquaeductu Urbis Romae*, Cambridge/New York (Cambridge Classical Texts and Commentaries 42).
Rodriguez-Almeida, E. (1994), "Marziale in Marmo," *MEFRA* 106, 197–217.
Roller, M. (2013), "On the Intersignification of Monuments in Augustan Rome," *AJPh* 134, 119–31.
Roman, L. (2010), "Martial and the City of Rome," *JRS* 100, 88–117.
Roman, L. (2014), *Poetic Autonomy in Ancient Rome*, Oxford.
Roscher, W.H. (1890), *Studien zur griechischen Mythologie und Kulturegeschichte. IV. Über Selene und Verwandtes*, Leipzig.
Rosati, G. (2009), "*Latrator Anubis*: Alien Divinities in Augustan Rome, and How to Tame Monsters through Aetiology," in: P. Hardie (ed.), *Paradox and the Marvellous in Augustan Literature and Culture*, Oxford, 268–87.
Rose, P.W. (2005), "Spectators and Spectator Comfort in Roman Entertainment Buildings: A Study in Functional Design," *PBSR* 73, 99–130.
Rosenberger, V. (1992), Bella et expeditiones. *Die antike Terminologie der Kriege Roms*, Stuttgart (Heidelberger althistorische Beiträge und epigraphische Studien 12).
Rosenmeyer, T.G. (1989), *Senecan Drama and Stoic Cosmology*, Berkeley.
Rossi, A. (2005), "*sine fine*: Caesar's Journey to Egypt and the End of Lucan's *Bellum Civile*," in: C. Walde (ed.), *Lucan im 21. Jahrhundert*, Munich, 237–60.
Rosso, E. (2008), "Les destins multiples de la *domus Aurea*: L'exploitation de la condamnation de Néron dans l'idéologie flavienne," in: S. Benoist/A. Daguet-Gagey (eds.) *Un discours en images de la condamnation de mémoire*, Metz (Publications du Centre régional universitaire lorrain d'histoire 34), 43–78.
Rosso, E. (2009), "Le theme de la *Res publica restituta* dans le monnayage de Vespasien: pérennité du 'modèle augustéen' entre citations, réinterprétations et dévoiements," in: F. Hurlet/B. Mineo (eds.), *Le principat d'Auguste*, Rennes, 209–42.
Rubin, G. (1975), "The traffic in women: notes toward a political economy of sex," in: R. Reiter (ed.), *Toward an Anthropology of Women*, New York, 157–210.
Rudd, N. (ed. and trans.) (2004), *Horace, Odes and Epodes*, Cambridge (MA) (LCL).
Rupprecht, H. (1995), "Flavius Josephus, eine bisher nicht beachtete Vorlage für Silius Italicus," *Gymnasium* 102, 497–500.
Sacerdoti, A. (2012), Novus unde furor. *Una lettura del dodicesimo libro della* Tebaide *di Stazio*, Pisa/Roma (Altera 2).
Sailor, D (2008), *Writing and Empire in Tacitus*, Cambridge.
Salemme, C. (1991), *Medea: un antico mito in Valerio Flacco*, Naples (Studi Latini 8).
Sallares, R. (2002), *Malaria and Rome*, Oxford.
Salles, R. (2009), "Chrysippus on Conflagration and the Indestructibility of the Cosmos," in: R. Salles (ed.), *God and Cosmos in Stoicism*, Oxford, 118–34.
Santini, C. (1991), *Silius Italicus and His View of the Past*, Amsterdam (London Studies in Classical Philology 25).
Santini, C. (1992), "Il prologo degli *Strategemata*," in: C. Santini/N. Scivoletto (eds.), *Prefazioni, prologhi, proemi di opera tecnico-scientifiche latine*, vol. 2, Rome, 983–90.
Scarborough, J. (1977), "Some Beetles in Pliny's *Natural History*," *The Coleopterists Bulletin* 31, 293–96.
Schenk, P. (1989), "Die Gesänge des Teuthras (Sil. It. 11, 288–302 u. 432–482)," *RhM* 132, 350–68.
Schenk, P. (1999), *Studien zur poetischen Kunst des Valerius Flaccus: Beobachtungen zur Ausgestaltung des Kriegsthemas in den Argonautica*, Munich (Zetemata 102).

Schenkl, K. (1871), *Studien zu den Argonautica des Valerius Flaccus*, Vienna.
Schiesaro, A. (2003), *The Passions in Play. Thyestes and the Dynamics of Senecan Drama*, Cambridge.
Schimann, F. (1997), "Feuer auf Lemnos: Feuer und Furie in den Argonautica des Valerius Flaccus," in: T. Baier/F. Schimann (eds.), *Fabrica: Studien zur antiken Literatur und ihrer Rezeption*, Stuttgart/Leipzig, 103–28.
Schmitz, C. (1993), *Die kosmische Dimension in den Tragödien Senecas*, Berlin (Untersuchungen zur antiken Literatur und Geschichte 39).
Scholz, U.W. (1993), "Consus und Consualia," in: J. Dalfen/G. Petersmann/F.F. Schwartz (eds.), *Religio Graeco-Romana. Festschrift für Walter Pötscher*, Horn/Graz (Grazer Beiträge Suppl. 5), 195–213.
Seal, C. (2014), "Civil War and the Apollonian Model in Valerius' *Argonautica*," in: A. Augoustakis (ed.), *Flavian Poetry and its Greek Past*, Leiden (Mnemosyne Suppl. 366), 113–35.
Secoy, D.M./Smith, A.E. (1977), "Superstition and Social Practices against Agricultural Pests," *Environmental Review* 2, 2–18.
Seewald, M. (2008), *Studien zum 9. Buch von Lucans* Bellum Civile: *Mit einem Kommentar zu den Versen 1–733*, Berlin (GFA 2).
Seo, J.M. (2013), *Exemplary Traits. Reading Characterization in Roman Poetry*, Oxford.
Severy, B. (2003), *Augustus and the Family at the Birth of the Roman Empire*, New York/London.
Shackleton Bailey, D.R. (ed.) (1988/1997²), *M. Annaei Lucani De Bello Civili Libri X*, Stuttgart.
Shackleton Bailey, D.R. (ed. and trans.) (2003), *Statius: Thebaid and Achilleid*, 2 vols, Cambridge (MA) (LCL).
Shackleton Bailey, D.R./Parrot, C.A. (eds.) (2015), *Statius: Silvae*, Cambridge (MA) (LCL).
Shaw, P. (2017), *The Sublime*, 2nd ed, London/New York.
Shelton, J.E. (1971), *A Narrative Commentary on the* Argonautica *of Valerius Flaccus*, PhD diss., Vanderbilt University.
Shey, H.J. (1968), *A Critical Study of the* Argonautica *of Valerius Flaccus*, PhD diss., University of Iowa.
Shotter, D.C.A. (1975), "A Time-Table for the *Bellum Neronis*," *Historia* 24, 59–74.
Siggelkow-Berner, B. (2011), *Die jüdischen Feste im* Bellum Judaicum *des Flavius Josephus*, Tübingen (Wissenschaftliche Untersuchungen zum Neuen Testament n.s. 306).
Skutsch, O. (1985), *The Annals of Quintus Ennius*, Oxford.
Slaney, H. (2009), "Flavian Medea: The Further Voice in Valerius' Argonautica," *Iris* 22, 2–21.
Slaney, H. (2014), "The Voyage of Rediscovery: Consuming Global Space in Valerius Flaccus' *Argonautica*," in: M. Skempis/I. Ziogas (eds.), *Geography, Topography, Landscape: Configurations of Space in Greek and Roman Epic*, Berlin (TiC Suppl. 22), 427–61.
Smelik, K.A.D./Hemelrijk, E.A. (1984), "'Who knows not what monsters demented Egypt worships?' Opinions on Egyptian animal worship in Antiquity as part of the ancient conception of Egypt," *ANRW* II.17.4, 1852–2000.
Smolenaars, J.J.L. (ed.) (1994), *Thebaid VII. A Commentary*, Leiden/New York/Köln (Mnemosyne Suppl. 134).
Smolenaars, J.J.L. (2008), "Statius *Thebaid* 1.72: is Jocasta dead or alive? The tradition of Jocasta's suicide in Greek and Roman drama and in Statius' *Thebaid*," in: J.J.L. Smolenaars/H.-J. van Dam/R.R. Nauta (eds.), *The Poetry of Statius*, Leiden/Boston (Mnemosyne Suppl. 306), 215–37.
Soerink, J. (2014), "Tragic/Epic: Statius' *Thebaid* and Euripides' *Hypsipyle*," in: A. Augoustakis (ed.), *Flavian Poetry and its Greek Past*, Leiden (Mnemosyne Suppl. 366), 171–91.

Soubiran, J. (1969), "De Coriolan à Polynice: Tite-Live modèle de Stace', in: J. Bibauw (ed.), *Hommages à Marcel Renard*, Brussels (Collection Latomus 101), 689–99.
Spaltenstein, F. (1986), *Commentaire des* Punica *de Silius Italicus (livres 1 à 8)*, Geneva.
Spaltenstein, F. (1990), *Commentaire des* Punica *de Silius Italicus (livres 9 à 17)*, Geneva.
Spaltenstein, F. (2004), *Commentaire des* Argonautica *de Valérius Flaccus (livres 3, 4, et 5)*, Brussels (Collection Latomus 281).
Spaltenstein, F. (2005), *Commentaire des* Argonautica *de Valérius Flaccus (livres 6, 7, et 8)*, Brussels (Collection Latomus 291).
Spilsbury, P. (2003), "Flavius Josephus on the Rise and Fall of the Roman Empire," *JThS* 54, 1–24.
Stadler, H. (1993), *Valerius Flaccus,* Argonautica *VII: Ein Kommentar*, Hildesheim.
Steele, C. (2013), *The End of the Roman Republic, 146-44 BC. Conquest and Crisis*, Edinburgh.
Steele, R.B. (1922), "The Method of Silius Italicus," *CPh* 17, 319–33.
Stem, R. (2007), "The Exemplary Lessons of Livy's Romulus," *TAPhA* 137, 435–71.
Stevenson, T. (2005), "Readings of Scipio's Dictatorship in Cicero's *De Re Publica* (6.12)," *CQ* 55, 140–52.
Stocks, C. (2014), *The Roman Hannibal: remembering the enemy in Silius Italicus'* Punica, Liverpool.
Stover, T. (2003), "Confronting Medea: Genre, Gender, and Allusion in the *Argonautica* of Valerius Flaccus," *CPh* 98, 123–47.
Stover, T. (2009), "Apollonius, Valerius Flaccus, and Statius: Argonautic Elements in *Thebaid* 3.499–647," *AJPh* 130, 439–55.
Stover, T. (2012), *Epic and Empire in Vespasianic Rome: A New Reading of Valerius Flaccus'* Argonautica, Oxford.
Stover, T. (2014), "Lucan and Valerius Flaccus: Rerouting the Vessel of Epic Song," in: M. Heerink/G. Manuwald (eds.), *Brill's Companion to Valerius Flaccus*, Leiden, 290–306.
Straumann, B. (2017), "Roman Ideas on the Loose," *Critical Analysis of Law* 4, 141–51.
Sullivan, J.P. (1991), *Martial – the Unexpected Classic: A Literary and Historical Study*, Cambridge.
Swain, S. (1996), *Hellenism and Empire: Language, Classicism, and Power in the Greek World, AD 50–250*, Oxford.
Swetnam Burland, M. (2015), *Egypt in Italy: Visions of Egypt in Roman Imperial Culture*, Cambridge/New York.
Takács, S. (2011), "Cleopatra, Isis, and the Formation of Augustan Rome," in: M.M. Miles (ed.), *Cleopatra: A Sphinx Revisited*, Berkeley, 78–95.
Taraporewalla, R. (2010), "The Templum Pacis: Construction of Memory under Vespasian," *AClass* 53, 145–63.
Tarrant, R.J. (1978), "Senecan Drama and Its Antecedents," *HSPh* 82, 213–63.
Tarrant, R.J. (1985), *Seneca's Thyestes*, Atlanta (GA).
Tarrant, R.J. (2002), "Chaos in Ovid's *Metamorphoses* and Its Neronian Influence," *Arethusa* 35, 349–60.
Taylor, P.R. (1994), "Valerius' Flavian *Argonautica*," *CQ* 44, 212–35.
Taylor-Briggs, P.R. (1995), "Critical Observations on the Text of the Fourth Book of Valerius Flaccus's *Argonautica*," *JAC* 10, 111–26.
Thackeray, H. St. J. (ed. and trans.) (1927), *Josephus: The Jewish War*, 3 vols, Cambridge (MA) (LCL).
Thackeray, H. St. J. (1929), *Josephus: The Man and the Historian*, New York.
Thalmann, W.G. (2011), *Apollonius of Rhodes and the Spaces of Hellenism*, Oxford.

Thomas, A. (1930), *Jean Gerson et l'éducation des dauphins de France: étude critique. Suivie du texte de deux de ses opuscules et de documents inédits sur Jean Majoris précepteur de Louis XI*, Paris.
Thomas, E. (2007), *Monumentality and the Roman Empire: Architecture in the Antonine Age*, Oxford.
Thomas, R.F. (1982), "Catullus and the Polemics of Poetic Reference (Poem 64.1–18)," *AJPh* 103, 144–64.
Thompson, D.W. (1932), "On the Greek Bird-Name Σελευκίς," *BSOS* 6, 1103–4.
Thonemann, P. (2011), *The Maeander Valley: A Historical Geography from Antiquity to Byzantium*, Cambridge.
Tipping, B. (2010), *Exemplary Epic: Silius Italicus' Punica*, Oxford.
Töchterle, K. (ed.) (1994), *Lucius Annaeus Seneca, Oedipus. Kommentar mit Einleitung, Text und Übersetzung*, Heidelberg.
Toohey, P. (1993), "Jason, Pallas and Domitian in Valerius Flaccus' *Argonautica*," *ICS* 18,191–201.
Touahri, O. (2009), "L'image politique du chef de guerre dans les *Punica* de Silius Italicus: les conseils de guerre avant Trasimène (V, 53-148) et Cannes (IX, 15-65)," in: O. Devillers/J. Meyers (eds.), *Pouvoirs des hommes, pouvoir des mots, des Gracques à Trajan. Hommages au Professeur Paul Marius Martin*, Leuven (Bibliothèque d'études classiques 54), 431–42.
Traina, A. (ed.) (1997), *Virgilio. L'utopia e la storia. Il libro XII dell'Eneide e antologia delle opere*, Torino (Testi e Crestomazie).
Trinacty, C.V. (2014), *Senecan Tragedy and the Reception of Augustan Poetry*, Oxford.
Tuck, S.L. (2016), "Imperial Image-Making," in: A. Zissos (ed.), *A Companion to the Flavian Age of Imperial Rome*, Chichester/Oxford/Malden (MA), 109–28.
Tupet, A.-M. (1976), *La magie dans la poésie latine*, Paris (Coll. Études Anciennes).
Turner, A. (2007), "Frontinus and Domitian: *Laus Principis* in the *Strategemata*," *HSPh* 103, 423–49.
Tyrrell, W.B. (1984), *Amazons: A Study in Athenian Mythmaking*, Baltimore (MD).
Van Noorden, H. (2015), *Playing Hesiod: The "Myth of the Races" in Classical Antiquity*, Cambridge.
Venini, P. (ed.) (1970), *P. Papini Stati Thebaidos Liber XI*, Florence.
Venturini, C. (2009), "Note in tema di '*Lex de imperio Vespasiani*' e di trasfigurazioni successive," in: L. Capogrossi Colognesi/E. Tassi Scandone (eds.), *La Lex de imperio Vespasiani e la Roma dei Flavi (Atti del Convegno, 20-22 novembre 2008)*, Rome (Acta Flaviana 1), 205–18.
Versluys, M.J. (2010), "Understanding Egypt in Egypt and Beyond," in: L. Bricault/M.J. Versluys (eds.), *Isis on the Nile: Egyptian Gods in Hellenistic and Roman Egypt. Proceedings of the IVth International Conference of Isis Studies, Liège, November 27–29 2008*, Leiden/Boston (Religions in the Greco-Roman World 171), 7–36.
Versluys, M.J. (2012), "Making Meaning with Egypt: Hadrian, Antinous, and Rome's Cultural Renaissance," in: L. Bricault/M.J. Versluys (eds.), *Egyptian Gods in the Hellenistic and Roman Mediterranean: Image and Reality Between Local and Global*, Caltanissetta/Palermo (Mythos Suppl. 3), 25–39.
Versluys, M.J. (2015), "Haunting Traditions. The (Material) Presence of Egypt in the Roman World," in: D. Boschung/A.W. Busch/M.J. Versluys (eds.), *Reinventing "The Invention of Tradition"? Indigenous Pasts and the Roman Present*, Paderborn (Morphomata 32), 127–58.
Vessey, D.W.T.C. (1970), "Varia Statiana," *CB* 46, 49–55; 64.
Vessey, D.W.T.C. (1973), *Statius and the Thebaid*, Cambridge.
Vessey, D.W.T.C. (1974), "Silius Italicus on the Fall of Saguntum," *CPh* 69, 28–36.

Vessey, D.W.T.C. (1985), "Lemnos Revisited: Some Aspects of Valerius Flaccus, *Argonautica* II.77–305*,*" *CJ* 80, 326–39.
Vessey, D.W.T.C. (1986), "*Pierius menti calor incidit*: Statius' Epic Style," *ANRW* II.32.5, 2965–3019.
von Albrecht, M. (1964), *Silius Italicus: Freiheit und Gebundenheit römischer Epik*, Amsterdam.
von Lieven, A. (2016), "Translating Gods, Interpreting Gods: On the Mechanisms behind the *Interpretatio Graeca* of Egyptian Gods," in: I. Rutherford (ed.), *Greco-Egyptian Interactions: Literature, Translation, and Culture, 500 BCE–300 CE*, Oxford, 61–82.
Wachsmuth, C. (1860), "Ueber die Unächtheit des vierten Buchs der Frontinschen Strategemata," *RhM* 15, 574–83.
Wacht, M. (1991), *Juppiters Weltenplan im Epos des Valerius Flaccus*, Mainz/Stuttgart (AAWM 10).
Walbank, F.W. (ed.) (1957), *A Historical Commentary on Polybius. Volume I: Commentary on Books I–VI*, Oxford.
Walter, A. (2013), "Beginning at the end: Silius Italicus and the desolation of Thebes," in: G. Manuwald/A. Voigt (eds.), *Flavian Epic Interactions*, Berlin (*TiC* Suppl. 21), 311–26.
Walter, A. (2014), *Erzählen und Gesang im flavischen Epos*, Berlin (GFA 5).
Ward, W.A. (1994), "Beetles in Stone: The Egyptian Scarab," *BiA* 57, 186–202.
Ward Perkins, J. (1956), "Nero's Golden House," *Antiquity* 30, 209–19.
Wardle, D. (1996), "Vespasian, Helvidius Priscus and the Restoration of the Capitol," *Historia* 45, 208–22.
Warmington, E.H. (ed. and trans.) (1956), *Remains of Old Latin I: Ennius, Caecilius*, rev. ed., Cambridge (MA).
Watson, L.C. (ed.) (2003), *A Commentary on Horace's* Epodes, Oxford.
Weber, W. (1921), *Josephus und Vespasian: Untersuchungen zu dem Jüdischen Krieg des Flavius Josephus*, Berlin/Stuttgart/Leipzig.
Weinreich, O. (1928), *Studien zu Martial: Literarhistorische und religionsgeschichtliche Untersuchungen*, Stuttgart (Tübinger Beiträge zur Altertumswissenschaft).
Welch, K.E. (2007), *The Roman Amphitheatre: From Its Origins to the Colosseum*, Cambridge/New York.
Welch, K. (ed.) (2015), *Appian's* Roman History: *Empire and Civil War*, Swansea.
Wellesley, K. (1956), "Three Historical Puzzles in *Histories* 3," *CQ* 6, 207–14.
Wellesley, K. (1981), "What Happened on the Capitol in December AD 69?," *AJAH* 6, 166–90.
Wellesley, K. (2000), *Year of the Four Emperors*, 3rd ed, Routledge.
West, M.L. (1966), *Hesiod,* Theogony: *Edited with Prolegomena and Commentary*, Oxford.
Wezel, E. (1873), *De C. Silii Italici cum fontibus tum exemplis*, PhD diss., Leipzig.
Wheeler, E.L. (1988), *Stratagem and the Vocabulary of Military Trickery*, Leiden (Mnemosyne Suppl. 108).
Wheeler, E.L. (2007), "The Army and the *Limes* in the East," in: P. Erdkamp (ed.), *A Companion to the Roman Army*, Malden (MA)/Oxford, 235–66.
Wienand, J. (2012), *Der Kaiser als Sieger. Metamorphosen triumphaler Herrschaft unter Constantin I*, Berlin (Klio Beih. 19).
Wijsman, H.J.W. (1996), *Valerius Flaccus,* Argonautica, *Book V: A Commentary*, Leiden (Mnemosyne Suppl. 158).
Wijsman, H.J.W. (2000), *Valerius Flaccus,* Argonautica, *Book VI: A Commentary*, Leiden (Mnemosyne Suppl. 204).
Willard, C.C. (1995), "Pilfering Vegetius? Christine de Pizan's Faits d'Armes et de Chevalrie," in: L. Smith/J.H.M. Taylor (eds.), *Women, the Book and the Worldly. Selected Proceedings of the St Hilda's Conference, 1993*. Volume II, Cambridge, 31–37.

Williams, G. (1994), "Nero, Seneca and Stoicism in the *Octavia*," in: J. Elsner/J. Masters (eds.), *Reflections of Nero: Culture, History & Representation*, London/Chapel Hill (NC), 178–95.
Williams, M.F. (1991), *Landscape in the Argonautica of Apollonius Rhodius*, Frankfurt am Main (Studien zur klassischen Philologie 63).
Williamson, G.A. (trans.) (1959), *The Jewish War*, Baltimore (MD).
Wilson, M. (2003), "After the Silence: Tacitus, Suetonius, Juvenal," in: A.J. Boyle/W.J. Dominik (eds.), *Flavian Rome: Culture, Image, Text*, Leiden, 523–42.
Wilson, M. (2013), "The Flavian *Punica*?" in: G. Manuwald & A. Voigt (eds.), *Flavian Epic Interactions*, Berlin, 13–28.
Winkes, R. (1995), *Livia, Octavia, Iulia: Porträts und Darstellungen*, Providence (RI)/Louvain-la-Neuve (Archaeologia transatlantica 13).
Wiseman, T.P. (1978), "Flavians on the Capitol," *AJAH* 3, 163–78.
Wiseman, T.P. (1995), *Remus: A Roman myth*, Cambridge.
Wiseman, T.P. (2010), "The Two-Headed State: How Romans Explained Civil War," in: B.W. Breed/C. Damon/A. Rossi (eds.), *Citizens of Discord: Rome and its Civil Wars*, Oxford, 25–44.
Wittig, M. (1986), "The Mark of Gender," in: N.K. Miller (ed.), *The Poetics of Gender*, New York, 63–73.
Wölfflin, E. von (1875), "Frontins Kriegslisten," *Hermes* 9, 72–92.
Wood, N. (1967), "Frontinus as a possible source for Machiavelli's method," *JHI* 28, 243–48.
Wood, S. (1999), *Imperial Women: A Study in Public Images, 40 BC – AD 68*, Leiden (Mnemosyne Suppl. 194).
Wood, S. (2016), "Public Images of the Flavian Dynasty: Sculpture and Coinage," in: A. Zissos (ed.) *A Companion to the Flavian Age of Imperial Rome*, Chichester/Oxford/Malden (MA), 129–47.
Woodman, A.J. (1988), *Rhetoric in Classical Historiography: Four Studies*, London/Portland (OR).
Woodman, A.J. (1997), "Tacitus," in: C. Kraus/A.J. Woodman (eds.), *Latin Historians*, Oxford/New York (*G&R* New Surveys in the Classics 27), 88–117.
Woodman, A.J./Martin, R.H. (1996), *The Annals of Tacitus. Book 3*, Cambridge (Cambridge Classical Texts and Commentaries 32).
Woolf, G. (1993), "Roman peace," in: J. Rich/G. Shipley (eds.), *War and Society in the Roman World*, London/New York (Leicester-Nottingham Studies in Ancient Society 5), 171–94.
Wyatt, J. (2013), "Ibis," *The Encyclopedia of Ancient History. Volume VI*, Malden (MA), 3382–83.
Wyke, M. (2002), *The Roman Mistress: Ancient and Modern Representations*, Oxford.
Yasumura, N. (2011), *Challenges to the Power of Zeus in Early Greek Poetry*, London.
Zadoks, J.C. (2007), "Fox and Fire – a Rusty Riddle," *Latomus* 66, 3–9.
Zanker, P. (2010), "By the emperor, for the people: 'popular' architecture at Rome," in: B.C. Ewald/C.F. Noreña (eds.), *The Emperor and Rome: Space, Representation and Ritual*, Cambridge/New York (*YCIS* 35), 45–87.
Zissos, A. (1999), "Allusion and Narrative Possibility in the *Argonautica* of Valerius Flaccus," *CPh* 94, 289–301.
Zissos, A. (2002), "Reading Models and the Homeric Program in Valerius Flaccus's *Argonautica*," *Helios* 29, 69–96.
Zissos, A. (2003), "Spectacle and Elite in the *Argonautica* of Valerius Flaccus," in: A.J. Boyle/W.J. Dominik (eds.), *Flavian Rome: Image, Culture, Text*, Leiden, 659–84.
Zissos, A. (2004a), "L'ironia allusiva: Lucan's *Bellum Civile* and the *Argonautica* of Valerius Flaccus," in: P. Esposito/E.M. Ariemma (eds.), *Lucano e la tradizione dell'epica latina*, Naples, 21–38.

Zissos, A. (2004b), "Terminal Middle: The *Argonautica* of Valerius Flaccus," in: S. Kyriakidis/F. De Martino (eds.), *Middles in Latin Poetry*, Bari (Rane 38), 311–44.

Zissos, A. (2006), "Sailing and Sea-Storm in Valerius Flaccus (*Argonautica* 1.574–642): The Rhetoric of Inundation," in: R.R. Nauta/H.-J. van Dam/J.J.L. Smolenaars (eds.), *Flavian Poetry* (Mnemosyne Suppl. 270), Leiden, 79–95.

Zissos, A. (ed. and trans.) (2008), *Valerius Flaccus'* Argonautica *Book 1: Edited with Introduction, Translation, and Commentary*, Oxford.

Zissos, A. (2009), "Navigating Power: Valerius Flaccus' *Argonautica*," in: W.J. Dominik/J. Garthwaite/P.A. Roche (eds.), *Writing Politics in Imperial Rome*, Leiden, 351–66.

Zissos, A. (2012), "The King's Daughter: Medea in Valerius Flaccus' *Argonautica*," in: A.J. Boyle (ed.), *Roman Medea*, Bendigo (*Ramus* 41), 94–118.

Zissos, A. (2014), "Stoic Thought and Homeric Reminiscence in Valerius Flaccus' *Argonautica*," in: M. Garani/D. Konstan (eds.), *The Philosophizing Muse: The Influence of Greek Philosophy on Roman Poetry*, Cambridge (Pierides 3), 269–97.

Zissos, A. (ed.) (2016), *A Companion to the Flavian Age of Imperial Rome*, Chichester/Oxford/Malden (MA).

Notes on Contributors

Neil W. Bernstein is Professor in the Department of Classics & World Religions at Ohio University (Athens, Ohio), where he has taught Latin language and literature since 2004. He is the author of *Seneca: Hercules Furens* (Bloomsbury, 2017); *Silius Italicus, Punica 2* (Oxford, 2017); *Ethics, Identity, and Community in Later Roman Declamation* (Oxford, 2013); and *In the Image of the Ancestors: Narratives of Kinship in Flavian Epic* (Toronto, 2008).

Federica Bessone is full professor of Latin language and literature at the University of Turin. She studied at the Scuola Normale Superiore and the University of Pisa. She is the author of *P. Ovidii Nasonis Heroidum Epistula XII. Medea Iasoni* (1997) and of *La 'Tebaide' di Stazio. Epica e potere* (2011); with Marco Fucecchi, she co-edited *The Literary Genres in the Flavian Age: Canons, Transformations, Reception* (2017); and she has published on Augustan and Flavian poetry, Seneca, Petronius. She is co-editor of the series "Millennium" (Alessandria, Edizioni dell'Orso) and a member of the scientific committee of "EuGeStA" and "RCCM."

Siobhan Chomse is Lecturer in Latin Language and Literature at Royal Holloway, University of London. She completed her PhD in 2015 at the University of Cambridge, where she taught for two years before joining the Department of Classics at Royal Holloway in September 2017. Siobhan's research focuses particularly on the idea of the sublime and its role in the literature of early imperial Rome. Her work has explored expressions of sublimity found in architecture, technology, and the natural world, from monuments to ruins, siege engines to earthquakes. At present, she is revising her doctoral thesis for publication.

William J. Dominik is Professor Emeritus of Classics at the University of Otago and Invited Full Professor and Integrated Researcher of Classics at the University of Lisbon. He has published numerous books, chapters, and articles on Roman literature and rhetoric (especially of the Flavian era), the classical tradition and reception, lexicography, and other topics. Among his books are *Brill's Companion to Statius* (co-ed., 2015), *Writing Politics in Imperial Rome* (co-ed., 2009), *Flavian Rome* (co-ed., 2003), *The Mythic Voice of Statius* (1994), and *Speech and Rhetoric in Statius' Thebaid* (1994). He is a committee member of the Epic Poetry Network (EPN). His webpage can be found at https://otago.academia.edu/WilliamJDominik.

Marco Fucecchi is Associate professor of Latin language and Literature at the University of Udine. He specializes in literature of the Augustan age and the early Empire, focusing on Flavian epic poetry. In this field he has published several papers, especially on Silius's *Punica*, and monographs including a commentary to Valerius Flaccus's *Argonautica* VI (1997 and 2006). Other studies on Augustan literature (Ovid's elegy from exile), Neronian literature (Seneca on Scipio's villa at *Liternum*), Flavian literature (intertextuality and *fides* in Silius's *Punica*), and late antique topics (divine personifications in Claudian) are forthcoming. He is currently preparing a commentary to Silius's *Punica* 17.

Lauren Donovan Ginsberg is Associate Professor of Classics at the University of Cincinnati. Her research focuses on Latin literature of the Neronian and Flavian ages, intertextuality, and cultural memory. In addition to articles on Seneca, Lucan, and other early Imperial poets, she is the author of *Staging Memory, Staging Strife: Empire and Civil War in the* Octavia (OUP 2017).

Jean-Michel Hulls completed a PhD at UCL in 2006 and has since published a number of chapters and articles on Flavian literature including studies of Statius, Silius Italicus, Martial, Suetonius and Josephus. He is currently working on a study of identity and selfhood in Statius's *Thebaid*. He teaches Classics at Dulwich College.

Alison Keith is Director of the Jackman Humanities Institute and Professor of Classics and Women's Studies at the University of Toronto. She is the author of *The Play of Fictions: Studies in Ovid's Metamorphoses II* (Ann Arbor 1992), *Engendering Rome* (Cambridge 2000), and *Propertius, Poet of Love and Leisure* (London 2008). Her research focuses on gender and genre in Latin literature and Roman culture. She is currently completing a book on Virgil for IB Tauris in their series "Understanding Classics."

Alice König is Senior Lecturer in Classics at the University of St Andrews. Her research focuses on ancient technical literature and the history of science and the relationship between literature, society, and politics in the early Principate. She is preparing a monograph on the author and statesman Sextus Julius Frontinus and has published a series of articles on Vitruvius, Frontinus, Martial, Pliny, and Tacitus. In 2011, she founded the Literary Interactions project (https://arts.st-andrews.ac.uk/literaryinteractions/), which has produced two edited volumes on different aspects of intertextuality. She also co-runs a collaborative research project entitled "Visualising War: Interplay between Battle Narratives in Ancient and Modern Cultures" (https://arts.st-andrews.ac.uk/visualising-war/). She directs the Centre for the Literatures of the Roman Empire at the University of St Andrews and is a member of the RSE Young Academy of Scotland.

Darcy Krasne is Lecturer in the Discipline of Classics at Columbia University in New York; she received her BA from the University of Oxford (Corpus Christi College) and her MA and PhD from UC Berkeley. Her research primarily focuses on the intersection of poetry, politics, and mythology in Latin poetry of the early Roman empire. She has published articles and book chapters on Valerius Flaccus and on Ovid's *Ibis*, *Metamorphoses*, and *Fasti*, and she was a Tytus Scholar at the University of Cincinnati in Spring 2017. Her current project is a monograph investigating ideas of cosmos, meteorology, and civil war in Valerius's *Argonautica*.

Leo Landrey is an independent scholar based in San Diego, California. He completed degrees from Bowdoin College and Brown University; his PhD dissertation, *Valerius Flaccus' Historical Epic*, explored the political dimensions of the societies depicted in the Flavian *Argonautica*. His research primarily focuses on Augustan, Neronian, and Flavian poetry, with a particular interest in the complicated status of epic heroism in texts with mutually contradictory discourses. He has published on Silius Italicus's *Punica* and has presented on Valerius Flaccus's *Argonautica* at numerous international conferences.

Eleni Hall Manolaraki is associate professor of Classics at the University of South Florida and the author of *Noscendi Nilum Cupido: Imagining Egypt from Lucan to Philostratus* (De Gruyter 2013). She has published articles and book chapters on geography, natural phenomena, animals, and plants in epic (Lucan, Statius, Silius Italicus), historiography (Tacitus), oratory (Pliny the Younger), and natural history (Pliny the Elder).

Raymond Marks is Associate Professor in the Department of Ancient Mediterranean Studies at the University of Missouri (Columbia, Missouri). He has published widely on Silius Italicus and is the author of *From Republic to Empire. Scipio Africanus in the Punica of Silius Italicus* (2005).

Steve Mason completed his BA and MA at McMaster University and his PhD at the University of St Michael's College, Toronto, after one year visiting in Jerusalem and another in Tübingen. After twenty-two years at Toronto's York University, the last eight as Canada Research Chair in Greco-Roman Cultural Interaction, he moved to Aberdeen and then to Groningen (2015). Mason edits the international project *Flavius Josephus: Translation and Commentary* (Brill, 2000–). His most recent monographs are *A History of the Jewish War, AD 66–74* (Cambridge) and *Orientation to the History of Roman Judaea* (Wipf and Stock), both from 2016.

John Penwill† passed away in April 2018. At the time of his death, he was honorary associate (formerly senior lecturer) in humanities at La Trobe University, Bendigo. He took his degrees from the University of Tasmania and Downing College, Cambridge. His research focused particularly on Roman literature of the late Republic and early Empire, and within that, the interface between literature and philosophy, principally in Lucretius's *De Rerum Natura* and Apuleius's *Metamorphoses*. He also published articles on Plato, the *Letters of Themistocles*, Vergil, Epicurean theology, Lactantius, Homer, Livy, Tacitus, Terence, Seneca, and the *Letters of Chion*, as well as contributing substantially to the field of Flavian epic poetry. He was a founding member of the Pacific Rim Roman Literature Seminar, a long-time editor of *Ramus*, and served in various capacities on the boards of the Australian Society for Classical Studies and the Classical Association of Victoria.

Claire Stocks is Lecturer for Classics at Newcastle University, UK. Her research interests include Augustan and post Augustan epic, especially Flavian epic. She is the author of *The Roman Hannibal: Remembering the Enemy in Silius Italicus' Punica* (Liverpool, 2014) and co-editor of *Horace's Epodes: Context, Intertexts, and Reception* (Oxford, 2016). She is currently working on a monograph on the representation of Jupiter in Flavian Poetry and Culture and a co-edited volume (with Antony Augoustakis and Emma Buckley) on *Fides* in Flavian Literature.

Tim Stover is Associate Professor of Classics at Florida State University (Tallahassee, Florida). He specializes in Latin literature, with a particular interest in epic poetry. In addition to articles on Lucretius, Vergil, Lucan, Valerius Flaccus, and Statius, he is the author of *Epic and Empire in Vespasianic Rome: A New Reading of Valerius Flaccus' Argonautica* (Oxford, 2012). He is also the co-editor, along with Laurel Fulkerson, of *Repeat Performances: Ovidian Repetition and the Metamorphoses* (University of Wisconsin Press, 2016). His current long term project is a book that examines the influence of Valerius's *Argonautica* on subsequent Flavian epic.

Marco van der Schuur is currently finishing his dissertation at the Rijksuniversiteit Groningen. This dissertation examines the role of Senecan tragedy in the Latin epic tradition and focuses both on Seneca's interpretation of Augustan epic in his tragedies and on Statius's reception of Senecan tragedy in his *Thebaid*.

Thematic Index

69 CE (*see* "Year of the Four Emperors")

Absyrtus (brother of Medea) 71ff., 77, 304f., 313, 385 n.92
Acastus (son of Pelias) 37 n.31, 38ff., 77 n.21, 247 n.68
acosmia (*see* "cosmos")
Actium 26, 48, 150 n.18, 208 n.24, 230, 297, 301, 353, 359, 375 n.43
Adrastus (king of Argos) 43, 46, 93f., 97, 253 n.2, 314
adultery 299ff.
Aeetes (king of Colchis) 28, 35, 41f., 69ff., 75 n.14, 79, 112, 305ff., 311
aegis 64, 121, 310f.
Aeneas 25f., 32 n.17, 33, 36, 48, 79, 83 n.36; n.38, 101, 128, 130, 134, 192f., 230, 232 n.22; n.25, 246 n.63, 273f., 290, 332 n.34, 375 n.43, 400 n.73
– Shield of (in Vergil's *Aeneid*) 26, 48, 230, 246 n.63, 375, 400 n.73
Aeson (father of Jason) 36ff., 69f., 246, 247 n.68, 304, 380 n.68
aesthetics 180, 185 n.17, 202, 319f., 341, 348, 394 n.46, 396
Africa 33, 66 n.33, 83, 165, 290, 344f., 370 n.28
Agrippa II (king of Judaea) 205f., 210 n.26, 220 n.39, 221
Ahl, Frederick 5 n.14, 26 n.2, 51, 92 n.11, 127 n.21, 204, 274 n.11, 276 n.23, 278 n.29, 291 n.68, 375 n.43
Alcimede (mother of Jason) 38, 304
Alexander the Great 163, 222, 263 n.31, 264 n.32, 341
Alexander, Ti. Julius (prefect of Egypt) 215, 218, 220, 222f.
Alexandria 20, 63 n.27, 73, 83, 204, 211, 215, 218, 219 n.38, 341, 345 n.18, 346
Allecto (a Fury; *see also* "Furies," "Megaera," "Tisiphone") 19, 120 n.37, 128, 136f., 184, 186, 327, 331
allegory 216, 357
– Homeric 372f.

alliances 42, 51, 60, 70, 150, 156 n.38, 158, 162, 164, 169ff., 175, 179f., 182ff., 196, 218, 221, 270, 277, 325 n.15
Alps 181, 188, 347
Amata (mother of Lavinia) 120 n.37, 130, 138 n.79, 184, 241 n.51, 327
Amazons 305f., 309f., 316
ambiguity 13, 27 n.3, 90, 95ff., 100, 107, 138 nn.78–79, 148f., 158, 187ff., 219, 257f., 287, 290, 326, 330, 366 n.13, 380 n.66, 382, 400
ambitiosa mors (*see* "suicide")
ambush 161 n.47, 165f., 173, 205, 323
Amphiaraus 122, 315
amulets 356ff.
Ananus II (chief priest of Jerusalem) 202
Anchises 92f., 106, 129 n.38, 327
Antaeus (opponent of Hercules) 66 n.33
Antigone 44, 47, 94, 129f., 134, 317ff.
Antioch 204, 219 n.37
Antiochus 262, 300
Antonius Primus, M. (Roman general of 69 CE) 287f.
Antonius, M. (*see also* "Cleopatra") 26, 48, 161 n.47, 163, 166, 168, 209, 212, 230
Aphrodite (*see* "Venus/Aphrodite")
Apion 356f.
Apollo 76, 259, 398
– cult titles and local cults of 355, 398
Apollonius Rhodius (*see also* index of passages) 28 n.8, 34ff., 71, 84 n.40, 114 n.20, 115 n.22, 116 n.25, 122, 227, 232 n.22, 363 nn.1–2
apostrophes 19, 90f., 93, 95, 231ff., 240, 248, 280, 282, 329f.
Appian 145 n.56, 148, 165 n.56, 256 n.9
Arabia 347, 355
Aratus 366 n.13, 376 n.50
Arch of Titus 207, 268 n.43, 396 n.51
architecture (*see also* "building programs") 387ff., 394, 406 n.99

448 —— Thematic Index

– architectural wonders 387ff., 399, 401, 407, 408 n.105
– cosmic 364, 389, 397f.
– Egyptian 342
– Flavian 207, 268 n.43, 303, 388ff., 396 n.51, 399ff., 408
– literary 30, 89, 90
– sublimity of 387–409 *passim*, 408 n.105
Ardea 182, 274, 276
Ares (*see* "Mars/Ares")
Argia (wife of Polynices) 18, 44ff., 99 n.25, 113ff., 120, 314f., 318f.
Argives 99 n.26, 134ff., 141, 314ff.
Argo 19, 35, 37 n.31, 38ff., 75 n.14, 77, 112, 120f., 234 n.30, 363 n.2, 367, 375 n.46, 384, 385 n.94
– as first ship 34 n.22, 35, 363, 367 n.19
– return route of 39, 84 n.40
– world-shaping voyage of 38f., 115, 363, 367, 384
Argonautic tradition 29, 34ff., 42f., 69 n.4, 71 n.8, 83 n.37, 112, 126 n.19, 228, 248, 305 n.31
Argonauts 38, 40ff., 65 n.31, 71, 73, 77, 82, 84 n.40, 247, 303ff., 306, 308, 310f., 312 n.42, 313, 316, 363
Argos (city) 91, 93f., 114, 133, 137, 314f.
Ariasmenus (character in Valerius Flaccus) 310f.
Arimaspoi (mythical Eastern people) 385 n.95
Aristotle (*see also* index of passages) 176, 352f.
Armenia 42
Armitage, David 1, 5 n.15, 7 n.18, 8, 126 n.20, 127 n.24, 148 n.9, 229 n.10, 230 n.11, 341 n.1, 385 n.92
Asia Minor 38, 77f., 82, 330 n.30
Astraea (*see also* "Dike") 366f.
Athena (*see* "Minerva/Athena")
Atreus 112 n.16, 124, 126ff., 137 n.72
augury 38 n.35, 98 n.23, 102, 256 n.7, 295ff.
Augustanism 11, 26, 29, 49, 267, 269 n.48, 297ff., 302f.

Augustus 1, 20, 26f., 29, 48, 79 n.26, 81, 153, 163, 171 n.67, 208f., 212f., 230, 255 n.6, 263 n.31, 269 n.48, 297, 301f., 341, 344, 375, 389, 406 n.99
autocracy (*see also* "tyrant") 14, 30, 146, 169f., 175, 177, 292
auxiliary troops
– of Hannibal 169
– Roman 16, 343

Bacchus 134, 135, 140f., 242
barbarians 114, 164 n.55, 166 n.60, 265 n.15, 342
Batavian revolt 161, 175
Bato (Carthaginian helmsman in Silius Italicus) 57ff.
battle narratives (*see also* "war"; *see also under individual battles*) 3, 8 n.21, 26, 30f., 52, 54, 60, 63, 150 n.22, 152, 155, 159, 170, 247, 253, 279, 290, 312 n.42
battles, naval 16f., 51–67 *passim*, 173, 183 n.11
Bedriacum, Battle of 209
Bellona 19, 35, 64, 77ff., 105 n.46, 311f.
bellum externum vs. *bellum internum* 16f., 26, 148f., 163f., 175 n.77, 211, 301, 329, 341, 343, 360
Berytus 204, 207, 215, 219 n.37
Black Sea 83, 304, 374
boundaries, violation and distortion of 131, 149, 162, 259, 274, 360, 363ff., 390, 401
Britain 83, 151 n.24, 152, 209, 233
Britannicus 256 n.9, 268 n.44, 269 nn.47 and 49, 283 n.46
brotherhood 17, 167 n.62, 253f., 255ff., 258 n.14, 260, 262f., 264ff., 267, 270
Brutus, D. Junius (naval commander) 54ff., 57, 59
Brutus, M. Junius (Caesar's assassin) 1, 161 nn.47–48
building program (*see also* "architecture")
– Augustan 153 n.31, 267 n.39, 389, 466 n.99
– Flavian 210, 267 n.39, 360, 387 n.7, 389, 390 n.22, 396f., 405
– Neronian 365 n.11, 388ff., 401, 408

Thematic Index — 449

- Pharaonic (*see* "architecture, Egyptian")
Burke, Edmund 390f., 393, 396 n.54, 398 n.66, 404

Cadmus 102, 105, 189, 314f.
Caesar, C. and L. (sons of Julia) 256 n.9, 267
Caesar, C. Julius 17, 20, 31, 44, 53ff., 59 n.19, 60ff., 64f., 70ff., 85, 91ff., 106, 129 n.38, 145 n.2, 150, 156ff., 162ff., 164, 166, 168ff., 172ff., 182f., 189, 209, 212, 256 n.8, 266, 269 n.47, 275ff., 278, 292, 375 n.43, 404f., 408
- literary works of (*see also* index of passages) 148 n.10, 150 n.19, 154, 161 n.48, 165 n.56, 167, 277
Caesarea 219, 221f.
Calderini, Domizio 257 n.13
Cannae 19, 28, 30ff., 51, 62, 168, 181, 264f., 273 n.10, 277f., 280ff., 291ff.
Canthus (an Argonaut) 39, 309f.
Capaneus (one of the Seven against Thebes) 99 n.27, 107
Capitoline 227–49 passim
- burning of 4, 13f., 21, 91, 228, 241, 246 n.62, 248, 287f., 337, 388
- Flavian occupation 4 n.11, 239
- in poetry 13, 236ff., 337 n.46
- rebuilding of temple 236, 239 n.42
- Temple of Jupiter Optimus Maximus 227f., 234ff., 241ff., 287, 388
Capua 51f., 52 n.6, 63 n.28, 181f., 183ff., 186f., 195, 274, 275 n.16, 276, 277 n.28, 291
Cartesian sense of self 321, 337
Carthage 28, 30f., 33, 51f., 64 n.30, 81, 136, 156, 162, 168 n.64, 169, 182, 210, 254, 256 n.8, 259, 262, 266, 270, 273ff., 280ff., 293, 298, 301, 313, 324, 328
Cassius Dio (*see also* index of passages) 165 n.56, 209
Cassius Longinus, C. (Caesar's assassin) 161 n.48, 212
Castor (*see also* "Dioscuri," "Pollux") 268, 283
catasterism 76, 81f., 375 n.49

Cato the Elder 154, 156, 158f.
Cato the Younger 44, 66 n.33, 234, 237f.
cattle of the Sun (*see also* "Sol/Helios") 79 n.25
Catullus (*see also* index of passages) 34f., 234 n.30, 363, 364 n.5, 366 n.14
Catulus Capitolinus, Q. Lutatius (cos. 78 BCE) 236
Ceres/Demeter 36 n.28, 45
cestos of Venus 117ff., 121, 122 n.41
Chaos 368ff., 371f., 369 n.27, 378
Chatti 173f., 268f.
Cicero (*see also* index of passages) 25 n.1, 31, 148, 232 n.24, 256 n.9, 261, 277, 278, 279, 355 n.49, 364 n.5
Cilicia 347, 354, 355
Circe 379f.
Citizens of Discord (ed. Breed/Damon/Rossi, 2010) 5, 149
city foundation 25f., 48, 105, 165 n.58, 188, 254ff., 256 n.9, 269, 276, 287f., 297, 314, 330 n.30
civil war (*see also* "*bellum internum*," "civil wars")
- "cultural imperative" to write about 149 n.17
- as inversion 95ff.
- as taboo 145f.
- as wound (*see* "trauma")
- chaos of 83, 150, 170, 391
- cyclicality of 81, 249, 276, 366 n.14
- definitions of 7ff., 148ff., 341 n.1
- distancing strategies 17, 29, 160, 272f., 319
- endings of 13, 19ff., 28, 30, 69 n.2, 208ff.
- origins of 19ff., 48, 277, 280ff., 385
- recent scholarship on 5f.
- *topoi* of 3 n.6, 9, 90ff., 100, 149, 168 n.64, 230, 231 n.16, 248, 272, 276, 341, 360, 385 n.92
civil wars (*see also* "civil war")
- between Caesar and Pompey 34, 51–67 *passim*, 70, 150 n.19, 164, 166, 172f., 256 n.8, 277, 404f.
- between Octavian and M. Antonius 26, 48, 163, 209, 230

- between Octavian/M. Antonius and Caesar's assassins 1, 161 n.48, 163, 212, 301
- between Sulla and Marius 33, 126, 148, 275f., 402
- in Egypt 73, 158 n.41, 341
- in Judea 18, 199ff.
- of 69 CE (see also "Year of the Four Emperors") 3f., 6, 20, 29, 69f., 75, 83, 146, 171, 208ff., 213ff., 227ff., 271ff., 285, 287f., 292, 295ff., 343, 387f.

Civilis, C. Julius (leader of Batavian revolt) 174f.

Clashing Rocks 84 n.40, 373, 375f., 378, 379 n.61, 385

Claudius (emperor of Rome) 145 n.2, 209, 212, 222

Cleopatra 26, 73, 209, 301, 341, 351, 360

Coastes (character in Valerius Flaccus) 112, 114

coinage (see also "personifications," "propaganda") 171 n.67, 203, 210ff., 225, 242 n.52, 267f., 268 n.45, 302, 394 n.46

Colchian dragon (see also "Sown Men (Colchian)") 71, 75 n.14, 102, 189, 311

Colchians 72 n.9, 77 n.21, 82, 84, 119 n.36, 247, 304, 313, 367 n.19

Colchis 19, 28, 35, 40f., 69f., 112, 114, 116, 118f., 272 n.7, 303ff., 308f., 311, 313, 363, 385 n.92

collapse (see also "cosmos," "instability," "ruins") 12, 14, 27, 29, 49, 146, 302, 364, 369–79, 389 n.13, 391, 406f.

Colosseum 15f., 387–408

commemoration (see also "memory") 15, 142, 190, 194ff., 236, 238 n.41, 242f.

Corinth 76, 116, 117 n.26, 121f., 210, 220

Coriolanus, C. Marcius 132, 134 n.57, 154, 164

Cornelia (mother of the Gracchi) 138 n.79

Cornelia (wife of Pompey) 44

cosmos 9, 11f., 14f., 19, 127f., 363–85 passim
- cosmic disorder 129, 133, 364 n.7, 375f., 378–80, 382–84

- cosmic dissolution 9, 124, 128, 282, 363–65, 369–73, 375–79, 385
- cosmic imagery 375, 395
- cosmic order 363f., 367f., 372f., 376, 378f., 384

Crassus, M. Licinius 157ff., 166 n.60, 212

Creon (king-regent of Thebes) 44, 105, 317ff.

Crete 346ff.

Creusa/Glauce (princess of Corinth) 76, 110 n.13, 116, 117 n.26, 380 n.68

Cupid/Eros 115 n.24

Curio, C. Scribonius (tr. 50 BCE) 33, 66 n.33

curses 2, 6, 25, 110, 137f., 210, 285, 298, 314, 316, 343

Cybele 312

Cyzicus (king of the Doliones) 65 n.31, 75 n.14, 83, 229, 244, 247, 272 n.7, 303f., 312 n.42

Danube 73

Daphnis (character in Silius Italicus) 66

deception 156 n.38, 164, 206, 224, 286, 297, 308, 330 n.31, 335, 380 n.68, 398

Decius Magius (see "Capua")

Deipyle (wife of Tydeus) 314

demagoguery 31, 203, 275 n.16, 281

despotism (see "tyrant")

deuotio (see also "suicide") 28, 32, 34, 43f.

didacticism (see also "Frontinus," "technical writing") 145, 152, 154 n.33, 157, 163, 170, 246 nn.62 and 65, 351

Dido 81, 246 nn.63–64, 247 n.65, 274, 331f.

Dike (see also "Astraea") 286 n.59, 366 n.14

Diodorus Siculus (see also index of passages) 234 n.30, 355

Dioscorides 348ff.

Dioscuri (see also "Castor," "Pollux") 39, 81f., 283
- as parallels for Titus and Domitian 75 n.14, 268 n.42

Discordia (see also "personifications") 2, 111, 120, 281, 315, 371

divine intervention (*see also* "gods") 35 n.26, 61 n.22, 72 n.9, 119, 141 n.92, 183, 186, 189ff., 310
Doliones (*see* "Cyzicus")
Domitian 13, 21, 42 n.38, 72 n.9, 76, 83 n.36, 146, 151 n.26, 152, 155, 157, 159, 160, 170, 172ff., 202, 207, 222, 228, 236ff., 263, 269, 293, 302f., 398 n.61, 408 n.105
– "Germanicus" as honorific *cognomen* 157, 173f., 267f.
– poetry of 81, 146 n.4, 236
– rivalry with Titus 75 n.14, 127, 255, 267ff., 282f., 283 n.45
Domitius Ahenobarbus, L. (cos. 54 BCE) 65f.
Domus Augusta 302
Domus aurea 365 n.11, 389ff., 395, 396 n.51, 397–400, 405, 408
Durkheim, Émile 321 n.1, 323 n.8, 325 n.15, 331 n.33
dux (*see* "leadership")

earthquakes 347, 374 n.40, 376ff., 391
East vs. West 210, 218, 343, 357, 378, 384f.
Eastern stereotypes 63
ecphrasis 10, 18, 26, 48, 109, 110 n.13, 111, 115 n.24, 116, 120ff., 244–47
Egypt (*see also* "Alexander, Ti. Julius," "Alexandria," "Vespasian") 220, 222, 341–61 *passim*
– *Aegyptiaca* 342ff., 346f., 360
– architecture of (*see* "architecture, Egyptian")
– as site of civil war 15f., 158 n.41, 218f., 341, 343, 360
– exports of (*see also* "trade") 344
– fauna of 342, 353ff.
– Flavian integration of 341 n.3, 342ff.
– flora of 346, 348ff.
– geography of 342
– gods of 353–59
– grain of (*see also* "grain supply," "trade") 344ff.
– history of (*see also* "Cleopatra") 342
– institutions of 342

– Julius Caesar in 156, 158f.
– marvels of 342, 347f., 351ff.
– monstrosity of 351ff.
– Othering of (*see also* "Otherness") 15f., 341ff., 347ff., 360f.
– religion of 355–59
– Vespasian's accession in (*see* "Vespasian")
Egyptians 26, 346ff., 355, 357ff.
ekpyrosis 365, 369, 370 n.29, 373, 378 n.57
Eleazar 334ff.
elites 214, 243, 248, 296, 336
Empedocles 371 n.33, 378 n.58
Enceladus (a giant) 45
encomium 20, 33, 75 n.13, 76, 83, 228, 292
Ennius 30 n.11, 296
epic heroism 28ff., 32 n.17, 35ff., 70ff., 75 n.14, 89, 102, 194, 196f., 248f., 290, 312, 314, 322, 338
epic language 89f., 95ff., 99, 101f., 106f., 194
epic tradition 125 n.12, 126, 181, 189, 192, 308
Erginus (second helmsman of Argo) 84
Erictho (*see also* "witches") 18, 46ff., 381ff.
Eriphyle 116, 120
Eteocles (*see also* "fratricide," "Polynices," "Thebes") 13, 43, 46f., 69 n.3, 92ff., 96, 101, 104, 124, 126f., 129, 131 n.44, 132ff., 136f., 139f., 142, 190, 193, 253 n.2, 258, 260, 266, 272 n.7, 278, 283, 288 n.62, 314f., 317, 322f., 328 n.23, 338
ethnicity (*see also* "Egypt, Othering of," "Otherness") 16f., 53, 327 n.21, 337, 343, 349, 351, 356, 360f.
ethnography 40, 342, 348, 351, 354 n.45, 359
Eudoxus of Cyzicus 354
Eumolpus (poet in Petronius's *Satyrica*) 2, 277
Euripides (*see also* index of passages) 124 n.9, 134 n.57, 135 n.60, 140, 188 n.30, 234 n.30, 241 n.50

Euryale (an Amazon) 309f.
Euryalus (character in Vergil's *Aeneid*) 95, 235, 310
Eurymedon (character in Silius Italicus; brother of Lycormas) 257, 329f.
exemplarity 11, Part III (145ff. *passim*), 261, 267f.
extremization 47

Fabius Maximus Cunctator, Q. 32, 65 n.32, 154, 265f., 277, 283f.
Fabius Pictor 255 n.5
Fama 19, 32 n.18, 91, 136, 314f.
familial strife 8f., 11, 13f., 18, 70 n.7, 85 n.42, 89, 93, 96, 104, 106, 114, 115, 121, 138 n.79, 186, 189, 230, 257ff., 263, 266, 278, 303–6, 308ff., 312, 315, 318f., 328, 367 n.17, 383
family (*see also* "brotherhood," "parricide," "sisterhood") 11, 20ff., 60, 71, 79, 95, 102, 104f., 120, 124, 127, 174 n.76, 175 n.78, 184, 188 n.30, 189, 197, 242, 248, Part IV (251ff. *passim*), 255, 261, 264, 267, 316, 320, 329, 388 n.10, 389
famine 182f., 186, 188 n.26, 195, 352
Fasti Triumphales 153
fertility
– of Egypt 345, 351f.
– of rivers 345, 352
– of Rome for civil war 277
– of women 101 n.31, 299ff.
fides 9, 11, 28, 52 n.6, 60f., 70, 179, 181, 183, 190, 194, 197, 337 n.46
– as personification (*see also* "personifications") 18f., 61, 180, 183ff., 196, 267 n.40, 286f., 314, 324 n.12, 325f., 329, 334, 336
Figulus, P. Nigidius (Roman intellectual) 76, 357 n.58
Flavian dynasty (*see also* "Domitian," "Titus," "Vespasian") 15, 20, 29, 71 n.8, 80 n.28, 148 n.12, 170, 207f., 210, 236, 254, 267ff., 387ff.
– rise to power of (*see also* "Vespasian, accession of") 1, 29, 148 n.12, 218ff., 236

Flavian Forum (*see* "*pax*, Templum Pacis")
Flavian literature, definitions of 4ff., 16, 151ff., 343
Flavian Rome (ed. Boyle/Dominik, 2003) 7 n.16, 151
Flavius Josephus (*see* "Josephus")
foreshadowing 27, 42, 77, 82 n.34, 116 n.25, 304
Fortuna Redux (*see* "coinage," "personifications")
fortune/misfortune
– as personification (*see also* "coinage," "personifications") 277, 359, 370 n.29
– reversals of 203, 222
Forum Augustum 153 n.31
Forum Romanum 153, 215
fratricide 9, 25, 83, 91, 196, 255 n.6, 256, 279, 295, 297, 299, 305, 308
– duel of Eteocles and Polynices 13, 43, 90, 92, 94 n.14, 96, 97, 99, 101ff., 141, 181, 190ff., 195, 317, 328 n.23
Frontinus (*see also* index of passages) 145–77 *passim*, 206 n.18
– military career of 151 n.24, 152
– political career of 151 n.24
– *Strategemata*
– – didactic goals of 145, 152, 157
– – readership and reception of 146f., 155, 170, 175f.
– – sources of 154, 167
– – structure of 150, 153, 161f.
Furies (*see also* "Allecto," "Megaera," "Tisiphone") 92, 98, 100, 120, 124, 125 n.12, 136f., 138f., 140f., 183, 185, 191, 193, 230f., 304, 332
– as catalysts of civil war 18, 124, 196, 314ff., 329
furor 9, 20, 43f., 91f., 100, 183, 188, 190, 221, 231 n.21, 246, 249, 257, 306, 312 n.42, 330, 374f., 403
– as personification (*see also* "personifications") 374 n.41, 375

Gaia 45
Galba, Servius Sulpicius 69, 197, 202, 209ff., 214f., 220f., 236, 292f., 302
Galilee 204f., 207, 209 n.26, 217, 224

games 262, 288 n.62, 354, 392, 394 n.46, 397 n.56, 401ff.
Ganymede, abduction of 244
Gates of Underworld (*see also* "Tartarus," "Underworld") 370
Gates of War 371
Gaul 174, 266, 346f.
Gauls 157, 168f.
gender (*see also* "Furies," "women") 11, 17ff., 25 n.1, 295–320 *passim*
– gendering of war 18, 104, 107, 295ff.
generalship, models of 147, 152, 165, 170, 172 n.70, 175 n.76, 203
genre (*see also* "epic language," "tragedy") 5f., 9, 10, 27, 29, 49, 75, 89f., 96, 103, 107, 125, 133f., 154, 181, 188, 191, 194, 296, 306, 313
– generic tensions 89f., 125, 134, 137 n.72, 141 n.96
geography 342f., 370
Germany 152, 157, 215f.
Gerson, Jean (tutor to the Dauphin of France) 176
Gesander 310, 385 n.94
Gigantomachy (*see also* "Enceladus") 27, 81, 366, 372 n.34
Glauce (*see* "Creusa")
gods
– agricultural deities 45, 355ff.
– divine quarrels 26, 141 n.92, 281 n.39, 308, 372
– Egyptian (*see* "Egypt, gods of")
– neglect of 122, 243, 367
– Olympians (*see individual entries*)
Golden Age (*see also* "Iron Age") 363, 366, 368, 385 n.94
Golden Fleece 28, 39, 41f., 70f., 75ff., 83f., 111ff., 303f., 307f., 311, 313, 384
Gorgons/Medusa 111, 310f., 315
Gracchi brothers 8, 25 n.1, 254, 256 n.9
grain supply 341, 344ff.

Hades (*see* "Pluto/Hades")
Haemonius 305f., 310, 379f., 382 n.75
Hammon 57f., 59 n.19, 356 n.51
Hannibal 17, 19, 31ff., 65, 154, 157, 163f., 167, 169, 172, 179, 181ff., 187f., 195f., 254, 256, 264ff., 267, 270, 273f., 277f., 280 n.37, 281, 284, 288, 293, 299f., 313, 323f., 326
Harmonia, necklace of 13, 15, 18, 109–22 *passim*, 315
Hasdrubal (brother of Hannibal) 17, 157, 168, 254, 264ff., 284 n.53
Haterii relief 396 n.53
Heinsius, Daniel 98, 368, 374, 378 n.59
Helen 70, 82, 110, 351
Helios (*see* "Sol/Helios")
Henry VIII 176
Hephaestus (*see* "Vulcan/Hephaestus")
Hera (*see* "Juno/Hera")
Hercules 81, 196
– cult titles and local cults of 354f.
– madness of 141, 192
– murderer of his family 192
– patron god of Saguntum 186, 188, 191, 326, 327 n.21
Herod (king of Judaea) 201, 212f.
Herodotus (*see also* index of passages) 38 n.33, 82 n.33, 208, 348, 360, 383
Hesiod 366 n.14, 367 n.16, 371
Hesperides 111, 315
Himilco (Carthaginian commander in Silius Italicus) 54ff., 156
Hippocrates (*medicus*) 352f.
Hirtius, Aulus 161 n.47, 396 n.53
historians, Flavian 4 n.12, 199–225 *passim*
Homer (*see also* index of passages) 47f., 75 n.14, 95f., 119, 290, 372 n.34, 372f.
– *Iliad* 70, 117ff., 372
– *Odyssey* 79 n.25, 115 n.22
Horace (*see also* index of passages) 9, 17, 25, 230 n.13, 234ff., 239, 297ff., 319, 330, 374
Hypsipyle (queen of Lemnos) 14, 121, 122 n.41, 227–49 *passim*, 304, 315f., 380 n.68
– as nurse of Opheltes 316
– cloak of 229, 244–49

Iapha 210 n.26
Iazyges (Eastern people in Valerius Flaccus) 309, 385 n.94

ibis 347, 353–58
Idmon 42, 75ff., 81
Imperator 21, 147, 150 n.21, 155, 157, 171, 174, 209, 215
imperialism 3, 12, 15f., 40, 43, 80, 209, 385 n.94
imperium 1, 12, 156f., 209, 215, 275f., 286, 388 n.10, 391
– *imperium sine fine* 15, 80, 239 n.47, 385
imports, Italian (*see* "trade")
incest 101ff., 124, 131, 138, 142, 299, 303, 314
India 346, 347, 360
ingens 36 n.27, 64, 101f., 104ff., 141, 192, 242 n.54, 310, 326
Ino 136
instability (*see also* "collapse," "cosmos," "ruins")
– architectural 360 n.69, 387–409 *passim*
– cosmic 15, 364, 368ff., 373, 377–79, 383
– dynastic 253ff., 267ff.
– imperial 4, 170f., 221
intertextuality 2f., 9f., 12f., 17, 47, 52, 58, 74 n.11, 76, 78, 93f., 114, 120, 124, 125 n.12, 127 n.21, 130f., 134 n.57, 135 n.60, 136 n.64, 150 n.19, 154, 167, 181, 184, 190f., 237f., 240, 241 n.49, 272, 278, 281, 282 n.43, 284, 288 n.62, 328 n.23, 337, 364, 369f., 383, 405
– antiphrastic 12, 44
– bidirectional 13, 191, 195
– competing models 234f., 240
– historical 227ff.
– incomplete models 129, 140
– stylistic 90, 95ff.
Iotapata (*see* "Jotapata")
Iris (goddess of the rainbow) 134, 189, 305f.
Iron Age (*see also* "Golden Age") 293, 363, 366f.
Isis 242, 345
Ismene (sister of Antigone) 317
Italians 164, 169, 301f., 310, 327, 351

Italy 16, 63f., 102, 136, 162 n.50, 169 n.65, 181, 186, 211, 215, 217, 234, 265, 277, 301, 342–47, 349, 351ff., 356, 357, 360, 388 n.11

Jal, Paul 1f., 3, 5, 9 n.26, 231 n.21, 374 nn.41–42, 403 n.83
Janus 371
Jason 19 n.39, 20, 28, 35ff., 69f., 71 n.9, 73, 75 n.14, 82ff., 113–18, 121, 229, 244ff., 248f., 303ff., 309, 311ff., 380 n.68, 383
Jerusalem 199, 201ff., 205, 207, 209 n.26, 210ff., 334
Jesus (chief priest of Jerusalem) 202
Jewish Wars (*see also* "war") 146 n.4, 199–225 *passim*, 332ff.
Jocasta 92f., 96 n.18, 102 n.34, 103ff., 120, 123 n.1, 126, 129ff., 137ff., 142 n.98, 316f.
John of Gischala 18, 217, 334 n.39
John of Salisbury 176 n.80
Josephus (*see also* index of passages)
– *Against Apion* 202
– *Bellum Judaicum* 11, 146, 148, 158, 201ff., 321ff., 332ff.
– Josephus Problem 200ff., 333
– *Judaean Antiquities* 202
Jotapata 205ff., 210, 224, 323, 332ff.
Judaea 81, 83, 200, 207f., 209 n.26, 210, 212, 214ff., 218f., 221, 337
Judaean War (*see* "Josephus, *Bellum Judaicum*")
Julia (daughter of Julius Caesar) 70
Julio-Claudian dynasty 30, 69, 80 n.28, 82, 84, 254, 255f., 267ff., 302, 319ff., 341, 389, 390 n.22, 391
Juno/Hera 19, 35 n.26, 41f., 45, 72 n.9, 117f., 130, 136f., 140f., 186, 188, 196, 247 n.68, 265, 289, 298f., 308, 313f., 326, 371f., 372, 383
Jupiter/Zeus 14f., 19, 27, 32, 35, 38, 40, 42f., 45, 69f., 77ff., 98 n.23, 107, 117, 134f., 140, 186ff., 230 n.15, 236, 239 n.47, 244, 263, 264 n.32, 268, 281, 290f., 298 n.7, 308, 331, 353ff., 356, 363, 364, 367ff., 372f., 378, 382ff., 398

– cult titles and local cults of 242, 244 n.59, 353–56
– Jupiter Optimus Maximus, temple of (see "Capitoline")
– prophecy of (see also "prophecy") 42, 70, 77–84, 236, 268
– shrines and temples dedicated by Flavians (see also "shrines") 238f., 242, 244 n.59
– supplication of (by Venus) 181f.
Juvenal (see also index of passages) 358

Kalyvas, Stathis 7f.
Kant, Immanuel 392f.
Khepri (see "Egypt, gods of"; see also "scarab," "sun")
kingship 70, 83 n.38, 95, 132, 212, 273, 286

Laelius, C. (Roman commander during Second Punic War) 156, 262
λαγνεία 216
Lake Trasimene, Battle of 51, 264
lament 9, 14, 33f., 46ff., 102 n.35, 203, 282, 319, 391
landscape 14, 47, 125 n.13, 322, 398
Laomedon 81 n.29
Larides and Thymber (characters in Vergil's *Aeneid*) 257 n.13, 258 n.14
Latins 25, 48, 128, 136, 301, 371
Latinus 101, 128, 192
Latium 26, 32, 128, 184, 192, 301
leadership 11, 36ff., 64 n.30, Part III (143ff. *passim*), 281, 283, 290, 343 n.11
legions, Roman 16, 172f., 203, 205, 207, 209, 211, 214f., 218f., 222f., 311, 341, 343
Lemnian women 122, 186, 189, 245, 272 n.7, 305, 315f., 346
Lemnos 13, 19, 82, 120ff., 227–49 *passim*, 272 n.7, 303f., 316, 372
lex de imperio Vespasiani (see "Vespasian, accession of")
Libya 34 n.20, 55, 63, 346, 404
lions 99 n.27, 298, 312, 336, 402, 403, 404, 405 n.91, 406

Livy (see also index of passages) 51 n.3, 148, 154, 157, 166f., 170, 176, 179, 181, 254, 256 n.8, 262, 263 n.31, 264f., 325ff.
locusts (see "pests, agricultural")
Lucan (see also index of passages) 3f., 10, 12f., 15, 18, Part I (23ff. *passim*), 90, 93, 95f., 126, 134 n.57, 138, 149, 160 n.46, 173, 180, 183, 195, 196, 231 nn.16–17, 237ff., 258, 271, 272f., 276, 364ff., 375, 379, 381 n.73, 404f.
– *Bellum Ciuile*
– – as paradigmatic for civil war literature 3, 10, 12, 18, 27, 42f., 48f., 95ff., 149, 375
– – ending of 71f. n.9
– suicide of 185
lunar spume 111, 117, 118 n.30
Lycormas (character in Silius Italicus; brother of Eurymedon) 257, 329f.
Lydia 145, 346

Macedonia 63, 168ff.
Maeon (character in Statius's *Thebaid*; see also "suicide") 322f., 338
Mago (brother of Hannibal) 17, 254, 264ff., 284
Mancinus (character in Silius Italicus) 31 n.15, 258, 284
manliness 18, 216f., 300, 312 n.42, 316, 335
Marcellus, M. Claudius (Roman general during Second Punic War) 31 n.12, 32, 51ff., 61, 62 nn.23–24, 63ff., 275 n.17, 281, 293
Marius, C. 33, 275f.
marriage (see "wedding")
Mars/Ares 63f., 102, 105, 111, 115ff., 119, 121, 140 n.92, 231, 263, 265, 281, 290, 304, 306ff., 315
Martial (see also index of passages) 12, 15, 151, 238 n.41, 387ff., 391f., 394, 397, 401, 404f., 407f.
Masada 214, 323, 332, 333ff.
Massilia 52f., 57, 58 n.19, 59f., 62ff., 66f., 163, 183 n.11, 196, 279f., 324 n.12

Massilians 17, 53ff., 56, 58 n.19, 59ff., 182f., 188f.
matrona (character in Lucan; *see also* "prophecy") 30 n.12, 76, 241 n.51
Mausoleum
– of Augustus 406 n.99
– of Halicarnassus 406 n.99
Medea 18, 19 n.39, 28, 35, 41f., 71, 73, 75 n.14, 76, 77 n.21, 82, 84, 103, 110, 112–22, 132, 141, 184, 246 n.64, 248, 304–8, 311ff., 351, 363, 366 n.14, 379–85
Megaera (a Fury; *see also* "Allecto," "Furies," "Tisiphone") 141 n.92, 191, 289
memory 1, 3f., 12, 94 n.14, 95, 133, 145, 146 n.4, 149, 153, 184, 233 n.26, 261, 293, 305, 311, 320 n.54, 390, 405 n.92
Mercury/Hermes 81
messengers 129, 134f., 232, 263
Metellus Pius, Q. Caecilius (cos. 80 BCE) 158, 161 n.49, 168
meteorology 381 n.74
Milky Way 370 n.28
Minerva/Athena 41, 42 n.38, 71f. n.9, 84 n.39, 113f., 308, 310
Minucius Rufus, M. (commander during Second Punic War) 283f.
Minyae (*see* "Argonauts")
Mithridates 159, 277, 351
moles 275, 395ff., 406 n.98, 407
monstrosity (*see* "Egypt, monstrosity of"; *see also* "gender")
monuments 15, 203, 225, 234 n.32, 342f., 387–409 *passim*
– monumentality 394, 406
– – Egyptian 342, 360
– – poetic 15, 343, 387f., 391f., 396, 408
– *monumentum*, derivation of 406 n.95
Mopsus 75, 76 n.17, 77, 82, 113f., 385 n.92
moralist tradition, Roman 2, 29, 33, 63, 164, 179f., 277, 303ff., 325
Morysine, Richard 176
motherhood 11, 45, 104ff., 131ff., 139 n.79, 299ff., 317
Mt. Carmel 219 n.37
Mt. Etna 45, 121, 246, 377
Mt. Vesuvius 337

Mucianus 219, 223
Murrus (character in Silius Italicus) 182, 189, 326
Mutina, siege of 1, 161 n.47, 163
Mycenae 78, 83 n.38, 128

Nature (personification; *see also* "personifications") 363, 366, 368
nefas 87ff., 90, 94, 95ff., 103 n.37, 104, 106, 109f., 112, 114ff., 120f., 123ff., 130f., 134 n.57, 138, 142 n.96, 192, 231, 316f., 328, 358, 370, 375, 384 n.87
Neikos (*see* "Discordia," "Empedocles")
Neptune/Poseidon 38, 76, 367 n.20
Nero (*see also* "building program, Neronian," "*Domus aurea*") 15, 25, 27 n.5, 42 n.39, 81, 84, 149 n.17, 180, 185, 197, 202, 204–7, 210, 212ff., 220, 256 n.9, 268 n.44, 269 n.49, 282, 283 n.46, 293, 302, 343, 351 n.37, 365 n.11, 388–92, 395, 397–401, 405
Nerva 4, 151 n.24, 199
New Carthage 262, 273
Nicanor (Roman military tribune) 205, 334
Nile 73, 341, 342 n.6, 344, 346, 349, 352, 359f.
Nisus (character in Vergil's *Aeneid*) 95, 235
numina (*see* "gods," "personifications")

obelisks 342
Octavian (*see also* "Augustus") 26, 48, 163, 208f., 212, 255 n.6, 297, 301, 341
Oedipus 8, 97ff., 101f., 104f., 123, 124 n.6, 129f., 132, 134, 137f., 141f., 258 n.14, 314, 316
Olympia (*see also* "games") 354
Olympus 74, 93, 134f., 191, 308, 372
onions 358
Opitergians (*see* "Vulteius," "suicide, mass")
optimism (*see also* "ambiguity," "pessimism") 75 n.14, 128 n.34, 131, 148 n.12, 396
Orpheus 401
Ostia (*see also* "grain supply," "trade") 346, 352

Otherness 15ff., 342f., 356, 359f.
Otho, M. Salvius 1, 202, 209ff., 220f., 293, 389 n.14
Ovid (*see also* index of passages) 9, 29 n.9, 91, 105, 125 n.14, 186, 189, 241 n.50, 255 n.6, 269 n.47, 282 n.43, 285, 363, 369
– *Metamorphoses* 27, 90, 368 n.22

Palatine 234ff., 359
palingenesis 365, 369
Pallas (epithet of Athena; see "Minerva/Athena")
Pallas (son of Evander) 188, 257 n.13, 290
Pan 183f., 187
paradox 9, 33, 48, 89, 95f., 99, 100, 106, 130, 133, 274, 304, 313, 321, 337, 338, 364 n.7, 368, 369 n.27, 378, 385 n.94, 387, 390, 394, 403 n.82, 407
parricide (*see also* "familial strife") 271ff., 278ff., 284ff., 293, 297, 309, 314, 329
Parthia
– Roman conflicts with 156, 159, 201
Parthians 298, 385 n.94
Paulus, L. Aemilius (cos. 216 BCE) 31ff., 281, 283
pax 69, 146 n.4, 320
– as personification (*see also* "personifications") 267
– *Templum Pacis* 207
pegmata 395f.
Pelias (uncle of Jason) 28, 35ff., 69ff., 77 n.21, 83, 185, 247 n.68, 380 n.68, 304, 383
Peloponnese 352
Penates 131, 182
Perperna Vento, M. (Roman general during Sertorian uprising) 166
Perses (character in Valerius Flaccus; brother of Aeetes) 28, 35, 41, 70, 112, 305, 308f.
personifications (*see also individual entries*) 11, 102, 120, 171 n.67, 180, 183, 185ff., 190f., 326, 355, 359
persuasion (*see also* "deception") 39f., 93, 140, 223, 332ff.
Perusia, siege of 1f.

perversion 13, 89, 95ff., 99ff., 106f., 125 n.13, 199, 254, 259, 263, 319, 329, 364 n.7, 365, 382
pessimism (*see also* "ambiguity," "optimism") 40f., 75 n.14, 138 n.79, 148 n.12, 270
pests, agricultural 353f., 356
Petronius (*see also* index of passages) 180, 185, 188, 195, 277
Peuce 71, 73, 77 n.21, 82ff.
Phaethon 282 n.43
Pharos 73, 76, 342 n.7
Pharsalia (see "Lucan, *Bellum Ciuile*"; see also "Pharsalus, Battle of")
Pharsalus, Battle of 1, 3, 30ff., 34, 43f., 46, 63f., 67, 169, 172ff., 232, 240
Philippi, Battle of 1, 3, 32, 106, 301
Phineus 84 n.40, 306, 373f., 376
Phrixus 69, 79, 111f., 306ff., 379f.
Phrygians 312
pietas 9, 11, 28, 38, 44, 46, 118f., 138, 187, 189, 227 n.3, 240, 248, 259, 260 n.20, 262ff., 268, 270, 319
– as personification (*see also* "personifications") 97, 187, 190f., 267 n.40, 286
Piso, L. Calpurnius (adopted son of Galba) 197
Pizan, Christine de 176 n.80
Plath, Sylvia 321ff., 338
Pliny the Elder (*see also* index of passages) 4 n.12, 12, 15f., 49 n.50, 151, 153 n.30, 158 n.41, 195, 337f., 341–61 *passim*, 398
Pliny the Younger (*see also* index of passages) 337, 387 n.3
Pluto/Hades (*see also* "Underworld") 79 n.25, 99, 314, 370 n.29, 372
Pollux (*see also* "Castor," "Dioscuri") 76, 243 n.55, 268, 283
Polybius (*see also* index of passages) 32, 154, 222, 324
Polynices (*see also* "Eteocles," "fratricide," "Thebes") 13, 19, 43ff., 69 n.3, 91f., 93ff., 98f., 101, 104, 113ff., 124, 126f., 129f., 131ff., 137–42, 190, 193, 253f., 258, 260, 266, 272 n.7, 278, 283, 288 n.62, 314f., 317f., 328 n.23

Polyxo (character in Statius's *Thebaid*; see also "Lemnian women") 19, 316
Pompeius Magnus, Cn. (Pompey the Great) 1, 31, 43f., 65f., 70f., 85, 92f., 106, 150, 156ff., 159, 161 nn.47–48, 162, 166, 168f., 172ff., 209 n.26, 210, 212f., 256 n.8, 266, 275ff., 375 n.43, 402, 404f.
Pomponia (mother of Scipio Africanus) 264 n.32, 291f.
Poseidon (*see* "Neptune/Poseidon")
Praetorian Guard 212, 222
Princeps (*see also* "Principate") 20, 25, 69, 212, 255 n.6, 262 n.27, 268, 302, 405
princeps iuuentutis 267, 268 nn.42 and 45
Principate 1, 127, 149, 157, 239, 247 n.67, 253, 255, 268 n.44, 271 n.2, 273 n.10, 293, 297, 302, 388, 390 n.23, 391
Procne 241 n.50, 316
propaganda (*see also* "building program," "coinage")
– Augustan 26, 297ff., 301
– Flavian 200ff., 239, 390, 397
– imperial 40, 300 n.9
prophecy 10, 27, 30 n.12, 38, 49, 69, 75–84, 107, 126, 236, 241 n.51, 275, 292, 296, 341 n.2, 373, 385
Punic Wars 156, 197, 254, 261, 301
– First Punic War 162, 168, 173
– Second Punic War 19, 28f., 30 n.11, 33, 49, 51–67 *passim*, 156, 163, 172, 179–97 *passim*, 253–70 *passim*, 272–93 *passim*, 325ff., 337
– Third Punic War 64 n.30
pyramids (*see also* "architecture, Egyptian," "monuments") 342, 393, 399, 408 n.105
Pyrrhus of Epirus 154, 172, 300

Quintilian 71 n.9, 151
Quirinus 268f.

readers 7, 15, 21, 27f., 31, 34, 36, 42, 49, 109, 117, 122, 127, 140, 146, 148ff., 152ff., 160f., 163ff., 167, 169ff., 172, 174–77, 185, 202f., 227ff., 233f., 236, 240, 242f., 245–49, 253, 320, 349
rebellion 91, 157, 162, 164, 166f., 170, 175, 316
recovery 27, 32, 70, 160, 171, 196, 209
recuperation 6, 343
Remus 4, 48, 85, 165 n.58, 254ff., 258, 282, 295ff.
repression 27
Republic, Roman 1–5, 11, 14, 16, 25, 27, 40, 43, 49, 126, 146, 158f., 162 n.51, 185, 197, 199, 208, 212, 220, 222f., 234, 238ff., 249, 253, 255, 267, 272, 274, 276, 278, 282, 298
Romanitas 327 n.21
Romanocentrism (*see also* "*urbs/orbis*") 344
Rome, city of 14f., 181, 204, 209, 211, 213, 216ff., 238f., 245, 254, 288, 344, 365 n.11, 387–92, 395, 398, 400f., 405f.
Romulus 4, 25, 48, 91, 165, 254ff., 258, 268f., 282, 295ff., 298
Rubicon 91, 404
ruins (*see also* "collapse," "instability") 234, 237f., 240, 245, 388 n.11, 390, 406
rus in urbem 390 n.20, 398

Sabinus, T. Flavius (brother of Vespasian) 222, 239
Sabratha (character in Silius Italicus) 57f.
Saguntum 17ff., 31 n.12, 51f., 61, 179–98, 256, 256 n.15, 270, 273–80, 285, 287f., 292f., 295, 313f., 323ff., 326ff., 329, 331 n.33, 332, 334–38
Sallust (*see also* index of passages) 25 n.1, 64 n.30, 148, 168 n.64, 176
Sanudo Torsello, Marino 176 n.80
satelles (character in Seneca's *Phoenissae*; *see also* "messengers") 129f.
Satricus (character in Silius Italicus) 31 n.15, 258f., 278, 284f.
Scaeva, M. Cassius (Roman centurion) 72, 85
scarab 356ff.
scepter 70, 94, 97, 273, 286–93

Scipios 17, 168, 179, 254, 260, 261ff., 281, 283 n.49, 291
– Scipio Aemilianus, P. Cornelius (grandson of Scipio Africanus) 261 n.24
– Scipio Africanus, P. Cornelius 20, 65 n.30, 28, 154, 168f., 172, 180, 196, 254, 261ff., 267, 269f., 276f., 280 n.37, 283, 288 n.62, 290–93
– – paternity of 264 n.32, 292
– Scipio Asiaticus, L. Cornelius (brother of Scipio Africanus) 254, 261ff., 270, 283
– Scipio Calvus, Cn. Cornelius (uncle of Scipio Africanus) 254, 256, 284, 288 n.62
– Scipio, P. Cornelius (father of Scipio Africanus) 254, 256, 264 n.32, 284, 288 n.62
Sciron (character in Silius Italicus) 57
seafaring, advent of (*see also* "Golden Age," "Iron Age") 304, 363, 366f., 385 n.95
seleucids 353ff.
self-destruction 61 n.22, 105, 107, 132, 134, 142 n.98, 165 n.58, 173, 321ff., 328, 330 n.30, 331f., 336ff., 385, 402, 404
self-sacrifice (*see* "suicide")
Senate, Carthaginian 277
Senate, Roman 32, 181, 197, 207, 210ff., 217f., 222, 290f., 302
Senate, Saguntine 325
Seneca the Younger (*see also* index of passages) 9, 13, 19, 37 n.32, 90, 93, 98, 123–42 *passim*, 188 n.30, 282, 364f., 366
– suicide of 185
serpents 111, 120 n.37, 136, 141, 184, 289, 291f., 311, 314, 326f., 353, 355
Sertorius, Q. (procos. of Spain) 157f., 161, 162, 165f., 168
Seven against Thebes 272, 315
shrines 25, 113, 236, 238ff., 244 n.59, 359
Sibyl (*see also* "prophecy") 275f., 289, 292, 355
Sicarii (occupants of Masada) 334, 336
Sicily 33, 51, 63, 67, 156, 327, 346, 348

Silius Italicus (*see also* index of passages) 14, 16f., 27, 29, 30–34, 49, 52ff, 56, 60, 66 n.33, 78, 146, 180, 253–71, 272–94, 303, 323–32
– political career of 196
simile 45, 95, 99 n.27, 115, 281, 311f., 316, 331, 371 n.30, 385 n.92, 402, 403 n.81, 404
Simon bar Giora 214f., 334 n.39
sisterhood 318f.
slaves 166, 210, 223, 302, 304, 324f., 337f., 405 n.91
Social War 161 n.47, 162
Sol/Helios 79, 116 n.25, 119, 121, 230 n.15, 383, 398
– Temple of the Sun (in Valerius Flaccus) 42, 116, 385 n.92
Solimus (character in Silius Italicus) 31 n.15, 258f., 284f.
Somnus (*see also* "personifications") 265
Sophocles 44, 104
sorcery (*see* "witches")
Sown Men (Colchian) 303, 305, 312f.
Sown Men (Theban) 102, 314
Spain 158, 161 n.49, 168f., 180, 292, 346
Spartacus 154, 162 n.50, 163, 166
Spartoi (*see* "Sown Men")
stasis 148, 202, 214f., 229, 330 n.30
Statius (*see also* index of passages)
– *Achilleid* 89f.
– *Siluae* 89, 152, 195, 238
– *Thebaid* 89f., 95, 98ff., 101f., 104, 106f., 123–44, 190ff., 236, 245 n.61, 272, 278f., 283, 289, 293, 314ff., 318, 327 n.21, 328 n.23, 338
– – Argonautic aspects of 109–22
– – style of 89ff.
Stoicism 358, 364ff., 365 n.8
Sublime, the (*see also* "architecture, sublimity of") 382, 387–410
Suetonius (*see also* index of passages) 151, 211, 218, 236, 242, 268 n.45, 283, 302, 338, 388, 397
suicide 28f., 32ff., 43, 58, 180, 192, 209, 214, 234, 247 n.68, 257f., 263, 279, 284f., 302, 321f., 323ff., 331f., 337f.
– *ambitiosa mors* 322

- as madness 141, 183, 192, 329ff., 336
- as metaphor for civil war 9, 11, 58 n.19, 141, 180 n.5, 195, 258 n.16, 278, 279 n.32, 287, 313f., 321–38, 404
- mass suicide 11, 17ff., 27, 51f., 179–97 *passim*, 224, 274, 278ff., 313, 321–38 *passim*

Sulla Felix, L. Cornelius 33, 126, 148, 162, 168, 275f., 402

sun (*see also* "Sol/Helios") 100, 103, 212, 296, 300, 356f., 379

sword 58, 93, 223, 229, 244, 246f., 257f., 272–94, 309, 312f., 316, 328f., 330ff., 383, 402

Syracuse 51ff., 60ff., 275f.

Syria 209, 218, 346ff.

Tacitus (*see also* index of passages) 1ff., 91, 127, 146, 148, 149 n.16, 151, 159, 170, 171, 175, 199f., 211, 217, 219 n.37, 220f., 223, 225, 231, 234, 243 n.58, 268 n.45, 269 n.49, 273, 279, 285, 288, 302, 388 n.12
- *Agricola* 171, 243 n.58

Tantalus 136ff.

Tartarus 99, 193, 331

technical writing (*see also* "didacticism," "Frontinus," "Pliny the Elder") 152, 154f.

teleology 15, 154f., 170, 210, 365 n.11

Telo (character in Lucan) 56ff.

Templum Pacis (*see* "pax")

terrigenae (*see* "Sown Men")

text as world 89f., 150, 155

textual tradition 73f. n.11, 98f., 126 n.15, 131–33, 369, 370 n.28, 378 n.59, 379 n.65, 380

Thebes 19, 102, 105, 107, 112, 120, 129, 131ff., 314ff., 323

Theophrastus (*see also* index of passages) 345, 348

theriomorphism 353, 355f., 359

Theseus 28, 44, 194

Thessaly 19, 35, 38, 47, 69ff., 304, 380, 383 n.79

Thoas (father of Hypsipyle) 13, 228, 240, 242, 244ff.

Thrace 304, 316

Thucydides 206, 208

Thyestes 103, 123–42, 284

Tiber 238, 242

Tiberias (Judaean town) 205f.

Tiberius (emperor of Rome) 149, 177, 256 n.9, 267, 293, 390 n.23

Tiburna (character in Silius) 18, 189, 313f., 326, 329, 331f.

Ticinus, Battle of the 51, 259, 288 n.62, 290

tigers 140f., 402, 404

Tisiphone (a Fury; *see also* "Allecto," "Furies," "Megaera") 18f., 97, 99, 111, 117, 123, 136ff., 183, 186ff., 195f., 231, 280, 311, 313ff., 326ff., 331, 334, 336

Titus 75 n.14, 83 n.36, 127, 146 n.4, 171 n.67, 199ff., 203, 205ff., 210f., 214f., 217, 220f., 255, 267–70, 283, 293, 389, 395

topoi (*see also* "civil war, *topoi* of") 3, 9, 100, 149, 150, 155, 165 n.56, 167, 168 n.64, 172, 230f., 239 n.47, 248, 271f., 276, 341, 343, 360, 371, 381, 385 n.92, 408 n.105

trade (*see also* "grain supply") 344ff.

tragedy (*see also* "genre") 28, 43ff., 71 n.9, 82 n.34, 90ff., 102ff., 116, 123–42 *passim*, 203, 232, 382

Trajan 4, 151 n.24, 199, 293

transgression 106, 363f., 390, 398

trauma 4, 8, 14f., 19, 27, 30, 148, 149, 160, 177, 227, 231ff., 240, 248, 343, 391

Trebia, Battle of the 33, 51, 290

triumph 153, 158, 167f., 180, 203, 207, 209f., 213, 225, 268f., 277, 290, 305f., 341, 350, 390 n.22, 400 n.73

Trojan War 25f., 79ff., 134

Trojans 25f., 48, 81, 91, 102, 128, 134, 137, 188, 193, 299, 301f., 310, 327, 371

Troy
- as mirror of Rome 80, 241 n.49, 274, 388 n.12
- fall of 25f., 33, 241 n.49, 388 n.12
- sacking of 32 n.17, 47 n.47, 188, 232 n.22, 301

Turnus 72 n.9, 101, 130, 136, 182, 187, 192, 290
Tydeus 140, 253, 314, 322f.
Tymbrenus 328f.
tyrants 28, 30, 36 n.27, 30, 37f., 40ff., 70, 81 n.29, 84, 175 n.78, 202f., 208, 213ff., 289, 292, 307ff., 322, 338, 389, 390f., 397f., 400f., 405, 408

uenationes (*see* "games")
uirtus (*see also* "virtues") 72f., 190, 237, 243, 286, 292, 326
– as personification (*see also* "personifications") 185, 190, 292 n.71
Underworld (*see also* "Pluto/Hades," "Tartarus") 110, 136, 185, 261, 322, 370f.
universalizing strategies 15f., 147, 158f., 176
urbs/orbis (*see also* "Romanocentrism") 12, 385 n.94

Valerius Flaccus (*see also* "Argonautic tradition," index of passages) 18, 27f., 34f., 49, 75 n.14, 146f., 160, 171 n.69, 185, 228, 230, 238, 243, 248f., 272, 303, 312, 363
– and Apollonius Rhodius 36, 84 n.40, 114 n.20, 116 n.25, 121f., 227, 233f.
– Statius's reception of (*see* "Statius")
Valerius Maximus (*see also* index of passages) 145f., 154, 157, 160, 167, 170f., 177, 179f., 195f., 261
Varro, C. Terentius (cos. 216 BCE) 31f., 34, 265, 280ff.
Varro, M. Terentius (Augustan intellectual) 25 n.1, 354 n.45
Velleius Paterculus (*see also* index of passages) 177, 279
Ventidius (*see also* "Parthia") 156, 158f., 166
Venus/Aphrodite 19, 32, 78f., 111, 115ff., 181, 184, 186, 189, 231, 241, 290, 308, 315f., 383
Vergil (*see also* index of passages) 9, 17, 25ff., 30, 33, 36, 44, 48f., 78ff., 80 n.28, 83 n.38, 89ff., 92f., 102, 125 n.14, 128ff., 136f., 141, 148, 181f., 186ff., 234ff., 238f., 272, 297ff., 301, 304, 308, 310, 313ff., 319, 327, 332, 364 n.7, 367 n.20, 370f., 375, 385, 388 n.12, 391
– *Georgics* 81, 282 n.43, 375 n.43
– Lucan's response to 12f., 27f., 49
Verginius Rufus, L. (cos. 63, 69, 97 CE) 209
Vespasian 20, 42 n.39, 71 n.8, 75f., 81, 83f., 146 n.4, 151 n.24, 199 n.1, 200, 203, 225, 227, 230 n.15, 233, 236, 242 n.54, 267, 268, 287, 302, 332ff., 343, 345f., 351, 359f., 395 n.49
– accession of (*see also* "Flavian dynasty, rise to power of") 15, 79 n.26, 202, 204, 207ff., 302, 341, 388f.
– acclamation of 218ff., 341
– and Judea 204ff., 332ff.
– as civil warrior 1, 20, 81, 84, 175, 199ff., 208ff., 213ff., 292f., 341
– representations of 20, 76, 83 n.36, 84, 170, 171 n.67, 200ff., 204ff., 220ff., 224f., 267, 292, 302
Veturia (mother of Coriolanus) 132, 138
Vindex, C. Julius (leader of revolt of 68 CE) 209
Virbius, Capys, and Albanus (brothers in Silius Italicus) 259, 288 n.62
Virgo (*see* "Astraea," "Dike")
virtues (*see also* "personifications," "*uirtus*") 30, 36, 43, 48, 248
– of an *imperator* 11, 65 n.30
Vitellians 91, 196, 215, 337, 345 n.18
Vitellius Germanicus, A. 1, 18, 20, 71, 175, 200, 202, 208–24, 293, 341, 345
Vulcan/Hephaestus 111f., 114ff., 119, 121f., 290, 315, 372f., 380 n.66
Vulteius (character in Lucan) 106, 186, 189f., 196, 324 n.12

war (*see also individual entries*)
– between Trojans and Latins 25f., 48, 137, 301, 371
– instigation of 18, 19, 186, 191, 193, 304, 305, 314, 316
– tactics of warfare 65 n.32, 151ff., 168, 311

weddings 110 n.13, 111, 117 n.26
– as catalyst for civil war 18, 115ff.
– of Jason and Medea 82, 84, 113ff., 121, 248
– of Polynices and Argia 91f., 113ff., 314
wild beasts (*see also* "lions," "tigers") 47, 188, 287, 298, 401–6
Winds 367 n.20, 368 n.21, 375 n.43, 379 n.65, 384
witches 46ff., 110ff., 356, 379ff.
women (*see also* "gender")
– as catalysts for civil strife 11, 301f., 304f., 313ff., 320
– Augustan discourse of "women out of control" 11, 189 n.32, 300, 302, 320
– fertility of 101 n.31, 299ff.
– imperial women 17, 302
– in opposition to men 301, 305ff., 315f.
– masculine qualities of 18, 315f.
– morality legislation 301ff.
– violence perpetrated by 47f., 120, 305, 315f.

Xanthippus, Eumachus, and Critias (brothers in Silius Italicus) 259f., 288 n.62

Year of the Four Emperors 3f., 6, 20, 25, 29, 69f., 75, 83, 84f., 146, 171, 208ff., 213ff, 227ff., 271ff., 285, 287f., 292, 295ff., 311, 343, 388

Zama, Battle of 51, 172, 280 n.37
Zeus (*see* "Jupiter/Zeus")

Index of Passages

Accius
– *trag.*
206–13 83 n.38

Aelian
– *NA*
17.19 354

Aelianus Tacticus
pr. 3 151 n.24

Aeschylus
– *Ch.*
631–38 234 n.30
– *Th.*
679–82 99 n.26
718 101 n.29
752–56 105 n.48

Aetna
171–74 377f.

Apollodorus
1.25 310 n.39

Apollonius Rhodius
1.609–26 234 n.30
1.609–39 227 n.1
1.614–15 122
2.421 84 n.40
3.531 380 n.67
3.531–33 380 n.68; 383 n.82
4.241–43 383 n.84
4.410–20 71 n.9
4.1165–67 114 n.20

Appian
– *BC*
1.1.1 256 n.9
1.2.4–5 256 n.9
1.7.58 148 n.8
4.3.14 208 n.21
– *Hisp.*
10–12 324 n.11

– *Mith.*
83.4 208 n.21

Apuleius
– *Met.*
1.3 381 n.72

Aristotle
– *Ath.*
5.2–3 208 n.21
13.1 208 n.21
– *HA*
6.37, 581a 347 n.25
7.4, 584b 352f.
– *Pol.*
1265d 208 n.21

Caesar
– *Ciu.*
1.72 161 n.48
3.88–89 173 n.71
3.98 173 n.73
3.99 173 n.73
3.101 161 n.48
3.107–12 158
– *Gal.*
1.35–44 277

Calpurnius Siculus
– *Ecl.*
1.46–50 105 n.46
7.23–72 397 n.56

Cato the Elder
– *hist.*
86–87 265 n.35

Catullus
64.11 34 n.22; 366 n.13
64.397 366 n.13
64.399 100 n.28
64.399–404 367 n.17

Cicero
– *Balb.*
34   254
– *Catil.*
1.7   279
3.10   278
– *Cons.*
fr. 10.41 (Courtney) 63 n.27
– *Leg.*
1.3   269 n.48
2.28   359 n.64
– *Mar.*
fr. 3.13 (Soubiran) 98 n.23
– *N.D.*
1.101   355
3.63   359 n.64
– *Off.*
2.8.26–29 277
3.47   32
– *Rep.*
1.31   148 n.8
6.12   261 n.24
– *Sul.*
2   279
– *Tusc.*
5.78   355
– *Ver.*
1.11   97 n.19
2.4.116 62 n.23
2.4.120–23 62 n.23

Clemens of Alexandria
– *Strom.*
1.21   202 n.9

Coelius Antipater
– *hist.*
fr. 25 265 n.35

Curtius Rufus
7.5.9–12 163 n.53

Dio Cassius
37–44   292
51.21.4 209
53.8.2 208 n.21
53.16.7–8 255 n.6
64   292
64.10.2–3 209 n.25
65.9.2a 345 n.18
66.26   283 n.45
67.2–3 303

Dio Chrysostom
1.82   208 n.21

Diodorus Siculus
1.87.6 355
2.24ff. 38 n.33
9.11.1 208 n.21
11.72.2 208 n.21
11.76.6 208 n.21
11.86.3 208 n.21
11.87.5 208 n.21
25.15   61 n.22; 324 n.11

Dionysius of Halicarnassus
– *Ant.Rom.*
1.2–4.1 38 n.33
2.11.2–3 256 n.9
– *Pomp.*
3   208

Dioscorides
– *Mat. Med.*
2.106.1 349
4.7.1   350

Ennius
– *Ann.* (Skutsch)
46–47   255 n.5
72–91   295ff.
78   296
80   297
82   297
92–95   295
220–21 371
225–26 371
268–86 38 n.34

Eratosthenes
– *Cat.*
32   310 n.39

Euripides
– *Hec.*
1035–55   47 n.47
– *Or.*
998–1000   83 n.38

Eusebius
– *Hist. eccl.*
3.9.2   202 n.9

Eutropius
7.13.2   209

Frontinus
– *Str.*
1.pr.1   152; 154
1.pr.2   152f.
1.1   156ff.
1.1.1   154; 156
1.1.2   156
1.1.3   156
1.1.4   156
1.1.5   158 n.41
1.1.5–7   158; 159f.; 173
1.1.8   157; 159
1.1.9   157; 159 n.44
1.1.10   157
1.1.11   157
1.1.11–13   157
1.1.12   158; 161 n.49
1.3.2   149
1.3.10   152
1.5   162
1.5.1   162 n.50
1.5.5   162 n.50
1.5.8   162 n.50
1.5.9   149; 162 n.50
1.5.17   162 n.50
1.5.20–22   162 n.50
1.7   162f.; 164
1.7.1–2   168
1.7.4   163
1.7.5   163
1.7.6   163
1.8   164
1.8.1   164
1.8.1–2   168
1.8.2   164
1.8.5–9   164
1.8.9   164
1.9   164f.
1.9.2–3   165 n.56
1.10   165
1.10.1   161 n.49; 165
1.10.4   149; 150 n.18; 165
2.1.2   161 n.49
2.1.3   161 n.49
2.1.11   149
2.2.11   169
2.3   167ff.
2.3.1   168f.
2.3.4   168
2.3.5   161 n.49; 168
2.3.6–7   173 n.72
2.3.7   168
2.3.8   168
2.3.9   168
2.3.10   168f.
2.3.11   168
2.3.12–13   169 n.66
2.3.14   168; 173 n.72
2.3.16   169; 172f.
2.3.17   172f.
2.3.18   172
2.3.20   172
2.3.21   172f.
2.3.22   169; 172f.
2.3.22–24   173
2.3.23   174
2.5   165ff.; 169
2.5.1   165
2.5.31   166f.
2.5.31–40   165; 167
2.5.32   166
2.5.36–37   166
2.5.38   166
2.5.39   166
2.5.40   149; 166
2.6.10   172 n.70
2.7.5   166 n.59
2.11.7   152
2.12.2   166 n.59
2.13.3   161 n.49; 166 n.59
3.13.7–8   161 n.47

3.14.1	149; 161 n.47	16.759–64	48 n.49
3.14.3	161 n.47	17.233–318	48 n.49
3.14.4	161 n.47	24.212–13	47 n.47
3.17.4	161 n.47	– *Od.*	
3.17.8	161 n.47	12.377–83	79 n.25
4.2.1	149; 150 n.18; 161 n.48		
4.3.14	161; 174	**Horace**	
4.5.2	149; 161 n.48	– *Carm.*	
4.7.1	161 n.48	1.2.29	25 n.1
4.7.6	161; 166 n.59	1.3.34	406 n.99
4.7.14	161 n.48	2.15.10–12	298
4.7.32	161 n.48	3.3	298f.
4.7.41	161 n.49	3.3.18–68	299
		3.3.25	299 n.8
[Hegesippus]		3.4.65	407 n.102
– *De excidio urbis Hierosolymitanae*		3.4.73–75	45 n.44
praef.	202 n.9	3.6.17	300
		3.6.17–48	299f.
Herodotus		3.6.18	300
1.59.3	208 n.21	3.6.20	300
1.60.2	208 n.21	3.6.21–24	300
1.150.1	208 n.21	3.6.25–28	300
2.75	355	3.24.25–26	289 n.62
3.82.3	208 n.21	3.30	409 n.110
4.192	347 n.25	3.30.1–2	408 n.105
5.28.1	208 n.21	3.30.6	235
6.109.5	208 n.21	3.30.6–9	235
		3.30.8–9	235
Hesiod		4.4.61–76	32
– *Th.*		4.8.22–24	298
276	310 n.39	– *Ep.*	
721–814	371	1.5.25–26	106 n.52
858	45 n.44	– *Epod.*	
– *Op.*		7	297ff.
135–36	367 n.16	7.1	9; 298
		7.1–2	90
Homer		7.3–4	92
– *Il.*		7.9–12	107 n.53
2.786–89	134	7.13	374 n.41
6.386–87	135	7.13–14	91
6.467–70	135	7.13–20	91 n.8
8.5–27	372	7.14	298
8.13–16	372	7.17–18	91
13.701–8	95	7.17–20	254; 255 n.7; 282 n.44
15.18–30	372	7.18	25 n.1; 298
15.19–20	373	7.19–20	298
16.508–683	48 n.49	7.20	298

Index of Passages

– S.
1.5.103 374 n.40
1.8 381 n.73

Hyginus
– Astr.
2.34 310 n.39

Isocrates
– Paneg.
4.79 208 n.21
4.114 208 n.21
4.174 208 n.21

Josephus
– AJ
1.6–7 202
19 212
19.216–20 222
20.267 202
– Ap.
1.50–51 201
1.50–53 199 n.1
– BJ
1.1–8 203
1.1–16 201
1.3 201
1.4–5 212
1.6 201
1.7 203f.
1.8 199 n.1
1.10 202
1.13–16 203
1.16 199 n.1
1.69 221 n.41
1.82 221 n.41
1.84 221 n.41
1.331 221 n.41
1.347 221 n.41
1.370 221 n.41
1.373 221 n.41
1.376 221 n.41
1.613 221 n.41
2.204 212; 222
2.204–14 212
2.210 212
2.455 221 n.41

2.457 221 n.41
3.1–8 205
3.29–30 205
3.29–34 205
3.59–69 205
3.65 205
3.127–34 205
3.132–34 205
3.141–43 205
3.340–91 332
3.341 221 n.41
3.342 224 n.45
3.344 205
3.345 205
3.346–51 205
3.350 205
3.350–54 224
3.351–54 206
3.352–53 219
3.360 224
3.361–82 224; 334 n.41
3.375–79 333
3.383–86 224
3.385 333; 335f.
3.385–86 333
3.387 224
3.387–91 279
3.392 334
3.397 206; 279
3.485 221 n.41
3.532–42 206
3.536 206
4.20–53 206
4.34 221 n.41
4.39 206
4.70 206
4.76 221 n.41
4.87–91 207
4.91 207
4.217 221 n.41
4.314–44 202
4.366–77 206
4.476–77 206
4.491–663 202
4.492–663 214ff.
4.498 221
4.501 221 n.41

4.501–2	221	7.148	207
4.502–3	215	7.152	207
4.502–44	215	7.157	213
4.545–46	215	7.158	207
4.546	212	7.159	221 n.41
4.550–55	210 n.26	7.161–62	207
4.560–63	217	7.185	221 n.41
4.586–87	216f.	7.259–75	334
4.588	217f.; 219	7.318	221 n.41
4.589	211; 221	7.318–36	335
4.590	221	7.319	335 n.42
4.591	221f.	7.322	335
4.592–93	216f.	7.331	335 n.42
4.592–600	222	7.338	335
4.596	216	7.339	335
4.601	222	7.341–88	334
4.602–4	219; 223	7.360	336 n.44
4.605	223	7.378	335
4.605–6	345 n.18	7.389	335f.
4.616	224	7.389–401	334
4.616–19	220	7.389–406	279
4.616–21	219	7.390	336
4.620	204	7.391–93	279
4.620–21	219 n.37	7.392	336
4.621	223	7.399	335
4.622	221 n.41	– *Vit.*	
4.622–29	207	13–16	205
4.625	207	22	206 n.19
4.630	204	39	206 n.19
4.649	221 n.41; 242 n.53	71	206 n.19
4.651	217	128–30	206 n.19
4.652	216	141	206 n.19
4.656	204	148	206 n.19
5.377	221 n.41	163	206 n.19
5.502	221 n.41	168–69	206 n.19
5.529	334	175–76	206 n.19
6.59	221 n.41	263	206 n.19
6.252	221 n.41	273–74	206 n.19
6.287–315	199 n.2	282	206 n.19
6.296	221 n.41	287–91	206 n.19
6.303	221 n.41	361	199 n.1
6.312–13	219	364–67	201
6.313	219	377–80	206 n.19
6.429	221 n.41	429	202
7.82	221 n.41		
7.120	221 n.41		
7.121	207		

Justin
– *Epit.*
1.3.5–6   38 n.33

Juvenal
15.9–11   358

Lactantius Placidus
Ad Theb. 11.393   96

Livy
1.6.3–7.3   255 n.7
1.6.4   255 n.7
1.6.4–2.7.3 282 n.44
1.7.2   256 n.7
1.20.2   269 n.48
2.39–40   132f.
2.40   134 n.57
21.14   61 n.22
21.14.1   325
21.14.1–4   179 n.1
21.14.3–4   325
21.15   326
21.16.2   181
22.43–44   31 n.15
22.51.2–4   265
25.27   51
25.31   62 n.23
26.19.6–9   263
27.43–49   157 n.39
28.4.2   262
29.3.15   265
30.44.8   256
30.45.6–7   269 n.47
38.56.8–9   262f.
– *Per.*
79   278f.
– *fr.*
49   156 n.37

Lucan
1.1–2   74; 92 n.10
1.2–3   93
1.2–4   258
1.3   278
1.5   375 n.45
1.6–7   106

1.8   9; 90ff.
1.13–14   40
1.33–38   27 n.5
1.33–45   81; 282
1.33–66   84
1.42   2
1.48   282
1.67–81   369
1.70–82   391 n.28
1.71   369
1.74   370 n.28
1.75–76   375f.
1.77   370 n.28
1.79–81   376
1.87–89   291
1.92–93   70
1.93–95   297 n.4
1.95   254; 255 n.7; 288 n.44
1.109   283
1.129   106
1.143–57   291
1.160–65   63 n.28
1.190–91   91
1.205–12   403f.
1.211   403 n.84
1.212   99 n.27
1.238   289 n.62
1.327–31   402; 404
1.328   402
1.377–78   279
1.432   54 n.9
1.494   53 n.7
1.522–83   30 n.12
1.547   59 n.20
1.584–695   76 n.17
1.673–95   30 n.12
1.674–95   75f.
1.676   241 n.51
1.680   3 n.6
1.681   9
1.681–82   188 n.28
1.692   59 n.20
1.695   3 n.6
2.43   284
2.45–46   33
2.67–232   91 n.7
2.67–233   232f. n.26

470 — Index of Passages

2.106	59 n.20	3.533–34	54
2.148–59	279	3.535–36	55 n.12
2.149–51	279	3.535–37	55
2.156–57	279	3.536	55 n.12
2.166–73	46 n.45	3.537	55 n.12
2.192	62 n.24	3.538–55	54
2.295	66 n.33	3.540	54 n.9
2.487–90	65	3.541	56 n.13
2.491	65	3.542	54 n.9
2.528–30	65f.	3.544	54 n.9
2.656	404 n.87	3.545–46	54 n.9
3.175	59 n.20	3.553	62 n.26
3.193–94	385 n.93	3.553–55	56
3.193–97	363 n.3	3.555	56
3.300–55	60	3.556–66	54
3.301–2	62 n.26	3.558	54 n.11
3.301–3	60f.	3.561	62 n.26
3.340	62 n.26	3.565–66	54 n.9
3.340–42	182f.	3.565–70	56 n.13
3.349–50	61	3.570–71	54 n.9
3.349–55	182f.; 279	3.574	56 n.13
3.350	61	3.578	56 n.13
3.351–55	61	3.583	62 n.26
3.354–55	183; 188	3.586	62 n.26
3.355	62 n.26	3.587–88	57
3.358	62 n.26	3.592	57f.
3.358–72	61	3.592–94	56
3.372–508	279	3.592–99	57
3.388	62 n.26	3.593	58 n.16
3.412–13	63 n.27	3.593–96	58
3.435	53 n.7	3.594	58 n.16
3.453–508	53	3.595	58 n.16
3.455–62	396 n.54	3.599	56
3.463	62 n.26	3.600	57 n.15
3.478	62 n.26	3.600–2	57
3.494	59 n.20	3.603–5	101 n.31
3.497	62 n.26	3.609–13	59
3.500–4	65	3.610	62 n.26
3.509–762	52; 279	3.613	57
3.514–15	59	3.627–33	59
3.516	62 n.26	3.635–36	59
3.521–37	53	3.647–50	56 n.13
3.525–27	55	3.648	54 n.9
3.525–37	55	3.652–61	57
3.526	62 n.26	3.660–61	56 n.13
3.530–31	55	3.661–69	59
3.532–33	54 n.10	3.667	62 n.26

Index of Passages

3.670–79	56 n.13	6.621–23	381
3.676–77	56 n.13	6.669	380 n.66; 381 n.72
3.681–88	56 n.13	6.693–94	382 n.75
3.691	56 n.13	7.39	62 n.24
3.694–96	56 n.13	7.62–85	31 n.15
3.697	62 n.26	7.95	9
3.728	62 n.26	7.95–96	91 n.9; 101 n.29
3.741–51	58 n.19	7.151–84	30 n.12
3.748–49	58 n.19	7.196	375 n.43
3.753	62 n.26	7.211	81 n.31
3.761–62	56	7.270–71	62 n.24
4.237–42	403 n.81	7.306	62 n.24
4.419–20	53 n.7	7.318–22	31
4.474–581	279	7.457–59	291f.
4.496–502	189 n.34	7.542–43	401f.
4.516–17	190	7.552–55	232
4.548–49	106	7.553–54	235 n.33
4.575–77	190 n.35	7.567–71	63f.
4.576	190	7.617–31	279
4.577–78	52 n.5	7.626–27	279
4.591	66 n.33	7.721–23	93 n.12
4.593–655	66 n.33	7.794	52 n.5
4.653	53 n.7	7.794–95	31
4.788–93	33f. n.20	7.794–99	44 n.40
5.67–236	76 n.17	7.799–801	256 n.8
5.135	53 n.7	8.8	59 n.20
6.17	53 n.7	8.445	73 n.10
6.31	53 n.7	8.702	59 n.20
6.42	59 n.20	8.872	291
6.137	59 n.20	9.149	59 n.20
6.232	59 n.20	9.349	59 n.20
6.294	59 n.20	9.379–85	237
6.400–1	74f.; 363 n.3	9.466–71	376 n.54
6.421	59 n.20	9.469–71	370 n.28
6.440–42	382 n.79	9.649	59 n.20
6.461–506	379 n.64	9.960	62 n.24
6.462–67	382	10.15–16	63 n.27
6.499–500	379 n.64	10.445–46	402ff.
6.500–5	381	10.535–46	72
6.506	381 n.72	10.546	85
6.506–8	381		
6.506–9	381	**Lucian**	
6.550–53	47	– Hist.Conscr.	
6.558–59	383 n.81	2	204
6.584–86	46	5–6	203 n.12
6.615	383 n.80	7	204
6.619–825	381	13	204

14–15	203 n.12	8.53.11	403 n.84
19	203 n.12	9.51	283 n.47
23	203 n.12	9.6	303
24	203 n.12; 204	– *Sp.*	
29	203 n.12	1	397 ; 399f.; 401; 406f.
		1.1	408 n.105

Lucretius

1.1052–113	370 n.28	1.5	406f.
2.1110–11	374 n.40	1.7	401; 407
3.72	100 n.28	1.8	392; 400; 407
3.642ff.	99 n.27	2	390; 394f.; 401; 405ff.
3.1034	254	2.1	395f.
5.75	63 n.27	2.2	395; 407
5.1293	286f.	2.4	395; 399f.; 401
5.1310–29	404 n.89	2.5–6	389 n.15; 396; 397 n.56; 407
6.419	63 n.27	2.6	395; 397; 406f.
6.535–607	391 n.28	2.7	395
6.546–49	376ff.	3	394; 399; 400; 401
6.568–74	376ff.	3.1–2	399f.
6.572–73	378	3.2	400; 401; 403
		3.3	401
		3.7	400 n.73

Manilius

– *Astr.*

		3.11	400 n.73
1.26	380 n.69	10.5–6	405
1.125–70	370 n.28	11.5	406
1.168–70	370 n.28	15.5	406
1.718	370 n.28	18	402f.; 404
1.907–14	3 n.6	18.2	402
2.46–52	379 n.64	18.3	404
2.118	374 n.40	18.6	403
2.778ff.	371 n.31	21.1–2	401
5.458–67	103	22	403
5.463–64	103	22.1–4	403
		22.2	404
		22.5–6	404 n.86

Martial

– *Ep.*

		22.9–10	404 n.86
1.36	283 n.47	22.11	403; 404 n.87
2.75	405 n.91	24.5	397 n.56
5.5.7	236		

Minucius Felix

– *Oct.*

5.5.7–8	81	33	202 n.9
5.8	303		
5.38	283 n.47		
6.2	303		

Origen

– *Contra Celsum*

6.4	303	1.47	202 n.9
6.7	303	2.13	202 n.9
7.1	72 n.9		
8.36	398 n.61; 408 n.105		

– In Ev. Matt.
10.17   202 n.9

Ovid
– Am.
1.15.21–22 34 n.22
– Ars
3.3   106 n.52
– Ep.
6.87–88   380 n.68
– Fast.
1.103–12   371
1.103–14   371 n.33
1.103–20   370 n.28
1.108   369 n.26
1.119–20   371 n.31
2.127–44   255 n.6
4.807ff.   255 n.6
– Met.
1.5–21   371 n.33
1.7–56   370 n.28
1.11   370 n.28
1.123–24   366 n.13
1.127–50   293
1.135–36   366 n.13
1.140–50   385 n.95
1.141   366 n.13
1.141–48   367 n.17
1.149–50   366 n.14
1.151–55   367 n.15
2.136   374 n.40
2.295–300 370 n.28
3.117   189
3.531   9
3.531–32   91 n.9
5.327–28   356 n.51
7.123–30   105 n.47
7.141–42   105 n.47
7.179–349 380 n.68
7.199–209 380 n.68
7.268   381 n.72
9.197   406 n.98
9.403–5   107
10.30   371 n.31
11.1–66   401
13.561–64 47 n.47
15.420–52 81 n.30

15.823–24 3 n.6
15.850–51 269 n.47
15.868–70 269 n.48

Pausanias
3.2.7   208 n.21
4.18.3   208 n.21
5.14.1   354
8.26.7   354

Petronius
– Sat.
108.14.1   9; 91 n.9
118.6   2
119–24   277
120.82–83 370 n.29
120–24   277
141   180 n.3
141.9   188 n.26

Pindar
– P.
4.251–57   84 n.40
4.251–53   233 n.30
12.20   310 n.39

Plato
– Lg.
1.628c   208 n.21
1.629c–d   208 n.21
– R.
5.470c–d   208 n.21

Pliny (the Elder)
– Nat.
2.14   358
2.14–15   358
2.14–27   358f.
2.16   359
2.27   338
2.107   342 n.6
2.132   350
2.195   347
3.20   180 n.3
5.60   360
5.118   354 n.43
6.1–2   379 n.61

Index of Passages

6.21–80	360 n.69	18.170	345f.
6.81–90	360 n.69	18.285–86	355
7.21–32	360 n.69	19.14	346
7.33	352	19.84	344; 347 n.26
7.33–52	351	19.101	358
7.35	342 n.6	19.110	344; 347 n.26
7.39	352	19.129	350
7.39–40	352	19.165	347 n.26
8.13	342 n.6	19.171	347 n.26
8.88	342 n.6	20.73	350
8.132	347	20.216	347 n.26
8.184	359 n.67	21.36	346
8.191	346	21.61	348
10.58–75	353	21.69	346
10.75	353ff.	21.87	349
10.79	354	21.88	350
10.134	347	21.90	346
10.186	347	21.102	347
11.97	357	21.117	346
11.105	355	21.142	350
11.272	342 n.6	21.176	348
12.108	346	23.134	348
12.109	347 n.26	23.158	350 n.35
12.111	346	24.88	347
12.129	346	24.109	347 n.26
12.134	346	24.138	350
13.26	346	24.138–40	350
13.38	347	24.141	350
13.56	348	24.141–42	350
13.58	348	25.11	342 n.6
13.66	347 n.26	26.4	342 n.6
13.73	347	26.8	342 n.6
13.113	346	27.53	347 n.26
13.126	347 n.26	27.145	347
14.74	348 n.29	28.10–17	352
14.117	348	28.17	352
14.149	342 n.6	28.104	357
15.20	156 n.37	28.175	357
15.25	348	29.76	357 n.57
18.8	355	29.93	357 n.57
18.63	345	29.106	354
18.63–70	345	29.110	357 n.57
18.76	351	29.132	357 n.57
18.77	346	29.140	357 n.57
18.82	345	30.18	348
18.95	346	30.39	357 n.57
18.109	345	30.75	357 n.57

30.81	357 n.57		– Mar.	
30.98–104	356		39	279
30.111	357 n.57		– Publ.	
30.122	357 n.57		15.5	388 n.12
30.138	357		– Mor.	
32.150	346		285e	354 n.45
33.161	347 n.26		351d–384c	356 n.52
34.45–46	395 n.49		381a	357
34.70	355		486b	283 n.47
34.77	355		813a	208 n.21
34.120	347 n.26		823f–825b	208 n.21
35.31	346			
35.35–36	347 n.26		**[Plutarch]**	
35.184	347 n.26		– Fluv.	
36.23	355		8	330 n.30
36.58	359			
36.64–74	342 n.7		**Polyaenus**	
36.64–89	342		4.3.25	163 n.53
36.68	342			
36.72	342		**Polybius**	
36.75	342		1.1.2	222 n.42
36.75–76	342 n.7		1.35.2	222 n.42
36.77	342 n.7		1.63.9	222 n.42
36.78–82	342 n.7		1.64.2	222 n.42
36.83	342 n.7		2.7.1–2	222 n.42
36.84	342 n.7		2.20.7–8	222 n.42
36.86–89	342 n.7		3.2.6	222 n.42
36.111	398		3.15.6–8	324 n.12
37.17	349		3.15.9	324
37.20	349		3.17.9–10	324
37.143	346f.		3.92.3–94	266
37.179	347		6.2.5–7	256 n.8
			6.2.5–8	222 n.42
Pliny (the Younger)			6.11.1	256 n.8
– Ep.			6.58	32
3.21.6	387 n.3		16.28.1	222 n.42
5.1	151 n.24		18.28.4–5	222 n.42
6.16	338		29.21	38 n.33
– Pan.			38.2.1–2	222 n.42
16.3	269			
20.24	269		**Pomponius Mela**	
			3.82.5	355
Plutarch				
– Alex.			**Propertius**	
42.4–6	163 n.53		4.4.91	59 n.20
– Cat.Ma.			4.11.9	54 n.9
26–27	156 n.37			

Quintilian
– *Inst.*
10.1.90   71 n.9

Res Gestae Divi Augusti
2–3.1   209
4   209
15   209
21.2–3   209
26–33   209
34.1   148; 209

Sallust
– *Cat.*
10–13   168 n.64
61.8–9   278
– *Hist.*
4.69.5–9   277
4.69.17   277
4.69.21   277
– *Iug.*
41   168 n.64

Scholia
Σ Ar. *Nu.* 749 382f. n.79

Seneca (the Elder)
– *Con.*
1.1.23   91

Seneca (the Younger)
– *Ag.*
611   237 n.38
622   135 n.64
– *Cl.*
1.26.4   107 n.53
– *Dial.*
6.2.6   378 n.57
6.26.5–6   370 n.28
11.14.4   262 n.27
– *Ep.*
88.22   396 n.52
– *Epigrams*
462 Riese   285 n.57
463 Riese   285 n.57
– *Her. F.*
84–85   105 n.46

85   141
86–88   141
87–88   141
258–61   102 n.35
662–79   371 n.31
1281–82   192
– *Med.*
35–36   384 n.89
309–39   367 n.18
335–39   363 n.3
361–79   384
373–79   363 n.3
454–56   84 n.40
570–74   117 n.26
694–770   380 n.68
739–70   382 n.79
771–844   110 n.13
961–62   141
1012–13   383
1027   383
– *Nat.*
2.1.1   382 n.77
6.1.4   378
6.1.4–5   377f.
6.1.12   377f.
6.22   377 n.55
– *Oed.*
73   237 n.38
237–38   105
371   104
548–658   381 n.73
949   123 n.3
951   123 n.3
965   123 n.2
1002   123 n.2
1038–39   104
– *Phoen.*
136–37   104 n.44
274–76   289 n.62
288–94   134
320–27   129
322   139 n.83
323   134f.
336–38   123f.
340   130
354–55   129
367–69   131 n.44

Index of Passages — 477

387–402	130 n.40; 133	**[Seneca]**	
388–93	129	– Her. O.	
402	129	874	289
406	129	– Oct.	
407–8	129	389	370 n.28
427–34	130	391	370 n.28
428–29	130	391–94	369
433	139	– Ad A.	
433–42	133	2.411	26 n.2
443	130	4.513	381 n.72
443–50	131		
458	130	**Servius/Servius Danielis**	
460	93	– Ad A.	
464–66	93	2.411	26 n.2
467–77	131	4.513	381 n.72
483	93		
528–30	102 n.34	**Silius**	
538–94	289 n.62	1.40–44	275 n.16
540–41	139 n.83	1.42–44	274
547–48	139 n.83	1.95	282
555–56	286	1.225–29	331 n.33
555–57	139 n.83	1.270	181
557	9; 91 n.9	1.296–2.692	279
565–66	139 n.83	1.384–85	182
599–600	289 n.62	1.665–69	182
648–49	289	1.679–89	277
653	132f.	1.767–86	283
660–64	131f.	2.11–14	277
664	124; 282	2.44–51	277
– Thy.		2.243–47	271
1–121	136	2.283–87	292
40–41	137	2.284	61
40–46	136	2.368–71	277
180–89	128	2.383–86	277
223–35	83 n.38	2.387–89	277
223–41	112 n.16	2.395–456	274
282–83	137 n.72	2.420–25	274
339	9; 91 n.9	2.457–525	326
546–622	128	2.457–707	180
552–59	128	2.475–525	61; 314
560–61	128	2.484–92	286
562	124; 128	2.488–89	191
563	128; 135	2.493	188 n.27
689–90	98 n.21	2.494–95	187f.
795	284	2.496–506	286
		2.498–505	286; 293
		2.513	188 n.27

2.513–25	183; 187	2.671–80	331f.
2.515–17	184	2.681–82	186 n.18; 280
2.520	188 n.27	2.683–88	335f.
2.522–23	188	2.692	332
2.526–52	313	2.696–98	193f.
2.526–91	326	2.700–1	194
2.526–707	61	3.2	196 n.46
2.528	188	3.30	63 n.27
2.551	329 n.29	3.66	61
2.553–79	313	3.238–40	264
2.558–79	189	3.564	181f.; 196 n.46
2.575–79	326	3.571–629	268
2.577	190	3.584–90	32
2.578	190	3.588–90	281f.
2.580–91	326	3.593–606	292
2.592	327	3.594–55	292
2.595	313	3.597	268
2.600	327	3.602	292
2.603	274	3.603	268
2.605–8	327	3.605–6	213 n.32
2.609–11	186	3.607	269
2.612–13	192	3.609	236
2.612–707	279	3.609–10	287
2.614–16	313	3.626–28	268
2.614–28	327f.	4.126–27	98 n.23
2.614–49	279f.; 285	4.217–19	290
2.614–91	271	4.230–31	290
2.614–707	274; 278; 287	4.231–47	290
2.617	186	4.355–95	288 n.62
2.617–19	192f.; 280	4.386	289 n.62
2.617–95	313	4.392–400	259f.
2.619–37	329 n.25	4.401–13	290
2.632–33	329	4.413–16	290
2.632–35	279; 327f.	4.416	290
2.633	329	4.417–44	290
2.633–34	329	4.445–53	290
2.634–35	329	4.454–71	290
2.636–49	257f.; 329ff.	4.457–59	263
2.639	330 n.30	4.622–37	290
2.648–49	329 n.26	4.638–99	290
2.654–55	271	4.674–75	261
2.654–57	313	5.160	196 n.46
2.654–58	287; 293	5.347	264
2.655–80	279f.; 285	5.370	264
2.659–95	274	5.423	59 n.20
2.665	331f.	7.106–7	291
2.665–80	329 n.27	7.151–52	65 n.32

7.244–45	277
7.280	196f. n.46
7.380–408	283
7.494–516	283
7.515	283
7.738–39	283 n.50
8.25–10.658	280ff.
8.50–201	274
8.243–57	168 n.64; 275 n.16; 280f.
8.243–350	283
8.253–57	281
8.278–83	281f.
8.332–36	281
8.349–50	283f.
8.349–621	292
8.384–85	261 n.26
8.468–69	293
8.468–71	292
8.546	291
8.622–76	30 n.12
8.648	281
9.1–7	31 n.15
9.12–14	284
9.66–177	31 n.15; 278
9.85–89	284
9.86	284
9.90–95	284
9.93–94	258
9.96–105	284
9.108–9	258
9.120	284
9.129–30	284
9.166–67	284
9.170	284
9.173	284 n.56
9.173–74	284
9.210–11	31
9.258	258
9.287–89	293
9.287–303	281 n.39
9.290–99	283 n.48
9.292	197 n.46
9.295	283 n.48
9.327	59 n.20
9.346ff.	32
9.350	32
9.351–52	32
9.353	32 n.18
10.341–42	265 n.36
10.343–71	265
10.373–87	284
10.382–87	265
10.450–51	31
10.608–12	32
10.657–58	32ff.; 168 n.64; 256 n.8; 280ff.
11.38–43	63 n.28
11.44–45	275 n.16
11.44–50	274f.; 293
11.48–50	275 n.16
11.143	61
11.292–97	275 n.16
12.431–32	197 n.46
12.622	59 n.20
13.99–103	275 n.16
13.256–98	277 n.28
13.261–98	185
13.263	185
13.271–72	185
13.314–20	183f.
13.351–56	63 n.28
13.369–80	277 n.28
13.601–12	289f.
13.615–49	263
13.637–44	291
13.638–39	292
13.643–44	292
13.645–46	291f.
13.650–51	261; 284
13.663–95	261 n.25
13.703	261
13.705–35	284
13.737–45	284
13.852–67	271
13.853–60	293
13.853–67	275f.; 292f.
13.853–69	274
13.861–67	293
13.868–69	280 n.37
14.1–2	63
14.3–8	63
14.9–10	63
14.33–34	289f.
14.39–44	62 n.25

14.50–54	62 n.25	14.384–407	54
14.85–98	289f.	14.387–88	55
14.85–109	52	14.390	55 n.12
14.93–95	62 n.25	14.392–93	55f.
14.100	52 n.5	14.393	56
14.106–7	52 n.5	14.394–561	56ff.
14.110–47	62 n.24	14.401	54 n.11
14.110–77	51	14.402–3	56f.
14.114	62 n.24	14.404	57 n.15
14.125	62 n.24	14.404–7	57
14.129	62 n.24	14.411	59 n.20
14.136–38	62 n.24	14.411–13	59
14.145	62 n.24	14.420	59 n.20
14.178–91	51	14.423ff.	57
14.180	53 n.7; 62 n.25	14.427–28	56 n.13
14.181–83	62	14.436–41	57
14.279–91	60	14.442–43	56f.
14.279–93	52	14.444–51	57
14.281–86	62 n.25	14.449	59 n.20
14.287–90	60	14.452–53	57
14.290–91	60	14.453–57	58
14.292–97	62	14.454	58 n.16
14.292–352	51; 53	14.455	58 n.16
14.296	53 n.7	14.456–57	58 n.16
14.301	62 n.25	14.458–61	58
14.315	53 n.7	14.460	58 n.19
14.328–29	53 n.7	14.462–76	66
14.335	53 n.7	14.474	59 n.20
14.338	62 n.25	14.476–80	56 n.13
14.341	62 n.25	14.481–82	57
14.353–59	53	14.481–87	57
14.353–93	53ff.	14.483	59 n.20
14.353–579	51f.	14.484	57 n.14
14.360–84	53f.	14.487–88	55 n.12
14.364–65	54 n.9	14.488	59 n.20
14.366–68	54 n.10	14.489–90	59
14.368	59 n.20	14.489–91	59
14.369	54 n.10	14.500	59
14.369–70	54	14.503–4	56 n.13
14.373	54 n.9	14.505–11	62 n.25
14.374	59 n.20	14.518–21	56 n.13
14.375–76	54 n.9	14.539–41	56 n.13
14.378	54 n.9	14.540	59 n.20
14.381	59 n.20	14.543–49	56 n.13
14.381–84	54 n.9	14.550	56 n.13
14.384–86	55	14.551	56 n.13
14.384–93	54f.	14.552–54	56 n.13

14.557–58	56 n.13	17.395	267
14.559–61	56	17.396–98	261
14.562	62 n.25	17.397–98	261 n.26
14.574	59 n.20	17.605–15	31 n.13
14.579	59 n.20	17.618–24	274f.
14.580–617	51	17.625–26	291
14.618–84	51	17.625–54	283
14.638	65	17.627	290
14.642	62 n.25	17.653–54	291
14.647–48	62 n.25		
14.654–65	63	**Sophocles**	
14.662–63	63 n.27	– *OT*	
14.665–75	62; 64	260	104 n.45
14.671–72	65	459–60	104 n.45
14.672–73	63 n.27	1208	104
14.676	275 n.17	1257	104
14.676–78	275		
14.679–83	62; 64	**Statius**	
14.683	66 n.33	– *Silu.*	
14.684–88	66 n.33	1.1.34	237
14.686–87	66 n.33	1.6.98–102	238
15.1–138	292	1.6.102	239 n.43
15.3–4	261	2.7.48–53	271
15.10–11	292	4.1.8	237
15.82–83	269 n.48	4.2.18–37	398 n.61
15.100	292 n.71	4.3.16	238 n.41
15.122–23	292	4.3.40–41	366 n.13
15.129–32	292	4.6.82–84	195
15.139–45	292	5.3.195–202	236 n.34
15.149–53	292	– *Theb.*	
15.205	263; 267	1.1	112; 272 n.7; 278; 308; 314
15.334–96	293	1.7	109; 232
15.341–42	293	1.7–8	105
15.403–5	291	1.16–33	152
15.411	266	1.21–22	236
15.585–87	266	1.33–37	272 n.7; 289 n.62
15.803–5	288	1.34	286
16.143–45	291	1.46	123 n.2
16.259–61	98 n.23	1.46–55	314
16.533–48	288 n.62	1.48	123 n.3
16.536	288 n.62	1.49	314
16.575–82	262	1.51–52	314
16.576	283	1.53–88	314
16.663–69	290	1.85–86	98f.
16.668	291	1.85–87	99; 123
17.266	288	1.121–22	135 n.64
17.328	61; 197 n.46	1.131–38	95

1.137–38	314	4.434–42	105 n.50
1.138–43	283	4.435	105 n.47
1.142–64	69 n.3	4.436	105 n.47
1.150	69 n.3	4.438	105 n.50
1.155–56	90	5.29–498	315
1.173–85	91 n.7	5.30–33	316
1.184–85	102 n.36	5.58–69	316
1.227–29	314	5.63	116 n.24; 122 n.41
1.402–3	253 n.2	5.75–89	316
1.504	98 n.23	5.90–142	316
2.201–7	314f.	5.92–94	316
2.211–13	91f.; 253 n.2; 315	5.97–103	316
2.113	253 n.2	5.120–22	316
2.249–64	113	5.144–46	316
2.265–67	315	5.157–58	316
2.265–68	113	5.190–240	272 n.7
2.265–305	315	5.200–39	316
2.266	111; 119	5.202–3	316
2.266–67	112	5.207–17	279
2.267	109	5.207–61	279
2.269–73	115	5.236–38	279
2.269–76	315	5.260	59 n.20
2.269–305	109–22 *passim*	5.280–83	241 n.51
2.276–88	111	5.303	316
2.277–85	315	5.335–85	234 n.30
2.281	111ff.	5.347–60	316
2.282–85	117f.	5.445–46	316
2.283–84	118	5.486–92	316
2.284	118; 380 n.66; 381 n.72	5.628	316
2.286–88	315	5.717	135 n.60
2.287	115f. n.24	6.197–201	98 n.22
2.287–88	120	6.783–84	99 n.27
2.289–305	120	6.943	59 n.20
2.294–95	109	7.227	135f.
2.299–305	315	7.227–42	134
2.303	116	7.228–29	134
2.319–62	315	7.240–42	135
2.415–41	283	7.452	135f.
2.640–41	279	7.452–69	135f.
3.82–91	322f.	7.465	136 n.65
3.83–84	322	7.466–69	136; 316
3.84–85	322	7.467–68	137 n.72
3.86	322	7.470–534	316
3.330–35	99 n.27	7.470–563	133
3.678–721	315	7.474–77	316f.
4.59–62	315	7.474–78	138
4.187–213	315	7.483	103

Index of Passages — **483**

7.483–84	96f. n.18; 138; 317	11.515	253 n.2
7.484–85	104 n.41	11.515–17	100
7.489	317	11.524–40	272 n.7
7.490–91	104 n.41	11.535–36	100
7.492–93	139	11.535–38	193
7.504–27	138	11.537–38	100
7.507–8	139	11.539–43	253 n.2
7.514	103 n.37; 138; 317	11.539–40	100
7.519–27	139	11.552–73	279
7.526–27	103 n.37	11.574–75	193
7.528–33	139	11.574–79	95
7.533	139	11.577–79	194
7.534–37	317	11.654–57	289
7.534–38	139	11.654–66	289
7.559–62	140	11.677–82	289
7.562–63	140	11.701–5	289
7.564–607	140f.	11.704–5	289
7.579	141	12.16	116 n.24
7.608–11	141	12.94–95	44 n.40
7.615–27	141	12.260–61	99 n.25
7.670–74	99 n.27	12.267–69	44f.
8.68	99	12.270–77	45 n.43
8.104–5	315	12.274–75	45
8.120–22	315	12.282–90	45
8.588–91	98 n.22	12.314–15	45
9.53	253	12.315–17	45
9.200–4	99 n.27	12.318–21	46
9.506–10	98 n.22	12.322	46
11.97–101	191	12.322ff.	46
11.110	99	12.336–39	46
11.232–33	97 n.19	12.341–43	46f.
11.248–49	98 n.22	12.349ff.	47
11.315–53	140	12.366–72	318
11.329–32	92	12.372–91	318
11.330–31	102 n.34	12.385–88	47f.
11.354–82	317	12.429–35	272 n.7
11.363–64	94	12.429–46	317f.
11.382–87	139 n.85	12.450–63	318f.
11.387–579	288 n.62		
11.390–91	96 n.18	**Suetonius**	
11.392–95	96	– *Aug.*	
11.407–8	101ff.; 141f.	7.2	255 n.6
11.408	106	– *Cl.*	
11.429–35	94f.	11	209
11.497–573	288 n.62	41	145 n.2
11.499–500	94 n.14	– *Dom.*	
11.499–508	97ff.	1	242

2.3	268; 283 n.45	13.36–38	42 n.39
8.3	303	15.37.1	389 n.17
8.3–4	303	15.38–43	388 n.11
15.3	72 n.9	15.42	390 n.20; 398
– Gal.		15.42.1	390 n.21; 398
2	236 n.35; 292	15.45.1	388 n.11
– Nero		– Hist.	
12	397 n.56	1.2	148f.; 199; 211
31	395 n.49; 397	1.2.2	234
31.1	397	1.3.2	231
31.2	389 n.14; 397f.	1.4	69
– Otho		1.10	220
7.1	389 n.14	1.30.7–8	197
9.3	209 n.25	1.47.2	197
– Tit.		1.50.2–4	1ff.
9.3	268; 283 n.45	1.50.3	220 n.40
10.2	283 n.45	1.76	221
– Ves.		2.1	220f.
1.1	388 n.10	2.1–7	221
4.5–6	199 n.2	2.6	221
5.6	199 n.2	2.38	148 n.8; 150 n.20
6.3	218; 219 n.36	2.38.2	231
7.1	211; 345 n.18	2.50–55	217
8.1	302; 388	2.56	217
8.5	388 n.10	2.73	217; 221
9.1	389 n.19	2.73.1	216 n.34
11	302	2.74	211; 221; 223
18	395 n.49	2.74–79	218
– Vit. Plin.	337f.	2.76.2	223
		2.79	218; 219 n.36; 219 n.37
Tacitus		2.81	219 n.37
– Ag.		2.82.3	345 n.18
2–3	199	2.89	218
17.2	151 n.24	2.101.1	199
21.2	403 n.82	3.8.2	345 n.18
39	269	3.25	285; 292 n.72
– Ann.		3.25.2–3	285
1.1–10	276	3.33.1–2	288
1.2	69 n.1	3.33.2	288
1.10.5	97 n.18	3.33–34	279
3.27–28	276	3.48.3	345 n.18
3.54.4	345 n.17	3.51	279
4.34–35	145 n.2	3.65	337
12.43.2	344	3.65.2	196
13.17	283 n.46	3.71–72	388 n.12
13.17.1	269 n.49	3.71–73	288
13.31	397 n.56	3.72	241 n.49; 288

3.72.1	4 n.11; 91; 231; 288	1.11–12	233
3.72.2	234 n.32	1.12–14	76
3.72–85	241 n.49	1.16	83
3.74	242	1.22–25	366
3.74.1	242 n.54; 244 n.59	1.26–30	36 n.27
3.82–86	287f.	1.26–37	69
3.83.2	288	1.33–34	303
3.83–85	279; 288	1.59	375 n.43
4	292	1.64–66	37
4–5	175 n.77	1.67–70	36 n.28; 366
4.1–3	276	1.70	366 n.13
4.22.2	175 n.77	1.71–73	37; 272 n.7; 367
4.38.1–2	345 n.18	1.73–78	70
4.52.2	345 n.18	1.76ff.	37
4.53	388 n.12	1.79–80	37
4.85–86	175 n.78	1.121–29	77 n.21
5.1–9	199 n.2	1.144	246f.
5.10–13	199 n.2	1.150ff.	37 n.31
5.13	199 n.2	1.154–55	38
		1.156–60	38 n.35
Tertullian		1.164–67	39
– *Apol.*		1.168–69	39
19.6	202 n.9	1.170–73	39
		1.194–202	37 n.31
Theophilus		1.207–39	75ff.
– *Ad Autol.*		1.211–17	367 n.20
3.23	202 n.9	1.224–25	366 n.14
		1.236	81
Theophrastus		1.244–47	38
– *HP*		1.245–47	367
1.1.7	348 n.28	1.485	40 n.36
		1.498–560	368
Thucydides		1.505–27	79
3.82	330 n.30	1.525	79 n.25
3.82–84	208 n.21	1.528–29	303f.
5.105	69 n.3	1.531–60	14; 38; 77ff.; 115
		1.531–67	239 n.47
Tibullus		1.542–51	383f.
1.10.33	9; 91 n.9	1.542–60	230 n.15
2.5.77	63 n.27	1.544–46	367
		1.545–46	19; 35; 79; 385
Valerius Flaccus		1.548–49	80
1.1	233	1.548–54	80
1.1–21	230 n.15; 234 n.31	1.555–56	79; 80 n.29; 239 n.47
1.1–4	74f.	1.556–57	367
1.7–9	83	1.557	81
1.7–21	151f.	1.558–60	79f.; 383f.

Index of Passages

1.563–65	69	2.208	231
1.563–67	38; 81	2.216–19	228; 231ff.; 304f.
1.568–73	82	2.220–30	367
1.586–93	368 n.21	2.227–28	230
1.598–607	367 n.20	2.229–31	279
1.605	375 n.46	2.231–32	230
1.630	375 n.43	2.237–38	230
1.641–50	367 n.20	2.239	231
1.644–45	76	2.242–46	228; 235ff.
1.693ff.	37 n.32	2.243	237f.; 244
1.693–99	71; 247 n.68	2.244–45	235 n.33
1.700–8	77 n.21	2.249–51	240f.
1.700–850	247 n.68	2.249–58	242
1.747–48	37	2.254–55	245
1.761	272 n.7	2.258	242
1.767–826	279	2.259–60	242
1.774–817	382 n.75	2.261–300	242f.
1.817	304	2.270–71	243f.
1.827	371 n.31	2.273	241
1.827–31	368ff.	2.274–75	366 n.14
1.829b	369	2.279	241
1.830	371	2.361–64	366
1.832–35	370f.	2.384–92	82
1.846–50	370	2.408–9	248
2.1	247 n.68	2.408–25	229; 244ff.
2.3	247 n.68	2.410–13	244ff.; 246f. n.65
2.16–18	366f.	2.418–21	246
2.82–91	371ff.	2.420	246f.
2.82–241	230	2.534	59 n.20
2.82–310	227; 229; 245f.	2.571–73	80f. n.29
2.87–88	373	2.613–20	367
2.95–100	121f.	3.14–18	234 n.31
2.98–99	367	3.14–248	247
2.101–2	231	3.15–332	272 n.7
2.101–6	120	3.15–458	303
2.101–310	304	3.17	312 n.42
2.106	231	3.19–31	312 n.42
2.107–14	304	3.30–31	312 n.42
2.107–310	272 n.7	3.80–86	75 n.14
2.111–14	304	3.81–82	247
2.174–85	189	3.186–89	283 n.47
2.184–85	279	3.214	304
2.184–241	279	3.224–28	371 n.30
2.191	231	3.225	373 n.38
2.192–95	231	3.229–30	65 n.31
2.196–98	120	3.230–34	312 n.42
2.204–8	120	3.235	312 n.42

3.239–42	247	5.684	70
3.340	247	6.1–760	272 n.7
3.340–42	246	6.28	54 n.9
3.341	247	6.122–28	309; 385 n.94
3.435	373 n.38	6.130–31	385 n.95
3.487–508	303	6.150	111
3.520	304	6.150–51	111f.
4.13	304	6.155–57	112
4.13–14	383 n.86	6.323–39	385 n.94
4.309–11	373 n.38	6.345–66	48 n.49
4.561–66	373ff.	6.369–80	309f.
4.563–66	376	6.394–403	310f.
4.564–65	373 n.38; 376	6.402–6	83
4.574–76	373ff.	6.403	304
4.582–83	373ff.	6.415	366 n.14
4.617	112	6.427–54	35 n.26
4.641	375	6.439–48	379ff.
4.642–43	375f.	6.442	383
4.692	375	6.443–44	380 n.67
4.695	375	6.445–46	380 n.70
4.708–10	84 n.40	6.447	118; 380 n.66
4.711–13	367	6.447–48	381
5.120–39	305f.	6.448	382 n.75
5.217–21	305	6.455ff.	118
5.217–25	234 n.31	6.467–68	116 n.25; 119; 122 n.41
5.221	62 n.24	6.467–69	383 n.85
5.224	233	6.469–74	118
5.228–30	303f.	6.575–760	75 n.14
5.231–40	306f.	6.668–71	118f.
5.236	70	7.255	184
5.250–55	307	7.329–30	380 n.68
5.256–58	307	7.330	381 n.72
5.259–62	70	7.370	373 n.38
5.259–77	112	7.569	373 n.38
5.265–66	308	7.607–43	303
5.265–6.760	303	7.625–40	311ff.
5.288–90	41	7.626	373 n.38
5.329–454	307 n.34	7.635–36	312
5.333–40	307f.	8.18–19	117 n.26
5.446–48	116	8.59	75 n.14
5.453–54	366 n.14	8.67	75 n.14
5.495–97	303	8.72–73	382 n.77
5.536	70	8.136–39	77 n.21
5.542–45	41	8.187	73 n.10
5.610–14	309	8.196	375 n.43
5.618–48	308	8.199	84
5.624–32	308	8.224	84 n.39; 113

8.225	116 n.24	2.624–33	391 n.28
8.228–29	115	2.689–91	98 n.23
8.229	116 n.24	4.296–629	274
8.234–36	116	4.333–61	246 n.63
8.236	248	4.495	332
8.247–51	113f.	4.666	136
8.257–58	113f.	5.84–96	327
8.259–84	77 n.21	5.604–40	189
8.259–467	304	5.605–79	301
8.261–63	72f.	5.670–71	9; 91 n.9
8.280–82	72 n.9	5.677–78	301
8.306	72f.	6.136–48	83 n.38
8.395–99	82	6.548–81	370
8.396	82f.	6.613	289 n.62
8.463	366 n.14	6.791–805	269 n.48
8.463b–67	72f.	6.826–27	106
8.467	84	6.832–35	92f.
		6.833	93

Valerius Maximus

		6.834	94
3.3.2	145	6.834–35	129 n.38
5.5.4	279	6.842	254
6.2.6	160 n.45	6.893	371
6.6.ext.1	61 n.22; 179f.; 325	6.893–96	370
7.4	146	7.44	232 n.25
7.4.4	157 n.39	7.45	192
9.5.ext.3	265 n.35	7.331	188 n.27
		7.335	137

Vegetius

– *Mil.*

		7.335–36	136
		7.341–56	327
2.3	154 n.34	7.351–52	120 n.37
		7.355	184

Velleius Paterculus

– *Hist.*

		7.376–405	301
		7.384	241 n.51
2.67.3	279	7.386	130
		7.461	374 n.42

Vergil

– *A.*

		7.518	128; 135
1.23–49	299	7.607	371
1.94–96	33 n.19	7.610	371
1.229–53	182 n.9	7.620–22	371
1.234–36	79	8.78	98 n.23
1.279	80; 239 n.47	8.675–713	276
1.291–96	79	8.675–728	26
1.292–93	269 n.48	8.678–81	230
1.459–63	246 n.63	8.685	26
2.361–62	232 n.22	8.685–88	230
2.410–12	25f.	8.692	375 n.43
		8.698–700	353

8.698–708	26	– *Ecl.*	
8.705–6	400 n.73	1.6	128
8.714–16	269 n.48	1.11–12	276
8.720–23	400 n.73	1.65–73	276
8.729–31	246 n.63	4.6	366 n.14
9.446	235	4.13	25 n.1
9.446–49	95; 235	4.33	366 n.13
9.447	235	9.2–6	276
9.448	235	– *G.*	
9.449	235	1.24–42	269 n.48
9.672–716	256	1.125–28	366 n.13
9.687	59 n.20	1.145–46	289 n.62
9.722–54	256	1.406	25 n.1
10.41	136	1.463–514	276
10.310–13	290	1.489–90	106
10.391–92	257 n.13	1.489–92	3 n.6
10.394–98	257 n.13	1.508	287
10.467	188	1.512–14	281
10.467–68	187	2.458–74	366 n.14
10.513–604	290	2.458–540	366 n.13
10.543–44	97 n.20	2.495–96	282 n.44
11.24–26	193f.	2.510–12	100
11.72–77	247 n.65	2.540	286f.
11.396	256	3.108–9	406 n.99
11.447–50	134	4.386	98 n.23
11.879–86	26	4.560–62	269 n.48
12.435–36	32 n.17		
12.707–9	101; 192	**Zonaras**	
12.856–60	130	8.21	324 n.11